JOURNAL FOR THE STUDY OF THE NEW TESTAMENT
SUPPLEMENT SERIES

272

Petr Pokorný

Testimony and Interpretation

Early Christology in Its Judeo-Hellenistic Milieu
Studies in Honour of Petr Pokorný

Edited by

Jiří Mrázek and Jan Roskovec

T & T CLARK INTERNATIONAL
A Continuum imprint
LONDON • NEW YORK

Published by T&T Clark International
The Tower Building, 11 York Road, London SE1 7NX
15 East 26th Street, Suite 1703, New York, NY 10010

www.tandtclark.com

British Library Cataloguing-in-Publication Data
A catalogue record for this book is available from the British Library.

Library of Congress Cataloging-in-Publication Data
A catalogue record for this book is available from the Library of Congress.

Typeset by ISB Typesetting, Sheffield
Printed on acid-free paper in Great Britain by CPI (Bath)

ISBN 0-567-08298-9

CONTENTS

LIST OF CONTRIBUTORS

Professor Dr Dale C. Allison, Jr is Errett M. Grable Professor of New Testament Exegesis and Early Christianity, Pittsburgh Theological Seminary, U.S.A.

Professor Dr János Bolyki is former Professor of New Testament Studies, Theological Faculty, Károli Gáspár Reformed University, Budapest, Hungary.

Professor Dr James H. Charlesworth is George L. Collord Professor of New Testament Language and Literature, Princeton Theological Seminary, U.S.A.

Dr John M. Court is Honorary Senior Research Fellow in Theology and Religious Studies, University of Kent, Canterbury, United Kingdom.

Dr Christoph Demke is former Bishop of Evangelical Church of the Province of Saxony, Magdeburg, Germany.

Professor Dr Karl P. Donfried is E. A. Woodson 1922 Professor, Department of Religion and Biblical Literature, Smith College, Northampton, Mass., U.S.A.

Professor Dr Detlev Dormeyer is Professor of New Testament Studies, Faculty of Humanities and Theology, University of Dortmund, Germany.

Dr Paul Ellingworth is Teaching Fellow, Department of Divinity with Religious Studies, King's College, University of Aberdeen, United Kingdom.

Professor Dr Martin Hengel was formerly Professor of New Testament Studies and Ancient Judaism, Faculty of Protestant Theology, Eberhard Karl University, Tübingen, Germany.

Professor Dr Rudolf Hoppe is Professor of New Testament Exegesis, Catholic-Theological Faculty, Rheinland Friedrich-Wilhelm University, Bonn, Germany.

Professor Dr Hans Hübner is former Professor of New Testament Studies, Faculty of Theology, Georg-August University, Göttingen, Germany.

Professor Dr Hans Klein is Professor of New Testament Studies, Institute of Protestant Theology, Sibiu, Romania.

Dr Larry J. Kreitzer is Tutor for Graduates and Tutor in New Testament, Regent's Park College, University of Oxford, United Kingdom.

Dr Matti Myllykoski is Docent of New Testament Studies, Faculty of Theology, University of Helsinki, Finland.

Dr Stanislaw Pisarek is Lecturer in New Testament Studies, Silesian Theological Seminary, Katowice, and St Johannes Cantius Theological Institute, Poland.

Professor Dr Stanley E. Porter is President, Dean and Professor of New Testament, McMaster Divinity College, Hamilton, Ontario, Canada.

Professor Dr Zdeněk Sázava is Professor of New Testament Studies, Hussite Theological Faculty, Charles University in Prague, Czech Republic.

Professor Dr Wolfgang Schrage is former Professor of New Testament, Protestant-Theological Faculty, Friedrich-Wilhelm University, Bonn, Germany.

Professor Dr Jens Schröter is Professor of New Testament Studies, University of Leipzig, Germany.

Professor Dr Kari Syreeni is Professor of New Testament Exegesis, University of Uppsala, Sweden.

Dr Ladislav Tichý is Docent of New Testament Studies, St. Cyril and Methodius Faculty of Theology, Palacký University in Olomouc, Czech Republic.

INTRODUCTION

Jan Roskovec

The two concepts that we have chosen for the title of this collection of essays represent important notions of modern hermeneutics and, at the same time, they seemed to us quite suitable for characterizing the inner course of thought and work of Prof. Dr Petr Pokorný, whose 70th birthday in May 2003 this volume should celebrate. After all, modern hermeneutics became in the recent years one of the focal points of his interests – but in that only came to the surface what earlier had been implicit inclination of his work, both as a scholar and teacher and as a minister of the church. The rehabilitation of testimony, notwithstanding its necessarily subjective disposition, as a valid and useful means of communicating 'truth' corresponds well to the scepticism that Pokorný had retained towards all kinds of hyper-sceptical conceptions of (un)reliability of the early Christian sources. At the same time, however, one of his constant emphases have been on interpretation, i.e. responsible effort to apprehend what is being witnessed, an effort that includes awareness of differing contexts as well as of necessity to respond to the testimony by taking one's own stance.

By the subtitle we have tried to delimit roughly the area of Pokorný's scholarly interests in terms of their subject matter. The early years of his studies are marked by the attention paid mainly to the 'milieu' of New Testament literature and theology, especially its 'Hellenistic' part. With his second doctoral dissertation he entered the discussion about the origins of gnosis[1] and carried on his explorations into the Coptic literature and gnosis by the commented translation of the *Gospel of Thomas* into Czech[2] and a comprehensive study about gnosticism with further translations of selected gnostic texts,[3] supplemented later on by a popular introduction into the hellenistic culture in general.[4] The utilization of the studies in that wider area for the proper task of biblical interpretation is reflected mainly in his two major commentaries to deutero-Pauline epistles: Colossians and Ephesinas.[5] Another link from the (gnostic-)Hellenistic culture that led

1. *Počátky gnose. Vznik gnostického mýtu o božstvu člověk (Origins of Gnosis. The Gnostic Myth about the Deity of Man*; Prague: Academia, 1968).

2. *Tomášovo evangelium*, Prague: Kalich 1981, reprinted within the edition of the New Testament Apocrypha: *Novozákonní apokryfy I., Neznámá evangelia*; Prague: Vyšehrad, 2001).

3. *Píseň o perle. Tajné knihy starověkých gnostiků* (*The Song of the Pearl. Secret Books of the Ancient Gnostics*; Prague: Vyšehrad, 1986).

4. *Řecké dědictví v Orientu. Helénismus v Egyptě a Sýrii* (*Greek Heritage in Orient: Hellenismus in Egypt and Syria*; Prague: OIKOYMENH, 1993).

5. Both written for the series Theologischer Handkommentar zum Neuen Testament, published

Pokorný into the very centre of the New Testament was the Jesus tradition (here the *Gospel of Thomas* may serve as a logical connective element). First he occupied himself with the tradition of Jesus' words,[6] but then turned to the earliest gospel and dealt with its general problems as well as its contents.[7] In recent years he contributed to the rehabilitation of Luke as a theologian[8] and is constantly following the new developments in the historical Jesus studies.

Though the overall character and method of Pokorný's work is clearly marked by the emphasis on linguistic accuracy and respect to the historical developments, he never loses interpretative – and that in his understanding means: theological – issues from his sight. As the main task of interpretation he sees enabling of understanding, and indeed, appropriation of the theological relevance of the biblical texts. He perceives clearly that in the Bible – and in the New Testament in particular – the historical issues are tightly linked with theological ones. This is most transparent in the way he tries to reconstruct 'unity within diversity' in the earliest times of Christian thought in general and of christology in particular.[9] The potential of Pokorný's scholarly work could be only briefly sketched here and may be followed in greater detail in the selected bibliography that is part of this volume. It is also reflected in the collected contributions of his colleagues and friends from all around the world.

This is not to say that the articles presented here were written as a direct reaction to Petr Pokorný's work. We decided not to set beforehand any strictly defined theme or topic, as it seemed quite difficult to choose just one to represent his main interest. However, we were pleased to find out that most of the contributions have at least a point of contact with some aspect of Pokorný's studies. In the following I will try to indicate these relationships that may bring out the coherence of the volume, otherwise naturally quite a diverse collection. The arrangement of the volume is quite simple: after some consideration we have decided to group the contributions according to the traditional pattern, following more or less the chronology of the respective subjects.

The Pauline section is opened up by *Karl Donfried*, who tries to ascertain more closely Paul's background in Judaism. The emphasis of the 'new perspective', that the apostle's critical attitude to his own Pharisaic past did not have to

in Berlin by Evangelische Verlagsanstalt (Col.: 1987, Eph.: 1992; ET of Colossians published by Hendrickson, Peabody, MA, 1991).

6. *Der Kern der Bergpredigt* (Hamburg: Bergstedt H. Reich, 1969).

7. *„Anfang des Evangeliums": Zum Problem des Anfangs und des Schlusses des Markusevangeliums*, in R. Schnackenburg, J. Ernst and J. Wanke (eds.), *Die Kirche des Anfangs* (FS H. Schürmann; Leipzig: St. Benno Verlag 1978), 115–32; Czech commentary to Mark: *Výklad evangelia podle Marka* (Prague: Kalich, 1974; article on Mark in *Aufstieg und Niedergang der römischen Welt*).

8. *Theologie der lukanischen Schriften* (FRLANT, 174; Göttingen: Vandenhoeck & Ruprecht 1998; abridged Czech version *Vznešený Teofile!*, Prague/Třebenice: Mlýn 1998).

9. *Die Entstehung der Christologie. Voraussetzungen einer Theologie des Neuen Testaments* (Berlin: Evangelische Verlagsanstalt; Stuttgart: Calwer Verlag, 1985. Later published in English (Edinburgh: T&T Clark, 1987) and restated in *Jesus in the Eyes of His Followers* (North Richland Hills,TX: BIBAL Press, 1998).

mean for him to give up Judaism as such, is taken further to the question of possible affiliations within the relatively complex spectrum of Judaism of the time. Donfried describes the common theological motifs that bring Paul close to the Essenes of *yahad*, the community of the Dead Sea Scrolls and that, at the same time, mark the distance of both Paul and the Essenes from the pharisaic streams.

This investigation into the possible 'pre-Christian roots of Paul' thought is followed by three studies that apply detailed exegesis of small parts in Paul's epistles to wider issues of Pauline and New Testament theology. *Rudolph Hoppe* tries to illuminate Paul's relationship with the Corinthian congregation from 1 Cor. 8.1–6. The main problem of this passage seems to be to discern precisely the position of Paul from the argumentation that he criticises. According to Hoppe, the core of the conflict is to be seen in different concepts of monotheism: Paul is refuting a mere monotheistic conviction that leads to indifference to others with the reminder of its Jewish and Christian connotations, viz. creation and the mediator of creation, that brings about the importance of love.

Ladislav Tichý takes up anew the question of Paul's 'mysticism' and asks over Gal. 2.20–21 about the precise meaning of the apostle's 'Christ in me' saying that has no parallel, but may be compared to similar construction in Pauline language. The same epistle, however with different questions, is approached by *Jens Schröter*. On the particular case of Paul's polemic he demonstrates support for Pokorný's methodological warning against the conclusion that the variety of formulations of early Christian confessions must imply the variety of contradictory christological concepts at the beginning. In Gal., Paul develops a polemic against what he sees as denying the very substance of the gospel that had been committed to him. Again, the problem is where precisely lies the point of controversy, in other words, what sort of difference is meant between 'the gospel of circumcision' and 'the gospel of foreskin' (Gal. 2.7) when Gal. 1.6–7 seems to assert that there is only one gospel. By careful semantical and syntactical analysis Schröter eliminates this seeming contradiction and describes Paul's position as the very opposite to the conception of the only possible form (expression) of the gospel. Paul seems to be realistically aware that there is a difference in the soteriological implications of the gospel for a Jew and a Gentile, because each has a different past, and that lifting the difference between the two is only the result of accepting the gospel on both sides.

The last two contributions concerning Pauline literature intersect directly with Pokorný's studies in this field, as they deal with the epistles to Ephesians, Colossians (and Philemon). Both concentrate on the background, or milieu, of the writings and both incline to reconsidering Pauline authorship of these epistles. *Stanley Porter* shows that the exhortation against drunkenness in Eph. 5.18–19, rather than just a general morality against alcoholism, might be directed against Dionysian practices, whose ecstatic frenzy, involving music, should be replaced by a joyful Christian worship in the Spirit. *Larry Kreitzer* surveys the archaeological and other information about the earthquakes in Lycus Valley and gathers possible allusions to this particular geographical and historical situation of the places where the mentioned epistles are addressed to. In the light of this evidence he argues for revising the issues of authorship, dating and destination (in the case of Eph.) of these letters.

Matti Myllykoski contemplates the singularity of the critical issues connected with the Gospel of Mark: as it is the first of its kind, the otherwise fruitful methods of literary criticism are of little avail here. A model that might help to understand the process of formation of the first Gospel is based on attention to the oral practice in that the tradition were used and modified before having been written down. The presented model is based on recognition, that there is no sharp divide between orality and literacy, and that the marks of literary techniques in the Marcan text cannot be denied. At the same time, some of the pecularities of the text, as well as the very formation of its overall structure, may be explained by the oral practice.

A critical revisiting of the question of how the relationship of the 'canonical' picture of Jesus to the 'historical' one should be evaluated is presented by *Dale Allison* on the example of Jesus' attitude to hell. After showing that a relatively strong case can be made for the assumption that Jesus' utterances mentioning the possibility of a postmortal punishment are generally a product of the later (church) tradition, Allison follows the line of argument pointing to the opposite.

One aspect of the motif of Jesus' ascension to heaven, developed particularly by Luke, is clearly a polemic against the pretensions of the deified Roman emperors. *Detlev Dormeyer* elucidates the philosophical critique of such claims as represented by Seneca's satirical comedy *Apocolocyntosis* – 'Marrowization'. After a survey of the history of apotheoses of the Roman rulers and of Seneca's career explaining the reasons for writing it, the basic contents of the play is summarized. In the conclusion, the question of possible points of contact of this play, written for the education of young Nero, to the Lucan work is asked.

An elaborate survey of the testimonies to Jesus from the sources other than the gospels is offered in the article by *Martin Hengel*. Among the early Christian witnesses, most part is devoted to Paul, in whose letters Hengel finds sufficient evidence of apostle's acquaintance with the traditions about the earthly Jesus. Similarly the rest of the New Testament and writings of the Apostolical Fathers show on closer examination that the tradition about Jesus' life was living, probably in oral form long after the literary fixation of the gospels. The non-Christian testimonies, scanty remarks in both Jewish and pagan writers of the first two centuries betray the diversity of the traditions and at least confirm clearly the historicity of Jesus.

The second section, too, is closed by two studies concentrating on the same text – the Gospel of Matthew. Both also have explicit christological direction. *Hans Klein* analyses the christology of the Matthean infancy narrative, with special attention to Mt. 1.18–25. In terms of redactional criticism he finds in the chs 1–2 two basic traditions: the one is characterized by Joseph's dreams and betrays still other Old Testament reminiscences, the other – the virginal conception by the Holy Spirit – carries marks of Hellenistic conceptions and is only retrospectively covered by an Old Testament quotation and the motif of Emmanuel. There is a christological development behind the passage, indeed, in its present state it is a cumulation of different christological concepts. The oldest may be the one of a 'saviour', connected to the name 'Jesus' and to the Old Testament birth of Samson (Judg. 13.5); the motif of 'Son of God' was originally also not connected to the virginal conception, but to the 'calling out of Egypt'.

Wolfgang Schrage is carefully treading the path between two traditional interpretations of the Matthean Sermon on the Mount. The christological emphasis (concentration on the sermonizer) has often been a way of mastering (or even avoiding) the uneasy moral claims of the text. Schrage sees the christological concentration as justified by the text (and context), but draws attention to the question of the precise contents and function of the christology in this respect. As the main accent of it he considers Jesus' role of the right interpreter of God's law, by God authorized teacher. There is no question about the validity of the Law and the Prophets, the real question is, how to understand them. In fact, it is only (this) right use of the Law and the Prophets that brings them to fulfilment. Besides being the right teacher of God's will, Jesus is also – from the very beginning of the Gospel – known as the one bringing about God's presence, and at the same time the one who himself, in a paradigmatical way, fulfils the requirements of the Sermon and remains together with his listeners subordained to the 'Father'.

Five contributions are devoted to the Gospel of John, a matter that Petr Pokorný touched in his work only marginally.[10] *János Bolyki* suggests an interesting analogy that might throw fresh light to the problem of history and 'myth' in the Fourth Gospel. The presence of the elements of drama in the Gospel is enhanced by the observation of the function that the drama had in the Graeco-Roman culture: retelling the myth in the way that makes them relevant to the contemporary audience.

The article of *Hans Hübner* confronts one of the basic notions of general hermeneutics, the notion of truth, in the perception of Heidegger (mainly in his later period) with the Johannine understanding of the concept (and its interpretation by Bultmann). Heidegger builds his concept of truth upon the classical Greek understanding of ἀ-λήθεια with the etymological explanation as 'disclosed' and conceives it, along the lines of his existentialist interpretation, in basically dynamic terms. If truth is a being that is perceptible, that discloses itself, one can only come to it by 'out-coming' from oneself, in an act of 'existence'. After surveying the antique references of the concept by Aristotle and Plato, Hübner confronts the heideggerian notion with two Johannine texts: already Jn 8.31–32 shows a dynamic understanding of truth that makes free, as well as its connection to word that has to be heard, Jn 14.6 makes for the personal character of truth (one reaches it in an encounter). As for Bultmann's utilization of this concept: it helps to avert the suspicion of mere subjectivism – coming to truth is a matter of encounter, not just of a new self-understanding.

10. In the study 'Der irdische Jesus im Johannesevangelium', *NTS*, 30 (1984), pp. 217–28; now also in: P. Pokorný, J.B. Souček, *Bibelauslegung als Theologie* (WUNT, 100; Tübingen: Mohr-Siebeck, 1997), pp. 327–39.

James Charlesworth, too, asks general questions about the 'purpose' of John's Gospel, in the foreground dealing with the interpretation of a particular place, Jn 3.13. He makes it a test case for the assumption that the anti-Jewish polemic of the Gospel might have been directed at circles influenced by apocalyptic Enoch literature. The formulation about the 'only one who ascended into heaven', as well as some other motifs in the Gospel (e.g. 'son of man' motif), may well be a statement contradicting the claim that Enoch was the one (or one of those) who entered heaven.

The Johannine parable of the vine and the branches (Jn 15) is explored by *Stanislaw Pisarek*, meticulously gathering parallels that may have inspired the metaphorical images used in the parable.

Kari Syreeni reveals his interests in hermeneutics and tackles the general questions of the purpose and composition of the Fourth Gospel with respect to the function of the Farewell Discourse in it (in a polemic with Käsemann). In Syreeni's view the inclusion of the farewell speech in the form of a literary testament served the theological linking of the earlier Johannine (enthusiastic?) christology of Jesus's continual presence with the tradition of the passion and death of Jesus. This is visible e.g. on the changed concept of Jesus' glory (glorification on the cross) and on the concept of the Paraclete, who – as the Spirit – represents Jesus, but at the same time reminds of the earthly Jesus. Within this process also the concept of parousia was revived.

The last section contains the contributions that in some way step over the bounds of exegesis to a more general reflection. *Christoph Demke* presents his 'historical imagination' about the earliest times of christological reflection, when the first steps towards the soteriological interpretation of Jesus' meaning were being taken. He defends the necessary role of imagination in trying to reconstruct the possible original questions of the people involved in the ancient events. According to Demke, the expiatory interpretation of Jesus' death on the cross was not initiated by the reflection of Jesus himself (as he made neither his person, nor his death a content of his message). The reaction of the disciples to Jesus' execution – their flight to Galilee – does not necessarily imply that they saw everything lost: a death of a righteous was not out of the bounds of their possible reflection. Quite probably they expected the imminent coming of God's wrath – his judgement as a reaction to what happened on Golgatha. The encounter with the risen Jesus that came instead must have been interpreted as a sign of mercy and forgiveness: the judgement had stayed away.

The contribution of *John Court* is also imaginative: an attempt to sketch a portrait of the 'seer of Patmos', the author of Revelation. Through the person of the author, his sense of authority, his possible historical situation, the nature of his visions, the concentration of his theology and his concept of witness/martyrdom, a concise introduction into the book is provided, that, interestingly enough, became characteristic for the western part of Christendom.

The section closes with two articles that offer a wider reflection about the role of christology. *Paul Ellingworth* introduces two – from our point of view – exotic conceptions of christology from mediaeval China and contemporary Africa and asks about the criteria that, in his opinion, cannot be simply (and only) a recourse to the biblical texts. *Zdeněk Sázava* brings in a reflection of a scholar who, for the most of his career, has also actively served as a church minister.

To all of the contributors of the volume the editors would like to express their sincere thanks – for their scholarly effort by which they expressed their congratulations to their colleague and friend, and for their Christian patience with which they waited for the publication of the book that has been delayed against our original plan and hope. Our special thanks go to Professor Stanley Porter who helped us to arrange the publication.

Part I

Paul, His Teachers and Pupils

PAUL THE JEW – BUT OF WHAT SORT?

Karl P. Donfried

1. *Some Introductory Observations*

a. *Paul's Self-Description as a Pharisee*

Although Paul self describes his life in Judaism at several points in his letters (Phil. 3.4b–6; 2 Cor. 11.22; Rom. 11.1), he refers to his relationship with the Pharisees only once. In Phil. 3.4b–6 we read:

> Εἴ τις δοκεῖ ἄλλος πεποιθέναι ἐν σαρκί, ἐγὼ μᾶλλον· περιτομῇ ὀκταήμερος, ἐκ γένους Ἰσραήλ, φυλῆς Βενιαμίν, Ἑβραῖος ἐκ Ἑβραίων, **κατὰ νόμον Φαρισαῖος**, κατὰ ζῆλος διώκων τὴν ἐκκλησίαν, κατὰ δικαιοσύνην τὴν ἐν νόμῳ γενόμενος ἄμεμπτος.

The final words in Phil. 3.5 (κατὰ νόμον Φαρισαῖος) cohere with several references in Acts in which Luke provides a description of Paul as a Pharisee (Acts 23.6; 26.5) and as one who studied with Gamaliel (Acts 22.3; see also 5.34). In Acts 22.3 Luke writes as follows:

> ἐγω εἰμι ἀνὴρ Ἰουδαῖος, γεγεννημένος ἐν Ταρσῷ τῆς Κιλικίας, ἀνατεθραμμένος δὲ ἐν τῇ πόλει ταύτῃ, παρὰ τοὺς πόδας Γαμαλιὴλ πεπαιδευμένος κατὰ ἀκρίβειαν τοῦ πατρῴου νόμου, ζηλωτὴς ὑπάρχων τοῦ θεοῦ καθὼς πάντεης ὑμεῖς ἐστε σήμερον·

As we will attempt to demonstrate, there are a variety of factors that suggest tension between Paul's views and those of the Pharisees. In fact, there are sufficient incompatibilities between the two to raise the urgent question whether Paul, at some point in his religious development, broke with his Pharisaic past without ever rejecting his identification as a Jew? In addition to significant incongruities between Pharisaic and Pauline thought, there are striking similarities between Pauline and Essene thought. If this is in fact the case, how might these apparent anomalies be explained?

In pursuing these matters I want to be very conscious of Pierre Benoit's warning 'against an imprudent tendency to accept as immediate contacts arising from direct influence what in fact may be no more than independent manifestations of a common trend of the time'[1] which is as appropriate today as when it was first written. In drawing certain analogies between the thought world of Paul and the Essenes, it is important to make clear at the outset that, from my perspective,

1. Pierre Benoit, 'Qumran and the New Testament', *NTS* 7 (1960–61), pp. 276–96.

Paul was never a member of the Essene community nor that there are not areas of substantial incongruities between Pauline and Essene ways of being Jewish.

b. *Discoveries in the Desert*

When a Bedouin shepherd threw a stone into a cave at Khirbet Qumran in 1947 our understanding of Judaism and Christianity in the first century CE changed dramatically. The last half of the twentieth century was responsible for publishing the vast majority of the 900 texts found in these caves; scholarship beginning in the twenty-first century will need to rewrite the complex phenomenon known as Second Temple Judaism, the history of the early Jesus movement and the interaction of the two. No longer can we speak about Judaism and Christianity in the first century as unified religions in sharp conflict with one another; rather we must recognize the enormous diversity of Judaism, a diversity so extensive that it included the earliest followers of Jesus. The interactions of these multiform Judaisms is far greater than previous generations of scholars have been able to recognize.

These 900 texts which have so dramatically altered our perception of this period were part of a broader Essene movement.[2] Shemaryahu Talmon of Hebrew University prefers to refer to this movement revealed in the Dead Sea Scrolls in terms of its own self-description, the Community of the Renewed Covenant or simply, the *yahad*.[3] Part of this group relocated itself from Jerusalem to Qumran in the second half of the second century and remained there until 68 CE when it was destroyed by the Romans marching on their way to Masada, fresh from having conquered and burned Jerusalem. Josephus, the first century Jewish historian, reminds us that some Essenes were resident in Jerusalem and that, in fact, there was an Essene quarter in the southwest corner of the city.[4] From the Damascus Document, one of the major texts found in Cave 4, we know that the Essene movement was spread throughout the land that we now know as Israel.[5] And it was not a small movement. Josephus tells us that, during his time, the Pharisees numbered 6,000 and the Essenes about 4,000.[6] Since 1947, we now have many original texts describing this community, thus shedding enormous light – sometimes directly and sometimes indirectly – on the entire shape of the Judaisms[7] of this period, including the Sadducees, the Pharisees, the Essenes and the early Jesus movement. The Dead Sea Scrolls have not only made available a large quantity

2. See Joseph A. Fitzmyer, *The Dead Sea Scrolls and Christian Origins* (Grand Rapids: Eerdmans, 2000), pp. 249–60.

3. Shemaryahu Talmon, 'The Community of the Renewed Covenant', in Eugene Ulrich and James VanderKam (eds.), *The Community of the Renewed Covenant: The Notre Dame Symposium on the Dead Sea Scrolls* (Christianity and Judaism in Antiquity Series, 10; Notre Dame, IN: University of Notre Dame Press, 1994), pp. 3–24, here 8.

4. Josephus, *War* 5.145.

5. For example, CD 7.6–9.

6. Josephus, *Ant.* 18.18–22.

7. The term 'Judaisms' is used intentionally in order to indicate the diversity and non-monolithic character of Second Temple Judaism.

of hitherto unknown texts but they have also provided, as a result of these documents, a new context for comprehending (1) the complexity of Second Temple Judaism, (2) the intention of Jesus of Nazareth and his movement and (3), especially for the focus of this conference, for understanding the great missionary of this movement, the Apostle Paul.

c. *The Older Understanding of Paul*

When I was a graduate student in the 1960s the dominant paradigm of the Apostle Paul present in leading academic centres went something like this:

1. That the major religious influences on Paul were those of the Graeco-Roman culture, not Judaism;[8]
2. that the centre of Paul's theology was justification by faith; as a result, Christ was considered to be the end, the termination of the Torah. This emphasis, it was argued, together with Paul's use of phrases such as 'works of the law', indicated his antipathy to Judaism; Judaism, in fact, had become a mere relic of his past.[9]

Further, for this long-reigning paradigm, Romans were viewed as the centre and summary of Pauline theology; it became the centre by which all other aspects of his thought were judged.[10] Simultaneously, the Acts of the Apostles, an admittedly secondary presentation of Paul written in the name of Luke, was viewed as flawed – except as we shall see in the area of chronology – precisely because it presents a very Jewish Paul in which the theme of justification by faith is virtually absent.[11]

The publications and subsequent interpretations of the Dead Sea Scrolls have lead an increasing number of New Testament scholars to question this older paradigm.[12] In the same way that the Second Vatican Council's Decree on Ecumenism, issued in 1964, brought to the fore the great text on Christian unity, John 17, and permitted it to be seen with fresh insight, so too the Dead Sea Scrolls have brought renewed emphasis to Paul's long neglected and repeated self-identification as a Jew throughout his letters. In Phil. 3.5–6, as already noted, the Apostle describes himself as: 'circumcised on the eighth day, a member of the people of Israel, of the tribe of Benjamin, a Hebrew born of Hebrews; as to the law, a Pharisee; as to zeal, a persecutor of the church; as to righteousness

8. See Rudolph Bultmann, 'Zur Geschichte der Paulus-Forschung', *ThR* 1 (1929), pp. 26–59.

9. See Hans Conzelmann, *An Outline of the Theology of the New Testament* (New York: Harper, 1969), pp. 155–61.

10. Günther Bornkamm, 'The Letter to the Romans as Paul's Last Will and Testament', in Karl P. Donfried (ed.), *The Romans Debate: Revised and Expanded Edition* (Peabody, MA: Hendrickson, 2001), pp. 16–28.

11. For example, Philipp Vielhauer, 'On the 'Paulinism' of Acts', in Leander E. Keck and J. Louis Martyn (eds.), *Studies in Luke–Acts* (Festschrift Paul Schubert; Nashville: Abingdon Press, 1966), pp. 33–50.

12. See, for example, Joseph A. Fitzmyer, 'Paul and the Dead Sea Scrolls', in Peter W. Flint and James C. Vanderkam (eds), *The Dead Sea Scrolls after Fifty Years* (Leiden: Brill, 1999), II, pp. 599–621.

under the law, blameless'. And in 2 Cor. 11.22 he asks, 'Are they Hebrews? So am I. Are they Israelites? So am I. Are they descendants of Abraham? So am I'. And in Rom. 11.1 the anguished Paul writes: 'I ask, then, has God rejected his people? By no means! I myself am an Israelite, a descendant of Abraham, a member of the tribe of Benjamin. God has not rejected his people whom he foreknew'.

Did Paul give up his Judaism once he was called – please notice that I have avoided the verb 'converted' – by the Risen Lord to be an apostle to the Gentiles or does he continue to consider himself a Jew? For those who argue the former, several texts are cited, especially, Rom. 10.4, that Christ is the end of the law; and a series of texts in Galatians and Romans dealing with 'the works of the law' which allegedly support such an interpretation of Rom. 10.4. Even so noted a scholar as Hans Joachim Schoeps, himself a Jew, comments that 'Paul furnished a solution to the problem of the law which in the last resort rested on a misunderstanding...'[13] And speaking of Paul's interpretation of the law in Gal. 3.19 he adds: 'The whole thing is, of course, pure speculation, and shows not the slightest dependence on scripture or reminiscence of rabbinical opinions'.[14] Of course, what Schoeps was largely unaware of was the huge body of literature that lies between Jewish scripture and the rabbis, that body of literature that is now so obvious to us – the Dead Sea Scrolls.

d. *The Dead Sea Scrolls and Paul*

Paul was active at least during the 30's, 40's, 50's and perhaps early 60's of the first century. All of this is relatively undisputed. What is disputed is how we date Paul's first letter, and thus the earliest extant document of Christianity, 1 Thess. The old paradigm had a vested interest in pushing the date late, around 50 CE, so that it could distance Paul from Jesus and claim a virtual abyss between the two and assert that Paul was the real founder of Christianity. If, aside from the fact that the current Pauline chronology which places all his writing activity between c. 50–56 is far too compressed, we find significant parallels between 1 Thess. and the thought world of the Dead Sea Scrolls, then we need to consider further the proposals of those scholars who wish to redate 1 Thess. to the earlier 40's.[15]

The old paradigm simply assumed the theological priority of Romans and, as a consequence, had little use for 1 Thess.; as a result 1 Thess. became the stepchild of Pauline studies precisely because it did not employ the concept of 'justification' and for this and other reasons appeared to be insufficiently 'Christian'. In turning more specifically to 1 Thess., a number of elements in this letter suggest

13. H.J. Schoeps, *Paul: The Theology of the Apostle in the Light of Jewish Religious History* (Philadelphia: Westminster Press, 1961), p. 200.

14. Schoeps, *Paul*, p. 183.

15. See further John Knox, *Chapters in a Life of Paul* (ed. D.A. Hare; Macon, GA: Mercer University, rev. edn, 1987), Gerd Lüdemann, *Paul, Apostle to the Gentiles: Studies in Chronology* (Philadelphia: Fortress Press, 1984) and K.P. Donfried, 'Chronology: The Apostolic and Pauline Period', in Karl P. Donfried, *Paul, Thessalonica and Early Christianity* (Grand Rapids: Eerdmans, 2002), pp. 99–117.

affinities with the *yahad*, the prophetic movement of the Community of the Renewed Covenant at Qumran and elsewhere. Some of the similarities between the two include:[16]

1. eschatological/apocalyptic similarities in their intense expectation of the final consummation of history;
2. the election and calling of God, as when Paul writes to the Thessalonians church that 'we know, brothers and sisters beloved by God, that he has chosen (ἐκλογή) you' (1.4);
3. holiness/sanctification, as in 1 Thess. 4.3, 'For this is the will of God, your sanctification' (literally, holiness [ἁγιασμός]);
4. the light/day, night/darkness contrasts and the use of the term 'sons of light'. In 1 Thess. 5.5 Paul writes: 'for you are all sons of light and sons of the day; we are not of the night or of darkness'. One of the major descriptors for the *yahad* is that they are 'sons of light;'[17]
5. the wrath/salvation dualism. 'For God has destined us not for wrath but for obtaining salvation…' are words found in 1 Thess. 5.9;
6. the phrase 'church of God' which has its direct parallel in the Qumran term קהל אל;[18]
7. ἄτακτος and the ethical order. It is now quite likely that the 'idlers' or 'loafers' of 1 Thess. 5.14, the ἄτακτοι in Greek, should, on the basis of parallel texts related to the Dead Sea Scrolls, be translated as those 'who are out of order', namely not following the סרך, the order of the community as described in 1 Thess. 4.1–12. One of the major documents of the Qumran library is *The Community Rule* (1QS), the סרך היחד and it, too, contains admonitions and encouragements to properly follow its order.

2. *Paul and the Essenes: Essential Agreements*

a. *ברית*

There is significant variance in the use of ברית between the conceptual frameworks of the Essene Community of Qumran and the Pharisees, with the Qumran community's understanding of ברית virtually absent from the latter. Talmon suggests that the Rabbis 'did not develop the notion that in their days, and with their community, God had renewed his covenant of old with the people of Israel. In contrast to the pointed *communal* thrust of the Covenanter's concept of ברית and specifically ברית חדשה, the noun ברית *per se* and in diverse word combinations, connotes in the Rabbinic vocabulary exclusively the act of circumcision.

16. For further details see Karl P. Donfried, 'Paul and Qumran: The Possible Influence of סרך on 1 Thessalonians', in Donfried, *Paul, Thessalonica and Early Christianity*, pp. 221–31; 'The Assembly of the Thessalonians: Reflections on the Ecclesiology of the Earliest Christian Letter', in Donfried, *Paul, Thessalonica and Early Christianity*, pp. 139–62.

17. For example, 1QS 2.16; 1QM 1.1; 13; 13.16.

18. See Donfried, 'The Assembly', pp. 405–7.

On the strength of this rite, every male infant is *individually* accepted into ברית אברהם אבינו, God's ancient covenant with all Israel'. This 'specific technical connotation of ברית', he continues, 'is not documented in *yahad* literature. On the other hand, the *communal* dimension of ברית which attaches to the concept of 'covenant renewal' in the Covenanters' theology, as reflected in the Foundation Documents, appears to be altogether absent from the Rabbinic world of thought'.[19]

In light of this strikingly different usage between these two Torah schools, it is of considerable interest to note Paul's evident affinity for the *yahad's* use of ברית, particularly in the context of an ecclesial comparison of the καινὴ διαθήκη with the old in 2 Cor. 3.6 and 3.14. For Paul there is correspondingly a communal thrust in the context of the new covenant. It is also remarkable that the only two communities that accentuate and interpret Jeremiah's ברית חדשה are the *yahad* and the early Jesus movement, especially as reflected in Paul.

b. *Biblical Hermeneutics*

In his comparison of the approaches to the Law represented by Qumran and the rabbis, Daniel Schwartz makes reference to 'the rabbinic refusal to grant normative importance to contemporary (since Sinai!) divine revelation, as opposed to Qumran which took it for granted'.[20] Such an assertion raises the entire issue of how biblical interpretation was practiced by the Qumran *yahad*, the Rabbis and the Jesus movement represented by Paul.

The *pesher* method of biblical interpretation used by the Qumran community has become well known as a result of the publication of the Dead Sea Scrolls. It is a contemporizing form of interpretation in which prophetic texts are understood as referring to present events in the life of the *yahad*. More specifically, in its use of biblical texts it divided the law into distinct categories, i.e., the revealed (*nigleh*) and hidden (*nistar*). The revealed law was known to all of Israel but the hidden was known only to the *yahad*. Representative of the former is 1QS 8.15–16: 'This (path) is the study of the Law which He commanded by the hand of Moses, that they may do according to all that has been revealed (*nigleh*) from age to age, and as the Prophets have revealed by His Holy Spirit'.[21] Thus, the 'hidden laws were thus progressively revealed and changed with the times'.[22] Both principles are also evident in 1QS 5.11–12: 'For they are not reckoned in His Covenant. They have neither inquired nor sought after Him concerning His laws

19. Shemaryahu Talmon, 'The Community', pp. 14–15.

20. Daniel Schwartz, 'Law and Truth: On Qumran-Sadducean and Rabbinic views of the Law', in Devorah Dimant and Uriel Rappaport (eds.), *The Dead Sea Scrolls: Forty Years of Research* (Leiden: E.J.Brill, 1992), pp. 229–40, here 238.

21. Translation Geza Vermes, *The Complete Dead Sea Scrolls in English* (New York: Penguin Books, 1997).

22. Lawrence H. Schiffman, *Reclaiming the Dead Sea Scrolls: The History of Judaism, the Background of Christianity, the Lost Library of Qumran* (Philadelphia and Jerusalem: The Jewish Publication Society, 1994), p. 248.

that they might know the hidden things [נסתרות] in which they have sinfully erred; and matters revealed [נגלות] they have treated with insolence'.

A further result of the *yahad's* prophetic hermeneutic is sharp criticism of Pharasaic rationalist interpretation. They are referred to as *dorshe halaqot*, meaning literally 'seekers after smooth things', but more properly understood as 'interpreters of false laws'.[23] In CD 4.19–20 they are called 'builders of the wall...', a phrase remarkably similar to the mishnaic tractate Avot 1.1 where it is taught that one should 'Build a fence around the Torah'. Similarly, in 1QH 4.10–11 it is stated that 'they planned evil [literally, 'Belial'] against me to replace your Torah which You taught in my heart with smooth things [i.e. false laws] (which they taught) to Your people'.[24] For Schiffman, the Pharisees are accused of following 'false laws, finding ways around the requirements of the law, and pronouncing false verdicts in legal cases – practices leading to the virtual annulment of Jewish law in the view of the sect. Indeed, the very existence of such laws constitutes an annulment of the Torah, because it replaces Torah laws with the laws of the Pharisees'.[25] Tradition could not be authoritative 'since all Israel had gone astray. The true way had only been rediscovered by the sect's teacher'.[26]

Shemaryahu Talmon largely supports such a reading of the dispute between the Qumran community and the Pharisees and maintains that we witness in the texts of the Dead Sea Scrolls a confrontation between a prophetically inspired movement inclined toward apocalypticism and a rationalist stream that will ultimately develop into Rabbinic Judaism.[27] He observes, further, that

> Rabbinic Judaism shelved prophetic inspiration and progressively developed a rationalist stance... By contrast, the *yahad* embrace unreservedly the Bible's high appreciation of prophetic teaching and continue to subject the life of the individual and the community to the guidance of personalities who were possessed of the divine spirit... In this respect, the Covenanters and nascent Christianity are on the save wave length. The acceptance of inspiration as the paramount principle of individual and communal life informs also the followers of Jesus.[28]

The words of Paul to the Corinthians echo such a perspective: 'And we speak of these things in words not taught by human wisdom but taught by the Spirit, interpreting spiritual things to those who are spiritual' (1 Cor. 2.13), and again, 'And I think that I too have the Spirit of God' (1 Cor. 7.40).

23. Schiffman, *Reclaiming*, p. 250.

24. Translation and comment by Schiffman, *Reclaiming*, p. 251.

25. Schiffman, *Reclaiming*, 251. Schiffman adds the following: 'Yet the matter is even more complex. In early rabbinic literature, the term 'talmud' referred to the Pharisaic-rabbinic method of study that allows the deduction of laws from one another. It is precisely that method of study that the sectarians are excoriating in this text... Apparently, a substantial difference did exist between these two modes of interpretation. Although the method, known as "talmud", used by the Pharisees in this period certainly seemed to yield laws derived from biblical exegesis, the Pharisees did not regard such exegesis as divinely inspired' (p. 252).

26. Schiffman, *Reclaiming*, p. 254.

27. Talmon, *Community*, p. 22.

28. Talmon, *Community*, pp. 20–21.

It should come as no great surprise that *yahad* and Paul cite biblical texts in ways not unrelated. Joseph Fitzmyer has made a careful comparison of the introductory formulas used by Paul to introduce the Old Testament with those used in the Dead Sea Scrolls.[29] He also makes references to the study by B.M. Metzger in which a comparison is made between the formulas used to cite 'Old Testament' quotations in the Mishnah and the New Testament.[30] Fitzmyer concludes his meticulous evaluation with the conclusion that Paul's introductory formulas are far closer to the *yahad's* method than to the Pharisaic-rabbinic approach of the Mishnah. He then raises two perceptive queries with regard to the mode of Pauline citation: 'Can the mode have so radically changed from the pre-70 Palestinian custom to that of the Mishnaic in the course of some 150 years? Or is a different custom being followed?'[31]

In this connection one other comment is in order. Otto Michel, in his important volume on Paul,[32] concluded that no collections similar to Paul's *testimonia* lists or *florilegia* (e.g. Rom. 3.10–18; 9.25–29; 15.9–12) could be found in the Jewish tradition.[33] The publication of 4QTestim in 1956 raises in yet another way the intriguing relationship between Paul and the *yahad* of Qumran.

c. *Justification and the Law*

John Reumann, critical of my article, 'Justification and Last Judgment in Paul'[34], states that 'Rom 2.6–11 is not discussed' and, further, that my interpretation is 'open to a synergistic on the third use of the law...'[35] Given the dialectical relationship between justification and last judgment in Paul for which I had argued, these verses in Romans both support and augment that understanding of Paul. Paul writes in Rom. 2:

> [5]But by your hard and impenitent heart you are storing up wrath for yourself on the day of wrath, when God's righteous judgment will be revealed. [6]For he will repay according to each one's deeds: [7]to those who by patiently doing good seek for glory and honour and immortality, he will give eternal life; [8]while for those who are self-seeking and who obey not the truth but wickedness, there will be wrath and fury. [9]There will be anguish and distress for everyone who does evil, the Jew first and also the Greek, [10]but glory and honour and peace for everyone who does good, the Jew first and also the Greek. [11]For God shows no partiality.

29. Joseph A. Fitzmyer, 'Paul's Jewish Background and the Deeds of the Law', in *According to Paul: Studies in the Theology of the Apostle* (New York: Paulist, 1993), pp. 18–35, here pp. 29–31. See also J.A. Fitzmyer, 'The Use of Explicit Old Testament Quotations in Qumran Literature and in the New Testament', *NTS* 7 (1960–61), pp. 297–333.

30. Bruce M. Metzger, 'The Formulas Introducing Quotations of Scripture in the New Testament and the Mishnah', *JBL* 70 (1951), pp. 297–307.

31. Fitzmyer, 'Paul's Jewish Background', p. 31.

32. Otto Michel, *Paulus und seine Bibel* (Gütersloh: Bertelsmann, 1929).

33. Michel, *Bibel*, p. 43.

34. Karl P. Donfried, 'Justification and Last Judgment in Paul', in *Paul, Thessalonica and Early Christianity*, pp. 253–78. For a response to John Reumann and other critics, see 'Justification and Last Judgment in Paul – Twenty-Five Years Later', pp. 279–92 in the same volume.

35. John Reumann, *Righteousness in the New Testament* (Philadelphia: Fortress Press; New York: Paulist Press, 1982), p. 82 ref. 84.

With Käsemann[36] and others one must recognize that the judgment Paul refers to in vv. 3 and 5 needs to be understood in light of his teaching on justification by grace through faith. When the Apostle argues in v. 6 that 'he will repay according to each one's deeds (τὰ ἔργα αὐτοῦ)...', the specific reference to the 'good deeds' (ἔργου ἀγαθοῦ) that follow in v. 7 are correctly understood as the result and fruit of faith. This is the case not only here and in v. 10 (τῷ ἐργαζομένῳ τὸ ἀγαθόν), but also in 2 Cor. 9.8 ('And God is able to provide you with every blessing in abundance, so that by always having enough of everything, you may share abundantly in every good work [πᾶν ἔργον ἀγαθόν]'), and Phil. 1.6 ('I am confident of this, that the one who began a good work among you will bring it to completion by the day of Jesus Christ [ἔργον ἀγαθὸν]').

With regard to Rom. 2.1–11, Fitzmyer comments that the 'Jews are no exception to the teaching of Paul's gospel that no one comes to salvation without God's grace; no one comes to justification on the basis of deeds only'.[37] In v. 6, 'For he will repay according to each one's deeds', by his direct reference to Ps. 62.12 (LXX 61.13) and Prov. 24.12, Paul, according to Fitzmeyer, is challenging an established principle of Judaism. One might appropriately ask whether there were precedents within Judaism that encouraged Paul and allowed him to hold concurrently his assertions about justification by faith and judgment according to deeds? We have already suggested that Paul seems to be influenced by elements of thought that are found in the scrolls found at Qumran.[38] Might that be the case here as well? In v. 5 ('But by your hard and impenitent heart you are storing up wrath for yourself on the day of wrath, when God's righteous judgment will be revealed'), the term that Paul uses for 'God's righteous judgment', δικαιοκρισίας τοῦ θεοῦ, a term quite different from his earlier use of δικαιοσύνη γὰρ θεοῦ, has the sense of God's distributive justice. It has been suggested that the phrase is equivalent to משפטי צדק ('just judgments') in 1QH 1.23, 30.[39] Further, Fitzmyer suggests that the Pauline clause that follows in v. 6, 'For he will repay

36. Ernst Käsemann, *Commentary on Romans* (Grand Rapids: Eerdmans, 1980), p. 58.

37. Joseph Fitzmyer, *Romans: A New Translation with Introduction and Commentary* (AB 33; New York: Doubleday), pp. 297–8. Fitzmyer, in a longer comment, affirms the major perspective of my original article on 'Justification and Last Judgment'. Fitzmyer maintains that 'it is precisely the motif of God's judgment that must be retained for the sake of the message of justification by grace through faith. God has the right to judge the world and to recompense humanity according to its deeds. This Pauline message of judgment is what the Christian needs to hear first (see 3.6), and in the light of that message, the message of justification by grace through faith takes on new meaning. It is only in the light of divine judgment according to human deeds that the justification of the sinner by grace through faith is rightly seen. Hence there is no real inconsistency in Paul's teaching about justification by faith and judgment according to deeds. Judgment according to deeds may be a relic of Paul's Jewish background, but it has become an important and integral element in his teaching' (p. 307).

38. 'Paul and Qumran: The Possible Influence of סרך on 1 Thessalonians', in Karl P. Donfried, *Paul, Thessalonica and Early Christianity*, pp. 221–31.

39. Joseph A. Fitzmyer, 'Paul and the Dead Sea Scrolls', in *The Dead Sea Scrolls after Fifty Years* (vol. 2; ed. Peter W. Flint and James C. Vanderkam; Leiden: Brill, 1999), pp. 599–621, here p. 615.

according to each one's deeds', is remarkably close to כיא את אל משפט כול חי והואה ישלם לאיש גמולו ('for with God resides the judgment of all the living, and He shall pay each man his recompense') in 1QS 10.18.[40]

In this immediate as well as in intimately related contexts, it appears that the Qumran scrolls may be a tributary to Paul's theological reflection. One need only listen to the following texts:

As for me,
I belong to wicked mankind,
to the company of unjust flesh.
My iniquities, rebellions, and sins,
together with the perversity of my heart,
belong to the assembly of perverse flesh
and to those who walk in darkness.
For mankind has no way,
And man is unable to establish his steps
since judgment is with God
and perfection of way is out of His hand.
All things come to pass by His knowledge;
He establishes all things by His design
and without Him nothing is done.

As for me,
if I stumble, the mercies of God
shall be my eternal salvation.
If I stagger because of the sin of flesh,
my judgment shall be
by the righteousness of God which endures for ever.
When my distress is unleashed
He will deliver my soul from the Pit
and will direct my steps to the way.
He will draw me near by His grace,
and by His mercy will He bring my judgment.
He will judge me in the righteousness of His truth
and in the greatness of His goodness
He will pardon all my sins.
Through His righteousness he will cleanse me
of the uncleanness of man
and of the sins of the children of men,
that I may confess to God His righteousness,
and His majesty to the Most High'.
(1QS 11.9-15)[41]

'I lean on Thy grace
and on the multitude of Thy mercies,
for Thou wilt pardon iniquity,
and through Thy righteousness
[Thou wilt pardon man] of his sin.

40. Michael O. Wise, Martin G. Abegg, Jr. and Edward M. Cook (eds.), *The Dead Sea Scrolls: A New Translation* (San Francisco: Harper, 1996).

41. Geza Vermes, *The Complete Dead Sea Scrolls in English* (New York: Penguin, 1997) with modification.

> Not for his sake wilt Thou do it,
> [but for the sake of Thy glory].
> For Thou hast created the just and the wicked'.
> (1QH 11.36-40)[42]

The theme of human sinfulness and wickedness, the assertion that 'judgment shall be by the righteousness of God' and the emphasis on the mercy of a gracious God in whom human righteousness is rooted are remarkably analogous to Paul's teaching about justification by grace. A closer examination of this terminology is revealing. The term δικαιοσύνη θεοῦ, 'the righteousness of God', is used by Paul in Rom. 1.17, 3.5, 21, 22; 10.3; and 2 Cor. 5.21, often in close connection with his comments on justification. It is not insignificant that the exact phrase 'the righteousness of God' is not found in the Old Testament but that it is found in 1QM 4.6 as צדק אל and in 1QS 10.25 and 11.12 [צדקת אל]. This prior usage of the concept by the *yahad* would indicate that it is not a Pauline creation. Further, at the beginning of the passage cited above, 1QS 11.9 there is a striking parallel to Paul's use of σαρκὸς ἁμαρτίας ('sinful flesh'; Rom. 8.3) and בשר עול (perverse flesh).[43] Also related to Paul's negative meanings for σὰρξ ἁμαρτίας, as in Rom. 8.5-8, is עוון בשר, 'the sin of flesh' in 1QS 11.9 and 12.

This Qumran perspective, by its very clustering of these themes into a consistent unity, moves beyond the Old Testament.[44] It is indeed possible that the *yahad* prepared the way for Paul to reformulate these emphases based on his encounter with the Risen Christ (Gal. 1.15–16). There are, of course, obvious differences between Paul and the *yahad*, the most notable is the centrality of the death and resurrection of Jesus Christ in his theology. Because messiah has come, the righteousness of God has already been revealed. For the *yahad*, who are still waiting for messiah(s), their radicalized obedience to Torah suggests that such a manifestation of the righteousness of God still remains a future expectation and goal. Thus Fitzmyer correctly recognizes that this community's emphasis on the mercy and the righteousness of God 'is transitional, because it is not yet the full-blown idea of Pauline justification by *grace through faith*'.[45] For this reason one should also follow his lead in translating משפט as 'judgment' and not as 'justification'.[46] 'Judgment' allows Qumran to influence Paul's thinking without suggesting the closer approximation that 'justification' implies. This same situation of similarity and dissimilarity is evident in the common yet different use of Hab. 2.4 in the *yahad* and in Paul (Rom. 1.17). Although 1QpHab. 8.10 goes beyond the Old Testament by connecting the words of Habakkuk to a person, as does Paul, yet for the Apostle πίστις/אמונה is not simply fidelity to a person but it is faith in the Risen Christ (Rom. 10.9-10).

42. Vermes, *Complete Dead Sea Scrolls*, with slight alterations.
43. Translations by Wise, Abegg, Cook, *A New Translation.*
44. For example, righteous [צדק], sin [חטאת] and mercy [חסד].
45. Fitzmyer, 'Paul and the Dead Sea Scrolls', p. 604.
46. Against, for example, S. Schulz, 'Zur Rechtfertigung aus Gnaden in Qumran und bei Paulus', *ZTK* 56 (1959), pp. 155–85, and Vermes, *Complete Dead Sea Scrolls*.

d. *The Works of the Law*

The examples just cited have suggested a proximity to Paul's theological formulations. There is yet another term that Paul uses, ἔργα νόμου, ('deeds of the law'), that has been now found in the Qumran scrolls. This phrase, ἔργα νόμου, has no parallel in the Jewish Bible. Close, but not exact, is the use of the noun מעשה ('deed') in Exod. 18.20: 'teach them the statutes and instructions and make known to them the way they are to go and the deed they are to do'. Referring to similar ideas, Num. 15.39 and Deut. 16.12, 30.8 use alternative terms, מצוות ('commandments') and חוקים ('laws'). However, the precise parallel phrase to Paul's ἔργα νόμου is found in the Qumran texts. In 4QMMT C27 one reads מקצת מעשי התורה ('some deeds of the law'), in 4QMMT C 30–31 the emphasis falls on the correct practice of these deeds ('in your deed [בעשותך] you may be reckoned as righteous') and in 1QS 5.21 and 6.18 one finds the phrase מעשיו בתורה ('his deeds in the law'). It is not unimportant to recognize that while the *yahad* does not use the typical pharisaic language, חלקות or מצוות, yet even when it makes lists of *serakhim*, it appears to be fully aware of the pharisaic terminology in creating the clever and polemical turn of phrase, דרשי חלקות, 'seekers of smooth things' (4Q 169.3–4).[47]

How is מעשי התורה to be understood in the Scrolls? Baumgarten observes that in 1QS 6.18 'a novice in the community is examined 'as to his intelligence *uma'asaw batorah* (in his deeds of the torah)'. The covenanters are themselves called *'ose ha-torah*. It is apparent that the phrase refers to scrupulous observance of the Law and particularly to the study of the Law in accordance with sectarian principles'.[48] The emphasis here is that one should act according to the Law, viz., to observe and practice it. This appears to be a sharply different tendency from the pharisaic, rabbinic branch of Second Temple Judaism described by Talmon.[49] To whom is Paul reacting by the use of this terminology? Although criticizing the context in which the Law is practiced there is no suggestion whatsoever in the Pauline letters that he is, as a result of this disapproval, rejecting the Torah. Once that is recognized, greater attention needs to be given to Paul's particular perspective with regard to the practice of the Law, insights that are not to be found in his negative assertions but rather in those places where he actually affirms the practice of the Law, as, for example, in 1 Thess. 4.1-12.[50] Significant in this regard is the recognition that Paul's polemic against the 'deeds of the Law' is frequently found within a broader apologetic context as is the case in Rom. 3.31 ('Do we then overthrow the law by this faith? By no means! On the contrary, we

47. Throughout the scrolls there are other variations of the theme לעשות תורה which require a separate, fuller treatment. See also Schiffman's discussion of *serakhim* in *Reclaiming*, pp. 247, 275, 280–81.

48. J.M. Baumgarten, *Studies in Qumran Law* (Leiden: Brill, 1977), pp. 82–83.

49. It is imperative for an accurate 'mapping' of the Law in Second Temple Judaism to recognize that these two 'theologies' of the Law are so different that they are, in fact, in fundamental conflict. In addition to the foundational article by Talmon cited in n. 10, see further Schiffmann, *Reclaiming*, pp. 245–55.

50. See further Donfried, 'Paul and Qumran'.

uphold the law') and Rom. 7.12 ('So the law is holy, and the commandment is holy and just and good'). While the 'deeds of the Law' are not the basis of righteousness – for Paul only Christ is – that does not deny a positive function for the Law, properly understood, in the life of those who are 'in Christ'. And for that very reason justification and last judgment are intimately bound to one another in Pauline theology; once they are loosed from one another the thought of Paul is easily converted into a form of antinomianism.

e. *Repentence and Predestination*

Schwartz understands repentance as 'a sinner's decision to be perfect, no longer to sin'.[51] For Paul, as can be seen in Romans 7,

> successful repentance is at least something of a fiction. As much as one tries, one really never really succeeds; the next day, or the next Day of Atonement, there is always a need to repent again... Similarly, Qumran writers who continually demanded 'perfection of way' were led to conclude that man cannot save himself; 'Man's way is not his own, and man shall not prepare his own steps, for the judgment is God's and perfection of way is in His hands' (1QS 11.10–11), 'I know that righteousness is not for man, and perfection of way is not for the son of man; unto the Most High are all works of righteousness, and the way of man cannot be established unless God creates for him a spirit to make perfect the way of the sons of man' (1QH 4.30–32).[52]

Schwartz continues that for the rabbis, in contrast,

> what is important is not so much what really happens as the human decision to repent (just as human decisions of courts are granted supreme importance); if it doesn't work out, in the end, then one should try again... And regarding the latter, human sin, God was considered to have allowed man an efficacious method of settling his account and starting anew – repentance.[53]

Paul's lack of repentance language and his virtual omission of forgiveness rhetoric suggest commonalities with the *yahad.* How can this be explained? A closer examination of these phenomena might indicate a coherent deep structure that underlies these connections. Relevant to a more detailed examination would be both Paul's analysis of sin in Rom. 3 is echoed in 1QS 11.9–15 and 1QH 11.36–40[54] and the fact that atonement at Qumran can only be viewed in light of the *yahad's* doctrine of predestination. Here, again, with regard to atonement language, Paul is considerably closer to the view reflected in the Dead Sea Scrolls (e.g., 1QS 3.15–23) than to that of the Pharisaic tradition. Precisely the *yahad's* confidence in predestination, within a context of dualism, differentiates them from the other Judaisms of the day.[55] Those predestined for righteousness have been given the knowledge of God as one reads in 1QH: 'And I, through my understanding, have come to know You, my God, through the spirit which You

51. Donfried, 'Paul and Qumran', p. 239.
52. Donfried, 'Paul and Qumran', p. 239.
53. Schwartz, 'Law and Truth', p. 239.
54. See previous citation of these texts in main body of paper.
55. See further Jacob Licht, 'The Doctrine of the Thanksgiving Scroll', *IEJ* 6 (1956), pp. 1–13.

placed within me... In Your holy spirit You have [o]pened to me knowledge of the mystery of Your understanding'.[56] As a result of this knowledge, as a consequence of the gift of "the spirit of the counsel of the truth of God" (1QS 3.6–9) the elect or chosen of God 'can discern the correct path and follow the divine will.'[57]

As mentioned earlier, Paul explicitly refers to the Thessalonians as ἐκλογή (1 Thess. 1.4) and speaks of predestination in Rom. 8.28–30. He reminds the Thessalonians that they are 'taught by God' (θεοδίδακτος; 1 Thess. 4.9) and to the Christians in Rome he writes emphatically that the Spirit of Life has set them free from the law of sin and death (Rom. 8.1–8). And as a result 'you are not in the flesh; you are in the Spirit, since the Spirit of God dwells in you' (Rom. 8.9). For a community such as this, repentance and forgiveness language becomes superfluous. Paul, for example, is so confident that the Thessalonian Christians had been taught by God that he can assure them that, despite the hindrances created by Satan, they are his 'crown of boasting' at the coming of Jesus; 'yes, you are our glory and joy!' (1 Thess. 3.18–20). A comparison with 1QS 4.6–8 is instructive: 'And as for the visitation of all who walk in this spirit, it shall be healing, great peace in a long life, and fruitfulness, together with every everlasting blessing and eternal joy in life without end, a crown of glory (כליל כבוד) and a garment of majesty in unending light'.

f. *Realism and Authority*

In Schwartz's analysis of the difference between the realism of Qumran and the nominalism of the Rabbis he notes that

> my basic thesis is that there is a symmetry between the respective natures of priests and rabbis themselves, on the one hand, and the natures of their respective attitudes toward law, on the other. Priests (in Judaism) are created by God, or by nature, if you will, and seem typically to have ascribed great authority to God or nature in the legal process. Rabbis, in contrast, created themselves, and even prided themselves on the lack of importance of pedigree among them; it is noteworthy that their approach to law leaves God and nature on the sidelines, objects of debate but not participants in it. It is interesting to wonder whether other legal systems have similar correlations between the jurists' qualifications and their attitudes toward realism and nominalism.[58]

Or as he puts it elsewhere, for priests, 'their authority did not, in fact, depend upon the law... Sages and rabbis, on the other hand, had authority only through the law'.[59]

This evaluation would clearly put Paul on the side of Qumran and raises the question as to how he understood his own authority not only in his relationship to proclamation but also with regard to the Law. Two issues immediately come to the surface: Paul's understanding of his being chosen by God to be an apostle and his priestly role, especially as he refers to it in Rom. 15.16:

56. Translation Schiffman, *Reclaiming*, p. 152 (*Thanksgiving Hymns* 12.11–13).
57. Schiffman, *Reclaiming*, p. 152.
58. Schiffman, *Reclaiming*, p. 240.
59. Schiffman, *Reclaiming*, p. 237.

> Nevertheless on some points I have written to you rather boldly by way of reminder, because of the grace given me by God to be a minister of Christ Jesus to the Gentiles in the priestly service of the gospel of God, so that the offering of the Gentiles may be acceptable, sanctified by the Holy Spirit.

In particular, what does Paul intend when he writes to the Romans about his 'priestly service' (εἰς τὸ εἶναί με λειτουργὸν Χριστοῦ Ἰησοῦ εἰς τὰ ἔθνη, ἱερουργοῦντα τὸ εὐαγγέλιον τοῦ θεοῦ, ἵνα γένηται ἡ προσφορὰ τῶν ἐθνῶν εὐπρόσδεκτος, ἡγιασμένη ἐν πνεύματι ἁγίῳ)?

The term λειτουργία is used in a distinctly liturgical setting in Phil. 2.17: 'But even if I am being poured out as a libation over the sacrifice and the offering of your faith, I am glad and rejoice with all of you' (Ἀλλὰ εἰ καὶ σπένδομαι ἐπὶ τῇ θυσίᾳ καὶ λειτουργίᾳ τῆς πίστεως ὑμῶν, χαίρω καὶ συγχαίρω πᾶσιν ὑμῖν) and it would appear that Paul is, in Rom. 15, describing himself as being involved in a distinctly liturgical act, viz., preaching the Gospel to the Gentiles, and this coheres well with his formulation at the opening of Romans: 'For God, whom I worship (λατρεύω) with my spirit in the proclamation of the gospel of his Son…' (1.9). Fitzmyer is to be followed when he concludes that in 'his mission to the Gentiles Paul sees his function to be like that of a Jewish priest dedicated to the service of God in his Temple'.[60] It is likely that for Paul in this context ἱερουργέω means 'to function as a priest', and that the 'service of the priests in the Jerusalem Temple provides the background of Paul's metaphorical language…'[61] The act of worship in this priestly offering is not that of animals but of repentant Gentiles.

The question that faces the interpreter in such a discussion is whether Paul, as a Pharisee according to the law, could have easily adapted the sacrificial language of the Temple cult in such a metaphorical way or whether a closer proximity to concepts situated within the *yahad* are at play here, and, particularly, whether the Apostle to the Gentiles could view his communities in Christ as replacements for the Temple much as did the covenanters at Qumran?

g. *The Language of Temple Purity and Sanctification*

There is sufficient language in the Pauline letters to suggest that Paul viewed his communities as being replacements for the Temple, a phenomenon also unmistakably evident in the Qumran literature. A few examples must suffice.

Most striking is the reference that 'we are the temple of the living God' in the broader context of 2 Cor. 6.14–7.1:

> [14]Do not be mismatched with unbelievers. For what partnership is there between righteousness and lawlessness? Or what fellowship is there between light and darkness? [15]What agreement does Christ have with Beliar? Or what does a believer share with an unbeliever? [16]What agreement has the temple of God with idols? For we are the temple of the living God; as God said,

60. Fitzmyer, *Romans*, p. 711.
61. Fitzmyer, *Romans*, p. 711.

> 'I will live in them and walk among them,
> and I will be their God,
> and they shall be my people.
> [17]Therefore come out from them,
> and be separate from them, says the Lord,
> and touch nothing unclean (ἀκαθάρτου μη ἅπτεσθε);
> then I will welcome you,
> [18]and I will be your father,
> and you shall be my sons and daughters,
> says the Lord Almighty'.

> [7.1]Since we have these promises, beloved, let us cleanse ourselves from every defilement of body and of spirit, making holiness perfect in the fear of God (καθαρίσωμεν ἑαυτοὺς ἀπὸ παντὸς μολυσμοῦ σαρκὸς καὶ πνεύματος, ἐπιτελοῦντες ἁγιωσύνην ἐν φόβῳ θεοῦ)'.

Almost identical is the use of 'temple' language in 1 Cor. 3.16 and 6.19, particularly with the 'you' references in the plural. The former is especially instructive: 'Do you not know that you are God's temple and that God's Spirit dwells in you? If anyone destroys God's temple, God will destroy that person. For God's temple is holy, and you are that temple'. The application of this way of thinking can also be found in 1 Cor. 5.1–13. This replacement temple community cannot tolerate immorality since the impurity of one will defile the entire church. Since 'our paschal lamb, Christ, has been sacrificed', the 'festival', presumably the sacred meal of the community, must be celebrated not with the old yeast of malice and evil but 'with the unleavened bread of sincerity and truth'. So that this can happen Deut. 17.7 is invoked: 'Drive out the wicked person from among you'. The presence of God in this sacred community demands purity. Paul's 'rule' in 1 Thess. 4.1–9, as we have observed, contains similar themes, including this equivalent pattern of uncleanness/impurity being opposed by the concepts of sanctification/holiness.[62]

3. *Paul and the Essene Community: Possible Contacts*

All of these diverse observations would suggest the possibility that Paul the Jew may have had some contact with the Essene world of thought. How does one explain these commonalties between the apostle to the Gentiles and the *yahad* of Qumran? Critical is the question raised by Fitzmyer: 'Where and how would he [Paul] have come into contact with this non-Pharisaic Palestinian Judaism, which some of the items in his theological teaching echo?'[63] Is the specific terminology and the broader conceptual similarities between the two mediated through earliest Christianity or was the pre-Christian Paul already influenced by the prophetic movement of the *yahad*?

Since the Community of the Renewed Covenant had a settlement in Jerusalem (by the Essene gate in the south of the city) as well as attracting followers

62. Donfried, 'Paul and Qumran', pp. 227–30.
63. Joseph A. Fitzmyer, 'Paul's Jewish Background', p. 35.

throughout Palestine, contact between Paul and this movement is possible.[64] In my judgment the contact took place in Jerusalem at approximately the time that Paul studied at the Pharisaic בית מדרש. In Josephus' *Vita* he shares a desire not only to study the teachings of the Pharisees and Sadducees, but also those of the Essenes.[65] Would Paul, the inquisitive and highly intelligent 'graduate student' in Jerusalem, be any less motivated to be in dialogue with the teachings of the Community of the Renewed Covenant than Josephus? Such a question brings to the forefront the issue of the pluralistic environment of Jerusalem prior to the 'progressive unification'[66] of Palestinian Judaism under the guidance of the rabbinic scribes after 70 CE.

The exploration of Paul's thought in the context of a pluralistic pre-70 CE Judaism raises a series of profoundly important issues. Paul, for example, self-describes himself as a Pharisee and yet, as we have had repeated occasion to analyse, breaks with that tradition at key points. Was there a predisposition to do so well before his call from the Risen Jesus on the road to Damascus? Could he have received encouragement for such a receptiveness as the result of his contact with the prophetic movement of the Community of the Renewed Covenant? Talmon's creative work (1994) is suggestive. He describes the Community of the Renewed Covenant as

> a third- or second-century crystallization of a major socio-religious movement which arose in the early post-exilic Judaism... The development of the movement runs parallel to that of the competing rationalist stream which first surfaces in the book of Ezra, and especially in the book of Nehemiah, and will ultimately crystallize in Rabbinic or normative Judaism.[67]

And, he adds, that the '*yahad*'s final dissent from the emerging brand of Pharisaic Judaism at the turn of the era constitutes the climax of the lengthy confrontation of these two streams'.[68] Does Paul's contact with the *yahad* Community of the Renewed Covenant facilitate his own dissent from that form of Pharisaic Judaism which had shaped his own spirituality? Does these tensions within the Judaisms of his period predispose him toward the Jesus movement and its proposed solution to the very issues that had been and were still central to Paul's own religious struggle?

64. See the discussion in Bargil Pixner, 'Jerusalem's Essene Gateway – Where the Community Lived in Jesus' Time', *BAR* 23 (1997), pp. 22–66 and the further literature cited there.

65. Josephus, *Vita*, pp. 10–11.

66. For this phrase and a broader discussion of this theme see Martin Hengel, *The Pre-Christian Paul* (London: SCM Press, 1991), p. 44.

67. Talmon, 'The Community', p. 22.

68. Talmon, 'The Community', p. 22.

1 Cor. 8.1–6 as Part of the Controversy between Paul and the Parish in Corinth

Rudolf Hoppe

1. *Introduction*

In his contribution 'Einer ist Gott – Einer ist der Herr', O. Hofius rightly draws attention to the particular exegetical importance of 1 Cor. 8.6.[1] Recent commentaries on the first letter to the Corinthians have taken this into account, without exception meticulously analysing the verse in its context.[2] In his thorough and ground-breaking study on Paul's monotheism,[3] W. Schrage pointed out even more distinctly than in his previously-published major commentary on the same subject, 'wie sehr Paulus in seiner Stellungnahme ... der skizzierten jüdischen Position nahe ist, und zwar nicht nur in der immer schon gesehenen Bestimmung Gottes als schöpferischem Ursprung von allem und in seiner im Sinne der Schöpfungsmacht verstandenen Vaterschaft'.[4] With this comment Schrage names an important aspect which has by no means been lacking in the discussion so far but which has not yet received the necessary focus it deserves. For this reason, I wish to further explore this dimension of Paul's creation theology in his argumentation in 1 Cor. This requires presenting Paul and the Corinthian parish as 'dialogue partners' and laying out their positions clearly. Having done so, I wish to draw attention to what each party emphasizes in the discussion and to identify where the cause for dissent between Paul and the congregation ultimately resides.

1. O. Hofius, ' "Einer ist Gott' – "Einer ist Herr" ', in M. Evang, H. Merklein and M. Wolter (eds.), *Eschatologie und Schöpfung* (Festschrift E. Gräßer; *BZNW* 89; Berlin/New York: de Gruyter, 1997), pp. 95–108; see O. Hofius, 'Christus als Schöpfungsmittler und Erlösungsmittler – Das Bekenntnis 1 Kor 8,6 im Kontext der paulinischen Theologie', in U. Schnelle and T. Söding (eds.), *Paulinische Christologie* (Göttingen: Vandenhoeck & Ruprecht, 2000), pp. 47–58.

2. W. Schrage, *Der erste Brief an die Korinther*. 2. Teilband (EKK VII/2; Solothurn/Düsseldorf and Neukirchen–Vluyn: Beuzinger/Neukirchener, 1995), pp. 215–51; H. Merklein, *Der erste Brief an die Korinther. Kapitel 5,1–11,1* (ÖTK 7/2; Gütersloh-Würzburg: Gütersloher/Edder, 2000), pp. 172–205; C. Wolff, *Der erste Brief des Paulus an die Korinther* (ThHKNT 7; Leipzig: EVA, 1996), pp. 165–77; A. Lindemann, *Der erste Korintherbrief* (HNT 9/1; Tübingen: Mohr-Siebeck, 2000), pp. 186–93; G. D. Fee, *The First Epistle to the Corinthians* (NICNT; Grand Rapids, MI: Eerdmans, 1987), pp. 357–76. See also the analysis of A. Denaux, 'Theology and Christology in 1 Cor 8,4–6', in R. Bieringer (ed.), *The Corinthian Correspondence* (Leuven: Peeters, 1996), pp. 593–606.

3. W. Schrage, *Unterwegs zur Einheit und Einzigkeit Gottes* (BThS 48; Neukirchen–Vluyn: Neukirchener, 2002).

4. *Unterwegs* (n. 4), p. 68.

The catalyst for Paul's discussion with the Corinthians is the question of whether to eat food that has been sacrificed to idols. That is the *occasion*. Yet there is reason to assume that behind this problem there are much *deeper questions* of an anthropological and theological nature. Is it not surprising – perhaps maybe even disproportionately – that Paul reacts to these practical – if also materially important – difficulties of the parish (eating food sacrificed to idols) with such a densely-packed and complex theological-christological statement like the one in 8.6? The question then is what anthropological and theological perspectives are hidden within this one verse.

2. *The Arrangement of 1 Cor. 8.1–6*[5]

In 1 Cor. 8.1–13, Paul first addresses the congregation's sexual-ethics questions (6.12–20) and then turns to a second problem which has also arisen from the tension between liberty and responsibility in Corinth: whether it is permissible to eat food offered to idols. On the whole, we can divide the section 8.1–13 into two subjects: γνῶσις and monotheism on the one hand (8.1–7a) and the application of this discussion to the problem of eating food offered to idols (8.7b–13) on the other. The goal of the first chain of reasoning is the acclamatory hymnic confession in v. 6,[6] where Paul declares first of all the uniqueness of God and his activity as creator and then proclaims the uniqueness of the Kyrios Jesus connected with terms of his pre-existence and his role as mediator of creation. This hymnic confession certainly was appropriated from tradition.[7]

The arrangement of 1 Cor. 8.1–6 is clear. 8.1a names the practical problem at hand while 8.1b gives a provisional answer to the question which has been raised (γνῶσιν ἔχωμεν). This answer provides the key word for the further development of the argument. For the time being, the train of thought is completed with ἔγνωσται in v. 3. With περὶ v. 4a echoes the key word of v. 1a (περὶ δὲ), thus opening the argument anew. At the same time, the term εἰδωλόθυτα of v. 4 refers back to εἰδωλοθύτων in v. 1. The expression οἴδαμεν ὅτι in v. 4 serves its function of connecting back to v. 1 too. In this way, vv. 4–5 widen the scope of the previous knowledge-argument by connecting it with the monotheistic confession. With v. 6 this idea finally achieves its purpose in the aforementioned acclamatory hymn. The differentiation between vv. 1–3 and vv. 4–6 is confirmed on the

5. Compare for the structuring Schrage, *1 Kor II* (n. 2), pp. 225–26.

6. For classifying the form of 1 Cor. 8.6 see J. Habermann, *Präexistenzaussagen im Neuen Testament* (EHS XXIII/362; Frankfurt am Main: Lang, 1990), p. 161; Schrage *1 Kor II* (n. 2), pp. 221–25.

7. See Habermann, *Präexistenzaussagen* (n. 6), pp. 159–60. The following had already voted in a similar way at the beginning of the 20th century: J. Weiß, *Der erste Korintherbrief* (KEK 5; Göttingen: Vandenhoeck & Ruprecht, 5th edn, 1910; reprint 1970), p. 223; E. Norden, *Agnostos Theos* (Darmstadt: WBG, 5th edn, 1971), pp. 240–41. The supposition of the authorship of the acclamation by Paul himself (so for example W. Thüsing, *Per Christum in Deum – Studien zum Verhältnis von Christozentrik und Theozentrik in den paulinischen Hauptbriefen* [NTA NF, 1; Münster: Aschendorff 1965], pp. 225–32) did not achieve recognition. See also Hofius, 'Einer ist Gott' (n. 1), p. 103: 'für sich zu nehmende(s) Bekenntnis'. But see Denaux, *Theology* (n. 2), who adheres to Paul as author of 1 Cor. 8.6: '…which probably has been created by Paul himself' (p. 605).

syntactical level.[8] Verse 7 then picks up the discussion about the γνῶσις again and directs the train of thought towards the practical level of behaviour within the parish.

3. *The Corinthian Position and the Pauline Chain of Reasoning*

The *trigger* for Paul's discourse is the question of whether it is possible for a Christian to eat food offered to idols. On the one hand, Paul and the Corinthian groups with which he is in contact[9] seem not to differ in the concrete factual issue, but on the other hand, the paragraph, especially with regard to the γνῶσις-slogan of v. 1a, by no means lacks a polemical edge.

Concerning the problem to be treated here the key question is how to imagine the constellation between the Corinthian position and the Pauline chain of reasoning. For where Paul possibly quotes the Corinthians and where he speaks himself is a matter of dispute among researchers.[10] Yet a decision on this question has serious consequences for evaluating the whole text 8.1–13, especially as to where the dissent over eating offered meat actually lies. At first glance, the dissent seems to be minimal.

It is not difficult to reach a consensus on the slogan πάντες γνῶσιν ἔχομεν (v. 1b) going back to the Corinthian correspondents. As early an exegete as J. Weiß regarded v. 1b as Paul's quote of a Corinthian slogan[11] to which the apostle agreed in principle – yet not without immediately subverting it and putting it to the test with the criterion of ἀγάπη.

It is not so decisive whether Paul precisely 'quotes' the position of Corinthian groups; at any rate, the founder of the parish is describing a position expressed this way or similarly in Achaia. The slogan grants top-priority to γνῶσις, even awarding it soteriological qualities. For the Corinthians, the claim to γνῶσις has a similar function to πάντα μοι ἔξεστιν, which in 6.12 serves as the basis for the claim of individual liberty. As over against this understanding of γνῶσις, Paul insists on the criterium of ἀγάπη which is fundamental for his argument and which is not ecclesially- or socially-limited either.[12] At any rate, the Corinthians

8. See Merklein, *1 Kor II* (n. 2), pp. 175–76.

9. Probably it is not the whole parish, but the adversaries are the representatives of the intellectual members of the educated classes. We find a similar constellation in 1 Cor. 1-4 within the dispute about the cross and wisdom.

10. See Hofius, 'Einer ist Gott' (n. 1), p. 101 and Schrage, *1 Kor II* (n. 2), pp. 220–21.

11. *1 Kor* (n. 7), p. 214; see Schrage, *1 Kor II* (n. 2), pp. 220–21, who points out the tension in v. 7a; Wolff, *1 Kor* (n. 2), p. 168. Merklein, *1 Kor II* (n. 2), p. 179, supposes a connection between the representatives of this slogan and the followers of the 'Apollos-party', 'die sich die soteriologische Relevanz Christi unter dem Stichwort der 'Weisheit' anzueignen versuchte', but without determining a direct identification. However Paul's adversaries, who are behind 1 Cor. 8.1ff., do not join up their position in the christology, but mainly in the theology. Nevertheless the advice throws light on the question of communication.

12. Although οἰκοδομεῖν expresses the relationship to the community, Paul in fact understands the ἀγάπη in v. 3 theologically as love to God, and this in a very fundamental way. Surely the ἀγάπη in 1 Cor. 13.4 is of great significance for the internal conditions in the Corinthian parish (ἡ ἀγάπη οὐ φυσιοῖ in regard to 1 Cor. 12 and 1 Cor. 14).

must already have combined the γνῶσις-theme with the problem of the meat offered to idols, justifying their eating practices with the knowledge they claim for themselves. They understood their ethos – which in this question evidently was controversial in the parish – based on their self-conception as those in possession of γνῶσις and thus felt free in their actions.

Paul argues just as basically by strictly tying γνῶσις to the criterion of election by God and love for God. This is in line with the fact that the ἐγνωκέναι τι in v. 2a cannot be limited to the topic of food offered to idols although this meaning at best may also be intended at the same time.[13] In short: Paul's Corinthian dialogue partners claim for themselves knowledge with soteriological qualities; Paul also attaches high value to γνῶσις without question but measures it against the criterion of love.[14]

While the description of the Pauline and Corinthian positions in v. 1 is quite evident, it is much more difficult to determine where the Corinthians and Paul part ways in the development of their own thought. We can give the best reasons for the opinion, that with περὶ τῆς βρώσεως Paul takes up with v. 4a to v. 1a and subsequently (οἴδαμεν ὅτι) continues to recapitulate the Corinthian position.[15] It can be left open, however, whether it is a quotation from the Corinthian letter again, with which the corresponding circles in the parish legitimated their consumption of food offered to idols theologically.[16] Certainly, Paul here reproduces with this a Corinthian argument again, because the mentioned οἴδαμεν ὅτι alludes to the one at the beginning of v. 4.[17] With v. 5, it may be that Paul again continues the argumentation with a construction of position and counter-position. If this is correct, then the result would be the following constellation of arguments:

> Corinthian representatives of parish: πάντες γνῶσιν ἔχομεν
>
> Paul: ἡ γνῶσις φυσιοῖ, ἡ δὲ ἀγάπη οἰκοδομεῖ
>
> Corinthian representatives of parish: περὶ τῆς βρώσεως τῶν εἰδωλοθύτων, οἴδαμεν ὅτι οὐδὲν εἴδωλον ἐν κόσμῳ καὶ ὅτι οὐδὲν θεὸς εἰ μὴ εἷς
>
> Paul: καὶ γὰρ εἴπερ εἰσὶν λεμόμενοι θεοὶ εἴτε ἐν οὐρανῷ εἴτε ἐπὶ γῆς, ὥσπερ εἰσὶν θεοὶ πολλοὶ καὶ κύριοι πολλοί, ἀλλ' ἡμῖν εἷς θεὸς ὁ πατὴρ ἐξ οὗ τὰ πάντα καὶ ἡμεῖς εἰς αὐτόν, καὶ εἷς κύριος Ἰησοῦς Χριστὸς δι' οὗ τὰ πάντα καὶ ἡμεῖς δι' αὐτοῦ.

13. See Schrage, *1 Kor. II* (n. 2), p. 232: 'mit anvisiert sein'.

14. See also 1 Cor. 13.4: ἡ ἀγάπη ... οὐ φυσιοῦται.

15. See Schrage, *1 Kor. II* (n. 2), pp. 220f; Wolff, *1 Kor.* (n. 2), pp. 168–69.

16. This is the position of Schrage, *Unterwegs* (n. 3), p. 68; *1 Kor. II* (n. 2), p. 221 (with the supposition of οὐδὲν εἴδωλον ἐν τῷ κόσμῳ and οὐδεὶς θεὸς εἰ μὴ εἷς being constituents of the Corinthian phraseology); see also Merklein, *1 Kor. II* (n. 2), p. 185; Wolff, *1 Kor.* (n. 2), p. 171; already Weiß, *1 Kor.* (n. 7), p. 219, had seen the tension between V. 4a und 4b ('Diese Auffassung [the whole rejecting an existence of gods] wird nun durch die Formulierung in V. 4a nicht völlig gedeckt') and consequently denied the Pauline authorship of the phraseology.

17. See οἴδαμεν in v. 1b; there it is most probably the introduction to the quotation.

That means the following: Paul reproduces two Corinthian formulas (v. 1.4), word-for-word or paraphrasing,[18] and in each case he challenges them with his own responses (vv. 2–3 and vv. 5–6) because he considers the Corinthians arguments as deficient. Given the parallelism of thesis and counter-thesis, it is most likely that these two Pauline positions are counter-positions against Corinthian slogans. Not only in the first case, but also in the second case (vv. 5–6) the same may be true.[19] To justify this thesis, we must clarify where Paul believes the deficits of the Corinthians arguments are to be found, particularly in the second case.[20]

In reconstructing the positions of both sides, O. Hofius chooses a completely different approach in reference to G. Heinrici. He ascribes the whole of vv. 4–6 to the Corinthian circles[21] and argues that in v. 7a (ἀλλ' οὐκ ἐν πᾶσιν ἡ γνῶσις) Paul is alluding to the Corinthian position and giving only a cautionary correction: 'Das Problem, auf das der Apostel eindringlich hinweist, liegt vielmehr einzig darin, ob diese Erkenntnis bereits für einen jeden Christen zum festen inneren Besitz geworden ist.'[22] Against such a summary of the conflict, however, significant objections may be raised. Schrage rightly indicates that such a quotation was uncommonly long and furthermore would have conflicted with the Corinthian 'realized eschatology'.[23]

In addition to this, two aspects speak against the proposal of Hofius. First, if vv. 4–6 are being collectively ascribed to the Corinthians, we must suppose that Paul – with the confessions in v. 4 and v. 6 as well as the limitation of v. 5 – was quoting or at least cross-referencing the Corinthians. But since the acclamation in v. 6 comes neither from the Corinthians nor from Paul, we should have to assume that Paul has reproduced a counter-position with a quotation, which belongs to it. But it would be singular for Paul to have cross-referenced such a counter-position together with its argument-base received from the parish-tradition. If it actually were so, the response with ἀλλ' οὐκ ἐν πᾶσιν ἡ γνῶσις would be very general and using little in the way of reasoned arguments. It is hardly possible to verify

18. Even though Paul does not quote the Corinthians verbatim in v. 4, he reports the argumentation by its central utterance.

19. Here I differ from most authors.

20. Most authors assume that vv. 5–6 continue the Pauline position. They suspect that the Pauline speech at best tones down the Corinthians' exaggerated confession and makes concessions to the real experiences of the community. This supposed, we would have to imagine that Paul does approach a step closer to the Corinthians and adopts the tradition, emphasizing the confession of monotheism, but interpreting it christologically. See Schrage, *1 Kor. II* (n. 2), p. 221; *Unterwegs* (n. 3), pp. 68–69; Wolff, *1 Kor.* (n. 2), pp. 171–72; H.J. Klauck, *1. Korintherbrief* (NEB 7; Würzburg: Echter, 2nd edn, 1987), p. 60; Merklein, *1 Kor. II* (n. 2), pp. 183–85; see also Weiß, *1 Kor.* (n. 7), pp. 219–20.

21. Hofius, 'Einer ist Gott' (n. 1), pp. 99–101; see Hofius, 'Schöpfungsmittler' (n. 1), p. 47; already G. Heinrici, *Der erste Brief an die Korinther* (KEK 5; Göttingen: Vandenhoeck & Ruprecht, 8th edn, 1896), p. 230, had interpreted vv. 4–6 as one comment.

22. Hofius, 'Einer ist Gott' (n. 1), p. 100.

23. *Unterwegs* (n. 3), p. 69 n. 160. Hofius, 'Einer ist Gott' (n. 1), p. 100 n. 21, substantiates his thesis grammatically, arguing that with καὶ γάρ can 'schlechterdings keine Richtigstellung oder Einschränkung eingeführt werden'. But Schrage, *Unterwegs* (n. 3), p. 69 n. 160, is able to give reasons for καὶ γάρ followed by ἀλλά in the sense of 'denn freilich' (referring to Bauer-Aland, *Wörterbuch zum Neuen Testament*, p. 798).

such a course of events. On the contrary, it is much more evident that Paul for his part is trying to convince using knowledge about tradition instead.[24]

Secondly and lastly, it is to be considered with respect to the content: If it is singular even for Paul to connect christological pre-existence-utterance and mediatorship of creation-utterance,[25] it is hardly conceivable that the Corinthian circles would have justified their γνῶσις according to a 'theology of creation' (or better a 'christology of creation'). We will see in fact that the relationship to creation is precisely the crucial area of dissent existing between Paul and the Corinthians (1 Cor. 1.18–25; 15).[26]

Hofius' reconstruction of the communication between Paul and the Corinthians is scarcely convincing. It can be assumed that the Corinthians, in addition to their γνῶσις-argument, justified eating food offered to idols based on their strict monotheism. In doing so, they could well have combined their monotheistic–philosophical image of God with the biblical monotheism of Deut. 6.4. Behind οὐδὲν θεὸς εἰ μὴ εἷς there is with no doubt the *sh^ema* of the Jewish tradition. When the Corinthian circles refer to Deut. 6.4 in their confession, they do so only for the εἷς θεός-statement excluding other gods, but not for the aspect of the love of God that belongs to Deut. 6.4 as well.

Most importantly, however, they have removed from their confession the creator-theme, which was characteristic – especially in connection with prophetic monotheism[27] – for the Hellenistic diaspora-Judaism.[28] Here is the crucial cause of dissent between the two confessions in 1 Cor. 8.4 and 1 Cor. 8.6 which makes it plausible to assign v. 4 to the Corinthians, but v. 6 to Paul, or rather to a tradition which he consciously assimilated.

4. *The Pauline Counter-Position in Verses 1b-3 and 5-6*

It is evident that in vv. 1b–3 Paul challenges the basic principles of the Corinthians' assertion. If we may presume that the Corinthian message to Paul comprised the emphatically represented conviction of their own γνῶσις and the avowal of the uniqueness of God in order to draw conclusions for individual freedom with regard to eating food sacrified to idols, then this context is the entity of

24. It is possible to find similar examples of quoting the early Christian Easter confession 1 Cor. 15.3–5 (in connection with denying of the resurrection) and the tradition of the Lord's Supper 1 Cor. 11.23–26 (in regard to the Corinthian misdoings at the eucharist). We encounter here the apostle's strategic and pragmatic attempts to convince the other side of his own point of view in a conflict, while looking for a consensus argued from the tradition that is shared by both sides.

25. That is at least *one* argument for the supposition of a tradition handed down; but the model of interpretation of the creation is accommodated by Paul.

26. See P. Lampe, *Ad Ecclesiae Unitatem. Eine exegetisch-theologische und sozialpsychologische Paulusstudie* (Habil.masch.; Bern: Evang.-Theol. Fakultät, 1989), p. 40; R. Hoppe, *Der Triumph des Kreuzes. Studien zum Verhältnis des Kolosserbriefs zur paulinischen Kreuzestheologie* (SBB, 28; Stuttgart: Kath. Bibelwerk, 1994), pp. 59–60.

27. Jes 45,6 (LXX): ὅτι οὐκ ἔστιν πλὴν ἐμοῦ ... ἐγὼ κύριος ὁ θεὸς ὁ ποιῶν ταῦτα πάντα.

28. See Habermann (n. 6), pp. 163f; G. Delling, *ΜΟΝΟΣ ΘΕΟΣ: Studien zum Neuen Testament und zum hellenistischen Judentum. Gesammelte Aufsätze 1950–1968* (Göttingen: Vandenhoeck & Ruprecht, 1970), pp. 391–400.

argumentation to which Paul has to respond. So if the Corinthian theses of v. 1a and v. 4 are to be seen together, this applies also to the Pauline reply. Therefore, Paul responds to both aspects with the keyword γνῶσις in vv. 1–3 and in his interpretation of the monotheistic avowal in v. 5 and v. 6. If this is evident, it is consequently not possible to assume a brusque antithesis in vv. 1b–3, but to see in vv. 5–6 a nearly consensus-statement by Paul with only a slight correction.

5. *The Pauline Antithesis in Verses 1b–3 and Verses 5–6*

Obviously, in Paul's opinion the statement of the Corinthians should be taken with a large pinch of salt in their self-assurance. We may suppose that the Corinthian statement to Paul included the firmly supported conviction of their own γνῶσις together with the profession that there is only one God as grounds for the conclusion of individual freedom in eating food sacrificed to idols. This is the context and background of argumentation, to which Paul has to respond. If the assumption of conjuction between v. 1a and v. 4 is correct, then it suggests a correlation between Paul's responses in vv. 1b–3 and vv. 5–6. Paul then reacts to both aspects with the cue γνῶσις in vv. 1–3 and his interpretation of the profession of monotheism in v. 5 and v. 6. If that is so, it is not possible to suppose in vv. 1b–3 a curt antithesis, while declaring nearly a consensus of Paul with the Corinthians with only insignificant corrections in vv. 5–6.[29]

In vv. 1b–3 Paul not only makes a correction of the Corinthian standpoint, but he almost turns the question upside down. The pointed theological articulation of the questionability of the γνῶσις is a reaction to both arguments 'knowledge' and 'monotheism': 'knowledge' is for Paul always firstly an acknowledgement of God. Especially if we connect the monotheistic profession of the Corinthians with the basic idea of Deut. 6.4, we have to suppose that the Corinthians did know Deut. 6.5 as well.[30] This correlation is obviously ignored by the interlocutors of Paul. For Paul the first question is not the 'knowledge', that there is only one God and there exist no idols. Important for him is only human subordination under God and acknowledgement of God as God, resulting from the γνῶσις. With this position Paul has at least indirectly introduced already in his first reply to the Corinthian argumentation the thought that we are all God's creatures.

6. *Corinthian and Pauline Monotheism*

With that we have to ask the question concerning the acclamation for itself and its correcting function, for this is the decisive 'more' in the strategy of the Pauline dialogue, to prove the deficiencies in the Corinthian concept of God. It is an acclamation with a character of a profession.[31] Formally, the profession is a *parallelismus membrorum*, developed in two lines:

29. This impression one gets from most publications; see e.g. Merklein, *1 Kor. II* (n. 2), p. 189.

30. καὶ ἀγαπήσεις τὸν θεόν σου...

31. See Habermann, *Präexistenzaussagen* (n. 6), p. 162; K. Wengst, *Christologische Formeln und Lieder des Urchristentums* (StNT 7; Gütersloh: Gerd Mohn, 1972), pp. 136–43.

ἀλλ᾽ ἡμῖν
εἷς θεὸς ὁ πατὴρ
ἐξ οὗ τὰ πάντα
καὶ ἡμεῖς εἰς αὐτόν,
καὶ εἷς κύριος Ἰησοῦς Χριστὸς
δι᾽ οὗ τὰ πάντα
καὶ ἡμεῖς δι᾽ αὐτοῦ.[32]

It is not possible to distinguish within the acclamation its basic form and expanded text, for the individual lines are related constitutively to one another: v. 6 is to be judged as a literary unity.[33] Only the beginning ἀλλ᾽ ἡμῖν was presumably added by Paul himself. With this beginning he emphasizes the community character of the profession. This relation to the community was already constitutive for the tradition, as the ἡμῖν and the ἡμεῖς in v. 6a.b.d indicate. The confession of the one God is a confession by believers, not a generalizing opinion. Therefore one should translate: 'For *us* is (in contrast to others)'.[34] This interpretation is supported by the preceding sentence, with which Paul – as is known – did not deny the existence of gods and κύριοι generally, but the importance of them for the believers in the Christian community. The 'one God' is an expression of faith from the Jewish and Christian point of view.

A different opinion is held by Hofius, who sees the dative as a *'dativus iudicantis'* and translates 'nach unserem Urteil'.[35] In this translation the sentence would have an objectified general character, but this does not lie in the intention of the context.[36] Paul gives an account of the consent of the believers and talks about the exclusive importance of the one God for the community. Therefore for the Corinthians the gods of the world (ἐν κόσμῳ[!]) are not important at all.

32. The graphical display of the text is adopted from Lindemann, *1 Kor.* (n. 2), p. 189; see also the text-presentations in *Novum Testamentum Graece* (Aland[27]) and in Hofius, 'Einer ist Gott' (n. 1), p. 103; Hofius, *Schöpfungsmittler* (n. 1), p. 48.

33. See also Habermann, *Präexistenzaussagen* (n. 6), p. 160, and his extensive references to the history of research (see pp. 172–77).

34. See Schrage, *1 Kor. II* (n. 2), p. 216: 'so ist doch für uns…', similarly Merklein, *1 Kor. II* (n. 2), p. 173; see also M. Hengel, 'Präexistenz bei Paulus?', in C. Landmesser, H.-J. Eckstein and H. Lichtenberger (eds.), *Jesus Christus als die Mitte der Schrift. Studien zur Hermeneutik des Evangeliums* (BZNW, 86; Berlin/New York: de Gruyter, 1997), p. 496 ('…spricht Paulus freilich nicht vom Sohn, sondern vom Kyrios, weil unmittelbar zuvor von den vielen Göttern und Kyrioi im weiten Raum von Himmel und Erde die Rede war, für die die Gemeinde – ἀλλ᾽ ἡμῖν – durch den einen Gott, der durch den einen Kyrios handelt, entmächtigt sind').

35. See Hofius, 'Einer ist Gott' (n. 1), pp. 102–103; see also Hofius, 'Schöpfungsmittler' (n. 1), p. 47.

36. The arguments which Hofius gives from the classical Greek ('Einer ist Gott' [n. 1]), p. 102, can hardly bear the burden of proof, for in *Soph Ai* and *Eur Med 580f* it is a question of a group-internal and subjective valuation, but not of a objectifying judgment. Against that, in favour of the confessional-subjective meaning, Schrage, *Unterwegs* (n. 3), p. 75, can refer to Jdt. 8.20 and Jub. 12.19; although in Jdt. 8.20 there is not a dative-construction as in 1 Cor. 8.6. An applicable line parallel to 1 Cor. 1.30 can be drawn with the preceding context 1.18–29: after Paul has spoken about the cross of Christ and the election of Christians by God – only offensive for the non-Christian world – the apostle concludes, 'for God has made him our wisdom; he is our righteousness; in him we are consecrated and set free'. That means that for the believers (ἡμῖν) Christ is the wisdom of God.

Irrespective of whether we understand the ἡμῖν in the way proposed here or follow the views of Hofius, it has a soteriological sense.[37]

7. *God as Creator*

If Paul receives the profession 1 Cor. 8.6 from his tradition and takes the avowal up, he adopts it and tries to have a correcting effect on the Corinthians with the εἷς θεός/εἷς κύριος-formula. In the pre-Pauline tradition the profession of monotheism would be first interpreted with the idea of God as Creator.[38] This characterization was lacking in the language of the Corinthian confession of the one God (v. 4), *for Paul, however, it has a central importance.* For with this interpretation it is possible for him to take up the anthropological aspect of creation and his definition of γνῶσις as appreciation of God as God or love to God in v. 3. Thus it is possible for Paul to argue theo-logically in the narrow sense and so to uncover the trouble area which is obviously not easy for the Corinthians to respond to. It is no accident that it was lacking in the Corinthian profession of the one God. To understand the constitution of man as creature constructively and to realize humankind in its continuing un-redeemed reality, that is a characteristic Corinthian problem. 1 Cor. 1.21 together with Rom. 1.18ff. provides us with illustrative material here.

1 Cor. 1.21 interprets the knowledge of God as acknowledgement, which is confiding in God. Rom. 1.18ff. places this confiding acknowledgement into the sphere of tension between the divine provision of the knowledge of God and the creature, which itself denies God. God answered to the human attempt to make God available in the paradox way of the cross of Jesus.[39] That God is the creator-God and that human beings owe their salvation to the creator and should accept their still incomplete nature and life reality, that is the truth that goes against the grain of the Corinthians and their self-assurance. Paul already had this fact in mind anthropologically in v. 4, and now he explains it theologically through the paternity of God.

The idea, that the Father-God is the creator, the creator of the universe or the father of the cosmos, is predetermined by hellenistic Judaism (Philo, Wisdom). But the formula with its eschatological orientation on those who believe in God, goes considerably beyond this Jewish-Hellenistic religious knowledge and so it shifts the emphasis from the cosmic reference to the human beings.[40] Here Paul

37. Otherwise see Lindemann, *1 Kor.*, p. 192, following H. Hübner, *Biblische Theologie des Neuen Testaments II* (Göttingen: Vandenhoeck & Ruprecht, 1993), p. 156 ('als Ausdruck existenzialen Denkens') and R. Bultmann, *Theologie des Neuen Testaments* (UTB, p. 630; Tübingen: Mohr-Siebeck, 9th edn, 1984), p. 229.

38. See Habermann, *Präexistenzaussagen* (n. 6), pp. 162–71; see also T. Söding, 'Gottes Sohn von Anfang an', in R. Laufen (ed.), *Gottes ewiger Sohn. Die Präexistenz Christi* (Paderborn: Schöningh, 1997), pp. 57–93.63.

39. See Lampe, 'Ad Unitatem' (n. 26), pp. 50–52; Hoppe, 'Triumph' (n. 26), pp. 58–62.

40. See A. Vögtle, *Das Neue Testament und die Zukunft des Kosmos* (Düsseldorf: Patmos, 1970), pp. 169–70. Söding, 'Gottes Sohn' (n. 38), p. 64 n. 33, misunderstands Vögtle saying in regard to Vögtle, that he (Vögtle) disputes a creation-related message (stellt 'in Abrede'). Vögtle only denies

applies his alternative point of view to the argumentation of the Corinthians: he confronts the soteriological interpretation of the γνῶσις with the eschatological orientation of the faithful. The defiance of the theological statement of the Corinthians therefore consists in a reflection of the sphere of tension between creation and eschatology.

8. *The Kyrios and Mediator of Creation*

More than ever now, the christological statement about the κύριος Ἰησοῦς, his pre-existence, his function as mediator of creation and as redeemer go beyond the Corinthian avowal of v. 4. Even if the acclamation is to be classified as an integrated literary whole and one is to assume that it was created as a whole, it has to be noted that christology (εἷς κύριος Ἰησοῦς Χριστός) is *attributed* to theology (εἷς θεὸς ὁ πατήρ), and not vice versa.[41] The objective priority has the εἷς θεός-denomination.[42] In the acclamation the christological κύριος-statement has an interpreting and determining function; God and Christ do not stand on the same level of significance. Through the theological knowledge the acclamation attempts to specify the idea of God, but at the same time it aims to define the serious role of Jesus in the relationship between God and the faithful through the christological interpretation. Just as fundamental as the fact that there is only one God is the fact that there is only one Christ, particularly functioning as the mediator of creation and redeemer.[43]

Through these two interpretations, in particular, the acclamation makes it clear that it conforms to the Jewish, more precisely to the Jewish-Hellenistic tradition. The primary accent therefore lies on these interpretations of Christ. The pre-existence is assumed, but it is not further emphasized as a central theme.[44] The significance of the avowal does not lie in the pre-existence, but in the mediatorship of creation and the eschatological orientation.[45]

The *leitmotif* of the mediator of creation is widely attested in the biblical tradition and Jewish literature outside the Bible: in the Hebrew Bible (Prov. 8.22ff.), in the LXX (Wis. 7.22; 9.1) and also in Philo.[46] Philo transmits the motif of the

that the creation in a salvation-history meaning becomes a New Creation because of the salvation of the believers (see 170: 'V. 6a will also doch wohl besagen: Gott der Vater ist der Schöpfer aller Dinge, und auch wir existieren, um ihm zu dienen und in ihm unser Ziel zu erreichen').

41. See Habermann, *Präexistenzaussagen* (n. 6), p. 171: 'Christus hat nur eine vermittelnde Funktion. Die Theologie umklammert die Christologie und bildet ihren Rahmen'.

42. Hofius can balance the distinction between God and the Kyrios Jesus only in identifying the determination of the father as father of Jesus Christ ('Einer ist Gott' [n. 1], pp. 105–106) and in connecting the christological interpretation with a son-of-God-christology, which is not to be founded in the text.

43. Διά has a soteriological meaning, see Schrage, *1 Kor. II* (n. 2), p. 244 n.197.

44. With regards to the Jewish context of the pre-existence interpretation see G. Schimanowski, 'Die frühjüdischen Voraussetzungen der urchristlichen Präexistenzchristologie', in *Gottes ewiger Sohn* (n. 38), pp. 31–55.

45. See n. 39.

46. Lit.: H. Hegermann, *Die Vorstellung vom Schöpfungsmittler im hellenistischen Judentum und*

mediator of creation both to σοφία and to λόγος. But while the σοφία is generally a transcendent idea dwelling at the side of God,[47] the λόγος faces towards the world. It has a particular function of holding up, represents God's devotion to the world, is the place of human experience with God despite the non-recognizability of his being (*det* 54). In the function of the δύναμις of God the λόγος is world-nourishing and world-directing and as a mediator of creation establishes the relationship between God and the world: in all *III*,96 the λόγος is instrument (ὄργανον) in God's creation, his image and therefore a model of human beings. As God's instrument it indubitably stands opposite the world and human beings, but as a link between God and the world it enables human beings for transcendental orientation to God (*Adv. Haer.* 230[48]). In addition to its cooperation at the creation the λόγος has the particular function of cohesion between God and the world. In *Migr.* 6–7 in the interpretation of Gen. 12.1–6 Abraham is advised to transcend the earthly,[49] but that is not tantamount to parting from the character of the world (*Migr.* 7). Rather it is demanded that he should be above it all and come via self-knowledge to the knowledge of whom it is necessary to follow (*Migr.* 8). Being unambigously differentiated from God, the mediator of creation has at all events the task of holding up the relationship between God and the world, of assuring the world of its transcendental orientation from God. The mediator of creation therefore has first and foremost the enabling function, on the one hand to conceive God as superior counterpart to the world, but on the other hand also to perceive and to realize his closeness to the world. For the utterance of the mediator of creation it is a matter of the relationship of God to humankind and vice versa. If these relations are left out of the idea of God, any eschatological perspective will disappear as well. The result would then be the 'philosophical monotheism', which the Corinthians know from their Hellenistic tradition,[50] but which falls short of the Jewish tradition, by which the Judaism left its indelible mark on the image of God.

9. *Consequences*

If one examines the differences between the Pauline and the Corinthian argumentation, it becomes clear that parting of the ways comes at the *creation-theology*.

Urchristentum (TU 82; Berlin: Akademie-Verl., 1961), H.F. Weiss, *Untersuchungen zur Kosmologie des palästinischen und hellenistischen Judentums* (Berlin: Akademie-Verl., 1966), pp. 181–211; B.L. Mack, *Logos und Sophia. Untersuchungen zur Weisheitstheologie im hellenistischen Judentum* (StUNT, 10; Göttingen: Vandenhoeck & Ruprecht, 1973), pp. 144–47; Hoppe, 'Triumph' (n. 27), pp. 167–75; Schrage, *Unterwegs* (n. 3), pp. 106–11.

47. See R. Hoppe, Art. Logos: NBL II (1995), pp. 659–66; Mack, *Logos* (n. 45).

48. There the λόγος has – without the function of mediator of the creation – the purpose of model for human beings.

49. In the allegorical interpretation Abraham is synonymous with the soul.

50. See to the hellenistic context of 1 Cor. 8.6 D. Zeller, 'Der eine Gott und der eine Herr Jesus Christus. Religionsgeschichtliche Überlegungen', in T. Söding (ed.), *Der lebendige Gott* (Festschrift Wilhelm Thüsing; NTA, 31; Münster: Aschendorff, 1996), pp. 34–58.

On the one hand there is the claim of γνῶσις, justified by the monotheistic avowal which – despite the adoption of Deut. 6.4 (LXX) – is moving in the Hellenistic sphere, on the other hand God as Creator and Christ as mediator of creation. That leads to the conclusion that Paul and the Corinthians disagreed in the crucial question: they shared the principal conviction that eating food offered to idols did not have to be taboo. Their ways part at the reasons for this: the Corinthians give as reasons for the γνῶσις and intellectual monotheism their *being* redeemed and therefore their individual freedom from the false gods. Paul reckons in his comprehension of God and his interpretation of Christ with humankind as created beings, and is also able to comprehend it constructively. In the acknowledgement of God and the orientation towards him, he is able to handle the question of eating food offered to idols more flexibly, more pragmatically and with social consideration. To a greater degree than the Corinthian representatives, Paul has a positive relationship to the reality of creation, because the interpretation of Christ as mediator of creation is an essential component of his christological message. The Corinthians' theoretical monotheism, which is lacking any specification, is overcome by an essential line in Paul's theology.[51]

51. With my reflections I thank Petr Pokorný for his existential striving for the sense of the biblical texts and his most important contributions to the exegesis of the New Testament. I thank Petr Pokorný too for his hospitality in Prague at his home over the last ten years. Ad multos annos! – For help in translating the German text I thank Jennifer Adams and Daniela Elter, students in Bonn, Germany.

Christ in Paul: The Apostle Paul's Relation to Christ Viewed Through Gal. 2.20a

Ladislav Tichý

Among all the New Testament authors it is undoubtedly the apostle Paul who expresses his close relation to Christ in a particularly impressive manner. One of the most powerful formulations are his words in Gal. 2.20a: ζῶ δὲ οὐκέτι ἐγώ ζῇ δὲ ἐν ἐμοὶ Χριστός. This assertion is certainly not isolated, it has numerous parallels in Paul and in the remaining New Testament. Primarily, we have several examples of the same grammatical construction (Christ or Jesus lives, abides, takes form, etc. in his faithful) in Paul (cf. 2 Cor. 13.5; Rom. 8.10; Gal. 4.19), in the Deutero-Pauline letters (cf. Col. 1.27; Eph. 3.16–19) and also elsewhere in the New Testament, esp. in John (cf. Jn 6.56; 17.23). However, the opposite construction (with 'Christ' or the 'Lord' as the object after the preposition ἐν) is much more frequent (about 165 times in Paul's letters apart from the Pastorals[1] and about 100 times in the undisputed letters of Paul,[2] not counting the passages in other New Testament books). In addition, there are also collocations with 'Spirit', either in the same perspective as Gal. 2.20a (the Spirit [of God] dwells or is active in the believers [Rom. 5.5; 8.9, 11, 15, 16, 23, 26; cf. Gal. 4.6]), or their opposites where Paul speaks of the believer's life or existence 'in (the) Spirit' (e.g. Rom. 8.9; 1 Cor. 12.3).

Does Gal. 2.20a represent only 'the other side of the equation',[3] the first side of which are Paul's ἐν κυρίῳ-formulations? Does this passage mean for Paul only the same experience that he expresses e.g. Rom. 8.9 by 'the Spirit of God dwells in you'?[4] Or can we see and find in Gal. 2.20a something more? Before we can answer these questions we must analyse Gal. 2.20a in its context. And before we can arrive at a conclusion, it will be useful to compare and evaluate other, both Pauline and non-Pauline, passages expressing the conviction that Christ dwells in those who belong to him.

1. Cf. R.N. Longenecker, *Galatians* (Word Biblical Commentary, 41, Dallas, TX: Word Books, 1990), p. 93 ('164 times'); J.A. Fitzmyer, 'Pauline Theology', in R.E. Brown *et al.* (eds.), *The New Jerome Biblical Commentary* (London: G. Chapman, 1991), pp. 1382–1416 (1409: '165 times').

2. Cf. M. Ryšková, *Jetzt gibt es keine Verurteilung mehr für die, welche in Christus Jesus sind* (St. Ottilien: EOS, 1994), p. 15.

3. Cf. Longenecker, *Galatians*.

4. Cf. E. de W. Burton, *A Critical and Exegetical Commentary on the Epistle to the Galatians* (International Critical Commentary; Edinburgh: T&T Clark, 1921), p. 137; also J.D.G. Dunn, *A Commentary on the Epistle to the Galatians* (London: A. & C. Black, 1993), p. 145.

1. *Gal. 2.20a in its context*

The fundamental significance of our phrase is already given by its presence in Paul's theologically very important epistle to the Galatians. The closer context only underscores the importance of this passage. Delimitation of this context, however, is not unanimous. Some commentators take Gal. 2.11–21 as one unit.[5] But most authors distinguish in this text two separate pericopes: 2.11–14 and 2.15–21.[6] In 2.11–14 Paul narrates his conflict with Peter at Antioch in Syria. Verses 15ff. seem to be the continuation of Paul's words to Peter in Antioch. But we cannot say it is a quotation of Paul's speech in the Syrian town. The connection with 2.11–14 is clear,[7] but 2.15–21 can be at most 'a reformulation of Paul's address to Cephas at Antioch'[8] and very probably Paul now turns to his readers.[9] We can therefore see Gal. 2.15–21 as the closer context of Gal. 2.20a.

In v. 15 Paul expresses a judgment with which not only Cephas (Peter), Barnabas and Jewish Christians, but also other Jews would agree: 'We are Jews by nature and not Gentile sinners'. The apostle is consonant here with Jewish self-confidence. Gentiles are called 'sinners' because they do not know the law. But in the next verse (2.16), Paul formulates the essence of the message he would like to communicate to the Galatians[10]: 'We know that a person is not justified by works of the law but through faith in Jesus Christ. So we, too, have believed in Christ Jesus, so that we might be justified by faith in Christ, and not by works of the law, because no one will be justified by works of the law'. This theological position would undoubtedly be accepted by Peter and other Jewish Christians, too. But according to Paul, it is very important to bear this truth in mind and also to accept fully its consequences. The adversative particle δέ after the participle εἰδότες is not found in a large number of Greek manuscripts[11], but its presence only underscores the importance of Paul's assertion in this verse. In the New Testament mainly Paul (25 times in the undisputed letters, from which 15 times

5. E.g. F. Mußner, *Der Galaterbrief* (HThKNT; Freiburg: Herder, 1974), pp. 132–33; J. Rohde, *Der Brief des Paulus an die Galater* (Berlin: Evang. Verl.-Anstalt, 1989), pp. 100–101.

6. E.g. Dunn, *Galatians*, pp. 115 and 131; U. Borse, *Der Brief an die Galater* (Regensburger Neues Testament; Regensburg: Pustet, 1984), pp. 101 and 111; Burton, *Galatians*, pp. 102 and 118; M. Zerwick, *Der Brief an die Galater* (Düsseldorf: Patmos, 1964), pp. 41 and 46.

7. E.g. H. Schlier, *Der Brief an die Galater* (Göttingen: Vandenhoeck & Ruprecht, 12th edn, 1962), pp. 81 and 87, separates both texts but he gives them only one heading.

8. J.A. Fitzmyer, 'Galatians', in *New Jerome Biblical Commentary*, pp. 780–90 (784).

9. Cf. Borse, *Galater* (1984), p. 112. Gal. 2.15-20 is by H.D. Betz and others considered as the *propositio* in the rhetorical division of the letter (cf. H.D. Betz, *Galatians. A Commentary on Paul's Letter to the Churches in Galatia* [Philadelphia: Fortress Press, 1979], pp. 113ff.). For a view against using rhetorical categories for New Testament letters cf. M. Reiser, *Sprache und literarische Formen des Neuen Testaments* (Paderborn: Schöningh, 2001), pp. 124–25.

10. 'This is the text on which all that follows in the Epistle is commentary', G.D. Duncan quoted by Dunn, *Galatians*, p. 134.

11. It is absent from the most Greek manuscripts beginning with P^{46}, but it is present in the uncials ℵ B C D* F G H 0278^{c} and some other manuscripts. The edition Nestle-Aland has this δέ in square brackets.

in Rom. and 8 times in Gal.) uses the verb δικαιόω (mostly in passive) to express the process by which the sinner becomes just 'and stands before God as "upright", "acquitted"'.[12] Paul emphasizes that this cannot be achieved by works of the law but only by the faith in Jesus Christ. Over the phrase πίστις ('Ιησοῦ) Χριστοῦ there is, as it is well known, a controverse among scholars. Grammatically, the genitive could be both subjective and objective. In my opinion, the reasons for understanding the genitive in this verse and in several other passages in Paul's letters (Gal. 2.20; 3.22; Rom. 3.22, 26; Phil. 3.9; cf. Eph. 3.12) as subjective may be seductive but are not really convincing. The main argument for the objective genitive in πίστις ('Ιησοῦ) Χριστοῦ is the context in this verse. As an antithesis to the 'works of the law' πίστις ('Ιησοῦ) Χριστοῦ must contain and involve something on the part of the human believer,[13] i.e. the faith in Jesus Christ. The opposite view is presented by the authors with different nuances. But if we look e.g. at two recent interpretations, neither that of J.L. Martyn ('Paul speaks of the faith of Christ, meaning his faithful death in our behalf'[14]) nor that of A. Vanhoye (he prefers two correlative senses of πίστις: 'affidabilità' and 'fede', the former on the part of Christ and the latter on the part of a Christian[15]) can entirely convince. The genitive construction can also underline the close connection of believers with Christ so that 'the faith in Christ Jesus is living as faith in him and through him'.[16] That is why Paul and other Jewish Christians have accepted the faith in Jesus Christ.

12. J.A. Fitzmyer, 'Pauline Theology', in *New Jerome Biblical Commentary*, pp. 1382–1416 (1397). Cf. also K. Kertelge, 'δικαιόω', in H. Balz and G. Schneider (eds.), *Exegetisches Wörterbuch zum Neuen Testament* (Stuttgart: Kohlhammer, 1980), I, coll. 796–807; C. Spiq, *Lexique théologique du Nouveau Testament* (Fribourg: Éditions Universitaires, 1991), pp. 346–52.

13. Dunn, *Galatians*, pp. 138–39, gives four reasons in favour of the usual view (i. e. 'faith in Jesus Christ') which are in my opinion more or less convincing: (1) faith as a religious term; (2) 'we never read in Paul of Christ "believing"'; (3) the text in Gen. 15.6; (4) the phrase is most naturally understood 'as posing alternative human responses to God's initiative of grace'. Cf. also J.A. Fitzmyer, *Romans. A New Translation with Commentary* (Anchor Bible 33, New York: Doubleday, 1993), pp. 345–46.

14. J. L. Martyn, *Galatians: A New Translation with Introduction and Commentary* (Anchor Bible 33A, New York: Doubleday, 1998), p. 251. Why did Paul not explain this understanding?

15. A. Vanhoye, Πίστις Χριστοῦ: fede in Cristo o affidabilità di Cristo?', *Biblica* 80 (1999), pp. 1–21 (19–20). Vanhoye's article is interesting but linguistically unconvincing. The Italian word 'affidabilità' (= reliability) is relatively very young. According to F. Sabatini and F. Coletti, *DISC Dizionario Italiano Sabatini-Coletti* (Firenze: Giunti, 1997), p. 57, it was coined in 1961 as a calque of the English noun 'reliability'. The English word is relatively not very old, either. It appears (see *The Oxford English Dictionary* [prep. by J.A. Simpson and E.S.C. Weiner; Oxford: Clarendon Press, 2nd edn, 1989], XIII, p. 562) for the first time in 1816. Its synonym 'trustworthiness' (used in the Summary of Vanhoye's article – *op. cit.*, p. 21) is documented for the first time in 1808 (cf. *Oxford English Dictionary*, XVIII, p. 626). Only the second synonym 'credibility' (also used in the Summary: *op. cit.*, ibid.) is older: the first example is from 1594 (cf. *Oxford English Dictionary*, III, p. 1137). It is clear that the idea of reliability was present in the noun πίστις. But in Antiquity and beyond one felt no need of an extra word for it. Therefore, this notion was hardly intended by Paul as (one of) the (two) dominant meaning(s).

16. Schlier, *Galater*, p. 93. Fitzmyer, *Romans*, p. 346, says about the understanding of the genitive as 'both the object and ground of faith' that it is 'idyllic dreaming revealing only the interpreter's embarrassment'. In the sense of a semantic balance, he is undoubtedly right.

The idea of the 'works of the law' must be understood in the Jewish context. Paul does not specify this concept more closely, but it should not be restricted 'to the ritual regulations of Judaism'.[17] J.G.D. Dunn sees 'works of the law' in this verse in connection with sectarian disputes over the interpretations of the Jewish law.[18] This may have been the background of Paul's thought. But on the other hand, Galatian readers would hardly understand Paul in this sense. Therefore, we must rather take 'works of the law' in a broader, less restricted and general sense. They are deeds that 'the Torah demands'.[19]

Paul feels confirmed in his conviction that there is no other way to justification by the Scripture itself. That is why he alludes to Ps. 143.2 ('before you no living being shall be justified') emphasizing the words by adding 'by works of the law'. Further passages from the Scripture will be quoted by him in Gal. 3–4.

In v. 17 Paul answers a possible objection: 'Is then Christ not a servant of sin?' His line of thought may be as follows: We (i.e. Jewish Christians) have abandoned the law and were seeking to be justified in Christ. We put ourselves on the same level as Gentiles who are sinners (cf. v. 15) and so increasing the number of them.[20] Paul's reply to this objection can be only resolute: 'Absolutely not.'

Then in v. 18 Paul seems to be more thinking of Peter's behaviour in Antioch: 'But if I build up again those things that I tore down, then I show myself to be a transgressor'. The 'I' here is rhetorical. A return to life according to and under the law would make Paul, Peter and other Jewish Christians sinners.

Paul's words in v. 19 'for through the law I died to the law so that I might live to God' may appear somehow enigmatic. Perhaps the best understanding is to see this formulation in connection with the role of the law as it is explained by Paul later in the letter (cf. Gal. 3.19–4.7). By faithfully observing the law Paul sought to please God and to achieve a closer relationship with him. But the crucified Christ showed him the only true way to this goal by demonstrating the insufficiency of the law. That is why Paul (and everyone who believes in Christ) must say: 'I have been crucified with Christ.'[21]

Gal. 2.20a, which is in the centre of our attention, continues[22] and deepens the line of thought in the preceding verse. The life of those who believe in Christ has gained a new dimension. Paul tries to express the newness of this life in the best possible way. Therefore he says 'it is no longer I who live, but it is Christ who lives in me'. Paul's life is now 'a life that Christ leads in him'.[23] This certainly

17. F. Mußner, *Galaterbrief*, p. 170.

18. Dunn, *Galatians*, pp. 135–39.

19. Schlier, *Galater*, p. 91.

20. It is possible that Paul had also in view libertine behaviour among some Galatian Christians (cf. Longenecker, *Galatians*, pp. 89–90).

21. Longenecker, *Galatians*, p. 92, sees Paul's fourfold argument in this verse: '(1) that it was the law's purpose to bring about its own demise in legislating the lives of God's people; (2) that such a jurisdictional demise was necessary in order that believers in Christ might live more fully in relationship with God; (3) that freedom from the law's jurisdiction is demanded by the death of Christ on the cross; and (4) that by identification with Christ we experience the freedom from the law that he accomplished'.

22. Cf. Burton, *Galatians*, p. 137: 'The first δέ is not adversative but continuative'.

23. Rohde, *Galater*, p. 116.

does not concern Paul alone. He undoubtedly 'speaks of himself on behalf of all the baptized'.[24] But on the other hand, Gal. 2.20a is not only a general and neutral description of the status of a Christian. Paul speaks about Christ living in him in this way by the strength of his life-experience, too. The 'I' here is not merely rhetorical. Already the 'I' in v. 19 was different from the rhetorical 'I' in v. 18.[25] The ἐγώ in 2.20 can also be hardly placed on the same level as the ἐγώ in Rom. 7.15–20.[26] This is confirmed by Paul's argumentation in Galatians, especially in 1.13–16. In Gal. 2.20a Paul does not speak only of himself, but he cannot be technically neutral, because he could not have forgotten what he had said earlier in the epistle about his special way to Christ.[27]

Paul must have been conscious of the metaphorical character of the statement about Christ living in him, therefore he sought to define more precisely the form of his life in this world. This is the sense of Gal. 2.20b: 'the life (ὅ in Greek) I now live in the flesh I live by faith in the Son of God, who loved me and gave himself for me'. Paul's life is a response to Christ's love, the clear and evident proof of which is to be seen in Jesus's death on the cross. What was this statement and confession of Paul based upon? Certainly it was the preaching of those who were apostles before Paul (cf. Gal. 1.17). But it was Paul's personal vocation by God, too (cf. Gal. 1.15–16). It is not possible to admit the former without the latter.[28] In Phil. 3.5–12 we can clearly see, too, how in a highly polemical passage – the whole of Galatians is polemical – Paul recalls his personal life of faith in Christ. Paul's response to Christ's love is his faith in the Son of God.[29] We cannot restrict Paul's own experience e.g. to emotional part only. It also involves his theological reflection of Christ's sacrificial death on the cross. In this event he recognized an unparalleled act of God's love.

Can or even should we speak in connection with Gal. 2.20 of Paul's mysticism? If we understand 'mysticism' in a broad and full sense then there can be no objection to applying this term to Paul's relation to Christ as it is expressed in this verse.[30] But very often 'mysticism' is understood just in a subjective or even

24. M. Zerwick, *Galater*, p. 51.

25. Cf. Longenecker, *Galatians*, p. 91; J. Lambrecht, 'The line of Thought in Gal.. 2.14*b*–21', *New Testament Studies* 24 (1978), pp. 484–95 (495); *pace* P.F. Ellis, *Seven Pauline Letters* (Collegeville, MN: Liturgical Press, 1982), p. 182.

26. *Pace* Burton, *Galatians*, p. 137.

27. Cf. Mußner, *Galaterbrief*, p. 182: 'nicht bloß als individuelle … Christusgemeinschaft verstanden werden darf, so sehr *dieser Aspekt mitbeachtet werden muß* (ἐν ἐμοί!)'; the italics are mine.

28. *Pace* P. Bonnard, *L'Épître de Saint Paul aux Galates* (Neuchâtel: Delachaux et Niestlé, 2nd edn, 1972), p. 56: 'Paul ne décrit pas son expérience individuelle mais la condition chrétienne générale'.

29. Τοῦ υἱοῦ τοῦ θεοῦ is here, too, an objective genitive. Several important manuscripts (p^{46} B D* G it$^{(b), d, g}$) and Victorinus-Rome read τοῦ θεοῦ καὶ Χριστοῦ. This reading is 'eine etwas pedantische Auffüllung' (Schlier, *Galater*, p. 102, n. 5). The reading τοῦ υἱοῦ τοῦ θεοῦ, which we must regard as original, need not be 'a higher, more formalized Christology' (H. Eshbaugh, 'Textual Variants and Theology: A Study of the Galatians Text of Papyrus 46', in S.E. Porter and C.A. Evans [eds.], *New Testament Text and Language. A Sheffield Reader* [Sheffield: Sheffield Academic Press, 1997], pp. 81–91 [89]).

30. The classical work is: A. Schweizer, *Die Mystik des Apostels Paulus* (Tübingen: J.C.B. Mohr, 1981 [1930]). He understands (*Die Mystik*, p. 2) mysticism as 'Denkmystik', i.e. mysticism

emotional sense. Because of this possible misunderstanding it is rather better to avoid this term. We can do without it in describing Paul's faith.

In v. 21 Paul first rejects another objection when he says: 'I do not nullify the grace of God'. We do not know whether such an objection was actually raised,[31] but Paul definitely turns down the thought that the life without law could mean overlooking or rejecting God's grace. He then explains why the life of faith is the very opposite of nullifying God's grace: 'If justification comes through the law, then Christ died for nothing'.

The important pericope Gal. 2.15–21 contains in v. 16 the kernel of Paul's message to the Galatians and in v. 20 we can find the concrete form of life according to the truth expressed in v. 16, exemplified by Paul's own life of faith.

2. *Parallel Passages in Paul*

There is no other passage in Paul's letters (undisputed or disputed) that would present the exact parallel to Gal. 2.20a, i.e. contain the formulation 'Christ lives in me'.[32] However, there are passages that have to be considered in this connection. As it was mentioned above, we can find some other formulations that speak about Christ's indwelling in those who believe in him. In the Proto-Pauline letters they are Rom. 8.10; 2 Cor. 13.5 (cf. also 2 Cor. 13.3, where Paul speaks of 'Christ speaking in me') and Gal. 4.19 (in this verse Paul says he is again in the pain of childbirth until Christ is formed in Galatians). These passages confirm that Paul referred to all believers in what he expressed in Gal. 2.20a.[33] Among the Deutero-Paulines, Eph. 3.17 (expressing the wish 'that Christ may dwell in your hearts through faith') and perhaps also Col. 1.27 ('mystery, which is Christ in you'[34]) show that this idea was current in Paul's school, too. Then there are

of thought, and Gal. 2.19–20 is the first text quoted by him (*Die Mystik*, p. 3) among 'Sprüche paulinischer Mystik'.

31. Cf. Betz, *Galatians*, p. 126.

32. It is, at any rate, worth noticing the relatively high frequency of the syntagma ἐν ἐμοί in the New Testament (41 occurrences, from which 15 in Paul's undisputed letters) in comparison with other ancient Greek authors (12 occurrences in Plato, 4 in Plutarch, 3 in Josephus Flavius, none in Epicurus and Marcus Aurelius – all data according to the *Thesaurus Linguae Graecae*). These numbers have no absolute value because the meanings of this syntactic unit are very different. Even in Gal. 1.16 (ἀποκαλύψαι τὸν υἱὸν αὐτοῦ ἐν ἐμοί), which is often compared with Gal. 2.20a (cf. e.g. Betz, *Galatians*, p. 124), this syntagma can be equivalent to a dative only (cf. W. Haubeck/H. von Siebenthal, *Neuer Sprachlicher Schlüssel zum griechischen Neuen Testament. Römer bis Offenbarung* [Giessen: Brunnen, 1994], p. 137). But it could be perhaps considered as a sign of the fact that in the New Testament the inner life of the person who speaks is more important than in other writings from Antiquity.

33. This is valid even though the preposition ἐν may have a wider sense and the phrase ἐν ὑμῖν can mean, e.g. in 2 Cor. 13.5, 'among you' (see e.g. Ch. Wolff, *Der Zweite Brief des Paulus an die Korinther* [Berlin: Evang. Verl.-Anstalt, 1989], p. 263).

34. This 'in you' (ἐν ὑμῖν) is often interpreted as 'among you'; see e.g. P. Pokorný, *Der Brief des Paulus an die Kolosser* (ThHNT 10/I; Berlin: Evang. Verl.-Anstalt, 2nd edn, 1990), pp. 86–87, and E. Schweizer, *Der Brief an die Kolosser* (EKK New Testament XII; Einsiedeln: Benziger; Neukirchen–Vluyn: Neukirchener Verlag, 3rd edn, 1990), p. 88. But cf. the comment to this verse

passages speaking of God's Spirit indwelling in the faithful. We have already asked the question whether these formulations say the same thing as those formulated by Paul e.g. in Gal. 2.20a. It is true that Paul can speak interchangeably about the abiding of Christ or the Spirit in the baptized (cf. e.g. Rom. 8.9–11). But it would be very simplistic if we asserted that Paul made a simple equation between Christ and God's Spirit.[35] Paul could clearly distinguish between Christ and the Spirit (cf. 1 Cor. 12.4–6; 2 Cor. 13.13). It is certainly appropriate to say that the mentioned expressions 'are for Paul different, generic ways of expressing the basic union of Christians with Christ. Christ dwells in Christians as his Spirit becomes the source of the new experience, empowering them in a new way and with a new vitality'.[36] But on the other hand, we must recognize that without his own experience with Christ, Paul would not have spoken of the Spirit in the way he did. This has to be considered in evaluating Gal. 2.20a.

What to say of those numerous passages where Paul uses the formula 'in Christ' or 'in the Lord'? Do they simply express the same thing as Gal. 2.20a? Before answering this question it is perhaps better to consider another one: Why are the passages containing 'in Christ' etc. much more numerous than the reverse formulations? It seems to me that it is caused by the fact that the formulations 'in Christ' etc. can have a more or less purely formal meaning, which can be compared with the later adjective 'Christian' (which the authentic Paul seems not to have known). As examples can serve e.g. Rom. 16.11,13; 1 Cor. 3.1; 4.10; 2 Cor. 12.2; Gal. 1.22; 1 Thess. 2.14; 4.16; 5.12).[37] With Gal. 2.20a and other parallels with the same grammatical construction it can hardly be the case. This answer can perhaps be at least a partial one, as it is clear that the exact meaning of the locution 'in Christ' etc. in Paul is controversial.[38] This may be true of the above-mentioned examples, too. But the possibility of a formal usage of these passages, without much emphasis on the inner quality of the relation to Christ, can hardly be denied.

3. *Other Parallels*

If we search in the New Testament outside the *Corpus Paulinum*, we can find parallels with the same grammatical construction as Gal. 2.20a only in the Johannine literature. In the Gospel of John, one of the main theological themes is a

in the commentary by P.T. O'Brien, *Colossians, Philemon* (Word Biblical Commentary, 44; Dallas, TX: Word Books, 1998).

35. 2 Cor. 3.17 ('Christ is the Spirit') cannot be a clue and a decisive instance because the phrase admits different interpretations (cf. e.g. Ch. Wolff, *Der Zweite Brief*, p. 76: 'ἐστιν ist nicht im Sinne einer Identitätsaussage zu verstehen' and J. Murphy O'Connor, 'The Second Letter to the Corinthians', in *New Jerome Biblical Commentary*, pp. 818–29 [820]: 'it is probable that Paul has God directly in view').

36. Fitzmyer, *Romans*, p. 490.

37. Cf. *Greek-English Lexicon of the New Testament and Other Early Christian Literature* (rev. and ed. by F.W. Danker; Chicago: University of Chicago Press, 3rd edn, 2000), p. 328, where e.g. 1 Thess. 5.12 is translated 'your Christian leaders (in the church)'.

38. Cf. the overview of the different interpretations: Ryšková, *Verurteilung*, pp. 32–48.

union – not only the one of Jesus with his Father, but also the union of believers with Jesus. In 6.56 Jesus says: 'Whoever eats my flesh and drinks my blood remains in me, and I in him (ἐν αὐτῷ)'. In Jn 15.4 Jesus, using in his speech the metaphor of vine, asks his disciples to remain in him so that he could remain in them (μείνατε ἐν ἐμοί κἀγὼ ἐν ὑμῖν). In Jn 17.23 Jesus prays, in the course of the so-called 'high priestly prayer', that his disciples might participate in his union with the Father and that he might be in them and the Father in him (ἐγὼ ἐν αὐτοῖς καὶ σὺ ἐν ἐμοί). From these passages the reciprocity of the relation of Jesus and his disciples is clearly visible. This reciprocity is the dominant thought and here it is not possible to make a distinction between the sides of the equation.[39] Further continuation and development of this theology can be found in the First Letter of John.[40] In 1 Jn 3.24 we read: 'Those who keep his commandments remain in him, and he in them'. It can be easily deduced from the context of this passage that the subject remaining in the faithful is God. But the distinction between God and Jesus is not clear-cut here.[41] Further, 1 Jn 4.15 is to be compared: 'Whoever confesses that Jesus is the Son of God, God remains in him and he in God' (cf. 4.13, too). These passages may suffice to demonstrate the theology of the Johannine community that stresses the close relation and association of the believers with Christ and with God through the faith in Christ that is and has to be manifest in the mutual love (cf. 1 Jn 3.23: 'that we should believe in the name of his Son Jesus Christ and love one another').[42]

This theological thinking can undoubtedly be described as high Christology. That is within the Johannine writings surely not surprising. But with respect to Gal. 2.20a we can see that Paul, writing several decades earlier, is not very much distant from this theology and Christology.

In other New Testament books (i.e. outside the *Corpus Paulinum* and the Johannine writings) we can find the relation to Christ expressed in correspondence with Paul's frequent usage (cf. 1 Pet. 3.16 speaks of good conduct of Christians in Christ [ἐν Χριστῷ] and in 1 Pet. 5.14 a greeting of peace is addressed to all who 'are in Christ' [ἐν Χριστῷ]). In our context we need not further pursue the

39. C.K. Barrett, *The Gospel according to St John. An Introduction with Commentary and Notes on the Greek Text* (London: SPCK, 2nd edn, 1978), p. 474 (to 15.4): 'we should take the two balanced clauses very closely together: let there be a mutual indwelling'.

40. It is disputed whether the Johannine letters are posterior or anterior to the Gospel of John. But it seems better to place the letters after the Gospel, at least after the main corpus of the Gospel of John. Cf. H.J. Klauck, *Die Johannesbriefe* (Darmstadt: Wissenschaftliche Buchgesellschaft, 1991), p. 126: 'Sie (= the three Johannine Epistles) sind entstanden, nachdem der Evangelist seine Tätigkeit schon beendet hatte'; R.E. Brown, *The Gospel and Epistles of John. A Concise Commentary* (Collegeville, MN: The Liturgical Press, 1988), p. 106: 'I would place them (= the Epistles of John) in the decade after the body of the Gospel was written'.

41. Cf. J. Beutler, *Die Johannesbriefe* (Regensburger Neues Testament, Regensburg: Pustet: 2000), p. 99; Brown, *Gospel and Epistles*, p. 117: 'Father and Son are not distinguished'; cf. also R.E. Brown, *The Epistles of John. Translation with Introduction, Notes, and Commentary* (Anchor Bible, 30, New York: Doubleday, 1982), p. 482.

42. This association with God and Christ can be expressed as the abiding of God's word in the believers, too (cf. 1 Jn 1.10).

significance of this theological language. It hardly goes beyond both Paul's mode of expression and his theology.

4. *Conclusion*

By way of summary we can say that Gal. 2.20a contains one way among others – in Paul specifically and in the New Testament generally – how a close relation of the baptized to Christ may be expressed. This expression is certainly an impressive one. We cannot overlook its personal element either. Although this fact is often neglected[43] or sometimes explicitly denied,[44] Paul was very probably relying on his own experience with Christ.[45] Christ took up the whole of his life (cf. 1 Cor. 5.14 and Phil. 3.12). In Gal. 2.20b Paul then tries to be more concrete. Last but not least, both statements in Gal. 2.20 have an important christological significance. In Christ's love expressed through his death on the cross Paul saw the unique expression of God's love towards him and towards all human beings who need justification before God. Paul does not say it in Gal. 2.20 explicitly, but he saw the love of Christ and the love of God as one. This is clearly confirmed by Rom. 5.7–8 and 8.32–39.[46] This is important because we are dealing here with quite early Christology. Paul was in his confession not isolated and certainly not in discord with the faith of Peter, James and others, but his testimony is too clear and powerful to be overlooked and it was handed over to us in a written form. The later New Testament writings (especially the Johannine literature) are then more specific in their mode of speaking about Christ. But the basis of this 'high' Christology is to be found already in Paul and specifically in Gal. 2.20, too.

For Christians, Paul's testimony about Christ and his love that is simultaneously God's love, as expressed in Gal. 2.20ab and at other places in his letters, has been a logical reason for the similar viewpoint and mode of life of faith. In this third millennium of the Christian era we are undoubtedly to encounter that this is not necessarily the viewpoint of all who read it or hear about it.[47] That is why the task of a comprehensible and persuasive interpretation of Paul's Christology and, in the end, of the message of the whole New Testament will not be easy. However, also today, Paul's example can be attractive and even engaging.

43. So perhaps the majority of the commentaries; cf. e.g. Schlier, *Galater*, pp. 101–103.

44. Cf. Bonnard, *Galates*, p. 56.

45. Cf. Dunn, *Galatians*, p. 145: 'the very radical nature of personal transformation effected by Paul's encounter with the risen Christ'.

46. See Dunn, *Galatians*, p. 147.

47. Cf. e.g. G. Martin-Chauffier who (reviewing a book about French Christian personages in history) writes (*Paris-Match*, no. 2784, 3 Oct. 2002, p. 29) about 'ce Dieu si obscure, confus et timoré qu'il a du envoyer son Fils sur terre pour expliciter son message'.

Die Einheit des Evangeliums: Erwägungen zur christologischen Kontroverse des Galaterbriefes und ihrem theologiegeschichtlichen Hintergrund

Jens Schröter

In seiner Studie „Die Entstehung der Christologie“[1] kommt Petr Pokorný im Abschnitt über „Die ältesten Glaubenszeugnisse“ zu dem Ergebnis, es sei „kaum möglich, mit den verschiedenen bekenntnishaften Äußerungen für die Existenz verschiedener urchristlicher Christologien zu argumentieren, die kontradiktorisch wären. Die festgeprägten Äußerungen unterscheiden sich voneinander durch ihren verschiedenen Sitz im Leben, aber es handelt sich nicht um theologische Alternativen.“ Wenig später wird dieses Verhältnis von Einheit und Vielfalt der urchristlichen Christologie wie folgt präzisiert: „Das Gesagte bedeutet nicht, daß die christliche Theologie einheitlich war. Es bedeutet nur, daß der Grund des Streits primär nicht Differenzen in der Ausprägung der christologischen Aussagen, sondern Differenzen in der Anwendung und Deutung sind.“ Zur Begründung verweist Pokorný auf den „Unterschied zwischen der paulinischen Deutung (Röm 1,17) des gemeinsamen Evangeliums (Röm 1,3f.) und seiner Anwendung durch Petrus (Gal 2,11–14), durch Jakobus (Gal 2,12), durch die hellenistischen Judenchristen in Antiochien (Barnabas), im Stephanus-Kreis“ sowie später in johanneischen und paulinischen Kreisen und durch Apollos in Alexandrien.[2]

Diesen knappen Bemerkungen genauer nachzugehen, würde sich nicht zuletzt deshalb lohnen, weil sie auf die Spur der im Untertitel angedeuteten „Voraussetzungen einer Theologie des Neuen Testaments“ führen. Pokorný zufolge führt eine Linie von der Entstehung der ältesten Glaubenszeugnisse über deren unterschiedliche Entfaltungen bis hin zur Kanonbildung. Darauf verweisen die im unmittelbaren Zusammenhang geäußerten Sätze: „Viel später haben die Gemeinsamkeiten die Bildung des christlichen Kanons ermöglicht. Erst dort, wo die neue Deutung praktisch die Leugnung der vorgegebenen Glaubensaussagen bedeutet hat, ist es zu einer Spaltung gekommen“.[3]

Im folgenden soll aus dieser größeren Perspektive ein Detail herausgegriffen werden.[4] Dabei interessiert uns die von Pokorný angedeutete Unterscheidung von

1. P. Pokorný, *Die Entstehung der Christologie. Voraussetzungen einer Theologie des Neuen Testaments* (Stuttgart: Calwer, 1985).

2. A. a. O., S. 81.

3. Ebd.

4. Eine Andeutung der im folgenden zu entfaltenden These findet sich bereits in: J. Schröter,

christologischen Aussagen und deren Anwendung in konkreten Situationen, die hier im Blick auf den Galaterbrief untersucht werden soll. Daß dieses Schreiben aufgrund der von Paulus in 2,11–21 ausgetragenen Kontroverse mit Kephas ein wichtiger Zeuge für die Geschichte der urchristlichen Christologie ist, liegt auf der Hand und wird auch durch die oben zitierten, hierauf Bezug nehmenden Sätze Pokornýs unterstrichen. Man kann die christologische Kontroverse des Galaterbriefes geradezu als Paradebeispiel für die Differenz von gemeinsamer Glaubensüberzeugung und je eigener Anwendung betrachten, denn der Dissens zwischen Paulus und Kephas liegt nicht im christologischen Bekenntnis selbst begründet, sondern in den Konsequenzen, die daraus zu ziehen sind.

Wenn Paulus im Anschluß an seine Schilderung des Zusammentreffens mit Kephas in Antiochien (Gal 2,11–14) zum christologischen Argument übergeht, setzt er bei der Unterscheidung zwischen „uns Juden" (also Petrus, Barnabas und sich selbst, auch anderen Judenchristen) und den „Sündern aus den Heiden" ein (2,15), um sodann (2,16f.) die gemeinsame Überzeugung der Judenchristen[5] in der Opposition von Gerechtigkeit ἐξ ἔργων νόμου und διὰ πίστεως Ἰησοῦ Χριστοῦ zu verankern. An dieser Stelle liegt also (zumindest für ihn) noch nicht der strittige Punkt,[6] wohl aber dann – wie die Fortsetzung zeigt – in der Frage, welche Konsequenzen hieraus zu ziehen sind.[7]

Hiervon ausgehend stellt sich die Frage, wie sich das Verhältnis von gemeinsamer Grundüberzeugung und unterschiedlichen Konsequenzen zum christologischen Gesamtargument des Briefes verhält. Dieses wird häufig so beschrieben, daß Paulus den in dem Brief bekämpften Gegnern die Legitimität ihrer Verkündigung abspreche und nur seine eigene Position als εὐαγγέλιον Χριστοῦ (1,7) gelten lasse. Von dorther finde auch der Vorwurf an Kephas seine Erklärung: Dessen sowie die der anderen Juden(christen) „Heuchelei" (2,13), von Paulus als Abweichung von der „Wahrheit des Evangeliums" (2,14) verurteilt, werde dem in 2,16 formulierten Grundsatz von der Rechtfertigung ohne des Gesetzes Werke

Die Universalisierung des Gesetzes im Galaterbrief. Ein Beitrag zum Gesetzesverständnis des Paulus, in: U. Kern (Hg.), *Das Verständnis des Gesetzes bei Juden, Christen und im Islam* (Rostocker Theologische Studien 5; Münster: LIT, 2000), S. 27–63.

5. Daß von diesen die Rede ist, geht aus dem εἰδότες hervor, das dann durch das ἐπιστεύσαμεν fortgesetzt wird. Das zweimalige betonte καὶ ἡμεῖς bzw. καὶ αὐτοί in V. 16f. hebt dabei hervor, daß *sogar Juden* wie Paulus, Kephas und Barnabas zu der Erkenntnis gelangt sind, daß außerhalb von Christus keine Gerechtigkeit zu erlangen ist, sie also ebenso wie die Heiden vor ihrer Bekehrung als in Christus zu rechtfertigende Sünder zu beurteilen waren. Das doppelte verstärkende καί nimmt also das ἡμεῖς φύσει Ἰουδαῖοι aus V. 15 auf und führt es weiter.

6. Vgl. C. Burchard, Nicht aus Werken des Gesetzes gerecht, sondern aus Glauben an Jesus Christus – seit wann?, in: H. Lichtenberger u. a. (Hg.), *Geschichte – Tradition – Reflexion*, B. 3: *Frühes Christentum* (FS M. Hengel; Tübingen: Mohr-Siebeck, 1996), S. 405–415, S. 406f., S. 409 und zuletzt C. Böttrich, Petrus und Paulus in Antiochien (Gal 2,11–21) BThZ 19 (2002), S. 224–239, S. 235.

7. Es kann dahingestellt bleiben, ob Paulus in 2,16 einen anerkannten Grundsatz zitiert oder ad hoc formuliert. Er geht jedenfalls davon aus, daß der Satz eine gemeinsame Basis darstellt, der auch Kephas nicht gut widersprechen kann, auch wenn dieser sich vielleicht nicht so zugespitzt ausgedrückt hätte.

nur aus Glauben nicht gerecht und reaktiviere stattdessen die in Christus überwundene Trennung von Juden und Heiden.

Eine wichtige Rolle spielt dabei das in 1,6 erwähnte ἕτερον εὐαγγέλιον, in der Fortsetzung durch ὃ οὐκ ἔστιν ἄλλο näher charakterisiert. Paulus mache, so eine häufig anzutreffende Sicht, mit dieser Wendung gleich zu Beginn des Briefes deutlich, daß es ein anderes Evangelium neben dem seinigen nicht geben könne,[8] sowohl die galatischen Gegner als auch Judenchristen wie Kephas sich deshalb den Vorwurf gefallen lassen müßten, ein Evangelium zu predigen, welches in Wahrheit keines ist.

Diese Rekonstruktion des paulinischen Argumentes greift jedoch, wie nunmehr zu zeigen ist, zu kurz. Wir setzen dazu bei einer Analyse der Verse 1,6 und 7 ein. Deren soeben angedeutete Interpretation ist nämlich, trotz des Konsenses der neueren Forschung,[9] keineswegs sicher. Zweifellos trifft zu, daß Paulus der Botschaft seiner Gegner die Legitimität abspricht. Die Intention des Satzes ist damit jedoch nicht hinreichend beschrieben. Paulus formuliert hier eine Aussage über die Einheit des von ihm verkündigten heidenchristlichen Evangeliums mit demjenigen, das den Juden bekanntzumachen sei. Erst auf dieser Basis wird die Tätigkeit seiner Gegner als Abweichung vom Evangelium Christi offenkundig. Dazu kommen weitere Indizien. Es fällt auf, daß Paulus im Galaterbrief des öfteren von *einer bestimmten Form* des Evangeliums spricht. Nicht zufällig urteilte deshalb schon Hans Dieter Betz, daß zwischen der in 1,6f. beschworenen Unteilbarkeit des εὐαγγέλιον Χριστοῦ und der Unterscheidung zwischen εὐαγγέλιον τῆς ἀκροβυστίας und τῆς περιτομῆς in 2,7 ein „strange disagreement" bestehe.[10] Die Frage, wie die dort erwähnte doppelte Gestalt des εὐαγγέλιον zu dessen in 1,6f. herausgestellter Einheit in Beziehung zu setzen ist, ist, wie Betz zu Recht betont hat, für das Verständnis der von Paulus vertretenen Position in der Tat von entscheidender Bedeutung. Schließlich begründet Paulus in K. 3 einerseits die Abrahamskindschaft der Heidenchristen und spricht andererseits vom Loskauf vom Fluch des Gesetzes, der sich schwerlich auf ehemalige Heiden beziehen kann, sondern die Befreiung der Judenchristen durch Christus beschreibt. Auch dies ist für die Frage nach der hinter dem Brief liegenden Kontroverse zu berücksichtigen. Diese verschiedenen Aspekte finden ihr gemeinsames Zentrum in der dem Galaterbrief eigenen Argumentationsstrategie, die ihre Basis in der Überzeugung von dem einen Evangelium in zweifacher Gestalt besitzt.

8. Vgl. etwa E. Gräßer, Das eine Evangelium. Hermeneutische Erwägungen zu Gal 1,6–10, *ZThK* 66 (1969), S. 306–344; F. Mußner, *Der Galaterbrief* (HThKNT IX) (Freiburg u. a.: Herder, 5th edn, 1988), S. 55–59.

9. Dieser bestand nicht immer. W.M. Ramsay, *A Historical Commentary on St. Paul's Epistle to the Galatians* (London: Hodder & Stoughton, 1899) und T. Zahn, *Der Brief des Paulus an die Galater* (KNT 9; Leipzig/Erlangen: Deichert, 1922), vertraten eine von der heute vorherrschenden abweichende Sicht, die inzwischen weithin in Vergessenheit geraten ist – zu Unrecht, wie sich zeigen wird.

10. H.D. Betz, *Galatians. A Commentary on Paul's Letter to the Churches in Galatia* (Hermeneia; Philadelphia: Fortress Pr., 1979), S. 49. Vgl. J.L. Martyn, *Galatians. A New Translation with Introduction and Commentary* (AnchB 33A; New York u. a.: Doubleday, 1997), S. 110: „A significant problem emerges when he seems at a later point to speak in fact of two gospels (2:7)."

Um dieses darzulegen, setzen wir (1) bei dem Interpretationsproblem der Verse 1,6f. ein, (2) zeichnen diese sodann in den weiteren Kontext des Briefes ein und (3) formulieren schließlich ein Fazit, das sich hieraus im Blick auf die Einheit des Evangeliums für Juden und Heiden ergibt. Dabei wird sich zeigen, daß das von Paulus entwickelte Argument mit einer Aufteilung in Wahrheit auf seiner und Täuschung auf der Gegner Seite – die er freilich vornimmt! – im Blick auf die hier entwickelte christologische Perspektive noch nicht ausreichend erfaßt ist.

1. *Zur Interpretation von Gal 1,6f.*

Unmittelbar nach dem Präskript wendet sich Paulus mit dem Vorwurf an die galatischen Gemeinden, sie würden sich abwenden von dem, der sie berufen hat (μετατίθεσθε ἀπὸ τοῦ καλέσαντος ὑμᾶς). Damit wird deutlich, daß er das Verhalten der Galater als Aufgabe ihrer Zugehörigkeit zur Abrahams- und Christusgemeinschaft betrachtet, zu der sie als Heiden von Gott ausersehen wurden.[11] Waren sie offenbar bereit, die Forderung der Kontrahenten des Paulus zu befolgen und die Integration ins Judentum durch die Beschneidung als Besiegelung ihrer Zugehörigkeit zu Christus zu vollziehen, so betrachtet Paulus dies gerade umgekehrt als Verrat an ihrer Berufung, die einem Rückfall in ihre heidnische Vergangenheit gleichkäme.[12]

Der Abwendung von Gott entspricht die Hinwendung εἰς ἕτερον εὐαγγέλιον, näher erläutert durch den Relativsatz ὃ οὐκ ἔστιν ἄλλο. Dieser Vorgang des Wechsels vom Stand ihrer Berufung zu einem anderen Evangelium[13] ist schließlich, wie der Konditionalsatz εἰ μή τινές εἰσιν οἱ ταράσσοντες ὑμᾶς καὶ θέλοντες μεταστρέψαι τὸ εὐαγγέλιον τοῦ Χριστοῦ anzeigt, durch Leute verursacht, die die Galater von ihrem bereits erreichten Glaubensstand[14] wieder abzubringen versuchen.

Der von Paulus in 1,6f. formulierte Satz, mit dem er diese Situation beschreibt, enthält einige Interpretationsprobleme. Wie noch deutlich werden wird, hängt das Verständnis der christologischen Kontroverse des Briefes nicht zuletzt davon ab, wie diese gelöst werden. Zu klären sind deshalb im folgenden (1) die Referenz des relativischen Anschlusses, (2) die semantische Beziehung von ἕτερος und ἄλλος sowie (3) die Interpretation des Konditionalsatzes εἰ μή τινές εἰσιν κτλ.

11. Darauf läuft dann die Argumentation in 3,6–29 hinaus: Die Galater sind als Heiden ebenso Erben der in Christus erfüllten Abrahamsverheißung wie die Juden. Damit ist die Distinktion Juden – Heiden, die in den Kapiteln 1–4 immer wieder eine Rolle spielt, in Christus aufgehoben.

12. Darum parallelisiert er die Versklavung der Juden unter dem Gesetz (3,10–14) und diejenige der Heiden unter den Götzen (4,8) als in Christus überwundene Spezialfälle der Existenz unter den στοιχεῖα τοῦ κόσμου (4,3.8).

13. Μετατίθεσθαι ἀπὸ ... εἰς bzw. ἐπί bezeichnet den Wechsel von einer Überzeugung zu einer anderen. Vgl. *MartPol 11,1:* καλὸν δὲ μετατίθεσθαι ἀπὸ τῶν χαλεπῶν ἐπὶ τὰ δίκαια. Bei *Diog Laert, 7,37* wird Dionysios als μεταθέμενος bezeichnet, weil er als Schüler Zenons das Ziel der Philosophie in die Lust (ἡδονή) verlegte.

14. Daß sich die Galater nach Auffassung des Paulus bereits im „rechten" Glaubensstand befanden, wird sowohl durch den Aorist καλέσας als auch durch das μετατίθεσθαι deutlich.

1) *Bezüglich des relativischen Anschlusses* sind drei syntaktische Bezüge möglich: Das ὅ kann sich (1) auf ἕτερον εὐαγγέλιον, (2) nur auf εὐαγγέλιον oder (3) auf den gesamten, mit dem ὅτι-Satz beschriebenen Vorgang des μετατίθεσθαι ἀπὸ ... εἰς beziehen.[15] Grammatisch legt sich die erste Option nahe, da sich das Relativum am besten als Aufnahme des zusammengehörigen Ausdrucks und nicht nur eines Teils desselben oder des gesamten vorangegangenen Satzes verstehen läßt. Sie wird deshalb auch von der überwiegenden Mehrheit der Ausleger favorisiert. Möglichkeit (2) wurde in der altkirchlichen und mittelalterlichen Auslegung (etwa von Johannes Chrysostomus, Martin Luther und Theodor Beza), später von Johann Albrecht Bengel, Wilhelm Martin Leberecht de Wette und Adolf Hilgenfeld vertreten.[16] Sie ist jedoch unwahrscheinlicher als die erste Möglichkeit, denn Paulus würde in diesem Fall von der Erwähnung des ἕτερον εὐαγγέλιον der Gegner unmittelbar zu einer Beschreibung des „wahren Evangeliums" übergehen, ohne das ἕτερον noch einmal aufzunehmen. Auch der folgende Konditionalsatz läßt sich besser integrieren, wenn sich das Relativum auf den gesamten Ausdruck ἕτερον εὐαγγέλιον bezieht. Richtig gesehen ist bei dieser Deutung indes, daß Paulus mit diesem Ausdruck tatsächlich von einer anderen, von seiner eigenen unterschiedenen Gestalt des Evangeliums spricht.

Möglichkeit (3) wird in den Kommentaren von Hugo Grotius und Heinrich Rückert vertreten und steht auch hinter der Übersetzung der Zürcher Bibel: „... was [doch] auf nichts anderes hinauskommt...". In diesem Fall würde sich der Relativsatz auf den von θαυμάζω abhängigen ὅτι-Satz, der das Verhalten der Galater zum Inhalt hat, beziehen, wogegen Paulus auf das ἕτερον εὐαγγέλιον und dessen Differenz zum εὐαγγέλιον τοῦ Χριστοῦ erst in dem anschließenden εἰ μή-Satz eingehen würde. Diese Deutung ist eher vorstellbar, legt sich letztlich jedoch auch nicht nahe. Man würde zum einen das Relativum ἅ bzw. ἅτινα, zum anderen eine Formulierung wie οὐδὲν ἄλλο ἔστιν oder aber ein τοῦτο γὰρ οὐκ ἔστιν ἄλλο erwarten. Auch müßte die εἰ μή-Konstruktion in diesem Fall durch ein ὅτι eingeleitet sein. Des weiteren ist es plausibler anzunehmen, daß Paulus hier seine dann in 2,11–21 näher entfaltete Auffassung von dem einen Evangelium vorbereitet, weshalb sich auch von daher die Referenz des Relativums auf ἕτερον εὐαγγέλιον näher legt. Dafür spricht schließlich auch die angedeutete Beziehung von ἕτερον εὐαγγέλιον und εὐαγγέλιον τοῦ Χριστοῦ.

Der Bezug des Relativpronomens auf ἕτερον εὐαγγέλιον ist deshalb die nächstliegende Möglichkeit und wird im folgenden vorausgesetzt.

15. Die verschiedenen Möglichkeiten werden diskutiert bei F. Sieffert, *Der Brief an die Galater* (KEK VII; Göttingen: Vandenhoeck & Ruprecht, 9th edn, 1899, S. 43f.; E. de Witt Burton, *The Epistle to the Galatians* (ICC; Edinburgh: T&T Clark, 1921, Nachdruck 1964), S. 22–24 sowie Zahn, *Galater*, S. 46f. Später werden sie gelegentlich noch erwähnt (so bei A. Oepke, *Der Brief des Paulus an die Galater* [ThKNT 9; Berlin: Evang. Verlaganstalt, 1957, 5th edn 1984], S. 49; H. Schlier, *Der Brief an die Galater* [KEK VII; Göttingen: Vandenhoeck & Ruprecht, 13th edn, 1965], S. 38, Anm. 1; Betz, *Galatians*, S. 49, Anm. 60 und Mußner, *Galaterbrief*, 56), aus neueren Kommentaren sind sie ganz verschwunden (so etwa bei Martyn, *Galatians*; F. Vouga, *An die Galater* [HNT 10; Tübingen: Mohr-Siebeck, 1998]; R.N. Longenecker, *Galatians* [WBC 41; Dallas: Word Books, 1990]).

16. Vgl. Sieffert, *Galater*, S. 43.

2) Zu besprechen ist des weiteren das auffällige *Nebeneinander von ἕτερος und ἄλλος*. Das Verhältnis beider Termini läßt sich wiederum auf dreierlei Weise bestimmen.

Bei der ersten, heute zumeist vertretenen Sicht werden beide Termini als Synonyme aufgefaßt: Paulus würde die Existenz eines anderen εὐαγγέλιον neben seinem eigenen zunächst hypothetisch einräumen, um sie sofort wieder zurückzunehmen, da es – enumerativ und qualitativ – nur ein einziges Evangelium geben könne. Das ἄλλο wird dabei als Pleonasmus verstanden, mit dessen Hilfe in V. 7 eine Korrektur des zuvor Gesagten vorgenommen und dem ἕτερον εὐαγγέλιον nunmehr abgesprochen würde, überhaupt εὐαγγέλιον zu sein. Die Formulierung wäre dann aufzufassen als „ein anderes Evangelium, welches es in Wahrheit gar nicht gibt" bzw. „welches in Wahrheit gar kein Evangelium ist".[17] Der folgende, durch εἰ μή eingeleitete Satz ist bei dieser Deutung als die positive Seite einer Alternative aufzufassen „es gibt nicht … sondern nur". Inhaltlich läuft diese Interpretation darauf hinaus, daß Paulus bereits zu Beginn des Briefes deutlich machen würde, es gebe nur *eine* Form der Verkündigung des εὐαγγέλιον τοῦ Χριστοῦ – nämlich die von ihm selbst vertretene. Mit dem ἕτερον εὐαγγέλιον werde dagegen die Botschaft der Gegner charakterisiert, die nicht Evangelium, sondern Verwirrung sei. Zur philologischen Begründung wird darauf verwiesen, daß ἕτερος und ἄλλος in der Koine nicht mehr streng unterschieden, sondern praktisch bedeutungsgleich verwandt würden. Dies entspricht der Auffassung, die auch in einschlägigen theologischen Lexika und Grammatiken zu dieser Stelle vermerkt wird.[18] Deshalb, so ist häufig zu lesen, könne auch der Relativsatz auf die genannte Weise übersetzt werden – obwohl, worauf bereits Brigitte Kahl zu Recht verwiesen hat, ὃ οὐκ ἔστιν ἄλλο genau genommen nicht heißt „welches es nicht gibt", sondern „welches kein anderes ist".[19]

17. So die Übersetzungen in den meisten deutschsprachigen Kommentaren. In dieselbe Richtung geht Martyn, *Galatians*, S. 106: „Not that there really is another gospel". Dagegen möchte J. D. G. Dunn, *The Epistle to the Galatians* (BNTC; Peabody: Hendrickson, 1993), S. 38 mit Anm. 2, dem Befund zweier griechischer Termini in seiner Übersetzung Ausdruck verleihen: „another gospel … which is not an other…"

18. Vgl. *ThWNT I*, s. v. ἄλλος κτλ. (Büchsel) und *II*, s. v. ἕτερος (Beyer); *EWNT I*, s. v. ἄλλος (K. Weiß); F. Blass/A. Debrunner, *Grammatik des neutestamentlichen Griechisch*, (bearbeitet von F. Rehkopf; Göttingen: Vandenhoeck & Ruprecht, 18th edn, 2001 [= BDR]), § 306,4 mit Anm. 8; W. Bauer, *Griechisch-deutsches Wörterbuch zu den Schriften des Neuen Testaments und der frühchristlichen Literatur* (hg. von K. und B. Aland; Berlin/New York: de Gruyter, 6th edn, 1988), s. v. ἕτερος. In der von F. W. Danker besorgten dritten Auflage der englischsprachigen Ausgabe dieses Wörterbuches (*A Greek-English Lexicon of the New Testament and Other Early Christian Literature* [Chicago/London: Univ. of Chicago Press, 3rd edn, 2000]) findet sich allerdings der Hinweis auf eine andere Interpretationsmöglichkeit von Gal 1,6 mit dem Verweis auf das Wörterbuch von Moulton/Milligan (dazu unten Näheres). Bei BDR wird im Blick auf den Konditionalsatz auf das lateinische „nihil aliud nisi" als Analogie verwiesen – was in der Tat eine Entsprechung zu οὐκ ἔστιν ἄλλο εἰ μή darstellt, nicht jedoch zu der dort gegebenen Übersetzung „welches es gar nicht gibt, außer daß".

19. B. Kahl, Der Brief an die Gemeinden in Galatien. Vom Unbehagen der Geschlechter und anderen Problemen des Andersseins, in: L. Schottroff/M.-T. Wacker (Hg.), *Kompendium feministische Bibelauslegung* (Gütersloh: Güterloher Verlagshaus, 1998), S. 603–611, S. 605: „Im griechischen Text steht gar nicht, daß es das ‚andere Evangelium' … nicht gibt. Sondern da steht wörtlich, daß es ‚kein

Faßt man die Termini in Gal 1,6f. als Synonyme auf, läßt sich der Gegensatz zwischen der Berufung durch Gott und dem ἕτερον εὐαγγέλιον mühelos erklären. Allerdings entstehen dadurch andere Schwierigkeiten. Ein erstes Problem ist, daß das ἄλλο bei dieser Deutung überflüssig wird und deshalb als pleonastische Ausdrucksweise erklärt werden muß.[20] Dies ist jedoch keineswegs die nächstliegende Erklärung für das Nebeneinander beider Termini. Wenn es Paulus um eine prinzipielle Bestreitung der Legitimität des ἕτερον εὐαγγέλιον *als εὐαγγέλιον* gegangen wäre, hätte er das ἄλλο weggelassen oder aber formuliert ὃ οὐκ ἔστιν εὐαγγέλιον. Mit dem ἄλλο wird dagegen nicht die *Existenz*, sondern die *Andersartigkeit* des ἕτερον εὐαγγέλιον bestritten.

Gegen die genannte Deutung spricht weiter, daß ἕτερος und ἄλλος hier in syntaktischer Opposition zueinander stehen. Interpretiert man sie als Synonyme, muß man deshalb davon ausgehen, daß Paulus die Botschaft der Gegner zunächst als Evangelium bezeichnet, um dies sofort im Anschluß mit einer jedenfalls nicht eindeutigen Formulierung wieder zurückzunehmen.[21] Der syntaktische Befund legt jedoch eine andere Interpretation der Termini nahe.

Ein drittes Problem ist schließlich, daß die zum Beleg der Synonymität von ἕτερος und ἄλλος herangezogenen Belege zur Deutung des in Frage stehenden Satzes nur bedingt tauglich sind. Daß die Bedeutungsfelder beider Termini nicht scharf voneinander zu trennen sind, steht dabei ebensowenig in Frage wie die Tatsache, daß sie in der Koine als referentielle Synonyme verwandt werden konnten.[22] Dieser austauschbare Gebrauch geht aus Textvarianten, in denen ein Terminus den anderen ersetzen kann,[23] ebenso hervor wie aus denjenigen Stellen, an denen sie im unmittelbaren Kontext oder innerhalb von Aufzählungen nebeneinander begegnen, denselben Sachverhalt also auf variierende Weise ausdrücken. Dies findet sich auch bei Paulus selbst, der die Termini in 1 Kor 12,8–10; 15,39–41

anderes ist'. Die Übersetzung des Relativsatzes ‚ο ουκ εστιν αλλο' ist grammatisch völlig unkompliziert. Theologisch ist das Gesagte aber offenbar so undenkbar, daß die Kommentare Paulus in der Regel auch hier einen lapsus linguae unterstellen."

20. Vgl. etwa Mußner, *Galaterbrief*, S. 57: „ἄλλο ist darum eigentlich in dem Relativsatz überflüssig und scheint nur pleonastisch zu stehen, um den folgenden εἰ μή-Satz besser einleiten zu können." Ähnlich Schlier, *Galater*, S. 38, Anm. 1.

21. Diese Schwierigkeit hat J. Rohde deutlich empfunden. Vgl. ders., *Der Brief des Paulus an die Galater* (ThKNT 9; Berlin: Evang. Verlagsanstalt, 1989), S. 41: „Evtl. hat Paulus selbst sofort gespürt, daß ihm eine problematische Formulierung entschlüpft war ... Es werden hier also zwei Gedanken zusammengefaßt: Auf der einen Seite ist die Predigt der Gegner kein Evangelium, und auf der anderen Seite gibt es kein Evangelium außer dem, welches Paulus verkündigt hat." Ob Paulus dies hier zum Ausdruck bringen wollte, ist durchaus zu hinterfragen.

22. Im Blick auf den ntl. Sprachgebrauch zeigt dies der knappe Überblick von J.K. Elliott, The Use of ἕτερος in the New Testament, *ZNW* 60 (1969), S. 140f. Es ist freilich problematisch, wenn dieser Artikel als Beleg für die Synonymität beider Termini in Gal 1,6f. zitiert wird, was mitunter geschieht. Elliott geht auf diese Stelle nur mit einem Satz ein: „Similarly, commentators on the importance of ἕτερον at Gal 1,6 (no v. l.) cannot argue from the word that a definite alternative Gospel was in the author's mind." Das Verhältnis beider Termini in Gal 1,6f. ist mit dieser Bemerkung nicht bestimmt, schon gar nicht in dem heute zumeist anzutreffenden Sinn einer Leugnung der Existenz eines anderen Evangeliums.

23. So etwa in Mt 10,23; 16,14; Lk 3,18; 10,1; 14,20; 16,18 u. ö.

und vermutlich auch in 2 Kor 11,4 synonym verwendet.[24] Die eigenen Bedeutungsmerkmale von ἕτερος und ἄλλος werden in diesen Fällen also vernachlässigt.

Die Austauschbarkeit von ἕτερος und ἄλλος, auch wenn sie sich bei Paulus selbst findet, besagt jedoch nicht, daß die bedeutungsspezifischen Merkmale der Termini verlorengegangen wären, also nicht nur von einer referentiellen, sondern auch von einer lexikalischen Synonymität auszugehen sei.[25] Hierauf weist schon der Umstand hin, daß in einigen neutestamentlichen Textvarianten ἕτερος durch eine Ordinalzahl ersetzt wurde,[26] ἄλλος dagegen nie. Ἕτερος hat in diesen Fällen also die Bedeutung „ein anderer, ein weiterer". Dies konnte an anderen Stellen auch durch ἄλλος ausgedrückt werden, was jedoch nicht besagt, daß die lexikalische Bedeutung von ἄλλος dadurch mit derjenigen von ἕτερος identisch geworden wäre. Besonders dort, wo, wie in Gal 1,6f., beide Termini außerhalb einer Aufzählung nebeneinander verwandt werden, um verschiedene Sachverhalte auszudrücken, kann nicht von einer Synonymität ausgegangen werden. In diesen Fällen kann vielmehr nur eine Analyse des konkreten Gebrauchs Aufschluß über die aktualisierten Bedeutungsmerkmale geben.

Im Blick auf den in Frage stehenden Satz ist hierzu von der syntaktischen Beobachtung auszugehen, daß ἕτερος durch ἄλλος negiert wird. Dies spricht dagegen, eine Synonymität anzunehmen oder ἄλλος in der Interpretation de facto durch εὐαγγέλιον zu ersetzen. Daß die semantische Differenz in diesem Fall vielmehr ernstzunehmen ist, wird von einigen Auslegern durchaus konstatiert, die darum die zweite, hier zu nennende Deutungsmöglichkeit vertreten.

Eine Bedeutungsdifferenz wurde zuerst im angelsächsischen Sprachraum von John B. Lightfoot notiert und so bestimmt, daß ἕτερος zur Unterscheidung, ἄλλος dagegen zur Aufzählung diene.[27] In derselben Richtung äußerten sich später Friedrich Sieffert,[28] Ernest de Witt Burton[29] und, ihm folgend, Richard N. Longenecker.[30] Im deutschen Sprachraum hat Klaus Haacker diese Position in

24. 1 Kor 12,8–10: ᾧ μεν ... λόγος σοφίας, ἄλλῳ δὲ λόγος γνώσεως ... ἑτέρῳ πίστις; 1 Kor 15,39–41: ἄλλη μὲν ... ἄλλη δὲ ... ἑτέρα μὲν ... ἑτέρα δὲ ... ἄλλη ... καὶ ἄλλη; 2 Kor 11,4: ἄλλον Ἰησοῦν ... ἢ πνεῦμα ἕτερον ... ἢ εὐαγγέλιον ἕτερον.

25. Vgl. C.K. Barrett, *A Commentary on the Second Epistle to the Corinthians* (BNTC; London: Black, 1973), S. 275: „That Paul could distinguish between *other* and *different* is shown by Gal. i. 6 f.; it does not, however, appear that he does so here [sc.: in II Cor xi. 4, J. S.]."

26. Mt 21,30: δευτέρῳ für ἑτέρῳ in א² B C² L Z u. a.; Lk 14,19f.: δεύτερος bzw. τρίτος für ἕτερος in 1675; Lk 16,7: δευτέρῳ für ἑτέρῳ in 157. Vgl. Elliott, *Use*, 140.

27. J.B. Lightfoot, *St. Paul's Epistle to the Galatians* (London/New York: MacMillan, 1887), S. 76: „Thus ἄλλος adds, while ἕτερος distinguishes."

28. *Galater*, S. 44: „Im Gegensatz zu ἕτερος andersartig ist also ἄλλο hier ein anderes der Zahl nach."

29. *Galatians*, S. 421: „...in so far as here is a distinction between the two words ἄλλος is enumerative and ἕτερος differentiative."

30. *Galatians*, S. 15: „Generally speaking, ἕτερον [sic] and ἄλλος are synonyms, with both words, usually denoting an enumerative sense ('an additional one') rather than a differentiative sense (‚another of a different kind') ... Yet here in context there seems little doubt that he means to suggest a qualitative difference, with ἕτερος signaling ‚another of a different kind' and ἄλλος ‚another of the same kind'."

dem Artikel ἕτερος für das EWNT vertreten.[31] Bei dieser Deutung wird zunächst zu Recht herausgestellt, daß beide Termini in ihrer Verwendung in Gal 1,6f. semantisch voneinander zu unterscheiden sind. Diese Differenz wird sodann so bestimmt, daß ἄλλος additiv, ἕτερος dagegen adversativ zu bestimmen sei. Paulus würde demzufolge argumentieren, daß die Botschaft der Gegner von der seinigen inhaltlich verschieden (ἕτερον) sei und deshalb keine zusätzliche, ergänzende Form der Evangeliumsverkündigung (οὐκ ἄλλο) darstellen könne.

Das entscheidende Problem dieser Sicht ist, daß sie die lexikalische Bedeutung der beiden Termini genau entgegengesetzt zu dem semantischen Unterschied, der sich zwischen ihnen feststellen läßt, bestimmt. Dieser besagt, daß ἕτερος ursprünglich zu den dualischen Pronomina gehört, durch welche das Andere/Entsprechende von zwei Dingen ausgedrückt wird (entsprechend dem lateinischen *alter*),[32] diese dualische Bedeutung sich in der späteren Verwendung jedoch abgeschliffen hat.[33] Ἄλλος unterscheidet sich hiervon dadurch, daß damit auf jeden Fall die Andersartigkeit zur Sprache gebracht wird (entsprechend dem lateinischen *alius*), die Alterität demnach nur eine, auf der Vernachlässigung der Differenz zu ἕτερος basierende Möglichkeit ist, dieses auszudrücken.[34]

Der Unterschied zwischen beiden Worten besteht demzufolge darin, daß ἕτερος ein relationaler, komparativischer, ἄλλος dagegen ein absoluter Terminus zur Bezeichnung der Andersartigkeit ist. Das spezifische Problem der Interpretation von Gal 1,6f. ist nun, wie die Bedeutung beider Termini vor diesem Hintergrund innerhalb der dortigen syntaktischen Konstruktion zu bestimmen ist. Daß sie in Opposition zueinander gestellt werden, läßt es dabei als unwahrscheinlich

31. K. Haacker, ἕτερος, *EWNT II*, S. 165–167. Ähnlich H. Windisch, *Der zweite Korintherbrief* (KEK VI; Göttingen: Vandenhoeck & Ruprecht, 9th edn, 1924), S. 327.

32. Vgl. W. Pape, *Griechisch-Deutsches Handwörterbuch* (Nachdruck der dritten Auflage bearbeitet von M. Sengebusch, I; Graz: Akademische Druck-u. Verlagsanstalt, 1954), s. v. ἕτερος: „1) einer von zweien, einer von beiden … bes.[onders] von paarweise vorkommenden Dingen … 2) wie schon bei den Aufzählungen mehrerer Dinge ἕτερος der zweite bedeutet, so wird damit auch Einer aus einer größern Menge herausgenommen u.[nd] einem Andern entgegengesetzt, so daß sogleich wieder eine Zweiheit eintritt … dah.[er] es auch dem ἄλλος entspricht u.[nd] ohne den Zusatz τις unbestimmter wird."

33. Vgl. E. Mayser, *Grammatik der griechischen Papyri aus der Ptolemäerzeit, mit Einschluß der gleichzeitigen Ostraka und der in Ägypten verfaßten Inschriften, Band II 2: Satzlehre, Analytischer Teil, Zweite Hälfte* (Berlin/Leipzig: de Gruyter, 1934), S. 88: „ἕτερος gehört zu den wenigen dualischen Pronomina, die sich im Hellenistischen bis spät erhalten haben (neben ἀμφότεροι, ἑκάτερος, μηδέτερος, ὁπότερος). Doch hat es diese Bedeutung der Dualität fast ganz verloren und unterscheidet sich kaum mehr von ἄλλος". Auch bei H. G.Liddell/R. Scott, *A Greek-English Lexicon. A New Edition Revised and Augmented throughout by Sir H.J. Jones with the Assistance of R. McKenzie and with the Co-Operation of many Scholars, With a Supplement* (Oxford: Clarendon, 9th edn, 1968, repr. 1992), wird als erste Bedeutung für ἕτερος „one or the other of two" angegeben. Niedergeschlagen hat sich diese Bedeutung in Termini wie οἱ ἕτεροι (die Gegenpartei = die Feinde), ἑτερόφθαλμος (einäugig) oder ἑτέρωθι (auf der anderen Seite).

34. Die von Burton genannten Belege aus der LXX und dem NT, mit denen er zeigen möchte, daß ἄλλος enumerative und ἕτερος differenzierende Bedeutung habe, belegen dagegen nur, daß sich die Bedeutungen beider Termini, *wenn sie einzeln begegnen*, aneinander annähern konnten. Daß ihre bedeutungsspezifischen Merkmale in der Weise, wie Burton behauptet, zu bestimmen seien, geht aus diesen Belegen indes nicht hervor.

erscheinen, daß ihre bedeutungsspezifischen Merkmale zu vernachlässigen seien. Noch unwahrscheinlicher ist, daß sich diese in ihr Gegenteil verkehrt hätten.[35]

Auf die Spur der korrekten semantischen Deutung des Befundes führt deshalb der, im deutschen Sprachraum offenbar unbemerkt gebliebene, Einspruch von William M. Ramsay gegen Lightfoot.[36] Ramsay stellt heraus, daß beide Termini die Bedeutung „verschieden" („different") annehmen könnten, dies jedoch nicht die Frage beantworte, welcher von beiden den höheren Grad an Differenz ausdrücke, wenn sie in syntaktische Opposition zueinander gestellt werden.[37] Der Befund stellt sich nach Ramsay in diesem Fall genau andersherum dar, als von Lightfoot angenommen.[38] Dies ergibt sich aus einem Blick auf diejenigen Verwendungen, in denen die bedeutungsspezifischen Merkmale beider Termini zum Ausdruck kommen.[39]

Im deutschen Sprachraum hat Theodor Zahn eine Interpretation vorgelegt, die dem dargestellten Befund gerecht wird. Seiner Auffassung zufolge haben die Gegner ein anderes, die Verkündigung des Paulus ersetzendes Evangelium in den galatischen Gemeinden verkündet, dem Paulus nunmehr mit dem Argument entgegentrete, daß das, was sie als rechtmäßiges Evangelium zu verkünden haben, nicht von dem seinigen abweiche, alles andere dagegen kein Evangelium sei.[40] Zahn beachtet also die semantische Differenz von ἕτερος und ἄλλος sehr genau, wenn er zwischen einem *weiteren* Evangelium und der Frage nach dessen *Andersartigkeit* unterscheidet.

Unter den neueren Auslegungen findet sich eine korrekte semantische Beschreibung des Befundes, soweit ich sehe, neben der bereits genannten Äußerung von Brigitte Kahl zu dem Relativsatz in 1,7,[41] lediglich bei François Vouga. Er schreibt: „Anders als Gal 1,19, aber wie in 2 Kor 11,4, werden ἕτερος und

35. Hierauf verweist auch der bei J.H. Moulton/G. Milligan, *Vocabulary of the Greek Testament* (London: Hodder & Stoughton, 1930, repr. 1997). s. v. ἕτερος dargestellte Befund: „ἕτερος and ἀμφότεροι are claimed by Blass ... as the only surviving words in the Hellenistic age which denote *duality* as distinct from plurality, and abundant evidence can be cited from the Κοινή of the correct use of ἕτερος in this sense." Es folgen etliche Beispiele aus Papyri, die die Verwendung von ἕτερος in dualischer Bedeutung für die Koine belegen.

36. Ramsay, *Galatians*, S. 260–266. Vgl. auch Moulton/Milligan, a. a. O. Dort findet sich am Ende des Artikels ἕτερος eine kurze Darstellung der Positionen von Lightfoot und Ramsay, die Ramsays Sicht aufgrund des zuvor angeführten Materials unterstützt.

37. A. a. O., S. 262: „But the point is: When ἕτερος and ἄλλος are pointedly contrasted with one another, which of the two indicates the greater degree of difference?"

38. Ebd.: „On the contrary, the truth is precisely the opposite. When the two words are pointedly contrasted with one another, ἕτερος means ‚a second', ‚another of the same kind', ‚new' [*e. g.*, ‚a new king succeeds in regular course to the throne'], while ἄλλος implies difference of kind."

39. Ein signifikantes Beispiel ist der von Ramsay (a. a. O., S. 263f.) angeführte Beleg aus Plato, *Prot. 330A–B*. Die Frage, ob sich die einzelnen Teile der Tugend so wie verschiedene Teile des Goldes zueinander verhalten, lautet οὐδὲν διαφέρει τὰ ἕτερα τῶν ἑτέρων, wogegen die jeweilige Besonderheit, durch die sie sich voneinander unterscheiden, formuliert ist als ἕκαστον δὲ αὔτων ἐστιν ... ἄλλο, τὸ δὲ ἄλλο.

40. Zahn, *Galater*, S. 48: „Sofern die Judaisten Ev[angelium] predigen, ist dies nichts anderes, als was P[au]l[us] gepredigt hat, und sofern sie etwas anderes lehren als er, ist dies nicht Ev[angelium]."

41. Siehe oben Anm. 19.

ἄλλος genau unterschieden: Die alternative Botschaft (*alter*), zu welcher sich die Galater hinwenden, kann deswegen kein Evangelium sein, weil es überhaupt kein anderes (*alius*) Evangelium geben kann".[42] Vouga zufolge kann also in der vorliegenden Konstruktion, anders als in anderen Fällen, nicht einfach davon ausgegangen werden, daß Paulus ἕτερος und ἄλλος synonym verwende. Vielmehr verbinde er mit beiden Ausdrücken einen je eigenen Aspekt. Trotz dieser zutreffenden Bestandsaufnahme kommt jedoch auch Vouga zu keiner anderen Lösung als die zuvor genannten Vorschläge, wenn er folgert, Paulus würde mit dem Relativsatz die *Existenz* des von den Gegnern verkündeten εὐαγγέλιον bestreiten. Dies kann er allerdings nur durch die Hinzunahme eines nicht im Text stehenden Kausalsatzes – „weil es überhaupt kein anderes (*alius*) Evangelium geben kann" – in die Auslegung erreichen. Paulus sagt jedoch nicht, daß es kein anderes (*aliud*) Evangelium *geben könne*, sondern daß das alternative (*alterum*) Evangelium kein anderes (*aliud*) *sei*! Damit ist die Pointe seines Argumentes etwas anders zu bestimmen.

Durch die syntaktisch unpräzise Bestimmung von ἕτερος und ἄλλος wird der Fokus des paulinischen Satzes demnach ebenso verschoben wie durch die semantisch unzutreffende Annahme, ἕτερος drücke eine qualitative, ἄλλος dagegen eine enumerative Differenz aus. Diese Positionen sind vielmehr bereits von der Annahme geleitet, Paulus würde im Galaterbrief die Existenz eines anderen Evangeliums grundsätzlich bestreiten. Auf die richtige Deutung, die dann auch die Pointe des paulinischen Argumentes etwas anders erscheinen läßt, führen dagegen die Interpretationen von Ramsay und Zahn sowie die Äußerungen von Kahl und Vouga. In diesen wird zum einen zu Recht herausgestellt, daß durch ἕτερος, wenn es in Opposition zu ἄλλος steht, nicht der größere Grad an Differenz, sondern ein enumerativer Sinn ausgedrückt wird, zum anderen wird darauf hingewiesen, daß ὃ οὐκ ἔστιν ἄλλο hier kaum als Negation der Existenz des ἕτερον εὐαγγέλιον zu deuten ist.

Paulus geht es in Gal 1,6f. demnach nicht darum, die Existenz einer zweiten Gestalt des εὐαγγέλιον zu bestreiten. Vielmehr räumt er ein, daß es eine solche weitere Form der Verkündigung des εὐαγγέλιον (ein ἕτερον εὐαγγέλιον) neben dem seinigen gibt. Dies ist freilich nicht im Sinne eines Zugeständnisses an seine Konkurrenten zu verstehen![43] Aus V. 7 geht stattdessen hervor, daß das ἕτερον

42. Vouga, *Galater*, S. 22. Ob diese semantische Differenz auch für 2 Kor 11,4 anzunehmen ist, wie Vouga voraussetzt, kann hier auf sich beruhen.

43. Kürzlich hat D. Sänger meine in dem genannten Beitrag (vgl. Anm. 4) angedeutete, dort jedoch nicht näher begründete Interpretation dadurch zu widerlegen versucht, daß er das ἕτερον εὐαγγέλιον als „keine gleichberechtigte Variante" bezeichnet, da es zu dem von Paulus selbst verkündigten εὐαγγέλιον in Konkurrenz stehe. Vgl. ders., Vergeblich bemüht (Gal 4,11)? Zur paulinischen Argumentationsstrategie im Galaterbrief, *NTS* 48 (2002), S. 377–399, hier S. 388, Anm. 52. Diese Kritik beruht auf einem völligen Mißverständnis meines Argumentes und läuft deshalb ins Leere. Niemand behauptet, daß Paulus die Verkündigung seiner Gegner als gleichwertige Alternative charakterisieren würde. Meine Position ist zudem mit dem Satz „Entgegen der mehrheitlich vertretenen Auffassung deutet J. Schröter den Relativsatz ὃ οὐκ ἔστιν ἄλλο als ein positives Zugeständnis..." völlig fehlgedeutet. Die Frage ist, *mit welchen Argumenten* Paulus die

εὐαγγέλιον erst durch die Verdrehung des εὐαγγέλιον τοῦ Χριστοῦ zu einem ἄλλο εὐαγγέλιον wird, dem zu folgen eine Abwendung von Gott darstellt.

3) Diese Deutung führt zu der dritten, hier zu besprechenden Frage, nämlich der *Deutung des Konditionalsatzes*. Bei der soeben dargelegten Interpretation fügt sich dieser derart ein, daß Paulus nunmehr zum Ausdruck bringt, das ἕτερον εὐαγγέλιον, welches in Wahrheit gar kein anderes (ἄλλο) sei, werde erst von seinen Gegnern zu einem solchen gemacht. Die Verdrehung des ἕτερον εὐαγγέλιον ist somit die Ausnahme von dem οὐκ ἔστιν ἄλλο, weil es nunmehr zu einer vom εὐαγγέλιον τοῦ Χριστοῦ abweichenden Form der Verkündigung gemacht wird. Indem die Gegner also die Einheit des Evangeliums bestreiten, verdrehen sie das εὐαγγέλιον τοῦ Χριστοῦ. Mit diesem zuletzt genannten Ausdruck charakterisiert Paulus das „wahre Evangelium" als die legitime Botschaft von Christus, die damit den Maßstab darstellt, an dem sich jede Form seiner Verkündigung messen lassen muß. Der Genitiv τοῦ Χριστοῦ ist demzufolge die entscheidende Qualifizierung des εὐαγγέλιον, was die Gegner verkennen, indem sie aus den verschiedenen Formen, in denen es sich manifestieren kann, eine grundsätzliche Differenz inhaltlicher Art ableiten. Paulus hält dagegen fest, daß trotz der verschiedenen Formen, in denen sich das Evangelium in der Verkündigung ereignet, an seiner grundsätzlichen Einheit kein Zweifel besteht. Indem die Gegner diese Einheit bestreiten, verlassen sie die durch die Berufung ἐν χάριτι von Gott eröffnete Gemeinschaft in Christus und versuchen sogar, andere dazu zu überreden, ihnen hierbei zu folgen.

Eine Paraphrase des analysierten Satzes lautet demnach: „Ich wundere mich, daß ihr euch so schnell von dem abwendet, der euch in der Gnade Christi berufen hat, hin zu einem anderen Evangelium. Dieses würde zu demjenigen, welches ich euch verkündet habe, gar nicht im Widerspruch stehen, würden euch nicht gewisse Leute verwirren und das Evangelium Christi verdrehen."

Als Ergebnis des ersten Teils läßt sich daher festhalten: Das Argument des Paulus in Gal 1,6f. lautet, seine Gegner behaupteten zu Unrecht, es gebe eine legitime Form der Verkündigung des Evangeliums (ἕτερος, alter), die sachlich von seiner eigenen verschieden (ἄλλος, alius) sei. Damit stellt er nicht grundsätzlich in Abrede, daß es *überhaupt* eine andere Form der Evangeliumsverkündigung gibt. Erst die Bestreitung der Einheit des Evangeliums macht diese alternative Form zu einer Verdrehung des εὐαγγέλιον τοῦ Χριστου und verleitet die Galater damit zur Abwendung von Gott.

2. *Das eine Evangelium in zweierlei Gestalt*

Die Pointe von Gal 1,6f. lautet, daß es neben der von Paulus verkündeten eine zweite Form des Evangeliums gibt, die nicht im Widerspruch zu der seinen steht.

Position der Gegner zurückweist! Diesbezüglich bietet der Beitrag Sängers keine weiterführenden Einsichten.

Der Vorwurf an die Gegner – und die diesen folgenden Galater – lautet demnach, daß sie die Einheit des Evangeliums verlassen, indem sie die je eigene Form, in der das Evangelium Gestalt gewinnt, verkennen, damit die Berufung durch Gott aufgeben und das Evangelium Christi verdrehen. Worin es sich bei den je eigenen Formen der Gestaltwerdung des Evangeliums handelt, wird im weiteren Verlauf des Briefes präzisiert. Dies soll zunächst anhand einiger Formulierungen in 1,10–2,21, sodann durch einen Blick auf 3,10–14 dargestellt werden.

Wenn Paulus in 1,11 wiederum auf das εὐαγγέλιον zu sprechen kommt, erläutert er es näher durch die Wendung τὸ εὐαγγελισθὲν ὑπ' ἐμοῦ. Wie der syntaktische Zusammenhang zeigt, handelt es sich dabei nicht um die Hinführung zu einer Aussage über den Inhalt des Evangeliums (wie in 1 Kor 15,3) oder um eine Reminiszenz an seine Erstverkündigung in den galatischen Gemeinden, sondern um eine Aussage über die Herkunft seines Evangeliums: Dieses ist Paulus nicht durch menschliche Unterweisung, sondern durch eine Offenbarung Jesu Christi zuteil geworden.[44] Es geht also um die spezifische Weise, in der das Evangelium, das Paulus den galatischen Gemeinden gebracht hat, an ihn selbst übermittelt wurde. Wenn er dessen göttlichen Ursprung herausstellt, so zielt dies auf die Legitimation seiner Verkündigung: Das von ihm verkündete Evangelium hat seinen Ursprung bei Gott selbst, weshalb seine Wahrheit sowie die Lauterkeit seines Verkündigers außer Frage stehen.

Mit der Aussage in 1,12 leitet Paulus demnach seine Ausführungen über eine bestimmte Gestalt des Evangeliums, nämlich die ihm durch eine ἀποκάλυψις von Gott bekanntgemachte, ein. Dies wird in 1,16 sachlich gefüllt: Inhalt der Offenbarung an Paulus sind der Sohn Gottes sowie der Auftrag, ihn ἐν τοῖς ἔθνεσιν bekanntzumachen. Wiederum geht es um eine Aussage, die sich auf eine spezifische Weise der Offenbarung des Evangeliums durch Gott sowie seine Proklamation unter den Menschen bezieht: Das Evangelium des Paulus ist dadurch charakterisiert, daß der Sohn Gottes unter den Heiden verkündet wird. Ein dabei ins Auge fallendes, für die inhaltliche Qualifizierung des εὐαγγέλιον τοῦ Χριστοῦ noch wichtig werdendes Merkmal ist die auffällige Herausstellung des Kontrastes zwischen dem außergewöhnlichen Eifer für die jüdischen Überlieferungen und der Verfolgung der Gemeinde Gottes durch den „vorchristlichen" Paulus einerseits, der Verkündigung des Evangeliums unter den Heiden andererseits. Dies weist voraus auf 2,15f., wo Paulus das aus dem Evangelium resultierende neue Selbstverständnis als allgemeine, auch von Kephas und den anderen Judenchristen geteilte Überzeugung ins Feld führen wird.

Der von Paulus nur an dieser Stelle verwandte (und auch ansonsten im Urchristentum vor Ignatius nicht begegnende) Terminus Ἰουδαϊσμός, in 2,14 durch die demselben Wortfeld angehörenden Ausdrücke Ἰουδαϊκῶς ζῆν und ἰουδαΐζειν ergänzt, weist auf eine Richtung hin, welche die Identitätsmerkmale des Judentums als exklusiv und das jüdische von anderen Völkern abgrenzend interpretierte.[45] Wenn gerade Paulus als ein

44. Der Genitiv Ἰησοῦ Χριστοῦ ist mit Mußner, *Galaterbrief*, S. 68, u. a. wohl im Zusammenhang mit 1,16 zu lesen und als objectivus zu verstehen (anders z. B. Vouga, *Galater*, S. 28).

45. Dies belegt die Verwendung dieser Terminologie in jüdischen Schriften. Zu ἰουδαΐζειν vgl. Est 8,17 LXX (περιετέμοντο καὶ ἰουδάϊζον); Theodotus, *Frg. 4* (Euseb, *PraepEv 9,22,4–6:*

dieser Auffassung zugehöriger Jude von Gott zum Heidenmissionar berufen wurde, dann ist unübersehbar, daß das Bekenntnis zu Jesus Christus zugleich eine Aufhebung der Trennung von Juden und Heiden bedeutet. Das Paulus von Gott anvertraute Evangelium ist damit zugleich inhaltlich präfiguriert.

Die so herausgestellte Tatsache einer spezifischen Form der Verkündigung des Evangeliums – seine Bekanntmachung unter den Heiden, die zugleich eine Reformulierung des Verhältnisses zu den jüdischen Überlieferung beinhaltet[46] – führt schließlich zu der Gegenüberstellung zweier Gestalten des Evangeliums im Bericht über das Treffen mit den Jerusalemer Autoritäten. Gal 2,2 zufolge zieht Paulus nach Jerusalem, um über „sein" Evangelium zu berichten. Wie bereits in 1,12 findet sich auch hier die Näherbeschreibung als τὸ εὐαγγέλιον ὃ κηρύσσω ἐν τοῖς ἔθνεσιν. Daß es neben dieser noch eine zweite Weise gibt, in der sich das Evangelium ereignet, zeigt sich daran, daß 2,7–9 zufolge τὸ εὐαγγέλιον τῆς ἀκροβυστίας und τῆς περιτομῆς als gleichwertige Gestalten des einen Evangeliums von allen Aposteln anerkannt werden. Das Evangelium des Paulus ist also nicht eine zweite, konkurrierende Verkündigung – aber auch nicht die einzige Form, in der es Gestalt gewinnt –, sondern eine mit der von den Jerusalemer Aposteln vertretenen *sachlich in Übereinstimmung befindliche* und von diesen deshalb vorbehaltlos akzeptierte, wenngleich in seiner konkreten Gestalt von deren *unterschiedene* Weise der Manifestation des einen Evangeliums.

Die Ausführungen des Paulus über „sein" Evangelium machen somit deutlich, daß es sich hierbei um eine spezifische Gestalt der Verkündigung des Gottessohnes handelt, die diesen unter den Heiden bekanntmacht. Durch seinen autobiographischen Bericht legt er dar, daß diese Gestalt des Evangeliums durch Gott selbst autorisiert ist und gleichwertig neben derjenigen steht, die von Petrus[47] und

περιτεμνομένους ἰουδαΐσαι); Jos, *Bell 2,454* (μέχρι περιτομῆς ἰουδαΐζειν), vgl. auch 463; zu Ἰουδαϊσμός 2 Makk 2,21; 8,1; 14,38; 4 Makk 4,26 sowie die Synagogeninschrift von Stobi (hierzu: H. Lietzmann, *ZNW* 32 [1933], S. 93f.; M. Hengel, Die Synagogeninschrift von Stobi, in: ders., *Judaica et Hellenistica. Kleine Schriften I* [WUNT 90; Tübingen: Mohr-Siebeck, 1996], S. 91–130, bes. 122f. [zuerst 1966]). Werden hier jüdische und heidnische Identität gegenübergestellt, so konfrontiert Ignatius in vergleichbarer Weise Ἰουδαϊσμός und Χριστιανισμός miteinander. Vgl. ders., *Magn 10,3* (vgl. 8,1); *Phld 6,1*.

46. Vgl. J.D.G. Dunn, Who Did Paul Think He Was? A Study of Jewish-Christian Identity, *NTS* 45 (1999), S. 174–193.

47. Die rätselhafte Verwendung dieses Namens im Unterschied zu dem ansonsten bei Paulus stets begegnenden Κηφᾶς (so bereits wieder in 2,9 und 11) hat zu der Vermutung geführt, Paulus zitiere hier aus einem in Jerusalem vereinbarten Dekret (so zuerst E. Dinkler, Der Brief an die Galater. Zum Kommentar von Heinrich Schlier, in: ders., *Signum Crucis. Aufsätze zum Neuen Testament und zur christlichen Archäologie* (Tübingen: Mohr-Siebeck, 1967), S. 270–282, 279 [zuerst 1953/55]; dann auch O. Cullmann, Πέτρος Κηφᾶς, *ThWNT 6* [1959], S. 99–112, S. 100, Anm. 6). Die Hypothese ist vielfach auf Widerspruch gestoßen und letztlich natürlich auch nicht beweisbar (zur Diskussion vgl. L. Wehr, *Petrus und Paulus – Kontrahenten und Partner. Die beiden Apostel im Spiegel des Neuen Testaments, der Apostolischen Väter und früher Zeugnisse ihrer Verehrung* [NTA NF 30; Münster: Aschendorf, 1996], S. 49–55). Die Vermutung, Paulus führe hier ein gewissermaßen „offizielles" Zitat an – oder gebe seiner Formulierung selbst einen „offiziellen" Anstrich – hat jedenfalls für sich, daß es ihm um eine förmliche Darlegung der Vereinbarung über die Weisen der Bekanntmachung des Evangeliums geht.

den übrigen Jerusalemer Aposteln vertreten wird. Daraus folgt, daß sich die zweifache Form, in der das eine Evangelium verkündigt wird und die in 1,6f. in der Erwähnung des neben dem seinen stehenden ἕτερον εὐαγγέλιον bereits zutage getreten war, auf seine Gestaltwerdung unter Juden und Heiden bezieht. Das in 2,7 erwähnte εὐαγγέλιον τῆς περιτομῆς kann deshalb auch nicht die Verkündigung seiner Gegner in den galatischen Gemeinden sein,[48] sondern es ist diejenige Gestalt des Evangeliums, die an die Juden ausgerichtet, von seinen Gegnern dagegen verfälscht wird.

Die für die Position des Paulus in der christologischen Kontroverse des Galaterbriefes zentrale Argumentationslinie tritt noch klarer hervor, wenn Paulus in 2,15f. zu dem Verhalten des Kephas Position bezieht. Wenn er hierfür bei der Unterscheidung von Juden auf der einen, Sündern aus den Heiden auf der anderen Seite ansetzt und für die christusgläubigen Juden sodann eine Erkenntnis reklamiert, die sie de facto mit den Heiden auf dieselbe Stufe stellt, dann führt dies seine bislang herausgearbeitete Argumentation weiter:[49] Paulus hat dargelegt, daß die Verkündigung des Gottessohnes an die Heiden eine von Gott selbst initiierte Weise der Verbreitung des Evangeliums ist. Dies führt ihn zu der christologischen – in ihren Konsequenzen dann auch ekklesiologischen – Einsicht der Aufhebung der Trennung von Juden und Heiden in der Christusgemeinschaft. In 2,15f. wird diese Tatsache als Erkenntnisprozeß aus judenchristlicher Perspektive beschrieben: Nicht nur Paulus, sondern die Judenchristen überhaupt,[50] haben erkannt, daß nur der Glaube an Christus zur Gerechtigkeit führt, mithin auch sie selbst in Christus als Sünder erfunden werden.[51] Die inhaltliche Grundlage der Gemeinschaft von Juden und Heiden in Christus besteht demnach darin, daß ihre gemeinsame Vergangenheit als Sünder sie auch als Partner in der Christusgemeinschaft einander gleichstellt.

48. Die diesbezügliche Formulierung von Dunn, *Galatians*, S. 42, ist deshalb missverständlich. Dunn schreibt zu Gal 1,6: „It is not immediately clear, how this 'gospel' relates to 'the gospel of circumcision' (ii.7): either it was the same ... or the incoming missionaries in Galatia represented a more traditional understanding of the gospel, a more strongly 'judaized' version of the gospel agreed at Jerusalem ...". Wenn es sich bei dem „Evangelium" der Gegner um das εὐαγγέλιον τῆς περιτομῆς aus 2,7 handeln würde, wäre die Betonung der Tatsache, daß sein eigenes diesem gegenüber als gleichwertig anerkannt worden war, für die Argumentation des Paulus nicht nur kontraproduktiv, sondern geradezu vernichtend.

49. Der Satz in 2,15 („Wir sind Juden und nicht Sünder aus den Heiden.") steht dabei für sich. Mit εἰδότες wird in V. 16 ein neuer Satz eingeleitet, der den Kontrast zwischen der Differenz aus V. 15 und der neuen Einsicht besonders herausstreicht. Vgl. Sieffert, *Galater*, S. 142f.

50. Es ist überaus bedeutsam, daß Paulus die in 1,13–16 noch mit seiner Berufung verbundene Neubewertung der jüdischen Identitätsmerkmale hier als Erkenntnisprozeß beschreibt, den er auch für Kephas, Barnabas, und wohl die Judenchristen überhaupt, reklamiert. Ob dies historisch zutreffend ist, läßt sich kaum noch überprüfen. Es kann aber wohl davon ausgegangen werden, daß Paulus Grund zu der Annahme hatte, es verhalte sich so, wie er es in 2,15f. beschreibt, da die Basis seiner Argumentation andernfalls hinfällig wäre.

51. Mit der Auffassung, daß die Gerechtigkeit nicht vom Menschen selbst hergestellt werden kann, steht Paulus in jüdischer Tradition, die etwa durch Ψ 142,2; 1QS XI,12–15; 1QH VI,30f.; IV,36f. u. ö.; 1Hen 81,5 belegt ist. Freilich wird sie dort nirgendwo den Weisungen der Tora programmatisch gegenübergestellt.

Die Anerkennung der Gleichwertigkeit des εὐαγγέλιον τῆς ἀκροβυστίας auf dem Jerusalemer Treffen stellt dann eine logische Konsequenz dieser Erkenntnis dar, denn die Judenchristen waren bereits zu der Einsicht gelangt, daß auch sie selbst – ebenso wie die Heiden – nur durch Christus zur Gerechtigkeit gelangen können. Paulus weitet dies in 2,15–17 dahingehend aus, daß er den Unterschied zwischen Juden und Heiden als in Christus grundsätzlich hinfällig beurteilt. Damit geht er über die Intention des in 2,16 formulierten Grundsatzes vermutlich hinaus. Dieser war ursprünglich wohl kaum als Beschreibung des Verhältnisses von Juden- und Heidenchristen formuliert worden, für die sie jetzt von Paulus herangezogen wird.[52] An dieser Stelle zeigt sich somit die Differenz zwischen gemeinsamer Überzeugung und unterschiedlicher Konkretion.

Damit kommen wir zu der letzten, hier zu besprechenden Frage, nämlich derjenigen, was sich Paulus unter den verschiedenen Formen des einen Evangeliums vorstellt. Auszugehen ist hierfür von dem Abschnitt 3,1–4,10, in dem er die Abrahams- und Christusgemeinschaft von Juden und Heiden beschreibt. Beide sind durch die πίστις mit Abraham sowie der an ihn ergangenen Verheißung miteinander verbunden. Deren Erfüllung geschieht in Christus, weshalb nunmehr die Anrechnung der Gerechtigkeit εἰς δικαιοσύνην erfolgt.

Im Zusammenhang des hier verfolgten Argumentes ist dabei von besonderem Interesse, daß Paulus von einem je eigenen Weg von Juden und Heiden zur Christusgemeinschaft ausgeht. Die Basis hierfür bezieht er aus der Schrift. Der Fluch über diejenigen aus dem Gesetz und der Segen für die ἔθνη sind dort ebenso vorgezeichnet wie die Befreiung der ersteren vom Fluch.[53] In 3,10–14 wird sodann deutlich, daß der Loskauf vom Fluch des Gesetzes und die Erlangung des Abrahamssegens durch die Heiden zwei einander korrespondierende Wege zur Christusgemeinschaft darstellen. Dies wird vornehmlich an dem Wechsel zwischen ἡμεῖς und τὰ ἔθνη in 3,13f. deutlich: Christus hat *uns* vom Fluch des Gesetzes losgekauft, damit der Abrahamssegen zu *den Heiden* gelange, damit *wir* die Verheißung des Geistes durch den Glauben erlangten. Dieser Wechsel läßt sich am besten so erklären, daß Paulus zunächst von Judenchristen spricht, die durch Christus vom Gesetz freigekommen sind, sodann zu den Heiden

52. Die These ist evtl. eine von Jesusanhängern in Auseinandersetzung mit ihren jüdischen Landsleuten entwickelte Auffassung, mit der sie ihre Sicht des Christusereignisses pointiert zusammenfaßten. Hierauf könnte die Formulierung ἔργα νόμου hinweisen, die Analogien in 1QS V,21.23.24; 4Q 258 (= 4QSd), Frg. 1, Kol. 2,1.3 sowie in 4Q 394–399 (= 4QMMT) besitzt. Die in 1QS V–VII aufgestellten Regelungen zur Einhaltung des Gesetzes geben möglicherweise Einblick in eine Form der Verpflichtung auf das Gesetz, die Paulus in Gal 2,16 kritisiert. Gal 2,16 könnte sich dann von einer Auffassung abgrenzen, die eine strenge Befolgung der Weisungen der Tora mit dem Erlangen der Gerechtigkeit verknüpfte und dies mit der neuen Erkenntnis der aus der πίστις resultierenden Gerechtigkeit begründen.

53. Paulus rekurriert in 3,8.10 und 13 explizit auf die Schrift. Damit sind also der Segen für die Heiden, der Fluch über die aus dem Gesetz sowie der Fluch über Christus, der den Loskauf bedeutet, mit Schriftargumenten begründet. Zwar werden auch in V.11 und 12 Schriftstellen zitiert, diese sind jedoch nicht als solche gekennzeichnet (es sei denn, man versteht das ὅτι in V.11 als Rezitativum) und liegen deshalb pragmatisch auf einer anderen Ebene.

übergeht, zu denen dadurch der Abrahamssegen gelangte, um schließlich beide in der Glaubensgemeinschaft zusammenzuschließen. Damit wird die Distinktion von Juden und Heiden aus 2,15 aufgegriffen und nunmehr auf den jeweiligen Weg zur Christusgemeinschaft bezogen.[54]

Paulus setzt also in den ersten beiden Argumentationsgängen des Galaterbriefes die in 1,6f. angezeigte Linie fort. Diese ist dadurch gekennzeichnet, daß es zwei Formen gibt, in denen das eine Evangelium Christi verkündet wird. Das Evangelium des Paulus geht auf eine Offenbarung Gottes zurück, wurde von den Jerusalemer Aposteln vorbehaltlos anerkannt und steht somit gleichwertig neben dem εὐαγγέλιον τῆς περιτομῆς. Die sachliche Grundlage der Einheit des Evangeliums besteht darin, daß „wir Judenchristen" zur Erkenntnis von der Aufhebung des Unterschieds zwischen Juden und Heiden in Christus gelangt sind, eine Erkenntnis, die Paulus nicht nur mit seiner Berufung verbindet, sondern als eine von den Judenchristen grundsätzlich akzeptierte Auffassung behauptet. Die beiden Gestalten des Evangeliums unterscheiden sich deshalb auch nicht in sachlicher Hinsicht, sondern durch die Adressaten, an die sie ausgerichtet werden, nämlich Juden und Heiden. Aus diesen ergeben sich die Unterschiede in der jeweiligen Gestaltwerdung des Evangeliums, insofern Juden und Heiden eine zwar in Christus vergleichbare, aber dennoch zu unterscheidende Vergangenheit haben: Für die Juden, die unter dem Gesetz versklavt waren, bedeutet das Evangelium den Freikauf vom Fluch des Gesetzes. Für die Heiden, die Göttern dienten, die in Wahrheit keine sind (4,8), bedeutet das Evangelium die Erfüllung der Verheißung, daß auch sie des Abrahamssegens teilhaftig werden sollen. Aus diesem je eigenen Weg zur Christusgemeinschaft folgt, daß es gegen das Evangelium Christi spräche, einer der beiden Gruppen diejenigen Identitätsmerkmale aufzwingen zu wollen, die für die Vergangenheit der jeweils anderen bestimmend waren.

Der Kritikpunkt, den Paulus sowohl gegen seine Kontrahenten in den galatischen Gemeinden als auch gegen Kephas geltend macht, richtet sich deshalb nicht dagegen, daß sie überhaupt eine andere Gestalt des Evangeliums verkünden. Indem sie jedoch behaupten, diese sei sachlich von der seinen verschieden, verlassen sie die Einheit des Evangeliums Christi in zweierlei Gestalt und bestreiten die Legitimität der auf eine Berufung Gottes zurückgehenden, auf dem Apostelkonvent anerkannten Gestalt der paulinischen Heidenmission ohne Übernahme der jüdischen Identitätsmerkmale. Wie dies konkret aussieht, geht zum einen aus dem Vorwurf an Kephas hervor, der durch seinen Rückzug von der Tischgemeinschaft mit den Heidenchristen von der Wahrheit des einen Evangeliums abgewichen ist, zum anderen aus demjenigen an die Galater, sie würden sich von den Gegnern zur Beschneidung bzw. zum Beachten von bestimmten Zeiten verführen lassen.

54. Vgl. hierzu auch T.L. Donaldson, The ‚Curse of the Law' and the Inclusion of the Gentiles: Galatians 3.13–14, *NTS* 32 (1986), S. 94–112.

3. *Die Einheit von Juden und Heiden in Christus*

Aus den angestellten Beobachtungen läßt sich folgendes Fazit ziehen: Paulus stellt im Galaterbrief nicht lediglich sein Evangelium als „Evangelium Christi" und der Gegner Botschaft als „Nicht-Evangelium" einander gegenüber. Seine Argumentation ist vielmehr differenzierter und führt zwei Formen, in denen das Evangelium verkündigt wird, auf eine gemeinsame Grundlage zurück. Das Ziel seiner Ausführungen ist dabei, die *ursprüngliche Einheit* dieser doppelten Gestaltwerdung des Evangeliums aufzuzeigen, welches von ihm, dem Heidenapostel, rechtmäßig verkündet, von den Gegnern und Kephas jedoch verdreht wird. Damit machen sie sich eines Verstoßes nicht nur gegen das Jerusalemer Abkommen, sondern gegen das von Gott autorisierte Evangelium selbst schuldig. Nicht daß es *kein anderes Evangelium gibt*, sondern daß die andere Gestalt des Evangeliums, wenn sie rechtmäßig verkündigt wird, *sachlich von der seinigen nicht verschieden ist*, ist demnach die Pointe der paulinischen Argumentation.

Dies ließ sich durch weitere Aspekte verstärken. Nirgendwo spricht Paulus so deutlich wie im Galaterbrief von *einer bestimmten Gestalt* des Evangeliums, die er verkündet, nirgendwo hebt er so prägnant hervor, daß es einen *je eigenen Weg* von Juden und Heiden zur gemeinsamen Abrahamskindschaft gibt. Ein Spezifikum des Galaterbriefes kann deshalb in dieser, auf die Einheit des Evangeliums ausgerichteten Argumentation des Paulus gesehen werden. Er ist darum bemüht, die doppelte Gestalt, in der sich das Evangelium manifestiert, nicht auseinanderbrechen zu lassen, sondern die Einheit von juden- und heidenchristlicher Ausformung des Evangeliums zu wahren. Freilich ist dies seiner Auffassung zufolge nur möglich, wenn der in 2,16 angeführte Grundsatz auch von Judenchristen weiterhin vorbehaltlos akzeptiert, die Aufrechterhaltung jüdischer Identitätsmerkmale innerhalb der Gemeinschaft der Glaubenden mithin sistiert wird. Man wird dabei davon auszugehen haben, daß sich Paulus zu Recht darauf beruft, dieser Grundsatz sei von Kephas und den anderen Judenchristen geteilt worden, auch wenn sie ihn vermutlich nicht in der schroffen Alternative von ἔργα νόμου und πίστις Χριστοῦ Ἰησοῦ formuliert hätten. Sie haben aus diesem Grundsatz jedoch andere Konsequenzen gezogen als Paulus und ihn nicht in derselben Weise gegen die Bewahrung jüdischer Identitätsmerkmale innerhalb der Gemeinschaft der Glaubenden geltend gemacht.

Die christologische Kontroverse des Galaterbriefes läßt sich somit als Differenz von gemeinsamer Grundüberzeugung und Unterschieden in der Konkretion gut erfassen. Daß die gemeinsame Überzeugung auch auf andere Weise umgesetzt werden konnte, ohne daß dies einen Verrat am Evangelium darstellen muß, hat Paulus im Galaterbrief nicht in Betracht gezogen. Freilich ist er an anderer Stelle ebenfalls darum bemüht, zwischen christologischer Überzeugung und gelebter Gemeinschaft von Juden- und Heidenchristen zu vermitteln, wie insonderheit seine Aufforderung zur Rücksicht auf die Beachtung von Speisevorschriften durch Judenchristen in Röm 14 belegt. Der von Petr Pokorný konstatierte Entfaltungsprozeß urchristlicher Glaubensaussagen läßt sich somit bei Paulus selbst beobachten, der im Galaterbrief die Einheit des Evangeliums gegen dessen von ihm befürchtete Verfälschung festhält, an anderer Stelle dagegen die Konkretion innerhalb der gelebten Gemeinschaft der Glaubenden diskutiert.

Ephesians 5.18–19 and Its Dionysian Background

Stanley E. Porter

I am greatly honoured to have been asked to contribute to this Festschrift for my esteemed colleague and friend, Petr Pokorný. I have known Petr for a number of years now, first through our common membership in SNTS (the 1995 meeting in Prague was my first one as a member, though I had been in attendance several times before), but more recently through our personal contacts brought about by our close institutional associations. The Protestant Theological Faculty of Charles University, no doubt through Petr's and others' instigation, formed a number of institutional ties in the years immediately following the Velvet Revolution, and I was pleased that mine at the time could be one of these. I had the honour of hosting Petr at a conference sponsored by that now former institution, and Petr honoured me by inviting me to give a lecture at the Symposium on the Historical Jesus, which inaugurated his Centre for Biblical Studies on 1 April 1999.[1] Everyone shared in the pride Petr took in instituting this Center on the occasion of the 650th anniversary of the founding of Charles University, as the fulfilment of a dream that he thought would never be realized – a place where free enquiry into the New Testament could occur within a university context.[2] Through the years, my wife and I have greatly enjoyed Petr's, as well as his wife's, hospitality on the occasion of our numerous visits. I realize that Petr has already once been honoured with a Festschrift, but a man of such vision and accomplishment deserves this further recognition, even though Petr would no doubt deny it. The major problem for a contributor is to decide in which area he dares to venture, since Petr's interests and publications have been so extensive. I trust that this brief contribution on a topic of my long-standing interest will intersect sufficiently with Petr's own scholarly concerns to be of some interest to him, as well as to others.

The passage that I wish to deal with is Eph. 5.18–19. The Greek text (Westcott and Hort edition), with my translation following, reads as follows:

1. S.E. Porter, 'Re-Assessing the Criteria of Authenticity'. Symposium on the Historical Jesus, in commemoration of the 650th anniversary of the founding of Charles University, and opening of the Centre for Biblical Studies, Protestant Theological Faculty, Prague, 1 April 1999. This paper was the impetus for writing my *The Criteria for Authenticity in Historical-Jesus Research: Previous Discussion and New Proposals* (JSNTSup, 191; Sheffield: Sheffield Academic Press, 2000).

2. I encourage everyone to ask Petr regarding the fortunes of the institute for atheism that once existed in Prague, that is, existed until the Velvet Revolution when it had to exist without being propped up by the government.

καὶ μὴ μεθύσκεσθε οἴνῳ, ἐν ᾧ ἐστιν ἀσωτία, ἀλλὰ πληροῦσθε ἐν πνεύματι, λαλοῦντες ἑαυτοῖς ψαλμοῖς καὶ ὕμνοις καὶ ᾠδαῖς πνευματικαῖς, ᾄδοντες καὶ ψάλλοντες τῇ καρδίᾳ ὑμῶν τῷ κυρίῳ.

Don't be drunk with wine, in which is dissipation, but be filled with the Spirit, speaking to each other in psalms and hymns and spiritual songs, singing and making psalms in your heart to the Lord.

It is worth noting the following features of the text, before attempting to come to some understanding of its exegetical background. The use of 'and' (καί) probably picks up a noteworthy or particular example of what v. 17 calls an example of being ἄφρονες or 'senseless'.[3] Grammatically, this passage is based upon a number of sets of parallel structures and both comparative and contrasting ideas.[4] There are two major imperative-based contrasting clauses, the first the negative clause regarding drunkenness with wine, and the second regarding being filled with the Spirit. Each imperative-based clause is modified, the first by a relative clause that reinforces the negative indication of the imperative, but the second by two parallel participle clauses (actually, there are two further participle clauses attached in vv. 20 and 21) reinforcing the positive features of being filled by the Spirit. There appears to be a quotation of Prov. 23.31 (LXX A) in Eph. 5.18 (μὴ μεθύσκεσθε οἴνῳ), although many commentators seem to want to dismiss this, either because it appears in other ethical traditions[5] or because it does not help to explain the rest of the verse.[6] I think that it is probable that this is indeed a quotation of the Old Testament in Greek, Paul's Bible,[7] rather than some coincidence, but that fact still does not mean that there is not more to explain as well. Indeed, I believe there is.

1. *Proposals for the Hellenistic Background of Ephesians 5.18–19*

Discussion of the Hellenistic background of Eph. 5.18–19 has been fairly extensive over the years, even if not highly productive or enlightening. Three major positions have been outlined. The first is that there is some influence from the Dionysian or Bacchanalian cult on the background of especially Eph. 5.18.[8] This view, which goes back to at least the nineteenth century, if not earlier in the

3. For this and other grammatical observations, among many commentators, see S.D.F. Salmond, 'The Epistle to the Ephesians', in W.R. Nicoll, *The Expositor's Greek Testament* (repr. Grand Rapids: Eerdmans, 1980), III, pp. 362–63.

4. Some of these are recognized by A.T. Lincoln, *Ephesians* (WBC, 42; Dallas, TX: Word Books, 1990), p. 338; T. Moritz, *A Profound Mystery: The Use of the Old Testament in Ephesians* (NovTSup, 85; Leiden: Brill, 1996), p. 94 n. 26.

5. See, e.g., A.T. Lincoln, 'The Use of the Old Testament in Ephesians', *JSNT* 14 (1982), pp. 16–57, esp. p. 43; *idem*, *Ephesians*, p. 340.

6. See Moritz, *Profound Mystery*, pp. 94–95.

7. See Lincoln, 'Use of the Old Testament in Ephesians', pp. 16–57.

8. Bacchus is a Lydian name for Dionysus (see M.P. Nilsson, H.J. Rose and C.M. Robertson, 'Dionysus', *OCD* [2nd edn], pp. 352–53, here p. 353), and the two are often used interchangeably.

critical literature,[9] has had a rough time in the recent critical discussion. There have been few sustained treatments,[10] but mostly suggestive comments.[11] The clear basis for this position is the reference to being drunk with wine (Eph. 5.18), one of the distinguishing characteristics of the Dionysian cult from its earliest recorded history.[12] However, for the most part, such a position is easily dismissed by recent commentators. For example, in the most recent major commentary on Ephesians, Hoehner says, 'Although this is possible, it is unlikely because Paul does not mention directly that this was their religious practice as he does in other places…'[13] I will return to this position below.

A recent view, propounded by Gosnell, is that the context of Ephesians 5 is of a mealtime.[14] These meals involved not only eating, but drinking, singing, discussion and the like. He sees parallels to what he posits as the background of Eph. 5.18–20 in other places in the New Testament, such as 1 Corinthians 11, if not the entirety of chs. 11–14, and Acts 20.7–12. Gosnell's suggestion is worth more serious attention than it has garnered, not least because at least one of the examples that he cites of such a meal in ancient times appears to contain Dionysian influence (Dio Chrysostom 2.63). Nevertheless, most commentators simply dismiss such an idea as well.[15]

A third view, and the current apparent majority position, is that Paul is simply moralizing about the undesirableness of an immoral life and the wisdom of an

9. I have not had the time to explore the exact origins of this viewpoint, but I try to show in this paper that the origin of the passage is to be found in this very situation.

10. The fullest that I have found is C.L. Rogers, Jr, 'The Dionysian Background of Ephesians 5.18', *BibSac* 136 (1979), pp. 249–57.

11. See E.J. Goodspeed, *The Meaning of Ephesians* (Chicago: University of Chicago Press, 1933), p. 59; H. Preisker, 'μέθη, κ.τ.λ.', *TDNT* 4 (1967), pp. 545–48, esp. p. 548; Moritz, *Profound Mystery*, pp. 94–95; H. Hübner, *An Philemon, An die Kolosser, An die Epheser* (HNT, 12; Tübingen: Mohr-Siebeck, 1997), p. 240. Cf. P. Pokorný, *Der Epheserbrief und die Gnosis* (Berlin: Evangelische Verlagsanstalt, 1965), pp. 91, 120 (non vid); *idem*, *Der Brief des Paulus an die Epheser* (THNT, 10/II; Berlin: Evangelische Verlagsanstalt, 1992), pp. 213–14, who examines the passage in the light of gnostic relationships.

12. See M.P. Nilsson, *Geschichte der Griechischen Religion*. I. *Bis zur Griechischen Weltherrschaft* (Handbuch der Altertumswissenschaft, 5.2.1; Munich: Beck, 1941), pp. 552–57.

13. H. Hoehner, *Ephesians: An Exegetical Commentary* (Grand Rapids: Baker, 2002), p. 701. See also M. Barth, *Ephesians* (AB, 34, 34A; Garden City, NY: Doubleday, 1974), II, pp. 580–81; Lincoln, *Ephesians*, p. 343; G.D. Fee, *God's Empowering Presence: The Holy Spirit in the Letters of Paul* (Peabody, MA: Hendrickson, 1994), pp. 720–21 n. 194; E. Best, *A Critical and Exegetical Commentary on Ephesians* (ICC; Edinburgh: T&T Clark, 1998), p. 507; P.T. O'Brien, *The Letter to the Ephesians* (Grand Rapids: Eerdmans, 1999), p. 389; M.Y. MacDonald, *Colossians, Ephesians* (SP, 17; Collegeville, MN: Liturgical Press, 2000), p. 318. Most commentators do not mention the Dionysian view as an option.

14. P.W. Gosnell, 'Ephesians 5.18–20 and Mealtime Propriety', *TynBul* 44.2 (1993), pp. 363–71. Gosnell simply says of the Dionysian view that 'many have, with reason, recognized such suggestions as basically insupportable', even though he does not mention what that reason is (p. 364).

15. E.g. O'Brien, *Ephesians*, p. 388 n. 12; Best, *Ephesians*, p. 509; Hoehner, *Ephesians*, pp. 701–702.

ordered life.[16] This is a position that wishes to link this section with other ethical or moral teaching in the book of Ephesians, including the *Haustafel* portion. Some commentators even go so far as to note that there is no indication from the context of any other immediate situation that elicited the author's comments, including no indications that there was in fact a problem with drunkenness in the Ephesian church.[17] This position, while wishing to respect the integrity of the text, perhaps does so at too large a price. That is the recognition that exegesis requires more than simply a blindered attention to the words alone of the text at the expense of the context that brought such words into existence.[18]

In fact, there are a number of historical, epigraphic, literary and even contextual factors that do indicate that the second and third positions above have neglected to appreciate fully the evidence to hand. Rogers's journal article failed to convince scholars that there was much of significance to the Dionysian hypothesis. Some of this reticence may have been precipitated by where the article was published – in a journal not known by reputation for having pushed the scholarly boundaries in critical circles. Another factor may have been that Rogers ventured pretty far and wide in his gathering of evidence, failing to focus upon specifically the Ephesian context so that that evidence was allowed to have its full weight. A last factor may have been that he was content to leave the issue of evidence to secondary scholarly opinion in a number of instances, when direct reference to primary sources, whether literary or epigraphic, would have helped to make his case more powerfully. In the light of this, I wish to argue that there are a number of factors that have not been fully considered but that indicate that the Dionysian cult, especially that cult as it was present in Ephesus (and by implication environs),[19] forms a very real and present background for the statements by Paul in Eph. 5.18–19. In fact, it appears to me that the more that we learn about this cult and its presence in Asia Minor, the more likely it becomes that Paul was responding directly to the influence of the cult in the church at Ephesus.[20]

16. I do not attempt to cite all who hold to this position. Representatives include: T.K. Abbott, *A Critical and Exegetical Commentary on the Epistles to the Ephesians and to the Colossians* (ICC; Edinburgh: T&T Clark, 1897), p. 161; C.L. Mitton, *Ephesians* (NCB; Grand Rapids: Eerdmans, 1973), pp. 188–90; Best, *Ephesians*, pp. 501–15.

17. Hoehner, *Ephesians*, p. 700.

18. To put this formulation in more Hallidayan linguistic terms, the register of usage points to a context of situation.

19. Much of the evidence cited below can be duplicated in many other cities of Asia Minor. The sources cited below can be examined for these specific references; cf. Rogers, 'Dionysian Background', pp. 250–55.

20. Hoehner (*Ephesians*, pp. 2–61) has clearly shown that it is entirely plausible (and has virtually always been) to argue for Pauline authorship of Ephesians. See L.M. McDonald and S.E. Porter, *Early Christianity and its Sacred Literature* (Peabody, MA: Hendrickson, 2000), pp. 482–88. There is certainly dispute over the destination of the letter, but by most accounts it ends up being sent to Ephesus, either originally or as part of a circular letter.

2. *Evidence for the Dionysian Background to Ephesians 5.18–19*

I will outline the evidence for the Dionysian background to Eph. 5.18–19 in four brief sections. The first is concerned with evidence from Euripides's *Bacchae*, the second with references to the cult of Dionysus at Ephesus, the third with ritual factors that link Ephesians to the Dionysus cult, and the fourth and final with theological commonalties between the Dionysian cult and Pauline Christianity.

a. *Euripides*, Bacchae

The first factor to consider is Euripides's *Bacchae*.[21] The subject of Dionysus was a very popular one in the literature of ancient Greece and Rome. However, the popularity of Euripides's rendering of the tale apparently overshadowed all others and led to the elimination of the other versions, so that this play by Euripides is the only extant Dionysian work of drama to remain from the ancient world.[22] It was so popular in fact that it became widely used as a schoolbook and was quoted in testimonia.[23] Nevertheless, this play rarely, if ever, is cited when Dionysus is the subject of discussion. I am not necessarily contending that Paul had direct knowledge of Euripides's play,[24] however, the play does go some way toward capturing at least some of the language that would have been associated with the figure of Dionysus, whether known directly or indirectly, language that may well therefore have been known to Paul.

The Dionysus cult, according to legend that appears to be regarded by contemporary scholarship as for the most part reliable,[25] originated in Thrace, or

21. I wish to thank my friend, Craig A. Evans, for his helpful discussion with me of the matter of this section, when I first broached to him my position on Eph. 5.18 nearly ten years ago.

22. See E.R. Dodds, *Euripides Bacchae* (Oxford: Clarendon Press, 1944), pp. xxv–xxx, for citation of Dionysian plays by other Greek and Roman authors.

23. See Dodds, *Euripides Bacchae*, p. xxvi. The tradition apparently culminates in the 48 books of Nonnos, the fifth century CE author. A convenient edition is found in: W.H.D. Rouse (trans.), *Nonnos* (LCL; 3 vols.; Cambridge, MA: Harvard University Press, 1940).

24. Nevertheless, I am convinced that today there is a tendency to underestimate the level of Paul's classical knowledge. See E.B. Howell, 'St Paul and the Greek World', *Greece & Rome* NS 11 (1964), pp. 7–29.

25. There are many accountings of the origins and spread of Dionysus and his cult. See the following, which I have drawn upon: Nilsson, Rose, and Robertson, 'Dionysus', pp. 352–53; M.P. Nilsson, *Griechische Feste von religiöser Bedeutung* (Leipzig: Teubner, 1906; repr. Milan: Cisalpino–Goliardica, 1975), esp. pp. 258–311; H.J. Rose, *A Handbook of Greek Mythology including its Extension to Rome* (London: Methuen, 1928), esp. pp. 149–56; M.P. Nilsson, *Greek Folk Religion* (Philadelphia: University of Pennsylvania Press, 1940); *idem*, *Geschichte*, pp. 532–68; H.J. Rose, *Ancient Greek Religion* (London: Hutchinson, 1946) *passim*; M.P. Nilsson, *A History of Greek Religion* (trans. F.J. Fielden; Oxford: Clarendon Press, 2nd edn, 1949), pp. 205–10, 293–94; W.K.C. Guthrie, *The Greeks and their Gods* (Boston: Beacon Press, 1950), pp. 145–82; M.P. Nilsson, *The Dionysiac Mysteries of the Hellenistic and Roman Age* (Lund: Gleerup, 1957; repr. Salem, NH: Ayer, 1985); cf. E. Rohde, *Psyche: The Cult of Souls and Belief in Immortality among the Greeks*

possibly Phrygia, the Phrygians being a tribe of Thracians. According to legend, Dionysus, after his birth (his mother's name, Semele, is from a Thracian-Phrygian root),[26] wandered in the east, which accounts for the accretion of oriental traits to the cult. Although the Dionysian cult apparently began as an ecstatic cult in Asia Minor, it early on penetrated the Greek mainland, where it was transformed from a vegetation cult to one of wine, wine being one of the identifying vegetative features. Thus, it is with wine that the cult was then identified from the earliest written records.[27]

This situation is what is reflected in Euripides's *Bacchae*. Wording from the drama especially significant for discussion of Eph. 5.18 occurs in a major speech of Teiresias that introduces Dionysus to Pentheus. There reference is made – to mortals being filled (πλησθῶσιν, line 281) with the juice of the grape, to the notion that Dionysus became a god who is poured out (σπένδεται, line 284) to or for the other gods so that on account of this humans have good things, to the god (ὁ δαίμων, line 298), Dionysus, being a prophet (μάντις, line 298) who produces prophecy (μαντικήν, line 299), and to the fact that whenever the god might enter fully into the body of a person, he makes those maddened speak of that which is coming (ὅταν γὰρ ὁ θεὸς ἐς το σῶμ' ἔλθῃ πολύς, λέγειν τὸ μέλλον τοὺς μεμηνότας ποιεῖ, lines 300–301).

A number of observations in terms of Ephesians 5, as well as other New Testament passages, can be made. The use of language of filling is the same in both instances. In Euripides, *Bacchae* 281 it refers to being filled with wine, while in Eph. 5.18 it is used in reference to being filled with the Spirit. Although some commentators have taken the anarthrous phrase in Eph. 5.18, ἐν πνεύματι, as referring to human spirit, most commentators now take it as referring to the divine Spirit.[28] That makes sense here with reference to the full contrast being between one being drunk with wine or being filled by the Spirit. Dionysus's being poured out (line 284) has perplexed commentators. Paley takes it thus: 'The obvious meaning is, that Bacchus himself, being a god, is offered in libations to the other gods. This, of course, is to identify the thing itself with the giver or inventor of it… Probably there is a play on the double sense of σπένδομαι, and the real sense is, "This god makes peace for us with the other gods", i.e. by giving us the means of appeasing them by offerings'.[29] This seems unnecessarily restricted in sense. Dodds, therefore, translates lines 284–85 and comments as follows: '"He, being god, is poured out in offering to the gods, so that to him men owe all their blessings" (because the libation of wine was a part of prayer)'.[30] He

(2 vols.; trans. W.B. Hillis; New York: Harper, 1966 [1928]), esp. pp. 282–303, plus notes, who disputes how much knowledge of Dionysus there was in Greece before the classical period.

26. Nilsson, *Feste*, p. 259.
27. See Nilsson, *Feste*, pp. 266–67; *idem*, *Geschichte*, pp. 552–57; *idem*, *Folk Religion*, p. 35.
28. Cf. Salmond, *Ephesians*, pp. 362–63; Hoehner, *Ephesians*, p. 705.
29. F.A. Paley, *Euripides* (3 vols.; London: Whittaker, 1874), II, p. 438.
30. Dodds, *Euripides Bacchae*, p. 100.

continues by saying that σπένδεται 'is quite certainly passive (not middle as L.S. 8), nor is there any play on the middle sense (as Paley, &c., fancied) – the statement that Dionysus "makes a truth with the gods" would have no meaning in the context'.[31] He admits, however, that 'The thought is curious, recalling Paul's mystical ἐγὼ γὰρ ἤδη σπένδομαι (2 Tim. 4.6), "I am poured out as an offering"'.[32] After citing an Indian parallel, he concludes that 'It is tempting to see here not merely the rediscovery but the survival of an ancient religious idea'.[33] Dodds may be correct that it is an ancient religious idea, but I believe that it is more than coincidence that Paul uses this language in 2 Tim. 4.6, in the light of what appears to be his knowledge of the Dionysian terminology. It appears that, in Ephesians, he is responding directly to the possible influence of the Dionysian cult, perhaps being practised there (see below), but that in writing to Timothy in 2 Timothy, who is still at Ephesus,[34] he utilizes language that directly echoes that used of the Dionysian cult. Lastly, there is the prophetic dimension to Dionysus, in which those who are in a Dionysian state of ecstasy prophecy the future.[35] The cult of Dionysus was apparently linked to mantic prophecy already before coming to Greece.[36] Commentators disagree whether line 300, with reference to the god entering into the body, refers to drinking too much wine or not. Paley thinks that Euripides 'confounds the effects of drunkenness with that of religious enthusiasm',[37] while Dodds disagrees.[38] However, as Dodds points out, Plutarch appears to have thought that was the case: 'wine, when it sends forth its vapors, reveals many unusual movements and words stored away and unperceived: "for bacchanalian frenzy and madness have much prophecy", according to Euripides [*Bacchae* 298–99]' (*De defectu oraculorum* [*Obsolescence of Oracles*] 432E LCL adapted). Nevertheless, as Dodds also indicates, in this section Dionysus

> is presented as the cause of two unaccountable modes of behaviour, second-sight and panic, two μανίαι (305) whose common characteristic is that in both of them human will and reason are submerged by a mysterious impulse coming from outside the individual consciousness, and therefore, in the belief of antiquity, from a higher power. All such psychological states, which could be neither explained nor controlled, were attributed to an external psychic interference.[39]

31. Dodds, *Euripides Bacchae*, p. 100.
32. Dodds, *Euripides Bacchae*, p. 100.
33. Dodds, *Euripides Bacchae*, p. 101.
34. See McDonald and Porter, *Early Christianity*, p. 488. Timothy was probably at Ephesus when both 1 and 2 Tim. were written. Here is not the place to enter into critical discussion of the many issues surrounding authorship of the Pastoral Epistles, except to say that the work above treats these issues.
35. There is a folk etymology that Plato cites, in which μανία and μαντική are commonly derived, the *tau* being attributed to an error (see Plato, *Phaedrus* 244c).
36. See Dodds, *Euripides Bacchae*, p. 103, who cites Herodotus 7.111, where Dionysus spoke through a priestess in a trance; and Euripides, *Hecuba* 1267, where Dionysus is referred to as 'the mantic from Thrace' (ὁ θρῃξὶ μάντις).
37. Paley, *Euripides*, II, p. 443.
38. Dodds, *Euripides Bacchae*, p. 103.
39. Dodds, *Euripides Bacchae*, p. 104.

The similarities in the language that Paul uses in his letters to that used to describe the Dionysian cult in Euripides's classic expression of it allow us to examine more closely what relationship there is between Paul's two commands (μεθύσκεσθε ... πληροῦσθε) and the possible behaviour of those in the Ephesian church.[40] Despite over a century of insightful discussion by scholars regarding the use of imperatives in Greek,[41] most grammarians and hence most commentators have retained a time-based estimation of the imperatives, such that the present tense-form imperative either commands the recipients to continue doing what they are doing or stop doing what they are currently doing. This older position is still found among a number of recent scholars and commentators.[42] However, the culmination of recent research into the imperative in Greek indicates that the notion of verbal aspect governs the use of the imperatives, and that context must decide whether an action is or is not underway.[43] In the context of Eph. 5.18–19, in the light of the strong evidence for a Dionysian background to the language that Paul uses, it may have been that some of those in Ephesus were continuing to be a part of Dionysian celebrations, or at least were tempted to return to them. Using the two present imperative forms, Paul firmly commands that they, first, not be drunk with wine, but that they, secondly, are to be filled with the Spirit.[44]

b. *The Cult of Dionysus at Ephesus*

There is much evidence that there was a cult of Dionysus that continued to exist at Ephesus. As noted above, one of the objections to Paul referring to Dionysian practice in Ephesians is that there is no direct reference to such a cult in the letter. However, if the cult were already well known to those in Ephesus, as well as to Paul, who had been in the city for some time, as well as traveling widely throughout Asia Minor, then it makes it unnecessary for Paul to have explained something that would have been known to his readers.[45] In fact, there is clear indication that the cult was very much a part of the heritage of Ephesus.

In 41 BCE, according to Plutarch in his life of Antony, Mark Antony crossed over from Greece to Asia, where he entered into the city of Ephesus. Plutarch records the following account:

40. There are many issues that might be raised regarding the terminology used. Besides the major commentaries, see Fee, *God's Empowering Presence*, pp. 720–23; A.J. Köstenberger, 'What Does It Mean to Be Filled with the Spirit? A Biblical Investigation', *JETS* 40.2 (1997), pp. 229–40, esp. pp. 231–35.

41. See S.E. Porter, *Verbal Aspect in the Greek of the New Testament, with Reference to Tense and Mood* (SBG, 1; New York: Lang, 1989), pp. 335–61; cf. D.B. Wallace, *Greek Grammar beyond the Basics: An Exegetical Syntax of the New Testament* (Grand Rapids: Zondervan, 1996), pp. 714–17.

42. E.g. Rogers, 'Dionysian Background', pp. 256–57; Lincoln, *Ephesians*, p. 344; Köstenberger, 'What Does It Mean', p. 233.

43. See Porter, *Verbal Aspect*, pp. 336–47.

44. Porter, *Verbal Aspect*, p. 357; cf. O'Brien, *Ephesians*, p. 390 n. 20; Hoehner, *Ephesians*, pp. 699–700. The implication is that God is the agent of this filling.

45. See Nilsson, *Dionysius*, *passim*, for reference to some of the evidence cited in this section.

> When Antony made his entry into Ephesus, women arrayed like Bacchanals, and men and boys like Satyrs and Pans, led the way before him, and the city was full of ivy and thyrsus-wands and harps and pipes and oboes,[46] the people hailing him as Dionysus giver of Joy and Beneficent. For he was such, undoubtedly, to some; but to the greater part he was Dionysus Carnivorous and Savage. For he took their property from well-born men and bestowed it on flatterers and scoundrels (*Antony* 24.3–4 LCL).

This passage indicates that, at the time Antony entered Ephesus, knowledge of the Dionysus cult was already firmly established in the city, since the people both knew how they should dress and behave, and had appropriate wording to greet Antony himself, who was apparently hailed as Dionysus. The characteristics attributed to him also conform to those that surround Dionysian behaviour as depicted in Euripides's account as well.

The material remains from Ephesus also support a firmly established Dionysian cult. The British Museum contains several Dionysian inscriptions from the Roman period that attest to the continued practice of the cult at Ephesus. The first is IBM 3.2 no. 595, dating to the Roman Antonine period (96–192 CE), which in lines 3–5 refers to initiates both of Demeter before the city and of Dionysus Phleus,[47] using one of Dionysus's many names. The inscription includes reference to a priest (line 2), a hierophant (lines 7–8) and an epimelete of the mysteries (lines 9–11), all as functionaries in the Dionysus cult. The linkage of Demeter and Dionysus is also similar to that in Euripides's *Bacchae* (see lines 272ff.). This inscription, according to the editor, is to be linked to another that mentions initiates of Demeter in Ephesus, IBM 3.2 no. 506 (138–61 CE).[48] Another inscription, IBM 3.2 no. 600, dating to the early second century CE, refers to the god Dionysus in line 1, and then appears to go on to equate the emperor Hadrian with the 'young Dionysus' in line 46. The inscription, according to the editor, apparently records a celebration of Dionysian mysteries in which Hadrian was worshiped as both Dionysus and Zeus Panhellenios, both titles which were used in worship of him.[49]

The effect of this evidence is to place the sending of the letter to the Ephesians, if it were sent to Ephesus by Paul, along the trajectory formed by these literary and inscriptional pieces of evidence. In fact, even if the letter were inauthentic, but sent to Ephesus or environs, the Dionysian cult would appear to be a known phenomenon for the audience, as well as author.

e. *Ritual Similarities*

Most of those scholars who treat Eph. 5.18 treat v. 18 in isolation when discussing the possible links to the Dionysian cult. The topic of this paper, however,

46. I change the translation of αὐλῶν from 'flutes' to 'oboes', according to the best of recent scholarship. See W.J. Porter, 'Λαλέω: A Word about Women, Music and Sensuality in the Church', in M.A. Hayes, W.J. Porter and D. Tombs (eds.), *Religion and Sexuality* (STT, 2; RILP, 4; Sheffield: Sheffield Academic Press, 1998), pp. 101–24, esp. pp. 114–21.

47. On this title, besides the notes to the inscription, see Nilsson, *Geschichte*, p. 552 n. 5.

48. E.L. Hicks, *The Collection of Ancient Greek Inscriptions in the British Museum*. 3.2. *Ephesos* (Oxford: Clarendon Press, 1890), p. 80.

49. Hicks, *Collection*, p. 222.

is Eph. 5.18–19. I believe that there are further indicators in the passage that Paul is addressing possible Dionysian cult connections of his audience. There are two further ritual elements to note that point in this direction.

The first takes into account reference in an inscription to a number of different functionaries in the Dionysian cult at Pergamon.[50] That inscription refers to there being two ὑμνοδιδάσκαλοι or 'hymn teachers', that is, those who taught the hymns or songs to the god, Dionysus. This is standard use of the term 'hymn' in Greek to refer to a song to a god. There is much debate in New Testament scholarship, however, regarding the reference by Paul in Eph. 5.19 (and Col. 3.16)[51] to ψαλμοῖς καὶ ὕμνοις καὶ ᾠδαῖς πνευματικαῖς (psalms and hymns and spiritual songs).[52] Although older scholars once distinguished these terms,[53] most scholars today take the terms as not differentiating different types of musical expressions, but as being what Dunn calls 'more or less synonymous'.[54] However, Wellesz has shown that this position reflects a later period but that our knowledge of Jewish and early Byzantine music points to there being a legitimate distinction among the three. He distinguishes between psalmody as cantillated Jewish psalms, hymns as syllabic songs of praise and spiritual songs as jubilant or ecstatic chants.[55] Thus, it appears that in the use of this language in Eph. 5.19 with regard to psalms, hymns and sacred songs, Paul may be making mention of some of the kinds of song-types that were used in Christian worship in relation to those that were used in the Dionysian cult. His use of the parallel participle phrasing[56] serves to reinforce that these Christian musical expressions are to emerge out of the one who is filled with the Spirit, rather than out of one who is drunk with wine.

50. See Nilsson, *Dionysius*, p. 52, where he cites *Mitteilungen des Deutschen archäeologischen Instituts, Athenische Abteilung* 24 (1899), p. 179 no. 31 = I. Pergamon 486a.

51. The reference in Colossians is thought by many scholars to be the source of the Ephesian reference. E.g. Lincoln, *Ephesians*, p. 345. This is not necessarily the case. See Best, *Ephesians*, p. 510, for differences.

52. For summaries of recent discussion, see R.P. Martin, 'Aspects of Worship in the New Testament Church', *Vox Evangelica* 2 (1963), pp. 6–32, esp. p. 11; W.J. Porter, 'Music', in C.A. Evans and S.E. Porter (eds.), *Dictionary of New Testament Background* (Downers Grove, IL: Inter-Varsity Press, 2000), pp. 711–19, esp. pp. 712–13. There are some textual variants in this phrase, which do not concern me here. See Hoehner, *Ephesians*, p. 707 nn. 5, 6, for recent discussion.

53. E.g. J.B. Lightfoot, *St Paul's Epistles to the Colossians and to Philemon* (London: Macmillan, 1875), pp. 290–91.

54. J.D.G. Dunn, *The Epistles to the Colossians and to Philemon* (NIGTC; Grand Rapids: Eerdmans, 1996), p. 238. He also uses the term 'near synonymity' (p. 238). There is a noteworthy looseness to his linguistic terminology, but the point is made nevertheless. See also M. Hengel, 'Hymn and Christology', in E.A. Livingstone (ed.), *Studia Biblica 1978*. III. *Papers on Paul and Other New Testament Authors* (JSNTSup, 3; Sheffield: JSOT Press, 1980), pp. 173–97, esp. p. 175; repr. in M. Hengel, *Between Jesus and Paul: Studies in the Earliest History of Christianity* (Philadelphia: Fortress Press, 1983), pp. 78–96, esp. p. 80; Mitton, *Ephesians*, p. 191; Lincoln, *Ephesians*, p. 345; Pokorný, *Der Brief des Paulus an die Epheser,* p. 214; Hoehner, *Ephesians*, pp. 709–10.

55. E. Wellesz, 'Early Christian Music', in D.A. Hughes (ed.), *Early Medieval Music up to 1300* (London: Oxford University Press, rev. edn, 1955), pp. 1–13. esp. pp. 2–6; *idem*, *A History of Byzantine Music and Hymnography* (Oxford: Clarendon Press, 2nd edn, 1961), pp. 33–34.

56. See Fee, *God's Empowering Presence*, p. 719.

The second ritual element to note that further confirms the distinction of the terms used in Eph. 5.19 and their place with regard to the Dionysian cult is in terms of the relation of this music to Jewish music. The position that is often maintained regarding the reference to psalms, hymns and sacred songs is that this music is clearly more Jewish than Greek in origin, especially with reference to the psalms. As a number of scholars note, the psalms may well have received their name from the fact that they were accompanied by plucked instruments such as harps, as ψάλλω implies.[57] More than that, however, as Braun notes, there may have been more cultural overlap between Jews and non-Jews than is sometimes realized. For example, Plutarch in his *Questiones Convivales* (*Table-Talk*) 671E (trans. LCL) notes that some Jews were involved in Dionysian celebrations. After the feast of Tabernacles, they celebrated another festival 'this time identified with Bacchus not through obscure hints but plainly called by his name, a festival that is a sort of "Procession of Branches" or "Thyrsus Procession", in which they enter the temple each carrying a thyrsus'. Plutarch says that they do not know what transpires in the temple, 'but it is probable that the rite is a Bacchic revelry, for in fact they use little trumpets to invoke their god as do the Argives at their Dionysia. Others of them advance playing harps'. Braun notes that Plutarch describes a number of other parallels between the Jews and Dionysian practices, such as the clothing of the high priest.[58] As Braun further comments:

> Certain features associated with the music played at such Jewish celebrations also reminded Tacitus of the Dionysian ritual; the priests, he recounts, sang psalms accompanied by tibia and tympanum, and he notes that 'because these priests sang accompanied by pipes and cymbals and wore wreaths of ivy, and because golden wine was found in their temple, one thought they actually worshiped the liber pater, the conqueror of the Orient, despite the contradictory nature of their customs' (*Hist.* v. 5).[59]

Thus, the music that Paul refers to in Eph. 5.19 may well be seen as reflecting Dionysian musical rituals, even if Jewish in origin, on the basis of their similarities in the ancient world.

d. *Theology of Eternal Life*

The last area of significant indication that Paul is addressing a situation in which Dionysian cult practices may form the backdrop is with regard to their respective theologies. This point is not as pronounced as the ones above, but is worth mentioning, nevertheless, since there are noteworthy theological similarities between Dionysian belief and Pauline belief regarding eternal life.

57. E.g. Hoehner, *Ephesians*, pp. 708, 711.

58. J. Braun, *Music in Ancient Israel/Palestine: Archaeological, Written, and Comparative Sources* (trans. D.W. Stott; Grand Rapids: Eerdmans, 2002), p. 273.

59. Braun, *Music*, pp. 273–74. It is also worth noting that, according to Cumont, some identified Jahweh Sabaoth with the Greek god Sabazios (who was seen to be identical with Dionysus) and as a result were expelled from Rome with the Chaldeans, in light of the Senate decree in 186 BCE that forbade Bacchanalian celebrations in Italy. See F. Cumont, *After Life in Roman Paganism* (New Haven: Yale University Press, 1922; repr. New York: Dover, 1959), p. 35.

The Dionysian belief seemed to be that the spirit of one who died went down to the afterworld, where one who was worthy participated in an eternal banquet. Drunkenness in the earthly life, therefore, was seen as in some way a foretaste of this eternal banquet. Cumont refers to this as 'sacred drunkenness',[60] in which the festal wine was consumed in anticipation of life after death. Cumont speculates that drunkenness, in which one is freed from human cares, was viewed as in some way a form of what he calls 'divine possession' for the individual by the god, wine. Wine, therefore, became the 'drink of immortality, which flowed for the sacred guests in the meals of the secret conventicles'.[61] Paul is not explicitly concerned in this passage with outlining his theology of the after-life.[62] However, two factors are noteworthy. The first is that in Eph. 5.14 he does cite a passage that is often thought to be hymnic in nature, that is possibly baptismal and that links Christ with rising from the dead. The second is that the structure of Paul's prohibition of drunkenness and his command of being filled with the Spirit has the direct implication of directing his audience – if they are knowledgeable of the Dionysian cult – away from any of its theological beliefs, including those related to wine and the after-life. It may be that the songs, rather than simply being musical, were a means by which instruction could be given, countering in some ways the prophetic tendencies of the Dionysian cult with both praise of Christ and instruction about him.[63]

3. *Conclusion*

There are a number of factors in this passage that I have not considered. What I have tried to bring to the fore are those elements that seem to indicate that there was knowledge on the part of both the author, Paul, and his audience, those in the Ephesian church, of Dionysian cult practices. The language of that cult has noteworthy similarities to Paul's language, as evidenced from the quotations in Euripides's *Bacchae*. More than that, such language would have been suitable and found a reception in the Ephesian context, where the Dionysian cult had been known from before and long after the letter to the Ephesians was written. There were also several other ritual similarities worth noting, as well as some theological indicators. Does this prove decisively that there is a Dionysian background to Eph. 5.18–19? Probably not, at least no more than many other such

60. Cumont, *After Life*, p. 35.

61. Cumont, *After Life*, p. 120.

62. For my perspective on this, in which I see many more similarities in Paul's theology of the resurrection to Greco-Roman thought than others do, see S.E. Porter, 'Resurrection, the Greeks and the New Testament', in S.E. Porter, M.A. Hayes and D. Tombs (eds.), *Resurrection* (JSNTSup, 186; RILP, 5; Sheffield: Sheffield Academic Press, 1999), pp. 52–81.

63. See J.D.G. Dunn, *Jesus and the Spirit: A Study of the Religious and Charismatic Experience of Jesus and the First Christians as Reflected in the New Testament* (Grand Rapids: Eerdmans, 1997 [1975]), pp. 238–39; cf. R.P. Martin, 'Some Reflections on New Testament Hymns', in H.H. Rowdon (ed.), *Christ the Lord: Studies in Christology presented to Donald Guthrie* (Downers Grove, IL: InterVarsity Press, 1982), pp. 37–49, esp. p. 44.

endeavors in establishing the background to a passage decisively prove such a fact. However, the evidence certainly appears strong enough to open up once more serious debate of such indicators in this context, and to raise further questions once more regarding the relationship of Paul to the Greco-Roman culture in which he lived.

LIVING IN THE LYCUS VALLEY: EARTHQUAKE IMAGERY IN COLOSSIANS, PHILEMON AND EPHESIANS

Larry J. Kreitzer

The historical circumstances surrounding the writing of the letter to the Colossians are among the most difficult to reconstruct within the Pauline corpus. Not only does the question of the (apparently) pseudepigraphal nature of the epistle have to be addressed, but so too do questions of its date and its relation to what we know about the history of the city of Colossae and the region of the Lycus river in Phrygia during the first century CE. Nowhere are such questions more acutely focused than when considering the great earthquake which struck the Lycus valley in 60 CE. A.J.M. Wedderburn frames the essential problem well:

> The idea of a later pseudonymous letter written to a city that was in ruins and to a church there that perhaps no longer existed and which Paul had never visited (Col. 2.1) seems too macabre to be likely, especially since the letter makes no mention of this disaster that had overtaken the city.[1]

However, is it correct to say that Paul's letters remain completely silent about the seismic activity?[2] Assuming that Colossians and Philemon were written by

1. *Baptism and Resurrection: Studies in Pauline Theology against Its Graeco-Roman Background* (WUNT, 44; Tübingen: J.C.B. Mohr [Paul Siebeck], 1987), p. 70. Wedderburn assumes that the earthquake that is known to have destroyed Laodicea in 60 CE also devastated Colossae. He bases his opinion primarily on the fact that Orosius *Historia Adversus Paganos* 7.7.12 records that an earthquake (in the singular!) affected Laodicea, Hierapolis and Colossae. Mention is also made of Eusebius' *Hieronymi Chronicon* 183.21–22 to this effect ('In Asia tres urbes terrae motu conciderunt Laodicea Hierapolis Colossae'), although it is noted that Eusebius dates the earthquake to 64 CE, thus associating it with events subsequent to the great fire of Nero's Rome.

2. The word σεισμός is generally used in the New Testament to refer to an actual earthquake; it is used 13 times in this sense (Mt. 24.7; 27.54; 28.2; Mk 13.8; Lk. 21.11; Acts 16.26; Rev. 6.12; 8.5; 11.13 [twice]; 11.19; 16.18 [twice]). It can also refer to a violent storm on the sea in which violent waves are whipped up by high winds, as is seen in Matthew 8.24. The cognate verb σείω is used 3 times to refer to an actual earthquake (Mt. 27.51; 28.4; Heb. 12.26). However, σεισμός can also be used figuratively, as in Mt. 21.10 when the city of Jerusalem is said to have been 'shaken up' (ἐσείσθη) by the triumphal entry of Jesus and the accompanying acclamation of the crowds; in Matthew 28.4 where the guards at Jesus' tomb are 'shaken' (ἐσείσθησαν) by the appearance of the angel of the Lord; and in Revelation 6.13 where the fruit of a fig tree is said to be 'shaken' (σειομένη) by a strong wind. The earthquake motif is especially significant within the book of Revelation. See Richard Bauckham, 'The Eschatological Earthquake in the Apocalypse of John', *Novum Testamentum* 19 (1977), pp. 224–33, for an interesting discussion of this.

Paul in about 64 CE during his Roman imprisonment, we certainly might expect that an event as significant as a recent earthquake in the very location that the letters were directed to would be noted.[3] Within this study I propose that in Colossians, Philemon and Ephesians there *are* veiled allusions to the great earthquake of 60 CE, allusions which together form an important piece of the puzzle about the relationship between the three letters. This becomes even more significant if, as I have suggested elsewhere, the letter we now know as Ephesians was originally intended for the church in Hierapolis, a daughter-church of the congregation at Colossae.[4]

I shall pursue this study under three headings: (1) Earthquakes in Asia: The Ancient Evidence; (2) The Earthquake of 60 CE: A Backdrop for the Epistles to the Churches of the Lycus Valley; (3) Earthquake Imagery in Colossians, Philemon and Ephesians.

1. *Earthquakes in Asia: The Ancient Evidence*

Several ancient historians refer to earthquakes which occurred in the province of Asia. Some also note the reaction of the Roman state to such natural disasters in what was one of the wealthiest and most important regions of the empire. A case in point is the historian Dio Cassius (circa 163/4–235 CE), a man who was well-placed to comment on imperial policy toward the province of Asia and (presumably) would have had access to official records and accounts. Dio was born in Nicaea in Bithynia, the son of a prominent diplomat within the Roman imperial court. Dio himself entered the Roman Senate in about 189 CE and was appointed as governor of Pergamum and Smyrna in 218 CE, a position which would have fostered an interest in the affairs of the province of Asia. Interestingly, he records in *Roman History* 54.30.3 how the Emperor Augustus (27 BCE–14 CE) responded creatively to the difficulties which befell Asia as a result of seismic activity.[5]

3. The fact that Paul (apparently) does not mention the earthquake is frequently invoked as proof that the letters were written before 60 CE, and are thus to be associated with the Caesarean imprisonment of Paul in 58–60. See E. Earle Ellis *The Making of the New Testament Documents* (Biblical Interpretation Series, 39; Leiden: Brill, 1999), p. 245, for example.

4. See *The Epistle to the Ephesians* (EC; London: Epworth Press, 1997). My original suggestion about the provenance of the letter has been furthered by a series of supplementary articles, including: 'The Plutonium of Hierapolis: A Geographical Solution for the Puzzle of Ephesians 2.8–9?', in Rut Dvořáková and Jiří Mrázek (eds.) *ΕΠΙΤΟΑΥΤΟ: Essays in Honour of Petr Pokorný* (Prague, 1998), pp. 218–33; 'The Plutonium of Hierapolis and the Descent of Christ into the 'Lowermost Parts of the Earth' (Ephesians 4,9)', *Biblica* 79 (1998), pp. 381–93 + Plates I and II; ' "Crude Language" and "Shameful Things Done in Secret" (Ephesians 5.4, 12): Allusions to the Cult of Demeter/Cybele in Hierapolis', *Journal for the Study of the New Testament* 71 (1998), pp. 51–77.

5. Unless otherwise indicated, the text and translation of the Greek and Latin texts are those contained within the Loeb Classical Library. Suetonius *Tiberius* 8.1 records that Tiberius made an appeal to the Senate on behalf of the citizens of Laodicea, Thyatira and Chios following an earthquake that shook their cities. It is likely that this is the earthquake which took place during the reign of Augustus.

When the province of Asia was in dire need of assistance on account of earthquakes, he paid into the public treasury from his private funds the amount of its annual tribute and assigned to it for two years a governor chosen by lot and not appointed.

Ἐπειδή τε ἡ Ἀσία τὸ ἔθνος ἐπικουρίας τιμὸς διὰ σεισμοὺς μάλιστα ἐδεῖτο, τόν τε φόρον αὐτῆς τὸν ἔτειον ἐκ τῶν ἑαυτοῦ χρημάτων τῷ κοινῷ ἐσήνεγκε, καὶ ἄρχοντά οἱ ἐκ τοῦ κλήρου, ἀλλ᾽ οὐχ αἱρετόν, ἐπὶ δύο ἔτη προσέταξε.

Augustus' successor, the Emperor Tiberius (14–37 CE), is also said to have been magnanimous in his support for many cities of the province of Asia which had been destroyed in an earthquake which took place one night in 17 CE. The catastrophe is recorded in a number of ancient sources, including Tacitus *Annals* 2.47; 13.3.5; 13.4.8; Strabo *Geography* 12.18.18; Dio Cassius *Roman History* 57.17.7; Seneca *Natural Questions* 6.1.13; Suetonius *Tiberius* 48.2; Velleius Paterculus *History of Rome* 2.126.4; and Pliny *Natural History* 2.86.[6] It is doubtful whether this earthquake affected the Lycus valley itself, as none of the twelve cities listed in Tacitus' account is located there. However, Tiberius' generosity to the region at large was marked by the issuing of a number of interesting coins, both from Roman imperial mints as well as local provincial issues.

One of the most important is an imperial sestertius which dates from 22–23 CE (Figure 1).[7] The obverse of the coin depicts the Emperor Tiberius seated on a curule chair and facing to the left, his feet resting on a stool. In his right hand he holds a patera, while in his left arm he crooks a long sceptre. The inscription around the edge of the coin reads CIVITATIBVS ASIAE RESTITVTIS ('Restoration of the communities of Asia'). The reverse of the coin has the letters SC (an abbreviation for 'Senatus Consulto') in the centre, and a surrounding inscription which reads TI(berius) CAESAR DIVI AVG(usti) F(ilius) AVGVST(us) P(ontifex) M(aximus) TR(ibunicia) POT(estate) XXIIII (meaning 'Tiberius Caesar, Son of the Divine Augustus, Augustus the High Priest, 24th period of Tribunicial Power').[8]

There is also a small bronze coin issued by the city of Magnesia at the foot of Mount Sipylus which is relevant here.[9] It was issued to commemorate Tiberius'

6. Pliny describes it as 'the greatest earthquake in human memory' (maximus terrae memoria morbatium).

7. The coin is listed in C.H.V. Sutherland *The Roman Imperial Coinage, Volume 1* (London: Spink and Son, Ltd, 1984), p. 97, as #48. For further discussion of the coin, see David Magie *Roman Rule in Asia Minor to the End of the Third Century After Christ* (Princeton, New Jersey: Princeton University Press, 1950), pp. 499–500, 1358–59; C.H.V. Sutherland *Roman History and Coinage 44 BC–AD 69* (Oxford: Clarendon Press, 1987), pp. 47–49.

8. See Michael Grant *Roman History from Coins* (Cambridge: Cambridge University Press, 1968), pp. 51–52 and Plate 18, Figure 1. Victor Ehrenberg and A.H.M. Jones *Documents Illustrating the Reigns of Augustus and Tiberius* (Oxford: Clarendon Press, 1955 second edition), p. 65, lists an important inscription (#50) from Puteoli, dated to 30 CE, which also commemorates Tiberius' restitution of a number of cities from Asia. The inscription is unintelligible at points but lists a dozen or so cities so assisted.

9. David Sear *Greek Imperial Coins and Their Values: The Local Coinages of the Roman*

(a.) obverse

(b.) reverse

Figure 1.

assistance to the city following its destruction in the great earthquake of 17 CE (Magnesia is one of the cities listed in Tacitus *Annals* 2.47). The obverse of the coin has a laureated bust of Tiberius facing right, a surrounding inscription reads ΤΙΒΕΡΙΟΝ ΣΕΒΑΣΤΟΝ ΚΤΙΣΤΗΝ ('Tiberius Augustus, Creator'). The reverse of the coin depicts a personification of the city of Magnesia greeting the figure of Tiberius with a clasp of hands. A surrounding inscription reads: ΜΑΓΝΗΤΩΝ ΑΠΟ ΣΙΠΥΛΟΥ ('Of the Magnesians at Sipylus'). In short, Tiberius appears to have dealt generously with the province of Asia following the disastrous earthquake of 17 CE, and this generosity is commemorated in both imperial and provincial coinage of the time.

Tiberius was certainly not alone in this regard, for other Emperors are also mentioned as following a disaster-relief policy with regard to areas affected by earthquakes. Nero demonstrated a similar spirit of compassion in connection with an earthquake which struck the city of Apameia in Phrygia in 53 CE. Thus, Tacitus *Annals* 12.58 says that the Emperor was kindly disposed to the city following this earthquake:

> And Apameia, which had suffered from an earthquake shock, was relieved from its tribute for the next five years.
>
> *tributumque Apamensibus terrae motu convolsis in quinquennium remissum.*[10]

More importantly for our consideration, the city of Laodicea within the Lycus valley was similarly hit by the severe earthquake of 60 CE which occurred during the reign of Nero. Mention of this destruction of Laodicea is found in a number

Empire (London: Seaby Publications, 1982), p. 25, lists this coin as #272; Andrew Burnett, Michael Amandry and Pere Pan Ripollés *Roman Provincial Coinage* (London: British Museum Press, 1992), p. 416, list it as coin #2451 (Plate #108).

10. Spartianus *Life of Hadrian* 21.5 records a similar comment concerning the Emperor Hadrian (117–138 CE), well known for his affinity towards the provinces of Greece and Asia.

of sources from antiquity, including Tacitus *Annals* 14.27 which records that the city took on the responsibility of its own rebuilding:

> In the same year, Laodicea, one of the famous Asiatic cities, was laid in ruins by an earthquake, but recovered by its own resources, without assistance from ourselves.
>
> *Eodum anno ex inlustribus Asiae urbibus Laodicea, tremore terrae prolapsa, nullo a nobis remedio propriis opibus revaluit.*

The *Sibylline Oracles* contain several passages which refer to the destruction of Laodicea and Hierapolis. Generally these are taken to refer to the earthquake of 60 CE, although given the oracular nature of the passages, it is always very difficult to date them precisely. Five specific passages are worth considering briefly in this regard.[11] We note, for example, *Sibylline Oracles* 4.107–108:

> Wretched Laodicea, at some time an earthquake will throw you headlong
> and spread you flat, but you will be founded again as a city, and stand.
>
> τλῆμον Λαοδίκεια, σὲ δὲ στρώσει ποτὲ σεισμός
> πρηνίξας, στήσῃ δὲ πάλιν πόλις ἱδρυνθεῖσα.

A related couplet is found in *Sibylline Oracles* 5.290–291, again with specific reference being made to the destructive power of earthquakes:

> Woe Laodicea, beautiful city, how you will perish
> destroyed by earthquakes and changed to dust.
>
> αἰαῖ, Λαοδίκεια, καλὴ πόλι· ὡς ἀπολεῖσθαι
> σεισμοῖς ὀλλύμεναί τε καὶ εἰς κόνιν ἀλλαχθεῖσαι.

The fall of Laodicea is also proclaimed in *Sibylline Oracles* 7.22–23, although in this instance there is no mention of earthquakes as such. In this case the image of destruction involves torrents of the Lycus river, possibly churned up by the effects of seismic activity:

> Alas, Laodicea, daring one, you will speak falsehood,
> you who have never seen God. The wave of Lycus will dash over you.
>
> αἰαῖ, Λαοδίκεια, σὺ δ᾽ αὖ θεὸν οὔποτ᾽ ἰδοῦσα
> ψεύσῃ, τολμηρή· κλύσσει δέ σε κῦμα Λύκοιο.

Mention is also made of earthquakes affecting both the cities of Laodicea and Hierapolis in *Sibylline Oracles* 12.279–281. This is an oracle which contains some material relating to the tumultuous reign of Severus Alexander (222–35 CE), and thus probably dates to that time period, at least in the final form that has come down to us. However, there is every possibility that the description of Laodicea and Hierapolis contained within these lines may date to a much earlier time. Given the fact that *Sibylline Oracles* 12 offers a review of imperial history from

11. The Greek text of the Sibylline Oracles is that of Johannes Geffcken *Die Oracula Sibyllina* (Leipzig: J.C. Hinrich'sche Buchhandlung, 1902). Translations are taken from J.J. Collins, 'Sibylline Oracles', in James H. Charlesworth (ed.) *The Old Testament Pseudepigrapha: Apocalyptic Literature and Testaments* (London: Darton, Londman & Todd, 1983), pp. 317–472.

the time of Augustus down to the death of Severus Alexander in 235 CE, these lines may have originated at any point in the 250 years under review. In other words, it is not impossible that the earthquake of 60 CE is what is being alluded to within these lines:

> Phrygia of many flocks will also groan with earthquakes.
> Alas, Laodicea, alas wretched Hierapolis,
> for you first did the yawning earth receive.
>
> καὶ Φρυγίη σεισμοῖσι πολυμήλη στοναχήσει
> αἰαῖ Λαοδίκεια, αἰαῖ Ἱεράπολι τλήμων·
> ὑμᾶς γὰρ πρώτας ποτ᾽ ἐδέξατο γαῖα χανοῦσα.

Finally, there is an interesting passage in *Sibylline Oracles* 5.318–20 which may also be of relevance in that it concentrates on the city of Hierapolis itself. The oracle comes within a larger section (5.286–327) in which the destruction of various cities of Asia is related, including the destruction of the city of Laodicea mentioned above (5.290–291). Most intriguing are the allusions to particular geographical features of the city of Hierapolis, including a veiled reference to the famous Plutonium near the temple of Apollo, and the travertine deposits formed by the hot springs which flowed through the area.

> Hierapolis also, the only land which has mingled with Pluton,
> you will have what you desired to have, a land of many tears,
> piling a mound on the earth by the streams of Thermodon.
>
> καὶ Ἱεράπολι, γαῖα μόνη Πλούτωνι μιγεῖσα,
> ἕξεις, ὅν πεπόθηκας ἔχειν, χῶρον πολύδακρυν
> ἐς γῆν χωσαμένη παρὰ χεύμασι Θερμώδοντος.

In summary, there are a number of pieces of evidence from antiquity which demonstrate the significant role that earthquakes played within the life of the province of Asia in general, and within the cities of the Lycus valley in particular.

2. *The Earthquake of 60 CE: A Backdrop for the Epistles to the Churches of the Lycus Valley*

Periodically, the fact that the Lycus valley was prone to earthquakes figures in attempts to reconstruct the historical circumstances of the letters written by Paul to the churches in the area. The suggestions of two interpreters in particular are worth noting briefly in this regard.

First, we have the reconstruction offered by P.N. Harrison. He builds on the interpretation of John Knox and Edgar J. Goodspeed about these matters, but instead of suggesting (as they do) that the lost letter to the Laodiceans is in fact what we now know as the letter to Philemon, he offers an altogether different proposal. Harrison thinks that Onesimus wrote what we now call the letter to the Ephesians to replace the letter to the Laodiceans which was lost during the earthquake, perhaps the one of 60 CE which was mentioned by Tacitus. He says:

> Onesimus must have known that it would have been hopeless to try and recover that letter thirty years later. There was only one thing to be done about that – and he if anyone was the man to do it – write another to take its place and represent it in the new collection.[12]

Second, we note an idea put forward by E.F. Scott, which has the merit of a textual anchor point within one of the letters itself. Commenting on the reference in Col. 4.13 to Epaphras' hard work' (πολὺν πόνον) on behalf of the Christians in Colossae and Laodicea, Scott offers an intriguing suggestion which connects Epaphras' efforts to events known to have taken place within the Lycus valley.

> It is tempting to read here a passing allusion to the great earthquake which must have happened just about this time, and on which Paul is so strangely silent throughout his letter. The historian Tacitus tells us that financial help was offered on a large scale to the afflicted cities, adding that Laodicea, with an admirable spirit of self-reliance, declined it. Epaphras may have come to Rome to enlist the sympathy of wealthy Christians for their brethren who had lost everything in the great disaster.[13]

3. *Earthquake Imagery in Colossians, Philemon and Ephesians*

Not only are the circumstances surrounding the production of both Philemon and Colossians seen by some interpreters as directly related to the severe earthquake of 60 CE, but some commentators detect veiled allusions to earthquakes within the Pauline letters themselves. For example, L.J. Baggott focused on the unusual expression in 1.23, μὴ μετακινούμενοι ἀπὸ τῆς ἐλπίδος τοῦ εὐαγγελίου (rendered by the RSV as 'not shifting from the hope of the gospel'), and suggested that Paul deliberately appeals to the Colossians' experience of seismic activity in the verse. Baggott remarks:

> Earthquakes have wrought havoc with the place, and one feels the force of the Apostle's plea in 1.23: 'Be not moved away (earth-quake-stricken) from the hope of the Gospel.[14]

There are several other similar allusions within Colossians and Ephesians which are worth noting in that they too could be viewed against the background of seismic activity in the Lycus valley. This is by no means the way that such allusions are generally interpreted, but it remains a fascinating variation worth considering. These seismic allusions fall into three distinct, but inter-related, categories. The imagery involved is concerned with: (a) Deep Roots, Stability and Firm Foundations, (b) Temple Building and Reconstruction, (c) Debt Cancellation and Tax Relief.

12. 'The Author of Ephesians', *Studia Evangelica* 2 (Berlin: Academie Verlag, 1964), pp. 603–604.

13. *The Epistles of Paul to the Colossians, to Philemon and to the Ephesians* (MNTC; London: Hodder & Stoughton, 1930), p. 90.

14. *A New Approach to Colossians* (London: Mowbray, 1961), p. 5.

a. *Deep Roots, Stability and Firm Foundations: Prevention against the Threat of Earthquakes*

It has often been noted that language about the power of God is a frequent feature in both Colossians and Ephesians (see Col. 1.11, 29; 2.12; Eph. 1.19; 3.7, 16, 20; 6.10). Perhaps this is as it must be, given the fact that there are fewer more powerful demonstrations of the raw power of nature known to the people of antiquity than that associated with earthquakes and geo-thermal activity. The congregations of the churches of the Lycus valley were certainly familiar with the physical manifestations of the power of nature. The language and imagery of 'power' (δύναμις) or 'energy' (ἐνέργεια) would not have been lost on them since they would have seen examples of it all around them each and every day. Indeed, it may well be that the curious reference in Eph. 4.14 to the believers as 'those who are being tossed around to and fro by waves' (κλυδωνιζόμενοι) is an illustration of precisely this point. Generally this is taken to be a nautical image, along the lines of James 1.6. However, it is equally possible that the writer of the letter is referring to the unsettling effects of seismic activity in much the same way that we today talk about the 'shock waves' of an earthquake.[15] Moreover, beyond the mere mention of 'power' itself, there are several other striking terms and phrases within Colossians and Ephesians whose semantic ranges might be extended legitimately to include seismic activity.

For example, it is worth noting the interesting use of ῥιζόω ('to take root'), a verb which appears only twice in the New Testament, once in Col. 2.7 and once in Eph. 3.17. Most commentators agree that the writer of Ephesians is reliant upon the passage in Colossians, building upon and expanding what is essentially an agricultural metaphor of planting much used by Paul elsewhere (as in 1 Cor. 3.6–9). Here in Col. 2.7 Paul exhorts the Christians in Colossae to walk in the Lord Christ Jesus, reminding them that they have already been 'rooted' (ἐρριζωμένοι) in him. The writer of Ephesians follows suit in 3.17, including within his prayer for the Christian believers that they might recognize the fact that they have been 'rooted and grounded in love' (ἐν ἀγάπῃ ἐρριζωμένοι καὶ τεθεμελιωμένοι). It is likely that both passages are dependent upon 1 Cor. 3.6–17, which combines the imagery of careful planting and gardening with that of wise temple-building. In any case, such imagery of trees, plants, and bushes setting down deep roots as a means of survival in a hostile environment is widespread. Not only is it a powerful image for a desert environment where water is scarce, but it also is suitable for an environment where the uprooting caused by earthquakes is an ever-present threat.

A related image is found in Col. 2.5 where Paul declares that he rejoices to see not only the good discipline of the congregation at Colossae, but also the 'stability of your faith in Christ' (τὸ στερέωμα τῆς εἰς Χριστὸν πίστεως ὑμῶν). The basic idea of 'stability' (στερέωμα) also appears in similar contexts in 1 Pet. 5.9 where the Christians are exhorted to 'stand firm in faith' (ἀντίστητε στερεοὶ τῇ πίστει), and Acts 16.5 where the churches are said to have been 'strengthened in

15. See my *The Epistle to the Ephesians* (EC; London: Epworth Press, 1997), p. 133, on this point.

the faith' (ἐστερεοῦντο τῇ πίστει). The point here is that 'stability' would be a very desirable quality to have in an earthquake-dominated environment. Indeed, the idea of 'standing' is especially significant within both Colossians and Ephesians, if the uses of the verb ἱστήμι and στήκω ('I stand') and their cognates is anything to go by. The verb itself occurs in Col. 4.12 and Eph. 6.11, 13 and 14, while the verb συνίστημι occurs in Col. 1.17 at a crucial point within the christological hymn of 1.15–20.[16] Generally these references to 'standing' are linked to language of 'maturity' and 'growth' and 'standing in battle' and thus are given a strongly ethical or moral sense. Yet the more literal sense of the verb is not to be neglected, particularly in an area where the effect of an earthquake is often to leave *nothing* standing. In a region well familiar with the devastation caused by earth tremors, the collapse of public buildings and the flattening of homes and shelters, such language of 'standing up' is all the more poignant. Even the use of the verbs βεβαιόω ('I confirm') in Col. 2.7 and συμβιβάζω ('I hold together') in Col. 1.29 can be read along these lines. In 2.7 Paul describes the Christian believers as 'those who have been confirmed (or strengthened) in the faith' (βεβαιούμενοι τῇ πίστει), effectively exhorting the members of the church in Colossae to live their lives in such a way that they show themselves confirmed in their faith. Similarly, in 1.29, Paul expresses his desire that the Christians in Colossae, together with the believers in Laodicea, may be encouraged, 'having had their hearts held together in love' (αἱ καρδίαι συμβιβασθέντες ἐν ἀγάπῃ). The same holds true of the body as a whole, as 2.19 demonstrates, where Paul describes the body as 'supplied and held together through its joints and ligaments' (διὰ τῶν ἁφῶν καὶ συνδέσμων ἐπιχορηγούμενον καὶ συμβιβαζόμενον). All of this is made possible, Paul says in 2.7, because they not only have secure roots which sink deep into the earth, but also they are 'people whose lives have been erected upon the firm foundation of Christ himself' (ἐποικοδομούμενοι ἐν αὐτῷ). This leads us on to consider further how the building metaphor is used in the letter to the Ephesians.

b. *Temple Building and Reconstruction: Repairing the Aftermath of Earthquakes*

Interestingly, the idea of 'building' upon Christ himself is extended significantly in the epistle we now know as Ephesians. This is most clearly seen in 2.19–22 where the believers are said to be 'members of the household of God' (οἰκεῖοι τοῦ θεοῦ), which 'has been built upon the foundation of the apostles and prophets' (ἐποικοδομηθέντες ἐπὶ τῷ θεμελίῳ τῶν ἀποστόλων καὶ προφητῶν). This whole 'structure' (οἰκοδομή) is said to be 'growing into a holy temple in the Lord' (αὔξει εἰς ναὸν ἅγιον ἐν κυρίῳ), and the church itself is 'being built

16. For more on the centrality of the line 'in him all things hold together' (καὶ τὰ πάντα ἐν αὐτῇ συνέστηκεν) in the hymn, see Paul Beasley-Murray, 'Colossians 1.15–20: An Early Christian Hymn Celebrating the Lordship of Christ', in Donald A. Hagner and Murray J. Harris (eds.), *Pauline Studies: Essays Presented to Professor F.F. Bruce on his 70th Birthday* (Grand Rapids, MI: Eerdmans, 1980), pp. 169–83.

together into a dwelling-place of God' (συνοικοδομεῖσθε εἰς κατοικητήριον τοῦ θεοῦ).[17] The language of inhabitation, or the construction of dwelling-places, is continued in several other places within the epistle. We see it in 3.17, where the writer expresses his hope that 'Christ might come to dwell in our hearts through faith' (κατοικῆσαι τὸν Χριστὸν διὰ τῆς πίστεως ἐν ταῖς καρδίαις ὑμῶν). Similarly, in 4.12 we read of the 'building up of the body of Christ' (οἰκοδομὴν τοῦ σώματος τοῦ Χριστοῦ), an image which is used again in 4.15–16 as the writer mixes his metaphors and describes both body-building and temple-growing, culminating in a declaration about the body's 'building up of itself in love' (οἰκοδομὴν ἑαυτοῦ ἐν ἀγάπῃ). Nowhere else in the Pauline corpus is there such a concentrated emphasis on imagery associated with the construction of buildings and dwelling-places. Only in Ephesians do we find the idea of the building up of the temple of God, the construction of Christ's own body, the church, alluded to in such a fashion. One cannot help but wonder if one of the reasons for the extended use of such a construction metaphor has to do with the background of the city to which the letter was first directed. It is on this particular point that familiarity with the history of the city of Hierapolis again becomes important.

Archaeology confirms that the city of Hierapolis underwent an extensive building programme during the reigns of Septimus Severus (193–211 CE), Caracalla (198–217 CE), Elagabalus (218–22 CE), and Severus Alexander (222–35 CE). Many of the ruins of the city presently visible date from this period. Not surprisingly, given the name of the city (*Hiera Polis* – the holy city), many of these ruins have been identified as temples or shrines. We should not assume, however, that Hierapolis only came to be a construction site of importance in the late-second and early-third centuries. In fact, much of the construction from this period was building upon long-established foundations and renovating temple complexes that had already been in existence for some time.

Hierapolis was renowned in the ancient world as a city filled with temples dedicated to a variety of gods, both central figures within the pantheon as well as local deities. Hierapolis also was an important centre for the Roman imperial cult, as the fascinating study by S.R.F. Price entitled *Rituals and Power* (1984) indicates. The importance of the imperial cultus within the religious life of the city is beyond doubt, and is amply witnessed to by the many temples which were located in Hierapolis. Price lists two imperial temples in Hierapolis, one from the time of Claudius (41–54 CE) and one from the time of Elagabalus (218–222 CE), as well as two in Laodicea, one from the time of Domitian (81–96 CE) and one from the time of Commodus (177–92 CE).[18] Occasionally we see evidence of these temples proudly proclaimed on the city's own coinage, with the provincial mints functioning like a well-oiled propaganda machine. Perhaps the best

17. Rudolf Schnackenburg, 'Die Kirche als Bau: Epheser 2.19–22 unter ökumenischem Aspekt', in M.D. Hooker and S.G. Wilson (eds.), *Paul and Paulinism: Essays in Honour of C.K. Barrett* (London: SPCK, 1982), pp. 258–71, offers an excellent introduction to this passage.

18. S.R.F. Price *Rituals and Power: The Roman Imperial Cult in Asia Minor* (Cambridge: Cambridge University Press, 1984), pp. 264–65.

example of this is to be seen in a small bronze coin type which was issued in 50–54 CE during the reign of the Emperor Claudius (41–54 CE) (Figure 2).[19] The coin has on its obverse a portrait of a bust of the god Apollo (or possibly Dionysus), draped and facing to the right. An inscription surrounds the bust which reads Μ ΣΥΙΛΛΙΟΣ ΑΝΤΙΟΧΟΣ ΙΕΡΑΠΟΛΙΤΩΝ ('M. Suillios Antiochus, of the Hierapolitans'). Generally the name is said to be that of a city official or magistrate responsible for the minting of coinage. The reverse of the coin depicts a temple with six columns, surrounded by an inscription which reads ΓΕΝΕΙ ΣΕΒΑΣΤΩΝ ('Genius of the Family of Augustus').

(a.) obverse

(b.) reverse

Figure 2.

The city's position as a neocorate, a later technical term used to denote a site containing a temple dedicated to the emperor cult,[20] probably dates to the time of Elagabalus. Certainly the extensive neocorate coinage issued by the city points in this direction, with the massive issue of 221 CE being particularly of note.[21]

19. Barclay V. Head *Catalogue of the Greek Coins of Phrygia* (London: Trustees of the British Museum, 1906), p. 229, lists this as coin #11; Andrew Burnett, Michael Amandry and Pere Pan Ripollés *Roman Provincial Coinage* (London: British Museum Press, 1992), p. 485, list it as coin #2973.

20. On the matter of neocorate coinage see, Von Papen, 'Die Spiele von Hierapolis', *Zeitschrift für Numismatik* 24 (1908), pp. 161–82; Leo Weber, 'Zur Münzprägung des phrygischen Hierapolis', in *XARITES: Friedrich Leo zum Sechzigsten Geburtstag* (Berlin: Weidmannsche Buchhandlung, 1911), pp. 466–90 + Plates VII and VIII; Leo Weber, 'Die Homoniemünzen des phrygischen Hierapolis', *JIAN* (1912), pp. 65–122; T.L. Donaldson *Ancient Architecture on Greek and Roman Coins and Medals* (Chicago: Argonaut Publishers, 1966 reprint of an 1859 original), pp. 21–32, 132–56; Barbara Burrell, 'Neokoroi: Greek Cities of the Roman East', *Harvard Studies in Classical Philology* 85 (1981), pp. 301–303.

21. The earlier opinion that the neocorate dated to the reign of Caracalla (198–217 CE) is no longer tenable. See Ann Johnston, 'Caracalla or Elagabalus? A Case of Unnecessarily Mistaken Identity', *ANSMN* 27 (1982), pp. 97–147; 'Hierapolis Revisited', *Numismatic Chronicle* 144 (1984), pp. 52–80 + Plates 12–16. The idea that the neocorate coins of Hierapolis were somehow connected with a visit of Caracalla to the city during a visit to Asia made in 214–15 CE is also called into question (the journey to Asia is mentioned in *Historia Augusta: Caracalla* 5.4–8; Dio Cassius,

Hierapolis appears to have been a neocorate four times over, a rare achievement which stands as some indication of the significance of the city in terms of its religious and political institutions. The title neocoros (νεωκόρος) speaks of a personal bond between the city and the emperor granting the privilege; it assumes a degree of loyalty and devotion to the emperor on the part of the city.

In other words, the fact that Hierapolis was a city well-known for its numerous temples means that the frequent references to temple-building in Ephesians makes perfect sense. This is particularly true if the city had suffered greatly during the earthquake of 60 CE which was known to have destroyed the city of Laodicea, a mere six miles away on the other side of the Lycus valley floor. Hierapolis would have been eager to rebuild and reestablish itself as a centre of cultic activity. Little wonder then that so much is made of the establishment of and up-building of the Church within the letter to the Ephesians. The writer is invoking an image with which the congregation in Hierapolis would have been very familiar.

c. *Debt Cancellation and Tax Relief: Easing the Financial Burden after Earthquakes*

Col. 2.14 contains a curious phrase concerning the cancellation of debt which may be relevant to our concerns. This phrase appears in a sentence describing what God has done through the death and resurrection of Christ. This divine act is said to involve God 'having cancelled out the certificate of debt which stood against us' (ἐξαλείψας τὸ καθ' ἡμῶν χειρόγραφον). This image is commonly interpreted as one drawn from the world of business and finance, one which is well-attested within both Jewish and Graeco-Roman circles.[22] The word translated as 'certificate of debt' (χειρόγραφον) occurs only here in the New Testament, and, not surprisingly given the context of the passage, it is almost universally taken to mean the debt of human sin and wickedness which is dealt with on the cross of Christ.[23] The verse thus invokes an image of the cancellation of debt as a metaphor of forgiveness. Such an image of debt-cancellation may be a deliberate allusion to the tax relief granted by the Roman state following the earthquake of 60 CE. As we noted above, Tiberius offered a five-year period of tax-remission in 17 CE following the great earthquake then.

There may also be a conceptual connection to Philemon 19 where Paul takes up the pen and himself writes to Philemon concerning the release of the slave

Roman History 78.16.8–78.17.4). Ann Johnston, 'Caracalla's Path: The Numismatic Evidence', *Historia* 32 (1983), pp. 58–76, discusses the chronological difficulties.

22. See Eduard Lohse *Colossians and Philemon* (HC; Philadelphia: Fortress Press, 1971), pp. 108–11; E. Lohse *TDNT* 9 (1974), pp. 435–36; Peter O'Brien *Colossians, Philemon* (WBC, 44; Waco, Texas: Word Books, 1982), pp. 124–26.

23. See Roy Yates, 'Colossians 2.14: Metaphor of Forgiveness', *Biblica* 71 (1990) pp. 248–59, for a helpful summary. Oliva A. Blanchette, 'Does the *cheirographon* of Col 2.14 Represent Christ Himself?', *CBQ* 23 (1961), pp. 306–12, and Wesley Carr *Angels and Principalities: The Background, Meaning and Development of the Pauline Phrase Hai Archai Kai Hai Exousiai* (SNTSMS, 42; Cambridge: Cambridge University Press, 1981), pp. 52–66, offer important discussions.

Onesimus.[24] He does not use the technical term χειρόγραφον in the verse, but he uses phrasing clearly reflective of it: 'I, Paul, write to you in my own hand: I will pay' (ἐγὼ Παῦλος ἔγραψα τῇ ἐμῇ χειρί. ἐγὼ ἀποτίσω). In other words, it may be that Paul is alluding here to the fact that the Roman Emperors remitted debts to the disaster-stricken inhabitants of the Lycus valley and is invoking the memory of that in his petition to Philemon. Effectively, he offers a hand-written certificate of indebtedness and offers to pay it himself, just as the Emperor Tiberius had done following the earthquake of 17 CE and, presumably, the Emperor Nero had done in 60 CE (we can safely assume that the reference in Tacitus *Annals* 14.27 to the city of Laodicea rebuilding without the help of the imperial treasury is an indication that such assistance had at least been offered by Nero).

4. *Summary*

This study began by noting some of the difficulties associated with establishing the historical circumstances surrounding the writing of the letter to the Colossians, particularly as regards the lack of reference to the great earthquake of 60 CE which was known to have devastated cities in the Lycus valley. The evidence for seismic activity within the province of Asia, particularly affecting the cities of Laodicea and Hierapolis, was surveyed, including key literary references such as Tacitus' *Annals* and various sections of the *Sibylline Oracles*. Several important numismatic issues relating to the imperial programmes of restoration and rebuilding following the earthquake were discussed; these included coins which were produced by both imperial and provincial mints.

Having established the importance of earthquakes within any discussion of the region of the Lycus valley, I moved on to consider some of the ways in which scholars have attempted to set the production of Ephesians and Colossians against the backdrop of the earthquake of 60 CE. This then led to an in-depth consideration of the three letters which I contend were directed to the Christians of the region (Colossians, Philemon and Ephesians); the aim here was to detect possible earthquake imagery within them. A number of terms and phrases within the three letters suggest that the writers of them were consciously alluding to imagery associated with seismic activity.

Such an assessment of the letters provides the basis for a reconsideration of two key questions arising from them. First, the assumption that Colossians makes no mention of the earthquake of 60 CE, so often asserted by scholars who build a case against Pauline authorship of the letter, needs to be challenged. If Colossians does indeed contain several deliberate allusions to the great earthquake of 60 CE, then questions about the genuineness of it as a Pauline letter are again legitimately raised. Second, the age-old conundrum about the provenance of the letter to the Ephesians, a difficulty which Ralph P. Martin once crystallized by

24. For more on Paul's handwritten remarks at the end of his letters, see Gordon J. Bahr, 'The Subscriptions in the Pauline Letters', *Journal of Biblical Literature* 87 (1968), pp. 27–41.

his provocatively entitled article 'An Epistle in Search of a Life-Setting',[25] may be one step closer to being resolved. My contention is that the letter to the Ephesians was originally directed to the Christian church in the city of Hierapolis. The earthquake imagery contained within the epistle, notably the language describing the (re-)building of the temple of God, provides an additional level of support for this theory.

25. *The Expository Times* 79 (1968), pp. 296–302.

Part II

JESUS IN THE SYNOPTIC TRADITION

Mark's Oral Practice and the Written Gospel of Mark

Matti Myllykoski

'All we have is the text'. This idea which has been so often brought up by Biblical scholars, particularly when criticizing other scholars' speculations, seems to befit the Gospel of Mark to a greater extent than any other early Christian document. Some hundred years ago the priority of the shortest gospel gradually became accepted by the majority of New Testament scholars, and ever since that time Matthew and Luke have predominantly been studied in relation to their assumed sources Mark and Q. The letters of Paul have been interpreted with help of other letters, and the deutero-Pauline letters have often been influenced by the authentic letters or by each other. The Gospel of John reveals either knowledge or use of the synoptic gospels or at least creative reinterpretation of traditions common or similar to all of them. Not so the Gospel of Mark. Here scholars who have nothing but the text must strongly disagree about the prehistory, sources, literary techniques, theology/ideology and socio-historical context of the document. It is only natural that the pioneer work of the gospel genre has remained a puzzle and a bone of contention for the whole community of scholars.

Diachronic studies in Mark have been bound not only to a variety of opinions and conclusions, but also to a partial scholarly consent and some sort of scientific optimism. Against this, some advocates of narrative criticism have emphasized that we cannot read the mind of the real author of the gospel and that the sources and traditions used by the Evangelists are irrecoverable and irrelevant. All we have is the narrative, an interwoven texture that is finally open to multiple contextual readings. Basically, it is not the narrative that makes sense, but its readers. It is certainly wishful thinking to assume that diachronic studies might someday produce the truth about Mark – definite, verifiable and generally accepted answers to the essential questions that have been posed in this century. And of course, even agreement would not guarantee the truth.

In the following essay, I will first briefly explore the development of methodology in the study of Mark's gospel in order to demonstrate that, in spite of the highly sophisticated discussion on various diachronic and synchronic aspects of the text and its prehistory, there is a huge gap in an area that should be of great interest: the oral practice of Mark as part of the process that led to the written gospel.

1. *From Herder to Kelber*

The Romantic movement in the late 18th century was fascinated by the folk cultures of the distant past and gave an impetus for hundreds of collectors to bring together pieces of oral tradition and traditions that seemed to belong to that category. The study of the oral tradition behind the gospels goes back to Johann Gottfried Herder (1744–1803) who regarded the works of the evangelists as products of Hebrew historiography.[1] Unlike the Greek and Roman historical writings, the Hebrew style of writing history reflected the infancy of humankind. Since the times of Isaiah, the Hebrew culture had not developed, but remained in the world of tales of supernatural events and prophetic utterances.[2] Herder further assumed that the rule of faith (*regula fidei*) was the basic content of the apostolic preaching: Jesus is the Messiah and the Son of God.[3] While he thought that this basic message can be traced back to Jesus himself, the differences between the letters of John, Peter and Paul proved to him that each one of them developed their own proclamation individually. In spite of that, in the beginning there was one gospel as the basis of all Christian proclamation. This gospel was the Hebrew Gospel of Matthew, which, however, was not necessarily identical with the canonical version of Matthew. Matthew and John were apostles and eyewitnesses, while Mark and Luke were evangelists. They all developed their respective stories freely and independently of each other. Herder heard within their witness the living voice of early Christian teaching.[4] However, he thought that Mark was very close to the oldest gospel. Because it is brief and concise and does not criticize the Jewish worship like Matthew, Herder drew the conclusion that it reflects the original Jewish views of the first Christians in Jerusalem.[5]

Herder accepted the tradition according to which Mark was a disciple and interpreter of Peter. He emphasized that 'no other gospel has so few literal qualities and so much living voice as that of a storyteller than this'.[6] The repetition of expressions like 'and', 'and immediately', 'and spoke to them', etc., reveal the popular

1. Herder, 'Vom Erlöser der Menschen: Nach unsern drei ersten Evangelien', *Sämmtliche Schriften XIX, Christliche Schriften II* (Riga: J.F. Hartknoch, 1796), pp. 135–252; 'Von Gottes Sohn, der Welt Heiland. Nach Johannes Evangelium: Nebst einer Regel der Zusammenstimmung unserer Evangelien aus ihrer Entstehung und Ordnung', *Sämtliche Schriften XIX, Christliche Schriften III* (Riga: J.F. Hartknoch, 1797), pp. 253–424. In the latter article, the 'Regel' that is relevant here in on pages 380–424.

2. Herder, 'Erlöser', pp. 194–96.

3. This gospel included materials that were designed to prove Jesus' messianity: God's proclamations about Christ at his baptism, transformation and resurrection; miracles; messianic speeches; the growth of the kingdom and the second coming of Christ. This gospel is guaranteed by the leading apostles Peter, James, and John. See Herder, 'Gottes Sohn', pp. 386–89.

4. Herder, 'Erlöser', pp. 202–15.

5. Herder, 'Gottes Sohn', pp. 391–96. Herder refers to the mentioning of names and embellishing stories with details as a sign of the individual originality of this gospel; he even speaks of it as an archetype of narrative (p. 394: 'ein Archetyp der Erzählung').

6. Herder, 'Erlöser', p. 216: 'Kein Evangelium hat so wenig Schriftstellerisches und so viel lebendigen Laut eines Erzählers wie dieses'.

tone of a Palestinian storyteller. Matthew and Luke, in contrast to Mark, did not speak, but wrote. Herder thought that as a storyteller Mark left a good deal of the teachings of Jesus out of his presentation, abbreviated parable and speeches, but rather transmitted many sayings in a repetitious style. All this served the needs of a listening audience. For Herder, the Gospel of Mark was an ecclesiastical gospel, a living story that was meant to be read aloud in front of the community.[7]

These views did not promote discussion about the oral character of the Gospel of Mark, because all the gospels were still directly connected to the apostolic authority. The living voice of the apostles and their disciples was in the service of one basic gospel. First the Griesbachian theory and then the two-source hypothesis dominated the scene of gospel studies. They were both explicitly literary theories that did not yield to discussion about oral tradition. Herder's lead was taken by the form-critics who followed William Wrede and rejected the idea of the Gospel of Mark as a historically reliable biography of Jesus. As they stripped the gospels into small units of traditions that were used in various ways in the early church, they also had to imagine that all these pieces of traditions – sayings, parables, miracle stories, and other units – were transmitted in oral form. However, they did not study the significance of the oral tradition as such. It was rather unimportant to them whether the sayings of Jesus were transmitted in an oral or written form.[8] There was basically no difference between the oral and written tradition, since in both the traditional units were connected into clusters by the same primitive principles. In the case of speech materials, the principles of connection were similarity of content and outward likeness (use of a catchword). In the narrative materials of Mark, Rudolf Bultmann points out the simple linking of succession, place composition, and temporal references.[9] The redaction criticism, in turn, did not focus on the question of oral tradition, but on the literary and theological achievement of the evangelists.

The revival of the theory of Homeric orality by the American classicist Milman Parry in the early 1930s was the starting point of modern oral studies.[10] He discovered that all early Greek poetry was originally oral. In order to know better the development of poetry in antiquity, it was meaningful to study living poetry, the stability of traditional poems and the changes they have gone through in the process of transmission. He and his student Albert Bates Lord collected and studied the performances of Yugoslav folksingers.[11] These singers, particularly the well-known Avdo Mededovic, could sing extremely long songs, opening a treasury of long oral tradition in personally memorized form. The performances revealed that the singers were accustomed to relying upon repetition of fixed formulas, metric conventions, standard story patterns and the like. The predictable

7. Herder, 'Erlöser', pp. 216–17.

8. See e.g. R. Bultmann, *History of the Synoptic Tradition* (ET, Rev. Ed.; New York: Harper & Row, 1968), p. 87.

9. Bultmann, *History*, pp. 322, 338–40.

10. M. Parry, *The Making of Homeric Verse* (ed. Adam Parry; Oxford: Clarendon Press, 1971).

11. A.B. Lord, *The Singer of Tales* (Harvard Studies in Comparative Literature, 24; Cambridge MA: Harvard University Press 1960).

and traditionally well known development of the themes in long songs was based on such requisites. The singers could use it – and had to use it – in order to reproduce the songs from their own memory, thereby creating a great deal of variation in the details, so that each of his performances is different from all others, not to speak of their difference to the performances of other singers. When the singers were asked whether they repeat the song always in precisely the same form, they were quite naturally inclined to claim so. Something like this must have happened with the performers of early Greek poetry as well.

It has not been easy to apply these findings to the gospel studies. Unlike the gospel tradition, the early Greek poetry and the poetry of the Yugoslav folksingers is metric and goes back to a long and standardized oral tradition. The problems of stability, change and variations in the small units and clusters in the gospel tradition must be approached differently. This becomes clear from Albert B. Lord's attempt to study the gospels as oral traditional literature and to survey them on the conditions of the methodology applied to the folksongs.[12] He finds in the gospels a mythic pattern very similar to the basic pattern that dominates the traditional lives of the heroes: birth, precocious childhood, investiture (Jesus' baptism and/or his triumphal entry into Jerusalem), death of the substitute (John the Baptist), death and resurrection.[13] Lord emphasizes that this pattern is only imperfectly, but independently, realized in the gospels of Matthew and Luke. In his survey of the parallel sequences and the verbal correspondences between the synoptic gospels Lord draws the conclusion that the great variations between them rules out the assumption that one could have been copied from another. Thus their stories are 'three oral traditional variants of the same narrative and non-narrative materials'. Lord regards chiastic variations in the arrangements of texts, elaboration of the individual episodes, duplications and multiforms (e.g. the sending of the seventy and the twelve in Luke) as characteristics of oral tradition.[14] In spite of these observations, it is very difficult to give up the theory of interrelations between the gospels. The characteristics named by Lord are known in the literary tradition of Greco-Roman literature as well.[15] However, the study of the gospel of Mark must include the quest for orality, the living voice of the early Christian storytellers.

In the past two decades, there has been a stimulating, but a still widely neglected discussion on the relationship between the oral and the written gospel in Mark. One of the first major studies in this field is *The Oral and Written Gospel* of Werner H. Kelber.[16] Kelber treats the oral legacy of Mark by dividing the gospel pericopes into heroic stories (healings), polarization stories (exorcisms), didactic

12. Lord, 'The Gospels as Oral Traditional Literature', in William O. Walker (ed.), *The Relationships among the Gospels: An Interdisciplinary Dialogue* (San Antonio: Trinity University Press, 1978), pp. 33–91.

13. Lord, 'Gospels', pp. 39–58.

14. Lord, 'Gospels', pp. 90–91 (conclusions drawn from the analysis on pp. 58–89).

15. C.H. Talbert, 'Oral and Independent or Literary and Interdependent?: A Response to Albert B. Lord', in W.O. Walker (ed.), *The Relationships among the Gospels: An Interdisciplinary Dialogue* (San Antonio: Trinity University Press 1978), pp. 93–102.

16. W. Kelber, *The Oral and Written Gospel: The Hermeneutics of Speaking and Writing in the Synoptic Tradition, Mark, Paul, and Q* (Philadelphia: Fortress Press, 1983).

stories (apophthegmatic tradition) and parabolic stories.[17] The heroic miracle stories have a commonplace structure, but they show a great variability in the use of commonplaces. Kelber evaluates both healings and exorcisms in terms of their variable basic structures, which allow a great variety in the details, but which keep the characters of the stories simple and undeveloped. He further emphasizes the basic simplicity of both didactic and parabolic stories. The former combine a story with a statement and make a striking word of Jesus vividly present, while the latter is non-argumentative, extravagant and ambiguous, bringing up rather something that it does not say. Kelber emphasizes the opposition between oral pluralism and oral gospel: since the little stories are self-sufficient, autonomous, and heterogeneous, the oral tradition by itself does not produce a need 'for telling of a single, comprehensive story about Jesus'.[18] The Gospel of Mark is thus a literary product that muted, decontextualized, and deconstructed the oral voices, drawing their pluralism onto a single path. Textuality works as disorientation and reorientation of oral tradition.[19]

For Kelber, the apocalypse in Mark 13 'touches most directly on the gospel's social matrix'.[20] In this text Mark directed his assault against 'politically committed Jewish-Christian prophets' who in their proclamation brought about an 'orally effected presence of Jesus'.[21] He has designed his treatment of the last events in the apocalypse in order to expose the errors of the self-reliant prophets and make clear the unpredictability of the future fulfilment. Mark's opposition to the oral proclamation of these prophets further explains the absence of the resurrection stories at the end of the gospel, which as a whole is 'a written alternative to the oral metaphysics of presence'.[22] Consequently, Kelber emphasizes that the written gospel is something completely different than the oral. In a written gospel, 'the kingdom is more paradox than a presence, and mystery rather than possession'.[23] The gospel is a written parable, in which the disciples who are insiders (4.11–12) become outsiders (4.35–8.21) and remain so to the end (16.1–8).[24]

The theory of Kelber is dependent on the traditional separation between oral tradition and written gospel, but more recent studies have demonstrated that the movement from oral tradition to a written document is not just antithetical. In recent times, the study of orality and literacy has led to the rejection of the sharp divide between these two, and has led instead to the tendency to pay attention to 'interactive' forms between them. In folklore, the creative input of oral performers has been recognized, and the interface between orality and literacy has been brought into the focus of research.[25] If we assume that Mark himself was a

17. Kelber, *Gospel*, pp. 44–64.

18. Kelber, *Gospel*, p. 79.

19. Kelber, *Gospel*, pp. 91-116. He thinks (pp. 96–105) that Mark in his gospel suffocated the voices of the first disciples as well as James and other members of Jesus' family (3.20–35).

20. Kelber, *Gospel*, p. 98.

21. Kelber, *Gospel*, p. 99.

22. Kelber, *Gospel*, p. 100.

23. Kelber, *Gospel*, p. 114.

24. Kelber, *Gospel*, pp. 117–29.

25. See e.g. J. Goody, *The Interface between the Written and the Oral* (Cambridge: Cambridge

storyteller, the interaction between his assumed oral performances and his written gospel must be taken seriously. It is difficult to imagine the author of the first gospel as a man who was an outsider to the transmission of oral traditions, as someone who merely listened to others and quietly wrote down notes, fragments and written sources. His notable experience with Jesus tradition rather hints at his role as an active oral performer who not only combined a great number of oral traditions for a written document, but first of all molded, combined, arranged and presented them in oral form. If this is true, all oral tradition that we find in the Gospel of Mark was first digested by Mark for his oral practice as a storyteller and a teacher. There must also have been other performers like Mark, and it is not that easy to imagine that the Christian communities did not try to unite the mass of oral traditions by means of performing them in wider clusters. Furthermore, it is difficult to perceive how Mark could have thought to overcome, or silence, the oral prophecy by a written gospel story, even though it is likely that he was fighting against 'false prophets'.

2. *The Theory of Horsley*

It is reasonable to assume that Mark himself came from the ranks of the oral performers and that his gospel reflects his oral usage. A seminal suggestion in this direction has come from J. Dewey who drew upon the work of W.J. Ong and E. Havelock. Dewey emphasizes that the Markan narrative bears oral characteristics because it is easily visualized and because it is not arranged in order. Instead, 'the happenings appear in an endless chain of association, based on the echo principle'.[26] Dewey further points out that there is no single linear outline in the Markan narrative, but 'rather it consists of forecasts and echoes, variation within repetition, for a listening audience'. However, she is not arguing that the gospel of Mark was composed orally, but it is very close to oral composition. Instead of the tight plot of a written novel, she recommends us to look for a 'much looser

University Press, 1987), pp. 80–91. See also L. Honko, 'Text as Process and Practice: The Textualization of Oral Epics', in L. Honko (ed.), *Textualization of Oral Epics* (Berlin: de Gruyter, 2000), pp. 1–54, especially pp. 6–9. Honko demonstrates (pp. 15–27) how the making of the 'oral text', viz. speech secondarily codified in the written letters, is a multifaceted process, in which the final product, the 'text', must actually be seen as an 'extended text'. First of all, the singer's ability to perform presupposes a 'pool of tradition' and an 'epic register' (a way of speaking which is valid for the performers), and 'multiforms' (a store of repeatable artistic expressions), which the singer uses in his tradition-oriented performances. Furthermore, the making of the oral text includes a notable amount of changes, replacements, substitutions and particularly variations in the units of the entire story. Some units are stable, while others are not. According to Honko, there is a 'mental text' in the mind of the singers that unites the actual performances of the epic in its cultural context. Concerning the performance itself, Honko speaks about the significance of performance strategy (choice of optional units, length of the performance), mode of performance (in solo or with instrumental accompaniment, use of different poetic categories), performative style (rhetorical means, gestures, pauses, etc.) and audience interaction.

26. J. Dewey, 'Oral Methods of Structuring Narrative in Mark', *Interpretation 43* (1989), pp. 32–44, especially p. 42.

and more additive aural plot structure'.[27] The vital question is, whether the plot of the whole gospel story can be plausibly interpreted in these terms. The tapestry of the Markan narrative seems to be overly rich and loaded with too many diverging meanings and interconnections to be a written version of one single oral performance.[28]

However, the interpretation of the written gospel of Mark as an original oral performance is one of the key elements in the theory presented by Richard A. Horsley. In his recent work, *Hearing the Whole Story*, Horsley questions the assumptions of many scholars reading Mark.[29] He emphasizes that Mark was neither produced nor originally read in pericopes, but heard as a whole story, presented by a gifted storyteller with a message that was simultaneously political and religious, since politics and religion were inseparable in first-century Palestine. So the message of Mark is not a theological treatise about non-political religious issues, like discipleship or Christology. The disciples are indeed no role model for the hearers of the story; on the contrary, they are subsequently presented as deserters, just as women of the gospel are portrayed as representative and exemplary.[30] The dominant plot of the gospel is about Jesus leading a renewal of Israel in opposition to its rulers, Roman and upper-class Jew alike.[31] Horsley argues that the Galilean peasants placed the oppression into the larger framework as that of a struggle between God and superhuman demonic forces. They also diverted their attention from the concrete political-economical realities of the Roman rule and channelled resistance into a battle against 'unclean spirits'.[32] The struggle against the Roman rule is visible in the exorcisms of Jesus, particularly as he drives the legion of demons into the sea: they stand for the legions of Romans that came from the sea and will be driven out to the sea where they came from. In Jerusalem Jesus' struggle becomes explicitly political as he attacks the temple and thus the upper class of the Jewish people. Horsley emphasizes the difference between the priestly and upper-class tradition in Jerusalem and the locally oriented tradition of the poor people in Galilee. He sees the Pharisees as representatives of the Judean Torah observance that tried to mediate the practical obedience of the Law to the Galileans. The Israelite little tradition was revived in the popular messianic and prophetic movement. Horsley sees this political resistance active in Jesus' confrontations with the scribes and Pharisees, and reads the conflicts surrounding the Sabbath (2.23–28), the food laws (7.1–23), and divorce (10.2–9) as demonstration of Jesus' adherence to the Galilean popular tradition

27. Dewey, 'Mark as Interwoven Tapestry: Forecasts and Echoes for a Listening Audience', *CBQ* 53 (1991), pp. 221–36; quotes are from pp. 234–35.

28. Cf. Dewey, 'Mark as Interwoven Tapestry', p. 235: 'There are developments in the flow of the narrative action – developments in christology, in discipleship, in relations with authorities, etc. But they do not occur at the same points; rather, developments in one will anticipate or recapitulate developments in others'.

29. R. Horsley, *Hearing the Whole Story: The Politics of the Plot in Mark's Gospel* (Louisville: Westminster John Knox Press, 2001).

30. Horsley, *Story*, pp. 79–97; 203–29.

31. Horsley, *Story*, pp. 99–120.

32. Horsley, *Story*, pp. 145–46.

against the tradition of the Law represented by the upper class of Jewish society.[33] Furthermore, the stability of marriage and family, restoration of households (10.17–31), and breaking with the ruler and servant relationship (10.42–44) are essential principles of Jesus' community, which for Horsley has a strongly covenantal character. This aspect of Mark's story reaches its climax in the ceremonial renewal of the covenant at the last supper.[34] The exemplary role of the women in Mark is connected with Jesus' rejection of the patriarchal pyramid of power and its substitution with a paradigm of leadership/service. Furthermore, the evangelist Mark cannot be compared to a modern scholar working with many books on his desk. He was rather an interpreter of living oral, prophetic and popular tradition, in contrast to the scribes of Jerusalem who controlled the Scriptures and their interpretation. Jesus is a prophetic leader and not a messianic figure. All references to him as a messiah are based on twisted meaning or misunderstanding. This reading naturally leaves no place for a messianic secret in Mark's gospel.[35]

The reconstruction of Horsley seeks to be comprehensive: everything in Mark is about the politics of the Galilean prophetic renewal movement against the Roman occupying power and the Jewish upper class in Jerusalem. Correspondingly, the Gospel of Mark as a whole was originally an oral presentation experienced by little people who knew quite well throughout the story what the storyteller Mark was talking about. While demonstrating blind spots of modern western scholarship in reading Mark, the interpretation of Horsley is not quite unproblematic.

First of all, the disciples in Mark are neither merely nor coherently presented as feeble followers who become deserters, but also as trusted recipients of divine mysteries. In 4.11–12 Mark portrays those who were around Jesus – reminding one of the doers of the will of God around Jesus in 3.34–35 – and the twelve as 'insiders', to whom is given 'the secret of the kingdom of God', in contrast to the outsiders who are so hardened that they cannot understand anything. Horsley plays down the role of the twelve in this passage by naming it as a smaller group within the disciples.[36] So they fail in spite of their inside position. However, the Markan Jesus puts his trust in the twelve even though they fail and lack understanding, even when their 'hearts are hardened' (6.37, 52; 8.4, 14–21). He knows about their weakness from the beginning and yet never ceases to entrust them with teachings that they are about to transmit to all later disciples, including the community of Mark. The Markan Jesus appoints the twelve 'to be with him, and to be sent out to proclaim the message, and to have authority to cast out demons' (3.14–15). As Jesus sends them out, they are successful in their task (6.7–13).[37]

The positive status of the twelve presented in these passages is never played down by the Markan Jesus. On the contrary, after all their failings and hard

33. Horsley, *Story*, pp. 156–76.

34. Horsley, *Story*, pp. 177–201.

35. Horsley, *Story*, pp. 231–53.

36. Horsley, *Story*, p. 80.

37. See also H. Räisänen, *The 'Messianic Secret' in Mark* (trans. C. Tuckett; Edinburgh: T&T Clark, 1990), p. 213.

lessons they are treated as those who have left everything and followed Jesus. In 10.28–31 Jesus answers the sincere statement of Peter with acknowledging words, and does not rebuke him as he did earlier in the story (8.31–33). In the light of the overall storyline in ch. 8–10, the Markan Jesus is confident, but outspokenly critical towards his disciples. Even though the disciples are quarrelling over who is the greatest among them, Jesus takes their unfailing witness and martyrdom for granted; the ideal role model of the servant does not contradict this presupposition (10.35–45). Jesus' instructions about prayer demonstrate natural confidence in the twelve (11.11, 14, 20–25). After the disputations in the temple, they are left on Jesus' side to receive his teaching about the great sacrifice of the poor widow (12.41–44). Jesus' detailed private teachings about the last events to Peter, James, John, and Andrew (ch. 13) point out that they had the task to transmit these instructions to the post-Easter communities. This, in turn, is in accord with the statement presented twice, that Jesus will go to Galilee ahead of Peter and the other disciples; their reunion will open the post-Easter mission that must become a success and not a failure. Mark mentions Peter especially because his denial is reconciled. Jesus, who had predicted his failure, trusts him and the other deserter disciples once again. Mark 16.7–8 is not about the final break with the disciples, since this would imply that Jesus had to wait for them in vain as he went ahead of them to Galilee. It is rather reasonable to assume that the Markan Jesus rejected Jerusalem as the place of reunion and the starting point of the mission of the disciples. For Mark, the silence of the women guaranteed that nothing happened in Jerusalem, which was the doomed city of the Jewish upper class – and for that matter, the seat of the Jewish Christian community that was led by James the brother of Jesus (cf. 3.20–21, 31–35).[38]

Even though Horsley's observations about anti-Roman aspects in miracle stories are insightful, they do not prove that the Markan story as a whole is directed against the Roman soldiers and their presence in Palestine. It is obvious that for Mark and his fellow Christians the Roman power was evil and that the coming of the Son of Man would soon end Rome's rule in God's land. It is also conceivable that the legion of demons, which was driven out of the Gerasene man and sank with the swineherds into the sea, has an associative connection with the Roman legions occupying the land. However, it is difficult to read the statement of the centurion in charge of Jesus' execution (15.39: 'truly, this man was God's Son' (NRSV); 'truly, this man was a son of god' [Horsley]) as ironical or as mockery and sarcasm.[39] It would have been easy for Mark to create an unambiguous statement that presents the centurion as a mocker and thus bring the mockery motif to a climax. In turn, the Roman centurion is a complete contrast to the mocking Jewish leaders, other Jews, whose words and actions are ominously responded to with darkness and the rupture of the veil of the temple. This impression is strengthened

38. For this theory, see M. Myllykoski, *Die letzten Tage Jesu II: Markus und Johannes, ihre traditionen und die historische Frage* (AASF Ser. B 272; Helsinki: Suomalainen Tiedeakatemia 1994), pp. 117–21.

39. Thus Horsley, *Story*, p. 252.

by the description of the centurion – in contrast to the mockers – as a sharp-sighted observer of Jesus' death ('stood facing him, saw that in this way he breathed his last'). He understands that divine powers were working in Jesus as he died. Just as the reluctant judge Pilate crucified Jesus with the title 'the king of the Jews' (15.26), so the centurion also makes an ambiguous confession to the truth that the Jewish leaders and crowds want to deny and mock.

The political undertones of the gospel of Mark are thus ambiguous. The communities close to Mark were in a war on two fronts: they were beaten in synagogues and brought before Gentile governors and kings (13.9), and it is very difficult to assume that they sympathized with the zealots or other rebellious Jews against the Roman power during, after, or even before the Jewish war. The community of Mark drew a particularly strict limit between the great number of outsiders and the little flock of insiders (4.10–12). The explicit confession to Jesus and his words 'in this adulterous and sinful generation' (8.38) will be the criterion judgement as the Son of Man comes. The political cause of these men and women who believed in Jesus and his gospel was qualified by the limits of their community, cult and confession.

The hypothesis of Horsley relies partly on traditional historical criticism and partly on modern narrative criticism. For him, Mark as an ideological whole finds its true expression in the oral performance and hearing of the whole story. Both are seamlessly connected with the historical situation of the original hearers of Mark. The oral presentation of the story was a political event that responded to the political situation of the hearers. In particular, the numerous miracle stories in Mark served a political purpose: deliverance from the Roman yoke. If the critique presented above is on a right track, a straightforward interpretation of Mark as a whole does not recommend itself. The plot of Mark reveals tensions and discrepancies, which speak for the presence of different traditions that originally made sense in different contexts. These signs of discontinuity in the gospel hint at the literary character of its making, since there is no seamless orality behind the text. Furthermore, it is important to imagine the oral practice of Mark in practical terms. It is difficult to envision that he appeared as a storyteller before his community, repeating each time the same three-hour long, intensively plotted and multifaceted story. As final product of the theological and compositional planning, the Gospel of Mark seems to be a too specific of presentation for a performer who was already accustomed to a looser composition with variations and changes. I find it reasonable to assume that Mark did not become a performer only as he planned the 'whole story', which he desired to present for a living audience. The process of learning and presenting the text of Mark can hardly be compared to the process of Mark the author.[40] This doubt is strengthened by the observation of Walter J. Ong about the disability of the oral culture to organize even shorter narrative 'in the studious, relentless climactic way that readers of

40. For presentation of the text of Mark, see the insightful article of a person who has been there for 25 years: D. Rhoads, 'Performing the Gospel of Mark', in *Body and Bible: Interpreting and Experiencing Biblical Narratives* (Philadelphia: Trinity International Press, 1992), pp. 102–19.

literature over the past 200 years have learned more and more to expect'.[41] The plot of the gospel of Mark can be seen as a dramatic story in Aristotelian terms, in which the dramatic elements – Jesus' mighty acts – are intensively developed (*dusis*) towards the recognition of his messianity by Peter (*peripeteia*), which, in turn, is followed by Jesus' proclamation of the necessity of his suffering, the dramatic conflicts with the Jewish authorities in Jerusalem, and his death (*lusis*).[42] Although working with traditions presupposes a strong output of orality, the production of this dramatic main plot of Mark was most likely a literary process.[43] Correspondingly we must ask what Mark told his audience before he became the author of the gospel – before he planned, composed, and wrote down or dictated the 'whole story'. If his story is made up of diverging traditional elements, how can this be seen in the light of Mark's oral practice?

3. *Mark's Oral Practice: A Hypothesis*

Like Dewey, Horsley and others, I find it reasonable to assume that Mark was a gifted and respected member of his community who neither just collected various Jesus traditions together (so form criticism),[44] nor was he an author and theologian who just sat at his desk and wrote down or dictated a thought-out gospel story that was based on oral fragments and some literary pieces (so redaction criticism).[45] I assume that Mark was practically trained to tell various clusters of Jesus stories, present them in new and different combinations and combine them

41. W. Ong, *Orality and Literacy: The Technologizing of the Word* (London: Routledge, 1982), p. 143.

42. F.G. Lang, 'Kompositionsanalyse des Markusevangeliums', ZThK 74 (1977), pp. 1–24; B. Standaert, *L'Évangile selon Marc: Composition et genre litteraire* (Nijmegen, 1978), pp. 64–106. For the role of orality in the composition of the Greek drama, see E. Havelock, *The Literate Revolution in Greece and Its Cultural Consequences* (Princeton, NJ: Princeton University Press, 1982), pp. 261–313. According to him, the Greek drama was born out of the need to provide all Hellenic audiences with the Homeric tradition presented didactically and in an entertaining way on the stage, p. 263. Havelock plausibly assumes that 'Greek tragedy was composed in a state of continuous physiological tension between the modes of oral and written communication', p. 265.

43. Cf. M. Hengel, 'Probleme des Markusevangeliums', in *Das Evangelium und die Evangelien: Vorträge vom Tübinger Symposium 1982* (WUNT, 28; Tübingen: Mohr-Siebeck, 1983), pp. 221–65, especially pp. 226–30. Hengel thinks that the Gospel of Mark grew out from the service of the Christian communities and was right from the beginning designed for serving such needs. The purpose of the gospel is something completely different than that of the Greek tragedy – to inspire and strengthen faith.

44. Cf. the revealing statement of Bultmann, *History*, p. 350: 'Mark is not sufficiently master of his material to be able to venture on a systematic construction himself'. The form critics basically wanted to finally turn down the idea that the gospels were lives of Jesus.

45. For redaction criticism, see the (extreme?) view of B. Mack, *A Myth of Innocence: Mark and Christian Origins,* Philadelphia: Fortress Press 1988, p. 321: 'Mark was a scholar. A reader of texts and a writer of texts. He was a scribe in the Jesus tradition of the synagogue reform movement'. And further, p. 323: 'In Mark's study there were chains of miracle stories, collections of pronouncement stories in various states of elaboration, some form of Q, memos on parables and proof texts, the scriptures, including the prophets, written materials from the Christ cult, and other literature representative of Hellenistic Judaism'. A modern New Testament scholar *par excellence*!

in a creative way. If this is true, the development of his theological ideas, his interpretation of the historical context of his community and his skill as a storyteller belong inseparably together. I assume that Mark developed the themes and narrative clusters present in the written gospel in the run of his long career as a storyteller. He must have mastered numerous other stories in addition to those that he articulated in his gospel. I suggest that the 'redaction' of individual stories started with his oral practice, but became a literary challenge as he began to shape his multifaceted oral repertory and select suitable sequences of stories in terms of a long narrative that should start with the coming of John the Baptist and end with the stories leading to the resurrection of Jesus. This process might or might not have been long, but it seems reasonable to assume that the process of writing was necessitated by an actual crisis that had something to do with the apocalyptic situation of persecution and expectation of the end described in ch. 13; it is rather difficult to think that this scenario was of no actual importance for Mark and his audience.[46]

Between the short oral units isolated by the form-critics and the whole story of Horsley there must have been a concrete development, in which the oral units of tradition were reflected against the background of what the first Christians assumed to be Jesus' career. To be sure, there was no overall organization of the material in the beginning.[47] What Jesus said and did could have been presented in various ways and in various contexts, but it seems clear that storytellers and teachers developed clusters of the smaller oral units for the needs of their communities. But is it more than mere guesswork to say anything about these developments? I think not.

In his study on memory in oral traditions, David C. Rubin surveys the mechanics of memory that underlie the oral genres, in particular epics, ballads, and counting-out rhymes.[48] Like many others before him, Rubin emphasizes that the singers do not recall their repertory verbally, but always with help of variations. Instead, it is essential to remember the structure of the different traditions and events; this is true, not only about epic singers but about everybody, including eye-witnesses of car-accidents. In his representation of themes in memory,[49] Rubin portrays themes like the young hero's first adventure as preservers of stability in the oral tradition. Having a relatively fixed pattern, these themes transcend any particular presentation and appear in different forms in various cultures. The memory of the singer or storyteller and the audience is oriented towards schemas that are basically general cognitive structures in which information is

46. On Mark 13, see particularly E. Brandenburger, *Markus 13 und die Apokalyptik* (FRLANT, 134; Göttingen: Vandenhoeck & Ruprecht, 1984). For my own reconstruction of the setting of ch. 13, see Myllykoski, *Tage II*, pp. 203–16.

47. The Markan studies of Wrede, Weiss, Wellhausen and Wendling in the early 20th century led to the programmatic thesis in the work of K.L. Schmidt, *Der Rahmen der Geschichte Jesu*, Berlin 1919; see particularly p. 17: 'The present study will demonstrate that Mark includes the earliest profile of the life of Jesus, but this profile is a schema just like that of the gospel of John…'

48. D. Rubin, *Memory in Oral Traditions: The Cognitive Psychology of Epic, Ballads, and Counting-out Rhymes* (New York/Oxford: Oxford University Press, 1995).

49. Rubin, *Memory*, pp. 15–38.

organized. Themes that fit the schemas are easier to remember, and so are such individual elements of the story that are important to the corresponding schema. Schemas enable the listeners to perceive the underlying structure of a piece more easily and complement the story with minor elements that are not explicitly mentioned in the performance. Rubin presents three sub-species of schema, by which the cognitive psychology has attempted to capture the thematic structure: script, story grammar, and associative networks. Script that describes a characteristic pattern of behaviour in a particular setting (e.g. going to a restaurant and ordering a meal) can be seen as a component in a larger narrative structure. Scripts consist of stereotyped sequence of actions that form a causal chain. Their contents are common knowledge, and therefore deviations from them are more likely to be recalled. They allow multiformity (e.g. in the restaurant example mentioned above, the change of the waiter into the waitress). 'A singer can substitute many different details, actions or series of actions, as long as they fill the same role in a script'.[50] Story grammars are global structures that attempt to capture the organization present in stories. They provide 'a hierarchical structure indicating which actions go together and what their relation is to the story as a whole'.[51] Themes are also learned as a network of associations. Each time two components of the story (e.g. journey and assembly) appear together, their node is strengthened, while the appearance of one of them without the other has a negative impact on their node.

These basic factors of representation of themes in memory may be helpful in our attempts to portray Mark as a storyteller. He and his audience had a theme that consisted of Jesus' actions in Galilee (and its surroundings), his journey to Jerusalem with his disciples, and his final conflict and death at the hands of his adversaries in Jerusalem. In this framework, it was possible to present different chains of short stories of Jesus' mighty acts and words, his teachings to his disciples, as well as his confrontations with his adversaries. It is not difficult to see that different forms of the Jesus tradition could be recalled by means of their schemas, which further helped to memorize e.g. different kinds of healing miracles and pronouncement stories and create variation in their details. Correspondingly, Jesus' actions basically follow some common scripts: he teaches the crowd or his disciples, heals the sick and the possessed, overcomes his adversaries in debate with his wisdom etc. Story grammar, in turn, indicates e.g. that the Markan Jesus heals a blind man on two specific occasions (8.22–26; 10.46–52), at which he has rebuked his disciples who lack understanding. The association of these and other similar themes is an important device in the communication between Mark the storyteller and his audience. Furthermore, Rubin observes that imagery aids memory, because it shares many properties with visual perception. Imagery in oral traditions works dynamically and spatially (not sequentially); it is specific and concrete.[52] In Markan Jesus traditions, episodes are often opened with a concrete,

50. Rubin, *Memory*, p. 25.
51. Rubin, *Memory*, p. 30.
52. Rubin, *Memory*, pp. 39–64.

spatial reference that immediately leads to action, teaching or dialogue.[53] I find it natural to assume that in many cases the Markan framing of the traditional 'pericopes' stems from his oral practice rather than literary processing of oral material.

All these factors in the story world of Mark's gospel hint at the presence of oral tradition and Mark's oral practice. I think that there are some further signs of oral practice in Mark's narrative. The phenomenon of duality in Mark stems most likely from the oral practice of the evangelist. Frans Neirynck, who first paid attention to duality as an overall feature in Mark, emphasized that often the first reference of a dual expression 'is a general statement and the second adds further precision'.[54] As Werner Kelber has noticed, such expressions readily serve both speaker and his audience.[55] Considering the extensive use of duality in Mark, particularly of double statements (temporal and local, general and special, repetition of the motif) and synonymous expressions and the like, it is impossible to see a barrier between orality and literacy in the narrative of Mark. Considering the unity of the Markan style demonstrated particularly by Neirynck and Peter Dschulnigg, it is somewhat problematic to peel out literary sources of the gospel on the basis of its language and style or even other criteria.[56] However, the orality of Mark's expressions does not rule out his use of literary sources, particularly in the case of the passion narrative. It must be assumed that Mark has transmitted the thought-content and plot of the oral and written traditions in the particular way that he had shaped in his oral practice.

Ernest Best has pointed out that the Gospel of Mark includes a number of instances, in which the evangelist uses the titles of Jesus inconsistently (1.24: the Holy One of God; 10.47, 48, 51: Son of David, Rabbouni; Son of Man curiously early in 2.10, 28), provides superfluous information (10.28 is in conflict with 1.29; 3.9; 4.1, 36, because according to these verses the disciples still have possessions; the dual expression in 1.16; useless information in 10.35 [sons of Zebedee] and 11.16), uses unmodified tradition (the suffering Son of Man in 8.31; 9.31; 10.33–34; summoning the twelve in 9.35), useless or irrelevant logia (11.22–25; 4.21–24), and finally unnecessary retention of names (Levi, Jairus, Barabbas, Simon of

53. Cf. Mark 1.16: 'As Jesus passed along the see of Galilee…'; 1.21: 'They went to Capernaum; and when the Sabbath came, he entered the synagogue and taught'.; and so on. Schmidt, *Rahmen*, p. 152 interprets the chronological and topographical references in the frames of the gospel pericopes as typical for popular stories. They can change or drop out. Schmidt thinks that the 'collectors' of the stories have mostly passed them on without notable changes.

54. F. Neirynck, *Duality in Mark: Contributions to the Study of the Markan Redaction* (BETL, 31; Leuven: Leuven University Press, 2nd edn, 1988), p. 71.

55. Kelber, *Gospel*, pp. 67–68. In his critique of Kelber's view, Neirynck (*Duality in Mark*, p. 227) pays attention to its inner inconsistency: Kelber asserts that 'Mark's use of orality does not give us full insight into the linguistic dynamics of the gospel's composition' and that the gospel arises 'out of the debris of deconstructed orality' (Kelber, *Gospel*, p. 95). Neirynck himself is inclined to regard the dual expressions in Mark as 'interpretive comments of the narrator' (*Duality in Mark*, p. 227).

56. P. Dschulnigg, *Sprache, Redaktion und Intention des Markus-Evangeliums: Eigentümlichkeiten der Sprache des Markus-Evangeliums und ihre Bedeutung für die Redaktionskritik* (SBB, 11; Stuttgart: Katholisches Bibelwerk, 1984), pp. 586–620.

Cyrene).[57] The titles of Jesus and the irrelevant logia as well as the unnecessary names go back to traditions used by Mark. However, because variation, extension and concrete details quite naturally enriched the oral tradition, it is not necessary to think that Mark was just preserving tradition at these points. Repetition serves storytelling, and the superfluous information can be understood as part of Mark's oral agenda. It is also reasonable to assume that unmodified tradition of the passion predictions merely reflects variants Mark used as a storyteller. The contradictory information about the disciples' possessions obviously stem from different traditions. But rather than proving that Mark was a conservative preserver of tradition – or a confused author – they demonstrate that in his oral practice these materials originally belonged to different contexts. Mark did not adopt contradictory traditions as a scribe who was making theological judgements as he was sitting at his desk, but rather as a storyteller who was used to all these traditions, and accustomed to speaking them out in his various presentations before his audience.

It is reasonable to assume that Mark's oral practice was the basis on which he built his written gospel. He most probably did not inherit the 'whole story' from the tradition nor did he make it out of scattered units or small clusters. If we consider the diversity and tension among the gospel materials, this basis most obviously consisted of larger narrative blocks that had a particular basic setting. The outline of Mark's gospel can be divided into three basic settings:

(1) Jesus' proclamation and mighty deeds in Galilee
(2) Jesus and his disciples on their way to Jerusalem
(3) Jesus' passion, death, and resurrection in Jerusalem (the passion narrative)

It was natural and convenient to articulate stories of Jesus' mighty deeds and relations to the crowd in setting (1), while setting (2) was more suitable for stories that expressed Jesus' role as the teacher of his disciples. Most likely these two basic settings were not created by Mark himself, but belonged to the Jesus tradition long before him. The passion narrative must have had a basic oral structure right from the beginning, and the diverging, tightly transmitted material in Mark 14–16 reveals that the development of the oral passion tradition and its molding into a written document was a long and complicated process.

It is possible to distinguish different themes whose development, partly within each other, led the story of Jesus through the three basic settings. As Mark told stories about Jesus' proclamation, disputations and mighty deeds in Galilee, he devoted himself to the enthusiasm shared by the disciples and the crowd that heard Jesus and saw what he did (1.16–3.6). However, the crowds must not understand Jesus' teachings. This is reserved for the disciples who must be prepared for their mission (3.7–4.41; 6.6b–13, 30); Jesus even allows to them understand that Gentiles are not unclean (7.1–37; cf. 5.1–43). Only after mighty miracles that are

57. E. Best, 'Mark's Preservation of Tradition', in M. Sabbe (ed.), *L'Évangile selon Marc: Tradition et redaction* (BETL, 34; Leuven: Leuven University Press, 1974), pp. 21–34.

greater than those performed by Moses and Elijah, the disciples of Jesus come to understand that Jesus is the Christ and the Son of God (6.14–8.30; 9.2–8). After Peter's confession, and on their way to Jerusalem, Jesus must teach them things that are related to his own exemplary suffering: they must not strive for power, but work for the good of the community (9.30–10.45). I assume that these and other themes have played an originally independent role in storytelling.

There is a tension between storytelling as performance before an audience and storytelling as something that aims to fulfill the needs of the community. It is not quite impossible to create a plausible image of the living situation of oral communication that was typical for Mark's oral practice. His audience consisted mostly of simple people who needed to be nourished with an ideologically unambiguous, entertaining and straightforward message. Mark certainly 'spoke the word to them as they were able to hear it' (cf. 4.33), and we can assume that his audience 'liked to listen to him' (cf. 6.20). Furthermore, it is not necessary to think that Mark was merely transmitting stories in long performances. If the first Christian storytellers began to appreciate the supernatural actions and authoritative words of Jesus as something that needed to be explained, they could most naturally use an extensive cluster of stories and teachings as a starting point for their actual address to the community. It is possible that they followed the practice of the synagogue sermon, not only for their reading of Jewish Scriptures, but also in use of their own Jesus traditions. For them Jesus was the Son of God who had divine authority, and many stories about him were modeled after Old Testament patterns.

It is plausible to assume that Mark received traditions from older storytellers who were his teachers. As an independent storyteller he could embrace the tradition valued by his community, but also use it in a creative way, reorganize and actualize it for particular situations, make changes, additions and omissions in each performance, but still imagine remaining faithful to the heritage he had received. To be sure, some of the original oral clusters used by Mark are only partially present in his written gospel.

It is difficult to demonstrate this theory in practice, but I think there is at least one good candidate for an old oral story cluster that Mark seems to have used in a creative way, first as a storyteller and later as an evangelist. This story that I assume to have existed in a traditional oral form presented Jesus as a divine man who is greater than Moses and Elijah. I assume that this story was also used by John who seems to have known it both from Mark and as an independent version.[58] Just like Moses, Jesus was first rejected by his own people (6.1–6; cf. Exod. 2.11–15). Facing a great crowd in 'a deserted place' (6.31, 35; 8.4; cf. Exod. 16.1–3), he has compassion for them and acts like a leader asked for by Moses, whose congregation was 'like sheep without a shepherd' (6.34; Num. 27.17).[59] After having taught them 'many things' to a late hour he leads his

58. The replacement of Peter with Judas Iscariot in Jesus' harsh word after the confession of Peter (Mk 8.31–33; Jn 6.70–71) is easiest to understand as a Johannine reaction against the text of Mark.

59. This seems to indicate the Jesus/Joshua typology. In Num. 27.18 Joshua is sorted out and commissioned as 'a man in whom is the spirit'.

disciples to doubt how to feed them – doubts similar to those of Moses (6.35–37; 8.1–4, hn 6.5; Num. 11.21–22). Jesus demonstrated his divine authority and saving power by feeding the enormous crowd (6.38–44; 8.5-9; Jn 6.6–13). According to the Christian tradition, this was even more than the rationed portions of manna in the desert (Exod. 16.4–21) and the miraculous multiplication of meal and oil through the hands of Elijah for the widow of Zarephath (1 Kgs 17.8–16). Like Moses, Jesus went 'up on the mountain to pray' (6.45–46; Exod. 24.15, 18; cf. Jn 6.3, 15) He did not divide the sea for his people, but he walked on the water in order to save his own in the storm (6.45–52; Jn 6.16–21; cf. Exod. 14.19–30).[60] When recognized as a powerful man people brought many sick people to him, whom he healed (6.53–56; cf. John 6.22–25).[61] Again, in the second feeding miracle told by Mark (8.1–9) Jesus' acts are set against the background of feeding the Israelites with manna, as numerous points of contact with Exod. 16–17 demonstrate.[62] As a miracle worker and healer, Jesus was tested like Moses (Exod. 17.1–7) and Elijah (1 Kgs 17.17–24), but he refused to give a sign to the Pharisees (8.11–12; Jn 6.30). After some events – perhaps after healing a blind man (8.22–26) – Peter confessed him to be the Christ (8.27–30; Jn 6.67–71).[63] I assume that the story ended with Jesus' transfiguration on the mountain (9.2–8), making him greater than Moses and Elijah (cf. Exod. 19–20; 34.27–33).

If Mark once told and interpreted stories like this, we can assume that he also developed skills in combining them. In this pursuit, he learned the art of weaving them together by taking several factors into consideration. He intended neither to break the tensions nor to reconcile the contradictions that came about as he composed the 'whole story'. He paid attention rather to those elements of the tradition that he found essential for the needs of his intended readers for whom he wrote 'the beginning of the gospel', the story of Jesus from his baptism to the empty tomb.

60. The idea of Jesus intending to pass his disciples (v. 48) is also related to Moses and Elijah stories (Exod. 33.17–34.8; 1 Kgs 19.11–13), and the time indication 'early in the morning' fits the exodus event (Exod. 14.24). Furthermore, the hardened hearts of the disciples (v. 52) are thematically related to the Exodus story.

61. The fringe of Jesus' garment seems to refer to fringes that God commanded the Israelites to make on the corners of their garments, in memory of the departure from Egypt (Num. 15.37–41).

62. J. Marcus, *Mark 1-8: A New Translation with Introduction and Commentary* (New York: Doubleday, 2000), pp. 483–85.

63. I think that the incomprehension of the disciples in the Markan cycle 6.14–8.30 tells more about Jesus than about the disciples whose incomprehension is used to highlight their realization that Jesus is the Messiah. Their hearts were hardened, because the secret of Jesus' person was too great to comprehend; see F.J. Matera, 'The Incomprehension of the Disciples and Peter's Confession (Mark 6,14–8,30)', *Biblica 70* (1989), pp. 153–72.

Jesus and Gehenna

Dale C. Allison, Jr

Given that so many people dislike hell but still like Jesus, it is not surprising that some modern reconstructions no longer depict him as a believer in eschatological or *post-mortem* punishment. One could here be cynical and wonder to what extent the wish has cultivated the conclusion, a conclusion which certainly goes against the impression that the canonical gospels leave. Maybe a Jesus who says nothing about hell is the artifact of interested biographers who themselves have nothing to say, or at least nothing good to say, about hell. Yet the matter is not resolved with this all-too-easy sort of *ad hominem* retort, for there are some interesting critical issues here. Those who doubt that Jesus believed in hell and employed it in his teaching are not without their arguments.

One motive for skepticism has to do with the coherence of Jesus's thought. Can it be that a mind which was profoundly enamoured of the love of God and which counseled charity toward enemies concurrently accepted and even promoted the dismal idea of a divinely-imposed, unending agony? If, as it seems, Jesus muted the element of vengeance in his eschatological language; if he proclaimed that God seeks the prodigal and graciously rains upon the unjust; and if he showed no interest in either Joshua or Judges, books featuring violent holy war, then surely we might wonder whether he would have been comfortable with a traditional hell. Jesus was an exorcist and healer; he sought to ameliorate human suffering, which an eternal hell, to the contrary, abets immeasurably. Do we not have here a conspicuous and *bona fide* contradiction? And should this contradiction not provoke misgiving about what goes back to Jesus and what does not?

The earliest argument along these lines is, to my imperfect knowledge, about two hundred years old. It comes not from a theologian or biblical scholar but from a Romantic poet, Percy Bysshe Shelley. In his essay, 'On Christianity', he argued that the evangelists 'impute sentiments to Jesus Christ which flatly contradict each other'.

According to Shelley, Jesus 'summoned his whole resources of persuasion to oppose' the idea of justice inherent in hell. Jesus believed in 'a gentle and beneficent and compassionate' God, not in a 'being who shall deliberately scheme to inflict on a large portion of the human race tortures indescribably intense and indefinitely protracted'. 'The absurd and execrable doctrine of vengeance seems to have been contemplated in all its shapes by this great moralist with the profoundest disapprobation'.[1]

Perhaps the most comprehensive case for this conclusion appears in an old book that, while still on the shelves of some libraries, has almost ceased to be remembered. In *The Lord of Thought* (1922), Lily Dougall and Cyril W. Emmet argued that the synoptic passages that depict a punishing God are additions to the true tradition.[2] Rejecting the possibility that Jesus had 'a confused mind, in which traditional beliefs existed unchallenged side by side with newer and more vital ideals which...contradict them',[3] the authors surmised that Jesus abandoned traditional conceptions of divine judgment. The discrepant tone of divine retribution is a regrettable 'accretion which has crept in during some of those various stages through which Christ's words passed before they reached their present form'.[4]

Is all this just reading between the lines and then dismissing half the lines because they do not fit with what we have read between them? Or does one part of the tradition demand, because of irreconcilable differences, a divorce from the other part? The verdict of Dougall and Cyril W. Emmet has this at least in its favour, that the feeling animating it is not confined to post-Enlightenment moderns. Origen, Didymus the Blind, Gregory of Nyssa, Diodore of Tarsus, Evagrius, Theodore of Mopsuestia, and Isaac of Nineveh all hoped for a universal reconciliation, and partly because of their conviction that God loves everyone, even the wicked – a conviction the canonical gospels implanted in them.[5] Isaac has the most arresting things to say on the subject and is the most eloquent. He contends that God has no anger, no wrath, no jealousy; that God is above retribution; and that God, being like a father, can never act out of vengeance or hatred. 'If it is a case of love, then it is not one of requital; and if it is a case of requital, then it is not one of love'.[6] Again, 'God is not one who requites evil, but He sets aright evil: the former is the characteristic of evil people, while the latter is characteristic of a father'.[7] In short, 'it is not (the way of) the compassionate Maker to create rational beings in order to deliver them over mercilessly to unending affliction (in

1. Percy Bysshe Shelley, 'On Christianity', in E.B. Murray (ed.), *The Prose Works of Percy Bysshe Shelley*, 1 (Oxford: Clarendon Press, 1993), pp. 260, 252–53.
2. Lily Dougall and Cyril W. Emmet, *The Lord of Thought: A Study of the Problems Which Confronted Jesus Christ and the Solution He Offered* (London: SCM Press, 1922).
3. Dougall and Emmet, *Lord of Thought*, p. 190.
4. Dougall and Emmet, *Lord of Thought*, p. 235.
5. Origen, *De prin.* 2.10.8; 3.6.3 GCS 22 (ed. Koetschau), pp. 181–83; *C. Cels.* 8.72 GCS 3, pp. 288–90; *John* 2.13 GCS 10 (ed. Preuschen), p. 68; Didymus, *1 Petr. ad* 1.12 PG 39.1759B, *ad* 3.22 1770B-C; *Ps. ad* 36.36 PG 39.1340C; Gregory of Nyssa, *Or. catech.* 26 SC 453 (ed. Winling), pp. 261–63; *Anim. et res.* PG 46.69C–72B, 88A, 100A–101A, 104B–105A; *Mort.* PG 46.524–25; *Vit. Mos.* 2.82 SC 1 (ed. Daniélou), p. 154; Diodore, *Frag. dog.* (see Abramowski, *ZNW* 42 [1949]), pp. 59–61, and cf. *Book of the Bee* ed. Budge, pp. 160–63); Evagrius, *Keph. gnost. Syr.* 2 2.84; 5.20; 6.27 PO 134/28.1 (ed. Guillaumont), pp. 95, 185, 229; *Ep.* 59 (ed. Frankenberg), pp. 608–609; Theodore of Mopsuestia, *Contra def. pec. orig.* PG 66.1005–1012 (cf. *Book of the Bee* 60 ed. Budge, pp. 161–62); Isaac of Nineveh, *Second* 39–40 CSCO 544 (ed. Brock), pp. 151–68.
6. Isaac of Nineveh, *Second* 39,17 CSCO 544 (ed. Brock), p. 160.
7. Isaac of Nineveh, *Second* 39.15 CSCO 544 (ed. Brock), p. 160.

punishment) for things of which He knew even before they were fashioned, (aware) how they would turn out when He created them – and whom (nonetheless) He created'.[8]

In view of Isaac and his predecessors, we cannot dismiss as peculiarly modern the sense of a tension between the God who makes the sun rise upon all and the God who destroys both body and soul in Gehenna. In line with this are old apocrypha, such as the *Greek Apocalypse of the Virgin*, in which God allows tormented sinners to get a respite during Pentecost or Lent or on Sundays.[9] Surely this happy thought was borne of the feeling that the divine goodness must ameliorate hell, at least a bit. It is the same with those popular apocalypses, such as the *Apocalypse of Peter* and the Armenian *Apocalypse of Paul*, in which saints pray sinners out of hell.[10] Here compassion vanquishes pain. Given texts such as these, as well as the rabbinic authorities who limit hell's duration[11] and the feeling of some early Christians, such as Marcion, that the God of compassion cannot be the God of vengeance, it is not unthinkable that Jesus the first-century Jew also had qualms about the matter.[12] Other Jews certainly had some misgivings. According to *2 Bar.* 55.7, when Baruch heard 'the announcement of the punishment of those who have transgressed', he did not rejoice in self-satisfaction but became 'wholly terrified'. 4 Ezra shows us the same horrified response and the seer's resultant feeling that human beings should not have been created (7.62–69; cf. 8.4–19; 10.9–17). Surely it is not, at least in theory, ahistorical to imagine that Jesus, who was, in Ed Sanders's words, 'a kind and generous man',[13] might have been equally distraught.

Source and redaction criticism supply another reason, one much less theoretical, for wondering whether Jesus really taught anything about divine punishment. The following are the synoptic texts that clearly presuppose a personal or collective judgment either after death or at the end of the present age.[14]

8. Isaac of Nineveh, *Second* 39.6 CSCO 544 (ed. Brock), p. 155.

9. *Gk. Apoc. BMV* 30 (ed. James), p. 126.

10. *Apoc. Pet.* 14 Rainer frag. (ed. James), *JTS* 32 (1931), p. 271; Arm. *Apoc. Paul* (form 4) 35 CCSA 3 trans. Lelair, pp. 171–72 (Mary and Paul pray everyone out of hell). Cf. *Sib. Or.* 2.330–39; *Ep. Apost.* 40 TU 43 (ed. Schmidt), pp. 18–19; Coptic *Apoc.* Elijah 5.28 TU 17 (ed. Steindorff), p. 102; *Tanna d. El.* p. 15 (Elyyahu Rab. 3).

11. *m. 'Ed.* 2.10; *t. Sanh.* 13.4; *b. Roš. Haš.* 17a; *y. Sanh.* 10.3; *Midr. Prov.* 17; *Tanna d. El.* p. 15 (Elyyahu Rab. 3).

12. See Richard Bauckham, 'The Conflict of Justice and Mercy: Attitudes to the Damned in Apocalyptic Literature', in *The Fate of the Dead: Studies on the Jewish and Christian Apocalypses*, *NovTSup* 93 (Leiden/Boston/Cologne: Brill, 1998), pp. 132–48.

13. E. P. Sanders, *The Historical Figure of Jesus* (Allen Lane: Penguin Press, 1993), p. 192.

14. I herein make no distinction between personal and collective eschatology, which exist side by side in the Jesus tradition (as in so much ancient Jewish and Christian literature), nor between Gehenna and Hades. On the equation of the latter two in the canonical gospels see W.J.P. Boyd, 'Gehenna – According to Jeremias', in E.A. Livingstone (ed.), *Studia Biblica 1978, II. Papers on the Gospels: Sixth International Congress on Biblical Studies*, *JSNTSup* 2 (Sheffield: JSOT Press, 1980), pp. 9–12. I pass over sayings, such as Lk. 19.41–44, that advert or may advert to historical and national judgement; for these see Marcus J. Borg, *Conflict, Holiness and Politics in the Teaching of Jesus* (Lewiston/Queenstown: Edwin Mellen Press, 1984), pp. 265–76.

Texts from Q

Lk. 10.12 = Mt. 10.15
Lk. 10.14 = Mt. 11.23
Lk. 10.15 = Mt. 11.24
Lk. 11.31 = Mt. 12.42
Lk. 11.32 = Mt. 12.41
Lk. 12.5 = Mt. 10.28 (cf. *2 Clem.* 5.4)
Lk. 12.8–9 = Mt. 10.32–33 (cf. Mk 8.38)
Lk. 12.10 = Mt. 12.31 (cf. Mk 3.28–29)
Lk. 12.46 = Mt. 24.50
Lk. 12.58–59 = Mt. 5.25–26
Lk. 13.24 = Mt. 7.13–14
Lk. 13.25, 27 = Mt. 7.22–23 (cf. Mt. 25.10–12; *Gos. Thom.* 75)
Lk. 13.28 = Mt. 8.12
Lk. 17.27, 30 = Mt. 24.38–39
Lk. 17.34–35 = Mt. 24.40–41 (cf. *Gos. Thom.* 61)
Lk. 19.26 = Mt. 25.29 (cf. Mk 4.25; *Gos. Thom.* 41)

Texts from Mark

Mk 9.43 (cf. Mt. 18.8)
Mk 9.45 (cf. Mt. 18.8)
Mk 9.47–48 (cf. Mt. 18.9)
Mk 12.40
Mk 13.27

Texts from Matthew alone

Mt. 5.19–20
Mt. 5.22
Mt. 7.19
Mt. 12.36–37
Mt. 13.42 (cf. *Gos. Thom.* 57)
Mt. 13.50
Mt. 15.13
Mt. 22.13
Mt. 23.15
Mt. 23.33
Mt. 24.51
Mt. 25.30 (contrast Lk. 19.27: Q)
Mt. 25.41 (cf. *2 Clem.* 4.5)
Mt. 25.46

Texts from Luke alone

Lk. 6.25
Lk. 12.20
Lk. 12.47–48
Lk. 16.23–24
Lk. 16.28

While sixteen of these texts come from Q, only five are from Mark; and Mark's three lines about Gehenna all belong to the same complex, 9.43–48. Eschatological punishment is most prominent in Matthew. Not only does Matthew, unlike

Luke, take over all of the relevant Markan texts, but he has many additional texts of his own, and almost half of the texts that name Gehenna in the synoptics are his alone. Assuming the priority of Mark and Q, Matthew has added about a dozen new references to eschatological punishment, and many are surely redactional. Furthermore, the Lukan parallels to Matthew 24.51 and 25.30 are much less developed in their eschatological imagery. Instead of 'He will cut him in pieces and put him with the hypocrites, where there will be weeping and gnashing of teeth', which we find in Mt. 24.51, Lk. 12.46 has the less elaborate: 'the master...will cut him in pieces, and put him with the unfaithful'. Similarly, whereas Mt. 25.30 has 'As for this worthless slave, throw him into the outer darkness, where there will be weeping and gnashing of teeth', Lk. 19.27 lacks both 'the outer darkness' and 'weeping and gnashing of teeth': 'But as for these enemies of mine who did not want me to be king over them – bring them here and slaughter them in my presence'. So it seems clear, at least for those of us who suppose that Matthew followed Mark, that the further we get from Jesus, the more hell we find. Consider the following chart, which is rather suggestive regarding Matthew's contribution to the words of Jesus.

Word or phrase	*Matthew*	*Mark*	*Luke*
ἀπώλεια (of eschatological punishment)	1	0	0
γέεννα	7	3	1
κλαυθμὸς καὶ ὁ βρυγμὸς των ὀδόντων	6	0	1
κόλασις (of eschatological punishment)	1	0	0
πῦρ (of eschatological punishment)	8	2	0
πῦρ αἰώνιον	2	0	0
σκότος ἐξώτερον	3	0	0

What one finds in Matthew when compared with Mark and Luke one can likewise find, if so motivated, in Q itself. John Kloppenborg has persuaded many that the Sayings Source contained two major types of sayings – prophetic sayings that announce the impending judgment of this generation on the one hand and, on the other hand, wisdom-like utterances addressed to the community that concern self-definition and general comportment toward the world.[15] The latter were, according to Kloppenborg, the formative component of Q. The prophetic sayings arrived later. This matters because such a reconstruction might encourage one so inclined to assign most or even all of Q's sayings about divine punishment to that source's second stage and then to deny them to Jesus. Kloppenborg himself would not argue so simply. He is quite careful not to identify the first stratification of Q with the historical Jesus and everything else with the church.[16] But others have been less circumspect, and acceptance of Kloppenborg's analysis would certainly be

15. John S. Kloppenborg, *The Formation of Q: Trajectories in Ancient Christian Wisdom Collections* (Studies in Antiquity and Christianity; Philadelphia: Fortress Press, 1987).

16. Kloppenborg, *Formation*, p. 245; *idem*, 'The Sayings Gospel Q and the Question of the Historical Jesus', *HTR* 89 (1996), p. 337.

consistent with scepticism about the originality of the sayings that announce eschatological or post-mortem judgment.

James Robinson has recently emphasized the contrast in Q between what he calls the 'judgmentalism' of a later redactional layer and the spirit of earlier materials.[17] 'Those parts of Q that have, over the years, been recognized as the archaic collections, seem to have been ignored by the redactor, where God passing judgment has replaced God taking pity on sinners!'[18] For Robinson, the tension between judgment and mercy in Q does not betray an inconsistency in Jesus's own mind but reflects rather the difference between Jesus himself and some of his interpreters. 'Jesus's vision of a caring Father who is infinitely forgiving and hence shockingly evenhanded in dealing with the bad as well as the good, may have been lost from sight a generation later, as a result of the grueling experience of the Jewish war, understood as God's quite judgmental punishment of Israel'.[19] Again, 'Jesus's basic insight into the ever-loving and forgiving nature of God would seem to have been lost from sight as the age-old view of God undergirding retaliatory justice again asserted itself.[20]

Such then are some of the arguments one might call upon to deny that Jesus said anything much about hell. What do we make of them? The argument from consistency is of great interest theologically. Speaking for myself, I see little prospect of harmonizing Jesus's God of catholic compassion with the God who tosses the lost into the eschatological incinerator. Isaac of Nineveh's musings make good sense to me. I nonetheless doubt that my being nonplussed about this issue is a suitable guide to the reconstruction of history. All of us are bundles of inconsistencies, from which generalization I see no reason to exempt Jesus. It would be unimaginative and foolhardy to subdue him with the straightjacket of consistency. It is useful to recollect the contradictions that a few older critics found in some of the old Jewish and Christian apocalypses, contradictions which have been the basis for dubious compositional theories, such as G.H. Box's analysis of 4 Ezra and R.H. Charles's analysis of Revelation.[21] We cannot infer, on the basis of our own logic, what someone else's logic must have dictated, especially someone from a very different time and place. Jesus's ways need not be our ways. We must distinguish between a tension that he might have tolerated – and that his followers did tolerate – from a contradiction that we personally may not abide. This is all the more so in the present case, for the Jesus tradition contains no explicit rejection of hell or related ideas. To go by the New Testament, if Jesus opposed divine judgment, his protest was stunningly ineffectual.

17. James M. Robinson, 'The Critical Edition of Q and the Study of Jesus', in A. Lindemann (ed.), *The Sayings Source Q and the Historical Jesus*, *BETL* 158 (Leuven: Leuven University Press, 2001), pp. 27–52.

18. Robinson, 'The Critical Edition of Q', p. 40.

19. Robinson,'The Critical Edition of Q', p. 43.

20. Robinson,'The Critical Edition of Q', pp. 42–43.

21. R.H. Charles, *A Critical and Exegetical Commentary on the Revelation of St. John* (2 vols.; ICC; Edinburgh: T&T Clark, 1920); G. H. Box, '4 Ezra', in R.H. Charles (ed.), *The Apocrypha and Pseudepigrapha of the Old Testament*, 2 (Edinburgh: T&T Clark, 1913), pp. 542–624.

We would do well to remember that the Christian tradition is full of people who have waxed eloquently about God's love one minute and then threatened people with divine vengeance the next. Paul penned 1 Cor. 13, yet he also spoke about 'the coming wrath' (1 Thess. 1.10; cf. 2.16; 5.9). The redactor of the sermon on the mount, with its glorious chapter 5, speaks of the weeping and gnashing of teeth fully six times; and Luke, who preserves Q's sermon on the plain, also passes down the tale of the rich man and Lazarus, with its flames of agony. From a later time I think of the curious case of Bernard of Clairvaux. He wrote exquisitely beautiful words about love and yet sponsored the Second Crusade with zest and had no qualms about consigning Abelard *ad inferos*. Even the wonderful Francis of Assisi warned of hell.

Furthermore, Gregory of Nyssa and Isaac of Nineveh and their kin, despite their qualms, retained a place for hell, albeit delimited. In my judgment, Gregory and Isaac would probably not have believed in hell if they had felt the freedom to do without it; post-mortem punishment remains foreign to their innermost and distinctive characters. Yet they did not do away with it, for they evidently felt obliged to make the best of what their tradition had handed them. They are a bit like the author of 4 Ezra. Despite his incisive scepticism and his profound conviction that God's dealings with humanity are unfair, he could not break with his tradition. Instead of giving up divine retribution, he put aside his feelings and, in the end, resigned himself to taking consolation from a Job-like ignorance and an apocalyptic worldview. We can imagine something similar with Jesus. If, as is likely enough, he had ever heard the end of Isaiah (66.24: 'And they shall go out and look at the dead bodies of the people who have rebelled against me; for their worm shall not die, their fire shall not be quenched, and they shall be an abhorrence to all flesh') or the last chapter of Daniel (12.2: 'Many of those who sleep in the dust of the earth shall awake, some to everlasting life, and some to shame and everlasting contempt'), or if he was familiar with the sort of eschatological expectations found in 1 En. and other apocalypses, he would have known about Gehenna; and he may well have accepted the prospect as carrying the authority of his divinely-inspired tradition. Dispensing with Gehenna may have been, given his social setting, something he seriously contemplated.

We must take full account of Jesus's Jewish and biblical heritage. After declaring that the Lord is 'a God merciful and gracious, slow to anger, abounding in steadfast love and faithfulness, keeping steadfast love for the thousandth generation, forgiving iniquity and transgression and sin', Exod. 34.6–7 immediately follows with this frightful and incongruent thought: God will 'by no means clear the guilty, but visits the iniquity of the parents upon the children, and the children's children, to the third and the fourth generation'. Deut. 32.39 says, much more succinctly, 'I kill and I make alive; I wound and I heal'. In like manner, the book of Wisdom castigates sinners and revels in their judgment while at the very same time offering this unsurpassed declaration of God's universal care: 'But you have compassion over all, because you can do all, and you overlook the sins of human beings with a view to their repentance. For you love all that exists, and loathe nothing which you have created; for if you had hated anything you would never have fashioned it. How could anything have endured, had it not been your will, or that which was undesignated by you have been preserved? But you spare all because they are yours, O Sovereign Lord, lover of all that lives; for your imperishable spirit is in them all' (11.23–12.1). It is beyond me how the person who wrote these remarkable words could also depict God as scornfully laughing at the unrighteous, as dashing them to the ground, as turning them into dishonoured corpses, as wrathfully assailing them with sword, lightning, and hailstorms (4.18–19; 5.17–23; cf. 16.15–24). But there it is.

What about the argument from source and redaction history, from the fact that sayings about hell attached themselves to the tradition as time moved on? This should indeed give us pause. Ultimately, however, it does not make up our minds, for the question is not whether tradents added references to divine punishment. They assuredly did. The issue is instead whether, in so doing, they were elaborating upon something that was there from the beginning or rather attaching a foreign element that altered the character of the tradition. That Christians contributed sayings about hell to the tradition is no proof that Jesus himself did not also do so.

If the arguments against eschatological punishment belonging to Jesus's proclamation do not force assent, what about the case on the other side? There is, to begin with, an argument from continuity. Many have urged that Jesus's position between John the Baptist, for whom the imminent judgment was central, and the early church, which longed for the *parousia*, makes most sense on the supposition that Jesus himself was much concerned with eschatology. One can construct an analogous argument about hell. John the Baptist, if we can trust Q, concerned himself with the salvation of individuals in the face of the coming judgment. Lk. 3.7 = Mt. 3.7 reports that he warned his hearers to flee from the wrath to come; and, in Lk. 3.17 = Mt. 3.12, we find the Baptist saying this: 'His winnowing fork is in his hand, and he will clear his threshing floor and gather the wheat into his granary, but the chaff he will burn with fire than can never be put out'. Paul too thought that if some were headed for life, others must be not so destined: Rom. 2.5 ('you are storing up wrath for yourself on the day of wrath'), 8–9 ('for those who are self-seeking and who obey not the truth but wickedness, there will be wrath and fury. There will be anguish and distress for everyone who does evil'); 14.10 ('we will all stand before the judgment seat of God'); 1 Thess. 1.10 (Jesus 'rescues us from the wrath that is coming'); etc. Now because Jesus submitted to John's baptism and praised him extravagantly (Lk. 7.24–35; Mt. 11.7–19: Q), and because Paul's letters are our earliest written witnesses to the Christian movement, is there not some presumption that Jesus, like his predecessor and his successor, fretted about people flunking the divine judgment? Jürgen Becker asks, 'What kind of historical view of Primitive Christianity would we be left with if we juxtapose a message of Jesus that was purified of all traces of judgment and a dark and brooding Primitive Christianity that so easily and in so many ways speaks of God's judgment?'[22]

22. Jürgen Becker, *Jesus of Nazareth* (New York/Berlin: Walter De Gruyter, 1998), p. 50.

In addition to the argument from continuity, one might appeal to the criterion of multiple attestation. Belief in hell or wrathful judgment appears, as already indicated, in all the synoptic sources. Furthermore, John's Gospel, while it nowhere mentions 'Hades' or 'Gehenna', also presupposes a divine judgment and recompense for the lost. That believers will 'not perish but have eternal life' (3.16; cf. 10.28; 11.26) implies that unbelievers will, to the contrary, perish and not have eternal life. Both 5.28–29 ('the hour is coming when all who are in their graves will hear his voice and will come out ... those who have done evil, to the resurrection of condemnation') and 12.48 ('The one who rejects me and does not receive my words has a judge; on the last day the word that I have spoken will serve as judge') confirm this. And 15.6 ('Whoever does not abide in me is thrown away like a branch and withers; such branches are gathered, thrown into the fire, and burned') probably, despite the doubts of many modern commentators, adverts to Gehenna.

Divine judgment does not appear in a mere isolated verse or two in the canonical gospels; it is rather a significant element of the Jesus tradition as we have it. The theme recurs in Matthew, Mark, Luke, and John, and it is central to the earliest source, Q. While Reiser's estimate, that 'more than a quarter of the traditional discourse material of Jesus is concerned with the theme of the final judgment',[23] seems overgenerous to me, one can hardly characterize the theme as marginal. It appears, moreover, in diverse genres – in parables (e.g. Q 13.25–27; Mt. 25.41, 46; Lk. 16.23–24, 28), in prophetic forecasts (Q 10.12–15; 11.31–32; Mt. 13.42, 50), in admonitions to insiders (Q 12.5; 13.24; Mk 9.43–48; Mt. 5.22), and in rebukes of outsiders (Q 13.28; Mt. 23.15, 23; Lk. 6.25). Some might think this evidence enough that divine judgment and Gehenna had a place in Jesus's proclamation. I myself am so inclined, for I am not sure how to find Jesus if we can altogether excise a theme or motif consistently attested over a wide range of material. In Gerd Theissen's words, 'All in all, there is no reason to deny that Jesus preached judgment. The tradition of this is too broad'.[24]

Others, however, would protest that this is too easy, and not without reason. The criterion of multiple attestation, although we usually neglect the fact, goes both ways. The more a motif is attested, the more reason we have to surmise its popularity among Christians; and how can early Christian fondness for something be, without further ado, evidence about Jesus? In the present case, why not regard the many references to judgment, some of which are clearly secondary, as proof of the popularity of the theme in the churches? And why not, with that in mind, then apply the criterion of dissimilarity to discredit attributing to Jesus words about the final judgment? In this way we could dissociate him from a belief that seems to so many to involve 'insane concentrated malignity on the part of God'.[25]

23. Marius Reiser, *Jesus and Judgment: The Eschatological Proclamation in Its Jewish Context* (Minneapolis: Fortress Press, 1997), p. 304.

24. Gerd Theissen and Annette Merz, *The Historical Jesus: A Comprehensive Guide* (Minneapolis: Fortress Press, 1998), p. 269.

25. W.M.W. Call, *Reverberations. Revised, with a Chapter from My Autobiography* (London: Trübe & Co., 1875), p. 12.

Although I do not commend this line of reasoning, our guild's tradition requires that we do more than just pile up units in the hope that somehow quantity will establish an origin with Jesus. Although we have a large number of sayings about the 'Son of man', that has settled nothing. One cannot expect it to be different with anything else. We want, in the end, to be able to cite some texts that plausibly give the sense of a few things Jesus said. So which, if any, of the many texts I have cited above satisfy on that score?

The older I get, the less I trust anyone's ability to answer this sort of question, to trace the history and origin of particular sayings. I have lost my youthful 'faith in the omnipotence of analytical decomposition'.[26] It is not so easy to establish that any particular saying goes back to Jesus, and it is not so easy to establish that any particular saying does not go back to him. Certainly a few sentences in a short space will not do the trick, and since the scope of this essay prohibits more than that, herein I shall content myself with citing three sayings that many have felt comfortable assigning to Jesus – one a threat to outsiders in Q, one an admonition to insiders in Mark, one a parable from L. The Q text is Lk. 13.28 = Mt. 8.12, which warns some group that it will be thrown into the outer darkness, where there will be weeping and gnashing of teeth. The Markan text is 9.43–48, which hyperbolically counsels cutting off hand, foot, and eye because being maimed is better than going to hell, to the unquenchable fire, where the worm never dies. The Lukan text is 16.19–31, the episode of the rich man and Lazarus, which has the former in Hades, a place of torment and agony. It would, admittedly, be silly to comb this morality tale, which takes up traditional elements and indeed comes ultimately from Egypt, for details about the afterlife. At the same time, and granting latitude in interpretation, one has difficulty imagining Jesus using this story if he did not believe in both an afterlife and in postmortem punishment. Indeed, 'one of the truths enshrined in the parable' is that 'death is not the end of the moral account, but its continuation, with the possibility of firm adjustment and even reversal'.[27]

If Q 13.28 or Mk 9.43–48 or Lk. 16.19–31 fairly reflects something Jesus said, then he spoke of some sort of hell. Now I shall attempt herein to establish the authenticity of these three sayings – none of which the Jesus Seminar colours red or pink.[28] I can, however, refer readers to others who would demur from the conclusions of the Seminar[29] and, beyond that, state that the case for Mk 9.43–48 in

26. Paul A. Weiss, *Inside the Gates of Science and Beyond: Science in its Cultural Commitments* (New York: Hafner, 1971), p. 214.

27. J. Gwyn Griffiths, 'Cross-Cultural Eschatology with Dives and Lazarus', *ExpTim* 105 (1993), p. 10.

28. Robert W. Funk, Roy W. Hoover, and the Jesus Seminar, *The Five Gospels: The Search for the Authentic Words of Jesus* (New York: Macmillan, 1993).

29. On Q 13.28–29 see John P. Meier, *A Marginal Jew: Rethinking the Historical Jesus, Volume Two: Mentor, Message, and Miracles* (ABRL; New York: Doubleday, 1994), pp. 311–17 (although his equation of the 'many' with Gentiles is problematic). For the authenticity of Mk 9.43–48 see Werner Zager, *Gottesherrschaft und Endgericht in der Verkündigung Jesu: Eine Untersuchung zur markinischen Jesusüberlieferung einschließlich der Q-Parallelen*, BZNW 82 (Berlin: Walter De Gruyter, 1996), pp. 210–13.

particular is strong. The vivid, hyperbolic language and shocking, even bloody images are designed to lodge in the memory. The moral earnestness is patent and surely characteristic of Jesus. So too the uncompromising demand for self-sacrifice. I cannot see any reason to deny this to him – unless it is the conviction that he could not have had Gehenna in his rhetorical arsenal.[30]

Having come to this conclusion and sided with those who think that Jesus spoke about hell, I am certain that my partial and imperfect outline of some of the relevant arguments will not, in the end, change anybody's mind. Little in our contentious field is clear to demonstration; and, regarding Jesus and Gehenna, we do not come to the question free of judgments about Jesus in general. Many of us, myself included, believe that the sort of eschatological or even apocalyptic Jesus that Johannes Weiss and Albert Schweitzer promoted, with his descendents in the works of Rudolf Bultmann, Joachim Jeremias and Ed Sanders, is close to the truth. Many others – most members of the Jesus Seminar, for example – believe that this line of research has not unearthed the truth, that the historical Jesus was somebody else. My point is that those who find more to applaud in Schweitzer than to boo will surely have greater sympathy for my arguments than those with another take on things. This is only natural. We do not and cannot evaluate the details apart from the big picture with which we begin. So if one's big picture is closer to, let us say, that of John Dominic Crossan or Marcus Borg or Stephen Patterson than to mine, my arguments will scarcely suffice to change one's paradigm. It is largely because I start with a Jesus who is a millenarian prophet, and because I know that millenarian prophets typically divide the world into two camps, the saved and the unsaved, that I give a hospitable reception to the case for affirming Jesus's belief in a God who will have bad news for some. In the end, then, the debate about Gehenna grows into a debate about the big picture we start with – a large subject which is, it goes without saying, fraught with complexity and so for another occasion.

30. Certainly the rejoinder that the cutting off of bodily members is excommunication and so reflects an ecclesiastical context does not carry conviction. Contrast. Funk *et al.*, *The Five Gospels*, p. 86. This Pauline interpretation, which goes back to Irenaeus, *Adv. haer.* 4.27.4 PG 7.1060C, and Origen, *Comm. in* Mt. 13.24–25, has nothing to do with the Markan context.

Die Apotheose in Seneca „Apocolocyntosis" und die Himmelfahrt Lk 24,50–53; Apg 1,9–11

Detlev Dormeyer

1. *Die Apotheose*

a. *Definition*

Der Begriff ἀποθέωσις = „Vergöttlichung" gehört zu den abstrakten Bildungen der hellenistischen Zeit. Einem bedeutenden Menschen wie Alexander dem Großen wird nach seinem Tod die Erhebung zum Gott zugesprochen (*Polyb.* 12,23,4). Für diese Vergöttlichung sind zugleich weitere Begriffe gebräuchlich. Der römische Senat entwickelt für den ermordeten Caesar das Apotheose-Ritual der *consecratio*, das grundlegend bleibt für die gesamte römisch-heidnische Kaiserzeit.[1] Die späteren griechischen Autoren übersetzen die *consecratio* mit ἀποθάνατασις (*Dio Cass.* 60,35,3). Bei der Heroisierung von historischen Wohltätern steht die „Unsterblichkeit", die ἀθανασία, im Mittelpunkt, aufgrund derer der Vergöttlichte seine Wohltaten weiter gewähren kann.

b. *Geschichte*

Apotheose gehört zu dem weiten Bedeutungsfeld der Verbindung einer Gottheit mit einem Menschen (Gen. 6,1–4). Der Mythenkreis um das Gottkönigtum des ägyptischen Pharao und der griechische Heroenglaube bilden die nahesten Analogien und Hintergründe. Die Anfänge der Apotheose im engen Sinne gehen auf das 6. und 5. Jh. v. Chr. zurück. Die Heroisierung vorgeschichtlicher Gestalten bei Homer und Hesiod wird weiter entwickelt zur Vergöttlichung aktueller, historischer Personen. Militärführer, Stadtherrscher, Priester, Dichter, Seher, Weise, Kulturschöpfer und Athleten werden nun nach ihrem Tod aufgrund ihrer Wohltaten für die Stadt heroisiert.[2] Mit der Wende zum 4. Jh. v. Chr. wird die lokale Heroisierung sogar auf die lebenden Wohltäter übertragen. Die Insel Samos erweist um 404 v. Chr. dem Spartaner Lysander als Sieger des Peloponnesischen Krieges göttliche Ehren (*Plut. Lys.* 18,3f.). Philipp II. von Makedonien (*Paus.* 5,20,110) und Dion von Syrakus (*Diod.* 16,20,6) folgen im 4. Jh. v. Chr. mit entsprechenden Ansprüchen nach. Alexander der Große (356–323 v. Chr.) ist bestrebt, die lokalen und regionalen Ansätze der Heroisierung (Vergottungs-Orakel

1. Apotheosis in: RE II.1 (1985), S. 184–88; Apotheosis in: KP 1 (1979), S. 458–60; Bickermann 1929, 1–34; Taeger 2, 1960, 50–474; Bremmer 1996, 12–31.

2. Roloff 1970, 3–102; Burkert 1977, 312–31; Betz 1983, 234–312.

im Ammon-Tempel im ägyptischen Siwa) in einem Reichskult der Apotheose zu vereinheitlichen. Die Diadochendynastien der Ptolemäer und später der Seleukiden führen diese Tendenz weiter; Ptolemäus II. (285–246 v. Chr.) läßt sich in Weiterführung der ägyptischen Königsmythologie zu Lebzeiten vergotten.[3]

Das römische Ritual der *consecratio* ist ursprünglich wie der griechische Heroenkult auf die Apotheose eines Verstorbenen bezogen, und zwar in engem Sinne auf das Herrscherhaus. Der Senat beschließt nach Caesars Tod, „Caesar alle göttlichen und menschlichen Ehren zu verleihen" (*Suet. Caes.* 84), und läßt diesen Beschluß öffentlich vor dem Scheiterhaufen verlesen. Nach der Verbrennung des Leichnams steigt die Seele des Julius Caesar auf und übernimmt die Herrschaft über einen Kometen (*Suet. Caes.* 88). Octavian, der *Divi filius* (= Sohn Gottes), läßt seinen vergöttlichten Adoptivvater als eine Statue im Tempel der Venus Genetrix, der Stammutter des Geschlechtes der Julier, aufstellen, jährlich Spiele zu ihrer und Caesars Ehren veranstalten und Münzen mit der Abbildung Caesars und des Kometen prägen. Der vom Senat zum Augustus erhobene Octavian verhält sich zwar distanziert zu Divinisierungsangeboten, die noch zu Lebzeiten vornehmlich aus dem Osten an ihn herangetragen werden, fördert aber den Kult der neuen Göttin „Dea Roma" und läßt sich gemeinsam mit ihr als ihr erster Anhänger und als eigenständiger „genius" verehren.[4] Nach seinem Tod wird das Ritual der *consecratio*-Apotheose erheblich erweitert. Bei der Verbrennung auf dem Marsfeld wird ein Adler als Symbol für die Auffahrt in den Götterhimmel freigelassen (*Dio Cass.* 56,42,3); zugleich muß ein Zeuge erklären, „er habe das Bild (*effigies*) des Verbrannten zum Himmel aufsteigen sehen" (*Suet. Aug.* 100).

Im 1. Jh. bleibt die Apotheose entgegen den mißlungenen Versuchen einer Selbstvergöttlichung von Caligula (37 – 41), Nero (54 – 68) und Domitian (81 – 96) strikt auf das mit der Verbrennung des toten Kaisers verbundene Ritual bezogen. Im 2. Jh. dagegen erfolgt ab Hadrian (117 – 138) die Vergöttlichung des lebenden Kaisers. Allerdings wird hauptsächlich zum Wohlergehen des Kaisers und weniger ihm selbst als Gott geopfert. Nach seinem Tode muß außerdem das Ritual der *consecratio*-Apotheose weiterhin durchgeführt werden. So nimmt der lebende Kaiser von Anfang an eine Zwischenstellung zwischen Sterblichkeit und Göttlichkeit ein;[5] die Göttlichkeit verstärkt sich ab dem 2. Jh., bleibt aber weiterhin für die philosophische Kritik zugänglich (*Lukian. dial. mort.* 13–14: Alexander; *Suet. Caes.*; *Tac. Ann.*; *Plin., Paneg.* 11). Frühester Text der Kritik ist Seneca's Apocolocyntosis aus dem 1. Jh.

Apotheose fehlt im AT und NT. Aber die atl. Mythen von der Zeugung der Riesen (Gen. 6,1–4), von der Entrückung des urgeschichtlichen Henoch (Gen. 5,21–24) und von der Himmelfahrt des Propheten Elija (2 Kön. 2,1–18) bieten Ansatzpunkte für die hellenistische und römische Apotheose. Auch das Frühjudentum bleibt zurückhaltend, deutet aber für Mose und verwandte Gestalten die

3. Habicht 1970, 3–124.
4. Price 1984, 54–57; Cineira 1999, 33–36.
5. Klauck 2, 1996, 62–71.

Apotheose nach dem Tode an (*Phil. Vit. Mos* 1,155–158; 4Q 482–520; *Jos. Ant.* 4,320–326). Die Evangelien statten den irdischen Jesus mit göttlichen Titeln und göttlicher Macht in Parallele zu göttlichen Menschen wie den Kaisern, Philosophen, Stadtgründern, Reformern, Wunderheilern, Propheten und Dichtern aus. Gleichzeitig liefern ihnen die atl. biographischen Berichte von den Propheten und Königen die Vorlagen, Jesu einmalige, eschatologische Gottesbeziehung von der Geschichte Israels her zu gestalten. Die göttliche Vollmacht und die Apotheose Jesu werden von den atl. formulierten Zeugnissen von der Auferweckung (Röm. 1,1–3; 1 Kor. 15,3–5), der Erhöhung (Phil. 2,6–11) und der Himmelfahrt (Lk. 24,50–55; Apg. 1,9–11) ausgeführt. Andererseits wird die Auswahl der atl. Bezüge von der antiken Apotheose und der ihr vorausgehenden Idealbiographie von der betreffenden Person bestimmt. Der Christus Jesus verkörpert in Lehre, Handeln, Herkunft und Apotheose den Gegenentwurf zu den Evangelien der Kaiser (Mk. 1,1; Mt. 1,1; Lk. 1,1–4; Joh. 1,1): Jesus erfährt als Verkünder der nur in ihm angebrochenen Königsherrschaft als einziger eine Apotheose. Diese erfolgt nach seinem Kreuzestod (Apg. 1,1–11) und bringt allein den Völkern Heil und Erlösung.

Diese ntl. Linie der Apotheose erfährt in der Offb eine besondere Ausformung.

2. *Senecas Satire Apocolocyntosis*

a. *Das Leben Senecas*

Lucius Annaeus Seneca lebte von 4 v. Chr. oder von der Zeitenwende an[6] bis 65 n. Chr. Der Vater L. Annaeus S. d. Ä. war in Corduba, Spanien, Rechtsanwalt oder römischer Beamter. Er gehörte dem Ritterstand an. In hohem Alter widmete er sich der Schriftstellerei; in jungen Jahren hatte er in Rom studiert. So sorgte er dafür, daß auch sein mittlerer Sohn Lucius in Rom studieren konnte. Die zwei Brüder Senecas waren ebenfalls sehr begabt. Der ältere Bruder Gallio wurde u.a. Prokonsul von Achaia, der jüngere Bruder Markus ließ seinen Sohn M. Annaeus Lucanus, der später ebenfalls als gefeierter Dichter dem Nero-Kreis angehörte, zum Rhetor und Philosophen ausbilden. L. Seneca ging mit dieser um die Philosophie erweiterten Rhetoren-Ausbildung voran. Zusätzlich zur üblichen sprachlichen Erziehung beim Grammaticus und Rhetor erhielt er eine Einführung in die Philosophie durch Sotion (Schule der Sextier) und den Stoiker Attalos. Ein längerer Ägyptenaufenthalt schloß sich an. Die Rückkehr nach Rom fand 31/32 statt. Jetzt, im Alter von 35 oder 30 Jahren, begann Seneca, sich um die Ämter des *cursus honorum* zu bewerben. Er erhielt die Quästur und wurde in den Senat aufgenommen (33–35). Unter Caligula (37–41) hatte er eine führende Stellung als Redner, Literat und Amtsinhaber (vermutlich Ädil) inne.

Von Claudius (41–54) wurde er 41 nach Korsika verbannt wegen angeblichen Ehebruchs mit Julia Livilla, einer Schwester Caligulas. Claudius war durch eine Intrige seiner Gattin Messalina zum Verbannungsurteil angestiftet worden.

6. Fuhrmann 1999, 10.

49 ließ Agrippina, die Nachfolgerin Messalinas, Seneca zurückrufen. Er erhielt die Oberaufsicht über die rednerische Ausbildung Neros, des Sohnes von Agrippina. Nero (37–68) war 12 Jahre alt. Im Jahre 50 wurde Seneca Prätor.

Nach Claudius Vergiftung (54) war er als Erzieher des 17-jährigen Nero gemeinsam mit dem Gardepräfekten Burrus faktisch Lenker des römischen Weltreichs. Diese goldene Zeit philosophischer Staatslenkung dauerte 5 Jahre. Sie wurde von drei Morden überschattet: Der Vergiftung von Claudius (54), der Vergiftung von Britannicus, dem jüngeren Stiefbruder Neros (55), der Ermordung Agrippinas (59), der Mutter Neros. Der letzte Mord beendete die Herrschaft Senecas. Obwohl dieser im Senat den Mord verteidigte, zog Nero von nun an die Herrschaftsgeschäfte direkt an sich. Nach Burrus Tod im Jahre 62 war Seneca völlig isoliert und zog sich aus dem Hofleben zurück. Im Jahre 65 nahm er sich auf Befehl Neros wegen angeblicher Beteiligung an der pisonischen Verschwörung das Leben.

Es ist anachronistisch, Seneca nach heutigen moralischen Maßstäben zu bewerten und ihn von den Morden völlig freizusprechen.[7] Doch der Frage der Beteiligung Senecas soll hier nicht weiter nachgegangen werden.

Es könnte sein, daß durch die Apocolocyntosis die Abstammung von Claudius abgewertet werden und die Mitregentenansprüche von Britannicus (41–55), dem Sohn des Claudius, geschmälert werden sollten.[8] So betont in der Apocolocyntosis der altitalische, bedeutungslose Unterwelts-Gott Diespiter (= Dispater) bei seinem Antrag auf Vergöttlichung die Blutsverwandtschaft des Claudius (*sanguine*) zu Augustus und zu der Augusta [Livia] (9,5). Livia war erst von ihrem Enkel Claudius divinisiert worden (*Dio Cass. 60,5*). Allerdings war Claudius auch durch Augustus Schwester Octavia, seiner Großmutter mütterlicherseits, mit Augustus blutsverwandt. Außerdem bestreitet Augustus dem Claudius nicht die Zugehörigkeit zum Caesar – und Augustus – Namen (*sub meo nomine latens* 10,4). Augustus entwertet vielmehr die Persönlichkeit des Claudius, wie es Seneca fortwährend im Erzählteil macht. Britannicus und Nero gehören beide zur Caesar-Großfamilie. Der eine hat nach Seneca den unfähigen Vater Claudius Caesar Augustus Germanicus, der andere den allseits anerkannten Germanicus Caesar zum Großvater. Neben dem Haß auf Claudius aufgrund achtjähriger Verbannung als ersten Grund[9] könnte also in dieser politischen Entwertung des Konkurrenten Britannicus der zweite Grund für die Schärfe der Satire liegen. Caligula rangiert am Schluß noch über Claudius, weil sein Vater der große Germanicus war.

So folgenreich wie die Morde war auch die Satire Apocolocyntosis, dt. „Verkürbissung". Diese Nachwirkung war ganz im moralpädagogischen Sinne Senecas. Seine Beteiligung an den Staatsmorden hingegen suchte er zu verschleiern.

7. So Schöne 1957, 39–41; Fuhrmann 1999, 177; 248–53; dagegen Weinreich 1923, 5: Seneca hat Tag- und Nachtseiten: „Die Nachtseite verrät die Satire und manches, was er in Korsika geschrieben hat."

8. So Bauer 1981, 85.

9. Weinreich 1923, 5–6.

Die Satire ist eine originäre, lateinische Gattung. Die Aussagen wollen weder als historisch gemäß der Geschichtsschreibung noch als ausgewogenes Charakterporträt gemäß der Biographieschreibung verstanden werden. Es geht um eine ganz persönliche Stellungnahme zu Tagesfragen verschiedenster Art.[10] Gesellschaftskritik, Verurteilung menschlicher Schwächen und Aufdeckung von Lastern bewegen in witziger Weise den Hörer zur Einsicht, zur Kontrolle eigenen und fremden Verhaltens und zur Veränderung von Fehlverhalten. Seneca, der Kaisererzieher, unterzieht die Apotheose der satirischen Kritik. Damit ist für den fünften Augustus, für den jungen Nero, von höchster Stelle ein Maßstab gesetzt, die Apotheose in ihrer Ambivalenz anzuerkennen und richtig zu gebrauchen. Die Lächerlichkeit vermag noch intensiver als der moralische Appell vor Mißbrauch zu warnen.

Die Satire kann unterschiedliche Gattungen in Dienst nehmen. Seneca wählt die Komödie.[11] Kaiser-Apotheose als Theater paßt hervorragend zum Mitbegründer der Apotheose, zu Oktavian Augustus. Er gestaltete seinen Sterbetag zum Abgang aus einer Komödie:

> „An seinem letzten Lebenstag erkundigte sich Augustus wiederholt danach, ob wegen seines Zustandes in den Städten bereits Unruhen entstanden seien, ließ sich einen Spiegel reichen, das Haar kämmen und die eingefallenen Wangen wieder herrichten. Dann richtete er an die vorgelassenen Freunde die Frage, ob sie nicht meinten, er habe das Schauspiel des Lebens gut gespielt, und fügte dann auf griechisch die übliche Schlußformel hinzu: ‚Hat das Ganze euch gefallen, nun so klatschet Beifall unserm Spiel, Und entlaßt uns alle nun mit Dank.' " (*Suet. Aug. 99*)

Wie das Leben des Augustus ist auch seine Apotheose ein Spiel. Es bildet die Götter nicht ab, sie stehen hinter ihm.

Obwohl später im 2. Jh. die Apotheose schon für den lebenden Kaiser aktuelle Bedeutung erhält, wird die satirische Sichtweise der Apocolocyntosis weiter rezipiert, wenn sie auch nur von Cassius Dio ausdrücklich genannt wird: „Seneca selbst schrieb ein Werk, dem er den Titel ‚Verkürbissung' gab, eine Bezeichnung, nachgebildet dem Worte Vergöttlichung" (*Dio Cass.* 60/61, 35, 3). Sueton läßt Nero ähnlich wie die Apocolocyntosis über die Dummheit und Grausamkeit des Claudius spotten; mit einem Wortwitz spielt Nero zusätzlich auf griechisch μωρός [„Tor"] (*Sen. Apoc.* 7,3) an (*Suet. Ner.* 33). Auch Plinius kennt den Spott Neros über die „Vergottung" von Claudius (*Plin. paneg.* 11). Alexander wird bereits vom 1. Jh. an zum negativen Prototyp des sich selbst vergöttlichenden Herrschers, der in seinem Zorn unmäßig und lächerlich die Göttlichkeit zu Lebzeiten verspielt (*Sen. de ira* 2,23,2–3; 3,17; *Curtius Rufus*; *Plutarch, Alex.*; *Arrian anab.*; *Lukian. dial. mort.: Alex.*).

Seneca lehnt die Apotheose nicht ab. Aber er warnt den jugendlichen Kaiser davor, sich selbst mit einer Gottheit gleichzusetzen. Nero ist Apollo „ähnlich" (5,9), aber nicht gleich. Die Apollo-Statue mit dem Gesicht Neros vor der domus aurea nach 64 mußte Seneca vielleicht nicht mehr erleben. Für Seneca hat die Apotheose die Doppelfunktion, dem regierenden Kaiser ein Ideal vor Augen zu

10. Weinreich 1923, 2.
11. Ähnlich Weinreich 1923: Parodie tragischer Szenen (S.10); Satyrspiel (S.19).

stellen und dem verstorbenen Kaiser die idealnahe Regentschaft zu- oder abzusprechen. Gegen die Senatsbeschlüsse entzieht Seneca Claudius die Apotheose (11,6) und spricht sie Tiberius zu (1,2). Doch es handelt sich bei diesem Spiel mit der Apotheose um eine Satire. Seneca übernimmt 55–56 das Konsulat, unterläßt es aber, dem Senat neue Anträge zur Abänderung der Apotheose-Beschlüsse zu unterbreiten und durchzusetzen. Es bleibt bei der Apotheose von Claudius und der Nicht-Apotheose von Tiberius. Die Nicht-Apotheose von Caligula war selbstverständlich und wird als Abschluß satirisch eingesetzt. In der Unterwelt wird Claudius dem völlig unfähigen Caligula als Sklave zugesprochen; der wiederum verschenkt ihn an den Unterweltsrichter Äackus; dort bleibt er für immer als Gerichtsdiener tätig (15,2).

Mit der satirischen Verurteilung des Menschen Claudius täuscht sich Seneca allerdings. In ernsthaften Schriften verurteilt Seneca natürlich nur Caligula (*de ira* 3.18,3–19,5), nicht Claudius (vgl. *consolatio ad Polybium*). Für die Nachwelt steht Claudius bis heute weit über Caligula. Die Rangfolge zwischen Augustus, Tiberius und Claudius bleibt Geschmackssache. Senecas Sichtweise war durch seine persönliche Verbannung getrübt. Doch ist es übertrieben, von „glühendem Haß“[12] und „literarischer Hinrichtung“[13] zu sprechen. Die römische Satire liebt die Isolierung und Übertreibung negativer Eigenschaften und erhebt nicht den Anspruch auf Wahrheit und Ausgewogenheit. Die Satire gleicht der Karikatur und dem politischen Witz. Fuhrmann führt zutreffend dazu aus:

> „Claudius hatte sich trotz mancher kluger Maßnahmen in den knapp vierzehn Jahren seiner Herrschaft kaum Freunde gemacht. Sein skurriles Wesen, seine Zerstreutheit und auch seine Gelehrsamkeit standen seiner kaiserlichen Autorität im Wege, und zumal am Hof sah man in ihm, wenn man ihn nicht geradezu verabscheute, gern eine Witzfigur. So ist es kein Zufall, daß sich gerade auf ihn – als einzigen römischen Kaiser – eine erbarmungslose Schmähschrift, eine böse Satire erhalten hat. Erstaunen ruft eher der Umstand hervor, daß kein anderer als Seneca, der Verfasser der beschönigenden Grabrede, das ebenso giftige wie geistvolle Pamphlet ersonnen hat. Man hat zu seiner Entschuldigung darauf verwiesen, daß er zu den Opfern der Willkürhandlungen des Claudius zählte; man kann noch hinzufügen, daß die Satire von Hause aus gewiß nur für einen engen Kreis von Hofangehörigen bestimmt war und daß nur die oft unerforschlichen Wege der Überlieferung auch die Nachwelt zum Zeugen einer literarischen Hinrichtung gemacht haben. Schließlich sei an den psychischen Druck erinnert, dem höfische Protokolle und Zeremonien die Beteiligten auszusetzen pflegen. Hier sind Ventile gefragt, und dazu zählen nicht nur Feste und Mummenschanz, sondern manchmal auch derbe, die sonst gültigen Hierarchien mißachtende Späße.“[14]

Die Apocolocyntosis will satirisch die gültigen Hierarchien umkehren und der Kritik zugänglich machen. Seneca behält darin recht, daß die Apotheose wie der olympische Götterhimmel metaphorisch zu verstehen ist. Die Form der Weiterexistenz nach dem Tode bleibt eine *terra incognita*, die Gegenwart für den regierenden Kaiser hingegen höchster moralischer Anspruch.

12. Schöne 1957, 38; Bauer 1981, 85; Binder 1999.
13. Fuhrmann 1999, 178.
14. Fuhrmann 1999, 178f.

b. *Elemente der Apotheose in der Satire Apocolocyntosis*

Die Apocolocyntosis, die „Verkürbissung“, gehört zu der menippeischen Satire, die eine Mischung aus Prosa und Metrum darstellt. Der Titel „Apocolocyntosis“ wird zwar von der einzigen antiken Belegstelle genannt und erklärt (*Dio Cass. 60/61, 35,3*), fehlt aber in den späteren Handschriften. Die meisten schlagen vor: *Ludus Senecae de morte Claudii Neronis* (Senecas Schauspiel vom Tode des Claudius Nero). Das Wortspiel, das Dio Cassius bietet (s.o.), überzeugt dagegen noch immer die Kommentatoren: „Der Titel enthält also den Vorwurf der Hohlköpfigkeit, da in der Antike wie auch in einigen neueren Sprachen noch heute der Kürbis Symbol und Schimpfwort für einen Dummkopf war.“[15] An der Autorschaft Senecas wird nicht gezweifelt. Die glänzende Beherrschung unterschiedlicher Stile und die moralphilosophischen Intentionen weisen deutlich einen Zusammenhang mit den anderen Schriften Senecas auf. Eine Parallele stellt das „Satyrikon“ des zeitgleichen Petronius (†66) dar. Die Satiren von Horaz, Persius und Juvenal dagegen tragen durchgehend ein poetisches Metrum.

Die Apocolocyntosis setzt mit einem Autor-Prolog ein:

> „Was im Himmel vor sich ging am 13. Oktober im neuen Kaiserjahre, zu Beginn der allerschönsten Zeit, das will ich zur Erinnerung berichten. Nichts soll mich dabei bestimmen, weder Haß noch Gunst. Es war wahrhaftig so, wie ich erzähle.
>
> Fragt einer nach der Quelle meines Wissens, so werde ich zunächst, wenn mir's nicht paßt, gar keine Antwort geben. Wer will mich auch zwingen? Ich weiß ja doch, ich bin ein freier Mann geworden seit dem Tag, da jener aus der Welt ging, an dem das Sprichwort Wahrheit wurde: zum König oder zum Trottel müsse man geboren sein.
>
> Gefällt mir's aber zu antworten, so will ich sagen, was mir gerade in den Schnabel kommt. Wer hat denn je von einem Historiker Zeugen zum Schwur gefordert? Ist's aber unvermeidlich, einen Bürgen anzuführen, dann mag man den fragen, der einst Drusilla zum Himmel fahren sah: der wird behaupten, er habe auch Claudius auf dieser Fahrt gesehen ‚mit humpelnden Schritten‘.
>
> Mag der wollen oder nicht, er muß doch alles merken, was im Himmel vor sich geht: er ist Aufseher der Via Appia, auf der bekanntlich auch der selige Augustus und Kaiser Tiberius zu den Göttern gingen. Nur unter vier Augen wird er freilich dir berichten, wenn du ihn fragst; sind mehrere dabei, läßt er kein Wort mehr hören. Denn seitdem er im Senate schwor, er habe Drusilla in den Himmel steigen sehen, und ihm zum Dank für diese *Freudenbotschaft* keine Seele glaubt, was er gesehen haben will – da hat er einen feierlichen Eid geleistet, nie wieder etwas anzuzeigen, auch dann nicht, wenn er mitten auf dem Forum einen totgeschlagenen Menschen fände.“ (*Sen. Apoc.* 1,1–3)

Der Prolog ist dem trockenen Stil eines Geschichtswerkes, einer historia, angeglichen.[16] Claudius hatte ja von Jugend an Geschichtswerke zu unterschiedlichen Völkern verfaßt (*Suet. Claud.* 41–42). Seneca wiederum hatte die Geschichtsschreibung gemieden.

Es fehlt ein Präskript (Verfasserangabe, Adressat, Widmung). Das Werk ist anonym verfaßt. Es setzt unmittelbar mit dem *Exordium*, der Beschreibung des

15. Bauer 1981, 85; vgl. Weinreich 1923, 11–12; Schöne 1957, 45; Fuhrmann 1999, 179.

16. Weinreich 1923, 10–30; „mit *in caelo* klingt erstmals die mythologisch-religiöse Komponente an… Die satirische Wirkung ergibt sich aus dem Zusammenspiel der Elemente“ (Binder 1999, 99).

Werkes, ein. Knapp wird die *Propositio*, das Thema, vorgestellt: 1,1,1–4. *Quid actum sit* verweist auf aktenmäßig bezeugte Vorgänge. Ort und Zeit werden deutlich eingegrenzt: „Himmel“ und „13. Oktober“. Ansprüche werden formuliert: Anbruch der allerglücklichsten Zeit, die das Evangelium von der Augustuszeit (1,1,3) noch einmal überhöht. Beteuerungen der kritischen Geschichtsschreibung ab Thukydides, das Gedächtnis durch Überlieferung zu sichern, ohne Haß und Gunst objektiv zu berichten und nur Wahres zu bringen, werden ironisch angehängt. Die späteren Vorworte Lk. 1,1–4; Apg. 1,1–2 bilden mit vielen anderen antiken Vorworten das ernsthafte Gegenstück.

Die *Argumentatio* 1,1,5–2,3a spielt ironisch mit dem Glaubwürdigkeitsbeweis der Quellen. Der Frager erhält keine Antwort, weil die Redefreiheit wieder eingekehrt ist. Ihre Einschränkung durch die Majestätsprozesse unter Claudius gibt ein Hauptthema der folgenden Komödie an. Das Sprichwort spitzt das Thema zu und verweist auf die anschließende satirische Ausarbeitung. Der Geburtsadel muß sich in der Weisheit bewähren, bei angeborener Dummheit verliert er seinen Anspruch auf den Prinzipat und die Apotheose. Schließlich wird sogar ein „Schwurzeuge“ eingeführt, den die Historiker nicht benötigen, wohl aber die Wundergeschichten. Die Apocolocyntosis ist eine höhere, lügenhafte Form der Geschichtsschreibung, weil sie eine wunderbare Himmelsreise enthält.[17] Daher erhält diese ja auch anschließend das Gewand der satirischen Komödie.

Die *Narratio* 1,2,3b–3,7 läßt den Zeugen seine Erlebnisse in Kurzform bringen, die dann im Folgenden breit entfaltet werden. Die Überhöhung durch den „Schwur“ wird mit dem Apotheose-Ritual begründet und zugleich entwertet. Der Zeuge wird als völlig unglaubwürdig entlarvt. Der von Livia eingeführte Zeugenbeweis führt notwendigerweise zum Falschzeugnis, so daß die folgende „Historia“ satirischer Unsinn, reine Komödie ist. Caligula hat für seine verstorbene Schwester Drusilla die Apotheose als Komödie inszeniert, dem Evangelium (*bonum nuntium*) ihrer Himmelfahrt (*caelum ascendens*) glaubt daher keiner.

Der Abschluß des *Exordiums* imitiert das *Postskript*, das an das Ende des Werkes gehört, dort aber fehlt. Die Beteuerungsformel wird zur überflüssigen Wiederholung der *Propositio* 1,1,1–4. Als *Postskript* würde sie dagegen Sinn machen (vgl. Joh. 20,30 f.; 21,24–25; Offb. 22,6–21) und die dialogische Struktur dieser Satire stilgerecht abschließen. Auch der Segenswunsch macht im Geschichtswerk keinen Sinn. Er gehört zur Briefliteratur. Allerdings hütet sich normalerweise der Briefschreiber, einem Falschzeugen „Heil und Glück“ zu wünschen. In dieser Satire sollen bewußt alle Stilarten durcheinander gehen: Geschichtsschreibung (*Acta und historia*), Satire (*rex und fatuus* = „Narr“), Komödie (*auctor* der Himmelsreise), Dialog und Brief.

Die Satire setzt mit der Bezeugung der Auffahrt des erhöhten Kaisers ein. Dieses Zeugnis fehlte bei Caesars *consecratio* und wurde erst von Livia für die Apotheose des Augustus eingeführt (*Suet. Aug.* 100). Dio Cassius bemerkt

17. Weinreich 1923, 19–25.

spöttisch, daß Livia den Zeugnis gebenden Prätor fürstlich entlohnte (*Dio Cass.* 56,46,2).

Caligula machte sich daraus ein Vergnügen, seine verstorbene Schwester Drusilla zu vergöttlichen und das Ritual der Livia pedantisch zu wiederholen (*Dio Cass.* 59,11). Außerdem läßt Seneca nicht nur den *divus Augustus* zu den Göttern aufsteigen, sondern auch den nicht vom Senat consecrierten Tiberius Caesar; d. i. eine Reverenz für Tiberius und eine Kritik an der Willkür der Senatsbeschlüsse zur Apotheose.

Claudius dagegen liegt im Sterben. Apollo singt einen Hymnus auf den Kaiser – allerdings nicht, wie zu erwarten wäre, auf den noch lebenden Kaiser, sondern auf seinen Nachfolger, den künftigen Kaiser. Claudius wird ironisch durch Nero ersetzt.

> „Fröhlich schlägt er die Laute und weist den Parzen die Arbeit,
> Hält sie mit Singen am Werk und täuscht sie über die Mühe.
> Während sie preisend rühmen das Spiel und die Lieder des Bruders,
> Spinnen sie weiter als sonst, und über menschliches Maß hin
> Geht das gepriesene Werk. ‚O macht kein Ende, ihr Parzen',
> So singt Phoebus, ‚er soll das Maß des irdischen Daseins
> Stolz besiegen, mir ähnlich im Antlitz, ähnlich an Schönheit,
> Und nicht schlechter beim Klange des Lieds. Glückselige Zeiten
> Wird er den Schwachen bringen und brechen das Schweigen des Rechtes.
> Gleichwie Lucifers Strahl die fliehenden Sterne verscheuchet,
> Oder wie Hesperus steigt beim Wiederkehren der Sterne,
> Gleichwie Helios – wenn das Dunkel lösend Aurora
> Purpurrot den Tag heraufführt – leuchtend die Erde
> Anschaut und das frische Gespann aus den Schranken hervorlenkt:
> Solch ein Kaiser ist da, so wird jetzt Rom einen *Nero*
> Schauen! Es leuchtet der strahlende Blick in milderem Glanze,
> Und das üppige Haar umwallt den stattlichen Nacken!'
> So sang Apollo." (*Sen. Apoc.* 4,1–2)[18]

Es liegt ein *Panegyrikus*, ein Herrscherpreis, vor. Nero ist Apoll ähnlich (*similis*), aber nicht mit ihm identisch. Ausführlich würdigt Weinreich diesen Herrscherpreis (*Laudes Neronis*). Seneca bietet für die prophetische Preisung des Augustus in der Aeneis (*Verg. Aen.* 6,792ff.) einen Ersatz „und bringt deshalb die mythologischen Vergleiche, die, abgesehen von Neros Gesangsleistungen, von seiner Schönheit den Ausgangspunkt nehmen, also sein Wesen angehen"[19]. Zum Wesen Neros gehören dann die Unterstützung der Schwachen und die Durchsetzung von Rechtssicherheit.[20]

Zu weit geht aber Weinreich mit seinem Schluß, daß der religiöse Hintergrund dieses *Panegyrikus* das Gottkaisertum sei, das bereits von Augustus geschaffen sei; die Nero-Münzen, die späten Selbstinszenierungen Neros als Gott, die Vergottungs-Sprache der ägyptischen Papyri[21] stellen Übergriffe dar, vor denen

18. Üb. Schöne, 1957, S. 13.
19. Weinreich, 1923, S. 39.
20. Weinreich, 1923, S. 38–43.
21. Weinreich 1923, 44–48.

Seneca ja gerade warnen will. Als von Apoll mit Kunst begnadeter, menschlicher Kaiser ergreift Nero die „Kithara" und besiegt mit seinen Liedern die Zeiten des sterblichen Lebens (*vincat mortalis tempora vitae*). Glückselige Zeiten (*felicia saecula*) und Rechtssicherheit bringt er den Schwachen. Gemeinsam mit Nero werden diese über Rom und das Weltall herrschen. In der Tat war Nero beim Volk beliebt und blieb beliebt nach seinem Selbstmord i. J. 68 (*Suet. Nero* 57; *Tac. Hist.* 2,8; Offb. 13,3). Die Rechtssicherheit knüpft an Claudius an (*Tac. Ann.* 13,43), auch wenn sie ihm im Verlauf der Apocolocyntosis wieder satirisch abgesprochen wird.

Nach dem Herrscherpreis Apolls stirbt Claudius einen schimpflichen Tod. Aufgrund der Pilzvergiftung erleidet er einen Durchfall. Auf diesen bezieht sich sein „letztes Wort" (*ultima vox*): „Wehe mir, ich glaube, ich habe mich beschissen" (*Sen. Apoc.* 4,3). Der Kommentar bezweifelt spöttisch die Richtigkeit dieser Aussage, da Claudius wie die Komödianten, die er beim Sterben um sich hat (*Sen. Apoc.* 4,2), einen Durchfall nur vortäuschen konnte. Bissig folgert der Autor-Kommentar: „sicher ist, er hat alles beschissen" (*Sen. Apoc.* 4,3), gemeint ist der Staat. Die Vorwürfe folgen erst später in der Rede des „Gottes" Augustus, der sich gegen die Vergöttlichung von Claudius ausspricht (*Sen. Apoc.* 10–11).

Inzwischen hat sich Claudius auf den Weg gemacht, von dem der Prolog gesprochen hat. Die Himmelfahrt umfaßt als Akt 1 die Kapitel 5–11, die Höllenfahrt als Akt 2 die Kapitel 13–15; Kapitel 12 bildet als Zwischenstation auf Erden ein Intermezzo.[22]

Jupiter erhält in Akt 1 die Meldung vom Herannahen eines seltsamen Wesens. Er schickt Hercules zum Empfang los. Der göttliche Mensch Hercules ist am besten in der Lage, zum Olymp aufsteigende Menschen auf ihre Würdigkeit hin zu prüfen. Claudius gelingt es auch mit vielen Umwegen, Hercules zum Fürsprecher der Vergöttlichung zu gewinnen (*Sen. Apoc.* 5–7). Er beeindruckt Hercules besonders damit, daß er dessen Reinigung des Augiasstalles auf seine Rechtssprechung anwendet (*Sen. Apoc.* 7,5). Die metaphorische Übertragung dieser Hercules-Tat auf Politik, Justiz und Verwaltung war schon damals ein beliebter Topos der Rhetorik.

An dieser Stelle bricht der Text ab. Die Textlücke kann nicht umfangreich gewesen sein. Der Text setzt mit der Götterversammlung in der Kurie wieder ein, zu der Hercules sich stürmisch begeben und der er den Antrag auf Vergöttlichung vorgetragen hat (*Sen. Apoc.* 8,1,1). Ein unbekannter Gott antwortet ablehnend auf den Antrag des Hercules.

> Kein Wunder, daß du in unser Rathaus hereinstürmst: vor dir gibt es ja weder Schloß noch Riegel. Nun sag' uns nur, was für einen Gott du aus dem Kerl da machen willst? ‚Ein epikureischer Gott' kann er nicht werden: ‚der hat ja weder selbst etwas zu leisten noch gibt er anderen etwas zu tun.' Lieber ein stoischer? Doch wie könnte er – um mit Varro zu reden – ‚kugelrund sein, ohne Kopf und ohne Vorhaut?' Und doch hat er etwas von einem stoischen Gotte an sich, ich sehe es schon: er hat weder Herz noch Kopf. Und sicher, wenn er Saturn um diese Gnade der Vergötterung gebeten hätte, dessen Monat er das ganze Jahr hindurch als Saturnalienprinz zu feiern pflegte, er hätte

22. Weinreich 1923, 56–120.

> es nicht erreicht, ja nicht einmal von Jupiter, den er doch, soviel an ihm lag, der Blutschande beschuldigte. Denn seinen Schwiegersohn Silanus ließ er hinrichten; und weshalb? weil er seine Schwester, ein allerliebstes Mädchen, das alle eine Venus nannten, lieber seine Juno nennen wollte. ‚Warum auch gerade seine Schwester?‘, wird er sagen, ‚das möchte ich gern wissen.‘ Bedenke doch, du Dummkopf: In Athen ist’s halb erlaubt, in Alexandria ganz. ‚Weil in Rom‘, sagst du, ‚die Mäuse die Mühlsteine lecken‘, deshalb wird der uns das Krumme gerade machen? Was man in seinem Schlafzimmer treibt, das weiß er nicht einmal, und jetzt ‚durchsucht er schon des Himmels Winkel?‘
>
> Ein Gott will er werden: ist’s ihm zu wenig, daß er in Britannien einen Tempel hat, daß die Barbaren ihn verehren und wie einen Gott anbeten, um ‚eines Trottels Gnade zu erlangen?‘“ (*Sen. Apoc.* 8,1–3)

Es wird die philosophische Apotheose nach der Schule der Epikuräer und Stoiker diskutiert. Den Anfang macht der Beginn der Hauptlehren Epikurs, der ähnlich bei Diogenes Laertius steht: „Ein epikuräischer Gott, der hat weder eine Handlung noch gewährleistet er sie anderen.“ (*Sen. Apoc.* 8,1; vgl. *Diog. Laert.* 10,139). Der Selbstgenügsamkeit des Epikuräers widerspricht das Streben nach olympischer Vergottung. „Denn es gibt Götter, eine Tatsache, deren Erkenntnis einleuchtend ist; doch sind sie nicht von der Art, wie die große Menge sie sich vorstellt… Gottlos aber ist nicht der, welcher mit den Göttern des gemeinen Volkes aufräumt, sondern der, welcher den Göttern die Vorstellungen des gemeinen Volkes andichtet“ (Epikur in *Diog. Laert.* 10,123). Das Ersuchen um Aufnahme in die homerische, olympische Götterwelt ist für einen Epikuräer höchst lächerlich. Der redende Gott ironisiert damit deren Scheinexistenz nach der Lehre der Epikuräer. Hinter den homerischen Göttern steht ein göttliches Prinzip, das den Philosophen nach ihrem Tode weiterhin eine Teilhabe gewähren wird, die sich aber der irdischen Beschreibung entzieht (Epikur in *Diog. Laert.* 10,124–126). Die Vergöttlichung der Epikuräer und die Vergöttlichung des Kaiserkults sind äquivoke Begriffe mit gegensätzlichen Vorstellungen.

Ähnlich äquivok ist der Gottesbegriff der Stoiker. Für die pantheistische, stoische Weltseele bedeutet die Kaiserapotheose keinen Vorsprung gegenüber der Vergottung der anderen, menschlichen Seelen. Die stoische Vorstellung vom Weltall als Kugel findet sich bei Cicero in ironischer Form.

> „Da sprach Velleius, ganz nach Art der Epikureer, natürlich sehr selbstbewußt, wobei er nichts so sehr fürchtete, wie den Anschein zu erwecken, er hege an irgend etwas einen Zweifel, und er redete so, als sei er gerade aus dem Rat der Götter und den Zwischenwelten Epikurs herabgestiegen: ‚So hört denn keine nichtssagenden und freierfundenen Behauptungen, nichts von einem Gestalter und Baumeister der Welt, Platons Gott aus dem *Timaios*, auch nichts von einer schicksalkündenden alten Frau, der Pronoia der Stoiker, die man lateinisch als *Providentia* (Vorsehung) bezeichnen kann, erst recht nichts davon, daß die Welt selbst, mit Geist und Empfindungen begabt, ein kugelrunder, feuriger und ständig kreisender Gott sei – Phantastereien und Wundermärchen von Philosophen, die nicht vernünftig diskutieren, sondern bloß so daherträumen.“ (*Cic. nat. deor.* 1,18)

Die Spannung zwischen philosophischem Atheismus und kultischer Kaiserideologie ist satirisch zugespitzt. Der philosophische Atheismus entmythologisiert die olympischen Götter zu anthropomorphen Vorstellungen des göttlichen

Kosmos. Der hellenistische und römische Herrscherkult vermehrt dagegen den anthropomorphen Götterhimmel um weitere, lächerliche, echt menschliche Gestalten wie Claudius. Die Götterberatung wird zu einer komödiantischen Senatsversammlung.

Die Nähe einzelner kultischer Gottheiten zum Regierungsstil von Claudius wird ironisch durchgemustert. Saturn macht den Anfang; denn Claudius dehnte die Saturnalien, die gewöhnlich vom 17.–22. Dezember stattfnden, auf das ganze Jahr aus. Die Sklaven übernahmen in diesem Fest die Rolle des Herrn. Da Claudius seinen Freigelassenen die Regierungsgeschäfte überließ, erwies er sich permanent als Saturnalienprinz. Er ist der eigentliche Sklave seiner Freigelassenen und hat nur scheinbar die Herrschaft inne. Die Reform des Claudius, mehrere Kammern für die Verwaltung des Reiches einzurichten und an ihre Spitze Freigelassene einzusetzen, bildet die Basis. Noch heute gehört der Topos vom Staatsführer als Faschingsprinz seiner Verwaltung zum Arsenal des politischen Kabaretts.

Jupiter kommt noch schlechter als Saturn weg; die Götterkritik der Vorsokratiker wirkt nach. Es wird auf den Fall des Silanus, des Verlobten von Octavia, der Tochter des Claudius, angespielt. Agrippina wollte die Ehe ihres Sohnes Nero mit der Stiefschwester Octavia. Daher wurde Silanus des Inzestes mit seiner Schwester beschuldigt und die Verlobung gelöst; Silanus beging am Tag der Heirat von Claudius und Agrippina Selbstmord (*Tac. Ann.* 12,3; *Suet. Claud.* 27.29). Claudius verurteilte aufgrund römischen Rechtes den angeblichen Inzest, der ja vom göttlichen Geschwisterpaar Zeus und Juno vorgelebt wurde, in Ägypten erlaubt und in Athen für Stiefgeschwister gestattet war. Was will Claudius mit seinen altrömischen Rechtsvorstellungen im lockeren, olympischen Götterhimmel? Nun folgt ein grimmiger Seitenhieb. Wie im Götterhimmel weiß Claudius nicht um das Treiben in seinem Schlafzimmer. Während im Olymp ein homerisches Gelächter ausbrach, als Hephaistos seine Gattin Aphrodite mit Ares beim Ehebruch festschmieden konnte (*Hom. Od.* 8,266–366), erzeugten die Liebschaften Agrippinas und ihrer Vorgängerin Messalina Intrigen und Morde. Das Ennius-Zitat (*Enn. Iphigenie frg.* 244) spielt darauf an, daß der ahnungslose Claudius auch im Himmel vergebens nach verbotener Liebe fahnden wird. Die Eitelkeit des Claudius ging soweit, daß er sich wie sein Vorgänger Caligula als Gott anbeten ließ (deum orant), allerdings im Unterschied zu Caligula nicht vom gesamten römischen Reich, sondern nur von den Barbaren im englischen Camulodonum (Colchester). Warum sucht er dann nicht den britannischen Götterhimmel auf? Weil er vom Autor und seiner Gemeinde als Garant der julisch-claudischen Kaiserherrschaft instrumentalisiert und den olympischen Göttern beigesellt werden muß – gegen alle philosophische Kritik. Der übliche Gebetsanruf wird durch den Austausch von Gott und Trottel (μωρός) zum philosophischen Seufzer, der pointiert den Abschluß der Rede bildet. Die Ausrufung von Kaisern als Götter ist eine unvermeidbare Trottelei zur Zähmung von Barbaren und römischen Bürgern. Im Blick auf Römer und Griechen legt später die Rede des vergöttlichten Augustus Kriterien der Auswahl vor (*Sen. Apoc.* 10). Jupiter läßt nach dieser kritischen Rede des unbekannten Gottes den Saal räumen und

Claudius draußen warten. Die Beratung geht weiter. Nach dem Gotte Janus ergreift der altitalische Gott Diespiter das Wort. Diespiter (etymologisch *dies* und *pater*) ist ein altitalischer Gott, der wie seine Mutter, Vica Pota, eine Siegesgöttin, im Kult bedeutungslos geworden war.[23]

> „Als nächster wird um seine Meinung gefragt Diespiter, der Vica Pota Sohn, auch er zum Konsul bestimmt, ein kleiner Winkelbankier: er lebte vom Profit, trieb einen schwunghaften Handel mit Bürgerrechten. An den machte sich Herkules freundlich heran und zupfte ihn am Ohrläppchen. Daher gab er seine Stimme in diesem Wortlaut ab:
> ‚Da der göttliche Claudius in Blutsverwandtschaft steht mit dem göttlichen Augustus und nicht minder mit der göttlichen Augusta, seiner Frau Großmutter, die er selber machen ließ zu einer Göttin, und da er alle Menschen weit übertrifft an Gescheitheit, und da es auch im Interesse des Staates liegen möchte, wenn einer da ist, der mit Romulus könnte ‚glühheiße Rüben verschlucken', so stelle ich den Antrag, der selige Claudius möchte vom heutigen Tage an ein Gott sein so gut wie jemand, der es vor ihm mit schönstem Recht wurde, und die Verfügung möchte eingetragen werden in Ovids Metamorphosen.'"
> (*Sen. Apoc.* 9,4–5)

Aufbau und Stil des Antrags sind von niederem, komödiantischem Stil. Die trockene Kanzleisprache ungewandter Rhetoren in Rechtssachen (*nummulariolus* = „Winkeladvokat") wird imitiert. Der Handel mit Bürgerrechten (*civitatula*) spielt auf die umstrittene Politik des Claudius an, mit der großzügigen Verleihung des Bürgerrechts die unterworfenen Peregrinen an die Stadt Rom und an das Kaiserhaus zu binden (*Sen. Apoc.* 3.3). Der Antrag hängt vier Begründungen unvermittelt aneinander: (1) Claudius ist blutsverwandt (*sanguine*) mit Augustus und Livia. (2) Seine Weisheit (*sapientia*) übertrifft alle Sterblichen. (3) Er lebt altitalischen Stil. (4) Er ist nach Verfahrensrecht (*optimo iure*) zum Gott vorgesehen. Da als Archiv der Apotheosen die *Metamorphosen* des Ovid fungieren, soll Claudius hinzugefügt werden, und zwar zu Hercules, Aeneas, von dem Julius Caesar sich ableitet, Romulus, Aesculap, Caesar, Augustus (*Ov. Met.* 10; 14; 15).

Von den vier Begründungen gehören drei in der Tat dem Apotheose-Ritual an:

(1) Die Zugehörigkeit zur Caesarfamilie, die sich von Venus herleitet; die Vergöttlichung von Aeneas, dem Sohn der Venus und des Anchises, von Caesar, Augustus und Livia verstärkt die göttliche Ahnenreihe.

(2) Die überragende Weisheit; der Senat mußte überprüfen, ob der Kaiser *sapientia* gezeigt hat; für Caligula entfiel offenkundig dieses Kriterium (*Sen. de ira 3,18,3–19,5*).

(3) Die altitalische Lebensweise nach Sitten der Väter (*mores maiorum*); Augustus restaurierte altitalische Gottheiten (Janus), Kulte und Bräuche;[24] Claudius schrieb eine tyrrhenische (= etruskische) Geschichte (*Suet. Claud.* 41–42); doch diese Restaurationsbemühungen gehören nicht zum Apotheose-Ritual.

(4) Der offizielle Senatsbeschluß der *consecratio*; der Senat hatte Claudius konsekriert; die Götter hatten die Konsekrierungen von Caesar und Augustus ausdrücklich durch Zeichen bestätigt.

23. Bauer 1981, 59.
24. Zanker 1987, 107–171.

Diespiter hat mit seinem hölzernen Antrag zunächst Erfolg. Da erhebt sich der göttliche Augustus und spricht gegen die Vergöttlichung seines Großneffen und Stiefenkels (*Sen. Apoc.* 10–11). Er nimmt Begründung (2), die *sapientia* des Claudius, aufs Korn und hält ihm ausführlich die Mordtaten vor, die von seinen Frauen ausgingen. Der Stil der Rede entspricht der Exempelreihe zu Caligula (*Sen. de ira* 3,18,3–19,5).

Hinzu kommt als neues Gegenargument die körperliche Mißgestalt und Stimmschwäche des Claudius. Dieses Argument gehört nicht zur *consecratio*, kann aber eine selbstverständliche Vorbedingung darstellen. Hier versäumt allerdings Seneca, zu erklären, weshalb ausgerechnet das sportlich trainierte Militär den unsportlichen Claudius zum Kaiser erhob. Seine *sapientia* zählte eben doch mehr als seine gebrechliche Gestalt. Nero stützte sich später bei der Rechtssprechung sogar auf die *commentarii „patris sui"* (*Tac. Ann.* 13,43). Mit seiner jugendlichen Gestalt und Stimmbegabung vermag Nero allerdings seinen Adoptiv-Vater Claudius und seinen jüngeren Stiefbruder Britannicus zu übertreffen. Satirische und staatspolitische Einschätzung der Weisheit des Claudius verlaufen mit Absicht getrennt. So erhält nur in der Satire der Antrag des Augustus auf Ausweisung des Claudius die Zustimmung aller Götter. Staatspolitisch wird die Apotheose nicht rückgängig gemacht.

Während in der Apocolocyntosis die Beschreibung der Rituale zwischen den Göttern fehlt, weil dieses Stück in den Handschriften verloren gegangen ist, lassen sich diese Informationen aus Homer und aus den satirischen Göttergesprächen Lukians holen. Nero selbst inszeniert nach seiner Rückkehr von den olympischen Spielen seine eigene Apotheose.

> „(1) Als der Kaiser nun in Rom einzog [68 n.Chr.] wurde ein Stück der Mauer niedergerissen und ein Teil der Tore ringsum eingebrochen; einige erklärten nämlich, beides sei so Sitte, wenn Wettkämpfer siegreich zurückkehrten. (2) Zuerst betraten Männer die Stadt, welche die von Nero gewonnenen Kränze trugen; ihnen folgten andere mit Holztafeln oben an den Speeren, darauf der Name des Spieles, die Art des Wettkampfes und die Angabe standen, daß Nero Caesar als erster aller Römer von Weltbeginn an diesen Sieg errungen habe. (3) Dann kam der Sieger selbst auf einem Triumphwagen, und zwar auf dem, den Augustus einstmals zur Feier seiner zahlreichen Siege benutzt hatte. Der Herrscher trug ein Purpurkleid mit Goldstickereien und auf dem Haupte einen Olivenkranz, während er in der Hand den pythischen Lorbeer hielt. Ihm zur Seite im Wagen fuhr der Leierspieler Diodoros. (4) Nachdem der Kaiser so, begleitet von den Soldaten, den Rittern und Senatoren, durch den Zirkus und über das Forum gezogen war, stieg er zum Kapitol empor und begab sich von dort in seinen Palast. Die ganze Stadt aber war mit Girlanden geschmückt, (5) während die gesamte Bevölkerung und besonders laut gerade die Senatoren im Chore riefen: ‚Heil dir, Olympiasieger, heil pythischer Sieger! Augustus! Augustus! Heil Nero, unserem Hercules! Heil Nero, unserem Apollo! Der einzige Sieger der Großen Tour! Der einzig Eine vom Beginn der Zeit! Augustus! Augustus! Göttliche Stimme! (6) Selig, welche dich hören dürfen!' Warum soll ich Umschreibungen gebrauchen und nicht die Worte, wie sie tatsächlich gesprochen wurden, wiedergeben? Die verwendeten Ausdrücke bringen doch meinem Geschichtswerk keine Schande! Im Gegenteil, daß ich nichts davon unterdrückte, verleiht ihm noch besonderen Schmuck." (*Dio Cass.* 63,20)

Mit Triumphzug und Seligpreisungen setzt Nero selbstvergessen die Satire Apocolocyntosis in die Realität um. Seneca fuhr mit der Apocolocyntosis eine dialektische Doppelstrategie. Zum einen unterstützte er Agrippina, ihren ermordeten Gatten vom Senat zum Gott erklären zu lassen und verfaßte für Nero die Grabrede (*laudatio funebris*) auf Claudius und die programmatische Antrittsrede vor dem Senat (*Tac. Ann.* 13, 3–4). Zum anderen entwertete Seneca die Apotheose durch seine anonym herausgebrachte Satire. In der Linie der Herrscherkritik ab Platon sollten die Gebildeten vor einer Mythisierung des Herrscheramtes gewarnt werden; nur die sorgfältige Ausbildung der Redner-, Philosophen- und Künstlerqualifikationen befähigt den Angehörigen eines divinisierten Hauses zum Herrscheramt. Auch die körperliche Statur, die sportliche Tüchtigkeit und die Ausbildung der Stimme gehören zu den notwendigen Fähigkeiten. Hinzutreten muß die Fähigkeit zur Herrschaft über das eigene Haus: über Frauen, Kinder und Freigelassene. Die größte Erbitterung zeigt Seneca darüber, daß Claudius sich von seinen Frauen und Freigelassenen hat regieren lassen; deshalb muß er in der Unterwelt zum Sklaven eines Freigelassenen werden (15,2).

Wie in den ntl. Haustafeln gehört die Führung des eigenen Hauses zur Basisqualifikation eines Mannes, der ein öffentliches Amt ausübt (Kol. 3, 18–4,1; Eph. 5, 22–6,9; 1 Petr. 2, 18–3,12; 2 Tim. 2,8 – 15; Tit. 2, 1–9; Sen.ep. 94,1–2).[25]

Wer wie Claudius diese Leistung nicht zu erbringen vermag, muß auf ein öffentliches Amt verzichten. Als Nero an dieser Aufgabe ebenfalls versagte, war die Erziehungsarbeit von Seneca gescheitert. Seine Lese-Tragödie zur Ermordung von Octavia (†62), der Tochter des Claudius und Frau des Nero, gibt deutlich die Resignation von Seneca zu erkennen. Auch wenn diese Tragödie Seneca abgesprochen wird, muß sie dem Kreis um Seneca zugeschrieben werden, so daß sie die Stimmung dieser Endphase der neronischen Herrschaft zutreffend wiedergibt.[26] Andererseits war die Apotheose des verstorbenen Herrschers unerläßlich, um das Leitungsamt der Caesar-Familie unanfechtbar zu machen und Bürgerkriege zwischen den mächtigen Familien oder Heerführern zu vermeiden. Der Mythos der Apotheose wurde instrumentalisiert zur Sicherung der zentralen Militärdiktatur des Julisch-Claudischen Kaiserhauses. Senecas Absicht war vermutlich, daß der Senat eine Kontrolle über den Apotheose-Mythos erhalten sollte. Er sollte innerhalb dieses Hauses nur den zum neuen Caesar und Augustus ausrufen, der der Idealvorstellung eines Herrschers am nahesten kam. Der Senat gebrauchte auch nach Senecas Selbstmord dieses Instrument, und zwar radikaler, als von Seneca angedacht. Der Senat verurteilte Nero zum Tode, erzwang seinen Selbstmord und wählte mit Galba einen Heerführer außerhalb der Caesar-Familie zum neuen Prinzeps.

Die erneute Adoption in die Caesar-Familie, die Galba und seine Nachfolger vornahmen, übertrug die Apotheose wieder auf die regierenden Prinzipes. Die Doppelfunktion der Apotheose blieb bis zur Christianisierung der Prinzipes erhalten. Der regierende Kaiser erhielt Göttlichkeit auf Vorschuß. Diese konnte ihm jederzeit vom Senat aberkannt werden. So erwies sich die Doppelstrategie Senecas als überaus erfolgreich. Mit ihr konnte auch das NT in Konkurrenz

25. Dazu Dormeyer 1993, 138–39.
26. Fuhrmann 1999, 342.

treten, da die Apotheose-Instrumentalisierung im Osten intensiver als im Westen betrieben wurde und dort außerdem die griechische Herrscherkritik bekannt war.[27] Der Kaiser ist Imperiumträger von Schwert und Steuern (Röm. 13,1–7; Mk. 12,13–17 parr.; Joh. 19,11); doch er muß diese Aufgaben im Dienst an den Untergebenen ausüben (Mk. 10, 41–45 parr.).[28] Versagt er, muß er sich vor der Nachwelt und vor dem auferweckten Menschensohn verantworten (Mk. 13,33–37; Offb. 19,11–21).

Die Apocolocyntosis bildet gemeinsam mit dem Satyricon einen Meilenstein der Herrschaftslegitimation und -kritik, ohne den die kritischen, z. T. satirischen Herrscherbiographien des 2.–4. Jh. nicht denkbar wären (*Sueton, Caes.*; *Lukian, dial. mort.*; *Historia Augusta*).

3. *Die Himmelfahrt Lk. 24,50–53; Apg. 1,9–11*

Das erste Buch des „Lukas", das Lukasevangelium, schließt mit einer Himmelfahrtserzählung im Stile atl. und altrömischer Biographien. Der Prophet Elija wird vor den Augen seines Schülers Elischa im Wirbelsturm zum Himmel getragen (2 Kön. 2,1–14), Romulus „verschwand unerwartet" und „erschien" einem vertrauenswürdigen Zeugen, dem er seinen letzten Auftrag für das römische Volk übergab (Plut. Rom. 27–28). Entsprechend erschien der Auferstandene seinen Jüngern, gab ihnen Aufträge für Jerusalem und die Völker, entfernte sich von ihnen beim abschließenden Segnen und wurde in den Himmel hinaufgehoben (Lk. 24,50–53). Der Vorgang der Himmelfahrt wird wie bei Romulus nicht beschrieben. Der Auferstandene entfernt sich und wird durch die Aufnahme in die himmlische Welt unsichtbar.

Im Prolog des zweiten Buches (Apg. 1,1–14) erzählt der Evangelist diese Himmelsaufnahmegeschichte noch einmal, nun aber im komödiantischen Ton.[29] Das Ritual der Kaiserapotheose wird nachgeahmt und karikiert (Apg. 1,9–11). Der Auferstandene gibt Verheißungen, die die Verheißungen in Lk. 24,44–49 präzisieren. Die Verkündigung der Umkehr für Jerusalem und die Völker mithilfe der Gabe aus dem Himmel (Lk. 24,47f.) erhält eine klare geographische Abfolge: „Aber ihr werdet die Kraft des Heiligen Geistes empfangen, der auf euch herabkommen wird; und ihr werdet meine Zeugen sein in Jerusalem und in ganz Judäa und Samarien und bis an die Grenzen der Erde." (Apg. 1,8). Die geographischen Stationen Jerusalem, Judäa, Samarien und Ökumene gliedert den Aufbau der Apg. Danach sehen die Apostel, daß der Auferstandene emporgehoben wird, eine Wolke ihn aufnimmt und ihren Blicken entzieht (Apg. 1,9). Da die Wolke für die Verklärung des irdischen Jesus das Symbol der Theophanie Gottes war (Lk. 9,34f.), hätten die Apostel voller Glauben den Ölberg verlassen können. Stattdessen starren sie unablässig in den Himmel, als ob ein Zeichen der Kaiserapotheose noch kommen müsse: ein Adler oder ein Komet. Tatsächlich

27. Wischmeier 1999; Fuchs 1964.
28. Dormeyer 1999, 73–85.
29. Dormeyer, 2003, 26–36.

erscheinen plötzlich zwei himmlische Gestalten in weißen Gewändern. Diese geleiten aber nicht den Auferstandenen in den Himmel, sondern machen den Aposteln Vorwürfe. Welches Himmelzeichen erwarten sie? Wollen sie etwa selbst eine Himmelsreise unternehmen, um den Himmel nach dem Auferstandenen zu durchsuchen und einem Triumphzug zu akklamieren? Der Auferstandene ist von ihnen weg in den Himmel aufgenommen, bleibt ihnen dort entzogen, behält dort seine Identität, handelt mit ihnen unsichtbar und manchmal sichtbar weiter und kehrt am Ende der Welt zurück, um die Schöpfung in Vollendung wiederherzustellen (Apg. 1,11.6f.).

Hat der Evangelist die Apocolocyntosis gekannt? Er hat von ihr hören können, und er hat sicherlich andere kaiserkritische Werke gekannt. Die Erklärung Neros zum Staatsfeind durch den Senat (*Suet. Ner. 49*) mußte Phantasien von dessen Hadesfahrt anstelle der Apotheose auslösen. Bereits für Caligula hatte Claudius alle Dekrete für nichtig erklärt (*Suet. Claud. 11*). Nicht nur Seneca, auch Plutarch setzte selbstverständlich die Höllenfahrt von Kaisern voraus, u.a. die andauernde Bestrafung Neros im Hades (*Plut. de sera numinis vindicta 30,567d–f*). Vom Auferstandenen Beweise seiner Apotheose zu erwarten, lag für die lukanische Gemeinde nahe. Die komödiantische Zweiterzählung macht deutlich, daß es diese Beweise nicht geben wird und geben darf. Allein die Lehre und Taten des irdischen Jesus „im ersten Buch" (Apg. 1,1) bilden die Grundlage für den Glauben an die Auferweckung und die herrschaftliche Erhöhung bis zur machtvollen Wiederkunft Jesu Christi. Am Faktum der Erhöhung kann nicht wie bei den römischen Kaisern gezweifelt werden.

Literaturverzeichnis

Bauer, A., *L. Annaeus Seneca, Apocolocyntosis. Die Verkürbissung des Kaisers Claudius* (üb. u. hg.; Stuttgart: Reclam 7676, 1981).

Betz, H.D., Gottmensch II. Griech.-röm. Antike und Urchristentum, *RAC* 12 (1983), S. 234–312.

Bickermann, E., Die römische Kaiserapotheose, *ARW* 27 (1929) 1–34.

Binder, G., *Seneca, Apokolokyntosis* (lat.-dt.; Darmstadt: Wissenschaftliche Buchgesellschaft, 1999).

Bremmer, J.N., *Götter, Mythen und Heiligtümer im antiken Griechenland* (Darmstadt: Wissenschaftliche Buchgesellschaft, 1996).

Burkert, W., *Griechische Religion der archaischen und klassischen Epoche* (Die Religionen der Menschheit; Stuttgart u. a.: Kohlhammer, 1977).

Cineira, D.A., *Die Religionspolitik des Kaisers Claudius und die paulinische Mission* (*HBS* 19; Freiburg u. a.: Herder, 1999).

Dormeyer, D., *Das Neue Testament im Rahmen der antiken Literaturgeschichte. Eine Einführung* (Darmstadt: Wissenschaftliche Buchgesellschaft, 1993).

Dormeyer, D., *Das Markusevangelium als Idealbiographie von Jesus Christus, dem Nazarener* (*SBB* 43; Stuttgart: Katholisches Bibelwerk, 1999).

Dormeyer, D./Galindo, F., *Die Apostelgeschichte. Ein Kommentar für die Praxis* (Stuttgart: Katholisches Bibelwerk, 2003).

Feldmann, L.H., *Flavius Josephus, Judean Antiquities 1–4* (Transl. and a Commentary; Leiden: Brill, 2000).

Fuchs, H., *Der geistige Widerstand gegen Rom in der antiken Welt* (Berlin: de Gruyter, 1938; 2nd edn, 1984).
Fuhrmann, M., *Seneca und Kaiser Nero. Eine Biographie* (Frankfurt: Fischer, 1999).
Habicht, C., *Gottmenschentum und griechische Städte* (Zetemata 14; München: Beck, 1970).
Klauck, H.J., *Die religiöse Umwelt des Urchristentums* (2 Bde; Stuttgart: Kohlhammer, 1995–1996).
Price, S.R.F., *Rituals and Power. The Roman imperial cult in Asia Minor* (Cambridge: Cambridge University Press, 1984).
Roloff, D., *Gottähnlichkeit, Vergöttlichung und Erhöhung zu seligem Leben* (Berlin: de Gruyter, 1970).
Schöne, W., Seneca, *Apocolocyntosis. Die Verkürbissung des Kaisers Claudius* (üb. u. hg.; München: Heimeran, 1957).
Taeger, F., *Charisma. Studien zur Geschichte des antiken Herrscherkultes* (2 Bde.; Stuttgart: Kohlhammer, 1957–1960).
Weinreich, O., *Senecas Apocolocyntosis. Die Satire auf Tod, Himmel- und Höllenfahrt des Kaisers Claudius. Einführung, Analyse und Untersuchung* (üb. v. o. w., Berlin: Weidmann, 1923).
Wischmeier, O., Herrschen als Dienen – Mk 10,41–45, *ZNW* 90 (1999) 28–44.
Zanker, P., *Augustus und die Macht der Bilder* (München: Beck, 1987).

Jesuszeugnisse ausserhalb der Evangelien

Martin Hengel

Wenn wir auf die urchristliche literarische Bezeugung Jesu schauen, so beginnt sie ca. 20 Jahre nach seiner Kreuzigung mit einem Außenseiter und ehemaligen Gegner, *Paulus*, der etwa um 50 seinen ersten, uns bekannten Brief an die neugegründete Gemeinde in Thessalonich schreibt, in dem er von Tod und Auferstehung Jesu und vom rettenden Glauben an diesen Jesus als den Messias, Kyrios und Gottessohn spricht, der vor dem kommenden Zornesgericht Gottes bewahren wird,[1] der ein apokalyptisches *„Wort des Herrn"* über dessen Parusie zitiert und betont, daß der Herr „wie ein Dieb in der Nacht" komme;[2] beides erinnert an apokalyptische Jesusworte bei den Synoptikern und wird wohl auf wirkliche Jesusüberlieferung[3] zurückgehen. In mehreren der echten Paulusbriefe, die im folgenden Jahrzehnt geschrieben werden, finden wir Hinweise auf den Menschen Jesus: in der Erwähnung von Jesu Geburt durch eine (jüdische) Frau, seiner Unterstellung unter das (mosaische) Gesetz (Gal 4,4), in seiner Herkunft aus dem Judentum (Röm 9,5), genauer aus dem Geschlecht Davids (Röm 1,3), des Sohnes Isais (Röm 15,12),[4] in seinem messianischen Dienst gegenüber Israel, dem eigenen Volk (Röm 9,3ff.; 15,8),[5] und vor allem in seinem Tod am Kreuz. D. h., Paulus weiß, daß Jesus vom römischen Statthalter in Jerusalem hingerichtet wurde.[6] In 1 Kor wird zweimal auf autoritative Worte des Kyrios, d. h. Aussprüche Jesu, verwiesen. Einmal handelt es sich um das Verbot der Ehescheidung und Wiederverheiratung nach der Scheidung[7] und zum anderen um das Gebot, daß die Verkündiger des Evangeliums von ihrer Verkündigungsarbeit auch leben sollen, das mit der synoptischen Tradition von der Aussendung der

1. 1 Thess 4,14 vgl. 5,10; 1,10. Zum Thema Jesustradition bei Paulus s. R. Riesner, Paulus und die Jesus-Überlieferung, in: *Evangelium – Schriftauslegung – Kirche* (Festschrift Peter Stuhlmacher zum 65. Geburtstag, hg. v. J. Ådna et alii; Göttingen: Vandenhoeck & Ruprecht, 1997), S. 347–65; F. Siegert, Jésus et Paul. Une relation contestée in D. Marguerat (Hg.), *Jésus de Nazareth* (Génève: Labor et fides, 1998), S. 439–57; D. Wenham, *Paulus. Jünger Jesu oder Begründer des Christentums?* (Paderborn: Schöningh, 1999).

2. 1 Thess 4,15–17; 5,2 vgl. Lk 12,39; Mt 24,30 parr.; 24,43; Apk 3,3; 16,15. Zu den „Worten des Herrn" s. M. Hengel, *The Four Gospels and the One Gospel of Jesus Christ* (London: SCM, 2000), S. 61–65.131ff.

3. S. dazu M. Hengel, *Paulus und Jakobus, Kleine Schriften III* (WUNT 141; Tübingen: Mohr-Siebeck, 2002), S. 346ff.

4. Vgl. Jes 11,10; Mt 1,5f.; Lk 3,32.

5. Vgl. Mk 10,45 = Mt 20,28; vgl. Lk 22,27; Jes 8,17; 53,10ff.

6. 1 Kor 1,17f.23; 2,2; Gal 3,1 etc.; s. dazu M. Hengel, *Crucifixion* (London: SCM, 1977).

7. 1 Kor 7,11.

zwölf Jünger zusammenhängt.[8] Bloße Anspielungen auf Logien der synoptischen Überlieferung ohne den Hinweis darauf, daß es sich um ein „Wort des Herrn" handelt, finden sich noch sehr viel häufiger, u.a. etwa mehrfach in der Paränese Röm 12,9–21; 13,8ff. oder 1 Kor 13,2. Grundlegend ist für Paulus auch die aramäische Anrufung Gottes als „lieber Vater", Ἀββᾶ, als Zeichen der Gotteskindschaft, die auf die Gebetsanrede Jesu zurückgeht und eine Abbreviatur des Vaterunsers darstellen könnte. Sie ist Paulus so wichtig, daß er das aramäische Wort seinen griechischen Missionsgemeinden vermittelt, wo es als Gebetsruf Zeichen für die Wirksamkeit von Gottes Geist wird.[9] Daß Paulus bei seiner Gemeindegründung die Passionsgeschichte *erzählte* und in seinen Gemeinden ihre detaillierte Kenntnis ganz selbstverständlich voraussetzt, ergibt sich aus 1 Kor 15,3–8 mit der „chronologischen" Aufzählung von Tod, Begräbnis, Auferstehung und den Erscheinungen Jesu in zeitlicher[10] Folge sowie aus der knappen Anspielung auf ein solches Wissen im Bericht über das letzte Mahl Jesu mit seinen Jüngern 1 Kor 11,23ff. Paulus spielt mit dem „der Herr Jesus in der Nacht, da er verraten wurde, nahm er das Brot, dankte, brach es und sagte..." nicht nur auf seine Einführung des Herrenmahls[11] bei der Gemeindegründung in Korinth an, sondern zugleich auch auf seine Erzählung der Passionsgeschichte in ihrem zeitlichen, man könnte auch sagen: „historischen" Verlauf. Sie enthielt ein konkretes Datum, sehr wahrscheinlich die Passanacht.[12] Er setzt dies alles bis hin zur Information über den Verrat Jesu in Korinth ganz selbstverständlich voraus.[13] Denn ohne einen solchen Bericht hätte die Gemeinde weder diesen Text, an den er sie erinnern will, noch seine Redewendung vom „Wort vom Kreuz", 1 Kor 1,18, oder eine Formulierung wie 1 Kor 5,7f. verstanden, wo es heißt: „denn unser Passalamm wurde geschlachtet, Christus. Darum laßt uns feiern nicht mit dem Sauerteig..., sondern dem ungesäuerten Teig..." Er erwähnt damit en passant in Korinth bereits Wohlbekanntes, d. h., man wußte dort auch von einer Kreuzigung Jesu in Jerusalem an einem Passafest, anderswo durften ja keine Passalämmer geschlachtet werden. Durch 1 Kor 11,23 und 15,3f. deutete Paulus auf eine „chronologische Kontinuität" im Leben Jesu hin, die über mehr als drei

8. 1 Kor 9,14 vgl. Lk 10,7 = Mt 10,10b: „Der Arbeiter ist seines Lohnes wert."

9. Röm 8,15f.; Gal 4,5f.; zum jesuanischen Ursprung und dem Anfang des Vaterunsers s. Lk 11,2; vgl. Mk 14,36.

10. S.M. Hengel, Das Begräbnis Jesu bei Paulus und die leibliche Auferstehung aus dem Grabe, in: F. Avemarie/H. Lichtenberger (Hgg.), *Auferstehung – Resurrection* (WUNT 135; Tübingen: Mohr-Siebeck, 2001), S. 119–83 u. ders., Das Mahl „in der Nacht, in der Jesus ausgeliefert wurde" 1 Kor 11,23, in: C. Grappe (ed.), *Le Repas de Dieu/Das Mahl Gottes* (WUNT 169; Tübingen: Mohr-Siebeck, 2004).

11. Zur Formulierung 1 Kor 11,20: κυριακὸν δεῖπνον.

12. Vgl. 1 Kor 5,6ff. und Lk 22,8.14f.: Ob er mit 1 Kor 5,5 indirekt auf den Vorgang Lk 22,3; Joh 13,2.27 anspielt? Vgl. auch Lk 22,30 und 1 Kor 6,1.9f. und Lk 22,28–30. Dazu M. Hengel, Mahl (Anm. 10).

13. Das ἐν τῇ νυκτὶ ᾗ παρεδίδετο deutet auf den nächtlichen Verrat des Judas hin. Die „Auslieferung" durch Gott (Röm 4,25; 8,32 vgl. Jes 53,6.12) wird im Hintergrund stehen. Man kann das παρεδίδετο wegen der eindeutigen Zeitangabe kaum auf die ganze Passion beziehen. Die zog sich über den darauffolgenden Tag bis zur „neunten Stunde" hin (Mk 15,33). Das besondere Ärgernis ist „der" Verrat durch den eigenen Jünger.

Tage von der Nacht des Gründonnerstags bis zum Ostermorgen reicht. Vermutlich wurde in der Osternacht in Korinth bereits das Herrenmahl gefeiert.[14] Auch mit den „Machthabern dieses Äons", 1 Kor 2,8, die Christus gekreuzigt haben, weil sie seine göttliche Würde (δόξα) nicht erkannten, sind zunächst einmal die politischen Mächte wie Pilatus und die Hohenpriester gemeint, selbst wenn sie wieder nur Handlanger dämonischer Mächte waren. Das vielgehörte Argument, Paulus habe keine oder nur ganz wenig Jesustradition gekannt, ja gar nicht kennen wollen, weil er daran überhaupt kein Interesse besaß, da er nur das „Kerygma" vom gekreuzigten und auferstandenen Kyrios verkündigt habe, ist irreführend und beruht auf dem bei Theologen beliebten Mißbrauch des argumentum e silentio, denn in seinen wenigen uns erhaltenen, mehr oder weniger zufälligen, durchweg situationsbedingten Briefen mußte er auf Dinge, die in der Gemeinde längst bekannt waren, nicht mehr eingehen. Daß sie uns erhalten sind, grenzt an ein Wunder. Wenn man das Weltende und Weltgericht in nächster Nähe erwartet, bräuchte man eigentlich keine literarisch festgehaltenen Erinnerungen mehr. Hinter den Briefen des Paulus stehen durchweg akute Konflikte. Das gilt selbst für den Römerbrief. Auf welche Weise er seine Gemeinde gegründet hat, erfahren wir aus ihnen bestenfalls in kurzen Randbemerkungen.[15] Der zeitlich geordnete Bericht über Jesu Wirken, seinen Tod und seine Auferstehung gehört in seine uns nahezu völlig unbekannte gemeindegründende Predigt (1 Kor 15,1–8). Es ist unsinnig zu glauben, der Apostel (und die anderen Heidenmissionare) hätte einen gekreuzigten Juden und Staatsverbrecher[16] als Messias, Gottessohn und Weltversöhner verkündigen können, ohne seinen jüdischen und heidnischen Hörern vom Leben, Wirken und Sterben dieses Jesus und von der damit verbundenen Erfüllung der prophetischen Verheißungen[17] zu berichten. Wenn er nach 1 Kor 2,2 in Korinth von „nichts anderem wissen wollte" als von dem gekreuzigten Jesus Christus, so schließt dies den Bericht über Jesu Passion und Tod selbstverständlich mit ein. Es begegnet uns hier wirkliches „Wissen" über den „Messias Jesus" und vor allem um seine Kreuzigung und nicht nur um eine bloße Formel ohne Realitätsbezug.[18] Der λόγος τοῦ σταυροῦ konnte ohne *Erzählung der Passionsgeschichte* überhaupt nicht verständlich verkündigt werden! Ähnliches gilt von dem „Evangelium" in 1 Kor 15,3f., das er als allererstes (ἐν πρώτοις) verkündigt oder besser erzählt hat; denn dieser Text ist – in äußerst verkürzter formelhafter Gestalt – nichts anderes als eine christologisch interpretierende Erzählung von einem Geschehen in Raum und Zeit. In Korinth wie in allen anderen neugegründeten Gemeinden wird man Paulus über diese Vorgänge zwischen der Nacht des „Herrenmahls" und Ostern die Seele aus dem Leib gefragt haben. Zur Predigt des gekreuzigten und auferstandenen Christus, der ja nicht nur eine „mythische, himmlische Gestalt",

14. Vgl. 1 Kor 16,2 in Verbindung mit Apg 20,7: Das κυριακὸν δεῖπνον 1 Kor 11,20 und die κυριακὴ ἡμέρα hängen zusammen.

15. 1 Thess 1,6.9; 2,1f.; 1 Kor 1,16; 2,1–5; Phil 4,15.

16. 1 Kor 2,7; vgl. auch *Tacitus, Ann. 48–51.*

17. 1 Kor 15,3f. vgl. Röm 1,1–4; 9,4f.; 1 Kor 10,1–11; Gal 3,13f. u.a.m.

18. οὐ γὰρ ἔκρινά *τι εἰδέναι* ἐν ὑμῖν εἰ μὴ Ἰησοῦν Χριστὸν καὶ τοῦτον ἐσταυρωμένον.

sondern gerade als der „gekreuzigte Messias", der Χριστὸς ἐσταυρωμένος,[19] eine konkrete menschliche Person war, die einen grausamen und schändlichen, ja abstoßenden Tod erlitt, gehörten auch Aussagen über dessen Person, Wirken und Schicksal. Man sollte Paulus noch keinen Doketismus unterstellen, als habe er die Menschheit Jesu nicht ernst genommen. Dagegen sprechen nicht nur Gal 4,4, sondern auch der Philipperhymnus, der sehr wohl vom Apostel selbst stammen kann. Seine Kreuzestheologie ist notwendigerweise antidoketisch. *2 Kor 5,16* darf man in diesem Zusammenhang nicht mehr zitieren. Hier geht es *nicht* um „Christus nach dem Fleisch" (κατὰ σάρκα) im Sinne des Menschen Jesus,[20] d. h., es handelt sich bei dem κατὰ σάρκα nicht um ein Attribut Christi, sondern darum, daß Paulus einst als Verfolger den gekreuzigten und darum „verfluchten"[21] „Christus auf fleischliche Weise" gekannt, man könnte auch sagen „verkannt" hatte, d. h. um eine *klare adverbielle Bestimmung*.[22] Man wird dies Paulus immer wieder vorgehalten haben, auch in Korinth.[23] Der Tag von Golgotha lag für den Briefschreiber ja nur 25 Jahre zurück. Augenzeugen waren noch in größerer Zahl vorhanden. 1 Kor 15,6 spricht er von einer Erscheinung Jesu vor etwa „500 Brüdern auf einmal, von denen die Mehrzahl bis heute lebt". Paulus hat die führenden Jesusjünger persönlich gekannt. Er nennt mehrfach Kephas/Petrus[24] und Jakobus, Jesu Bruder, und je einmal Johannes, „die Zwölf" und „die Brüder

19. 1 Kor 1,23; 2,2; Gal 3,1. Zum abstoßenden Charakter der Kreuzigung s. M. Hengel, *Crucifixion* (Anm. 6).

20. So Röm 9,5: ἐξ ὧν (d. h. Israel) ὁ Χριστὸς ὁ κατὰ σάρκα; man beachte die Nachstellung. Auch Röm 1,3 (γενομένου ἐκ σπέρματος Δαυὶδ κατὰ σάρκα) ist eine positive Aussage, ebenso Röm 4,1 zu Abraham. Beide Sätze Röm 9,5 und 1,3 sind für ihn nicht bedeutungslos!

21. Gal 3,13 und Dtn 27,26.

22. Εἰ καὶ *ἐγνώκαμεν* κατὰ σάρκα Χριστόν... Selbst R. Bultmann, *Theologie des Neuen Testaments* (Tübingen: Mohr-Siebeck, 9. Aufl., 1984), S. 239 gibt zu, daß die adverbielle Bedeutung „wahrscheinlicher" sei, verwischt dann aber diese klare Bedeutung durch eine unsinnige Umkehrung: „denn ein κατὰ σάρκα gekannter Christus ist eben ein Χριστὸς κατὰ σάρκα." S. schon ders., in: *Glauben und Verstehen I.* (Tübingen: Mohr-Siebeck, 1933), S. 185.259: „Der alte Streit, ob ‚dem Fleische nach' zu ‚Christus' oder zu ‚wen wir gekannt haben' gehört, ist gleichgültig." Hier wird ein Text dem eigenen dogmatischen Vorurteil gefügig gemacht. Paulus meint in diesem Zusammenhang gerade nicht eine „menschliche Persönlichkeit", die „vergangen ist", sondern ein zutiefst *sündiges* Erkennen Jesu, das am κατὰ σάρκα Gekreuzigten Anstoß nimmt. Jesus wurde ja nicht aus einem Menschen in einen Gott verwandelt. Er ist schon für Paulus der *menschgewordene* präexistente Gottessohn (Gal 4,4; 1 Kor 8,6; Phil 2,6ff.); wie könnte da das Menschsein Jesu für ihn gleichgültig sein! Dazu M. Hengel, *Kleine Schriften III* (Anm. 3), S. 261–301. Hier zeigt sich das christologische Defizit Bultmanns. P. Althaus, *Das sogenannte Kerygma und der historische Jesus* (BFCT 48; Gütersloh: Mohn, 1963), S. 20 weist diesen Mißbrauch von 2 Kor 5,16 mit Recht zurück. Zum adverbiellen Gebrauch von κατὰ σάρκα in 2 Kor S. 1,17; 10,2. Selbst G. Theissen/A. Merz, *Der historische Jesus* (Göttingen: Vandenhoeck & Ruprecht, 2. Aufl., 1997), S. 100 wollen in 2 Kor 5,16 eine Abwertung des Rückgriffs auf den historischen Jesus sehen: Diese schwerwiegende Fehlinterpretation ist offenbar nicht auszurotten. S. dazu den grundlegenden Aufsatz von O. Betz in: *Aufsätze zur biblischen Theologie, Bd. 2: Jesus, der Herr der Kirche* (WUNT 52; Tübingen: Mohr-Siebeck, 1990), S. 114–28.

23. Vgl. 1 Kor 15,9f. und 9,2.

24. Beide Namen, der aramäische und der griechische, sind ihm bekannt; vgl. Gal 2,7.9. D. h., er wird auch die Umstände der Entstehung dieses Namens gekannt haben. Vielleicht spielt er 1 Kor 3,11 indirekt darauf an.

des Herrn".[25] In Galatien und Korinth wußte man genau, wer diese Leute waren: Paulus selbst muß dort relativ ausführlich davon berichtet haben, sonst hätte es z. B. in Korinth keine „Kephaspartei" gegeben. Vielleicht hat Kephas-Petrus die Gemeinde in Korinth nach ihrer Gründung durch den Heidenapostel besucht und dort einen starken Eindruck hinterlassen.[26] Sollte Paulus dort zwar über Kephas, Jakobus, die anderen Brüder und Jünger Jesu und Apostel Christi in vielfacher Weise geredet, über den Menschen Jesus selbst jedoch beharrlich geschwiegen haben? Das wäre eine absurde Idee.

Man kann natürlich annehmen, daß Kephas-Petrus, der Apostel für die Judenmission und wohl auch zeitweiliger Kontrahent des Paulus, als ehemaliger Sprecher der Jünger Jesu und Augenzeuge in sehr viel reicherem Maße und souveränerer Weise über Jesustradition verfügte, eben darin Paulus überlegen war und daß er, u. a. auch deshalb, von den Gegnern des Apostels in Korinth mehr geschätzt wurde als dieser. Bei der Kephaspartei in Korinth geht es nicht um die Gesetzesfrage, wie F. C. Baur und seine Schule meinten, sondern wohl eher um die Christusbeziehung,[27] bei der die „Kephas-Anhänger" Paulus gegenüber den Jerusalemer Aposteln und hier vor allem gegenüber Kephas-Petrus zurückstellten, weil er gar nicht wirklicher Jünger Jesu und Augenzeuge, sondern zunächst Verfolger gewesen sei. Dennoch hat Paulus auf Jesuserzählung und -überlieferung bei seiner Gemeindegründung *ganz sicher* nicht verzichtet. Er hätte sonst seinen Zuhörern bei der Gründung neuer Gemeinden Jesus als den Gekreuzigten, den am Fluchholz „Gehenkten"[28], der das Verdammungsurteil des Gesetzes beseitigt, überhaupt nicht verkündigen können. *Die Erzählung der Passionsgeschichte ist eine Voraussetzung für seine Theologia crucis.*

Auch die Missionspredigten vor Juden und Heiden in der *Apostelgeschichte* enthalten eine – kompakt-rudimentäre – Erzählung von Wirken, Tod und Auferstehung Jesu eng verbunden mit dem alttestamentlichen Schriftbeweis.[29] Dahinter steht ein Geschehen, das „von Galiläa und der Taufe, die Johannes verkündigte, seinen Ausgang nahm",[30] verbunden mit einem von der Situation

25. 1 Kor 9,5; 15,6f. vgl. Gal 1 und 2.

26. Auf diese Weise würde sich die „Kephaspartei" 1 Kor 1,12 am besten erklären; s. auch Dionysios von Korinth in seinem Brief an Soter von Rom um 170 bei *Euseb, h.e. 2,25,8*: „beide haben in unserer Stadt Korinth die Pflanzung (1 Kor 3,6ff.) begonnen."

27. Vgl. 1 Kor 1,12f.; 2 Kor 10,7; 11,23.

28. Gal 3,13.

29. Da Lk im Evangelium eine ausführliche Darstellung gebracht hatte, konnte er sich in den Kurzpredigten der Apostelgeschichte längere Ausführungen ersparen. Umso erstaunlicher ist es, wie viel er dort über Jesus berichtet. Wahrscheinlich wurde in den Jahrzehnten vor seinem Werk von den Missionaren in ähnlicher Weise gepredigt. Am ausführlichsten kommt dies zum Ausdruck in der Petruspredigt vor Cornelius und seinen Freunden (Cornelius bildet eine Parallele zu Theophilus Lk 1,3) Apg 10,24.36–43; vgl. auch Petrus in Jerusalem zu Pfingsten 2,22f. und 3,13ff.; 4,10; 5,30f.: Bei den Ansprachen vor den Juden wird das Wirken Jesu situationsgemäß als bekannt vorausgesetzt und werden Passion und Auferstehung in den Mittelpunkt gestellt; eine wesentliche Rolle spielt dabei der Schriftbeweis; s. auch den Hinweis auf die Augenzeugenschaft der Jünger 2,32; 4,20. Zu Paulus s. 13,23–31. Der Schwerpunkt liegt dabei auf der Erfüllung der Väterverheißungen und bei der Passion.

30. Apg 10,37f.

her notwendigen Schema, das noch den Aufbau des Mk beherrscht, wo der Schwerpunkt ebenfalls bei der Passion liegt. Die Actareden des Lk sind dabei sicher vom Autor gestaltet, aber nach älteren Vorbildern, wie sie in der Missionspredigt vor Juden und Heiden üblich waren. Man hat hier mit Recht auf das bekannte Geständnis des Thukydides über die Schwierigkeit der exakten Wiedergabe von Reden aus dem Gedächtnis hingewiesen: Er habe sie so formuliert, „wie meiner Meinung nach ein jeder in seiner Lage etwa sprechen müßte",[31] wobei Lk diese „Redeentwürfe" aus Raumgründen noch stark verkürzte. Interessant ist, daß er ganz selbstverständlich in seinen Actareden und -dialogen voraussetzt, daß das Wirken und Schicksal Jesu in Judäa allgemein bekannt war, selbst bei Cornelius und seinem Freundeskreis[32] und bei König Agrippa II.:[33] Diese Ereignisse sind „nicht in einem Winkel geschehen." Er gibt hier die geschichtliche Wirklichkeit zutreffend wieder.

Das eigentliche *Rätsel der paulinischen Predigt*, die wir ja nicht direkt kennen, – Gelegenheitsbriefe, wo alles in äußerster Breviloquenz und in Andeutungen gesagt werden muß, sind etwas ganz anderes als ein jahrzehntelang geübter freier mündlicher Vortrag[34] – ist die Frage, wie es möglich war, daß schon kurze Zeit nach Ostern, als noch zahlreiche Augenzeugen lebten, der gekreuzigte Galiläer Jesus von Nazareth als der zur Rechten Gottes Erhöhte, ja selbst als „gottgleicher"[35] präexistenter Schöpfungsmittler[36] verkündigt werden konnte. Dieser Vorgang ist einzigartig in der antiken Religionsgeschichte. Die zweite Frage ist, ob diese fast explosionsartige Entwicklung der Christologie irgendwelche Anhaltspunkte im Wirken Jesu hat oder ob sie dieser *völlig* widerspricht. Das letztere glaube, wer mag. Wir glauben es nicht.[37]

Die bereits bei Paulus sichtbare Tendenz der gelegentlichen Andeutungen auf wohlbekannte Jesustradition setzt sich in späteren Briefen fort. Der *Hebräerbrief*[38] spielt auf die Verkündigung Jesu und auf seine Hörer, die seine Botschaft „an uns" weitersagten, sowie auf die damit verbundenen Wunder an (2,3f.). Der unbekannte Autor erweist sich damit (wie Mk und Lk) als Angehöriger der zweiten

31. *Hist. 1,22,1.*

32. Apg 10,37: ὑμεῖς οἴδατε τὸ γενόμενον ῥῆμα καθ᾽ ὅλης τῆς ᾽Ιουδαίας.

33. Apg 26,26. Das ἐν γωνίᾳ mochte für Rom gelten, aber nicht für Judäa und Syrien.

34. Ein Beispiel gibt Lk Apg 20,7ff.; vgl. 13,16–41 und 19,9 die Lehrvorträge des Apostels in der von ihm gemieteten Schule des Tyrannos von Ephesus mit der interessanten „novellistischen" Ergänzung von Codex D.

35. Phil 2,6; 1 Kor 8,6; vgl. Kol 1,15.

36. M. Hengel, *Kleine Schriften III* (Anm. 3), S. 262–301.

37. S. dazu M. Hengel/A. M. Schwemer, *Der messianische Anspruch Jesu und die Anfänge der Christologie* (WUNT 138; Tübingen: Mohr-Siebeck, 2002), S. 1–80. Vgl. auch u. Hengel, *Kleine Schriften III* (Anm. 3), S. 240–60.

38. Er ist noch vor dem ersten Clemensbrief, der ihn verwendet, und vor der Paulusbriefsammlung, die ihn aufnimmt, ca. 75–85 n. Chr. (oder aber ca. 60–65 n. Chr., d. h. noch vor der Tempelzerstörung) entstanden. Eine Abfassung vor der Zerstörung Jerusalems halten wir fast für wahrscheinlicher. Der Sammler der Paulusbriefe nahm ihn doch wohl als traditionelles, anerkanntes Schreiben in seine Sammlung auf, vielleicht weil er wußte, daß der Brief von einem Paulusschüler (oder einer Schülerin) stammte. Dies könnte den Wegfall des Präskripts erklären.

Generation. Der Eingangssatz des Briefes, daß Gott, nachdem er einst auf vielfältige Weise durch die Propheten geredet hatte, „am Ende dieser Tage zu uns durch den Sohn geredet habe", schließt selbstverständlich die Verkündigung des irdischen Jesus mit ein. Dasselbe gilt von Hebr 12,2, wo Jesus als „Urheber und Vollender des Glaubens" bezeichnet wird, der „das Kreuz erduldete und die Schande geringachtete". Der *auctor ad Hebraeos* erwähnt auch Jesu tiefe Anfechtung angesichts des bevorstehenden Todes, d. h. die Gethsemaneszene (5,7–9), und seinen Tod außerhalb der Tore Jerusalems (13,12). Auch er hat die Passionsgeschichte gekannt.

Der erste *Clemensbrief* gegen Ende des 1. Jhs., der den Hebräerbrief kennt, beruft sich mehrfach auf Worte des Kyrios, die mit der synoptischen Tradition verwandt sind[39] und die vermutlich aus der katechetisch fixierten mündlichen Gemeindeparänese stammen, aber auch schon die Kenntnis eines schriftlichen Evangeliums, etwa des Mk, voraussetzen können. Der *Jakobusbrief* enthält – ohne Hinweis auf den Ursprung – vielfach paränetische Jesusüberlieferung z. T. in altertümlicher Form,[40] ähnliches gilt von den Briefen des *Ignatius*, der den Bericht über die Taufe Jesu durch Johannes in der Fassung des Mt-Evangeliums kennt, dreimal Pontius Pilatus und einmal den Tetrarchen Herodes (Antipas) erwähnt, um die Annagelung bei der Kreuzigung weiß und eine Auferstehungsgeschichte mit Petrus und den Jüngern erzählt.[41] Wenn 1 Tim 6,13 etwa zeitgleich mit Ignatius von dem „guten Bekenntnis" spricht, das Jesus vor Pontius Pilatus „bezeugt hat", dann spielt er auf Jesu Bekenntnis zu seinem messianischen Auftrag vor dem römischen Präfekten vielleicht schon in der erweiterten Tradition an, die auch hinter dem vierten Evangelium[42] steht. Auffallend ist, daß Ignatius und die Pastoralbriefe den Doppelnamen Pontius Pilatus kennen, den wir nur noch bei Lk 3,2,[43] Apg 4,27 und Mt 27,2 finden, wobei Mt den Namen bei Lk gefunden haben könnte.[44]

Es werden hier in den Briefen des Neuen Testaments, mehr oder weniger zufällig, vor und später auch neben den Evangelien Spuren eines mündlichen Überlieferungsstromes sichtbar, der sich weit bis ins 2. Jh. hinein nachweisen läßt,

39. *1 Clem 13,1–7* vgl. dazu Lk 6,31.36–38; Mt 5,7; 6,12.14; 7,1.12; weiter *Polycarp, Phil 2,3* und *Clem. Alex., strom. 2,91*; 1 Clem 46,7f. vgl. Mk 14,21 und 9,42; Lk 17,1f.; Mt 26,24; 18,6f.; *1 Clem 24,5* vgl. Mk 4,3 parr; S. auch das mit Mk 7,6 (Mt 15,8) verwandte Jesajazitat 29,13 in *1 Clem 24,5*. Vgl. auch M. Hengel, *Gospels* (Anm. 2), S. 129ff.; 285ff.

40. S. z. B.P.J. Hartin, *James and the Q Sayings of Jesus* (JSNT Suppl. Ser. 74; Sheffield: Academic Press, 1991). Zur Datierung M. Hengel, *Kleine Schriften III* (Anm. 3), S. 511–48.

41. *Eph 11,1* = Mt 3,7; *Smyr 1,1* = Mt 3,15; *Po 2,2* = Mt 10,16; *Eph 14,2* = Mt 12,33; Pontius Pilatus: *Mag 11,1*; *Trall 9,1*; Pontius Pilatus, der Tetrarch Herodes (vgl. Lk 3,1; 23,6ff.) und Annagelung *Smyr 1,1f.*; Erscheinung des Auferstandenen: *Smyr 3,1* vgl. Lk 24,39–43 und Apg 1,4; 10,41. Vermutlich kannte er schon wie auch die Pastoralbriefe das lukanische Werk.

42. Joh 18,29–19,19; zum Stichwort μαρτυρεῖν s. 18,37. Dazu H. Stettler, *Die Christologie der Pastoralbriefe* (WUNT II/105; Tübingen: Mohr-Siebeck, 1998), S. 118–22. Aber auch ein Bezug auf Mk 15,2parr. ist möglich.

43. Dort wie bei *Ignatius Smyr 1,1f.* zusammen mit dem Tetrarchen Herodes.

44. Mt kannte wahrscheinlich Lk; s. M. Hengel, *Gospels* (Anm. 2), S. 169–207. Diese Möglichkeit wird völlig übersehen, obwohl ich noch kein wirkliches Argument dagegen gefunden habe. Man ist heute allzu sehr „Q-gläubig" geworden.

sich dabei mehr und mehr mit Traditionen aus schriftlichen Evangelien vermischt und – wie das Werk des Papias um 130 und die „apokryphen" Evangelien, etwa das Thomas- und Petrusevangelium, zeigen – allmählich verwildert.[45]

1. *Außerchristliche Zeugnisse*

Auf Grund der Tatsache, daß das Urchristentum zunächst für die römischen Behörden eine absonderliche jüdische Sekte von Schwärmern aus einer abgelegenen Provinz war, in der man erst allmählich eine Gefahr witterte und deren Texte auf Gebildete eher abstoßend wirkten, ist es verständlich, daß es in den uns erhaltenen jüdischen oder paganen römischen und griechischen Quellen des 1. und 2. Jhs. nur relativ selten und eher am Rande erschien. Man hatte anderes zu berichten. Doch selbst unter dieser Voraussetzung zeigt ein Vergleich zu anderen Persönlichkeiten der antiken Welt, die keine eigenen schriftlichen Zeugnisse hinterlassen haben, daß die Historizität Jesu *erstaunlich gut* bezeugt ist: Wenn seit der radikalen Tendenzkritik des vorigen Jahrhunderts, etwa bei Bruno Bauer und bis hin zu Rudolf Augsteins „Jesus-Menschensohn",[46] immer wieder die Geschichtlichkeit Jesu ganz oder halbherzig bezweifelt wurde, so deutet dies nur auf einen völligen Mangel an historisch-kritischem Denken bei den jeweiligen Verfassern hin. Gerne wird im Streit um Jesus die Behauptung aufgestellt, daß wir ja nur christliche, d. h. durchweg tendenziöse und unzuverlässige Zeugnisse besäßen, und dabei übersehen, daß es in den ersten 150 Jahren Christentum[47] für antike Verhältnisse eine beträchtliche Zahl sehr verschiedenartiger nichtchristlicher Zeugnisse gibt. Auch das Urteil von John Bowden, „that their information could easily be written on a postcard and they do not tell us anything of substantial interest",[48] ist so vielleicht doch etwas zu einseitig.

In seinen ca. 93/4 veröffentlichten Ἰουδαικὴ ἀρχαιολογία, deren 20 Bücher von der Weltschöpfung (Gen 1,1) bis zur Zeit kurz vor Ausbruch des Jüdischen Krieges reichen, erwähnt der jüdische Historiker, ehemalige Jerusalemer Priester und kaiserliche Freigelassene in Rom, *Flavius Josephus,* zweimal die Person Jesu. Im letzten Buch *ant.* 20,200 berichtet er von der Hinrichtung des Jakobus, des „Bruders des sogenannten Christus". Der Hohepriester Hannas II. (Sohn des Hannas der Leidensgeschichte) habe Jakobus zusammen mit einer größeren Zahl von Judenchristen als „Gesetzesbrecher" durch ein von ihm einberufenes „Synhedrium" zum Tod durch Steinigung verurteilen und hinrichten lassen.[49] Mit der neutralen Formel τοῦ λεγομένου Χριστοῦ weist Josephus zurück auf eine frühere Erwähnung im Zusammenhang seiner Darstellung der Wirksamkeit des

45. Dazu M. Hengel, *Gospels* (Anm. 2), S. 57–73, 116–41. Zum Thomasevangelium s. J. Schröter, *Erinnerung an Jesu Worte* (WMANT 76; Neukirchen-Vluyn: Neukirchener, 1997), *passim.*

46. S. M. Hengel, EvKomm 11 (1972), S. 666–70; und zur Neubearbeitung 1999 ders., ThBeitr 32 (2001), S. 158–63. In der Neubearbeitung schwächt A. seine These erheblich ab. Die Absurdität seiner Behauptungen wird dadurch nicht geringer.

47. Von Jesus bis Irenäus ca 30–180 n. Chr.

48. *Jesus. The Unanswered Question* (London: SCM, 1988), S. 34.

49. Nach dem Tod des Prokurators Festus und vor der Anreise seines Nachfolgers Albinus ca. 62 n. Chr.

Pilatus,[50] das *Testimonium Flavianum*, das freilich in der Vergangenheit sehr umstritten war, da man es für eine christliche Fälschung hielt. Heute, nach eingehenden sprachlichen Analysen, neigt man eher dazu, anzunehmen, daß die ursprüngliche feindliche bis distanzierte Charakterisierung Jesu durch Josephus durch einen christlichen Abschreiber mit Hilfe einiger leichter Retuschen in eine positive verwandelt wurde, d. h., daß der wesentliche Bestand echt ist. Man hat mehrfach versucht, durch wenige Änderungen die ursprüngliche Form zu rekonstruieren, so jetzt wieder G. Theissen und A. Merz im Anschluß an W. Bienert und R. Eisler.[51] Die ursprüngliche Form läßt sich zwar nur noch hypothetisch erschließen, für die Ursprünglichkeit einer solchen – überwiegend negativen – Jesusnotiz bei Josephus sprechen jedoch mehrere Argumente: So vor allem, daß der Jesus-Bericht des Josephus[52] sachgemäß eingeordnet auf zwei Berichte von jüdischen Unruhen z. Zt. des Pilatus[53] folgt. Jesus erscheint so als Unruhestifter. Darüber hinaus lassen sich die christlichen „Korrekturen" leicht beseitigen. R. Eisler vermutete, daß man ein ursprünglich negatives σοφιστὴς ἀνήρ in ein σοφὸς ἀνήρ verwandelt und aus einem ἀπηγάγετο, „er verführte", ein positives ἐπηγάγετο gemacht hat. Mit anderen Worten, Josephus habe Jesus so als einen Volksverführer dargestellt, und ein christlicher Abschreiber versuchte, durch kleine Änderungen das negative Bild zu beschönigen. Andere Formulierungen blieben unverändert, so der Hinweis auf seine „außergewöhnlichen Taten" (παράδοξα ἔργα) und seine Tätigkeit als Lehrer (διδάσκαλος ἀνθρώπων), vor allem aber die entscheidende Aussage: „und als auf eine Anzeige unserer Volksführer Pilatus ihn zur Kreuzigung verurteilt hatte, hörten seine früheren Anhänger nicht auf..." Ähnliches gilt von dem Schlußsatz: „Bis heute hat diese nach ihm benannte Sippschaft (τὸ φῦλον) der Christianoi nicht aufgehört zu existieren." Für die Echtheit dieses Grundbestandes spricht auch die Übereinstimmung mit dem sonstigen Stil des Josephus. Daß Josephus nur so wenig über Jesus und die Christen sagt, nimmt nicht Wunder, er schweigt ebenso über den essenischen Lehrer der Gerechtigkeit wie auch über die berühmtesten frühen pharisäischen Lehrer Hillel, Schammai oder Jochanan ben Zakkai.[54]

Etwa um 116/7 beschreibt *Tacitus*[55] mit tiefer Verachtung für ihren „abscheulichen Aberglauben" (*exitiabilis superstitio*) die Verfolgung der „Chrestiani"

50. *Ant.* 18,63f. S. dazu M. Hengel, Paulus und Jakobus, *Kleine Schriften III*, WUNT 141 (2002), S. 551ff.

51. G. Theissen/A. Merz, *Jesus* (Anm. 22), S. 74–82.

52. *Ant.* 18,63.

53. *Ant.* 18,55–62: Die Kaisermedaillons in den Feldzeichen beim Einzug der Kohorten in die Antonia und die Inanspruchnahme des Tempelschatzes für die Wiederherstellung der Wasserversorgung von Jerusalem. Es folgen religiöse Betrügereien von Isispriestern und zwei Juden in Rom (18,65) mit der Kreuzigung der Schuldigen (18,79) und die Unruhen in Samarien, die zur Absetzung des Pilatus führen (18,85–87).

54. Er nennt nur einen führenden Pharisäer Samaias aus der Frühzeit des Herodes *ant.* 14,172–176 und dessen Schüler Pollion 15,3f.370. Auch Gamaliel, der berühmteste Schriftgelehrte im 2. Viertel des 1. Jh.s und Lehrer des Paulus (Apg 22,3; vgl. 5,34), wird nur als Vater seines Sohnes Simeon *bell.* 4,159 und *vita* 190 genannt. Von seiner Bedeutung sagt er kein Wort.

55. *Ann.* 15,44.

durch Nero in Rom 64 n. Chr. Dabei geht er auch auf den Begründer dieses Aberglaubens ein: „Der Urheber der so benannten Sekte, Christus, wurde unter der Herrschaft des Tiberius durch den Prokurator Pontius Pilatus mit dem Tode bestraft, für den Augenblick unterdrückt, brach dieser abscheuliche Aberglaube (s. o.) jedoch wieder hervor, nicht nur in Judäa, dem Ursprungsort dieses Übels, sondern auch in Rom, wo alle abscheulichen Kloaken von überallher zusammenströmen und gefeiert werden."[56] Vermutlich hat Tacitus als römischer Prokonsul unter Trajan (112) in der Provinz Asia die Christen näher kennengelernt und auch Prozesse gegen sie geführt. Er sieht in ihnen „Verbrecher, die die härtesten Strafen verdient haben".[57] Etwa gleichzeitig hat auch sein Freund Plinius in Bithynien/Pontus die dortigen Christen verfolgt. Wie Josephus setzt Tacitus selbstverständlich die Realität der Hinrichtung Jesu voraus, und er weiß, daß sie unter dem Prokurator Pontius Pilatus in Judäa geschah.[58] Leider fehlen in den Annalen nicht nur die Bücher 7–10 über die Zeit vom Tode des Tiberius (16.3. 37 n. Chr.) bis zur Mitte der Regierungszeit des Claudius (bis ca. 47), sondern auch der größte Teil des 5. Buches über die Jahre 29 bis Herbst 31. Es ist durchaus möglich, daß Tacitus darin kurz über den Tod Jesu und vielleicht auch über die Christen berichtet hatte und dieser Bericht so negativ war, daß diese Teile seines Werks nicht überliefert wurden. Nach *Sulpicius Severus*, der die bis auf Buch 1–5 verlorenen Historien ausschreibt, soll Titus im Kriegsrat für die Zerstörung des Tempels eingetreten sein, weil dadurch mit den Juden auch die Christen ausgerottet würden.[59]

Wenige Jahre zuvor, um ca. 110/111, schreibt der *jüngere Plinius* den berühmten *Brief an Trajan*.[60] Er geht nicht weiter auf den Ursprung der Sekte ein, sondern betont nur, daß er bei den Verhören in den Christenprozessen erfahren habe, daß diese an einem bestimmten Tag vor Tagesanbruch zusammenkommen, um Christus, als sei er ein Gott, Hymnen zu singen.[61] Er selbst forderte von den Delinquenten, daß sie den Göttern opferten und diesen Christus verfluchten.[62] In dem Brief wird als selbstverständlich vorausgesetzt, daß der Kaiser weiß, wer dieser Christus war. Die Verfluchung eines gekreuzigten Staatsverbrechers

56. 15,44,3: *auctor nominis eius Christus Tiberio imperitante per procuratorem Pontium Pilatum supplicio adfectus erat; repressaque in praesens exitiabilis superstitio rursum erumpebat, non modo per Iudaeam, originem eius mali, sed per urbem etiam, quo cuncta undique atrocia aut pudenda confluunt celebranturque.*

57. 15,44,5: *sontes et novissima exemplos meritos*. Vgl. A. M. Schwemer in M. Hengel/A. M. Schwemer, *Anspruch* (Anm. 37), S. 134ff.

58. Pilatus hatte noch den Titel *praefectus Iudaeae*, seit Claudius wurden die Statthalter dort *procurator* genannt.

59. *Sulp. Sev., Chronica II* 3,6f. s. dazu M. Stern, *Greek and Latin Authors on Jews and Judaism*, II (Jerusalem: Israel Academy of Sciences and Humanities, 1974), S. 64ff. mit Kommentar. Hier ist die Frage, ob der Hinweis auf die Christen auf Tacitus zurückgeht oder von dem christlichen Autor hinzugefügt wurde. Dies muß durchaus nicht der Fall sein. Die Christen betrachteten ja die Tempelzerstörung später eher als ein Positivum und als Strafe für die Juden.

60. Ep. 10,96.

61. 96,7: *carmenque Christo quasi deo dicere.*

62. 96,5: *maledicerent Christo*; vgl. Bar Kochba bei Justin, *apol.* 31,6.

entsprach der Staatsräson und war zugleich ein untrügliches Zeichen dafür, daß der Delinquent mit diesem „verwerflichen, maßlosen Aberglauben“[63] gebrochen hatte.

Kurze Zeit nach Tacitus erwähnt auch *Sueton*[64] die neronische Verfolgung der Christen, spricht aber nicht über den Begründer „dieses neuen und verfluchten Aberglaubens“[65]; sehr wahrscheinlich erwähnt er ihn jedoch schon vorher in seinem Claudiusbericht: Claudius habe die Juden, die auf Veranlassung eines gewissen Chrestos ständig Unruhen anstifteten, aus Rom vertrieben.[66] Da Christus ein für griechische Ohren unverständlicher Name war,[67] verstanden ihn griechische Hörer wegen des Itazismus, in dem ἦτα als ἰῶτα ausgesprochen wird, im Sinne von „Chrestos“[68], einem beliebten Sklavennamen. Tacitus schreibt deshalb in den *Annalen* 15,44,2 von „Chrestiani“[69]. Auch Tertullian, *apol.* 3,5, bestätigt diese Fehldeutung. Bei der Claudiusnotiz Suetons wird wohl auf Streitigkeiten in den jüdischen Synagogengemeinden in Rom in der Zeit etwa um 47/48 n. Chr. angespielt, die durch das Eindringen der Christusbotschaft verursacht wurden und, wie auch Lk Apg 18,2 andeutet, zur Ausweisung der Unruhestifter führten. Alle diese Nachrichten präsentieren uns zugleich das Grundproblem der Christologie: *Wie konnte* aus einem hingerichteten jüdischen Verbrecher ein Gott werden? Wie kommt es zu diesem „Skandalon“[70] für Juden, Griechen und Römer?

Wesentlich ist in diesem Zusammenhang auch die Tatsache, daß Tacitus, Sueton und Plinius die einzigen uns erhaltenen römischen Historiker bzw. politischen Autoren nach Claudius sind, bei denen wir einen Hinweis auf Christus und die Christen überhaupt erwarten durften. Größere historische Texte zwischen der Spätzeit des Tiberius bzw. Claudius und Trajan, die Jesus und seine Bewegung erwähnen konnten, sind uns nicht erhalten geblieben. An griechischen Texten wäre nur Josephus zu nennen, und er erwähnt Jesus, Jakobus und die Judenchristen. Hier werden ganz falsche Vorwürfe erhoben.

In der Mitte des 2. Jhs. erfahren wir aus der Feder *Lukians* von dem in Palästina gekreuzigten „Sophisten“ und den von ihm gegebenen Gesetzen,[71] während der

63. 96,8: *superstitionem pravam, immodicam.*

64. Nero 16,3.

65. *Superstitio nova ac malefica. Maleficus* kann auch die Bedeutung von magisch haben. Zur Judenpolitik des Claudius und der Ausweisung der Juden(christen) s. R. Riesner, *Die Frühzeit des Apostels Paulus* (WUNT 71; Tübingen: Mohr-Siebeck, 1994), S. 139–80 (142–48 zur Suetonnotiz).

66. *Claud. 25,3* vgl. Apg 18,2; s. dazu ausführlich R. Riesner, op. cit., S. 139–80.

67. Man kannte im Griechischen außerhalb der LXX und verwandter Texte nur das Verbaladjektiv im Sinne von „aufstreichbar, aufgestrichen, gesalbt“ bzw. das Substantiv im Neutrum „Salbe, Aufstreichmittel“. W. Grundmann, ThWNT IX, S. 485; vgl. Liddell/Scott, *Lexicon* 1996, 2007; vgl. S. 1170: νεοχριστός/όν „newly plastered“. Als Bezeichnung einer Person im Sinne von „der Gesalbte“ war es völlig unbekannt.

68. „Der Brave, Brauchbare, Rechtschaffene“.

69. *Ann. 15,44,2*; vielleicht in leichter Ironie: das Volk habe die wegen Verbrechen verhaßten (*propter flagitia invisos*) Chrestiani „Anhänger eines Rechtschaffenen“ genannt.

70. Vgl. 1 Kor 1,23; vgl. Gal 6,12; Phil 3,18f.

71. Lukian, *Peregr.* 11–13.16. Vermutlich spielt er auch bei der Schilderung der Selbsttötung des Peregrinus Proteus in Olympia (167 n. Chr.) auf die Passionsgeschichte an. Peregrinus wird selbst in Palästina und Syrien eine Zeit lang Christ, legt die Bücher der Christen (d. h. wohl vor

Arzt *Galen* mehrfach Moses und Christus als Lehrer nebeneinanderstellt, die beide für ihre Lehren Glauben fordern. Gleichzeitig spricht er mit einem gewissen Respekt von ihrer Todesverachtung und ihrem ethischen Lebenswandel.[72] Hier wie dort begegnen wir Christus als autoritativem Lehrer. Viel zu wenig bedacht ist in der Forschung schließlich der wirkliche oder fiktive jüdische Gewährsmann des *Celsus*[73] in seiner Schrift gegen die Christen um 170, der, wie auch Celsus selbst, nicht nur alle Evangelien kennt,[74] sondern so etwas wie ein jüdisches „Antievangelium" voraussetzt, der von der Verstoßung der Mutter Jesu wegen Ehebruchs mit dem Soldaten Panthera weiß, Jesus als Räuberhauptmann darstellt und von dessen Zauberkünsten berichtet, die er in Ägypten gelernt hat. Die Strafe seines schimpflichen Todes traf ihn als Volksverführer zu Recht; es handelt sich um Überlieferungen, deren erste Spuren bei Mt angedeutet werden[75] und die uns viel später wieder in den Toledot Jeschu begegnen.[76] Bereits diese so verschiedenartigen nichtchristlichen Nachrichtensplitter weisen auf einige wesentliche Grundlinien hin; sie könnten, wenn wir nur sie besäßen, in einer Enzyklopädie wie Pauly-Wissowa mit einigem Recht mehrere Spalten beanspruchen.

Ein weiteres weniger bekanntes, aber auch rätselhaftes Zeugnis ist der syrisch erhaltene Brief des *Mara bar Sarapion*, der freilich kaum vor der zweiten Hälfte des 2. Jhs. angesetzt werden darf, da sich keine frühere syrische Literatur nachweisen läßt.[77] Wenn ihm ein griechischer Text zugrunde läge, könnte er älter sein. Der Verfasser schreibt darin an seinen Sohn, möglicherweise im Zusammenhang mit dem Leiden der Bevölkerung von Samosata bei der Besetzung der Kommagene durch Vespasian 72 n. Chr., und erwähnt die Juden, die Verwüstung und Vertreibung erlitten, weil sie ihren weisen König töteten, so wie die Athener für den Tod des Sokrates bestraft wurden. Sokrates lebe durch Plato weiter und

allem die Evangelien) aus und läßt sich im Gefängnis von ihnen versorgen. Dagegen bezeichnet „Alexander der Lügenprophet" die Christen als ἄθεοι (25.38). Zu Lukian und den folgenden Autoren s. M. Hengel, Die ersten heidnischen Leser der Evangelien, in *Hyperboreus, Studia Classica Petropolitana* 9,1 (FS A. Gavrilov, 2003), S. 89–111.

72. W. den Boers, *Scriptorum paganorum I–IV, Saec. de Christianis Testimonia, Textus Minores II*, Leiden ²1965, 12; R. Walzer, *Galen on Jews and Christians* (Oxford: University Press, 1949); ders., Art. Galenos, *RAC 8*, S. 777–86.

73. Dazu E. Bammel, *Judaica. Kleine Schriften I* (WUNT 37; Tübingen: Mohr-Siebeck, 1986), S. 265–83.

74. Auch der Jude Tryphon hat das Evangelium des Mt (und hier vor allem die Bergpredigt) gelesen, Justin, *dialogus* 10,2, und ist von seinen rigorosen unhaltbaren Forderungen beeindruckt.

75. Mt 2,15; 27,62–66: ἐκεῖνος ὁ πλάνος (62); 28,11–15; vgl. auch Tertullian, *de spectaculis* 30,5f.

76. *Orig., c. Cels.* 1,28–2,79 s. dazu R. Bader, *Der ΑΛΗΘΗΣ ΛΟΓΟΣ des Kelsos* (Stuttgart/Berlin: Kohlhammer, 1940), S. 52–84. W. Horbury, *Jews and Christians in Contact and Controversy*, (Edinburgh: T&T Clark, 1998), S. 162–75. Zu den Toledot Jeschu s. Samuel Krauss, *Das Leben Jesu nach jüdischen Quellen* (Berlin: Calvary, 1902; Nachdruck Hildesheim: Olms, 1977); G. Schlichting, *Ein jüdisches Leben Jesu* (WUNT 24; Tübingen: Mohr-Siebeck, 1982). Zu Celsus und den Christen s. jetzt J. G. Cook, *The Interpretation of the New Testament in Greco-Roman Paganism* (STAC 3; Tübingen: Mohr-Siebeck, 2000), S. 17–102.

77. Sie beginnt erst mit Tatians Diatessaron und Bardesanes; s. A. Baumstark, *Geschichte der syrischen Literatur* (Bonn: Marcus u. Weber, 1922).

„der weise König wegen der neuen Gesetze, die er gegeben hat". Der Brief ist von einem Heiden geschrieben, vermutlich einem Stoiker, der freilich dem Christentum positiv gegenübersteht.[78]

Etwa um 110 n. Chr. hörte der junge *Arrian* den stoischen Philosophen *Epiktet* (ca. 50–130) in Nikopolis in Epirus. Später bringt er dessen Vorträge in die uns vertraute literarische Form. Epiktet erwähnt darin einmal die Christen und ihre Todesverachtung, die freilich die Todesfurcht nicht wie der Philosoph durch die Kraft einer vernunftgemäßen Argumentation überwinden, sondern, darin Verrückten (ὑπὸ μανίας) vergleichbar, „durch Gewohnheit" (ὑπὸ ἔθους). Sonderbarerweise nennt er die Christen „Galiläer", eine Bezeichnung, die – vielleicht von ihm abhängig – erst wieder bei *Julian Apostata* erscheint. Sie kann m. E. nur aus christlichen Quellen, etwa dem Kontakt mit Christen stammen, denn nur sie wußten, daß Jesus und seine Jünger „Galiläer" gewesen waren. Als Bezeichnung für die Christen ist sie vor Julian weder für Griechen noch Juden bezeugt.[79]

Nach dem christlichen Universalgelehrten und Chronographen *Julius Africanus* (ca. 160–240), der Bibliothekar des Kaisers Alexander Severus war, soll ein unbekannter Chronograph des 1. oder 2. Jhs., *Thallos*, in seiner Weltgeschichte die durch ein Wunder bewirkte Finsternis bei der Kreuzigung Jesu auf natürliche Weise als Sonnenfinsternis erklärt haben.[80] *Phlegon von Tralles*, ein an Wundergeschichten interessierter Historiker und Freigelassener Hadrians (117–138 n. Chr.), identifizierte diese Finsternis vermutlich mit der am 24.11.29 n. Chr., d. h. im 15. Jahr des Tiberius, stattgefundenen Eklipse der Sonne. Er scheint nach Origenes auch in konfuser Weise von eingetroffenen Voraussagen Jesu (bzw. von Petrus) berichtet zu haben,[81] während eine Generation später Celsus nur von

78. Cureton, *Spicilegium Syriacum* (London, 1855), 43; Übersetzung bei J. B. Aufheuser, *Antike Jesuszeugnisse* (Bonn: Marcus u. Weber, 2 Aufl., 1925); Theissen/Merz, *Jesus* (Anm. 22), S. 84–86, die den Brief zu früh ansetzen. Die Vertreibung der Juden aus ihrer Heimat könnte auch zugleich auf die Folgen des Bar-Kochba-Aufstandes 132–136 hinweisen, die „neuen Gesetze" auf Mt und die Apologeten. Mit Recht heben G. Theissen/A. Merz eine „deutliche *Außenperspektive* in der Bewertung Jesu und des Christentums" hervor (S. 85).

79. *Diss. 4,7,6* s. dazu M. Hengel, *Leser* (Anm. 71). Zur μανία der Christen vgl. Justin, *apol.* I,13,4 und die Vorwürfe der *amentia* bei *Plinius d. J.* 10,96,4 und der ψιλὴ παράταθις *Mark Aurel* 11,32. Zu den „Galiläern" s. Mk 14,70 = Lk 22,59 = Mt 26,69; vgl. Lk 23,6; Mt 26,71; Apg 1,11; 2,7. Die Bezeichnung geht auf die Kenntnis der Evangelien zurück.

80. Jacoby *FGrHist* 256F 1 = A.A. Mosshammer (Hg.), *Georgii Syncelli Ecloga chronographica* (BT; Leipzig: Teubner, 1984), S. 391. Seine Identifizierung mit einem samaritanischen Freigelassenen des Tiberius beruht auf einer Konjektur des Josephus, *ant.* 18,167 und ist sehr fraglich (conj. Hudson Θάλλος statt ἄλλος Σαμαρεύς; dazu H. Windisch, *ThR 1 NF* [1929], S. 285ff.); Theissen/Merz, *Jesus* (Anm. 22), S. 91. Kritisch dazu Jacoby im Kommentar und M. Hengel, *Leser* (o. Anm. 71); die Sonnenfinsternis sei nach Origenes, *c. Cels.* 2,33.59 und anderen s. *FGrHist* 257F 16 auch von Phlegon berichtet worden.

81. *C. Cels. 2,14* = *FGrHist* 257F 16d: „im 13. oder 14. Buch der Chroniken … gestand er Christus das Vorauswissen (πρόγνωσιν) über gewisse zukünftige Ereignisse zu; er brachte freilich Dinge, die Petrus betrafen, mit solchen, die sich auf Christus beziehen, durcheinander (συγχυθείς) er bezeugt aber, daß das von Jesus gesagte Wort wörtlich eingetroffen sei." Es könnte hier der früheste Hinweis eines heidnischen Autors auf einen Evangelientext vorliegen, vgl. Mk 8,31ff.; 14,29f.; Joh 13,36ff.; 21,18ff. Nach Photius *bibl. 97,1–5* = *FGrHist* T3 war er ein sehr

den „Wundern“ Jesu erzählt und diese dessen magischen Künsten zuschreibt. Phlegon könnte so der erste Heide sein, bei dem wir annehmen dürfen, daß er eine oberflächliche Kenntnis von Aussagen der Evangelien besaß. Auch sein Zeitgenosse, der berühmte Rhetor *M. Cornelius Fronto*, der Erzieher Mark Aurels, erging sich in einer schriftlich verbreiteten oratio in scheußlichen Anklagen gegen die Christen und hat dabei wohl auch deren Stifter eingeschlossen. U. a. warf er ihnen nächtliche Ausschweifungen und Kannibalismus vor.[82]

Eine ganz andere Gattung sind die relativ zahlreichen – im einzelnen freilich nicht unumstrittenen, z. T. verzerrten – *talmudischen Jesuszeugnisse*, deren älteste Traditionen ebenfalls bis in das Ende des 1. bzw. Anfang des 2. Jhs. zurückgehen können.[83] Sie sind verständlicherweise schroff antichristlich. Jesus erscheint hier als eine „Unperson“, deren Namen man gerne umschreibt: er sei der illegitime Sohn Marias, sein Vater sei ein gewisser Panthera gewesen. Nach einer alten Tradition (Baraita) aus dem babylonischen Talmud[84] „wurde Jesus, der *Nôsri*,[85] am Vorabend des Passafestes aufgehängt, ...weil er Zauberei getrieben, Israel verleitet und abtrünnig gemacht hat“. Auch fünf Jünger Jesu, Matthai, Naqaj, Neser, Buni und Thoda, seien hingerichtet worden. Der berühmte und eigenwillige frührabbinische Lehrer Eliezer ben Hyrkanos wurde etwa um 90 n. Chr. von der römischen Behörde angeklagt, er sei Judenchrist, da er früher positive Kontakte zu Judenchristen, besonders einem Jakob aus Sichnin besaß[86] und u. a. eine sonderbare Gesetzesauslegung des Jesus ben Panthera positiv beurteilt habe.[87] Aus etwas späterer Zeit, um 100 n. Chr., stammt die Nachricht, daß

mittelmäßiger Autor, der vor allem an sensationellen Orakeln interessiert war. In seinem Milieu konnten auch die Evangelien Aufmerksamkeit erregen. Möglicherweise hat er über die Passion Jesu oder das Martyrium des Petrus berichtet. U. a. verfaßte er eine Sammlung von „Wundergeschichten“; s. die neue Textausgabe mit Übersetzung von K. Brodersen (TZF; Darmstadt: Wissenschaftliche Buchgesellschaft, 2002).

82. Minucius Felix, *Oct.* 31,2; 9,6 (Fronto wurde etwa zwischen 100 und 110 im afrikanischen Cirta geboren). Zur selben Zeit traten die ersten christlichen Religionsphilosophen und Apologeten auf und bezeugten das Interesse einzelner Gebildeter für die neue Religion. Die Streitschrift des Celsus ist wohl eine Antwort auf dieselben.

83. H. Strack, *Jesus, die Häretiker und die Christen nach den ältesten jüdischen Angaben*. J. Klausner, *Jesus von Nazareth. Seine Zeit, sein Leben und seine Lehre* (SIJB 37; Leipzig: Hinrich, 1910) (orig. hebr. 1922; Berlin: Jüdischer Verl., 1930; Jerusalem: Jewish Publ. House, 3 erw. Aufl., 1952), S. 17–66. Dagegen urteilt J. Maier, *Jesus von Nazareth in der talmudischen Überlieferung* (ETF 82; Darmstadt: Wissenschaftliche Buchgesellschaft, 1978) extrem negativ apologetisch und ohne wirkliches historisches Verständnis für diese eigenartigen Texte.

84. *bSanh 43a*; Strack 18* §1a) und 43f* §13. Zum Namen Panthera s. auch zu Celsus.

85. *Nosrîm* war die gängige jüdische Bezeichnung für die Christen, abgeleitet von dem Herkunftsort Jesu, Nazareth. H. H. Schaeder, *ThWNT* 4, S. 879–84.

86. J. Klausner, *Jesus*, 48f. vermutet hier (zu Unrecht) den Herrenbruder Jakobus; doch könnte es sich um einen späteren Herrenverwandten handeln. Hegesipp nennt einen Jakobus als Großneffen Jesu und Enkel des Jesusbruders Judas (nach einem Fragment aus der Kirchengeschichte des Philippus von Side, Text bei E. Preuschen, *Antilegomena* (Gießen: Töpelmann, 1905, S. 111 Z. 17), der wegen seines Zeugnisses vor Domitian zusammen mit seinem Bruder Zoker bei den Judenchristen in Galiläa hoch angesehen war.

87. Vgl. *jShab* 14,4; Strack 45* §15. Die Jesus-Halacha leitet dieser Jakob mit der Formel ein:

ein berühmter Rabbi seinen Neffen, der von einer Schlange gebissen war, lieber sterben lassen wollte, als daß er duldete, daß ein (anderer?) charismatischer Judenchrist, Jakob aus Kefar Sama, den man schon gerufen hatte, den Verletzten im Namen „*Jeshû'a ben Pantera*" heile.[88] Die – klügere – Frau des Eliezer ben Hyrkanos, Imma Shalom, die Schwester R. Gamaliels II., der zwischen 90 und 110 die höchste schriftgelehrte Autorität und Haupt des Lehrhauses von Jabne war, soll zusammen mit ihrem Bruder einen (judenchristlichen) „Philosophen", der sich auf Mt 5,17 berief, der Bestechlichkeit überführt haben.[89] Diese Erzählungen mögen legendären Charakter haben, sie geben uns jedoch – trotz der grundlegenden Feindschaft – einen Einblick in das zunächst noch ambivalente Verhältnis früher tannaitischer Lehrer zum frühen Judenchristentum und zu Jesus selbst.

Diese extrem verschiedenartigen, durchaus zufälligen, ganz überwiegend polemischen, ja z. T. extrem christenfeindlichen außerchristlichen Nachrichten über Jesus und das früheste Christentum *machen an sich schon die Historizität Jesu völlig gewiß*. Er erscheint als äußerst umstrittener jüdischer Lehrer, der von Pontius Pilatus wegen Verbrechen gegen den römischen Staat bzw. als falscher Prophet und Verführer hingerichtet wurde, eine allseits bekannte gemeingefährliche Sekte begründete und von seinen Anhängern zum Gott erhoben wurde. Die bis heute nicht verstummende Polemik, bei der ganzen Jesusüberlieferung handle es sich um eine Fälschung früher christlicher Kreise, scheitert schon an der Vielfältigkeit dieser nichtchristlichen Traditionen über Jesus, die ursprünglich sehr viel reicher waren, aber weitgehend verlorengingen, weil man diese polemischen Zeugnisse auf christlicher Seite natürlich nicht bewahrte. Dies gilt z. B. für die kaiserlichen Erlasse gegen Christen[90] außer dem Trajanedikt, das durch den Briefwechsel des jüngeren Plinius erhalten blieb, und dem Reskript des Statthalters von Asia Minucius Fundanus[91]. Man muß dabei bedenken, wie wenig die antike Welt zunächst an den Vorgängen im abgelegenen Galiläa oder Judäa interessiert war. Interessant war, was in Rom passierte. Weiter muß man beachten, daß man in den Kreisen der Gebildeten über 200 Jahre lang die Existenz der Christen häufig totschwieg oder völlig verzeichnete. Dies gilt auch für die talmudische Tradition. Noch der wichtigste Verfasser einer Römischen Geschichte in griechischer Sprache, *Cassius Dio* (um 200–230), nennt die Christen kein einziges Mal und spielt nur indirekt auf sie an; so, wenn er in einer Rede des Mäcenas den Kaiser Augustus auffordern läßt, gewaltsam gegen subversive neue Gottheiten vorzugehen.[92] Aber derartige Phänomene finden wir in der antiken Welt öfter: Der

„So lehrte mich Jesus der *nôsri* (Tosefta: *ben Panterî*)." Der Vorgang soll sich am oberen Markt in Sepphoris abgespielt haben.

88. *tChullin* 2,22f.; Strack 21* §3a).

89. *bShab* 116a/b; Strack 19*ff. §2.

90. Nach Lactanz, *inst. 5,11,19* sammelte Domitius Ulpianus am Anfang des 3. Jhs. im 7. Buch seines Werkes *de officio proconsulis* die *rescripta principum nefaria* gegen die Christen. Diese Sammlung ist uns – verständlicherweise – nicht erhalten.

91. Justin, *apol.* I, 68; dazu M. Hengel, *Judaica et Hellenistica, Kleine Schriften I* (WUNT 90; Tübingen: Mohr-Siebeck, 1990), S. 367–78.

92. 52,36,1–3: Er soll seine Untertanen zwingen (ἀνάγκαζε), die „göttliche Macht (τὸ θεῖον)

Begründer der jüdischen Freiheitsbewegung, Judas der Galiläer, wird nur von Josephus und in der Apostelgeschichte erwähnt, in den sonstigen antiken und talmudischen Texten überhaupt nicht. Die erhaltenen römischen Quellen schweigen auch über den jüdischen Führer im Aufstand von 132–136, der mehr als drei Jahre lang das römische Reich erschütterte; seinen Namen Simon bar Kochba bzw. Kosiba kennen wir nur aus christlichen (Justin und Euseb) und talmudischen Quellen, aus Aufstandsmünzen und jetzt in Originalzeugnissen plötzlich aus den Schriftenfunden der Wüste Juda.[93] Man muß die verstreuten außerchristlichen frühen heidnischen und jüdischen Nachrichten über Jesus auf dem Hintergrund der für die Alte Geschichte durchaus üblichen fragmentarisch-zufälligen Quellensituation sehen. Sie ist im Blick auf den galiläischen Handwerker aus Nazareth und seine Bewegung an antiken Maßstäben gemessen erstaunlich vielfältig und instruktiv.

Zusammen mit den Hinweisen auf Jesus in der frühesten christlichen Literatur außerhalb der Evangelien ergeben sie trotz aller Polemik bereits ein relativ vielschichtiges und erstaunliches Bild, das mit den Grundaussagen der Evangelien weitgehend übereinstimmt. Wir haben keinen Grund, diese Überlieferungen geringzuschätzen.

nach der väterlichen Tradition zu verehren" und der Verbreitung „neuer Gottheiten" (καινά τινα δαιμόνια) wehren, da diese den Staat bedrohten.

93. P. Schäfer, *Der Bar-Kochba-Aufstand* (TSAJ 1; Tübingen: Mohr-Siebeck, 1981); L. Mildenberg, *The Coinage of the Bar Kokhba War* (Aarau/Frankfurt am Main: Sauerländer, 1984); M. Hengel, *Kleine Schriften I* (Anm. 91), S. 344–50 und 379–91.

Die Christologie in der Kindheitsgeschichte des Matthäus am Beispiel von Mt 1,18–25

Hans Klein

Die Kindheitsgeschichten des Mt und des Lk beinhalten geballte Christologie, geht es doch den ersten Erzählern derselben wie den Evangelisten um die Wiedergabe dessen, wer Jesus aus der Sicht der Christen ist, aus dem Wissen heraus, daß Jesus von Anfang an der Gleiche war, als der er später wirkte.

Die Kindheitsgeschichte des Mt enthält eine Fülle von christologischen Aussagen, die weitgehend auf vorgegebene Tradition zurückgehen. Jesus gilt als der im AT Verheißene, wie die fünf als solche heraus gehobenen Zitate (1,23; 2,6.15; 18,23) deutlich machen. Darum wird er bereits in 1,1 als Christus, Sohn Davids und Abrahams eingeführt, er wird zudem in den berichtenden Texten als Sohn Josephs Davidsohn (Mt 1,20), Gottessohn (2,15), Christus (1,18; 2,4) und Retter seines Volkes (1,21) bezeichnet. Motive aus der zeitgenössischen Literatur Israels werden übernommen, um auszusagen, daß sich in ihm alle Erwartungen und Verheißungen erfüllen.[1]

Diese Christologie soll im folgenden an dem ersten dieser Berichte, Mt 1,18–25, näher betrachtet werden, wobei Tradition und Redaktion gleicherweise ins Blickfeld kommen werden. Ebenso wird der Frage nachzugehen sein, welche Kreise an den verschiedenen Aussagen Interesse hatten. Der schwierigen Frage der Klärung, welche Funktion die Traditionen vor ihrer Aufnahme in das Evangelium hatte, werden wir uns nur nähern können. Eine an Wahrscheinlichkeit grenzende Antwort ist von der heutigen Gestalt des Textes her kaum möglich, denn Mt hat ihn vermutlich als erster aufgeschrieben,[2] und dabei kräftig redigiert.

1. *Der Zusammenhang Mt 1,1–2,23*

Der Bericht Mt 1,18–25 ist eine midraschartige Erläuterung[3] zum Geschlechtsregister 1,1–17, wie bereits die Überschrift 1,18a zeigt, die auf V. 16 zurückweist.

1. Vgl. U. Luz, *Das Evangelium nach Matthäus (Mt 1–7)* (EKK I,1; Düsseldorf: Benzinger Verlag u.a., 5th edn, 2002), S. 144f.

2. Vgl. E. Schweizer, *Das Evangelium nach Matthäus* (NTD 2; Göttingen: Vandehoeck & Ruprecht, 1973), S. 12; U. Luz, *Mt* (s. Anm. 1), S. 143. Auf S. 142 weist er darauf hin, daß „hier die Zahl ausgesprochener Matthäismen weit größer ist als im Durchschnitt des Evangeliums".

3. So H. Frankemölle, *Jahwe-Bund und Kirche Christi. Studien zur Form- und Traditionsgeschichte des „Evangeliums" nach Matthäus* (NTA NF 10; Münster: Aschendorff, 2nd edn, 1974), S. 14. K. Stendahl, Quis et unde. An Analysis of Mt 1–2, in: W. Eltester (Hg.), *Judentum –*

Die Fülle der Namen, die mit ganz geringen Erläuterungen bei einzelnen Personen aneinander gereiht werden, wollen deutlich machen, was bereits in 1,1 festgehalten ist: Jesus ist der Christus, und als solcher Sohn Davids und Abrahams, d.h. der, in dem das mit Abraham einsetzende segensvolle Wirken Gottes seinen krönenden Abschluß findet. Wer Jesus verstehen will, muß also mit der Geschichte der Führung Gottes beginnen, die mit Abraham, dem Stammvater einsetzt und über David, dem Urtyp des Königs Israels, führt.

Seiner Form als Bericht entsprechend gehört 1,18–25 aber auch in den größeren Zusammenhang von 1,18–2,23. Das zeigen die fünf Zitate aus dem AT, die jeweils den Abschnitt beherrschen. Das sieht nach einheitlicher Komposition aus. Bei näherem Betrachten zeigt sich allerdings, daß differenziert werden muß. Die Erzählung von den Magiern (2,1–12) setzt den vorhergehenden Bericht über die Verheißung der Geburt Jesu nicht voraus.[4] Es ist eine eigenständige Perikope, die das Zitat auch nicht wie die übrigen vier Texte am Ende hat, sondern in der Mitte (2,6). Sie setzt die Messianität Jesu (2,1), im Verständnis eines „Königs der Juden" (2,2) voraus und zeigt auf, daß diese Sicht nur für den König Herodes und die Stadt Jerusalem gefährlich erscheint. Die Magier als Vertreter der außerisraelitischen Welt beten den „König" an (2,11), „König der Juden" ist eine religiöse Größe. Der folgende Bericht von der Flucht nach Ägypten (2,13–15) hängt mit dem vorhergehenden nur lose, aber nicht innerlich zusammen.[5] Hingegen zeigt der Bericht über den Kindermord (2,16–18) die Auswirkungen der irdisch verstandenen Messianität auf den König und die Bevölkerung. Daß hier eine sekundäre Verbindung vorliegt, ergibt schon die Frage, warum Herodes nicht gleich mit den Magiern Soldaten oder zumindest Spione geschickt hat, die dafür sorgen, daß das geschieht, was er wünscht.

Hingegen scheinen drei Berichte zusammenzugehören, jene von der Verheißung und Geburt (1,18–25), von der Flucht nach Ägypten (2,13–15) und von der Ansiedlung in Nazareth (2,19–23). Sie sind alle drei dadurch gekennzeichnet, daß Joseph im Traum Weisung von einem Engel erhält, die nicht als Redaktion des Mt angesehen werden kann,[6] und die Durchführung dieser Weisung in genauer Übereinstimmung mit dem Wort berichtet wird. Diese Art des Berichtes ist vom AT her geprägt. Eine ähnliche Darstellung begegnet noch in den Eliaerzählungen,

Urchristentum – Kirche (FS J. Jeremias; BZNW 26; Berlin: De Gruyter,1960), Ss. 94–105, (102) sprach von einer „enlarged footnote" (S. 102).

4. Vgl. A. Vögtle, Die matthäische Kindheitsgeschichte, in: M. Didier (Hg.), *L'Évangile selon Matthieu. Redaction et théologie* (BEThL XXIX; Gembloux: Ducolot, 1972), Ss. 153–83 (158): „Notwendig setzt die Erzählung Mt II jedenfalls nur die Vorstellung der Bethlehemgeburt Jesu voraus, nicht aber die der geistlichen Empfängnis" (S. 158).

5. Anders G. Strecker, *Der Weg der Gerechtigkeit. Untersuchung zur Theologie des Matthäus* (FRLANT 82; Göttingen: Vandehoeck & Ruprecht, 3rd edn, 1971), S. 51 mit Anm. 5, der den Zusammenhang von V. 7 und V. 16 betont und für die Zusammengehörigkeit der Texte auf die Mosetradition hinweist, wie sie Josephus, *Antiquitates* II, 205–23 schildert. S. auch S. 170 mit Anm. 39.

6. So bei Mt nur noch 2.12 als Aufnahme des Motivs durch Mt und 27.19 in einem redaktionellen Text, vgl. E. Schweizer, *Mt* (s. Anm. 2), S. 12.

wo allerdings nicht ein Engel das Wort im Traum[7] spricht, das Wort ergeht direkt an den Propheten:

> „Es erging das Wort Jahwes an ihn (Elia) also: Geh fort von hier und wende dich ostwärts und verbirg dich am Bache Krith, der östlich vom Jordan fließt. Da ging er hin und tat, wie Jahwe befohlen hatte und blieb am Bache Krith, der östlich vom Jordan fließt." (1 Kön 17,3–5, vgl. 17,8–10)[8]

Durch diese Erzähltechnik soll der Gehorsam des Joseph gegenüber Gottes Weisung gekennzeichnet werden. Neu gegenüber dem Bericht des AT ist allerdings, daß dieses Geschehen zusätzlich als Erfüllung alttestamentlicher Prophetie gesehen wird. Darauf ist noch einzugehen.

Zeigt sich somit durch die Art und Weise der Erzählungen, daß sie der Tradition des AT verpflichtet sind, so ist damit wahrscheinlich, daß zumindest die zugrundeliegenden Überlieferungen dem Judenchristentum entstammen. Das gilt, zumindest partiell auch für den Inhalt. Denn die Deutung des Namens Jesus mit „er wird sein Volk retten" (1,21) ist nur einem Hörer bzw. einem Leser direkt verständlich, der hebräisch oder aramäisch mitdenkt. Im Hebräischen würde die Wendung „Jesus, denn er wird sein Volk retten" lauten: יְהוֹשׁוּעַ כִּי יוֹשִׁיעַ אֶת עַמּוֹ,[9] eine echte Deutung des Namens und zugleich ein Wortspiel. Sie müßte im Deutschen wiedergegeben werden mit: (nenne ihn) „Gottesrettung, denn er wird sein Volk retten". Daß der Name Jesus bei der Übersetzung nicht erklärt wird, etwa mit ὅ ἐστιν μεθερμηνευόμενον σωτηρία κυρίου,[10] hängt wohl damit zusammen, daß der erste Übersetzer damit rechnen konnte, daß das Wortspiel verstanden wird. In dem zweiten Bericht (2,13–15) ist das Zitat in 2,15 nicht der LXX, sondern dem MT entnommen, denn die LXX spricht von Söhnen (pl.), die aus Ägypten gerufen wurden, nicht vom „Sohn" (sing.), wie es der masoretische Text tut. Endlich ergibt das nicht genau identifizierbare Zitat „er soll Nazoräer heißen" (2,23), ein Wortspiel mit Nazareth-Nazara, und setzt voraus, daß Jesus als נָזִיר (*nazir*) gesehen wurde.[11]

7. Die Frage, wo die Tradition einer Offenbarung im Traum durch einen Engel liegt, ist kaum zu klären. Offenbarungen im Traum gibt es in der Gen. 20,6f; 28.11f; 37,5–10 u.ö., Gesichter in der Nacht mit Engeldeutung und Ergehen des Wortes Jahwes Sach 1–6, eine Erscheinung des Herrn in der Nacht Apg 18. 9f; 23. 11, der Engels Gottes Apg 27,23. Vgl. auch B.M. Nolan, *The Royal Son of God. The Christology of Matthew 1–2 in the Setting of the Gospel* (OBO 233; Fribourg: Universitätsverlag u.a. 1979), S. 31.

8. R. E. Brown, *The Birth of the Messiah* (London: G. Chapman, 1993), S. 139, Anm. 17 weist noch auf Mt 21,4–6 hin, wonach die Jünger genau dem Befehl Jesu entsprechen. Ähnliche Texte gäbe es Hi 42,9, vgl. Ex 1,17; Nu 20,27 und meint diese Entsprechung von Befehl und Ausführung sei ein LXX-ismus.

9. Vgl. dazu H. L. Strack, P. Billerbeck, *Kommentar zum Neuen Testament aus Talmud und Midrasch* (München: C.H. Beck, 3rd edn, 1951), S. 64; sowie E. Klostermann, *Das Matthäusevangelium* (HNT 1; Tübingen: Mohr-Siebeck, 2nd edn, 1927), S. 8.

10. So mit Philo, *De mut.nom.* 121, der den Namens Josua so deutet.

11. H. Schaeder, *ThWNT* IV, 883, der auf Ri 13,5 (vgl. 16,17) als Grundtext hinweist. R. Bartelmus, *Heroentum in Israel und seiner Umwelt*, (AThANT 65; Zürich: Zwingli Verlag, 1979), S. 81 Anm. 15, ist sicher, daß Mt 2,23 auf Ri 13,5 angespielt wird. Ähnlich E.Schweizer, Er soll Nazoräer heißen, in W. Eltester (Hg.), *Judentum – Urchristentum – Kirche* (FS J.Jeremias; BZNW 26;

Man könnte also davon ausgehen, daß in den drei Berichten judenchristliche Tradition mit einer dafür spezifischen Christologie vorliegt. Aber:

(a) Der letzte Bericht ist so sehr von Mt gestaltet,[12] daß nicht erkennbar wird, inwieweit Mt einer Tradition folgt. Nur γῆ Ἰσραηλ läßt sich als Rest einer Tradition erkennen.[13] Indes, der „Herausführung aus Ägypten" (2,15) mußte die Angabe eines neuen Wohnortes folgen und dieser konnte nur Nazareth sein. So muß man auch hinter 2,19–23 eine Tradition vermuten, die davon berichtete, daß Joseph mit Maria und dem Kind aus Ägypten ins Land Israel und nach Nazareth zogen. Aber Genaueres läßt sich nicht wahrscheinlich machen.

(b) Der Gedanke der Geburt aus dem Geist in 1,18–20 ist nur im hellenistischen Judenchristentum denkbar. Das bedeutet, daß man aufgrund von 1,21; 2,15 und 2,23, mit einem aramäisch sprechendem Judenchristentum als Träger der Überlieferung rechnen kann, zumindest in 1,18–20 aber mit hellenistisch geprägtem Judenchristentum als Überlieferungsträger gerechnet werden muß. Es lohnt sich darum der Versuch, hinter den Text des Mt zurückzufragen. Bei 1,18–25 scheint dies möglich zu sein, bei den anderen beiden Texten ist die Wahrscheinlichkeit dazu sehr gering. Man kann zwar versuchen, durch Streichung von ἀνεχωρησάντων δὲ αὐτῶν (2,13aa), μέλλει δὲ Ἡρῴδης ζητεῖν τὸ παιδίον καὶ ἀπολέσαι αὐτό (2,13b) und von καὶ ἦν ἐκεῖ ἕως τῆς τελευτῆς Ἡρῴδου (2,15a) sowie von τελευτήσαντος δὲ τοῦ Ἡρῴδου (2,19aa), τεθνήκασιν γὰρ οἱ ζετοῦντες τὴν ψυχὴν τοῦ παιδίου (2,20c) und 2,22.23a (Ναζαρέτ κτλ.) einen sehr kurzen Bericht als Vorlage des Mt zu rekonstruieren, aber wir wissen nicht, was Mt selbst aus seiner Vorlage entfernt, und wie er sie gekürzt hat. Das Zitat 2,15 steht zudem am falschen Platz. Man erwartet es hinter 2,21. So scheint mir eine Rekonstruktion der vormatthäischen Tradition nicht möglich.

2. *Der Text Mt 1,18–25*

Die Erzählung ist auf ein Minimum reduziert. Die beiden Hauptpersonen werden nicht vorgestellt, und sie sind weitgehend passiv.[14] Wer Maria und Josef sind,

Berlin: De Gruyter, 1960), Ss. 90–93, (93), der aber das Wortspiel im hellenistischen Millieu entstanden denkt. Dies ist natürlich möglich, ebenso aber auch eine Herleitung aus dem aramäisch sprechenden Judentum. Der Unterschied zwischen den Worten ist nicht so groß, daß ein Wortspiel nicht möglich gewesen wäre. Die Ableitung von נצר *(näzär)* Jes 11,1 erscheint mir sehr weither geholt. Dagegen auch W. Rothfuchs, *Die Erfüllungszitate des Matthäusevangeliums. Eine biblisch-theologische Untersuchung* (BWANT 88; Stuttgart u.a: Kohlhammer 1969), 65.

12. Vgl. die Parallele zwischen 2,22f und 4,12 ἀκούσας δὲ ὅτι mit folgendem Namen; ἀνεχώρησεν εἰς mit Angabe des Landes, sowie καὶ … ἐλθὼν κατῴκησεν εἰς mit Angabe der Stadt. Die sprachliche Entsprechung, von V. 13–14 mit V. 19–21 geht in dieser Form wohl auf Matthäus zurück.

13. Sonst nicht mehr im New Testament, in der LXX noch in 1 Sam 13,19; 1 Chr 13,2; 22,2; 2 Chr 2,16; 30,25; 24,7, vgl. γῆ τοῦ Ἰσραηλ, 17 mal bei Ez. Γῆ mit Namen begegnet in den beiden Zitaten 2,6 und 4,15 und 10,15; 11,24. Bei den letzten beiden Texten ist nicht eindeutig festzustellen, ob die Wendung, die im Paralleltext bei Lk nicht begegnet, Mt vorgegeben war. Daher erscheint mir die Formulierung γῆ Ἰσραηλ (2,19) traditionell zu sein.

14. J. Weiß, W. Bousset, *Matthäusevangelium* (SNT 1; Göttingen: Vandenhoeck & Ruprecht, 4th edn, 1929), S. 231.

weiß die christliche Leserin oder der gläubige Leser. 1,17 war dazu allerdings auch nur einiges Bruchstückhafte und unter der Voraussetzung gesagt, daß Christen über die Eltern Jesu Bescheid wissen. Daß die beiden in Bethlehem zu Hause sind, ergibt sich aus dem folgenden Bericht (2,1–12). Mt spart an Worten und reduziert alles auf das Notwendigste. So berichtet er auch nicht, woher Joseph weiß, daß Maria schwanger ist. Man kann vermuten, daß es ihm zugetragen wurde oder daß es an ihrem Körper erkennbar war, aber solche Vermutungen führen ab, daran hat der Evangelist kein Interesse. Ein solches hat er nur an der Feststellung, daß Joseph ein δίκαιος (Gerechter 1,19) ist. Denn dieses einzige Adjektiv innerhalb der Erzählung ist überschießend und darum bewußt gesetzt.

Der Aufbau des Berichtes ist aufschlußreich:[15]

V. 18a: Überschrift
  V. 18b: Darstellung des Konfliktes: Joseph ist mit Maria verlobt, Maria ist schwanger.
    V. 19: Absicht des Joseph, den Konflikt zu lösen
      V. 20: Engelerscheinung und Handlungsanweisung an Joseph
        V. 21: Zusätzliche Erklärung des Engels
          V. 22f: Deutung des Geschehens vom AT her
      V. 24: Tat des Joseph nach der Anweisung des Engels (vgl. V. 20)
          V. 25a: Vermerk, daß Joseph Maria nicht berührt
        V. 25b: Tat des Joseph entsprechend der Erklärung (vgl. V. 21)

Die Deutung des Geschehens in V. 22f vom AT her ist sichtlich sekundär. Das Zitat zerreißt den Zusammenhang,[16] der darin besteht, daß die Tat des Joseph der Anweisung des Engels in seiner doppelten Gestalt, als Anleitung zur Tat und Erklärung derselben entspricht. Es kommt hinzu, daß es nicht den Namen Jesu deutet, wie das Wort des Engels, sondern die Person Jesu als Emmanuel – Gott ist mit uns. Das Wort weist auf 11,27 voraus, wonach Jesus der einzige Offenbarer Gottes ist, und dieses Wort hat bereits den Schluß mit seiner kräftigen Aussage und 28,18 im Blick: „Mir ist alle Gewalt gegeben…“ Man wird daraus schließen müssen, daß das Zitat von Mt eingeführt wurde. Dabei hat er an einer Stelle den Wortlaut verändert. Statt καλέσεις schreibt er καλέσουσιν und hat dabei bereits die christliche Gemeinde im Blick.[17] Entfernt man dasselbe, dann erscheint die Erzählung zunächst einheitlich: Ein zu Beginn beschriebener Konflikt wird nicht auf menschliche Weise, sondern Gott gemäß gelöst. Der Engel gibt die Art und Weise an, was zu tun und wie die Sache zu verstehen ist. Dementsprechend ist Joseph in der Erzählung der Einzige, der aktiv ist. Er wird von einer falschen Tat abgehalten und zur richtigen Tat angewiesen, die er genau dem Wort des Engels folgend ausrichtet. Dennoch wird die Erzählung durch die Entnahme von V. 22f nur in ihrer Struktur, nicht insgesamt einheitlich. Denn

15. E. Lohmeyer, *Das Evangelium des Matthäus*, (KEK; Göttingen: Vandenhoeck & Ruprecht, 4th edn, 1967), S. 12 gliedert in drei Teile: Konflikt (V. 18f); Lösung (20–23); Ausgang (V. 24f).

16. Vgl. F. Hahn, *Christologische Hoheitstitel. Ihre Geschichte im frühen Christentum* (FRLANT 83; Göttingen: Vandenhoeck & Ruprecht, 3rd edn, 1966), S. 274. Es ist wie 21. 4f eingeschoben, vgl. E. Klostemann, *Mt* (s. Anm. 9), S. 10.

17. Vgl. W. Rothfuchs, *Erfüllungszitate* (s. Anm. 11), S. 60.

durch sie hat die Aussage, Maria sei durch den Geist schwanger geworden, sowohl im Bericht V. 18, als auch im Engelwort V. 20 festgehalten, keinen Bezug mehr. Das Zitat aus Jes 7,14 ist es, das die Jungfrauenschwangerschaft und damit jene aus dem Geist erklärt. Es kommt hinzu, daß der Befehl, dem Kinde den Namen „Jesus" zu geben und die dazugehörige Erklärung mit der Geburt aus dem Geist nicht zusammenhängt. Die Parallelen aus dem AT, die eine gottgewollte Schwangerschaft bringen, kennen den Gedanken der Geburt aus dem Geist nicht, während die Verheißung des Kindes mit Namensgebung und Namensdeutung fest in entsprechenden Erzählungen verankert sind (vgl. Gen 16,11; Jes 7,14). Dasselbe gilt für die Ankündigung der Geburt durch einen Engel (vgl. Gen 16,11; Ri 13,3.5). Die nächste strukturelle Parallele zu unserm Text ist Gen 16,11, denn sie enthält Engelerscheinung, Ankündigung der Schwangerschaft und Geburt, sowie Anweisung zur Namensgebung und Namensdeutung. Inhaltlich ist aber Ri 13,3.5 näher vor allem wegen der Aussage des Engels dort, daß der angekündigte Sohn „Israel retten wird" (Ri 13,5).

Man erwartet von der Aussage V. 18 her ein Wort, eventuell aus dem Munde des Engels, daß das aus dem Geist geborene Kind „Gottessohn" genannt wird. Tatsächlich ist dies 2,15 mit dem Zitat aus Hos 11,1 vorausgesetzt. Der Titel kommt dort völlig unvorbereitet. So erscheint mir der Schluß unumgänglich, daß Mt seine Vorlage nicht nur durch V. 22f ergänzt hat, sondern gleichzeitig eine Aussage entfernte, die davon sprach, daß Jesus durch die Geburt aus dem Geist zum Gottessohn wird, wie es Lk 1,35 gesagt wird.[18] Er konnte dies tun, weil er später in 2,15 die Gottessohnschaft Jesu zu erwähnen gedachte, und er wollte es vermutlich tun, um mit Gen 6,1–4 nicht in Konflikt zu kommen. Nach Mt ist Jesus nicht kraft der Geburt durch den Geist Gottessohn,[19] die Gottessohnschaft ergibt sich durch den Ruf heraus aus Ägypten, bzw. überhaupt durch den Ruf Gottes, wie Mt es in der Taufgeschichte des Mk (1,11) las. Die Gottessohnschaft ist auch bei Mt adoptianisch verstanden, die Jungfrauengeburt bzw. jene aus Gottes Geist sagt in seinem Verständnis aus, daß Gott in ihm mit uns ist.

Ist einmal der begründete Verdacht vorhanden, daß Mt seine Tradition verändert hat, dann lassen sich weitere Elemente finden, die wahrscheinlich von Mt abgeändert wurden. Merkwürdig ist besonders das Wort des Engels an Joseph 1,20. Er weist Joseph an, sich nicht zu fürchten, aber nicht, wie sonst bei Engelerscheinungen über die Gegenwart des Göttlichen, sondern davor, Maria zu sich zu nehmen, wobei nicht deutlich wird, wovor er sich wirklich fürchtet, denn Maria

18. Vgl. A. Vögtle, Die Genealogie Mt 1,2–16 und die matthäische Kindheitsgeschichte, in: Ders, *Das Evangelium und die Evangelien. Beiträge zur Evangelienforschung* (Düsseldorf: Patmos, 1971), Ss. 57–102 (66): „Er setzt mit dem Passus (1,18–25) sehr wohl sachlich Lk 1,26–38 voraus."

19. Zu rasch formuliert R. Pesch, Der Gottessohn im matthäischen Evangelienprolog. Beobachtungen zu den Zitationsformeln der Reflexionszitate, *Bibl* 4 (1967), Ss. 395–420 (410): „...als Sohn einer Jungfrau stammt Jesus aber ἐκ πνεύματος ἁγίου, d.h. er ist Sohn Gottes" und ebenso U. Luz, *Die Jesusgeschichte des Matthäus* (Neukirchen-Vluyn: Neukirchner, 1993), S. 41f: Gerade diese Identifizierung will Mt vermieden wissen. Dasselbe gilt für die Aussage von J. D. Kingsbury, *Matthew. Structure, Christology, Kingdom* (Philadelphia: Fortress, 2nd edn, 1978), S. 43: „Matthew is equally intent upon showing that Mary's child can be called the Son of God: he is conceived by the Holy Spirit (mentioned twice 1,18.20)."

zu sich zu nehmen, ist in keiner Weise gefährlich, es ist das Normale bei einer Verlobung. In Frage kommt darum im Sinne des Mt nur das Verständnis von „sich scheuen", ein sehr seltener Gebrauch.[20] Man möchte darum annehmen, daß Mt hier eine urtümlichere Aussage verändert wiedergegeben hat.[21] Die Wendung muß allen Parallelen entsprechend sachgemäß etwa gelautet haben: „Joseph ... fürchte dich nicht, nimm Maria zu dir." Der Beschwichtigungsformel „fürchte dich nicht", die zur Engelerscheinung gehört, wäre die Anweisung zur Tat gefolgt.

Eine vergleichbare Veränderung der Tradition dürfte in der Bezeichnung Josephs als Davidsohn (1,20) liegen. Man erwartet daß Jesus als υἱός Δαυιδ gekennzeichnet wird. Auch hier dürfte Mt etwas verändert haben. Wie der Text seiner Tradition lautete, läßt sich nicht mehr eruieren.

Es kommt ein Letztes hinzu: V. 25a wird berichtet, daß Joseph Maria nach ihrer Heimführung nicht berührt. Das ist gegenüber dem Engelwort zusätzlich. So wird man fragen, ob es nicht in dem Engelwort enthalten war und weggelassen wurde, weil durch die Einfügung der Namensdeutung in V. 21 die Konstruktion zu überladen wurde.

Diesen Beobachtungen zufolge kann das Engelwort in der Vorlage des Mt etwa gelautet haben: „Fürchte dich nicht, Joseph (Sohn Davids), nimm Maria zu dir, erkenne sie aber nicht, denn sie ist schwanger vom Heiligen Geist. Das von ihr Geborene wird Gottes Sohn genannt werden." Es handelt sich hier um einen Bericht, der eine Geburt aus Gott voraussetzt[22] und erklären will, wieso Jesus dann doch Josephs Sohn ist. Joseph, der Empfänger einer Information durch einen Engel dürfte im Mittelpunkt gestanden haben.[23] In den Versen 1,18b–20.24.25a wäre die alte Erzählung verarbeitet.

Übrig bleibt das Engelwort V. 21. Es ist einer anderen Tradition entnommen.[24] Wie diese ausgesehen haben muß, kann man freilich nur vermuten. Meist wird

20. Vgl. W. Bauer, B. und K. Aland, *Griechisch-deutsches Wörterbuch zu den Schriften des Neuen Testaments und der frühchristlichen Literatur* (Berlin u.a: De Gruyter, 6th edn, 1988), S. 1721.

21. In diesem Sinne auch R.E. Brown, *Birth* (s. Anm. 8), S. 158. Vgl. G.Strecker, *Weg* (s. Anm. 5), 54 Anm. 2: „Bezeichnend ist auch, daß das Furchtmotiv, ursprünglich die menschliche Entsprechung zur himmlischen Epiphanie (Lk 1,30), auf die Absicht Josephs seine Braut zu verlassen, umgedeutet ist."

22. So mit Recht bereits M. Dibelius, *Jungfrauensohn und Krippenkind. Untersuchungen zur Geburtsgeschichte Jesu im Lukasevangelium* (SHAW phil.-hist. Kl. 4; Heidelberg: Winter 1932), Ss. 25f; E. Schweizer, *Mt* (s. Anm. 2), S. 11. Daß diese, wie Dibelius meint, apologetischen Charakter hatte und die Jungfrauengeburt verteidigen wollte, ist weniger wahrscheinlich, vgl. G. Strecker, *Weg* (s. Anm. 5), S. 54. Als Parallele aus der Welt der Griechen vgl. den Bericht über die Zeugung des Plato, *Diog. Laertios, III,2*, wonach Apollo dem Ariston im Traum erscheint und dieser daraufhin verzichtet, sich der (bis dahin unberührten) künftigen Mutter zu nähern, bis sie das Kind geboren hatte.

23. Das entspricht der Ankündigung der Geburt des Isaak an Abraham Gen 18,10.

24. Auch R.E. Brown, *Birth* (s. Anm. 8), S. 162 rechnet mit zwei vormatthäischen Traditionen, eine mit der Ankündigung der Geburt des davidischen Messias nach dem Modell alttestamentlicher Erzählungen und einer betreffend die Botschaft von Jesus als Gottessohn geworden durch Heiligen Geist. Die Erzählung von der Ankündigung sei der vorlukanischen Tradition in Lk 1 nahegestanden. Ähnlich W.D. Davies, D.C. Allison, *The Gospel According to Saint Matthew* (ICC I; Edinburgh: T&T Clark, 1988), S. 194f rechnet mit einer primären Erzählung über die Ankündigung der Geburt

angenommen, daß V. 21 das ursprüngliche Kernstück des jetzigen Berichtes bildete, der durch das Motiv der Geburt aus dem Geist angereichert wurde.[25] Das ist nach dem oben Gesagten nicht wahrscheinlich. Darum muß der Versuch gemacht werden, diese Tradition inhaltlich näher zu kennzeichnen.

Geht man von der Parallele des AT aus, kann man eine Erzählung postulieren, der zufolge Maria, als Verlobte Josephs die Erscheinung eines Engels erlebte (vgl. Gen 16,11; Ri 13,3; Lk 1,26f), der die Geburt eines Kindes ankündigte. An den vergleichbaren Stellen erscheint der Engel immer der werdenden Mutter. Der wichtigste Teil dieser Erzählung war das Engelwort (V. 21), das seiner Form nach Gen 16,11 nahestand. Es deutete den Namen Jesu und beschrieb damit sein Werk, sprach also davon, wer Jesus ist und was er tat. Der Bericht geht in das aramäisch sprechende Judenchristentum zurück.[26] Seine Funktion war vermutlich, das ungewöhnliche Wesen Jesu auf Gottes Eingriff bereits im Mutterleib zurückzuführen.[27]

Die Erzählung hat möglicherweise eine christologische Auslegung von Ri 13,5 zur Grundlage, wo der Passus: „er wird anfangen, Israel zu retten“, etwa im Stile des Habakuk-Kommentars von Qumran so kommentiert wurde: „Dies bezieht sich auf Jeschu, der sein Volk retten wird“.[28] Der Zusatz „von allen Sünden“ spezifiziert, daß es sich nicht um eine Rettung im Sinne einer Befreiung von den Feinden geht, wie es Ri 13,5 mit seinem „aus der Hand der Philister“ ausspricht und noch im Benediktus des Zacharias (Lk 1,74) erwartet wird, sondern um eine Befreiung von den Sünden als neue Möglichkeit des Gehorsams vor Gott.[29]

Trifft diese Rekonstruktion im Wesentlichen zu, dann darf man damit rechnen, daß es diese Tradition ist, die der Bericht Mt 1,18b–20.24–25a voraussetzt, und wo darum die Personen nicht mehr eingeführt werden und das Problem der Schwangerschaft gleich am Anfang berichtet wird, für eine Erzählung etwas

an Joseph in Farben der Mosetradition, die durch eine davidische Christologie angereichert wurde, in der auch die Empfängnis durch den Geist ausgesprochen war.

25. So viele im Gefolge von R. Bultmann, *Geschichte der synoptischen Tradition* (Göttingen: Vandenhoeck & Ruprecht, 4th edn, 1961), S. 316f.

26. Die These von M. Karrer, Jesus der Retter (Soter). Zur Aufnahme eines hellenistischen Prädikats im Neuen Testament, *ZNW* 93 (2002), S. 155f, Mt 1,21 bilde „einen Schlußpunkt“ anderweitig aufgezeigter Linien im New Testament, kann ich nicht teilen. Über das Alter eines Textes kann ohne diachronische Analyse nicht entschieden werden.

27. Es wäre somit das erzählerische Pendant zur Aussage der Propheten über die Bildung der Auserwählten Gottes von Mutterleib an (Jes 44,24; 49,1.5; Jer 1,5; vgl. Gal 1,15).

28. Vgl, 1QpHab VII 3–7 : „und wenn es heißt: *damit eilen kann, wer liest,* so bezieht sich seine Deutung auf den Lehrer der Gerechtigkeit, dem Gott kundgetan hat alle Geheimnisse…*denn noch ist eine Schau auf Frist, sie eilt dem Ende zu und lügt nich.* Seine Deutung ist, daß sich die letzte Zeit in die Länge zieht. 4Q161Frg. 10 zu Jes 11,1: „Seine Deutung bezieht sich auf den Sproß Davids, der auftritt am Ende der Tage“, Text bei J. Meier, *Die Qumran-Essener: Die Texte vom Toten Meer I,* (UTB 1862; München u.a: Reinhardt, 1995), S. 161. Der Text Ri 13 ist zu jener Zeit messianisch gelesen worden. Das zeigt die Wiedergabe von „Philistern“ mit ἀλλόφυλοι, Fremdstämmige, in der LXX.

29. Ps 130,8 steht dabei kaum im Hintergrund. Anders nach vielen Vorgängern M. Karrer, *Jesus* (s. Anm. 28), Ss. 153–76 (156 mit Anm. 17).

eigentümlich. Denn im hellenistischen Judenchristentum dürfte der rekonstruierte Bericht über die Ankündigung an Maria, dessen Kernstück 1,21 ist, im Sinne einer Geburt aus dem Geist, gemeint ist durch die göttliche Schöpferkraft,[30] verstanden und ausgelegt worden sein. Dieser Gedanke legte sich nahe, weil der ältere Bericht nur von der Zusage des Engels an Maria, die Mutter sprach. Der neue Bericht, der im Text von Mt 1,18b–20.24–25a enthalten ist, will auf die Frage antworten, wieso Joseph noch bei Maria blieb, wenn sie bereits in der Verlobungszeit schwanger war. Nach israelitischem Recht (Dt 22,23f) sollte eine Braut Jungfrau sein. Mit der Verlobung war sie bereits rechtlich an den künftigen Ehemann gebunden, eine Schwangerschaft in dieser Zeit mußte dementsprechend auf einen Ehebruch zurückgehen und darauf stand eine hohe Strafe, auch wenn jene der Steinigung bei Bräuten zur Zeit Jesu in Israel nicht mehr vollzogen wurde.[31] In der hellenistischen Welt war man weit toleranter. In eine solche Situation dürfte Mt 1,19 hinein sprechen, wenn es heißt, daß Joseph Maria nicht „durch Anzeige beim Gerichtshof in die Öffentlichkeit bringen und *bloßstellen*" wollte.[32] Das Wort δειγματίζειν ist in der hellenistischen Welt als „Bloßstellung" einer Ehebrecherin belegt.[33]

Demnach wäre der Vorgang des Überlieferungswachstums ähnlich zu denken wie in der Kindheitsgeschichte des Lukas, wo zunächst auch und zwar ebenfalls im palästinischen Judentum von einer Engelsbotschaft an Maria berichtet wurde (Lk 1,26*.31–33), die Jesu Größe kundtat, woraufhin im hellenistischen Judenchristentum die Geburt aus dem Geist ausgesagt wurde (Lk 1,34f).[34] Dort hatte die Aussage von der Geburt aus dem Geist ebenfalls erläuternden Charakter, doch sollte damit erklärt werden, „wie" eine solche Geburt denkbar ist. Der Bericht des Mt will die Frage beantworten, wieso Joseph bei Maria blieb und zum rechtlichen Vater Jesu wurde. Seine Funktion war es, die Davidsohnschaft Jesu bei Voraussetzung seiner Geburt aus Gottes Geist fest zu schreiben. Mt ist von dieser Tendenz noch beeinflußt, insofern er die Davidsohnschaft Jesu bereits 1,1 betont. Sie hat erst die Voranstellung der Genealogie Jesu in 1,1–17 ermöglicht, weil die Linie zu Joseph führt. In der Tradition vor Mt entstand somit ein zweiter Bericht, der den ersten voraussetzt.[35]

30. Vgl. W. Grundmann, *Das Evangelium nach Matthäus* (ThHKNT I; Berlin: EVA, 1968), p. 67, der mit Recht darauf hinweist, daß רוח hebr. Feminin ist, πνεῦμα ist neutrisch.

31. Vgl. U. Luz, *Mt* (s. Anm. 1), 147, Anm. 36. Auch Mt 5,32; 19,9 setzt Todesstrafe bei Ehebruch nicht mehr voraus, wohl aber Joh 8,5. Die Praxis dürfte also zur Zeit des Neuen Testament nicht überall gleich gewesen sein. Das lassen auch die Texte bei Strack-Billerbeck I (s. Anm. 9), p. 53 erkennen.

32. So H. Schlier, ThWNT II, pp. 31, 37f, dort auch die Hervorhebung.

33. Vgl. W. Bauer, B. und K. Aland, *Wörterbruch* (s. Anm. 20), p. 344. Dies wird durch die von Davies/Allison, *Mt* (s.Anm.24), p. 204 angeführten hebräischen Belege für das im selben Sinn gebrauchte hebräische Lehwort *di(u)gma*[a] bestätigt.

34. Vgl. dazu meinen Beitrag, Die Legitimation der Täufer- und der Jesusbewegung nach den Kindheitsgeschichten des Lukas, in *ΕΠΙΤΟΑΥΤΟ, Studies in Honour of Petr Pokorný on his Sixty-fifth Birthday* (Třebenice: Mlýn, 1998), Ss.. 208–17 (213).

35. Bei Lk lief der Prozeß etwas anders, hier wurde die erste Fassung Lk 1,26*.31–33 durch V. 34f ergänzt.

Mt hätte demnach zwei Erzählungen zur Geburt Jesu vorgefunden und miteinander verbunden.[36] Eine solche These läßt sich von seiner Arbeitsmethode her begründen. Denn er hat auch sonst aus zwei ähnlichen Traditionen einen einzigen Bericht erstellt. Das bekannteste Beispiel ist die Kombination zwischen dem markinischen Bericht über die Versuchung Jesu (Mk 1,12f) und jenem aus Q in Mt 4,1–11. Hier benützt er Mk 1,12f als Rahmen, die Q-Tradition als Inhalt.[37] Ähnlich geht er auch Mt 1,18–25 vor, wo er in den Grundbestand eines Berichtes V. 21 ein- und V. 25b anfügt, wobei er wahrscheinlich, eine Aussage in V. 20, wonach aus dem Geist der „Gottessohn" zur Welt kommt, ausgelassen wurde.

Die Frage, warum Mt den zweiten Bericht und nicht den ersten als Rahmen wählte und aus dem ersten nur einige Bruchstücke übernahm, ist relativ leicht zu beantworten: Der zweite Bericht war der weiterführende, weil der jüngere. Er konnte an die Genealogie (1,17) angeschlossen werden. Es kommt hinzu, daß Mt in der gesamten Kindheitsgeschichte Joseph und nicht Maria im Mittelpunkt stehen und handeln läßt. Er entscheidet sich damit für eine patriarchalische Struktur, die bereits das Geschlechtsregister (1,1–17) prägt. Maria wird zur Nebenperson, sie ist Objekt des Handelns Gottes und des Joseph. Daß Gott sie ausersehen hat, Jesus zur Welt zu bringen, erfahren die Leser jetzt fast nur noch nebenbei, aber dort, wo es ihm möglich war, gibt er Maria dennoch eine gewichtige Position: in 2,11 berichtet er, daß die Weisen aus dem Osten „das Kind und seine Mutter" sehen, von Joseph schweigt er. Ebenso stehen 2,13 und 2,20 „Kind und Mutter" im Auftrag des Engels an Joseph. Sosehr Joseph der Handelnde ist, sind Mutter und Kind die zentralen Personen, er nur deren Beschützer.

Es ergibt sich somit:

(a) Die Deutung des Namens Jesu als „er wird sein Volk von den Sünden retten" war verankert in einer alten Erzählung. Sie enthält eine urtümliche Christologie. Der Name Jesu wird zum Anlaß des Nachdenkens darüber gemacht, wer er ist. Jesus wird als „Retter seines Volkes" gefeiert, eine messianische Aussage, die im Sinne des uralten Bekenntnisses „Christus starb für uns, d.h. für unsere Sünden"[38] gedeutet wird. Rettung bringt Jesus danach nicht von den Feinden, die das Volk von außen bedrohen, wie noch das Benedictus des Zacharias ausspricht (Lk 1,74), sondern von dem, was das Volk von Gott trennt, von den Sünden.

(b) Die Aussage, daß die Schwangerschaft der Maria auf den Geist Gottes zurückgeht, ist Erläuterung des ersten Berichtes in der Gestalt eines zweiten. Damit wird Gottes Initiative bei der Geburt Jesu verstärkt hervorgehoben. Mehr noch, es wird ausgesagt, daß Jesus eigentlich ein himmlisches Wesen in Menschengestalt ist. Er hat in Joseph keinen natürlichen, aber einen rechtmäßigen Vater und ist damit Gottessohn und Davidsohn.

36. Vgl. Anm. 25.

37. Vgl. dazu meine Feststellungen in: *Bewährung im Glauben. Studien zum Sondergut des Evangelisten Matthäus* (BThSt 26; Neukirchen-Vluyn: Neukirchner Verlag 1996), S. 29f; 28–34 weitere Beispiele von Zusammenlegungen von Texten durch Mt.

38. Röm 5,8; 14,14 u. ö. bzw. 1 Kor 15,3, vgl. Gal 1,4. Zur Formel und ihrem Alter vgl. P. Vielhauer, *Geschichte der urchristlichen Literatur* (Berlin u.a: De Gruyter 1975), Ss. 16–18.

(c) Der Hinweis auf Jes 7,14 expliziert die Zeugung aus dem Geist als Jungfrauengeburt, die implizit in der Aussage von der Schwangerschaft durch den Geist vorausgesetzt ist. Dabei wird der Schwerpunkt von der Jungfrauengeburt und seiner ontologischen Aussage über Jesus weg auf seine Eigenart und Bedeutung verlegt, die in dem Namen Emmanuel ausgesprochen ist: „in ihm ist Gott mit uns." Die Gottesohnschaft Jesu ergibt sich für Mt nicht mehr aus der Zeugung durch den Geist und somit ontologisch, sie beruht auf dem Rechtsakt, wonach Gott Jesus als Sohn aus Aegypten ruft (2,15). Mt ist damit der alttestamentlich-jüdischen Tradition wieder näher als seine Vorlage.

3. *Die Christologie der Kindheitsgeschichte des Mt*

Stellt man diese Aussagen in den Zusammenhang, so ergibt sich:

(a) Die ältesten christologischen Aussagen der Kindheitsgeschichte des Mt kreisen um den Namen „Jesus" und die Näherbestimmung „aus Nazareth". Sie gehören ins aramäisch sprechende Judenchristentum.

(b) Die Deutung der Namen wird in beiden Fällen auf Grund des damals messianisch gedeuteten Textes Ri 13,5 gemacht, sie entspringt offensichtlich einem christlichen Kommentar dieser Bibelstelle. Ri 13,3–5 und Gen 16,11 machen eine erste Erzählung über Jesu Geburt möglich. Die Bibel der ersten Christen, das AT, ist somit bereits für die palästinischen Christen Quelle für Aussagen über Jesu.

(c) Die Suche nach geeigneten Texten zur Interpretation Jesu weitet sich aus. Hos 11,1 wird auf Jesus gedeutet, Jesus als Gottessohn verstanden, eine Gottessohnschaft, die als Messianität begriffen wurde. Weil nach Hos 11,1 der Gottessohn aus Ägypten gerufen wird, muß ein Aufenthalt Jesu in Ägypten berichtet werden, ebenso eine Rückkehr ins Land Israel, konkret nach Nazareth. Dies alles geschieht noch in der aramäisch sprechenden Urgemeinde.

(d) Beim Übergang in die hellenistiche Welt, wird die Gottessohnschaft Jesu als Wirken Gottes durch seinen Geist ausgelegt. Nicht das AT hilft zur Deutung des Wesens Jesu, sondern bereits die aufgrund des AT geprägte Geschichte über die Anfänge Jesu. Die Erzählung über die Engelerscheinung an Maria wird um eine von der Engelerscheinung an Joseph ergänzt. Die Gottessohnschaft Jesu wird ontologisch verstanden.

(e) Darum muß die Davidsohnschaft Jesu neu verankert werden. Sie läuft über Joseph, der als Davidsohn angesprochen wird (1,20). Indem Joseph Maria zu sich nimmt, ist Jesus rechtlich Davidsohn. Wie Röm 1,3f; Lk 1,31–33 sind Gottessohnschaft und Davidsohnschaft miteinander kombiniert.

(f) In vergleichbarer Umwelt entsteht auch die Erzählung von den Magiern (2,1–12). Sie setzt die Messianität Jesu voraus, wie bereits der Anfang (2,1) zeigt. Der Titel „Christus" wird als „König der Juden" ausgelegt (2,2) und seine Geburt in Bethlehem von Mi 5,1–4; 2 Sam 5,2 her begründet. Daraus ergibt sich die Feindschaft des Herodes zum Neugeborenen Kind. Die Erzähler haben bei dieser Feindschaft, die neben Herodes auch ganz Jerusalem erfaßt, bereits die Erfahrungen bei Jesu Kreuzigung und die Ablehnung der Botschaft von Jesus als dem Christus durch die Stadt im Auge. Jesus ist für diejenigen, die an irdischer Macht und Sicherheit haften, ein Dorn im Auge, der verschwinden muß. Für die frommen Außenstehenden ist der Titel „Christus" und „König der Juden" eine religiöse Bezeichnung. Sie beten den „Christus" an (2,11).

(g) Die Erzählung vom Kindermord (2,16–18) enthält eigentlich keine christologische Aussage, zeigt aber die Angst auf, in der die Mächtigen angesichts der Botschaft von Jesu Messianität leben und wie sie sich auswirkt. Das Weinen Rahels setzt das Wissen voraus, daß Rahel in Bethlehem begraben ist. An dieser Stelle fließen Motive der Mosetradition ein, die verstreut auch sonst in der Kindheitsgeschichte eine Rolle spielen, die aber zusammen genommen kaum zur These führen können, daß Jesus als neuer Mose dargestellt werden soll.[39]

(h) Mt bringt selbständig das Zitat aus Jes 7,14 ein und eliminiert gleichzeitig die Aussage, wonach Jesus durch den Geist zum Gottessohn wird. Durch die Zeugung aus dem Geist wird Jesus im Verständnis des Mt zum Emmanuel – Gott mit uns. Das ist die steilste, aber auch vom AT her begründbare Christologie: in Jesus ist Gott mit uns, d.h. Jesus repräsentiert die Gegenwart Gottes und wirkt im Namen Gottes, uns zum Heil. Die Gottessohnschaft versteht Mt nicht mehr ontologisch, sondern wieder vom Rechtsakt Gottes her.

Zugespitzt kann man sagen, daß die Christologie der Kindheitsgeschichten des Mt weitgehend im Gespräch mit dem AT entstanden ist. Vorausgesetzt ist immer, daß die Christen bereits wissen, daß Jesus das Heil Gottes gebracht hat. Sie artikulieren es aufgrund alttestamentlicher Texte neu. Das Wissen um Jesus prägt somit die Christologie, im Gespräch mit dem AT wird sie neu formuliert.

39. So allerdings D. M. Crossan, Structure & Theology of Mt 1,18–2,23, in: *Cahiers de Joséphologie 16* (1968), Ss. 119–35. Zu den einzelnen Motiven, die Moseüberlieferung aufnehmen können vgl. U. Luz, *Mt I* (s. Anm. 1), Ss. 145, 182.

BERGPREDIGT UND CHRISTOLOGIE

Wolfgang Schrage

Die Frage nach dem rechten Verhältnis der Bergpredigt zur matthäischen Christologie hat unterschiedliche Antworten gefunden. Diese sollen hier zu Ehren des verehrten Jubilars und Freundes wegen des vorgegebenen Titels der Festschrift noch einmal kritisch gemustert und diskutiert werden. Entgegen manchen anderen Thesen ist die Bergpredigt im Sinne des Matthäus m.E. nur recht zu verstehen und zu praktizieren, wenn man sie prononciert mit der Christologie des ersten Evangeliums verklammert. Zwar wird diese nur *in nuce* erkennbar. Insofern bedarf es nicht der Akzeptanz einer ausgebildeten Christologie über Person und Werk Jesu, um von der Bergpredigt angesprochen zu werden. Wohl aber hat man im Sinne des Matthäus auch bei den drei Kapiteln der Bergpredigt in Mt 5–7 im Ohr zu behalten, was schon in den ersten vier Kapiteln über den Christus gesagt worden ist, d.h. primär, daß sich in Jesus als dem Messias die alttestamentlichen Verheißungen Gottes erfüllen.

1. Methodische Grundvoraussetzung ist dabei, daß eine überzeugende Lösung für die hier zur Diskussion stehende Thematik nur im Rahmen der Konzeption des Gesamtevangeliums gefunden werden kann, also bei Einordnung der Bergpredigt in deren Makrokontext. Auch wenn eine Sicht „von hinten her" in einer leserorientierten Auslegung problematisch sein mag,[1] kann z.B. von der ausdrücklichen Bezugnahme in 28,19f auf „alles" das, was Jesus im vorangehenden Evangelium gelehrt und geboten hat, kaum abstrahiert werden, ja das erste Evangelium „ist eine Geschichte, die von Anfang bis zum Schluß gelesen werden will" und sich erst einer „Lektüre des Ganzen" erschließt,[2] zumal auf der redaktionsgeschichtlichen Ebene.[3] Zu einer adäquaten Beurteilung der Bergpredigt

1. Vgl. M. Mayordomo-Marín, *Den Anfang hören. Leserorientierte Evangelienexegese am Beispiel von Matthäus 1–2* (FRLANT 180; Göttingen: Vandenhoeck & Ruprecht, 1997).

2. So U. Luz, Eine thetische Skizze der matthäischen Christologie, in C. Breytenbach (Hg.), *Anfänge der Christologie* (FS F. Hahn; Göttingen: Vandenhoeck & Ruprecht, 1991), S. 221–35, hier 221; vgl. schon G. Eichholz, *Auslegung der Bergpredigt* (BSt 46; Neukirchen-Vluyn: Neukirchener Verl., 2nd edn, 1970), S. 14, nach dem es nahe liegt, „immer wieder über den Text der Bergpredigt *hinauszugreifen* und das Matthäusevangelium *als ganzes* zu bedenken"; P. Stuhlmacher, Jesu vollkommenes Gesetz der Freiheit. Zum Verständnis der Bergpredigt, *ZThK* 79 (1982), S. 283–322, hier 292: „*Matthäus will die Kap. 5–7 im Rahmen seiner Gesamtdarstellung des Wirkens Jesu gelesen sehen!*"; E. Schweizer, Die Bergpredigt im Kontext des Matthäusevangeliums, in: C. P. Mayer (Hg.), *Nach den Anfängen fragen* (FS G. Dautzenberg; Giessen: Selbstverlag d. Fachbereichs 07, 1994), S. 607–617, hier 607f, 616; anders Mayordomo-Marín, a.a.O. (Anm. 1), S. 367.

3. Darin liegt einer der Unterschiede zu früheren Bergpredigtexegesen, etwa der von H. Windisch,

genügt im wesentlichen aber schon das, was in Kap. 1–4 vorangeht und von Jesus als dem Subjekt der Rede in Mt 5–7 erkennbar werden läßt,[4] um die Bergpredigt nicht beziehungslos zu verselbständigen, vor allem nicht vom Bergprediger. Schon darum bleibt ein Verständnis der Bergpredigt im Sinne eines bloßen Kompendiums urchristlicher Moral ebenso ein unhaltbares Konstrukt wie ein sog. Bergpredigtchristentum, sosehr die größere Gefahr in der Kirchen- und Theologiegeschichte auch immer von der anderen Seite drohen mag, nämlich Matthäus und Jesus von der Bergpredigt zu isolieren.

2.1. Die Einsicht in diesen konstitutiven Konnex von Bergpredigt und Bergprediger hat nun freilich auch zu einer radikalen Christologisierung der Bergpredigt geführt, etwa in der wirkungsgeschichtlich einflußreichen Arbeit von E. Thurneysen,[5] der an die Spitze seiner Auslegung den programmatischen Satz stellt: „Wie das ganze Evangelium muß auch die Bergpredigt in grundsätzlicher Weise christologisch aufgefaßt werden. Wer sie anders auffaßt, hört an ihr vorbei" (S. 7). Nach Matthäus sei Jesus der einzige und der ganze Inhalt des Evangeliums. Wenn aber „Jesus selber und allein der wirkliche Inhalt des Evangeliums

Der Sinn der Bergpredigt. Ein Beitrag zum Problem der richtigen Exegese (UNT 16; Leipzig: J.C. Hinrichs, 1929, S. 101), der gegen eine „Zusammenhangsexegese" und für eine „Perikopen- und Einzelspruchexegese" plädiert, was auf der Ebene des historischen Jesus sein Recht behält. Auf der Ebene des 1. Evangeliums müssen dann aber die von U. Luz, *Die Jesusgeschichte des Matthäus* (Neukirchen-Vluyn: Neukirchener Verl., 1993), S. 12–17 genannten „Signale", „Weissagungen", „Schlüsselworte", „Repetitionen", „Inklusionen", „Querverweise und Wiederaufnahmen" übergangen werden. Zur These von *H.D. Betz* von der ursprünglichen Selbständigkeit der Bergpredigt vgl. unten Anm. 25.

4. Natürlich ist die Bergpredigt keine Rede im Sinne der antiken Rhetorik. Immerhin ist es interessant, daß nach Quintilian in den symbuleutischen Reden viel darauf ankommt, welche Person hier redet, ob sie z.B. durch ihr früheres Leben berühmt geworden ist, aus einer angesehenen Familie stammt oder durch ihr Alter oder ihre Stellung große Erwartung erweckt (Instit. Orat. 3,8,48). Rhetorische Kategorien für die Struktur der Bergpredigt verwendet H.D. Betz, *The Sermon on the Mount* (Minneapolis: Fortress Pr., 1995), S. 50–58; vgl. zur Rhetorik der Bergpredigt weiter W. Petersen, *Zur Eigenart des Matthäus. Untersuchung zur Rhetorik in der Bergpredigt* (Osnabrück: Rasch, 2001; vgl. dazu M. Meiser, ThLZ 127 [2002], S. 762–64). Jedenfalls hat gerade der Prolog als „christologischer Schlüsseltext" zu gelten (Luz, a.a.O. [Anm. 3], S. 41, der 1,1–4,22 dazu rechnet [ebd., 5.33]).

5. Die Bergpredigt, *TEH* 46 (1936) bzw. (danach wird hier zitiert) *TEH* 105 (1963); vgl. auch K. Barth, *KD* II/2, S. 766f. Thurneysen beruft sich ebd. 14 auf A. Tholuck, A. Bengel, den älteren Blumhardt und A. Schlatter. Noch dogmatischer interpretiert C.G. Vaught, *The Sermon on the Mount: A Theological Interpretation* (Albany, NY: State University of New York Press, 1986), S. 8f, nach dem Jesus seine Jünger als „Living Logos" lehren soll. Eine andere Frage ist, ob Matthäus Jesus als Person gewordene Tora (so m.E. wenig überzeugend J.M. Gibbs, The Son of God as the Torah Incarnate in Matthew, *StEv* 4 [1968], S. 36–46) oder inkarnierte Weisheit versteht (so M.J. Suggs, *Wisdom, Christology, and Law in Matthew's Gospel* (Cambridge/Mass: Harvard University Pr., 1970), wobei sich die letztere Annahme vor allem auf die Parallelität von 11,2 („Werke des Christus") und 11,19 („Werke der Weisheit") stützt (ebd. 56f.118), doch ist die Inkarnation der göttlichen Weisheit „*nicht* das Zentrum der mt Christologie. 11,19e bleibt eine Zusatzbemerkung, mit der Matthäus auf den grundlegenden Charakter der *Taten* des Christus, die er in seinem Buch erzählt, hinweisen will" (U. Luz, *Das Evangelium nach Matthäus, Teilbd. 2* [EKK I/2; Zürich u.a.: Beuzinger/Neukirchener Verl., 1990], S. 189 Anm. 45).

ist", dann – so folgert Thurneysen – „dann ist dieser Jesus und Jesus allein auch der ganze Inhalt der Bergpredigt", was in dem berühmten Satz gipfelt: „Dann ist der Bergprediger die Bergpredigt" (ebd.).

2.2. Schon die erste Probe dieser Auslegung, die sich von dem Ansatz leiten läßt, die Bergpredigt enthalte „lauter Worte, die nicht nur als von Jesus gesagte gehört werden wollen, sondern die als diese von ihm gesagten auch, und zwar in ausschließlicher Weise von ihm handeln" (ebd.), ist alles andere als beweiskräftig. Nach Thurneysen soll nämlich die Antithesenreihe in 5,17–48 Jesu eigene stellvertretende Erfüllung des Gesetzes im Blick haben: „das, was er getan hat und tut, um Gesetz und Propheten zu verwirklichen, das ist es, worum es nach der Bergpredigt selber in diesen Beispielen der Antithesen geht" (S. 8). Schon die simple Frage, wie das etwa mit 5,27f, die von der Ehe handeln, zu vereinbaren sein soll, zeigt das reichlich Gezwungene und Einseitige dieser „exklusiv christologischen" Erklärung. Ebensowenig überzeugend sind die anderen Beispiele. Wenn in Mt 7,21.24.26 von einem „Tun" die Rede ist, bedeutet das nach Thurneysen „gerade nicht eine Erfüllung des Gesetzes durch den Menschen", sondern „sich mit seinem ganzen Leben in die in Christus geschehene Erfüllung hineinstellen" (S. 27). Daß damit nicht das Eigentliche der Bergpredigt getroffen ist, liegt auf der Hand.[6]

3. Immerhin wird hier bei aller Überinterpretation als grundlegende Perspektive doch mit Recht und Nachdruck herausgestellt, daß die Bergpredigt nicht ohne den Bergprediger zu verstehen ist, Jesus in ihr als „der Bringer des messianischen Reiches mit seiner neuen Gerechtigkeit" (S. 14) dargestellt und dieser Jesus für Matthäus mit dem gegenwärtigen Herrn identisch ist. Auch andere Exegeten betonen darum, daß die Leser des Evangeliums den Bergprediger bereits als Messias kennengelernt haben[7]. Das soll nicht den Eindruck erwecken, bei den

6. Vgl. etwa P. Pokorný, *Der Kern der Bergpredigt* (Hamburg: H. Reich, 1969), S. 29: „Das christologische Moment der ‚neuen Moral' Jesu besteht nicht in der Begrenzung der Forderungen auf Jesus Christus, der Vorstellung gemäß, daß nur Jesus die Aufrufe der Bergpredigt erfüllt habe und daß kein anderer dies wiederholen könne. Im Gegenteil: Das Christliche besteht in dem Bekenntnis, daß Jesus uns einen Weg gebahnt, auf welchem wir ihm nachfolgen dürfen"; vgl. auch 56. W.D. Davies/D.C. Allison, ‚Reflections on the Sermon on the Mount', *SJTh* 44 (1991), S. 283–309, hier 292: „the christological interpretation does not exclude the imperative character of the SM but rather confirms it".

7. Vgl. u.a. C. Stange, ‚Zur Ethik der Bergpredigt', *ZSyTh* 2 (1924/25), S. 37–74, hier S. 70f, und G. Kittel, Die Bergpredigt und die Ethik des Judentums, ebd. Ss. 555–94, hier 586f („das Neue und Andere" sei „nicht die Lehre Jesu, sondern die Person Jesu"); J.P. Meier, *The Vision of Matthew. Christ, Church, and Morality in the First Gospel* (New York u.a.: Paulist Pr., 1979), S. 42–51 („Christ and Church as the Basis of Morality"); Schweizer, a.a.O. (Anm. 2), S. 613–16, der das vor allem am inneren Aufbau der Bergpredigt zu verifizieren sucht, die „vom Zuspruch Jesu, in dem Gott selbst sich dem Hörer zuspricht", umrahmt sei (614), was für 5,3–10 zutrifft, für 7,24–27 m.E. allerdings nicht unproblematisch ist. Die Deutung von H. Weder, *Die „Rede der Reden". Eine Auslegung der Bergpredigt heute* (Zürich: Theol. Verlag, 1985), S. 36 dürfte eine Überinterpretation sein, wenn aus dem Herantreten der Jünger an Jesus in 5,2 geschlossen wird, die Bergpredigt richte sich „in erster Linie an solche, die sich von diesem Jesus ganz bestimmen lassen", auch wenn dem in der Sache zuzustimmen ist.

christologischen Titeln in den ersten vier Kapiteln seien alle späteren Aspekte dieser Titel im Evangeliums oder gar deren traditionsgeschichtliche Implikationen präsent oder den Titeln kämen in seiner Christologie eine herausragende Bedeutung zu,[8] auch wenn sie umgekehrt nicht als eine *quantité négligable* herunterzuspielen sind.[9] Zutreffend aber ist in der Tat, daß schon die ersten vier Kapitel Jesus als Christus und Sohn Gottes erweisen, wie schon die unübliche Fülle der christologischen Titel mit ihrer Akzentuierung der heilsgeschichtlichen Kontinuität und Erfüllung illustriert.[10]

3.1. Schon im ersten Vers des Stammbaums in 1,1 wird Jesus Christus[11] als Abrahams- und Davidsohn qualifiziert,[12] und 1,18–25 erzählt dann, wie der von der Jungfrau Geborene durch die Anerkennung Jesu durch Josef zum Davididen wird. Als Sohn wird er als vom Geist gezeugt und von der Schrift verheißen

8. Vgl. Luz, a.a.O. (Anm. 2), S. 223. „Während ursprünglich die christologischen Hoheitstitel als Prädikativ funktionierten, um auszusagen, wer Jesus ist, scheint es bei Mt vor allem umgekehrt: Die mt Jesusgeschichte funktioniert als Prädikativ und bestimmt den Inhalt der traditionellen Hoheitstitel neu"; zustimmend zitiert auch bei Mayordomo-Marín, a.a.O. (Anm. 1), S. 215 Anm. 67; vgl. auch J.D. Kingsbury, *Matthew as Story* (Philadelphia: Fortress Pr., 1986), S. 41–56; M. Müller, The Theological Interpretation of the Figure of Jesus in the Gospel of Matthew: Some Principal Features in Matthean Christology, *NTS* 45 (1999), S. 157–73, hier 157f, 161f u.ö.

9. Vgl. unten Anm. 11.12 u. 52 und etwa R.T. France, *Matthew: Evangelist and Teacher* (Exeter: Paternoster Pr., 1989), S. 279–98; auch J. Ernst, *Matthäus. Ein theologisches Portrait* (Düsseldorf: Patmos, 1989), S. 21 plädiert für „ein Ineinander und Miteinander von indirekter und direkter Christologie"; H. Frankemölle, *Jahwebund und Kirche Christi. Studien zur Form- und Traditionsgeschichte des „Evangeliums" nach Matthäus* (NTA 10; Münster: Aschendorff, 1984), S. 262 betont dabei mit Recht, daß die wichtigsten Würdetitel des Evangeliums verdeutlichen, daß „in Jesus sich alle messianischen Erwartungen des AT erfüllten"; vgl. auch Ernst, *Matthäus*, S. 37.

10. Vgl. z.B. J.D. Kingsbury, The Place, Structure, and Meaning of the Sermon on the Mount Within Matthew, *Interp.* 41 (1987), S. 131–43; Davies/Allison, a.a.O. (Anm. 6), S. 284f (zu konkreten Verzahnungen von Mt 5–7 mit anderen Teilen des Evangeliums vgl. S. 299–302); Meier, a.a.O. (Anm. 7), S. 52–62; U. Luz, *Das Evangelium nach Matthäus, Teilbd. 1* (EKK I/1; Zürich u.a.: Beuzinger/Neukirchener Verl., 2nd edn, 2002), S. 293: „Der erzählende Rahmen des ganzen Evangeliums ist für Matthäus ein Ausdruck des Vorsprungs der Gnade"; J. Gnilka, *Das Matthäusevangelium* (HThK I/1; Freiburg u.a.: Herder, 1986), S. 292: „Im Gesamtkonzept des Mt ist das vorausgreifende Heilsangebot nicht zu übersehen"; anders aber z.B. M. Hengel, ‚Zur matthäischen Bergpredigt und ihrem jüdischen Hintergrund', *ThRu* 52 (1987), S. 327–400, hier 358 Anm. 52; vgl. auch G. Barth, *TRE* 5, S. 608: Vor 4,23 bringe Matthäus nur das „unbedingt Notwendige"; die Szene werde „gewissermaßen nur mit der notwendigsten Staffage ausgerüstet, um nun programmatisch Jesu Lehre zeigen zu können".

11. Zu (ὁ) Χριστός hier und in 1,16.18 u.ö. vgl. W. Grundmann, *ThWNT* IX, S. 522–24; France, a.a.O. (Anm. 9), S. 281–83; E.P. Blair, *Jesus in the Gospel of Matthew* (New York: Abingdon Press, 1960).

12. Vgl. zum Stammbaum K.-H. Ostmeyer, Der Stammbaum des Verheißenen: Theologische Implikationen der Namen und Zahlen in Mt 1,1–17, *NTS* 46 (2000), S. 175–92, z.B. S. 189f: „Christus wird zum Kulminationspunkt aller Verheißungen, indem er mittels seiner Abstammung und durch sein Leben ihre wesentlichen Epochen und Aspekte verkörpert und rekapituliert"; zum Davidssohn, der vor allem in Heilungsberichten vorkommt, vgl. E. Lohse, *ThWNT* VIII, S. 489f, der 490 Anm. 52 im matthäischen Bezug auf die Davidsohnschaft keine Historisierungstendenz erkennt, sondern J.M. Gibbs (Purpose and Pattern in Matthew's Use of the Title „Son of David", *NTS* 10 [1963/64], S. 446–64, hier 463) zitiert: „Matthew emphasizes Jesus as the Son of David, in whom are fulfilled all legitimate Jewish Messianic hopes"; France, a.a.O. (Anm. 9), S. 284–86; Luz, a.a.O. (Anm. 2.), S. 223–26.

(1,22f), durch einen Engel angekündigt (1,21–23), ja von Gott selbst öffentlich proklamiert (3,17; vgl. gegenüber σὺ εἶ in Mk 1,11 das οὗτος ἐστιν)[13]. Von besonderem Gewicht sowohl im Blick auf die im engeren Sinn theologischen Aussagen der Bergpredigt als auch auf das gesamte Evangelium ist die Erfüllung der Immanuelweissagung von Jes 7,14 in 1,23 (μεθ' ὑμῶν ὁ θεός), die einen unübersehbaren Bogen über 18,20 zum ἐγὼ μεθ' ὑμῶν εἰμι (28,20) schlägt[14] (vgl. auch das die österliche Reaktion der Jünger in 28,17 antizipierende προσκυνεῖν der Magier in 2,11 vor dem nach 2,6 in Bethlehem geborenen Messias und die Deutung des Jesusnamens in 1,21: „Er wird sein Volk von ihren Sünden erlösen", was schon auf 9,16; 20,28 und 26,28 vorausverweist.

3.2. Auch die schon vor der Bergpredigt skizzierte Wirksamkeit läßt Jesus als den Erwarteten erkennen. So erhellt das matthäische Verständnis des Gottes- bzw. Himmelreiches (5,3.10.19f; 6,10.13.33; 7,21) aus der knappen Zusammenfassung der Botschaft Jesu in 4,17: „Kehrt um, denn das Reich der Himmel ist nahe gekommen" (vgl. auch 4,23 „Evangelium vom Reich"), wobei speziell das begründende γάρ zu beachten bleibt. Hier wird zwar die Predigt Jesu der des Täufers aufs stärkste angeglichen (vgl. 3,2), andererseits aber wird durch das in 4,15f vorangestellte Erfüllungszitat aus Jes 8,23–9,1 der Unterschied markiert: Dem Volk, das in Finsternis und Todesschatten sitzt, ist ein Licht aufgestrahlt. Weiterhin wird schon vor der Bergpredigt die die messianische Heilszeit heraufführende Heilungstätigkeit Jesu nicht nur im Summarium berichtet (4,23–24a), sondern auch in 4,24b–c konkretisiert und damit zugleich „das ‚Zuvor' des Heils" angezeigt.[15]

13. E. Schweizer, *ThWNT* VIII, S. 381f will 3,17 durch 3,15 „im Sinne des leidenden Gerechten korrigiert" sehen; vgl. auch ders., a.a.O. (Anm. 2), S. 608 zur Beziehung von 4,17 zu 16,21. Vgl. zum Gottessohn weiter Luz, a.a.O. (Anm. 2), S. 231–34 und vor allem J.D. Kingsbury, *Matthew: Structure, Christology, Kingdom* (Philadelphia: Fortress Pr., 1975), S. 40–83, der dem Sohn Gottes bei Mt die Prävalenz zuschreibt; ähnlich R. Schnackenburg, *Die Person Jesu Christi im Spiegel der vier Evangelien* (HThK Suppl. 4; Freiburg u.a.: Herder, 1993), S. 115f; zurückhaltend im einzelnen z.B. Meier, a.a.O. (Anm.7) S. 56 Anm. 21f und S. 92 Anm. 77; anders zu Mt 1,18ff auch J. Nolland, No Son-of-God Christology in Matthew 1:18–25, *JSNT* 62 (1996), S. 3–12.

14. Luz, a.a.O. (Anm. 10), S. 150 sowie a.a.O. (Anm. 3), S. 43.45 und Frankemölle, a.a.O. (Anm. 9), S. 267 sprechen von Inklusion; zu 1,23 vgl. Frankemölle 7–83, z.B. 18: „Gott ist in Jesus seinem Volke gegenwärtig; in Jesus als dem Emmanuel ist der Gemeinde Jesu ‚mit der Gegenwart des Christus Gottes gnädige Gegenwart gegeben'" (Zitat von A. Schlatter). Vgl. auch M. Müller, Proskynese und Christologie nach Matthäus, in: M. Karrer (Hg.), *Kirche und Volk Gottes* (FS J. Roloff; Neukirchen-Vluyn: Neukirchener Verl., 2000), S. 210–24, hier S. 223f: „Weil in der Person Jesu Gott gegenwärtig ist und auch nach Ostern nicht entschwindet (28,20b), haben narrativ gesprochen, die Magier richtig gehandelt, und fallen alle weiteren Huldigungsbezeugungen gegenüber Jesus … nicht unter das Verdikt von Mt 4,10, weil sie einerseits die Gottheit Gottes belassen und andererseits die *Unmittelbarkeit Jesu zu Gott* nicht verleugnen".

15. Vgl. zu diesem „Zuvor" G. Lohfink, *Wem gilt die Bergpredigt? Beiträge zu einer christlichen Ethik* (Freiburg u.a.: Herder, 1988), S. 29–31; vgl. ders., Wem gilt die Bergpredigt?, *ThQ* 163 (1983), S. 264–84, der auf die Anwesenheit ganz Israels abhebt (s. 273–76), und dann im Blick auf 4,23. 24b–e erklärt: „Diese Volksscharen repräsentieren nicht nur das von Jesus zu sammelnde Gesamt-Israel, sondern sie repräsentieren darüber hinaus das Israel, dem die Befreiung schon geschenkt ist, dem das Evangelium schon angeboten ist und dem sich die messianische Heilszeit bereits erfüllt".

Zudem gehört Mt 5–7 mit Mt 8–9 in besonders enger Weise zusammen (vgl. die übereinstimmende Rahmung bzw. Schlußnotiz in 4,23 und 9,35).[16] Damit aber gehören auch das διδάσκειν Jesu auf der einen Seite und sein θεραπεύειν auf der anderen Seite unlöslich zusammen.[17] Beides ist Ausdruck von Jesu σπλαγχνιζέσθαι (9,36). Die Bergpredigt ist insofern konstitutiv Teil des Evangeliums vom Reich (4,23).

3.3. Schon die hier nur kurz skizzierte Einbindung der Bergpredigt in den Gesamtrahmen der Jesusgeschichte und deren Einordnung in den heilsgeschichtlichen Kontext deutet zugleich an, daß der Bergprediger auch im Sinne des Matthäus nicht einfach als *Mosissimus Mose* eines gesetzlichen Moralkodex anzusehen ist, dessen Imperative ohne den Heilsindikativ in der Luft hängen. Auch wenn man die notwendige Verknüpfung kaum so zuspitzen darf, daß in jedem Wort der Bergpredigt ein „Nachsatz" zu sehen sei, dem etwas voranging, weil die Worte z.T. aus ihren ursprünglichen Zusammenhängen herausgelöst worden sind,[18] ist es in der Tat korrekt, daß auch bei Matthäus die Verkündigung der Gottesherrschaft und damit das Evangelium vorangeht (4,23).[19]

Gerade für Matthäus wird zwar zutreffen, daß der Zuspruch sofort einen Anspruch in sich schließt[20]. Umgekehrt aber sind Gebote für ihn immer auch Angebote, können auch Imperative eine Gestalt der Gnade sein.[21] Die üblichen Verhältnisbestimmungen von Indikativ und Imperativ im Schema von Grund und Folge sind viel zu starr und schematisch, um das von Matthäus Intendierte zu erfassen. Matthäus hat erstaunlicherweise z.B. zwischen 6,14f in der Bergpredigt, wo unser Vergeben die Voraussetzung für Gottes Vergeben ist, und 18,23ff, wo unser Vergeben die Konsequenz und Entsprechung zu Gottes vorausgehender Vergebung bildet, offenbar keinen Widerspruch empfunden[22]. Auch die „Gerechtigkeit" ist anders als an den anderen Stellen in 5,6 und 6,33 „Gabe und

16. Meier, a.a.O. (Anm. 7), S. 46 Anm. 3 spricht von einem christologischen Diptychon.

17. Die oft zu lesende Vorordnung des „Messias der Lehre" vor den „Messias der Tat" (J. Schniewind), die sich auf die Abfolge der Kap. 5–7 und 8–9 beruft (vgl. z.B. G. Barth, *TRE* 5, s. 608), ist durchaus zu hinterfragen.

18. So J. Jeremias, *Die Bergpredigt* (CwH 27; Stuttgart: Calwer Verl., 1963), jetzt in ders., *Abba* (Göttingen: Vandenhoeck & Ruprecht, 1966), S. 171–89, hier S. 186f. Das kann freilich allenfalls für die Rekonstruktion der Worte des irdischen Jesus von Bedeutung sein, doch trifft es nicht einmal hier zu, daß *jedem* Wort der Bergpredigt ein Vordersatz vorangehe (so ebd. S. 186).

19. Vgl. z.B. D.C. Allison, The Structure of the Sermon on the Mount, *JBL* 106 (1987), S. 423–45, hier S. 441: „Before the crowds hear the Messiah's word they are the object of his compassion and healing. Having done nothing, nothing at all, they are benefitted".

20. G. Strecker, *Der Weg der Gerechtigkeit. Untersuchung zur Theologie des Matthäus* (FRLANT 82; Göttingen: Vandenhoeck & Ruprecht, 1962), S. 175, nach dem Indikativ und Imperativ sogar „identisch" sein sollen; zutreffender U. Luz, RGG^4 I, S. 1309: „‚Indikativ' und ‚Imperativ' liegen ineinander"; vgl. weitere Stimmen bei G. Barth, *TRE* 5, S. 611.

21. Vgl. Luz, a.a.O. (Anm. 10), S. 293: „Schließlich ist für Matthäus Gottes fordernder Wille selbst ein Stück Gnade" mit Verweis auf G. Strecker, Die Makarismen der Bergpredigt, *NTS* 17 (1970/71), S. 255–75, hier S. 274: Matthäus „übereignet dem Menschen seine Forderung als Gabe".

22. Vgl. z.B. Pokorný, a.a.O. (Anm. 6), S. 45. Überhaupt wird man den systemischen Charakter zu beachten haben, in der bestimmte Aussagen andere vor Ideologisierung schützen; vgl. ders., Die

Forderung zugleich".[23] Wenn bei diesem Ineinander von Indikativ und Imperativ in der Bergpredigt der Imperativ fokussiert wird, so ist dieser doch nicht knechtendes Joch und unerträgliche Last (vgl. 23,4), sondern Jesu „sanftes Joch und leichte Last" (11,30). Die von Matthäus so stark herausgestellte Kritik an aller Frucht- und Werklosigkeit des Glaubens berechtigt jedenfalls nicht dazu, von einer durchgängigen Ethisierung des Evangeliums und seiner Bergpredigt zu sprechen und aus dem matthäischen Jesus einen Tugend- und Gesetzeslehrer oder Propheten von radikalen „Einlaßbedingungen" zu machen[24]. Auch wenn Matthäus die Bergpredigt bereits übernommen[25] und sie vorsynoptisch in sich keinerlei Christologie hätte,[26] wäre im Sinne des Matthäus diese Sicht zu korrigieren.

4. Der Akzent in der matthäischen Christologie im Rahmen der Bergpredigt ruht freilich unzweifelhaft auf seiner Rolle als vollmächtiger Lehrer und endgültiger Ausleger des Willens Gottes, der durch niemanden zu überbieten oder auszutauschen ist.

Bergpredigt/Feldrede als supra-ethisches System, in: K. Wengst (Hg.), *Ja und Nein: Christliche Theologie im Angesicht Israels* (FS W. Schrage; Neukirchen-Vluyn: Neukirchener Verl., 1998), S. 183–93.

23. Stuhlmacher, a.a.O. [Anm. 2], S. 287 Anm. 9 im Anschluß an R.A. Guelich, *The Sermon on the Mount* (Waco: Word Books, 1982), S. 84–88; zu Jes 61 vgl. auch ebd. das Stellenregister 435 und H. Giesen, *Christliches Handeln. Eine redaktionskritische Untersuchung zum δικαιοσύνη-Begriff im Matthäus-Evangelium* (EHS.T 181; Frankfurt a.M.: Lang, 1982); anders freilich z.B. Strecker, a.a.O. (Anm. 20), S. 157f, der an sämtlichen Stellen „die ethische Haltung der Jünger, eine Rechtschaffenheit" finden will; Luz, a.a.O. (Anm. 10), S. 212f, 283f; Hengel, a.a.O. (Anm. 10), S. 359–62; Betz, a.a.O. (Anm. 4), S. 130f.

24. Es ist m.E. durchaus zweifelhaft, die Makarismenreihe einfach als Katalog ethischer Maximen zu interpretieren und als Heilsrufe im Anschluß an die Prophetie (Jes 61) zu überhören; vgl. schon Windisch, a.a.O. (Anm. 3), S. 150f, der in der ersten Viererreihe „prophetische Heilsverkündigung" und „Evangeliumsklänge" heraushört; Ch. Burchard, Versuch, das Thema der Bergpredigt zu finden, in: G. Strecker (Hg.), *Jesus Christus in Historie und Theologie* (FS H. Conzelmann; Tübingen: Mohr-Siebeck, 1975), S. 409–32, hier S. 418; R. Guelich, The Matthean Beatitudes: ‚Entrance Requirements' or Eschatological Blessings?, *JBL* 95 (1976), S. 415–34; Allison, a.a.O. (Anm. 19), S. 429f; I. Broer, *Die Seligpreisungen der Bergpredigt: Studien zu ihrer Überlieferung und Interpretation* (BBB 61; Königstein/Ts.: Hanstein, 1986); Gnilka, a.a.O. (Anm. 10), S. 115; Weder, a.a.O. (Anm. 7), S. 44f. Nach T. Holtz, Grundzüge einer Auslegung der Bergpredigt, *ZZ* 31 (1977), S. 8–16, hier S. 11 sollen die Makarismen sogar „als reines Evangelium programmatisch am Eingang der Bergpredigt" stehen.

25. So H.D. Betz, Die Bergpredigt: Ihre literarische Gattung und Funktion, in: ders., *Studien zur Bergpredigt* (Tübingen: Mohr-Siebeck, 1985), S. 1–16; vgl. aber z.B. die berechtigte Kritik von Ch.E Carlston, Betz on the Sermon on the Mount – A Critique, *CBQ* 50 (1988), S. 47–57; D.C. Allison, A New Approach to the Sermon on the Mount, *ETL* 64 (1988), S. 405–14 und die beiden Responses von E.W. Saunders und K. Snodgrass, *BR* 36 (1991), S. 81–87 bzw. 88–94; anders die Verteidigung von Betz (The Sermon on the Mount: In Defense of a Hypothesis) ebd. S. 74–80.

26. So Betz, a.a.O. (Anm. 25; Defense), S. 76f und etwa ders., The Problem of Christology in the Sermon on the Mount, in: Th.W. Jennings (Hg.), *Text and Logos: The Humanistic Interpretation of the New Testament* (FS H. Boers; Atlanta: Scholars Pr., 1990), S. 191–209, der aus dem Fehlen des Kerygmas von Tod und Auferstehung Jesu in der Bergpredigt schließt, daß dieses verworfen wurde und die Soteriologie auf der von Jesus interpretierten Tora basiert. Vgl. auch unten Anm. 62.

4.1. Kontrovers ist dabei, ob eine Mose-Typologie vorliegt, was vor allem bei der sog. Pentateuchtheorie und dem Bergmotiv diskutiert wird. Doch die These, nach der die fünf Reden des Matthäus den fünf Büchern des Pentateuch entsprechen, wird man trotz der parallelen Abschluß- und Überleitungsformeln (7,28; 11,1; 13,53; 19,1; 26,1) kaum gelten lassen, denn es gibt auch fünf Psalmbücher, fünf Abschnitte im Prediger, fünf in den Sprüchen und im *äthHen*, d.h. die Fünfteilung ist traditionell.[27] Erwägenswerter ist die Annahme, daß Matthäus im Unterschied zur lukanischen Feldrede die Jesusrede nicht zufällig auf einen Berg plaziert und damit an den Sinai erinnern bzw. auf einen neuen Sinai verweisen will. Eine solche indirekte Charakterisierung Jesu als neuer Mose durch die Bergszene in 5,1 könnte durch die Parallelität zwischen Herodes in der Kindheitsgeschichte Jesu und Pharao in der Mosegeschichte gestützt werden.[28] Aber schon, daß Matthäus die Wendungen „neuer Mose", „neuer Sinai" und „neues Gesetz" vermeidet,[29] warnt vor einem Überziehen dieser Analogien.[30] Matthäus hat tatsächlich nicht ein neues vom alten verschiedenes Gesetz im Sinn, sondern die Auslegung und Transzendierung des mosaischen. Zudem läßt sich das Bergmotiv auch anders denn als Gegenstück zum Berg der mosaischen Gesetzgebung erklären, da das Bergmotiv auch in Mt 14,23 beim Gebet Jesu, 15,29 bei den Heilungen und 17,1 bei der Verklärung wiederkehrt und der Berg in 28,16 Ort der Ostererscheinungen ist. Der Berg hätte dann eher als Offenbarungsort zu gelten[31]. Das Verhältnis Jesu zu Mose ist jedenfalls für Matthäus nicht das der Antithese und Überholung, sondern das der Entsprechung und Überbietung.[32]

27. So W.D. Davies, die hier zitierte deutsche Fassung *Die Bergpredigt* (München: Claudius, 1970) ist eine Zusammenfassung des voluminösen Werkes *The Setting of the Sermon on the Mount* (Cambridge: Cambridge University Pr., 1966); zur Pentateuchtheorie vgl. S. 18–22 bzw. engl. S. 14–25.

28. Vgl. das Massaker an den Kindern in Ex 1,22 und den Kindermord in Bethlehem Mt 2,16ff, die wunderbare Errettung des Mose und Jesu (Ex 2,1ff/Mt 2,13ff), ferner die 40-tägige Versuchung (Ex 34,28/Mt 4,2), wobei Jesus nach Luz, a.a.O. (Anm. 3), S. 36 jedoch als „neuer Mose und Umkehrung des Mose zugleich" erscheint; vgl. weiter etwa F. Hahn, *Christologische Hoheitstitel* (FRLANT 83; Göttingen: Vandenhoeck & Ruprecht, 1963), S. 400f; D.C. Allison, *The New Moses: A Matthean Typology* (Minneapolis u.a.: Fortress Pr., 1993).

29. Das hindert freilich nicht, daß manche Ausleger die Bergpredigt als „das neue Gesetz" oder als „die neue Gesetzgebung" und Jesus als „neuen Gesetzgeber" ausgeben (so z.B. Windisch, a.a.O. [Anm. 3], S. 10.45); zur Problematik einer *nova lex* vgl. aber G. Barth, Das Gesetzesverständnis des Evangelisten Matthäus, in: G. Bornkamm u.a., *Überlieferung und Auslegung im Matthäusevangelium* (WMANT 1; Neukirchen: Neukirchener Verl., 1960), S. 54–154, hier S. 143–49.

30. Vgl. Davies, a.a.O. (Anm. 27; Bergpredigt), S. 20–22; Guelich, a.a.O. (Anm. 23), S. 58 u.ö.

31. So z.B. Strecker, a.a.O. (Anm. 20), S. 98; vgl. auch Kingsbury, a.a.O. (Anm. 13), S. 56f; Luz, a.a.O. (Anm. 10), S. 266: „Eine feststehende Bedeutung hat er nicht"; vgl. weiter T.L. Donaldson, *Jesus on the Mountain. A Study of Matthean Theology*, JSNT Supp. 8 (Sheffield: Sheffield Ac. Pr., 1985), der zu 5,1 von frühjüdischen Texten ausgeht (51–83), wo der Berg und besonders der Zion als Ort eschatologischer Ereignisse begegnet, so daß 5,1 den Ort nennen soll, „where Jesus calls people into eschatological fellowship and gives them the διδαχή which provides the basis for and prescribes the characteristics of that fellowship" (116), mit spezieller Berufung auf 5,14b (S. 117f).

32. Wahrscheinlich geht die Antithesenform in 5,21–48 nicht auf den Evangelisten zurück, sondern ist ihm schon aus den 3 Antithesen des Sonderguts vorgegeben; vgl. etwa G. Barth, *TRE* 5, S. 606; I. Broer, *Freiheit vom Gesetz und Radikalisierung des Gesetzes. Ein Beitrag zur Theologie des*

4.2. Bedeutsamer als die Mosetypologie ist, daß Jesus primär als von Gott autorisierter Lehrer und verbindlicher Ausleger des Gesetzes erscheint.[33] Dieser Zug wird zwar noch besonders unterstrichen durch auf eine rabbinische Sitte rekurrierende Notiz in 5,1, daß Jesus sich vor Beginn seiner Rede hingesetzt, also die übliche Haltung des Toralehrers eingenommen haben soll (vgl. Mt 23,2). Seine Autorität jedoch ist unvergleichlich und unüberbietbar (7,29), wie auch das einleitende Amen,[34] „Ich aber sage euch“[35] und der fehlende Rekurs auf andere Schriftstellen bei Jesu eigener Auslegung bestätigt. Jesus erscheint also als *der*, nicht als ein Lehrer unter anderen[36] (vgl. 23,10: καθηγητὴς ὑμῶν ἐστιν εἷς ὁ Χριστός). Wie sehr Matthäus daran lag, diesen Charakter der Bergpredigt als Didache Jesu, als Unterweisung im Gehorsam in der christlichen Halacha herauszustellen, dokumentieren die beiden Schlußverse in 7,28–29, und an diesem Punkt besteht im Unterschied zu den unterschiedlichen Hörerkreisen auch keinerlei Differenz zwischen Anfang und Ende der Bergpredigt.[37] Inhaltlich aber geht

Evangelisten Matthäus, SBS 98 (Stuttgart: Katholisches Bibelwerk, 1980), S. 11–74; G. Strecker, *Die Bergpredigt. Ein exegetischer Kommentar* (Göttingen: Vandenhoeck & Ruprecht, 1984), S. 65f; vgl. aber Suggs, a.a.O. (Anm. 5), S. 110 sowie ders., The Antitheses as Redactional Products, in: Strecker, a.a.O. (Anm. 24), S. 433–44 u.a.

33. Vgl. G. Bornkamm, Enderwartung und Kirche im Matthäusevangelium, in: ders. a.a.O. (Anm. 29), S. 13–47, hier S. 32, wonach vor allem in der Auslegung des Gesetzes „die eigentlich matthäische Christologie greifbar“ wird.

34. 5,18.26; 6,2.5.13.16. Ob man in diesem nichtresponsorischen Amen als Einleitung der Worte Jesu „einen den Gottesnamen meidenden Ausdruck der Vollmacht Jesu“ zu erblicken hat (so J. Jeremias, *TRE* 2, S.389) oder eine bloße Bekräftigung (vgl. H.-W. Kuhn, *EWNT* I, S. 167: „Beteuerungs- und evtl. auch Vollmachtsformel“; ähnlich H. Hübner, *EWNT* II, S. 855), ändert nicht viel.

35. 5,22.28.32.34.39.44. Vgl. E. Lohse, „Ich aber sage euch“, in: ders., *Die Einheit des Neuen Testaments* (Göttingen: Vandenhoeck & Ruprecht, 1973), S. 73–87. Danach gibt es im Rabbinat nur formale Parallelen, die die eigne Auslegung der anderer Gelehrten entgegenstellen. Vgl. jetzt aber auch den Vergleich mit 4Q393–399 bei K.-W. Niebuhr, Die Antithesen des Matthäus. Jesus als Toralehrer und die frühjüdisch-weisheitlich geprägte Torarezeption, in: Ch. Kähler (Hg.), *Gedenkt an das Wort* (FS W. Vogler; Leipzig: Evang. Verlagsanstalt, 1999), S. 175–200, hier S. 180f.

36. Offenbar darum wird Jesus von den Seinen nicht mit den für Schriftgelehrte geläufigen διδάσκαλος tituliert (so 8,19 von einem der Schriftgelehrten; 9,11 in der Anrede der Jünger durch die Pharisäer „euer Lehrer“, was eine Distanz konnotiert: er ißt mit Zöllnern und Sündern; 19,16 im Munde des reichen Jünglings und 22,19 von Anhängern des Herodes). Ähnlich steht es mit ῥαββί so nur 26,25.49 im Munde des Judas. Wo Mt entsprechende Anreden bei Markus vorfand, hat er sie geändert und durch κύριε ersetzt: 17,4 gegenüber Mk 9,5; 8,25 gegenüber Mk 4,30; 20,33 gegenüber Mk 10,51 ῥαββουνί; vgl. Hahn, a.a.O. (Anm. 28), S. 74f; E. Lohse, *ThWNT* VI, S. 966; H.F. Weiss, *EWNT* I, S. 767; Meier, a.a.O. (Anm. 7), S. 50 „The title ‚teacher‘ is inadequate because it carries the idea of *merely* a teacher, *only* a human being“. Allerdings wird man in das Gesamtbild auch die narrativen Strukturen einzubeziehen haben; vgl. S. Byrskog, Jesus the Only Teacher. Didactic Authority and Transmission in Ancient Israel, Ancient Judaism and the Matthean Community, *CB.New Testament* 24 (1994), S. 200–18; ebd. S. 200 Anm. 1 weitere Literatur. Man sollte hier jedenfalls keine falschen Alternativen konstruieren und etwa mit Kingsbury, a.a.O. (Anm. 10), S. 134 erklären, der Bergprediger „is not the ‚Teacher‘ but the ‚Son of God‘“.

37. Vermutlich darf man aus dem Vorliegen konzentrischer Hörerkreise schließen, daß Jesu Lehre nicht nur als Jünger- und Gemeindeunterweisung konzipiert ist; vgl. Luz, a.a.O. (Anm. 10), S. 266, 540 und a.a.O. (Anm. 3), S. 55–57 und auch Betz, a.a.O. (Anm. 4), S. 81.

es um die Tora und ihre messianische Auslegung. Darauf weist auch der spezifische Gebrauch des Wortes διδάσκειν. Während Markus das Verbum nämlich ohne Unterschied für Jesu Lehren überhaupt verwendet, wird der Begriff Lehren bei Matthäus speziell für die Gesetzeslehre reserviert, wenn Jesus also eindeutig als Toralehrer gekennzeichnet werden soll.[38] Gerade dieser halachische Gesichtspunkt der Lehre Jesu wird von Matthäus in der Christologie der Bergpredigt in den Vordergrund gerückt, nicht dagegen der kerygmatische, auch wenn man sich vor Überinterpretation im Sinn einer scharfen Trennung hüten sollte (vgl. 4,17.23).[39]

4.3. Die Funktion Jesu als messianischer Ausleger der Tora könnte jüdischen Erwartungen entsprechen, die dem Messias die Rolle des gültigen Auslegers der Tora und eine neue Belehrung in der Tora zuschreiben[40], doch ob Matthäus mit solchen Gedanken vertraut war, muß offen bleiben. Wahrscheinlicher reagiert Matthäus (nach Jamnia!) auf Vorwürfe jüdischer Seite, daß Jesu Toraauslegung nicht die des wahren Lehrers ist und nicht der der Pharisäer und Schriftgelehrten entspricht,[41] möglicherweise aber zugleich auf ein antinomistisches Mißverständnis über den Sinn von Jesu Sendung bzw. eine jüdisch-hellenistische gesetzesfreie Praxis,[42] doch kann das hier auf sich beruhen. Jedenfalls aber hat er die Funktion des irdischen Messias Jesus wesentlich als Auslegung des Gesetzes verstanden[43]. Matthäus stellt Jesu Leben und Lehre darum programmatisch unter das Leitwort – es ist das erste Wort Jesu überhaupt im Evangelium – von der Erfüllung aller Gerechtigkeit (3,15) bzw. von der Erfüllung des Gesetzes und der Propheten (5,17). Das Verständnis von 5,17 ist freilich äußerst umstritten.[44]

38. Vgl. Bornkamm, a.a.O. (Anm. 33), 35 Anm. 1; W. Schenk, *Die Sprache des Matthäus. Die Text-Konstituenten in ihren makro- und mikrostrukturellen Relationen* (Göttingen: Vandenhoeck & Ruprecht, 1987), S. 184f; A.F. Zimmermann, *Die urchristlichen Lehrer* (WUNT2, 12; Tübingen: Mohr-Siebeck, 1984), S. 150–57.

39. Nach Strecker, a.a.O. (Anm. 20), S. 175 „trägt die Didache kerygmatische, wie umgekehrt das Kerygma belehrenden Charakter" (vgl. auch, S. 127f); auch Luz, a.a.O. (Anm. 10), S. 247–50 rückt beide Begriffe nahe aneinander. Im übrigen darf man διδάσκειν nicht intellektualistisch verstehen (vgl. Frankemölle, a.a.O. [Anm. 9], S. 96f).

40. Nach allerdings singulären und mehr peripheren Äußerungen sollen in der kommenden Welt trotz der prinzipiellen ewigen Gültigkeit der Tora einige der Speisevorschriften wegfallen bzw. einige der Zeremonialgesetze, die unverständlich waren, vom Messias interpretiert werden. Vgl. *Billerbeck IV* 1–3; Davies, a.a.O. (Anm. 27; Bergpredigt), S. 51–78; Barth, a.a.O. (Anm. 29), S. 144–46; P. Schäfer, Die Torah in der messianischen Zeit, *ZNW* 65 (1974), S. 27–42; Hengel, a.a.O. (Anm. 10), S. 377f und R. Riesner, *Jesus als Lehrer* (WUNT 2, 7; Tübingen: Mohr-Siebeck, 1981), S. 304–30.

41. Vgl. zur „Sprechsituation" des Matthäus z.B. H. Frankemölle, Die sogenannten Antithesen des Matthäus (Mt 5,21ff), Hebt Matthäus für Christen das „Alte" Testament auf?, in: ders. (hg.), *Die Bibel: das bekannte Buch – das fremde Buch* (Paderborn u.a.: Schöningh, 1994), S. 61–92, hier, S. 82–85; Davies, a.a.O. (Anm. 27; Bergpredigt), S. 98–106; Davies/Allison, a.a.O. (Anm. 6), S. 294–97.

42. Barth, a.a.O. (Anm. 29), S. 88 geht z.B. von einer „doppelten Frontstellung gegen Antinomismus und Rabbinat" aus; vgl. aber z.B. K. Pantle-Schieber, Anmerkungen zur Auseinandersetzung von ἐκκλήσια und Judentum im Matthäusevangelium, *ZNW* 80 (1989), S. 145–62: gegenwärtige Konflikte mit dem zeitgenössischen, vor allem rabbinischen Judentum werden von Matthäus zurückprojiziert.

43. Barth, a.a.O. (Anm. 29), *passim*.

44. Vgl. die Kommentare z.St.

4.4. Was Matthäus unter der fast nur (d.h. mit Ausnahme von Lk 16,16) bei ihm begegnenden Koordinierung von *Gesetz und/oder Propheten* versteht, die Jesus erfüllt, zeigen besonders 7,12[45] und 22,40, die der matthäischen Redaktion angehören, auch wenn in 5,17 „oder" statt „und" gebraucht wird. Daß damit zunächst die zusammenfassende Umschreibung für das Alte Testament bzw. deren beiden wichtigsten Bestandteile genannt sind, ist nur eine vorläufige Antwort. 7,12 und 22,40 machen nämlich deutlich, daß Matthäus vor allem die halachisch-ethischen Partien des Alten Testaments im Auge hat (vgl. auch die Schlußstellung der Feindesliebe in der sechsten Antithese und die Zitierung von Hos 6,6 in Mt 9,13 und 12,7). Wie stark Matthäus Jesus am Doppelgebot der Liebe als Auslegungs- und Beurteilungskriterium des Gesetzes gelegen sein läßt, erweist besonders deutlich Mt 22,39: Während bei Markus das Gebot der Nächstenliebe als das „zweite" Gebot nach dem Gebot zur Liebe Gottes gilt, ist es nach Matthäus dem ersten „gleich", d.h. gleichrangig.[46] Vor allem aber fügt Matthäus den Satz hinzu, daß in diesen beiden Geboten das ganze Gesetz und die Propheten hängen (22,40). Das Gesetz ist nach Matthäus zwar bis zu Jota und Häkchen verbindlich (5,18f), aber nicht ohne Auslegung.[47]

4.5. Damit ist schon eine wichtige Vorentscheidung für das Verständnis des viel umstrittenen πληρῶσαι in 5,17 gefallen, das der Annullierung von Gesetz und Propheten gegenübergestellt wird. Rein von der Wortbedeutung her sind verschiedene Deutungen möglich: a. das Gesetz auffüllen, ausbauen, komplettieren; b. es durch die Tat erfüllen, es tun und danach handeln; c. es eschatologisch bestätigen, zur Geltung bringen, in seiner wahren Bedeutung herausstellen. Die rechte Entscheidung über den in Mt 5,17 vorliegenden Sinn kann zwar nur vom Mikro- und Makrokontext her fallen, doch schon von den genannten Stellen her, die die Vorrangigkeit des Liebesgebotes als Zentrum, Schlüssel und Maßstab der Interpretation betonten, legt sich am ehesten ein Verständnis von πληρῶσαι im unter c genannten Sinne der Aufrichtung durch rechte *Auslegung* von Gesetz und Propheten nahe. Hätte Matthäus freilich die Propheten zusätzlich in ein schon umlaufendes Logion eingebracht,[48] wäre von den anderen matthäischen Belegen für Erfüllung her wohl auch an die heilsgeschichtliche Erfüllung von

45. Zur Goldenen Regel vgl. A. Dihle, *RAC* 11, S. 930–40, 937 zu Mt 7,12; A. Sand, *Das Gesetz und die Propheten. Untersuchungen zur Theologie des Evangeliums nach Matthäus* (BU 11; Regensburg: Pustet, 1974), S. 187–89.

46. Vgl. Barth, a.a.O. (Anm. 29), S. 70–80; Sand, a.a.O. (Anm. 45), S. 189–93; W. Schrage, *Ethik des Neuen Testaments* (NTD.E 4; Gottingen: Vandenhoeck & Ruprecht, 2. Aufl., 1989), S. 152f; Luz, a.a.O. (Anm. 3), S. 64–66; Weder, a.a.O. (Anm. 7), S. 95–98; vgl. weiter, auch zu den religions- und traditionsgeschichtlichen Fragen H.W. Kuhn, Das Liebesgebot Jesu als Tora und als Evangelium. Zur Feindesliebe und zur christlichen und jüdischen Auslegung der Bergpredigt, in: H. Frankemölle u. K. Kertelge (Hg.), *Vom Urchristentum zu Jesus* (FS J. Gnilka; Freiburg i. B.: Herder, 1989), S. 194–230, hier S. 204–20.

47. Daß die Frage nach der rechten Auslegung, genauer: die nach ihrer Quintessenz bzw. dem Verständnis dessen, worin Gesetz und Propheten zusammenzufassen sind, für Matthäus die Kardinalfrage ist, bestätigt die Beobachtung, daß alle hierfür einschlägigen Stellen sich nur bei ihm finden (7,12; 9,13; 12,7; 22,40; 23,33). Allerdings ist das Liebesgebot das größte, aber nicht das einzige Gebot.

48. So Guelich, a.a.O. (Anm. 23), S. 137.

Gottes Heilsverheißung zu denken. Πληροῦν in diesem Sinne erscheint bekanntlich oft bei den sog. Reflexions- bzw. Erfüllungszitaten, nach denen Gott sein Verheißungswort in Christus erfüllt (1,22; 2,15.17.23; 4,14 usw.[49]). Auch Gesetz und Propheten zusammen können offenbarungs- bzw. verheißungsgeschichtlich gebraucht werden, so vor allem in 11,13, wo die Propheten dem Gesetz voranstehen („Alle Propheten und das Gesetz haben bis Johannes geweissagt") und die prophetische Dimension der Erfüllung zutage tritt. Daß Matthäus auch in der Bergpredigt an *solcher* Erfüllung der prophetischen Heilsverheißung liegt, veranschaulichen die Makarismen mit ihren Anspielungen auf Jes 61. Doch vom Folgenden, speziell den Antithesen her, muß die Tora im Vordergrund stehen. Das bestätigt der Übergang von V 16 (Forderung der guten Werke) zu V 17: Werke sind eben das, was schon Gesetz und Propheten gebieten. Auch Propheten können nicht nur weissagen, sondern auch den Willen Gottes gebieten (vgl. die beiden genannten Hosea-Zitate). Kurzum: Auch wenn ein heilsgeschichtliches Moment in πληροῦν mitschwingen wird, so hat das Übergewicht doch die Herausstellung der wahren Bedeutung von Gesetz und Propheten, und zwar durch den messianischen Interpreten Jesus.[50]

5. Auch die Verwendung des Kyriostitels läßt erkennen, wie entscheidend die Ausrichtung an Jesu eschatologisch gültiger Auslegung ist. Das zeigt der Schluß der Bergpredigt in 7,24–27, wo Jesus nun die höchste Würde zugesprochen wird und er einerseits als Herr der Christen, andererseits als eschatologischer Weltenrichter erscheint.[51] Hier wird dem Enthusiasmus mit seiner falschen Inanspruchnahme der Vollmacht Jesu eine Abfuhr erteilt: Falsche Christen und Propheten sind solche, die Jesus als „Herr, Herr" akklamieren, aber nicht den Willen Gottes

49. Vgl. W. Rothfuchs, *Die Erfüllungszitate des Matthäus-Evangeliums* (BWANT 88; Stuttgart: Kohlhammer, 1969); Luz, a.a.O. (Anm. 3), S. 50–53.

50. Vgl. Barth, a.a.O. (Anm. 29), S. 64; Strecker, a.a.O. (Anm. 32), S. 57 (Jesus bringt Gesetz und Propheten „zum vollen Maß", d.h. bestätigt sie „in ihrer eigentlichen Bedeutung"); I. Broer, a.a.O. (Anm. 32), S. 34.71 („Zur-Fülle-Bringen"); Sand, a.a.O. (Anm. 45), S. 185; Kuhn, a.a.O. (Anm. 46), S. 220 („Das Liebesgebot bestimmt inhaltlich die ‚Fülle' von Tora und Propheten und ist das Kriterium für solche ‚Fülle'"); Weder, a.a.O. (Anm. 7), S. 94f; Betz, a.a.O. (Anm. 4), S. 178f. Anders z.B. U. Luz, Die Erfüllung des Gesetzes bei Matthäus (Mt 5,17–20), *ZThK* 75 (1978), S. 398–435, hier S. 416f, der für Tun plädiert, wofür das vor διδάσκει stehende ποιεῖν in V 19 sowie V 20 sprechen könnte; vgl. ders., a.a.O. (Anm. 10), S. 314, wo Lehre als „Nebengedanke" gelten gelassen, aber der Praxis der „Vorrang" eingeräumt wird. F. Hahn, Mt 5,17 – Anmerkungen zum Erfüllungsgedanken bei Matthäus, in: U. Luz u. H. Weder (Hg.), *Die Mitte des Neuen Testaments: Einheit und Vielfalt neutestamentlicher Theologie* (FS E. Schweizer; Göttingen: Vandenhoeck & Ruprecht, 1983), S. 42–54 stellt die Verwirklichung durch das messianische Geschehen in den Vordergrund und schließt darin Lehre und Tun mit ein.

51. H.D. Betz, Eine Episode im Jüngsten Gericht (Mt 7,21–23), in: ders., a.a.O. (Anm. 25), S. 111–40, hier S. 134 kommt Mt 7,21–23 „einer expliziten Christologie am nächsten", wobei freilich „die Christologie hier nur eingebettet in die Eschatologie" vorliege. Eine andere Frage ist, ob Jesus hier tatsächlich nur als Anwalt seiner Anhänger fungiert (ebd. S. 135). Eher ist hier von Jesus „als dem eschatologischen Zeugen und Richter" zu reden (G. Bornkamm, *ThWNT* V, S. 208; vgl. auch Gnilka, a.a.O. [Anm. 10], S. 277).

tun.[52] Bei Matthäus läßt das nur hier und jetzt dringliche Tun des Willens Gottes als Oppositum zur Herr-Herr-Akklamation für V 21 keinen Zweifel daran, daß auch dieses Herr-Herr-Sagen *vor* dem Gericht geschieht, also nicht erst wie in V 22 eschatologische Anrede im Gericht ist. Daß auch in V 21 Christen, und zwar hier und jetzt, im Blick sind, bestätigt auch V 22b–d, wo sich die Enthusiasten auf ihre charismatische Wirksamkeit berufen, die natürlich ebenfalls auf Erden ihren Ort hat: „Herr, Herr, haben wir nicht in deinem Namen Dämonen ausgetrieben und in deinem Namen viele Machttaten vollbracht?" Jesus wird also von den Seinen schon hier und jetzt als Kyrios respektiert, während sein Herrsein über Nichtchristen gar nicht zur Debatte steht. Das steht auch im Einklang mit dem sonstigen Gebrauch des Kyrios-Titels bei Matthäus.[53]

Zwar wird Kyrios abgesehen von den auf Gott bezogenen Beispielen (1,20.22.24; 2,13.15.19; 4,7.19; 5,33 u.ö.) auch in den eschatologischen Gleichnissen gebraucht, charakteristischer ist aber, daß die Kyrios-Anrede an den irdischen Jesus uns nur im Munde der Jünger begegnet. Für die Jünger ist Jesus also bereits hier und jetzt der Kyrios. In V 22 dagegen fungiert Jesus als eschatologischer Richter, der mit seinem Urteilsspruch eine Reserve, ja Kritik an Prophetie, Exorzismus und Machttaten zu erkennen gibt. Das ist umso erstaunlicher, als solche Phänomene sonst in den urchristlichen Gemeinden weithin als besondere Auszeichnung gelten und auf den Geist selbst zurückgeführt werden (vgl. z.B. 1 Kor 12 und 14), ja auch bei Matthäus die Austreibung der Dämonen als Anbruch des Reiches Gottes verstanden (12,28) und den Jüngern ebenfalls ausdrücklich aufgetragen wird (10,8). Aber mit solchen spektakulären Aktionen hat man sich nach Matthäus noch nicht ganz dem Kyrios und der besseren Gerechtigkeit ausgeliefert. Vor allem aber ist nicht das Tun als solches belangreich, sondern dasjenige, was sich an den Worten Jesu orientiert. Hier findet nicht nur die Orthodoxie ihr Maß an der Orthopraxie, sondern die Orthopraxie als solche ist strittig. Gewiß werden Inspiration und Wunder in Jesu Namen nicht bestritten (7,29), wohl aber eigentümlich relativiert. Wer sich auf den erhöhten Christus oder den Geist beruft und Außergewöhnliches zu wirken weiß, ist damit noch

52. Ob die Lukasform in Lk 6,46 („Was nennt ihr mich Herr, Herr und tut nicht, was ich euch sage") ursprünglicher ist und die Beziehung auf das durch Jesus ausgeübte eschatologische Gericht von Matthäus stammt, braucht hier ebensowenig zu interessieren wie die Frage, ob Lukas beim Herr-Herr-Sagen an den Kult denkt oder nur die Anrede an den Lehrer sei. Jedenfalls darf die Gerichtsszene von V 22 nicht auch in V 21 eingetragen werden.

53. Auch wenn Kyrios fast ausnahmslos im Vokativ erscheint, erklärt Bornkamm, a.a.O. (Anm. 33), S. 39 zu Recht: „Titel und Anrede Jesu als des κύριος haben bei Matth. also durchaus den Charakter eines göttlichen Hoheitsnamens"; ebs. Hahn, a.a.O. (Anm. 28), S. 85; vgl. trotz Zustimmung aber die Zurückhaltung gegenüber einer von Kyrios her entwickelten matthäischen Christologie bei Kingsbury, a.a.O. (Anm. 13), S. 103–13 (z.B. 105: „an auxiliary christological title"); vgl. auch France, a.a.O. (Anm. 9), S. 287f. An unserer Stelle ist κύριε jedenfalls eine Hoheitsbezeichnung und nicht nur respektvolle Höflichkeitsanrede (so auch Kingsbury, S. 107, nach dem κύριος sich hier nach Mt auf den Menschensohn bezieht); vgl. weiter Strecker, a.a.O. (Anm. 20), S. 123–25, der wie Hahn S. 97f (Gebetsruf an den Weltenrichter) die eschatologische Dimension betont, auch wenn der kommende Kyrios „als der Gekommene dargestellt" ist (S. 125); vgl. auch H. Geist, *Menschensohn und Gemeinde. Eine redaktionskritische Untersuchung zur Menschensohnprädikation im Matthäusevangelium* (fzb 57; Würzburg: Echter Verl.,1986), S. 351–67.

längst nicht legitimiert und gerettet. Der Christus fragt als Weltenrichter nicht nur nach Früchten, sondern nach guten Früchten, und dessen Kriterium sind Jesu Worte. Es geht um das Tun des Willens *Gottes*, wobei der Unterschied zu Lk 6,46 („Tut, was *ich* euch sage“) gewiß kein Gegensatz ist, denn auch für Matthäus ist der Wille Gottes der durch Jesus proklamierte und ausgelegte Wille Gottes (vgl. 7,24 „*meine* Worte“).

6. Weitere Akzente in der matthäischen Christologie ruhen auf drei anderen Punkten: Zum einen ist, wie schon angedeutet, auch bei der für die Bergpredigt relevanten Christologie auszugehen vom Schluß des Evangeliums in Kap. 28, wo eine Art Summarium des Evangeliums geboten wird und der Auferstandene seine Worte als irdischer Jesus für alle Zeiten neu in Geltung setzt und verpflichtend macht: „Geht hin in alle Welt und macht zu Jüngern alle Völker, und lehrt sie halten alles, was ich euch befohlen habe“ (28,19f).[54] Die Unterweisung in dem, was Jesus gelehrt hat, und zwar inklusive der Bergpredigt, wird zu Ostern neu autorisiert und universalisiert. Die in der Bergpredigt geforderte bessere Gerechtigkeit gilt nun für alle, die zu Jüngern werden, und zwar, weil der Prediger der Bergpredigt nun der erhöhte und inthronisierte Herr ist, dem alle Macht gegeben ist im Himmel und auf Erden (Mt 28,18).[55] D.h. das Wort des irdischen Jesus ist seit Ostern das Wort des auferweckten Gekreuzigten und die eschatologische Gottesherrschaft nun nicht mehr zu trennen von der Herrschaft Jesu Christi. Anders als Lukas läßt Matthäus darum auch inhaltlich keinen Bruch im Gebotenen zwischen dem, was der Irdische und dem, was der Erhöhte gebietet, erkennen, allenfalls implizit in der möglichen Korrektur der ausschließlichen Israelmission (10,5.23) durch den universalen Missionsauftrag (28,19).[56] Sonst aber ist der Weg der besseren Gerechtigkeit vor und nach Ostern inhaltlich wesentlich derselbe. Dieser Weg der besseren Gerechtigkeit aber wird jetzt von

54. Vgl. *Eichholz*, a.a.O. (Anm. 2), S. 15; G. Bornkamm, Der Auferstandene und der Irdische. Mt 28,16–20, in: E. Dinkler (Hg.), *Zeit und Geschichte* (FS R. Bultmann; Tübingen: Mohr-Siebeck, 1964), S. 171–91, hier S. 186f; Barth, a.a.O. (Anm. 29), S. 122–28; W. Trilling, *Das wahre Israel. Studien zur Theologie des Matthäus-Evangeliums* (StANT 10; Kösel: München, 3. Aufl., 1964), S. 21–51; J. Lange, *Das Erscheinen des Auferstandenen im Evangelium nach Matthäus. Eine traditions- und redaktionsgeschichtliche Untersuchung zu Mt 28,16–20* (fzb 11; Würzburg: Echter Verl., 1973), 342f; France, a.a.O. (Anm. 9), S. 312–17.

55. E. Fuchs, Jesu Selbstzeugnis nach Matthäus 5, in: ders., *Zur Frage nach dem historischen Jesus. Ges. Aufsätze II* (Tübingen: Mohr-Siebeck, 1960), S. 100–25, hier S. 116 hebt aber auch auf den Tod Jesu ab: „Der erhöhte Jesus, der in der Bergpredigt spricht, ist derselbe, der im Gehorsam gegen Gottes Richterwillen ans Kreuz ging, um alle Gerechtigkeit zu erfüllen. Nur aufgrund dieses vollendeten, in Jesu Auferstehung bzw. Erhöhung sogar als Sieg über Sünde, Tod und Teufel (Matth 4,1–11) geoffenbarten Gehorsams Jesu kann die Gemeinde zusammen mit ihrem Evangelisten wagen, die Gewißheit der Hoffnung für sich in Anspruch zu nehmen“; vgl. auch ebd. 119 und Schweizer oben Anm. 13.

56. Vgl. dazu aber A. v. Dobbeler, Die Restitution Israels und die Bekehrung der Heiden. Das Verhältnis von Mt 10,5b.6 und Mt 28,18–20 unter dem Aspekt der Komplementarität. Erwägungen zum Standort des Matthäusevangeliums, *ZNW* 91 (2000), S. 18–44, der in den genannten Texten keinen Widerspruch und kein geschichtliches Nacheinander findet, erst recht keine Substitution, sondern unterschiedlich akzentuierte Aufträge.

der Nähe des Auferstandenen begleitet (28,20). Dem korrespondieren Nachfolge und Jüngerschaft, auch wenn in der Bergpredigt der Nachfolgegedanke allenfalls ansatzweise in dem „um meinetwillen“ in 5,11 angedeutet ist[57] (vgl. immerhin 4,18ff). Der, der seit Ostern seine Nähe erweist, ist aber niemand anderes als der verheißene Immanuel (1,23), als der Retter und Helfer der Armen und Kranken, der Recht- und Gewaltlosen (11,2ff u.ö.). Noch einmal ergibt sich aus der matthäischen Christologie, daß die Herrschaft Jesu Christi auch für Matthäus kein Oktroy ist, die Bergpredigt nicht allein imperativisch begründet und der Heilsindikativ keineswegs vergessen oder beiseite gedrängt ist.

7. Zum zweiten ist es wohl Absicht, wenn Matthäus andeutet, daß der irdische Jesus auch selbst das verwirklicht, was er lehrt, daß Jesus also sein eigenes Gesetz praktiziert und auch in seiner Lebensweise als Vorbild der Jünger erscheint. So ist der Verweis von 26,52 („Stecke dein Schwert in die Scheide“) zweifellos in Beziehung zur fünften Antithese der Bergpredigt, also der Mahnung zur Gewaltlosigkeit zu sehen. Dieses vorbildhafte Moment in der matthäischen Christologie erweist ebenso die Gethsemaneperikope, in der das Gebet Jesu („Nicht mein, sondern dein Wille geschehe“) deutlich genug im Anschluß an die dritte Vaterunser-Bitte der Bergpredigt in 6,10b formuliert ist. Auch die Korrespondenz der Versuchung Jesu in Mt 4 und seiner Mahnung in Gethsemane (Mt 26,41) zur sechsten Vaterunser-Bitte in 6,13 („führe uns nicht in Versuchung“) ist kaum zu übersehen.[58] Ferner findet der herausragende Zug der Niedrigkeit (πραΰς) des Messias und seine Einladung an die Mühseligen und Beladenen (vgl. 11,28f; 21,5) seine Entsprechung in der Seligpreisung der πραεῖς in 5,5:[59] So wie er sanftmütig und niedrig ist, so sollen auch die Jünger dieses „Joch“ auf sich nehmen (vgl. 11,28)[60] und Brüder der Geringsten werden (25,31ff). Ebenso entspricht die Mahnung in 6,24, Gott allein zu dienen (δουλεύειν), dem Beispiel Jesu, der Gott allein verehrt (λατρεύειν) in 4,10. Weiter hat das Erbarmen Jesu (vgl. die von Jesus erhörten Rufe „Erbarme dich meiner bzw. unser“ 9,27; 17,15; 20,31) seine Analogie in der Seligpreisung der Barmherzigen (5,7; vgl. auch die Zitation von Hos 6,6 in 9,12 und 12,7), und endlich ist auch der als δίκαιος leidende Jesus (27,19.24) Vorbild der Jünger,[61] wie die Seligpreisung der Verfolgten „um der Gerechtigkeit willen“ (5,10) deutlich macht (vgl. auch 5,5 mit 3,15).[62] Auch ohne einen ausdrücklich formulierten μίμησις-Gedanken ist

57. Vgl. G. Lohfink, Gesetzeserfüllung und Nachfolge. Zur Radikalität des Ethischen im Matthäusevangelium, in: H. Weber (hg.), *Der ethische Kompromiß* (Freiburg u.a: Herder, 1984), S. 15–58, hier S. 23: „Allerdings wird in der Bergpredigt ein entscheidender Aspekt vollkommener Tora-Erfüllung noch nicht genügend deutlich: nämlich die Nachfolge Jesu“; vgl. Mt 19,16–30.

58. Vgl. M. Gielen, „Und führe uns nicht in Versuchung“. Die 6. Vater-Unser-Bitte – eine Anfechtung für das biblische Gottesbild?, *ZNW* 89 (1998), S. 201–16, hier S. 211.

59. Vgl. Barth, a.a.O. (Anm. 29), S. 97, 117–22.

60. Vgl. Müller, a.a.O. (Anm. 8), S. 168.

61. Zum Vorbild in Taufe und Passion vgl. Strecker, a.a.O. (Anm. 20), S. 177–84: Jesu Passion sei „Vorabbildung des Leidens der Gemeinde“ (S. 182).

62. Noch weiter geht Meier, a.a.O. (Anm. 7), S. 63: „the beatitudes mirror Jesus himself, the truly happy man, the embodiment of the joy the Kingdom brings“. Betz, a.a.O. (Anm. 26; Problem),

also die Orientierung an Jesus ein gerade auch in der Bergpredigt unverkennbares Moment der matthäischen Christologie.[63]

8. Ein letzter Punkt, der weiterer Ausarbeitung bedürfte, ist das Verhältnis der Bergpredigtchristologie zur Theologie im engeren Sinn, was in den Arbeiten zur matthäischen Christologie zugunsten einer Christologisierung manchmal zu kurz kommt,[64] obschon der theozentrische Grundzug mit der Hinordnung auf und der Unterordnung unter Gott nicht gut zu übersehen ist.[65]

8.1. Es fällt auf, daß Aussagen, die Jesus als Lehrer und Ausleger mit Vollmacht bezeichnen, vor allem in den jeweiligen Einleitungen von Jesu Worten stehen: „Ich aber (ohne adversatives δέ 5,18.20) sage euch" (5,22.27.32.34.39.44), „Amen, ich sage dir bzw. euch (5,26; 6,2.5). Innerhalb der Redestücke selbst aber kommen im christologisch relevanten Sinn nur vor: die Verfolgung „um meinetwegen", d.h. um der Zugehörigkeit zu Christus willen in 5,11, das zurückblickende und den Zweck seiner Sendung resümierende „ich bin gekommen" in 5,17[66] und das zweimalige doppelte Kyrie (vgl. oben) sowie τοῦ πατρός μου in 7,21f (vgl. dazu unten).

S. 199–206 hat Ähnliches unter Voraussetzung einer ursprünglichen Selbständigkeit der Bergpredigt im Anschluß an A. Schlatter (Der Einzige und wir anderen, in: *Gesunde Lehre: Reden und Aufsätze* [Velbert: Freizeiten Verl., 1929], S. 149–62) für die gesamten 3 Kapitel in die Diskussion gebracht: Jesus porträtiere sich hier indirekt und unchristologisch selbst (vgl. Schlatter, S. 149f: „Was er als Sollen uns auferlegt, ist in ihm als Wille und Wahrheit lebendig. Indem Jesus das Bild des Jüngers zeichnet, wie er ihn haben will, wird uns sein eigener Weg wahrnehmbar"). Für Betz, S. 206f ist das eine mögliche Erklärung für das Fehlen einer Christologie in der Bergpredigt, doch fügt auf S. 208 mit Recht den Hinweis auf „genre and function" hinzu.

63. Vielleicht darf man erwägen, ob sich nicht auch das christologische μεῖζον gegenüber dem Tempel (12,6) und πλεῖον gegenüber Jona (12,41) und Salomo (12,42) bei den Jüngern im πλεῖον gegenüber den Schriftgelehrten und Pharisäern (5,20) reflektiert; vgl. auch das περισσόν gegenüber den Heiden (5,47).

64. Die Einwände von D. Hill, The Figure of Jesus in Matthew's Story: A Response to Professor Kingsbury's Literary-Critical Probe, *JSNT* 21 (1984), S. 37–52 gegen Kingsbury (a.a.O. [Anm. 13]), daß „God's point of view is the determinative one for Matthew's story" (S. 39), während in Wahrheit gelte „The God's orientation of the story is background, not foreground" (S. 42), dürfte für die Bergpredigt in dieser Zuspitzung jedenfalls problematisch sein.

65. Das betont zu Recht Frankemölle: Matthäus habe die „Denkökonomie" des Deuteronomisten und Chronisten „aufgenommen und dem ihm überkommenen Traditionsstoff aufgeprägt; denn auch er denkt theozentrisch, wenn diese Linie auch stark christologisch überlagert oder sogar ansatzweise verdrängt bzw. parallelisiert wird" (a.a.O. [Anm. 9], S. 84); vgl. auch S. 388–400. Gleichwohl bleibt es dabei: „Jesus ist auf Erden der mit Gottes Autorität auftretende und Gottes Funktionen übernehmende Gesandte, so daß in seiner Person Gott selbst gegenwärtig ist" (S. 20). Mit Luz, a.a.O. (Anm. 2), S. 223 wird man vor allem in der Immanuel-Formel „die theologische Dimension matthäischer Christologie" sehen; vgl. ders., a.a.O. (Anm. 20), S. 150 (Mt habe „zwar nicht Jesus mit Gott identifiziert, wohl aber angedeutet, daß für ihn Jesus die Gestalt ist, in der Gott bei seinem Volk und später bei allen Völkern gegenwärtig sein wird") sowie Müller, a.a.O. (Anm. 8), S. 166 und France, a.a.O. (Anm. 9), S. 311f.

66. Vgl. dazu E. Arens, The *ΗΛΘΟΝ-Sayings in the Synoptic Tradition* (OBO 10; Freiburg/Göttingen: Universitätsverlag. Freiburg/Vandenhoeck & Ruprecht, 1976); T. Schramm, *EWNT* II, S. 142; W. Carter, Jesus' „I have come" Statements in Matthew's Gospel, *CBQ* 60 (1998), S. 44–62.

8.2. Statt dessen dominieren im Inhalt der Worte Jesu zahlenmäßig wie sachlich eindeutig Gottesaussagen. Sie bilden das theologische Zentrum. Zu nennen sind vor allem der theologische Zentralbegriff „Reich der Himmel bzw. Gottes" (5,3.10.19f; 6,10.13.33; 7,21)[67] und die zahlreichen in Kap. 1–4 noch fehlenden Vaterprädikate Gottes wie „euer himmlischer Vater" oder „euer Vater in den Himmeln" (5,16.45f.48; 6,1.8.14.26.32; 7,11.21), „dein himmlischer Vater" (6,4.5.18) und „unser Vater im Himmel" (6,9), doch gehört hierher auch das häufige passivum divinum (5,4.6f; 7,1.7; vgl. auch unten zu ἐρρέθη). Es geht der Bergpredigt vor allem (πρῶτον), so könnte man sagen, um das Aussein auf *Gottes* Reich und *seine* Gerechtigkeit (6,33), deren eschatologischer Repräsentant und Vermittler Jesus ist.

Gott erscheint zumal in Worten über die Schöpfung, Eschatologie und Ethik: Er läßt „seine" Sonne aufgehen und regnen (5,45), und zwar in grenzenloser Güte auch über Böse und Ungerechte; der Himmel ist sein Thron und die Erde sein Schemel (5,34f); er gibt das tägliche Brot (6,11), sorgt für seine Geschöpfe und die Seinen (6,26.32), weiß um deren Bedürfnisse (6,8.32), gibt gute Gaben (7,11) und sieht ins Verborgene (6,4.5.18). Zu ihm wird gebetet (6,6.8ff), und er wird gepriesen (5,16). Er allein kann auch eschatologisch definitiv die Heiligung seines Namens, das Kommen seines Reiches und die Realisierung seines Willens im Himmel und auf Erden bewirken (6,9f). Gott allein kann Lohn gewähren (5,12; 6,1f.5.16), wird von denen, die reinen Herzens sind, geschaut werden (5,8), und die Friedensstifter werden υἱοὶ θεοῦ heißen (5,9; vgl. auch 5,45). Statt von Nachfolge ist in der Bergpredigt vom θεῷ δουλεύειν die Rede: Gott ungeteilt zu dienen ist nach 6,24 das Oppositum zum Mammonsdienst. Erscheint Jesus als Vorbild (vgl. oben), so eben in der Praktizierung des Willens *Gottes*. Auch die im Schlußsatz der Antithesen hervorgehobene Orientierung des Verhaltens der Jünger soll in Entsprechung zu Gott selbst geschehen: „Werdet vollkommen, wie euer Vater im Himmel vollkommen ist" (5,48). Man kann zwar darüber streiten, ob τέλειος hier inhaltlich die Liebe im intensiven oder extensiven Sinn oder noch anderes meint,[68] doch heißt es jedenfalls nicht „wie *ich* vollkommen bin". Tritt Jesus an die Seite des Mose, so doch nicht an die Stelle Gottes.[69] Seine Autorität ist zwar keine von Mose, wohl aber von Gott abgeleitete.

67. Die Frage, ob die „Herrschaft des Menschensohns" (13,41; vgl. auch 16,28; 20,21) eher „ekklesiologisch" zu deuten (vgl. Bornkamm, a.a.O. [Anm. 33], S. 40f und Barth, a.a.O. [Anm. 29], S. 125 Anm. 6, wobei 16,28 Probleme macht) oder mit der Herrschaft Gottes zu identifizieren ist (vgl. Strecker, a.a.O. [Anm. 20], S. 166 Anm. 7), ist zwar umstritten, jedenfalls aber ist βασιλεία bis auf 11,12 und 12,28 eine futurische Größe (vgl. Strecker, S. 166; Luz, a.a.O. [Anm. 10], S. 237f); vgl. auch Trilling, a.a.O. (Anm. 54), S. 153: „Die auf Erden vorhandene Herschaft Christi, sein ‚Reich', ist die Gestalt der gegenwärtigen Herrschaft Gottes über die Welt". Das sollte freilich nicht zu einer solch starken Christologisierung führen wie bei Kingsbury, a.a.O. (Anm. 13), S. 137 u.ö.

68. Vgl. *Schrage*, a.a.O. (Anm. 46), S. 152. Zur *imitatio dei* vgl. die Literatur bei E. Larsson, *EWNT* II, S. 1053f und Betz, a.a.O. (Anm. 4), S. 325f.

69. Das schließt zwar nicht aus, daß er dem göttlichen Wort auch gegenüberteten kann, denn die Nichtnennung des Redenden bei ἐρρέθη (S. 5,21ff) ist kein Versuch, „die polemische Beziehung auf Gott oder Moses zu vermeiden", sondern es ist an „ein Gotteswort" zu denken (G. Kittel, *ThWNT* IV, S. 112); vgl. auch Luz, a.a.O. (Anm. 10), S. 330: ἐρρέθη sei „sowohl vom rabbinisch exegetischen als

Gerade wenn das Vaterunser (6,9–14) die Mitte der Bergpredigt bildet,[70] steht das Gottesverhältnis der Jünger im Zentrum.

8.3. Die besondere Relation Jesu zu Gott wird wie schon in den vorangehenden Kap. 1–4 (vgl. oben) vor allem durch seine Sohnschaft qualifiziert. Jesus ist der Sohn seines Vaters im Himmel (7,21f), woran zweifellos auch eine Unterscheidung und eine Überlegenheit des Vaters, vor allem aber die Gewißheit Jesu um seine besondere Nähe und sein einzigartiges Verhältnis zu Gott deutlich wird, das auch sonst stark hervortritt (10,32f; 11,25ff; 12,50 u.ö.).[71] Das impliziert auch bestimmte Parallelitäten: Ist es in der Bergpredigt Gott selbst, der um Vergebung gebeten wird (6,12) und der sie gewähren kann (6,14f), so eignet nach 9,16 auch dem Menschensohn die Vollmacht zur Sündenvergebung, was nicht ohne 1,21 und 26,28 zu verstehen ist. Auch das Gericht steht einerseits nach 6,15 Gott zu, andererseits fungiert nach dem Schlußabschnitt offenbar Jesus als der, der den Gerichtsspruch spricht (7,23). Das ändert nichts daran, daß sein Verhältnis zu Gott das des Gehorsams und des Vertrauens ist und er den Auftrag und Willen Gottes zu erfüllen hat.[72]

Festzuhalten ist somit: Die Bergpredigt ist auf intensive und vielfältige Weise mit der Christologie verknüpft. Jesu einzigartige, sich auch in der Bergpredigt manifestierende ἐξουσία (7,29),[73] die ihm nach 28,18 von Gott verliehen ist, korrespondiert zumal den Christusprädikaten der Eingangskapitel des Evangeliums. So wie er selbst seinen Ursprung im Geist Gottes hat, so hat ihn auch seine Bergpredigt. Auch wenn man trotz aller Funktionseinheit die Autorität und Würde Jesu und diejenige Gottes nicht einfach identifizieren kann, sind seine Worte in der Auslegung des Willens *Gottes* im Horizont des heilvoll nahen Reiches und der Barmherzigkeit Jesu die entscheidende Begründung und Richtschnur für das Leben seiner Jünger, und daß in Jesus Gott selbst präsent und mit ihnen ist (1,23), ist seit Ostern auch in der Bergpredigt das alles entscheidende Vorzeichen.

auch vom matthäischen Sprachgebrauch her am ehesten als *Passivum divinum* für Gottes Sprechen in der Schrift zu deuten"; ähnlich Meier, a.a.O. (Anm. 7), S. 243; Broer, a.a.O. (Anm. 32), S. 78, 108f; Guelich, a.a.O. (Anm. 23), S. 180; anders Barth, a.a.O. (Anm. 29), S. 87 („es ist als Tradition gelehrt worden"). Eine andere Frage ist, ob auch Matthäus bei den Antithesen wirklich an ein Gegenüber oder nicht doch eher an eine Verschärfung denkt; vgl. oben und etwa Luz, a.a.O. (Anm. 3), S. 69f und G. Röhser, Jesus – der wahre „Schriftgelehrte". Ein Beitrag zum Problem der „Toraverschärfung" in den Antithesen der Bergpredigt, *ZNW* 86 (1995), S. 20–33.

70. So schon K. Barth, *KD* II/2, S. 777; W. Grundmann, *Das Evangelium nach Matthäus* (ThHK 1; Berlin: Evang. Verlagsanstalt, 1968), S. 205; Luz, a.a.O. (Anm. 3), S. 61.

71. Vgl. Frankemölle, a.a.O. (Anm. 9), S. 160, nach dem die Christologie „gleichsam die Klammer" zwischen „mein Vater" und „euer Vater" bildet bzw. (S. 161) „Mittler zum Vater" ist; Schnackenburg, a.a.O. (Anm. 13), S. 117: „Der ‚Sohn' wird durch seine Relation zum Vater als der Offenbarungs- und Heilsmittler gesehen"; France, a.a.O. (Anm. 9), S. 294.

72. Vgl. schon die Versuchungsgeschichte, wo der Teufel „Sohn Gottes" im Sinne eines Wundertäters versteht, der seine Macht zum eigenen Vorteil mißbraucht (4,6).

73. Vgl. auch Windisch, a.a.O. (Anm. 3), S. 145. Nach E.P. Blair, a.a.O. (Anm. 11), S. 46 hat das matthäische Jesusportrait sein Zentrum überhaupt in der ἐξουσία (8,5ff; 11,25ff u.ö.)

Part III

Jesus in the Johannine Perception

CHRISTOLOGY IN THE GOSPEL OF JOHN: A NEW APPROACH

János Bolyki

One of the most renowned 20th century discussions concerning Johannine Christology was Käsemann's and Borknamm's controversy over whether John's Gospel (JG) portrayed the historical Jesus one-sidedly as 'a God striding along above the earth', or, in other words, whether 'a naive docetism' could be discovered in it.[1] This controversy certainly pointed to the very heart of Johannine Christology, and revolved around the issue of whether John's Gospel overemphasized the divine nature of Jesus at the expense of his human nature, or whether it maintained a punctilious balance between the natures, as presented in the 'complementary' formula of the Chalcedon dogma. This issue, brought up by German scholars, has continued to draw the attention of Anglo-American researchers to our day.[2] A quite recent study, however, confutes the hypothesis that JG portrayed Jesus as a Christian refutation of Roman Caesarean state propaganda, calling him the Christian 'Saviour of the World' (Jn 4.42).[3] According to another opinion, the historicity of the Johannine narrative 'seems to be...rather positive when it comes to things like the chronological framework of Jesus' public career'.[4]

Thus the study of Johannine Christology is far from lacking in new or renewed perspectives. It was only recently that Peter Pokorný wrote of Johannine Christology: 'It is not a secondary development, but an interpretation of Jesus' message in another literary form'.[5] The present paper is related to this idea and, accordingly, attempts *to study Johannine Christology as an interpretation of Jesus' preaching in another literary form – a form that is close to antique drama.*

1. E. Käsemann, *Jesu letzter Wille nach Johannes 17* (Tübingen: Mohr-Siebeck, 3rd edn, 1971), pp. 13ff.; G. Bornkamm, 'Towards the Interpretation of John's Gospel: A discussion of *The Testament of Jesus* by Ernst Käsemann', in: J. Ashton, *The Interpretation of John* (Philadelphia: Fortress, 1986), pp. 79–98.

2. J.D.G. Dunn, *Christology in the Making* (London: SCM Press, 1980); and its critique: John A.T. Robinson, *Johannes. Das Evangelium der Ursprünge* (Wuppertal: Brockhaus, 1999), pp. 374ff.

3. M. Labahn, 'Heiland der Welt'. Der gesandte Gottessohn und der römischer Kaiser – ein Thema johanneischer Christologie?', in: M. Labahn and J. Zangenberg, *Zwischen den Reichen: Neues Testament und Römische Herrschaft* (Tübingen: Mohr-Siebeck, 2000), pp. 147–73.

4. A. Ekenberg, 'The Fourth Gospel and the History of Jesus', in *Communio Viatorum* XLIV (2002), pp. 182–91.

5. P. Pokorný, *Jesus in the Eyes of His Followers* (North Richland Hills: Bibal Press, 1998), p. 82.

In antiquity, tragedies constituted a genre interpreting an older (epic) tradition. Though JG is no tragedy, it does bear elements of drama, and some of its aspects do have analogies with the genre of tragedy. As Greek tragedy interpreted Homeric myth,[6] so JG re-interpreted the earlier oral or written traditions of Jesus. This is why it is legitimate to try to understand some aspects of Johannine Christology by comparing the interpretative functions of tragedy and JG. In the following, we shall attempt such an approach.

What was the interpretative role of tragedy? According to Zsigmond Ritoók,[7] Greek tragedy, with all but a few exceptions, interpreted myths. Why did it do so, he asks. And his answer can be summarized in four points. (1) Myths are the expressions of human relations, they thus present human experience in the form of stories. Should these relations or experiences recur in history, they can be generalized, be made to appear as examples or *paradeigmata*, as 'eternal truths'. These *paradeigmata* can become ethical examples, 'organizing factors in self-interpretation', insofar as they help the understanding and contextualization of similar relations and experiences in newer ages. (2) Certain human relations and experiences can continue to exist through several periods; people living in particular periods take up their positions with regard to these according to their historical conditions, and they 'retell the myth' in which they have recognized themselves concerning these issues 'as befits their period'; in other words, they shape myth according to their consciousness. This re-telling is the phenomenon of re-interpretation. For this to take place, however, people of newer periods have to reduce the myth to a formula that pertains to actual questions, that carries messages for them – this being possible if the plot of the myth so allows. 'A myth can only become the carrier of a message (truth), if a period is capable of discovering a message or truth addressed to it by way of the reduction mentioned above'.[8] The choice of the possibilities of reduction depend on the social experiences and scale of values in a given period. (3) As a consequence, there can be several, even *contradictory interpretations* of a myth. It is in these very different or contradictory interpretations that the different or contradictory experiences or scales of value are manifest. An example would be Euripides' two tragedies: *Trojan Women* and *Helen*. In the first play, Helen appears as the cause of the Trojan war, and therefore deserves her death; in the second one, she is a positive heroine, and suffers innocently. (4) The dramatic interpretation of a myth can also be studied from the point of view of the community, too. Viewers of the plays could more readily identify the exemplary or general aspects of myths if they could compare them not so much 'with immediate experience but an image that had already been made common'.[9]

6. In Aristotle's *Poetics* (47a9; 51b24), the word 'myth' simply means story or narrative, and that not in an ideological-religious but in a literary-generic sense. Its other meaning is an explanation of the world which attributes phenomena rationally inexplicable at the given time to transcendent forces.

7. Ritoók Z., in Ritoók Z., J. Sarkady and J. Szilágyi, *A görög kultúra aranykora Homérostól Nagy Sándorig* ([The Golden Age of the Greek Culture from Homer to Alexander the Great]; Budapest: Gondolat, 1984), pp. 284–86.

8. Ritoók, p. 283.

9. Ritoók, p. 286.

The interpretation, the continued re-interpretation of myth therefore took place in the framework of a historical process, giving old myths new life (lifelikeness) and meaning (newer and newer possibilities of interpretation), and, in a changed period, letting them have a message in which a newer generation could recognize itself, and moreover understand its world in the light of myth re-interpreted.

1. *The Re-interpretation of the Person and Story of Jesus in John's Gospel*

Among other things, JG differs from the Synoptic gospels in that it not only wishes to repeat or enlarge the Jesus tradition, the oral and written traditions about Jesus' life – for which we could use the term *myth*, retold story, as applied by Aristotle in his *Poetics* –, but also to reflect on them, to interpret them in a new situation calling for decisions.[10] Let us have a look at some of the obvious proofs of this.[11] First of all, this is proven by the interpretative, even dramaturgical comments of the gospel. The disciples do not only witness to the words and deeds of Jesus, they also remember them subsequently, after Jesus' glorification. Consequently, the story of Jesus can only be interpreted in the light of Easter (2.22; 12.26; 15.20)!

Another proof is the final comment by the author (20.30–31) that he knew many other deeds of Jesus, but his aim was not to present an abundance of material but to lead his readers and hearers to belief in Jesus. What he wanted to interpret with his gospel was that Jesus was the one he had got to know. The third group of proofs concerns the fact that Jesus regarded himself as the true interpreter of the tradition. Already in the prologue, the evangelist portrays Jesus as the Logos embodied, that he was the one who revealed (ἐξηγήσατο) the invisible God. The root meaning of the verb is to list facts, to relate and explain hidden divine matters. In other words, the evangelist explained and interpreted him. The author deems his own role analogous with that of Jesus: as Jesus, 'the only begotten Son', who was 'in the bosom of the Father' (being an expression of intimate trust and adequate knowledge), creditably declared the invisible God, so the author of JG, who at the last supper leaned on Jesus' bosom, declared the genuine nature of Jesus (1.18; 13.23; 21.20). The two 'bosom leanings' and the two declarations constitute an inclusion at each end of the gospel, providing the whole work with a framework, and thus proving that the gospel *reveals the God-revealing Jesus, that is, it interprets him*. Finally, one of the names John uses for the Holy Spirit is *Paraclete*, whose role is to interpret Jesus for both the disciples and the world (14.26; 15.26). It is this very interpretative power of the Holy Ghost that provides

10. A fine observation by Hübner is pertinent here: 'There never is a tradition in itself; there can only be tradition as interpreted' (J. Hübner, *Biblische Theologie des Neuen Testaments* [Göttingen: Vandenhoeck & Ruprecht, 1995], III, p. 244).

11. W.E. Sproston, 'Witnesses to what was: ἀπ' ἀρχῆς I John's Contribution to our Knowledge of Tradition in the Fourth Gospel', in: S. Porter and C. Evans (ed.), *The Johannine Writings*, (Sheffield: Sheffield Academic Press, 1995), pp. 138–60.

our author with his particular vision of Jesus. In the following we wish to present one aspect of this interpretation.

JG is radically different from the other gospels in that it does not present the *crucifixion* as suffering and defeat, but interprets it as the beginning of Jesus' 'reception above', of his glorification (12.24, 32; 13.1, 3; 14.2b-3, 12b; 17.1). A soldier pierces the side of the dead Jesus, water and blood comes out forthwith, and whoever saw this bears true witness in order that 'ye', readers and hearers of all times, 'might believe' (19.34–35). Here is *Johannine interpretation*! The myth, the story or plot of the drama concludes with the disgraceful fall of the hero – but only without interpretation. So the interpreter comes along, and explains that Jesus' death on the cross is not a tragic fall but a *victory*. A particular element of Johannine style, the use of ambiguity, is also at the service of interpreting the crucifixion. For example, in 12.32 the verb ὑψόω (to lift up, or, in the passive, to be lifted up) means, on the one hand, that Jesus is lifted up on to the cross by soldiers, and, on the other, that, through the crucifixion and the inseparable resurrection, the Father lifts him up into heavenly glory. The narrative has three great prolepses anticipating the future event of the death on the cross. These are 'the hour' (i.e. when the time of Jesus' death comes: 2.4; 7.6, 30; 8.20; 12.23, 27; 13.1), the 'lifting up' (3.14; 8.28; 12.32-34) and the 'glorification' (7.39; 8.54; 11.4; 12.16, 23, 28). Furthermore, JG uses the means of misunderstanding, irony and symbol to be able to continually comment on the importance of the death on the cross in a concealed manner. An example for the motif of misunderstanding is in 7.33–36 where Jesus' 'going' to the Father is misunderstood as his going to the dispersed Jewry. The motif of irony appears when the mockery of Jesus' enemies proves him right. For example, when Caiaphas says: 'Ye know nothing at all…, it is expedient for us, that one man should die for the people, and that the whole nation perish not' (11.50), by which he means that it is better for Jesus to die than them to lose their authority over the people. The reader however thinks that Caiaphas, in spite of himself, has said the truth, for 'Jesus should die for that nation; and not for that nation only, but that also he should gather together in one the children of God that were scattered abroad' (11.52). For an example of symbols we can mention 3.14–15 where the brass serpent on the pole in the wilderness that healed those who looked on it from the bites of the snakes symbolizes the crucified Jesus, who will heal sinners from the mortal bite of sin, if they look on him.

In the Johannine outlook, the last word is not death on the cross, just as it is not the staggering death of the hero that concludes Greek tragedy. To bring up a few examples of the latter: Aeschylus' *Prometheus Bound*: 'let me lie / Plunged in the black Tartarean gloom; / Yet – yet his sentence shall not doom / This deathless self to die!' (1050–52); his *The Choephori*: 'the god thy friend / Guard thee and aid with chances favouring' (1063–64); Sophocles' *Philoktetes*: 'Piety does not die with men; / whether they live or die, piety remains' (1440–41); or his *Oedipus at Colonus*: 'It was a messenger from heaven, or else / Some gentle, painless cleaving of earth's base; / For without wailing or disease or pain / He passed away – an end most marvellous' (1658–62); and Euripides' *Alcestis*: 'She died for her lord; / A blessed spirit she is now. / Hail, O sacred lady, be our friend!'; or his *Iphigenia at Aulis:* 'thy child is living still, among the gods' (1608). In JG, the death on the cross is followed by resurrection and glorification, and it is looking back from these that the former can be understood.

2. *The Interpretation of Christ's Sacrifice: (Soteriological and Sacramental Aspects)*

The question we now seek to answer is what role self-sacrifice and expiatory death had in Greek tragedy and in the New Testament, and JG in particular.

As far as the intellectual history of vicarious sacrifice is concerned,[12] the deaths of Jewish martyrs also point beyond their own fates. They died out of fidelity to Mosaic law. Pertinent deuterocanonical and intertestamental texts can be found in *Test. Mos.* 9; *2 Macc.* 6–7; Dan. LXX 3.38-40 (the Prayer of Azariah). No immediate relation can be demonstrated, however, between the sacrifices and prayers of Jewish martyrs and the idea of vicarious satisfaction.

Second, let us have a brief look at the role of vicarious sacrifice in Greek and Roman culture. The 'devotio pro principe', the willingness of soldiers or civilians to sacrifice themselves for the emperor, is well-known. Interestingly enough, Anthony and Cleopatra called themselves 'Συναποθανουμένοι, after a Greek comedy bearing that name. It was common practice in the first century A.D. to refer to Alcestis, Euripides' heroine who died instead of her husband, on the inscriptions of gravestones of pious women who had done some great sacrifice for their husbands. We have no evidence of the sacrificial death of anyone influencing the wider community in this period of Hellenism.

The world of ideas of *4 Macc.* 6–7 was in an important phase in the development of the idea of expiatory sacrifice. This is how the priest Eleazar prays in this book: 'Be merciful to your people, and let my punishment be sufficient for their sake. Make my blood an expiation (καθάρσιον)!' for them, and take my life as a ransom (ἀντίψυχον) for theirs' (6.28–29). The concept of vicarious sacrifice is quite clear in this plea. The idea of cleansing by blood on the altar (Lev. 4.26b, 31b, 35b) and on the ark of the covenant (Lev. 17.22) derives from the Old Testament cult, but that is not about human sacrifice, and it therefore has little to do with vicarious satisfaction. It is on this basis that some scholars have explained Eleazar's prayer through the influence of Euripides rather than that of the cult.[13] Since the language of the tragedies, Greek, was spoken throughout Palestine, especially among the scattered Jewry, and since theatres performed throughout the empire, thus in Palestine and Asia Minor, too, the influence of Euripides on the tragedian Ezechielos, Philo (*Omnis probus 141*) and even Acts (26.14) is undeniable. All this has led J. Bremmer to draw the conclusion that the motif of

12. J.N. Bremmer, 'The Atonement in the Interaction of Jews, Greeks, and Christians', in J. Bremmer and F.G. Martinez (editors), *Sacred History and Sacred Texts in Early Judaism* (Kampen: Kok Pharos, 1992), pp. 75–93.

13. Bremmer, 'The Atonement', p. 87.

accepting death for the sake of the people in Euripides probably influenced those Jewish Christians who sought to interpret the expiatory effect of Jesus' death.[14]

Having briefly looked at the history of intellectual development, let us now dwell on the *function of death as expiatory sacrifice* in the world of the tragedies and the New Testament. In respect of the scope of death accepted for the sake of others or even as an expiatory sacrifice, we can find several examples. Alcestis dies only for one single man, her husband: 'To show you honour and – at the cost of my life – that you may still behold the light, I die' (ll. 282–84). In *Phoenician Women*, prince Menoeceus does so to save his town (ll. 997ff.). Sophocles has Ismene die for thousands in *Oedipus in Colonus* (ll. 498ff.; 503–504), and has Antigone, in spite of it being forbidden, lay her unburied brother to rest out of sisterly love, clinging on to an ideal and faithfulness to the divine commandment (ll. 457ff.). On the basis of Pokorný's study on the comparison of the sacrifice of Antigone (Sophocles) and Jesus,[15] we may point out four differences between them: (1) Jesus' death was for the whole cosmos; it was not for the continuation of others' earthly lives but in order to take away the sin of the cosmos that he died; his death therefore is an expiatory, atonement making and saving sacrifice; (2) it was not the force of fate but the will of God that he obeyed in it; (3) his death has an eschatological significance and begins a new era; (4) his death rendered all other expiatory sacrifices pointless. In JG, however, the death of Jesus is not only an expiatory sacrifice but also the restoration of a spoiled relationship on the basis of 12.20–36. The sacrifice of Antigone thus has at least two highly significant bearings on the New Testament. One is the fact that she calls her premature death a 'gain' (κέρδος, l. 461), and the fact that Paul also uses the same word with respect to his own death in Phil. 1.21. And the second one is Antigone's often-cited confession: 'My nature is for mutual love, not hate' (l. 523). This has its parallel in Jesus' saying: 'For even the Son of man came not to be ministered unto, but to minister, and to give his life as a ransom (λύτρον) for many' (Mk 10.45 par.). Λύτρον was paid especially for freeing slaves and prisoners of war, but in New Testament usage the concept of 'redemption' was founded on Jesus' expiatory and saving death even in the earliest formulations of faith. For example: 'God delivered him up (= to death, as a sacrifice to atone) for us all' (Rom. 8.32); the Lord Jesus Christ 'gave himself for our sins' (Gal. 1.4); the Son of God 'hath loved us, and hath given himself for us' (or: 'in our stead'); Christ 'loved us, and gave himself for us' (Eph. 5.2, 25). What is important to know about this so-called 'self-giving' formula is that it understands Jesus' death as an expiation or a vicarious satisfaction, or so it interprets it theologically.[16] The majority of the tragedies were born at the time of the crisis of Greek theism. Tragic death seen as expiatory sacrifice reinterprets divine things: fate is at liberty to make the hero suffer anything, but the hero – and the tragedian! – so interprets his own mortal suffering as to see a new manifestation of the divine world

14. Bremmer, 'The Atonement', pp. 92–93.

15. Pokorný, op. cit.

16. Ph. Vielhauer, *Geschichte der urchristlichen Literatur* (New York/Berlin: de Gruyter, 1975), p. 17.

in it. So, in the Christian kerygma, the death of Jesus does not conceal the divine world, but actually presents or reveals its reality. The death of Jesus is the very heart of God's self-revelation and love for man![17]

Coming to JG, it is well worth mentioning that not all tragedies have their heroes sacrifice themselves, as in the examples mentioned above; they might die for reasons of blood feud, obsession, suicide, the whims of the gods. In JG, however, there is but one death: the death of Jesus. Perhaps consciously differing from the other gospels, JG has nothing to say about the deaths of John the Baptist or Judas, and it has the dead Lazarus be resurrected. *JG does not wish to acknowledge any other death but Jesus' self-sacrificing and expiating death!* Jesus' death is a triumph in JG. But not only a triumph. In connection to interpreting his death as sacrifice, it is instructive to follow through all the signals built into the structure of the gospel, as Zumstein has done.[18] Accordingly, what the Baptist foretells in the first minutes of the drama ('Behold the Lamb of God, which taketh away the sin of the world', 1.29), the evangelist repeats in retrospective summary at the tragic conclusion (19.14, 31b–33) by saying that 'it was the preparation of the Passover' (that is Jesus died as a Passover lamb) and that 'they brake not his legs' (on the cross, as soldiers did with the two others, because the bones of the Passover lamb were not to be broken). Putting or including the gospel in between the same initial and conclusive idea calls our attention to the fact that Jesus is the Lamb of God that, by its death, takes away the sin of the world. A part of the so-called 'bread sermon' in 6.53–56 declares that without the 'drinking' of Jesus' blood, i.e. without his faithful acceptance, no one can have everlasting life. The blood of Jesus here refers to the sacrificial nature of his death. In his High Priest prayer, Jesus, facing his death, says to God about his disciples that 'for their sakes I sanctify myself' (17.19). The phrase 'for their sakes' (ὑπέρ αὐτῶν) recalls the words used by the other evangelists and Paul in the institution of the Lord's Supper (Mk 14.24 par.; 1 Cor. 11.24), the roots of which go back to Isaiah's prophecy (53.11, LXX), who had foretold that the so-called 'suffering servant of God' suffered for us and because of us, and we would be healed by his wounds. In 10.11, Jesus proclaims: 'I am the good shepherd: the good shepherd giveth his life for the sheep' (ὑπέρ τῶν προβάτων).[19]

When a soldier pierces the side of the dead Jesus, 'forthwith came there out blood and water' (19.34). The image probably refers to the sacraments, the Eucharist and baptism, deriving from Jesus' saving death. Several students have observed that the evangelist does not explicitly speak of baptism in the name of the Holy Trinity and the institution of the Lord's Supper. But there are other things he does not name – things important to him (e.g. the names of 'the beloved disciple' and

17. P. Pokorný, 'Antigone und Jesus (Opfer und Hoffnung)', in *Geschichte–Tradition–Reflexion III* (FS M. Hengel; Tübingen: Mohr-Siebeck, 1996), pp. 49–62.

18. J. Zumstein, 'Die johanneische Interpretation des Todes Jesu', in his *Kreative Erinnerung. Relecture und Auslegung im Johannesevangelium* (Zürich: Pano Verlag, 1999), pp. 125–44.

19. Considering the texts reviewed, it is rather odd for Bultmann to deny that JG teaches the saving death of Jesus: 'Sacrifice is alien to the life work of Christ', see R. Bultmann, *Az Újszövetség teológiája* ([Theology of the NT]; Budapest: Osiris, 1998), pp. 326ff.

the mother of Jesus). The author of JG may have feared that the rites of the two sacraments would be separated from their source – the death of Jesus – and become ends in themselves. Nonetheless, the being 'born of water and of the Spirit' in 3.5 and the scene in which Peter casts himself into the sea and swims to his Master standing on the shore in 21.7 both refer to the sacrament or, if you will, the rite of baptism. But the 'bread speech' in chapter 6 and the washing of the feet scene in chapter 13 are wholly about the Lord's Supper, and are consciously related to Jesus' saving death and its power to cleanse from sin (13.10). When the Master performing the rite of feet washing asks his disciples: 'Know ye what I have done to you?' (13.12), and he himself answers, he is actually giving the interpretation of the rite, namely the sacrificial rite (13.7–11) and its ethical, paradigmatic consequences (13.13–17). Furthermore we could go as far as to say that 7.37 ('In the last day, that great day of the feast, Jesus stood and cried, saying, "If any man thirst, let him come unto me, and drink. He that believeth on me, as the scripture hath said, out of his belly shall flow rivers of living water"') is 'a drama within the rite'. As the fixed liturgy of the feast of tabernacles (e.g. pouring out water in memory of the water miracles of the wanderings in the wilderness) was going on, Jesus, so to speak, disturbing it, but actually interpreting it, shouted to the crowd partaking of the rite that it was actually about himself, that it reached its final meaning in Him, specifically after his sacrificial death, when His people have received the gift of the Spirit in themselves, outpouring like water. This is particularly confirmed by the editorial or narrator's comment of the evangelist in 7.39. *This unity of myth rite and interpretation has no parallel in the literature of antiquity*!

3. *The Existential Interpretation of Christology*

Greek tragedy is a good example of how it is possible to explain and interpret in an existential sense the myths of an earlier period. From among the many possible examples, let us take a look at a work by each of the three great tragedians. First, Aeschylus' *Prometheus Bound*, the tragedy of the titan who helped men and who was therefore mercilessly punished by Zeus. The author first uses the myth to interpret the *conditions of human life*. This he traces to the three presents men got from Prometheus. The first one is the pure existence of men, which had been endangered by the wrath of Zeus, but the titan had intervened ('To wipe out man and rear another race: / And these designs none contravened but me. / I risked the bold attempt, and saved mankind / From stark destruction and the road to hell'; ll. 234–38). In other words, human life is fundamentally fragile and contingent. The second is another human condition of life, 'blind hope', whereby man downcast because of finite life is protected from knowing the time of his death, which would make him give up all plans and designs, and wait only for his death ('I took from man expectancy of death… I planted blind hope in the heart of him', ll. 248, 250). In other words, a positive unreality can have a beneficent effect on 'real' life. Finally, it was fire, another factor ensuring human life, that Prometheus obtained from the gods, and together with it he also gave men inventions and culture ('I conferred the gift of fire...and [they] shall master many arts thereby... Senseless as beasts I gave men sense... I taught them...of the plumpness of the inward parts / What colour is acceptable to the Gods', ll. 252, 254, 494–95). In other words, human life cannot near fulfilment without reason, the use and understanding of the forces of nature, and without communing with the powers above. Seemingly, the form of human co-existence, society, is not mentioned. But it is only the list which leaves it out. Actually, however, the representation and critique of social forms run through the whole drama. The first form was the rule of titans by brute force. The second was ascension to power by Zeus, who put an end to the chaotic dealings of the titans, but inaugurated a forceful tyranny. And then came Prometheus attempting to establish freedom and protect mankind. Finally, after the clash of Zeus and Prometheus, a new era comes, when Zeus renounces the use of force and establishes the rule of law. Though all this has its background in Athenian history,[20] in it we encounter an abstraction of fact in terms of a philosophy of history, indeed, an ontology.

In Athens, everyone knew the Oedipus legend,[21] and in his *Oedipus the King*, Sophocles dramatized not only the story of the hero who had killed his father and unknowingly married his mother, but also the tragedy of a man who in seeking the reasons why misfortune befell his town is questing for his genuine existence. 'He is looking for his own self. And how passionately!'[22] He had answered the riddle asked by the Sphinx: 'Who is man?', now he is to answer the question: 'Who is he?' What is more, as he seeks the unknown cause of his town's plight, and, as king, he wants to pass judgment over the unknown cause, he is unconsciously preparing his change of position from being a judge to become the accused. With this, he touches upon existential issues, such as man and his roles (masks), the possibility of a tragic exchange of roles, the tension between being and appearance, and the voluntary acceptance of suffering. He interprets the dependence of a man on his lot, the possibilities of gaining and losing power, the heavy price to be paid for self-knowledge: the acceptance of guilt and suffering, and also how one can survive a desperate attainment of self-knowledge (as he was the unwitting cause of his town's affliction).

The third example is Euripides' *Bacchants*. King Pentheus of Thebes abhors the cult of Dionysus and the related debauchery, and prohibits it even when the deity visits Thebes to oversee his own cult. The king does not recognize the god coming incognito and orders his capture, but Dionysus stirs up the women of the town, who, in their cultic frenzy, discover the disguised king among themselves and tear him apart – with his mother taking the lead. With a bit of exaggeration, we might call this play 'an ancient forerunner of deep psychology'. The tragedian might have tried to solve the puzzle of why the ecstasy or frenzy of Dionysiac mysteries and initiation rituals have an appeal even for otherwise 'sober' people. Contrary to modern deep psychology, the final catastrophe does not justify bridling uncontrolled human instincts and passions by bringing them to consciousness, but

20. Ritoók Z., *op.cit*, pp. 545–49.
21. Ibid., p. 546.
22. Ibid., p. 571.

presents their eruption like in a novel by Dostoevsky. It demonstrates the fact that 'there are irrational forces exerting their influence in the world that cannot be put under the control of reason, it would be futile for reason to resist..., the world falls from under the influence of reason, and becomes prey to impulses'.[23] Only a critic suffering from an incurably optimistic rationalism would deem this tragedy retrograde, but in cases of massive historical hysteria, we have to acknowledge that man can act upon not only the guidance of reason but upon impulse, too.

In the following we shall attempt to answer the question how *far the dramatic-tragic traits of JG assert themselves in the existential interpretation of the mythic traditions it treats*. Almost all the subjects brought up by the tragedies mentioned above are broached by the fourth gospel. Let us take the seven well-known 'I am' formulas,[24] that have a decisive significance not only from the point of view of Jesus' self-revelation, but also from that of man's own existential needs. The formulas are as follows: 'I am the bread of life..., the light of the world..., the door..., the good shepherd..., the resurrection and the life..., the way, the truth, and the life..., the true vine' (6.35; 8.12; 10.7; 10.11; 11.25; 14.6; 15.1). What is man really in need of? Bread, light, leadership, the knowledge of the way of genuine life and truth, a fruitful life, and the continuation of life after death. Man is a being that has an existential need for nourishment, guiding, a qualified earthly life and an ensured afterlife. Let us think of *Prometheus Bound*, according to which, beyond sheer being, man needs blind hope and fire, in other words, the knowledge of the visible and invisible world. After half a millennium, JG offered answers similar to those of Aeschylus, though in a different culture.

In the second example, Sophocles' *Oedipus the King*, we have similarly found existential explanations of the human condition parallel to those of JG. Oedipus faces two questions: 'Who is man?' (the Sphinx's riddle) and 'Who am I?' (his own tragic problem). In JG, the author has Pilate join these two questions when he points to the scourged Jesus wearing the crown of thorns, and says to the crowd in front of the building of the Praetorium: 'Behold the man!' (19.5). Already in the Gospel of Mark, the context is an antique coronation ceremony (*praesentatio* – presentation, *inthronisatio* – enthronement, *acclamatio* – acclamation), but in parody form. This is far more complicated in JG. What was meant by Pilate to arouse compassion, was taken as provocation by the crowd, and was understood literally as well as manifoldly by the evangelist. 'Behold the man!' – so miserable at the mercy of dazzled crowds and self-seeking authority. He is so majestic: a king soon to be enthroned on the cross; at the same time, he suffers all the humiliation and affliction with profound dignity. He is so human amid inhumanity, and so divine amid godlessness. Beyond tragic condensation, the text also involves a theological position in this situation, namely that we can discover genuine man in Jesus only because God is present in him. Who then is man? Is

23. Jonas H., *Gnosis und Spätantiker Geist*, I–II (Göttingen: Vandenhoeck & Ruprecht, 1993), II, p. 4.

24. R. Bultmann, *Theologie des Neuen Testaments* (Tübingen: Mohr-Siebeck, 9th edn, 1984), 48/2. Where Jesus uses the 'I am' formula without adding.

he who his clothes show him to be? No, by that criterion he is a provincial criminal sentenced to death and rigged out fancily for punishment's sake. Who is this man? Is he a king, as he called himself, or a deceiver, as he is charged with being? The Johannine drama is heightened to a paradox, for it says: *Who is this man? This man is God!* God subdued by man stands here facing condemnation so that man, who deserves to be condemned, might not have to face such condemnation!

JG has Pilate utter another basic human or existential question, similarly during Jesus' trial. When as judge he tries to establish whether Jesus calls himself the King of the Jews (18.33, 35, 37) and thereby rebels against Caesar, Jesus answers that he came to the world with the mission to witness to the truth (18.37b). Then comes Pilate's disillusioned, agnostic question: 'What is truth?' (The Greek noun ἀλήθεια here means not justice in a legal sense, but reality asserted in the order of the universe.) Why does the question about truth pertain to the being of man? According to the context, because human existence is truthful – Bultmann might have said 'eigentliche' – if it is a testimony, a witness to truth. And, as in *Oedipus the King*, so in JG: truth is revealed in suffering. Is it not a genuinely tragic idea that the truth and reality of human existence is revealed only in the suffering that bereaves man of his historical existence? JG does state this paradox, but, being an evangelical, not a Greek tragedy, it also speaks of the existence beyond history, the Easter existence: resurrection.

WAHRHEIT UND WORT: HEIDEGGERS „VOM WESEN DER WAHRHEIT" UND WAHRHEIT IM JOHANNES-EVANGELIUM

Hans Hübner

1. *Hinführung zur Thematik*

Erneut habe ich die Gelegenheit, Petr Pokorný mit einem Aufsatz in einer Festschrift zu gratulieren, diesmal zu seinem 70. Geburtstag. Dabei möchte ich wieder, gerade auch um des zu Ehrenden willen, ein hermeneutisches Thema bedenken, und zwar ein Thema, das seine Wurzeln in der Antike – nämlich im Neuen Testament und in der griechischen Philosophie – hat und das bis heute theologisch und philosophisch von höchster Bedeutung und Bedeutsamkeit ist. Vor fünf Jahren habe ich zu seinem 65. Geburtstag den hermeneutischen Akzent dadurch gesetzt, daß ich anhand von Eph 3,14–19 zu zeigen versuchte, wie es in der *Erkenntnis Gottes* um den Zugang zur *Wirklichkeit Gottes* geht.[1] Auf dem im Herbst 2001 von der Tschechischen Akademie der Wissenschaften und der Evangelisch-Theologischen Fakultät der Karls-Universität in Prag veranstalteten und maßgeblich von Petr Pokorný gestalteten Hermeneutik-Symposium habe ich mich, auch im Blick auf den späteren Heidegger, bemüht, theologische und hermeneutische Fragen in einer bewußt grundsätzlichen und somit programmatischen Weise weiterzudenken[2]: Dem Ineinander von Ereignis, Seyn, Da-sein und Wort bei *Martin Heidegger*, zugleich auch der bei ihm aufweisbaren Korrespondenz von Zuspruch und Hören des Seyns, entspricht im *Neuen Testament*, vor allem bei Paulus und Johannes, das Ineinander von Evangelium als Macht Gottes – genauer: von Evangelium als worthafter Präsenz des mächtigen Gottes – und Hören Gottes (*genetivus obiectivus*) bzw. Hören des sich im menschlichen Wort des göttlichen Evangeliums aussprechenden Gottes. Der einerseits im Zuspruch des Seyns und der andererseits im Zuspruch Gottes (diesmal: *genetivus subiectivus*) angesprochene Mensch ist durch solchen Zuspruch ein anderer geworden. Im Neuen Testament finden wir für diese Sicht vor allem zwei hervorragende Aussagen, nämlich Röm 1,16f. und Joh 1,1. Wenn ich diesmal meinen Beitrag zu Ehren Petr Pokornýs unter die Überschrift „Wahrheit und Wort" stelle, so bleibe ich ganz auf der eben skizzierten Linie.

Ich expliziere einen früher geäußerten Gedanken, den ich 1978 in meinem ἀλήθεια-Artikel des „Exegetischen Wörterbuchs zum Neuen Testament"[3] nur

1. H. Hübner, Erkenntnis Gottes und Wirklichkeit Gottes. Theologisch-hermeneutische Gedanken zu Eph 3,14–19, in: *ΕΠΙΤΟΑΥΤΟ. Studies in Honour of Petr Pokorný* (Třebenice, Mlýn, 1998), S. 176–84.

2. Ders., Zuspruch des Seyns und Zuspruch Gottes. Die Spätphilosophie Martin Heideggers und die Hermeneutik des Neuen Testaments, in: P. Pokorný, J. Roskovec (Hg.), *Philosophical Hermeneutics and Biblical Exegesis* (WUNT 153; Tübingen: Mohr-Siebeck, 2002), S. 144–75.

3. Ders., Art. ἀλήθεια κτλ., in: EWNT I, Stuttgart 1980 (Art. in 1. Lieferung August 1978), S. 138–45.

angedeutet habe: „Freilich läßt sich fragen, ob Bultmanns Verständnis der johanneischen ἀλήθεια nicht schon näher bei bestimmten Gedanken aus Heideggers ‚Vom Wesen der Wahrheit' [...] steht als bei der existenzialen Interpretation der Wahrheit in ‚Sein und Zeit' § 44." Es ist sicherlich nur ein Teilaspekt der neutestamentlichen Hermeneutik, um den es im folgenden geht. Aber gerade dieser Teilaspekt umfaßt in entscheidender Weise den zentralen Gehalt der neutestamentlichen Grundaussage. Es ist die alte Pilatus-Frage, freilich anders verstanden, als der römische Prokurator sie verstehen konnte (Joh 18,38): *„Was ist Wahrheit?"* Und es ist zugleich die damit verbundene Frage: *„Was ist das Wort?"*

Der genannte Aufsatz *„Vom Wesen der Wahrheit"* (im folgenden: WW) geht auf einen Vortrag zurück, den Heidegger 1930 in Bremen, Marburg und Freiburg und 1932 in Dresden gehalten hat. Gedruckt wurde er aber erst 1943, und zwar in einer überarbeiteten Fassung. In der 2. Auflage 1949 wurde der Schlußanmerkung der erste Absatz hinzugefügt. Jetzt liegt WW in Band 9 der Gesamtausgabe der Werke Heideggers vor.[4] Warum schreibe ich aber jetzt ausgerechnet über diesen Aufsatz? Bin ich nicht sogar selbst in meinen Publikationen zur Wahrheitsfrage bei Heidegger über diesen Aufsatz hinausgekommen? Gerade in den letzten Jahren habe ich mich doch mit seinen so wichtigen, erst postum publizierten Schriften ab 1936 beschäftigt, in denen er auf seinem Denkweg gegenüber der Schrift von 1930 erheblich weitergekommen ist, nämlich mit GA 65, Beiträge zur Philosophie (Vom Ereignis)[5], GA 66, Besinnung[6], und GA 67, Überwindung der Metaphysik[7]. Warum also heute noch einmal die Thematisierung von WW? Hat nicht schon 1952 Walter Biemel zusammen mit A. de Waelhens dazu das Nötige gesagt?[8] Kann man nicht heute noch in Biemels rororo-Monographie „Heidegger" diese Gedanken nachlesen?[9] In der Tat, das kann man. Aber gerade in den letzten Jahren hat WW wieder die besondere Aufmerksamkeit in der Heidegger-Forschung der Philosophen gefunden. Ich nenne hier nur zwei wichtige Monographien: *Martin Brasser*, Wahrheit und Verborgenheit.[10] Der Untertitel zeigt, daß es der

4. M. Heidegger, Vom Wesen der Wahrheit, in: ders., *Wegmarken*, Gesamtausgabe [im folgenden: GA], Bd. 9 (hg. von F.-W. von Herrmann; Frankfurt a.M.: V. Klostermann, 2. Aufl. 1996), S.177–202 (hiernach zitiert); Einzelausgabe: ders., *Vom Wesen der Wahrheit* (Frankfurt a.M.: V. Klostermann, 8., ergänzte Aufl. 1997; nicht ganz identischer Text mit dem in GA 9).

5. M. Heidegger, *Beiträge zur Philosophie (Vom Ereignis)*, GA 65 (1989, 1994); dazu: H. Hübner, „Vom Ereignis" und vom Ereignis Gott. Ein theologischer Beitrag zu Martin Heideggers „Beiträgen zur Philosophie", in: P.-L. Coriando (Hg.), *„Herkunft aber bleibt Zukunft". Martin Heidegger und die Gottesfrage*, Martin-Heidegger-Gesellschaft. Schriftenreihe, Band 5, Frankfurt a.M.: V. Klostemann, 1998).

6. M. Heidegger, *Besinnung* (GA 66; Frankfurt a.M.: V. Klostermann, 1997); dazu: H. Hübner, Martin Heideggers Götter und der christliche Gott. Theologische Besinnung über Heideggers „Besinnung", *Heidegger Studien* 15 (1999), S.127–51.

7. M. Heidegger, *Metaphysik und Nihilismus. I. Die Überwindung des Metaphysik. 2. Das Wesen des Nihilismus* (GA 67, Frankfurt a.M.: V. Klostermann, 1999); dazu: H. Hübner, ‚Seynsgeschichtliches und theologisches Denken. Kritische und unkritische Anmerkungen zu „Die Überwindung der Metaphysik"', *Heidegger Studien* 18 (2002), S. 59–87.

8. W. Biemel, A. de Waelhens, Heideggers Schrift „Vom Wesen der Wahrheit", *Symposion* 3 (1952), S. 471–508.

9. W. Biemel, *Martin Heidegger mit Selbstzeugnissen und Bilddokumenten* (rowohlts monographien Nr. 200; Hamburg: Rowohlt, 1973 u.ö.), S.66–78.

10. M. Brasser, *Wahrheit und Verborgenheit. Interpretionen zu Heideggers Wahrheitsverständnis von „Sein und Zeit" bis „Vom Wesen der Wahrheit"* (Epistemata. Würzburger Wissenschaftliche Schriften. Reihe Philosophie, Bd. 203; Würzburg, 1997).

Verfasser für sinnvoll gehalten hat, nur den Denkweg Heideggers von SuZ bis WW unter Leitfrage nach der Wahrheit zu untersuchen. Und soeben ist von *Friedrich-Wilhelm von Herrmann* eine Monographie erschienen, die nur WW gewidmet ist: Wahrheit – Freiheit – Geschichte.[11] Einmal abgesehen von diesem neuen Interesse der Philosophen an WW: Diese Wahrheitsschrift ist auch deshalb noch von besonderem Interesse, weil sie dasjenige Dokument der sogenannten Kehre Heideggers ist, das die bemerkenswerte Modifikation seines Denkens im Blick auf die Wahrheitsfrage ist. Und ich hoffe, daß die im folgenden gebotenen Ausführungen zeigen, wie es gerade diese Modifikation ist, die für den Theologen von besonderer Wichtigkeit ist.

Auch zum *theologischen Horizont* der folgenden Ausführungen einige einführende Worte: Gott ist nach dem Zeugnis des Neuen Testaments, basierend auch auf Aussagen des Alten Testaments, als *Deus hermeneuticus*[12] der sich dem Menschen erschließende Gott. Das Sich-Erschließen gehört also zum *Wesen* Gottes. *Per definitionem* ist Offenbarung dann *Wesens*-Äußerung Gottes. Gilt jedoch zugleich, daß Gott der Unergründliche, der in seinem Wesen begrifflich nicht Erfaßbare ist, dann ist Gott als *Deus revelatus* gerade nicht der in seiner totalen Wesenheit erkannte und erkennbare Gott. Auch als *Deus revelatus* bleibt er der *Deus absconditus*.[13] Doch ist der *Deus hermeneuticus* damit nicht im geringsten minimiert. Denn die Rede vom *Deus hermeneuticus* als *Deus revelatus* will ja zum Ausdruck bringen, daß er sich dem Menschen nach *dessen* Erkenntnismöglichkeiten erschließt, also im Blick darauf, daß der Mensch sein nur begrenzt erkenntnisfähiges Geschöpf ist und eben nicht – Gott!

2. *Martin Heideggers Schrift „Vom Wesen der Wahrheit"*

An dieser Stelle unserer Überlegungen stellt sich bereits die Frage nach einer möglichen und hilfreichen Parallele zur biblisch-theologischen Bedeutung von „Wahrheit" in *Martin Heideggers* Philosophie.[14] Schon in seinem fundamentalontologischen Werk *„Sein und Zeit"* (im folgenden: SuZ; Erstauflage 1927)[15] hat er im viel diskutierten § 44, Dasein, Erschlossenheit und Wahrheit, die *Aussagewahrheit* von der *Wahrheit als Erschlossenheit des Daseins* unterschieden.[16] Wahrheit ist nicht primär die Richtigkeit einer Aussage. Vielmehr *gründet* die *Aussagewahrheit* in der als Existenzial der

11. F.-W. von Herrmann, *Wahrheit – Freiheit – Geschichte. Eine systematische Untersuchung zu Heideggers Schrift „Vom Wesen der Wahrheit"* (Frankfurt a.M.: V. Klostermann, 2002).

12. H. Hübner, Deus hermeneuticus, in: Th. Söding (Hg.), *Der lebendige Gott. Studien zur Theologie des Neuen Testaments* (Festschrift W. Thüsing; Münster: Aschendorff, 1996), S. 50–58.

13. P. Althaus, *Die Theologie Martin Luthers* (Gütersloh: Gerd Mohn, 1962), S. 238–43.

14. Zur Wahrheit in der Theologie s. u.a.: E.M. Pausch, *Wahrheit zwischen Erschlossenheit und Verantwortung. Die Rezeption und Transformation der Wahrheitskonzeption Martin Heideggers in der Theologie Rudolf Bultmanns* (TBT 64; Berlin/New York: de Gruyter, 1995); Ch. Landmesser, *Wahrheit als Grundbegriff neutestamentlicher Wissenschaft* (WMNT 113; Tübingen: Mohr-Siebeck, 1999); zu beiden Werken: H. Hübner, Der Begriff „Wahrheit" in der Theologie (Literaturbericht), *ThLZ* 127 (2002), S. 576–86.

15. M. Heidegger, *Sein und Zeit* (Tübingen: Mohr-Siebeck,18. Aufl., 2000).

16. Ib. S. 226: „Nicht die Aussage ist der primäre ‚Ort' der Wahrheit, sondern *umgekehrt*, die Aussage als Aneignungsmodus der Entdecktheit und als Weise des In-der-Welt-Seins gründet im Entdecken bzw. der *Erschlossenheit* des Daseins."

Erschlossenheit aufgewiesenen Wahrheit. Die eigentliche Wahrheit ist somit die Wahrheit im *existenzialen* Sinne, nämlich das menschliche Dasein, das sich seine existenzial verstandene Welt – also sein *In-der-Welt-sein* – und in diesem seinen In-der-Welt-sein sich selbst erschlossen hat. Konstitutiv für die Wahrheit als Erschlossenheit sind *Geworfenheit* und *Entwurf*. Es geht mir hier nicht darum, Heideggers Fundamentalontologie oder irgendeinen zeitlichen Abschnitt seines Philosophierens als Theologie zu verkaufen. Aber wollen wir zugunsten der Theologie diese so verstehen, daß sie ihren *Grund* in ihrem Wesen als *hermeneutische* Wissenschaft besitzt, so kommen wir nicht um den Tatbestand herum, daß Heidegger – wie immer man auch zu seinem Philosophieren steht – hermeneutische Einsichten gewonnen hat, an denen eine sich hermeneutisch verstehende Theologie nicht vorbeikommt.[17] Und zu diesen Einsichten gehört nach meinem Verständnis von Hermeneutik die Sekundarität der Aussagewahrheit (*veritas est adaequatio rei et intellectus*) gegenüber dem Primat der existenzial verstandenen Wahrheit: *Der Mensch ist seine Wahrheit*.[18] Wörtlich heißt es in SuZ: „Die ursprünglichste und zwar eigentlichste Erschlossenheit, in der Dasein als Seinkönnen sein kann, ist die *Wahrheit der Existenz*."[19]

Bereits 1930, also nur drei Jahre nach dem Erscheinen von SuZ, hält Heidegger seinen Vortrag *„Vom Wesen der Wahrheit"*.[20] Er steht noch ganz in der Tradition von SuZ.[21] Insofern aber diese Schrift ein Dokument der sogenannten Kehre und somit des Beginns des seinsgeschichtlichen Denkens ist, bekundet sich in ihm bereits eine neue Denk-*Richtung* des Philosophierens. Gewisse Aspekte des in SuZ Gesagten werden nun in einen erweiterten und gerade dadurch auch etwas modifizierten Horizont gestellt (s. Anm. 21). Ebenso erfährt die Terminologie gewisse Änderungen; und mit eben dieser veränderten Terminologie ergeben sich interessante Weiterführungen des in „Sein und Zeit" Gedachten und Gesagten. Begleiten wir also Heidegger auf seinem Denkweg[22] in WW.

17. Welche philosophisch-hermeneutische Terminologie man am Ende in theologisch-hermeneutischen Aussagen verwendet, ist nicht entscheidend. Ich bleibe einstweilen in dieser Frage bei *Heideggers* Terminologie, weil sie im philosophischen Diskurs verständlich ist und mir zur Zeit keine bessere bekannt ist.

18. Was von Herrmann, *Wahrheit – Freiheit – Geschicht*e, S. 106, von der Wahrheit in WW sagt, gilt im Prinzip auch von SuZ, § 44 (Kursiven durch mich): „Im Horizont des daseinsmäßigen Menschenwesens geht es nicht um den Ausschluß und auch nicht um die Abwertung der *Aussagewahrheit*, sondern nur um deren *ontologische Verwurzelung* und Neuinterpretation." Auch der nächste Satz verdient unsere besondere Aufmerksamkeit: „Wenn man sich vergegenwärtigt, daß z.B. *Kant* in der ‚Kritik der reinen Vernunft' die *Urteilswahrheit in* der *transzendentalen Wahrheit fundiert sein läßt*, dann erscheint die fundamentalontologische und auch die seinsgeschichtliche Gründung der Aussagewahrheit in einem ontologisch früheren Bereich nicht mehr als etwas Außergewöhnliches."

19. Heidegger, SuZ, S. 221.

20. Jetzt in: Ders., *Wegmarken*,GA 9 (s. Anm. 4).

21. Auch später bleibt für Heidegger SuZ grundlegend, er erweitert aber die Frage nach dem Dasein in seinsgeschichtlicher Weise. Doch ist bekanntlich auch schon in SuZ die Frage nach Dasein um der Frage nach dem Sein willen gestellt, s. z.B. ib. 17: „Die so gefaßte Analytik des Daseins bleibt ganz auf die leitende Aufgabe der Ausarbeitung der Seinsfrage orientiert." S. auch F.-W. von Herrmann, *Wege ins Ereignis. Zu Heideggers „Beiträgen zur Philosophie"* (Frankfurt a.M.: V. Klostermann, 1994), S. 6: „Der *zweite* Ausarbeitungsweg in den ‚Beiträgen' bleibt insofern auf den *ersten* [in SuZ; H.H.] rückbezogen, als sich der *Ereignis-Charakter* des Seins aus dem gewandelten Sichzeigen des in ‚Sein und Zeit' eröffneten Bereichs bekundet."

22. Ich verwende jetzt einmal den Terminus „Denkweg" etwas anders, als ihn O. Pöggeler in seiner bahnbrechenden Monographie *Der Denkweg Martin Heideggers* (Tübingen: Mohr-Siebeck, 3. Aufl.,1983), intendiert hat. Er meint nämlich den Weg, den Heidegger im Laufe seiner philosophi-

Auch in WW geht Heidegger von der *Aussagewahrheit* aus. Er wählt das Beispiel eines Geldstücks (S. 183): „Wie kann das völlig Ungleiche, die Aussage, an das Geldstück sich angleichen? Sie müßte ja zum Geldstück werden und dergestalt ganz und gar sich aufgeben." Seine Antwort (S. 183f.): „Die Aussage über das Geldstück bezieht ‚sich' aber auf dieses Ding, indem sie es vor-stellt und vom Vor-gestellten sagt, wie es mit ihm selbst nach der je leitenden Hinsicht bestellt sei. Die vorstellende Aussage sagt ihr Gesagtes so vom vorgestellten Ding, *wie* es als dieses ist." Dieses Vor-stellen versteht er als „das Entgegenstehenlassen des Dinges als Gegenstand". Der entscheidende Begriff ist für ihn die *Offenheit eines Offenen*, der gegenüber sich der Mensch in *Offenständigkeit* verhält (S. 184). So gibt sich das Dasein frei als „*Freisein* zum Offenbaren eines Offenen" (S. 186). Eine solche Freiheit, also das freie Dasein, „läßt das jeweilige Seiende das Seiende sein, das es ist" (S. 188). Das Seinlassen seinerseits faßt Heidegger aber als „das Sicheinlassen auf das Seiende", also auf das Offene (S. 188). Seine Kernaussage ist in diesem Zusammenhang (S. 188): „Dieses Offene hat das abendländische Denken in seinem Anfang begriffen als τὰ ἀληθέα, das Unverborgene.[23] Wenn wir ἀληθεία statt mit ‚Wahrheit' durch ‚Unverborgenheit' übersetzen, dann ist diese Übersetzung nicht nur ‚wörtlicher', sondern sie enthält die Weisung, den gewohnten Begriff der Wahrheit im Sinne der Richtigkeit der Aussage um- und zurückzudenken in jenes noch Unbegriffene der Entborgenheit und der Entbergung des Seienden." Heidegger fordert also ein Umdenken, ein Zurückdenken, und zwar hinsichtlich der Richtigkeit der Aussage. Das entspricht durchaus SuZ § 44, in dem ja auch der Primat der Aussagewahrheit bestritten ist. Im Begriff der *Unverborgenheit* (s.u.) ist aber wiederum das Dasein impliziert. Aus der Perspektive von SuZ gesagt, geht Heidegger auch hier wieder auf die existenziale Bedeutsamkeit von Wahrheit zu.[24]

Aber Denk-*Bewegung* und Denk-*Richtung* haben sich gegenüber SuZ in WW merklich verändert. Denn so sehr es in beiden Werken letztlich um das existenziale Wesen der Wahrheit geht, so ist doch die Existenz in WW aus neuer

schen Entwicklungen gegangen ist. Ich meine hier den Weg der Argumentation, den Heidegger Schritt für Schritt in WW geht.

23. Dazu von Herrmann, *Wahrheit – Freiheit – Geschichte*, S. 112: „Vom Offenen wird gesagt, daß es im Anfang des abendländischen Denkens begriffen sei als τὰ ἀληθέα, als das Unverborgene. Diese Bemerkung darf nicht dahingehend mißverstanden werden, als solle gesagt werden, im frühgriechischen Denken sei das jetzt in Abgrenzung gegen die Offenbarkeit des Seienden aufgezeigte Offene in seiner Offenbarkeit bereits gedacht worden. Vielmehr soll der Hinweis auf τὰ ἀληθέα besagen: Was sich jetzt als Offenheit des Offenen gezeigt hat, worin das Seiende als Seiendes allererst offenbar wird, sei im griechischen Anfang als die Offenheit des Seienden, als das Seiende in seiner Unverborgenheit erfahren. Das soll aber nicht besagen, die frühen griechischen Denker hätten die Unverborgenheit des Seienden schon aus der Offenheit als der Unverborgenheit gedacht."

24. S. auch von Herrmann, *Wahrheit – Freiheit – Geschichte*, S. 107: „Die Frage nach dem Wesen der Wahrheit ist hier in ‚Vom Wesen der Wahrheit' der Zugangsweg zur Erfahrung des Daseins. Denn es wird sich auf diesem Weg zeigen, daß das ursprünglichere Wesen des Menschen [...] das Innestehen im ursprünglich wesenden Bereich der Wahrheit ist, das Innestehen als die eigenste Seinsweise (Existenz) des Menschen."

Perspektive gesehen. Schon die Orthographie ist bezeichnend: *Ek-sistenz* statt *Existenz*. Läßt sich das Dasein als Freiheit auf Seiendes im Sinne des Seinlassens ein, so ist es, „in sich aus-setzend, ek-sistent“ (S. 189). Versteht Heidegger die Freiheit als „die Eingelassenheit in die Entbergung des Seienden als eines solchen“, so folgert er (S. 189): „Die in der Wahrheit als Freiheit gewurzelte Eksistenz ist die Aus-setzung in die Entborgenheit des Seienden als eines solchen.“ Deutlich ist auf jeden Fall, daß Heidegger eine *doppelte Bewegung* beschreibt: 1. *die Offenheit des offenbaren Offenen hin zur Offenständigkeit des Daseins*, 2. *die Offenständigkeit des Daseins hin zur Offenheit des offenbaren Offenen*. Somit entspricht dem Ek-sistieren auf seiten des Daseins das Sich-Offenbaren des Seienden. Heidegger hat so in neuer Terminologie die Überwindung der sogenannten Subjekt-Objekt-Spaltung ausgesagt, also seinen Widerspruch gegen Descartes.

Freiheit ist hier anders verstanden als im üblichen Sprachgebrauch. Sie als „eine Eigenschaft des Menschen“ zu sehen sei eine der hartnäckigsten Vormeinungen (S. 187). Das menschliche Belieben, so heißt es pointiert, verfügt nicht über die Freiheit (S. 190): „die *Freiheit*, das ek-sistente, entbergende Dasein *besitzt den Menschen* und das so ursprünglich, daß einzig *sie* einem Menschentum den alle Geschichte erst begründenden und auszeichnenden Bezug zu einem Seienden im Ganzen als einem solchen gewährt.“[25] Also: *„Nur der eksistente Mensch ist geschichtlich.“*[26] Freiheit ist also mehr als die dem Menschen freistehende Möglichkeit, dieses zu tun oder jenes zu lassen. Heidegger verweist auf den Wesenszusammenhang von Wahrheit und Freiheit, der uns dahin bringe, „die Frage nach dem Wesen des Menschen in einer Hinsicht zu verfolgen, die uns die Erfahrung eines verborgenen Wesensgrundes des Menschen (des Daseins) verbürgt, so zwar, daß sie uns zuvor in den ursprünglich wesenden Bereich der Wahrheit versetzt“ (S. 187). Hier ist von *Erfahrung* die Rede, und zwar von der „Erfahrung eines verborgenen Wesensgrundes des Menschen“. Der Grund, das Gegründet-Sein des oberflächlich nicht zu erfahrenden Mensch-Seins ist der Mensch nämlich als Wahrheit seiner Existenz und Ek-sistenz, also die ihm *geschenkte Freiheit*. Ich paraphrasiere: Die Existenzwahrheit des Menschen ist der verborgene Grund der Freiheit. Ich spitze zu: Der Mensch als Wahrheit gibt dem Menschen die Freiheit – natürlich ist es ein und desselbe Mensch! –, so daß der Mensch der Wahrheit die Freiheit ist. Dieser Satz ist nur im Denkrahmen Heideggers verständlich und unterliegt in der Optik bestimmter philosophischer Konzeptionen dem Sinnlosigkeitsverdacht.[27]

25. *Freiheit* und *besitzt den Menschen* durch mich kursiv.

26. Kursive durch mich.

27. Meine Interpretation Heideggers dürfte nicht ganz fern von der liegen, die von Herrmann, *Wahrheit – Freiheit – Geschichte*, S. 105, zu diesem Problem gibt: „Innerhalb dieser, gegenüber der überlieferten Denkungsart bereits grundlegend gewandelten Fragebahn kommt es zur denkenden ‚Erfahrung eines verborgenen Wesensgrundes des Menschen‘ [...]. Diesen Wesensgrund nennt Heidegger das ‚Dasein‘. ‚Erfahrung‘ besagt hier, daß dem Denken das zu Denkende widerfährt. Das ihm so Widerfahrende ist solches, was sich dem Denken von ihm selbst her zeigt.“ Vor allem mit dem Begriff *„Widerfahrnis“* ist das, worum es Heidegger geht, bestens ausgesagt. Denn das Offenbare eines Offenen ist ja in der Tat Widerfahrnis des Daseins als eines Offenständigen.

Vom Wesen der Wahrheit aus kommt Heidegger auf die *Unwahrheit* zu sprechen. Für den mit SuZ Vertrauten ist das keine Überraschung. Denn dort sind in § 44 bereits Wahrheit und Unwahrheit im Zusammenhang genannt. Nach SuZ gehört das *Verfallen*[28] zur Seinsverfassung des Daseins, das Verfallen nämlich an die jeweilige Welt, an das „Man". Das *ontologische* Urteil[29]: *„Das Dasein ist, weil wesenhaft verfallend, seiner Seinsverfassung nach in der ‚Unwahrheit'."* Und: „Der volle existenzial-ontologische Sinn des Satzes: ‚Dasein ist in der Wahrheit' sagt gleichursprünglich mit: ‚Dasein ist in der Unwahrheit'."

Auch in WW nennt Heidegger einen Zusammenhang von Wahrheit und Unwahrheit. Aber er redet nicht mehr wie in SuZ von der Gleichursprünglichkeit beider. Der „geschichtliche Mensch [kann; H.H.] im Seinlassen des Seienden das Seiende auch *nicht* sein lassen", und so werde dieses Seiende verdeckt und verstellt. So gelange im zur Macht gekommenen Schein „das Unwesen der Wahrheit zum Vorschein" (S. 191). Heidegger sieht also den *Ursprung des Unwesens der Wahrheit nicht im Menschen gelegen*, weil die *ek-sistente Freiheit als Wesen der Wahrheit keine Eigenschaft des Menschen* sei. Er folgert (S. 191): „Die Unwahrheit muß vielmehr aus dem Wesen der Wahrheit kommen." Dann aber sind Wahrheit und Unwahrheit nicht, wie in SuZ, „gleichursprünglich".[30] Die Priorität der Wahrheit ist eindeutig ausgesagt. Ist aber die Wahrheit der Ursprung der Unwahrheit und erschöpft sich das Wesen der Wahrheit nicht in der Richtigkeit der Aussage, „dann kann auch die Unwahrheit nicht mit der Unrichtigkeit des Urteils gleichgesetzt werden" (S. 191). Sieht man nun mit Heidegger die Aussagewahrheit als für das Wesen der Wahrheit sekundär, dann ist in der Tat Unwahrheit *primär* etwas anderes als die Unrichtigkeit des Urteils.

Interpretiert man die ἀληθεία als *Unverborgenheit*, dann kann man mit Heidegger die Unwahrheit als *Verbergung* deuten. Folglich ist seine Argumentation in sich schlüssig (S. 193): „Die Verborgenheit ist dann, von der Wahrheit als Entborgenheit her gedacht, die Un-entborgenheit und somit die dem Wahrheitswesen eigenste und eigentliche Un-wahrheit." Dann stellt sich „die Verborgenheit des Seienden *im Ganzen*[31] [...] nie erst nachträglich ein als Folge der immer stückhaften Erkenntnis des Seienden" (S. 193). Also ist diese Verborgenheit des Seienden im Ganzen, verstanden als die eigentliche Un-wahrheit, „älter als jede Offenbarkeit von diesem und jenem Seienden" (S. 193f.). Vordringlich wichtig ist für unsere Fragestellung das Verständnis der Unwahrheit, der Verbergung und des Un-wesens der Wahrheit vom Da-sein her. Denn es ist dieses Da-sein als Eksistenz, das die eigentliche Un-wahrheit verwahrt. Von gleichem Gewicht ist, daß Heidegger in diesem Zusammenhang das *Sein* nennt (S. 194): „Für den Wissenden allerdings deutet das ‚Un-' des anfänglichen Un-wesens der Wahrheit als

S. auch ib. S. 107: „Die *Freiheit* als Grund für das offenständige Verhalten zum offenbaren Seienden *empfängt ihr eigenes Wesen aus dem ursprünglich wesenden Bereich der Wahrheit, in das sie versetzt ist.*"

28. Heidegger, SuZ, S. 221, s. auch § 27.
29. Ib. S. 222; Kursive durch Heidegger.
30. Anders von Herrmann, *Wahrheit – Freiheit – Geschichte*, S. 136.
31. Kursive durch mich.

der Un-wahrheit in den noch nicht erfahrenen Bereich der Wahrheit des Seins (nicht erst des Seienden)." Un-wahrheit ist demnach das Verfehlen des Seins. Und *wer das Sein verfehlt, die Wahrheit des Seins verfehlt, verfehlt auch das Dasein, verfehlt den Menschen.* Des Menschen Defizienz: Er läßt es zumeist bei diesem oder jenem Seienden bewenden, das Sein jedoch kommt nicht in seinen Blick.

Das eigentliche Un-wesen der Wahrheit ist das *Geheimnis*. Indem sich aber das vergessene Geheimnis des Daseins „in der Vergessenheit und für sie versagt, läßt es den geschichtlichen Menschen in seinem Gangbaren bei seinen Gemächten stehen" (S. 195). Das also läßt sich vom Menschen aussagen: seine *Gemächte*. Pöggeler verdeutlicht dies, indem er unsere Stelle so ergänzt, daß „die sich selbst verbergende Verborgenheit [...] den Menschen beim Gängigen *und Verfügbaren*, bei den Gemächten *seines Tuns* stehen" läßt[32]: Der Mensch verfügt über das Seiende; seine Gemächte sind die Gemächte seines Tuns. Es ist nach Heidegger die vom Menschentum ergänzte „Welt" – Welt als Existenzial, somit eben *seine* Welt! –, es sind die je neuesten Bedürfnisse und Absichten des Menschen, es sind seine Vorhaben und Planungen, denen er seine Maße entnimmt, dabei aber das Seiende im Ganzen vergißt. Erneut meldet sich der alte Protagoras: „Der Mensch ist das Maß aller Dinge." Das Sein ist in seiner Wahrheit vergessen; der Mensch aber ist wieder einmal in seiner Selbst- und Seinsvergessenheit der „Macher" seiner Gemächte. Er ist der sich selbst destruierende Mensch! Heideggers Terminologie lautet (S. 196): *„Ek-sistent ist das Dasein insistent."*[33] Er expliziert (S. 196): „Insistent ist der Mensch der je nächsten Gangbarkeit des Seienden zugewendet. Aber er insistiert nur als der schon ek-sistente, indem er doch das Seiende als ein solches Richtmaß nimmt." „Die Umgetriebenheit des Menschen weg vom Geheimnis hin zum Gangbaren" nennt Heidegger das *Irren* (S. 196). Wer sich daher in Seinsvergessenheit an das bloß Seiende als seine eigenen Gemächte hält, ist der Irrende. Kommt der Mensch nach SuZ immer schon vom Verfallen her, so heißt dieses Geschehen nun in WW (S. 196f.): „Der Mensch irrt. Der Mensch geht nicht erst in die Irre. Er geht nur immer in der Irre, weil er ek-sistent in-sistiert und so schon in der Irre steht. Die Irre [...] gehört zur inneren Verfassung des Da-seins, in das der geschichtliche Mensch eingelassen ist. Die Irre ist der Spielraum jener Wende, in der die in-sistente Ek-sistenz wendig sich stets neu vergißt und vermißt."

Die Aussagen über die Irre lesen wir in Abschnitt 7, überschrieben *Die Unwahrheit als die Irre.*[34] Sie führen zur Frage des *Seins*. Im *Zugleich* der *Entbergung* und *Verbergung* waltet die Irre (S. 198): „Die Entbergung des Seienden als eines solchen ist in sich zugleich die Verbergung des Seienden im Ganzen." Heidegger stellt den „Ausblick in das Geheimnis aus der Irre" dar als „das Fragen im Sinne der einzigen Frage, was das Seiende als solches im Ganzen" sei und erklärt dann (S. 198): „Diese Frage denkt die wesentlich beirrende und daher

32. Pöggeler, *Der Denkweg Martin Heideggers*, S. 97; Kursive durch mich.
33. Hervorhebung durch Heidegger.
34. Bisher habe ich die Zählungen und Überschriften der einzelnen Abschnitte nicht genannt. Wegen der Wichtigkeitkeit der Abschnitte 7–9 soll dies aber nun geschehen.

in ihrer Mehrdeutigkeit noch nicht gemeisterte Frage nach dem *Sein* des Seienden." Dieses *Denken des Seins* begreife sich seit Platon als „Philosophie".[35]

Der Anfang von Abschnitt 8, überschrieben *Die Wahrheitsfrage und die Philosophie* zeigt, daß dieses Denken des Seins darauf hinausläuft, was er in den „Beiträgen zur Philosophie" unter dem „Denken des Seyns" verstanden hat (s.u.). Bereits der erste Satz ist bezeichnend (S. 198f.): „Im Denken des Seins kommt die geschichtegründende Befreiung des Menschen zur Ek-sistenz ins Wort, das nicht erst der ‚Ausdruck' einer Meinung, sondern je schon das gutverwahrte Gefüge der Wahrheit des Seienden im Ganzen ist." Hier ist das Denken des *Seins* im Kontext des *Wortes* genannt. Denken des Seins und Wort gehören in dasselbe Ereignis. Ist doch das Wort nicht bloßer *Aus*-Druck einer Meinung und somit nichts *Äus*-serliches; es *ist* „je schon das gutverwahrte Gefüge der Wahrheit des Seienden im Ganzen". Wort und Wahrheit sind eines, wenn „Wort" im Vollsinn seiner Bedeutsamkeit verstanden wird. Das gesprochene Wort ist somit die sich *aus*-sprechende Wahrheit als die sich *aus*-sprechende Ek-sistenz. Mit dem Instrumentarium einer sezierenden Analytik läßt sich freilich der Kumulus dieser Termini nicht be-*griff*-lich be-*greif*-en.

Das zeigt sich auch an dem, was Heidegger zum hermeneutisch zentralen Verb „*hören*" im Anschluß an das letzte Zitat sagt: Es ist uninteressant, wie viele für dieses Wort das Ohr haben. Anders gesagt: Wie viele auf dieses Wort hören können. Und so unterscheidet er zwischen denen, die von dem Weltaugenblick an, den der Anfang der Philosophie erfüllt, *denkend* fragen können, und den Vertretern der „*ausgeprägten* Herrschaft [!] des gemeinen Verstandes (die Sophistik)" (S. 199). Dieser *gemeine Verstand* – seine Vertreter sind taub gegenüber der Seinsfrage und stumpf gegenüber philosophischem Denken – beruft sich in oberflächlichem Denken „auf die Fraglosigkeit des offenbaren Seienden". Er ist nicht in der Lage, auf das Sein hin zu *fragen*. Er wird sogar in seiner Frageunfähigkeit aggressiv gegenüber der Fragefähigkeit der Philosophie; denn er deutet in unglücklicher Gereiztheit „jedes denkende Fragen als einen Angriff auf den gesunden Menschenverstand" (S. 199). Die brutalen weltanschaulichen Diktaturen der letzten hundert Jahre, seien sie linker oder rechter Couleur, sind die Realisierung solcher Gereiztheit. Politische, auch religiöse Fanatismen wehren sich bekanntlich aus uneingestandener Angst und Unsicherheit hinsichtlich eigener Überzeugungen gegen jegliches denkende Fragen. Lenin, Stalin, Hitler oder Bin Laden konnten oder können kein Hinterfragen ihrer zementierten Positionen zulassen, weil sie sonst von der Freiheit des Denkens hinweggeschwemmt würden.[36]

35. Freilich versteht Heidegger hier unter „Philosophie" noch jenes Denken, das im ersten Anfang den Titel „Metaphysik" erhalten habe. Und es ist ja gerade die Metaphysik, deren Überwindung er später als konstitutiv für den anderen Anfang sah, der in gewisser Weise mit Nietzsche beginne. Also ist das hier genannte „Denken des Seins" noch das in den Anfängen des anderen Anfangs begriffene Denkbemühen um die Frage nach dem Sein.

36. von Herrmann, *Wahrheit – Freiheit – Geschichte*, S. 201, deutet diese Stelle auf folgende Weise: „Gesagt ist nur, daß die andersanfängliche Philosophie [...] das Seiende und dessen Offenbarkeit *vom Wesen des Seins her* denkt. Auf diesem ihr zugewiesenen Wege hält sie sich aber frei von jedem ‚Machtanspruch von außen', d.h. von einer Weisung, die nicht aus ihrer eigensten Sache, dem Wesen des Seins (als des Seins des Seienden), an sie ergeht."

Heidegger ist sich dessen bewußt, daß „das volle Wesen der Wahrheit das Unwesen einschließt und allem zuvor als Verbergung waltet", und somit „die Philosophie als das Erfragen dieser Wahrheit in sich zwiespältig" ist. In ihrem Fragen kann sich die Philosophie also „nicht einzig an das Seiende halten, aber auch keinen Machtanspruch von außen zulassen" (S. 199).

In Abschnitt 9, überschrieben *Anmerkung*, fügte Heidegger in der 2. Auflage 1949 den ersten Absatz noch ein. Dessen Kernaussage lautet (S. 201): „Die Frage nach dem Wesen der Wahrheit findet ihre Anwort in dem Satz: *das Wesen der Wahrheit ist die Wahrheit des Wesens*." In der Wendung „Wahrheit des Wesens" versteht er „Wesen verbal und denkt in diesem Wort, noch innerhalb der Metaphysik bleibend [s.o.], das Seyn als den waltenden Unterschied von Sein und Seiendem". Jetzt also spricht Heidegger in diesem überarbeiteten Vortrag – endlich! – vom *Seyn*. Wahrheit interpretiert er jetzt als „lichtendes Bergen als Grundzug des Seyns". Sie ist in ihrem lichtenden Seyn ein hermeneutisches Geschehen, mit den „Beiträgen zur Philosophie" gesprochen: Er-eignis. Also: *Wahrheit ist entweder hermeneutisch oder sie ist keine Wahrheit!* Und so sagt er (S. 201): „Weil zu ihm [dem Seyn; H.H.] lichtendes Bergen gehört, erscheint Seyn anfänglich im Licht des verbergenden Entzugs. Der Namen dieser Lichtung ist ἀλήθεια." Der Schlußsatz der ganzen Studie ist aussagekräftig genug (S. 202)[37]: „Die Schrittfolge des Fragens ist in sich der Weg [!] eines Denkens, das, *statt Vorstellungen und Begriffe zu liefern*, sich als Wandlung des Bezugs zum Sein erfährt und erprobt."

3. *Wahrheit in der griechischen Philosophie*

So manches, was Heidegger in WW sagt, ist bestens geeignet, mit neutestamentlichen Aussagen zur Wahrheit[38], besonders aus dem Joh, konfrontiert zu werden, „konfrontieren" hier im neutralen, nicht im antithetischen Sinn gemeint. Aber für einen solchen Vergleich gewinnen wir ein besseres Fundament, wenn wir zunächst in die philosophische Literatur der Griechen schauen, zumal Heidegger und Bultmann, also der Philosoph und auch der Theologe, beim Durchdenken der Frage nach der Wahrheit auf das profane griechischen Wahrheitsverständnis rekurrierten. Zu bedenken ist die Etymologie von ἀλήθεια; von den Autoren dürfen wir Platon und Aristoteles nicht übergehen. Und unverzichtbar ist auch der Blick auf die Stoa.

Zunächst zur *Etymologie*: Als bekannt darf hier vorausgesetzt werden, daß ἀλήθεια eine α-*privativum*-Konstruktion ist: ἀ-λήθεια ist das *Nicht*-Vergessene, das *Nicht*-Verborgene. Daß Heidegger ἀλήθεια sehr bewußt als *Unverborgenheit* interpretiert hat, wurde bereits ausführlich dargelegt. Doch ist zu fragen, wie weit Griechen bei diesem Wort etymologisch gedacht haben. Aber daß doch manche bei ἀλήθεια den Fluß Lethe in der griechischen Unterwelt, den Fluß des Vergessens, zuweilen vor Augen hatten, darf man vermuten. Daß diese Assoziation bei Platon und Aristoteles zumindest unterschwellig gegeben war, sei hier angenommen.

37. Kursive durch mich.
38. Ich sage bewußt nicht „über die Wahrheit"!

a. *Aristoteles*

Aristoteles war Schüler Platons. Und so sollte eigentlich zuerst Platons Auffassung von der Wahrheit thematisiert werden, ehe Aristoteles bedacht wird. Doch aus Gründen, die sich auf Heideggers Aristoteles-Interpretation stützen, scheint es mir sinnvoll, diesmal zuerst den Schüler und dann erst den Lehrer zu behandeln.

Seine Deutung des Wahrheitsverständnisses bei Aristoteles hat Heidegger besonders einprägsam in seiner Marburger Vorlesung vom Wintersemester 1925/26 vorgetragen.[39] Kann man, wenn man nicht einer phänomenologischen Denkweise grundlegend widerspricht, wichtigen Aussagen aus SuZ und WW zustimmen, so auch im Blick auf diese Vorlesung. Ihre Argumentation überzeugte mich bereits nach Erscheinen von GA 21 (1976), zumindest ihrer inhaltlichen Tendenz nach, und das nicht nur in der Wahrheitsfrage.[40]

Von zentraler Bedeutung war für Heidegger vor allem Aristoteles, *De interpretatione 4, 17a, 1–3*: ἔστι δὲ λόγος ἅπας μὲν σημαντικός, ... ἀποφαντικὸς δὲ οὐ πᾶς, ἀλλ᾽ ἐν ᾧ τὸ ἀληθεύειν ἢ ψεύδεσθαι ὑπάρχει. Heidegger übersetzt zunächst: „‚Jedes Reden weist zwar auf etwas hin (bedeutet überhaupt etwas) – aufweisend, sehenlassend dagegen ist nicht jedes Reden, sondern nur das, darin das Wahrsein oder Falschsein vorkommt' (als die Weise des Redens).“[41] Spezifisch für Heidegger, auf jeden Fall aber sachlich zutreffend ist seine Übersetzung von ἀποφαντικὸς mit *„sehenlassend“* oder kurz danach mit *„aufweisend sehen lassend“*.[42] Das entspricht ganz seiner phänomenologischen Grundkonzeption. Heidegger präzisiert dann gemäß dieser Intention seine Ausgangsübersetzung in folgender Weise: „aufweisend sehen lassend (Aussage) ist nur das Reden, darin das Entdecken oder Verdecken die eigentliche Redeabsicht trägt und bestimmt“. Auf diese Art kann er die „auszeichnende Möglichkeit des Redens im Sehenlassen“ zum Ausdruck bringen: der λόγος ist σημαντικός bzw. ἀποφαντικός.[43] Damit sind wir aber wieder bei der Wahrheitsfrage, und zwar im Zusammenhang von *Wahrheit und Wort*, von ἀλήθεια und λόγος: Die Aussage – und das heißt: das Wort – läßt Gesagtes von der Sache selbst her sehen. Heidegger folgert: „Der Satz ist nicht das, darin Wahrheit erst möglich wird, sondern umgekehrt, der Satz ist erst in der Wahrheit möglich, sofern man das Phänomen gesehen hat, das die Griechen mit Wahrheit meinten und das Aristoteles zum ersten Mal begrifflich scharf gefaßt hat.“ Und dann die entscheidende Formulierung, uns der Sache nach aus SuZ und WW vertraut: „[Der] Satz ist nicht der Ort der Wahrheit, sondern Wahrheit ist der Ort des Satzes.“[44] Zu Recht wehrt sich Heidegger dagegen, daß Aristoteles behauptet habe, der Satz sei der Ort der Wahrheit.[45] Was dieser gerade in dem eben zitierten Satz aus *De interpretatione* über das Wahr-Sein, τὸ ἀληθεύειν gesagt hat, lautet ja: Das Wahr-Sein befindet sich (ὑπάρχει) – neben dem Falsch-Sein – in einem „sehenlassenden“ Logos. Und dieser Logos, dieser Satz läßt also sehen, ob seine Aussage wahr oder falsch ist. Die Behauptung, „der Satz *ist* der Ort der Wahrheit“, ist zumindest eine sinnverzerrende Überspitzung dessen, was Aristoteles sagen wollte. Der Satz ist vielmehr der Ort (ἐν ᾧ), an dem sich *die dem Satz vorgegebene Wahrheit* sehen läßt.

39. M. Heidegger, *Logik. Die Frage nach der Wahrheit. Marburger Vorlesung Wintersemester 1925/26* (hg. von W. Biemel [GA 21]; Frankfurt a.M.: V. Klostermann, 1976).

40. Zu dieser Vorlesung H. Hübner, *Biblische Theologie des Neuen Testaments. Bd. 3. Hebräerbrief, Evangelien und Offenbarung; Epilegomena* (Göttingen: Vandenhoeck & Ruprecht, 1995), S. 233ff.

41. Heidegger, GA 21, S. 129.

42. *Ib.* S. 131.

43. *Ib.* S. 133.

44. *Ib.* S.135; Wegfall des Artikels wahrscheinlich Druckfehler.

45. *Ib.* S. 128.

Kann man also sagen, daß schon für Aristoteles Wahrheit ein phänomenologischer Begriff war? Natürlich war dieser kein Phänomenologe in dem Sinn, wie wir es heute in philosophischer Terminologie verstehen. Aber seine Philosophie ist in ihrem Innern so angelegt, daß sie phänomenologisch verstanden und interpretiert werden kann. Die ἀλήθεια wurde von Aristoteles so gedacht, daß wir ihr von unserem heutigen Verständnis von Phänomenologie her das Prädikat „phänomenologisch" geben und sie als hermeneutischen „Begriff" fassen können. Denn sie ist das Sich-Zeigen des von ihrem Logos Ausgesagten. Zugespitzt gesagt: Wahrheit, ἀλήθεια, ist der Gehalt des Wortes, des λόγος. Kraft dieses Wortes läßt sie sehen, was sie jeweils als ihr je Eigenes sehen lassen will.

Eine für Heidegger wichtige Stelle war *Metaphysik Γ 7, 1011b 26*: τὸ μὲν γὰρ λέγειν τὸ ὂν μὴ εἶναι ἢ τὸ μὴ ὂν εἶναι ψεῦδος, τὸ δὲ τὸ ὂν εἶναι καὶ τὸ μὴ ὂν μὴ εἶναι ἀληθές. In Heideggers Übersetzung: „Denn das redende Sehenlassen des Seienden als Nichtsein oder des Nichtseienden als Sein ist Verdeckung, das Sehenlassen aber des Seienden als Sein und des Nichtseienden als Nichtsein ist Entdeckung." Das Adjektiv ἀληθές hat er also mit „Entdeckung" wiedergegeben. Erinnern wir uns daran, daß für Heidegger nach SuZ § 44 „Wahrsein als Entdeckendsein" ein Existenzial ist.[46] Heidegger vermutet, daß für einen Europäer des 20. Jahrhunderts, der diese Bestimmung liest, das doch sehr trivial sei. Aber[47]: „Diese Definition [ist] das Resultat der größten philosophischen Anstrengung, die Plato und Aristoteles gemacht haben."

Im folgenden Abschnitt, überschrieben „Wahrheit und Sein", interpretiert er *Metaphysik Θ*. Hier nur eine bezeichnende Ausssage Heideggers aus dem Schlußteil dieser Interpretation[48]: „Aristoteles sagt: das Sein ‚ist' die Entdecktheit. Er läßt die primär im θιγεῖν liegende Entdecktheit vikariieren mit dem Sein. b 24 bestimmt er das ἀληθές des Einfachen durch das θιγεῖν und 1052 a 1, wo er nach dem Sein des Einfachen fragt, rekurriert er wiederum auf das schlichte νοεῖν – θιγεῖν. Entdecktheit also übernimmt die Antwort auf die Frage nach dem Sein. Ein Seinscharakter des Seienden, und zwar der des eigentlich Seienden, des Einfachen, ist durch Entdecktheit bestimmt."

Um es noch einmal in Erinnerung zu rufen: Es ging uns hier nicht um Heidegger, sondern um Aristoteles. Heidegger wurde herangezogen, weil seine Aristoteles-Interpretation zumindest in die richtige Richtung zielt. Und als Resultat zeigte sich: Der λόγος läßt uns das sehen, was in der ἀλήθεια anwesend ist. Somit ist das *Zusammensein von λόγος und ἀλήθεια* ein *phänomenologisch-hermeneutisches Geschehen.*

b. *Platon (und Stoa)*

Nun von der gedanklichen Klarheit des Schülers zur leidenschaftlichen Unbedingtheit des Lehrers, der aufgrund der *Begegnung* mit einem Philosophen *philosophisch existentiell zu denken* gelernt hatte! Konkret: Von Aristoteles zu Platon, und von Platon zu Sokrates. Man muß die Einführung von *Ottomar Wichmann* in seinem Platon-Buch lesen, um etwas davon mitzubekommen, wie ein Platonforscher ob der begeisternden Philosophie Platons selber begeistert wird und begeisternd wirkt. Er will Platon seiner Gegenwart vermitteln; er will einer „rein" wissenschaftlichen Platonforschung, der alle Versuche, Platon dem heutigen Menschen nahezubringen, zuwider sind, eine radikale Absage erteilen – mit Recht! Die Idee des Guten war Platon durch seine *Begegnung* mit Sokrates aufgegangen. Dieses Ideelle „wurde *als Wahrheit, als sittliche Pflicht und*

46. Ders., SuZ, S. 219.
47. Ders., GA 21, S.163.
48. *Ib.* S. 190.

als Wesensgrund sein ‚Anliegen' für Zeit und Ewigkeit".[49] In diesem Einführungskapitel ist laufend von Wahrheit – dem Thema unserer Studie – im Blick auf Platon *und zugleich* im Blick und den heutigen Menschen die Rede, und zwar „*in der aufs Wesenhafte, Werthafte und Sinnhafte gehenden Unbedingtheitswertung*, die Platon mit aller Entschiedenheit zum höchsten Anliegen seiner Philosophie macht"[50]. *Helmut Meinhardt* stellt heraus, daß Platon in seiner durch die Ideenlehre bestimmten Philosophie „einen ausgezeichneten Terminus ἰδέα noch nicht kennt". Und so erklärt er: „Diese erst sehr viel spätere Terminusbildung muß hermeneutisch reflektiert werden, wenn wir heute Platons Texte daraufhin befragen, was in ihnen ‚die Ideen' bedeuten."[51] Erfreulich, daß er die Notwendigkeit einer *hermeneutischen* Reflexion so klar aussagt!

Es ist hier nicht der Ort, der Frage nachzugehen, ob und inwiefern Platon seine *Ideenlehre* im Laufe seines Nachdenkens weiterentwickelte oder gar entscheidend modifizierte. Es genügt, die Wahrheitsfrage bei Platon im Rahmen der Grundkonstituenten dieser Ideenlehre zu skizzieren. Meinhardt hat völlig recht, wenn er auf die Gefahr hinweist, „diese Frage einengend nur als ‚logische' zu hören, als lediglich logisch-methodisches Problem der Definition".[52] So meine die Frage etwa nach der „Idee" des Frommen im *Euthyphron* „nicht nur deren ‚Begriff' als widerspruchsfreie Merkmalskombination, sondern die *Wesenheit* Frömmigkeit selbst, durch welche alles Fromme fromm ist, das Urbild (παράδειγμα), durch dessen Nachahmung eine Handlung fromm wird".[53]

Ein terminologischer Tatbestand ist auffällig: Im *Staat* heißt es, daß „die Wahrheit *gesehen* werde", ἀλήθεια *ὁρᾶται*, jedoch *nicht* im *direkten* Zusammenhang der Wiedererinnerungslehre. Im *Phaidros* ist jedoch vom Sehen unmittelbar in diesem Zusammenhang die Rede, und zwar von den Seelen vor ihrem Eingang in einen Leib. Jede Seele habe vor ihrer Geburt *das Seiende geschaut*, Phaidr 249e: πᾶσα μὲν ἀνθρώπου ψυχὴ φύσει *τεθέαται* τὰ ὄντα. Nach ihrer Geburt kam es aber für die meisten zum Vergessen des Gesehenen; diese vergaßen sogar das Heilige, Phaidr 250a: λήθην ὧν τότε εἶδον ἱερῶν ἔχειν. Nur wenige Seelen wären entzückt, wenn sie die irdischen Abbilder der Ideen sähen: αὗται δέ, ὅταν τι τῶν ἐκεῖ ὁμοίωμα *ἴδωσιν*, ἐκπλήττονται καὶ οὐκέθ' αὑτῶν γίγνονται. Diese aber bekannten[54]: „Die Schönheit aber strahlte uns einstmals in hellem Lichte, als wir mit dem seligen Reigen in Gefolgschaft des Zeus oder anderer Götter beglückende Gesichte sahen und betrachteten und eingeweiht wurden in die Weihen [...]; herantretend zu dem Geheimnis vollkommener und unverfälschter, wandelloser und seliger Erscheinungen, die sich uns enthüllten im reinen Lichte; rein und unbefleckt von dem, was wir jetzt als unseren sogenannten Leib an uns tragen, in den wir eingesperrt sind wie die Auster in ihre Schale." Daraus im griechischen Original nur Phaidr 250b: κάλλος δὲ τότε ἦν *ἰδεῖν* λαμπρόν. Es war die *Schau der Idee der Schönheit*, und in der Schau dieser Idee ereignete sich die *Schau des ewigen Seins*, die *Schau der sich selbst enthüllenden Wahrheit*.

Wahrheit ist aber dann im Denken Platons nicht eine Sache der Logik, jedenfalls nicht primär; darin hat Meinhardt recht. Man kann an Platons Philosophie überhaupt nicht den Maßstab der Klassifikation unserer philosophischen Disziplinen anlegen.

49. O. Wichmann, *Platon. Ideelle Gesamtdarstellung und Studienwerk* (Darmstadt: Wissenschaftliche Buchgesellschaft, 1966), S. 7f.

50. *Ib.* S. 11.

51. H. Meinhardt, Art. Idee, I. Antike, in: *Historisches Wörterbuch der Philosophie*, Bd. 4 (Darmstadt: Wissenschaftliche Buchgesellschaft, 1976), S. (55–65)55.

52. *Ib.* S. 56.

53. *Ib.* S. 56; Kursive durch mich.

54. Platon, *Sämtliche Dialoge, Bd. II: Phaidros* (übers. von O. Apelt; Philosophische Bibliothek; Bd. 80; Hamburg, 1988 = Leipzig: Meiner, 1923), S. 64.

Wollte man bei ihm Erkenntnistheorie und Ontologie unterscheiden, so würde man sein Denken auseinanderreißen, das doch das Denken aus einer Ganzheit heraus ist. Er denkt – ich sage es einmal ein wenig anachronistisch – *ontologisch*, denn es geht ihm ja um *das Sein*. Aber natürlich impliziert für ihn das Sein auch die Dimension des Erkenntnismäßigen. Doch unterscheidet er nicht zwischen Ontologie und Erkenntnistheorie, er unterscheidet nicht zwischen Ontologie und Logik. So gibt es für ihn durchaus auch – noch einmal in unserer Terminologie – die Wahrheit einer Aussage. Genannt sei hier nur *Politeia 582*. Sokrates fragt Adeimantos[55]: „Wird denn ein Gott lügen mögen, indem er uns in Wort oder Tat ein Trugbild vorführt?" (ψεύδεσθαι θεὸς ἐδέλοι ἂν ἢ λόγῳ ἢ ἔργῳ φάντασμα προτείνων). Aber wahr ist für Platon im primären und eigentlichen Sinne des Denkens die *Wirklichkeit*, das also, was *ist*, das *Seiende* bzw. das *Sein*. Deshalb *sieht* derjenige die Wahrheit, der sieht, was ist, also der die Wirklichkeit erfaßt. Und da nach Platons Ideenlehre die Idee den höchsten Wirklichkeitsgrad besitzt, ist das Sehen der Idee das eigentliche Sehen dessen, was ist. Indem *sich* aber die Wirklichkeit vom Menschen *sehen läßt*, vor allem die höchste Wirklichkeit, indem sich die Idee und Wirklichkeit Gottes, also die Wahrheit als Wirklichkeit dem Menschen erschließt, sind wir in inhaltlicher Hinsicht nahe bei Heideggers WW. Und da das Prädikat „wahr" im Sinne des platonischen Ganzheitsdenken auch dem Menschen im konkreten Fall zugesprochen werden kann, ist Wahrheit, wo immer sich dieser ihr öffnet, auch eine *Seinsweise* des *menschlichen Daseins*, der Existenz. Und es geht aus diesen Überlegungen auch hervor, daß im platonischen Denken zumindest anfangsweise der Mensch als Ek-sistenz gesehen wird.[56]

So fragmentarisch auch sein mag, was soeben zum platonischen Wahrheitsdenken gesagt wurde, so hinreichend mag es für unsere Gesamtthematik sein. Schauen wir jetzt nur noch kurz auf die *Stoa*, weil diese philosophische Richtung in neutestamentlicher Zeit dominant war. In ihrer Terminologie spielt die Wahrheit, ἀλήθεια, keine maßgebende Rolle. Im Sachregister des Standardwerks über die Stoa von Max Pohlenz findet sich weder das Stichwort „Wahrheit" noch das griechische Äquivalent ἀλήθεια.[57] Wohl sind einige Stellen im Indexband in *Stoicorum veterum fragmenta* genannt.[58] Ich nenne hier nur Stobaeus, *eclog. I 79,1 W.*: Chrysipp bringt als Synonyme für ἀλήθεια vor allem Εἱμαρμένη, ὁ λόγος, ἡ αἰτία und ἡ φύσις. Demnach ist auch an dieser Stelle die Wahrheit als λόγος die sich erschließende göttliche (freilich im Sinne des Pantheismus!) Realität.

c. *Wahrheit im Johannes-Evangelium*

Unsere eingangs gestellte Frage war, ob Bultmanns Interpretation der johanneischen ἀλήθεια eine größere Affinität zur Wahrheitskonzeption von WW besäße als zu der von SuZ § 44, mehr noch, ob wir nicht auf diesem Wege zu einer Deutung des Johannes-Evangeliums kämen, die dessen theologisches Denken adäquat wiedergibt. Ehe wir nun im letzten Kapitel unserer Überlegungen zur Beantwortung dieser Doppelfrage kommen, sollten wir aber einem Aspekt Beachtung schenken, den *Martin*

55. *Ib. Bd. V: Der Staat*, übers. von O. Apelt (Philosophische Bibliothek, Bd. 152, Hamburg, 1988, Leipzig: Meiner, 1922), S. 84.

56. Für die *hellenistische Literatur* sei auf den auch heute noch unverzichtbaren Aufsatz von R. Bultmann, Untersuchungen zum Johannesevangelium, verwiesen, zunächst erschienen in ZNW 27 (1928) und 29 (1930), jetzt in: ders., *Exegetica. Aufsätze zur Erforschung des Neuen Testaments* (hg. von E. Dinkler (Tübingen: Mohr-Siebeck, 1967), S. 124–97. In ihr findet sich wie bei Platon ἀλήθεια auch im Sinne von Wirklichkeit. Bultmann verweist vor allem auf das *Corpus Hermeticum*, ib. S. 165ff.

57. M. Pohlenz, *Die Stoa. Geschichte einer geistigen Bewegung* (Göttingen: Vandenhoeck & Ruprecht, 4 Aufl., 1970–72).

58. *SVT* IV, S. 265, nr. 913.

Brasser in seinem Wahrheitsbuch thematisiert: Wollte Heidegger 1930 in der ursprünglichen Fassung seines Vortrags bewußt alles Theologische aus der Wahrheitsfrage ausschalten? In GA 9 ist WW in der 2. Auflage der überarbeiteten Fassung von 1943 gedruckt; in dieser 2. Auflage wurde, wie schon gesagt, der erste Absatz der Schlußbemerkung hinzugefügt. In diesen beiden Auflagen befindet sich ein längerer Abschnitt über die Wahrheit als *adaequatio rei et intellectus*, also über die berühmte Definition der *veritas* des Thomas von Aquin, die er seinerseits von Isaak Israeli übernommen hatte. Da Heidegger 1930 erklärt hat, er wolle in seinem Vortrag über den Glauben schweigen, gibt es nach Brasser Grund zur Vermutung, daß dieser Thomas-Abschnitt im ursprünglichen Text von 1930[59] noch nicht stand.[60] Daß Heidegger 1943, einerlei wie man seine zu dieser Zeit geäußerten Ausführungen zur *veritas* als *adaequatio rei et intellectus* beurteilt, theologische Aussagen innerhalb seiner philosophischen Darlegungen bringt, kann nicht verwundern, da er bereits in den „Beiträgen zur Philosophie" (1936–1938; allerdings erst 1989 postum publiziert) die theologische Frage[61] behandelt und sie dann vor allem im Humanismusbrief (Erstauflage 1947, zusammen mit Platons Lehre von der Wahrheit) thematisiert. Auf jeden Fall ist Brassers Beobachtung richtig, daß es von der Urfassung zur 1. Auflage eine Verschiebung zur Beachtung des theologischen Denkens hin gibt. Bezeichnend ist die im Original von 1930 enthaltene und seit 1943 gestrichene (polemische?) Umkehrung von Joh 8,32: „Im Philosophieren geschieht das, was wir mit dem Satz fassen können: die Freiheit wird euch wahr machen."[62, 63]

Von WW (und SuZ) aus ist zu fragen, ob ἀλήθεια auch im Joh primär nicht die Aussagewahrheit meint, sondern Wahrheit als *Unverborgenheit*. Ist also auch im Joh Wahrheit als Existenzial zu denken, als *existenziale Wahrheit*? Zugespitzt: Ist der Mensch *als Existenz* seine Wahrheit? WW ging ja insofern über SuZ hinaus, als der Mensch aufgrund seines ek-sistenten Wesens als *Ek-sistenz* gedacht ist. Und so lauten nun die entscheidenden Fragen: Ist auch im Joh existenziale Wahrheit als *ek-sistenziale Wahrheit* gedacht? Geht im Joh die Frage nach der Existenz als Ek-sistenz in ihrem inneren Gefüge, wie in WW, auf die Frage nach dem *Sein* zu? Meint Wahrheit dann auch *Wirklichkeit, Wirklichkeit Gottes*?

Beginnen wir mit *Joh 8,31f.*![64] Dort ist sowohl von Jesu *Wort* als auch von der *Wahrheit* die Rede. An die ihm glaubenden Juden ergeht sein mit göttlicher Autorität verkündeter Zu-Spruch: „Wenn ihr *in meinem Wort* (ἐν τῷ λόγῳ τῷ ἐμῷ) bleibt, seid ihr in Wahrheit (ἀληθῶς), meine Jünger." Der gehörte Glaube bringt sie also in den „Raum" des Wortes, in den Raum der Gnade, χάρις, in

59. Leider gibt es bis heute noch keine Edition des Textes von 1930. Er ist nur partiell verfügbar in: F. Fränzki, *Heideggers Schrift „Vom Wesen der Wahrheit". Urfassung und Druckfassungen* (Pfaffenweiler: Pfaffenweiler Presse, 2. Aufl. 1987).

60. Brasser, *Wahrheit*, S. 254.

61. Dazu P.-L. Coriando, *Der letzte Gott als Anfang. Zur ab-gründigen Zeit-Räumlichkeit des Übergangs in Heideggers „Beiträgen zur Philosophie"* (München: Fink, 1998); s. Rezension H. Hübner, Der Begriff „Wahrheit" in der Theologie, *ThLZ* 127 (2002), S. (576–86), 583–86.

62. Zitiert bei Brasser, *Wahrheit*, S. 333.

63. Dann ist aber auch in Betracht zu ziehen, daß R. Bultmann, *Das Evangelium des Johannes* (KEK II; Göttingen: Vandenhoeck & Ruprecht, 19. Aufl. 1968), in 1. Aufl. bereits 1941 vorlag, also noch vor der Publikation des Humanismusbriefs und WW; Bultmann konnte somit vor 1941 die Äußerungen Heideggers nach der sogenannten Kehre über die Wahrheit noch gar nicht zur Kenntnis nehmen.

64. Wegen des eingeschränkten Platzes, der mir zur Verfügung steht, nenne ich keine exegetische Sekundärlit. zum Joh. Es versteht sich aber von selbst, daß ich mich aufgrund der Thematik dieses Aufsatzes auf Bultmanns Joh-Kommentar beziehen werde.

Joh 1,14 zusammen mit der ἀλήθεια in einem Hendiadyoin genannt. Gnade und Wahrheit sind somit der *eine* Raum der Erlösung. Das Wort ist als Zu-Spruch das gesprochene Wort. Als *verbum efficax* gesprochen, bewirkt es das *neue Sein* des Glaubenden als „Sein in Christus", z.B. Joh 15,4–7.[65] Der Logos des Joh ist in entscheidender Hinsicht gleichbedeutend mit dem *Evangelium* des Paulus; dies zeigt die programmatische theologische Überschrift des Römerbriefs, Röm 1,16f.: Das Evangelium ist die Macht Gottes, δύναμις θεοῦ. *Das Evangelium ist Gott selbst* in seiner Dynamik, es ist ὁ θεὸς ὁ δυνατός. Es ist also *der mächtige Gott in seinem machtvollen Wort* und somit die *Präsenz* des seinen Zu-Spruch sprechenden *Gottes*. Kurz: Das Evangelium gehört zum *Wesen* des lebendigen, lebendigmachenden Gottes.[66] Wer dieses Evangelium glaubend hört, existiert im Raum der Erlösung. Die Metapher des Raumes[67] vermittelt nach Joh 8 und Röm 1 den *Wirk*-Bereich Gottes: Kraft seines Wortes bewirkt Gott das neue Sein der Glaubenden. Paulinisch gesprochen: Das Wort bewirkt die Rechtfertigung als Gerechtsprechung und Gerechtmachung. Diesem *ontischen* Geschehen entspricht freilich auch ein *noetisches* Geschehen: Der Glaubende *erkennt* die Wahrheit. Aber es ist eben kein bloß theoretisches Erkennen, sondern ein *existenzänderndes* Verstehen – mit *Ernst Käsemann*: Existenzwandel durch Herrschaftswechsel.[68]

Joh 8,32 führt die Jesus-Rede in diesem „noetisch-ontischen" Sinn weiter: καὶ γνώσεσθε τὴν ἀλήθειαν, καὶ ἡ ἀλήθεια ἐλευθερώσει ὑμᾶς. Der Glaubende erkennt die Wahrheit. Und es ist diese Wahrheit, die die Freiheit des Glaubenden wirkt. Das *„Objekt"* der Glaubenserkenntnis ist das *„Subjekt"* der Befreiung des Glaubenden. Die Wahrheit ist aber dann kein nur zu akzeptierender Glaubens-„Satz", ist gerade keine Aussagewahrheit über den Glauben. Ist Gott mit der Wahrheit identisch, dann wirkt die Wahrheit die Freiheit, weil *Gott als die Wahrheit* die *Freiheit wirkt*. Dann aber heißt „die Wahrheit erkennen" nichts anderes als „Gott erkennen". Gott *als* den von der Sklaverei der Sündenmacht befreienden Gott zu erkennen bedeutet dann, Gott als Befreier zu glauben. Und das heißt: *zu* ihm – und zwar *durch* ihn – in ein lebendiges Verhältnis zu kommen. Das Sklavenverhältnis wird beseitigt. Der Sklave wird zum Freien. Von dieser Knechtschaft sagt Jesus, Joh 8,34: „Jeder, der die Sünde, ἁμαρτία, tut, ist Sklave der Sünde." Ein Satz von der Wucht paulinischer Theologie! Man wird an Röm 3,9 erinnert: „Alle befinden sich unter der Macht der Sünde."

Vom glaubenden Hören war eben die Rede. Glaubend hört, wer „*aus* Gott" existierend Gottes Worte hört, nicht aber, wer „*aus* dem Teufel ist", Joh 8,44.47. Von solchen gilt der Vorwurf Jesu, Joh 8,43: „*Ihr könnt* mein Wort *nicht hören*!" Wer sich im Machtbereich der ἁμαρτία befindet, kann Jesu befreiendes Wort

65. Theologisch relevant ist in Joh 15,7 die Explikation von ἐὰν … τὰ ῥήματα μου ἐν ὑμῖν μένῃ durch ἐὰν μείνητε ἐν ἐμοί.

66. Hübner, Zuspruch des Seyns und Zuspruch Gottes (s. Amn. 2), S. 165f.

67. Ders., *Theologie des Neuen Testaments, 2. Bd.: Die Theologie des Paulus* (Göttingen: Vandenhoeck & Ruprecht, 1993), S. 179–89: Exkurs: Theologische Zwischenbilanz (Exkurs über die *hermeneutische Relevanz* des *theologischen Denkens in Räumlichkeiten*; auch Bezug auf Ernst Cassirer).

68. E. Käsemann, Gottesgerechtigkeit bei Paulus, in: ders., *Exegetische Versuche und Besinnungen* (2. Bd.; Göttingen: Vandenhoeck & Ruprecht, 3 Aufl., 1970), S. 181–93.

nicht „hören". Wohl *öffnet* sich Gott im Worte Jesu dem Menschen. Wenn sich aber dieser dem Worte Jesu nicht *öffnet*, bleibt er dem sich offenbarenden, sich öffnenden Gott gegenüber „*ver*-schlossen". Denn Gott *er*-schließt sich ihm nicht; er bleibt, mit Luther gesprochen, *homo incurvatus in seipsum*, bleibt in der Sklaverei des Mißverstehens seiner selbst. Er macht sich zum Gefängnis seiner selbst – ohne zu wissen, daß er sich im selbstgebauten Gefängnis befindet!

Jetzt zu *Joh 14,6*! Dem unverständigen Thomas sagt Jesus: „Ich bin der Weg, die Wahrheit und das Leben" (ἐγώ εἰμι ἡ ὁδὸς καὶ ἡ ἀλήθεια καὶ ἡ ζωή). Die Wahrheit, ἀλήθεια, ist also hier in ganz besonderer Weise *Existenz*-Wahrheit, ist *Wahrheit als Person*. Eine geschichtliche Person *ist* die Wahrheit! Sie ist personale Wahrheit *für* andere. Der *Logos*, als der Ewige geschichtliche Existenz geworden, sagt, er sei die Wahrheit. Die zum *geschichtlichen* Logos gewordene göttliche Wahrheit ist als die *sich* aus der Ewigkeit *„Heraus-stellende"* und sich in den Kosmos (= Menschenwelt) *„Hinein-stellende"* und somit die in diesen Kosmos hinein *Ek-sistierende* in ihrer *geschichtlichen Existenz Ek-sistenz* geworden. Paraphrasieren wir in diesem Sinne *Joh 1,14*: *„Und das Wort ist geschichtliche Ek-sistenz geworden."* Er ist ja in die Menschenwelt hinein ek-sistierend deren Leben geworden. Er ist *Wahrheit als Ek-sistenz*. Γενόμενος in Joh 1,14 sagt die Geschichtlichkeit der Wahrheit als Logos, der *Wahrheit* als *Wort* aus. Wort und Wahrheit sind das das *eine* Heil wirkende *Ereignis*, wobei Wort und Wahrheit sozusagen ein Hendiadyoin ausmachen: *Die Wahrheit erschließt sich in dem Wort, das ihr ureigenes Wort ist.* Ist der Logos nach Joh 1,1 θεός, so auch die Wahrheit – ich präzisiere: als die Wahrheit des Vaters ὁ θεός, als die Wahrheit des Logos, θεός.

Schauen wir also jetzt wieder auf WW! Auch in dieser Schrift sind Wort und Wahrheit als Einheit ausgesagt, als Hendiadyoin. 1930 hat Heidegger zwar noch nicht vom *„Ereignis"* im Sinne der weiterdenkenden „Beiträge zur Philosophie" von 1936–1938 mit dem bezeichnenden Untertitel „Vom Ereignis" gesprochen. Aber als der von ihm überarbeitete[69] Vortrag in 1. Auflage 1943 erschien, lagen die postum herausgegebenen Schriften GA 65–67 auf seinem Denkweg schon hinter ihm. Sicherlich hat er bei der Überarbeitung mitbedacht, was er in GA 65–67, vor allem in GA 65, mit „Ereignis" bzw. „Er-eignis" sagen wollte.[70]

In diesem Zusammenhang sei auf den Anfang des wichtigen 8. Abschnitts, überschrieben *Die Wahrheitsfrage und die Philosophie*, verwiesen. Der erste Satz lautet (S. 198f.): „Im Denken des Seins kommt die geschichtegründende

69. Fränzki (s. Anm. 59), dürfte aber zu weit gehen, wenn er in dieser Überarbeitung zwar keinen Rückfall in die vorkehrig-transzendentale Grundstellung sieht, wohl aber eine fundamentale Umdeutung des Vortrags von 1930, nämlich einen „Rückfall in das Denken der uneigentlichen Kehre, das dadurch ausgezeichnet ist, daß es das Sein am Leitfaden der Unverborgenheit denkt", *ib.* S. 108; s. dazu die Kritik von Brasser, *Wahrheit*, S. 295–303.

70. S. auch Heideggers wichtige Bemerkung im *Brief über den ‚Humanismus'*, GA 9, S. 328: „Der Vortrag ‚Vom Wesen der Wahrheit', der 1930 gedacht und mitgeteilt, aber erst 1943 gedruckt wurde, gibt einen gewissen Einblick in das Denken [!] der Kehre von ‚Sein und Zeit'. Diese Kehre ist nicht eine Änderung des Standpunktes von ‚Sein und Zeit', sondern in ihr gelangt das versuchte Denken erst in die Ortschaft der Dimension, aus der ‚Sein und Zeit' erfahren ist, und zwar erfahren in der Grunderfahrung der Seinsvergessenheit." S. auch *ib.* S. 313, Anm. 1.

Befreiung des Menschen zur Ek-sistenz ins Wort, das nicht erst der ‚Ausdruck' einer Meinung, sondern je schon das gutverwahrte Gefüge der Wahrheit des Seienden im Ganzen ist." Ist mit „Denken des Seins" gemeint, daß der Mensch das Sein denkt (*genetivus obiectivus*) oder daß das Sein denkt (*genetivus subiectivus*)? Ist nun die 1. Auflage von WW wenige Jahre nach den „Beiträgen zur Philosophie" erschienen und wurde für sie der Text von 1930 überarbeitet, so sollten wir die „Beiträge" da heranziehen, wo sie helfen könnten, offene Fragen von WW zu beantworten. Und das dürfte hier der Fall sein. In den „Beiträgen" ist laufend vom Seyn, Denken und der Wahrheit die Rede. In Nr. 267 *Das Seyn (Ereignis)* heißt es von der „Sage ‚das Seyn ist'": „[...] das Sagen sagt nicht *vom* Seyn etwas ihm allgemein Zu-kommendes, an ihm Vorhandenes aus, sondern sagt das Seyn selbst aus ihm selbst [...]."[71] Man kann die letzten Worte in einer Kurzformel so paraphrasieren: *Das Seyn sagt sich selbst aus.* Kurz danach ist die Rede vom λόγος, der nicht mehr „als Aussage Leitfaden des Vorstellens des Seins bleiben kann"; dadurch werde „das Denken ‚des' Seyns [...] *wesentlich* schwerer".[72] In Nr. 267 ist die Rede davon, daß der Mensch das Seyn denkt.[73] Diese Stellen sind Indiz dafür, daß nach WW das *menschliche Denken des Seins* vom *Denken des Seins von sich selbst her* geschieht. Kurz danach heißt es[74]: „‚Der Mensch' und ‚der Gott' sind geschichtslose Worthülsen, wenn nicht *die Wahrheit des Seyns in ihnen sich zur Sprache bringt.*" Deuten wir den ersten Satz des 8. Abschnitts von WW in diesem Sinne: Es ist der befreite Mensch, der im Denken des Seins „zur Ek-sistenz ins Wort" kommt. Dieses Wort ist aber „das gutverwahrte Gefüge der Wahrheit des Seienden im Ganzen". Das also ist das Wortfeld dieser Stelle: *Denken, Sein, Ek-sistenz, Wort, Wahrheit.* Es ist zugleich eines der wichtigsten Wortfelder in Joh. Unbestreitbar sind beide Wortfelder aus unterschiedlichen Richtungen gedacht. Dennoch treffen sich ihre Gehalte in auffälliger und bezeichnender Weise: Die Wahrheit ist *Wahrheit des Seins* bzw. *des Seins Gottes* und zugleich *Existenz-Wahrheit.*[75]

Auch *Friedrich-Wilhelm von Herrmann* widmet dem 8. Abschnitt von WW und dem darin ausgesagten „Denken des Seins" besondere Aufmerksamkeit. Er bemüht sich hier – wie in seiner ganzen Studie – in möglichst enger Anlehnung an Heideggers Terminologie dessen Text in hermeneutischer Absicht zu explizieren. In dieser Intention schreibt er[76]: „Denn die Ek-sistenz ist das andersanfängliche Wesen des Menschen als das Sein des Da, d.h. als das ausgesetzte Sichaussetzen dem vollen Wesen der Wahrheit, zu der die beiden Weisen der Un-wahrheit (Verbergung und Irre) gehören." Ich möchte diesen Satz so interpretieren: Zum „Sichaussetzen dem vollen Wesen der Wahrheit" ist auch das „Denken des Seins" durch das Da-sein zu rechnen.

71. Heidegger, GA 67, S. 475.
72. *Ib.* S. 474.
73. Z.B. *ib.* S. 476.
74. *Ib.* S. 476; Kursive durch mich.
75. Eigentlich hätte ich beim Vergleich von WW und Joh auch die Frage nach dem Verhältnis von *Wahrheit* und *Un-wahrheit* (Problem von *Verborgenheit* und *Un*-verborgenheit) und ebenso nach der *Freiheitsproblematik* erörtern müssen. Aus Platzgründen habe ich hier auf beide Themen verzichtet. Ich werde sie in einer späteren Publikation ausführlich behandeln.
76. von Herrmann, *Wahrheit – Freiheit – Geschichte*, S. 197.

Es ist die dem Wesen der Wahrheit ausgesetzte *Ek*-sistenz, die als solche das Sein interpretiert. Mit dieser Deutung von WW dürfte er in der Nähe derjenigen Deutung stehen, nach der im menschlichen Denken des Seins das Sein selbst waltet. Schließt nämlich, wie er sagt, das „denkerische Wort [...] das gewandelte Wesen der Wahrheit, des Seins, des Menschen und der Sprache ein“[77], ist also, wenn wir so interpretieren dürfen, die so gewandelte Wahrheit des Seins *im* menschlichen Denken des Seins, so ist es doch wohl eben diese *Wahrheit*, die *im Denken des menschlichen Denkens denkt.* Wenn von Herrmann sagt, „das Gehaltenwerden der Philosophie durch [!] die von ihr zu denkende Wahrheit meint das ‚Geworfensein‘, das im seinsgeschichtlichen Denken als das *Ereignetsein* aus dem ereignenden Walten der Wahrheit erfahren wird“, so geht m.E auch diese Aussage in die von mir eingeschlagene Richtung.[78] Auch er bezieht sich wie ich auf Nr. 267 der „Beiträge“, wenn auch nicht auf die von mir zitierten Stellen.

Heideggers Aussage, daß der gemeine Menschenverstand *nicht hören kann* (S. 199), wurde bereits genannt, ebenso die anklagende Rede Jesu vom Nicht-hören-Können derer, die nicht an ihn glauben (Joh 8,43). Eine auffällige Übereinstimmung der Terminologie! Darüber hinaus: In WW wie auch im Joh findet sich der Topos vom Nicht-hören-Können im Kontext der Wahrheit, die die Freiheit wirkt, im Joh die berühmte Stelle Joh 8,31f. Beide Male ist dieses Nicht-hören-Können ein defizientes Hören aufgrund des Sich-nicht-Öffnens, sei es gegenüber der Wahrheit des Seyns, sei es gegenüber dem Geist der Wahrheit (Joh 14,17). Dort heißt es unmißverständlich, daß der Kosmos (hier die glaubensunwillige Menschheit) das durch den Geist vermittelte Gotteswort nicht erfassen kann, es nicht „sieht“ und auch nicht erkennt.

Was also führt nach dem Joh zum Hören-Können? Sagen wir es mit der Terminologie von WW: Es ist das offenständige Verhalten gegenüber einem Offenen, *theologisch konkretisiert*: Das *offen*-ständige, d.h. glauben wollende Verhalten gegenüber dem sich in seiner *Offen*-barung *öffnenden* Gott. Es ist die glaubende *Ek*-sistenz gegenüber dem aus dem „von oben kommenden“, dem ἄνωθεν ἐρχόμενος, der seinerseits der *ἐκ* τοῦ οὐρανοῦ ἐρχόμενος ist. Insofern ist es im Sinne der johanneischen Theologie möglich, auch von Gott bzw. vom Logos die *Ek*-sistenz auszusagen. Gott bzw. der Logos stellt sich „heraus“ (ἐκ!). In Gott und somit in seinem Wort erschließt sich, was von Gott und Wort ausgesagt werden kann, nämlich die Wahrheit schlechthin, die identisch mit der *Wirklichkeit* Gottes ist.

Kommen wir auf *Rudolf Bultmann* und auf meine eingangs erwähnte Bemerkung im EWNT zurück! In seinem Joh-Kommentar von 1941[79] hat er eine *existentiale Interpretation* von ἀλήθεια in Joh 8,32 vorgelegt. Hier sei ἀλήθεια „nicht die ‚Wahrheit‘ überhaupt [...], die Erschlossenheit alles Seienden schlechthin im Sinne des griechischen Fragens nach der ἀλήθεια“.[80] Was ist aber dann ἀλήθεια im Joh? Seine Antwort: „Vielmehr ist die Frage nach der ἀλήθεια orientiert an der Frage nach der ζωή als dem eigentlichen Sein des um sein Sein

77. *Ib.* S. 198.
78. *Ib.* S. 203.
79. Und allen darauf folgenden Auflagen.
80. Bultmann, KEK II, S. 332.

besorgten Menschen, dem diese Frage aufgegeben ist, da er Geschöpf ist. Gottes ἀλήθεια ist also Gottes Wirklichkeit, die allein Wirklichkeit ist, weil sie Leben ist und Leben gibt [...]."[81] In dieser existentialen Interpretation ist ἀλήθεια als das Bestimmtsein des menschlichen Daseins gedeutet. Dabei geht es aber um mehr als um das Selbstverständnis des Menschen. Der Text wird zwar daraufhin befragt. Aber die den Menschen betreffende Aussage über die ἀλήθεια betrifft auch Gott: *Gottes Wahrheit* ist *Gottes Wirklichkeit*. In Jesu Kommen in die Welt erschließt sich Gott als Wahrheit und Wirklichkeit. Gott als ek-sistente Wirklichkeit offenbart seine Wahrheit als seine im Logos dem Menschen geschenkte Offenbarkeit. Als der sich offenbarende Gott ist er im Logos der lebendige, Leben schenkende Gott, Joh 1,4.

Damit vertrat Bultmann bereits 1941, also zwei Jahre vor der 1. Auflage von WW, eine Interpretation der Wahrheit, die über die existenziale Interpretation in SuZ hinausgeht, nämlich einen substanzhaft in WW nachweisbaren Gedanken.[82] So stellt sich die Frage: Hat er also 1941 in seinem Denken *vorweggenommen*, was Heidegger erst 1943 publizierte? Nein, er hatte doch dessen Wahrheitsvortrag schon 1930 in Marburg gehört!

Wie ist nun *WW aus theologischer Perspektive* zu bewerten! Wir fragen: Hat Heidegger mit seinem Vortrag von 1930 und folglich mit seiner Kehre insofern eine weitere Rezeptionsmöglichkeit seiner Philosophie für Bultmann geschaffen, als dadurch Einwände gegen dessen *existentiale Interpretation* – seien sie berechtigt oder nicht – als eine zu sehr auf den Menschen bezogene Interpretation zumindest abgeschwächt werden könnten? Um nicht falsch verstanden zu werden: Ich bin der letzte, der grundsätzliche Einwände gegen die existentiale Interpretation erhebt. Es dürfte bekannt sein, daß ich sie immer wieder gegen horrende Mißverständnisse verteidigt habe – freilich auch in kritischer Sicht von Bultmanns Rezeption dieser Methode.[83] Doch sehe ich in seinem Rekurs auf Grundgedanken von WW einen substantiellen Fortschritt der *kritischen* Heidegger-Rezeption durch die Theologie. Denn in WW sind Gedanken ausgesprochen, die – als theologisch modifizierte! – besser ermöglichen, Gott als Offenbarenden *theologisch verantwortlich zu denken*. Daß die Rezeption des späten Heidegger sinnvoll ist, wurde mir anhand seiner postum publizierten Schriften klar.[84]

Und in genau diesem Zusammenhang möchte ich dem von mir im geringen Maße kritisierten Bultmann im hohen Maße zustimmen. Er hat Heideggers Gedanken in SuZ unter Berücksichtigung des Wahrheitsvortrags von 1930 *theologisch* so weitergedacht, daß er *Gottes Wahrheit* als *Gottes Wirklichkeit*

81. *Ib*. S. 333.

82. Dieses Wahrheitsverständnis finden wir später auch im Joh-Teil von Bultmanns *Theologie des Neuen Testaments*, S. 370f. In seinen *Untersuchungen zum Joh* (1928–30), S. 165, verweist er für ἀλήθεια als „Wirklichkeit"auf das Corpus Hermeticum und noch nicht auf das Neue Testament.

83. S. meinen Aufsatz „Was ist existentiale Interpretation?" in: Hübner, *Biblische Theologie als Hermeneutik* (Göttingen: Vandenhoeck & Ruprecht, 1995), S. 229–51.

84. S. meine in Anm. 5–7 genannten Aufsätze zu GA 65–67. In ihnen erörtere ich das *eigentliche*, hier nicht genannte Kernproblem der Heidegger-Rezeption in der Theologie: Heideggers Verständnis des *Seyns* ist mit dem *biblischen Gottesgedanken* inkompatibel. Wie ist dennoch im Grundsätzlichen der Dialog möglich?

interpretierte. Gehe ich zu weit, wenn ich sage, daß er damit – theologischer reflektierend! – Heideggers *fundamentalontologisches Denken* in Richtung *Seinsdenken* weitergedacht hat? Dann wäre er aber doch einen wichtigen Schritt auf dem weiteren Denkweg Heideggers mitgegangen[85] und sein Verdienst weit größer, als man es bisher gesehen hat! Hat also Bultmann mit seiner *neuen* existentialen Interpretation im Joh-Kommentar einen *neuen hermeneutischen Parameter* geschaffen?

85. Insofern muß ich mich auch selber korrigieren. Noch in meinem in Anm. 2 genannten Prager Vortrag auf dem Hermeneutik-Syposium habe ich im November 2001 erklärt, Bultmann sei den Denkweg Heideggers nach dessen Kehre nicht mitgegangen. Freilich hat bezeichnenderweise keiner der Teilnehmer oder Teilnehmerinnen mir hierbei widersprochen.

DID THE FOURTH EVANGELIST KNOW THE ENOCH TRADITION?

James H. Charlesworth

It is a pleasure to contribute to this book published in honour of Professor Petr Pokorný, a close friend and admired colleague for over thirty years. For decades he has focused his research on not only the New Testament corpus but also on the sacred documents not eventually collected into the Christian canon. Since he has shown keen interest in both the *Books of Enoch*, which are in the Ethiopic canon but not in his or mine, and the Gospel of John, that is a hallmark of the Christian canon, I can imagine he will be interested in my central question. I am asking: Is it possible that John 3.13 ('No one has ascended into heaven except he who descended from heaven, the Son of Man'.[1]) is a polemic against Jewish apocalyptic thought; and is it conceivable that he is specifically targeting the claims in the Enoch group? I shall conclude by answering, 'probably yes', to each section of this question.

1. *Prefatory Remarks*

Recently, I was asked, 'What is the purpose of the Fourth Gospel' [4G]? I replied, that first, I would begin by asking if this is the proper question. Did the Fourth Evangelist begin by thinking, 'What is my purpose?'

What errors in the past were caused by asking the wrong or imprecise question? Even through irony the Fourth Evangelist, especially in the presentation of Nicodemus, suggests the problems inherent in the wrong questions (see, viz., Jn 3.4). Today, we agree that questions about the 4G are better couched in light of what we have learned rather recently about Early Judaism (especially between 167 BCE and 132 CE).[2]

When one reads the 4G (which represents more than one author), one learns that the original author intends to proclaim to those who are already believers that the way to understand Jesus is to hear the full story. It begins at creation and has not yet ended. His readers, it seems, need theological sophistication and correction from erroneous thoughts (i.e., that Jesus' death revealed he was a failure and perhaps that he was not really human).[3] The answers are in the story of the One

1. Some early manuscripts add at the end of the sentence 'he who is in heaven'.

2. I attempted to follow this principle in my *The Beloved Disciple: Whose Witness Validates the Gospel of John?* (Valley Forge: Trinity Press International, 1995).

3. I am not implying that the Fourth Evangelist is intentionally anti-gnostic (but in its final form

who has been sent from Above, but paradoxically is never called 'the one from above'. The One is the fleshly human Jesus who brings proof of God's love for his world (creation) and shows the way to the Father Above.

If, therefore, the implied readers of the 4G are sophisticated and learned in traditions about Jesus and know, even believe, that he is the Christ the Son of God and the Son of Man, and if they – or most of them – are Jews, then one may assume, at least at the outset, that they knew about, and perhaps some had memorized portions of, the *Books of Enoch* or *1 (Ethiopic) Enoch* (i.e., the Aramaic traditions behind Greek and Ethiopic Enoch).[4] These books of Enoch circulated in more than one scroll – as we know from the Qumran caves – and were composed over three centuries (c. 300 BCE to c. 4 BCE).[5] While the purposes of the 4G are many, one seems to be the need to elevate Jesus in contrast to others, especially the ideal figures like Enoch who was revered by numerous early Jews and not only by the Qumranites and the Enoch group. Let us now turn to the texts.

2. *Selected Parallels*

According to Jn 1.51, Jesus tells Nathanael that he will see 'heaven opened, and the angels of God ascending and descending upon the Son of Man'.[6] According to Gen. 28.12, Jacob has a dream at Bethel and sees 'a ladder fixed on the earth, whose top reached to heaven, and the angels of God ascended and descended on it' [LXX]. Scholars need to explore what is the parallel between this Johannine passage and the traditions preserved in or mirrored by the *Ladder of Jacob*. The mere order of verbs, *ana-* before *kata-* prove some connection with the Jacob traditions, and perhaps through them to Genesis.[7]

More importantly now for us is the Fourth Evangelist's affirmation that Jesus is apocalyptically heralded the Son of Man. That means 1.51 may reflect a polemic against the Jews who had by the time of the Fourth Evangelist arrived at

some passages do seem to be anti-docetic). Some scholars conclude that the 4G is naively docetic; I find it difficult to call the genius of Jn naive; perhaps incipiently docetic might be a better term. The Fourth Evangelist does clearly hold, perhaps in intentional tension, Jesus' identity with God and his humanity. See esp. E. Käsemann, *The Testament of Jesus* (trans. G. Krodel; Philadelphia: Fortress Press, 2nd edn, 1968); M.M. Thompson, *The Humanity of Jesus* (Philadelphia: Fortress Press, 1988); and P.N. Anderson, *The Christology of the Fourth Gospel* (Valley Forge: Trinity Press International, 1996).

4. In the fourth century CE Christian missionaries created *Ge'ez* or Ethiopic in order to translate the scriptures; hence, some forms of the Son of Man mirror the Hebrew word for Eve חַוָּה, 'the mother of all the living' (Gen 3.20).

5. See the report of an agreement reached at an international gathering of Enoch scholars in Charlesworth, 'A Rare Consensus Among Enoch Specialists: The Date of the Earliest Enoch Books', *Henoch* 24 (2002), pp. 225–34.

6. The Son of Man is mentioned for the first time in Jn in 1.51. The *epi* with the accusative indicates that the comparison is not between the Son of Man (or Jesus) and the ladder (which would indicate Jesus is the bridge between heaven and earth). Jesus is the one who brings God's word to humans.

7. R. Bultmann pointed to the mystical interpretation of Gen. 28.10-17. See his *The Gospel of John* (trans. G.R. Beasley-Murray; Oxford: Blackwell, 1971), p. 105 n. 3.

the conclusion that Enoch is 'that Son of Man'.[8] Note, that while the 'Son of Man' is not associated with Enoch in the chapters prior to 71.14, the *Parables of Enoch* conclude with the elevation and declaration that none other than Enoch is the Son of Man (71.14):

> And that angel came to me (Enoch), and greeted me with his voice, and said to me: 'You are the Son of Man (*we'etu walda be'si*)[9] who was born to righteousness, and righteousness remains over you, and the righteousness of the Head of Days will not leave you'.[10]
>
> Und er kam zu mir and grüßte mich mit seiner Stimme und sprach zu mir: 'Du bist der Menschensohn, der zur Gerechtigkeit geboren ist, und Gerechtigkeit wohnt über dir, und die Gerechtigkeit des Hauptes der Tage verläßt dich nicht'.[11]
>
> Il [*var.* L'ange] est venu vers moi, et m'a salué de la voix. Il m'a dit: 'Tu es le Fils d'homme, toi qui es né pour [*var.* selon] la justice, la justice a demeuré sur toi, la justice du Principe des jours ne te quittera pas'.[12]
>
> E venne presso me quell'angelo, mi salutò con la sua voce e mi disse: 'Tu sei il figlio dell'uomo nato per la giustizia e la giustizia ha dimorato in te e la giustizia del Capo dei Giorni non ti abbandonerà'.[13]
>
> Llegó a mí aquel ángel, me saludó y me dijo: 'Tú eres el Hijo del hombre que naciste para la justicia; ella ha morado en ti, y la justicia del 'Principio de días' no te dejará'.[14]

It is easy to imagine the Hebrew (and, of course, Aramaic) and Greek that is conceivably behind *1 En.* 71.14; they would be somewhat similar to the modern translations:

> Οὗτος (Μιχαὴλ) ἦλθε πρὸς ἐμέ, μὲ ἐχαιρέτισε μὲ τὴν φωνήν του καὶ μοῦ εἶπε· Σὺ εἶσαι Υἱὸς τοῦ Ἀνθρώπου, ὁ γεννηθεὶς διὰ δικαιοσύνην· δικαιοσύνη κατοικεῖ ἐπὶ σὲ καὶ ἡ δικαιοσύνη τοῦ Παλαιοῦ τῶν Ἡμερῶν δὲν σὲ ἐγκαταλείπει.[15]
>
> והוא נגש אלי וישאל לי לשלום בקלו ויאמר אלי אתה הוא בן־האדם אשר נולד לצדקה וצדקה תנוח עליך וצדקת ראש־הימים לא תעזבך [16]

8. R. Bultmann rightly saw that the Johannine discourses lead us to speculate 'the relationship in which the Gospel of John and Gnosticism stand to each other'. Today, I am convinced, that Gnosticism needs to be defined broadly so that it includes the proto-gnostic thoughts found in the Jewish apocalypses. See Bultmann, *The Gospel of John*, translated by G.R. Beasley-Murray (Oxford: Blackwell, 1971), p. 7.

9. For the Ethiopic, see the photographs published by M. A. Knibb in *The Books of Enoch* (Oxford: At the Clarendon Press, 1978), 1.214 [fol. 9rc]. The Ethiopic noun *wald* means 'son' but also 'boy' (as in Arabic). The noun *be'si* means 'man' but also 'husband' and 'person'.

10. M.A. Knibb, *The Ethiopic Book of Enoch* (Oxford: At the Clarendon Press, 1978), 2.166.

11. S. Uhlig, *Das Äthiopische Henochbuch* (Jüdische Schriften aus hellenistisch-römischer Zeit 5.6; Gütersloh: Gerd Mohn, 1984), p. 634.

12. A. Caquot in *La Bible: Écrits intertestamentaires*, ed. A. Dupont-Sommer and M. Philonenko, et al. (Paris: Gallimard, 1987), p. 551.

13. L. Fusella in *Apocrifi dell'Antico Testamento*, ed. P. Sacchi (Turin: Unione Tipografico-Editrice Torinese, 1981), pp. 571–72.

14. A. de Santo Otero in *Apocrifos del Antiguo Testamento*, ed. A. Diez Macho, et al. (Madrid: Ediciones Cristiandad, 1984), p. 4.95.

15. S. Agourides in *ΤΑ ΑΠΟΚΡΥΦΑ ΤΗΣ ΠΑΛΑΙΑΣ ΔΙΑΘΗΚΗΣ*, ed. Agourides (Athens, 1973), 1.334.

16. A. Kahana, ed., הספרים החיצונים (Jerusalem: Makor Publishing Ltd., 1978) vol. 1, p. סו.

The *angelus interpres* is probably Michael (as the Greek translation indicates).[17] Enoch has been elevated above even Michael and the other archangels, namely Gabriel, Raphael, and Phanuel. He is enthroned (see esp. 69.29). The chapter is a fitting climax to the elevation of Enoch throughout the *Books of Enoch*.[18]

M. Black rightly claimed that 'the plain meaning' of 71.14 is 'that Enoch himself is divinely designated or called to an even higher celestial role than he already enjoys as immortalized Patriarch, 'scribe of righteousness', namely, the role of the heavenly Man of his earlier visions (46,48)'.[19] Virtually no scholar has seen that Jn 3.13 is a polemical statement, and that it was directed against Enoch. D.R.A. Hare rightly perceives that 3.13 'has polemical import', but he errs by claiming that the polemic is directed against a human 'who claims to have ascended to heaven and to have returned with heavenly information'.[20] The major problem with Hare's analysis is he assumes that humans and angels were distinct categories for Jews, and he fails to cite one person who made such a claim during the time, or before, the time of the 4G.[21] The possibility that the Fourth Evangelist intends to prove that Jesus, and not Enoch, is the Son of Man is increased by the following observations.

At the outset there is the *Tendenz* in *1 Enoch* that helps us perceive the types of Judaism against which the Fourth Evangelist is competing, intermittently. Note these selected examples:

> '...the elect one (shall be) in the light of eternal life. ...For the sun has shined upon the earth and darkness is over'. (*1 En.* 58.2, 5; Isaac in *OTP* 1.39–40)
> 'The light shines in darkness' (Jn 1.5)
> '...the light has come into the world...' (Jn 3.29)
> 'I am the light of the world' (Jn 8.12 and 9.5)
> 'How can you say that the Son of Man must be lifted up: Who is this Son of Man?' Jesus said to them, 'the light is with you for a little longer' (Jn 12.34–35)

17. Although Michael, Raphael, Gabriel, and Phanuel are mentioned twice before 71.14, Michael is always listed first and he is the one who guides Enoch; see 71.3. The first one to clarify this identification seems to be A. Dillmann: '*jener Engel* kann nur Michael, der höchste Engel, sein nach V. 3'. Dillmann, *Das Buch Henoch* (Leipzig: Fr. Chr. Wilh. Vogel, 1853), p. 218.

18. C.P. Van Andel argues that *1 En.* 70 and 71 lead to a clear 'climax. Hier is het Henoch zelf, die tot de waardigheid van de Zoon des mensen verheven wordt'. See his *De Structuur van de Henoch-Traditie en het Nieuwe Testament* (Studia Theologica Rheno-Traiectina 2; Utrecht: Kemink en Zoon N.V., 1955), p. 37.

19. M. Black, *The Book of Enoch* (Studia in Veteris Testamenti Pseudepigrapha 7; Leiden: Brill, 1985), p. 18.

20. D.A.R. Hare, *The Son of Man Tradition* (Minneapolis: Fortress Press, 1990), p. 85.

21. According to 2 Cor. 12.1-10 Paul does claim to ascent into the third heaven and have a vision of Paradise, but unlike Enoch he does not claim this as the source of his authority or bring back 'heavenly' knowledge. For humans as angels, see Charlesworth, 'The Portrayal of the Righteous as an Angel', in J.J. Collins and G.W.E. Nickelsburg (eds.), *Ideal Figures in Ancient Judaism* (SBL Septuagint and Cognate Studies, 12; Chico, CA: Scholars Press, 1980) pp. 135–51. In translating the Qumran Scrolls, we cannot discern if *elim* and 'the most holy of holy ones' denote Qumranites or angels. The future resurrected body, form, or state seems to be superior to those of angels: 'and the excellence of the righteous will then be greater than that of the angels' (2Bar 51.12 [Klijn in *OTP* 1.638; cf. *1 En.* 104.4–6; ctr. *1 En.* 51.1, 5, 10). Also, see *2 En.* 30.11 J, 'And on the earth I assigned him (man) to be a second angel, honored and great and glorious' (Andersen in *OTP* 1).

‘And this is eternal life, that they know you the only true God, and Jesus Christ whom you have sent’ (Jn 17.3)

‘(So) I, Enoch, I saw the vision of the end of everything alone; and none among human beings will see as I have seen’. (*1 En.* 19.3; Isaac in *OTP* 1.23)
κἀγὼ Ἐνὼχ ἴδον τὰ θεωρήματα μόνος, τὰ πέρατα πάντων, καὶ οὐ μὴ ἴδῃ οὐδὲ εἷς ἀνθρώπων ὡς ἐγὼ ἴδον. [one of the passages extant in Greek][22]
[Jesus to Nicodemus.] ‘How can you believe if I tell you heavenly things (τὰ ἐπουράνια)?’ (Jn 3.12)

‘Wisdom could not find a place in which she could dwell; but a place was found for (for her) in the heavens’. (*1 En.* 42.1; Isaac in *OTP* 1.33)
‘And the Word became flesh and dwelt among us …’. (Jn 1.14)[23]

‘For I know this mystery; I have read the tablets of heaven and have seen the holy writings, and I have understood the writing in them; and they are inscribed concerning you’. (*1 En.* 103.2; Isaac in *OTP* 1.83)[24]
[According to the Fourth Evangelist, only Jesus has such knowledge.[25] Jesus:‘If you believed Moses, you would believe me, for he wrote of me. But if you do not believe his writings, how will you believe my words?’ (Jn 5.47)][26]

Recall Enoch’s vision of the ‘Lord of the sheep’ ([מ]רא ענא][27]; ὁ κύριος τῶν προβάτων [*1 En.* 89.42])[28] and the 70 evil shepherds in *1 En.* 89–90.[29]
[Jesus.] ‘I am the door of the sheep (ἡ θὺρα τῶν προβάτων) … I am the good shepherd’ (Jn 10.7, 11).
I would add *1 En.* 89.36, ‘[And I watched in that dream until] that [Sh]ee[p] was changed; and he became a man…’
[30] [וחזית בחלמא דן עד די א]מר[א] דן אתהפך והוא אנוש

…the name of that (Son of) Man was revealed to them. (*1 En.* 69.27; Isaac in *OTP* 1.49)
Now is the Son of Man glorified (Jn 13.31)

22. M. Black, *Apocalypsis Henochi Graece* (Pseudepigrapha Veteris Testamenti Graece 3; Leiden: Brill, 1970), p. 32.

23. The noun ‘wisdom’ does not occur in the 4G; but ‘Word’ seems in many ways to be synonymous with ‘wisdom’.

24. Why does none of the canonical evangelists use the word ‘mystery’ or mention ‘Enoch’ (except Luke in 3.37)?

25. See esp. Jn 2.25; 3.11; 7.29; 8.14, 32; 17.7–8, 25; 21.17.

26. I include this quotation not so much because of the appearance of ‘writing’ in each document but to caution against thinking that the Fourth Evangelist is arguing primarily against the Enoch groups. The main opponents are Jews who follow Moses; yet, the Enoch traditions may have also been revered by many of these selfsame Jews.

27. The *mem* is uncertain; the text is preserved on 4QEn^{e} 4 ii line 21 (Plate XX); see J.T. Milik, *The Books of Enoch* (Oxford: At the Clarendon Press, 1976), pp. 240–41. See 4QEn^{e} 4 iii lines 19–20, [ומ]רא ענא] (the *mem* is uncertain). Also, see the restoration in 4QEn^{d} 2 ii line 27.

28. The Greek is from the margins of the tachygraphical manuscript Vat. Gr. 1809. I am grateful to the librarian of the Biblioteca Apostolica Vaticana for permission to study this unusual manuscript. For some facsimiles and a description of Vat. Gr. 1809, see S. Lilla, *Il testo tachigrafico del ‘de divinis nominibus’* (Studi e Testi 263; Vatican: Biblioteca Apostolica Vaticana, 1970).

29. The reference to ‘shepherds’ appears in *1 En.* 89.59–90.22; this section is not preserved in Greek.

30. 4QEn^{c} 4 line 10. Some of the consonants are dubious; see Milik, *Books of Enoch*, p. 205 (Plate XIV).

> All the days of the righteous 'shall be completed in peace' (בשלם ית]מליון;[31] *1 En.* 10.17)
> ...he shall proclaim peace to you... (*1 En.* 71.15; Isaac in *OTP* 1.50)
> [Jesus to his disciples.] Peace be with you ... Peace be with you. (Jn 20.19,21)

Given the intermittent polemical nature of *1 Enoch* and of the 4G, I am convinced that it is fruitful to ponder to what extent the Enoch traditions have given rise to some expressions and thoughts in the 4G. Would not the Fourth Evangelist have strongly disagreed with the Jews who claimed that Enoch (חנוך) was 'the wisest of men' (ו[ח]כים אנושא)[32] or that he should be celebrated as the one who at the judgment will be 'the scribe of righteousness' (ЄNѠX ПЄГPⲀMMⲀTЄYC̄ H̄T̄ⲀΪKⲀΪ-ŌCYNH)[33] which is a thought rather contemporaneous with the 4G since it appears in the *Testament of Abraham*: 'And the one who produces (the evidence) is the teacher of heaven and earth and the scribe of righteousness, Enoch (ὁ διδάσκαλος τοῦ οὐρανοῦ καὶ τῆς γῆς καὶ γραμματεὺς τῆς δικαιοσύνης)'.[34]

Four passages are most important: First, in Jn 3.12 Jesus tells Nicodemus, 'If I have told you earthly things and you do not believe, how can you believe if I tell you heavenly things?' Second, in Jn 3.13 the reader is informed that 'No one has ascended into heaven but he who descended from heaven, the Son of Man'. Third, in Jn 7.27 the reader is told that 'when the Christ appears, no one will know where he comes from'. Finally, in Jn 9.35-37 the Fourth Evangelist places in Jesus' mouth this self-disclosure: 'the Son of Man...is he who speaks to you' (9.35-37; cf. 12.34-36). One does not need to read Bultmann to know that for the Fourth Evangelist the Son of Man is a 'Messianic title for Jesus'.[35]

Taken together, Jn 3.12-13 and 9.35-37 suggest that the Fourth Evangelist may be reacting against the Jews who claim that Enoch ascended into heaven and had been named 'that Son of Man'. Note *1 En.* 48:

> And at that hour that Son of man (*zeku walda sab'*)[36] was named in the presence of the Lord of Spirits, and his name (was named) before the Head of Days. Even before the sun and the constellations were created, before the stars of heaven were made, his name was named before the Lord of Spirits. (48.2–3)[37]

31. 4QEn[c] 1 ii line 6 (Plate X). The *taw* is dubious, but probable because of context. Cf. the Greek (μετὰ εἰρήνης) and Ethiopic (*basalâm*).

32. 4QEn[g] 1 ii line 23 (Plate XXI). The *kaph* is not certain but probable.

33. The expression is found in numerous texts; see Milik, *Books of Enoch*, pp. 103–106.

34. TAb 11.3 [Recension B]; translated by E.P. Sanders in *OTP* 1.900. The Greek text has been republished by M.E. Stone; see his *The Testament of Abraham: The Greek Recensions* (Texts and Translations 2; Pseudepigrapha Series 2; Missoula: Society of Biblical Literature, 1972), p. 78.

35. Bultmann, *John*, p. 150.

36. Knibb, *The Ethiopic Book of Enoch*, 1.123 [fol. 6rb]. There are more examples of the *pronomina demonstrativa* in Ethiopic than in Hebrew or Aramaic (or for that matter in Greek). The demonstrative *'zeku'* is a compound of *ze-* and *ku* (from *ka* 'there') that denotes 'this there' which means 'that'. See A. Dillmann, *Ethiopic Grammar*, expanded by C. Bezold and translated by J.A. Crichton (London: Williams & Norgate, 1907), p. 330. The noun *sab'* is the plural form of *be'si*, 'man' or 'person'.

37. Knibb, *The Ethiopic Book of Enoch*, 2.133-34.

Why would some Jews choose Enoch above Noah, Abraham, Moses, David, Solomon, and others? Enoch was a good choice.[38] First, he was 'seventh' after Adam (according to P; J makes 'Lemech' seventh). Second, he was perfect because 'he walked (ויתהלך) with God'. Third, he did not die (ואיננו) because 'God took (לקח) him'. Fourth, these cryptic words in Gen. 5.24 probably suggested to the Enoch group that Enoch was still alive (perhaps in heaven) to inspire and guide the elect ones on the earth (cf. Gen. 5.21-24). More than the Qumranites who revered Enoch, at least originally, believed Enoch was unusually special. While some books of Enoch were being composed a Jew, who represented another segment of Early Judaism, claimed that Enoch had indeed ascended into heaven (μετετέθη; *WisSol.* 4.10).[39]

Such veneration of Enoch would have elicited polemics from other Jews.[40] We find evidence of such polemics in Jewish texts. We have clear textual evidence that Enoch was a threat and there was a need to polemicize against his adoration. Such a denigration of Enoch is preserved in *Genesis Rabba*. As J. Dan states, in his forthcoming monograph on *Jewish Mysticism and the Dead Sea Scrolls*, the traditions preserved in this text explain that Enoch was 'taken by God not as a result of his righteousness, but as following from his frequent movement from righteousness to evil-doing; so God decided to 'remove' him as long as he is righteous'. Let us review the evidence.

Reflecting on Gen. 5.24, 'Enoch walked with God, and he was not, for God took him', R. Hama bar Hoshaia interpreted the text to mean that Enoch was inscribed 'in the scroll of the wicked'. R. Aibu argued that 'Enoch was a dissembler'. R. Abbahu claimed that Enoch was not 'translated into heaven', but died 'a quite ordinary death'. These Rabbis refused to elevate Enoch. They denigrated him, claiming that he was not special for God 'removed' him, because he was about to be unrighteous. Their opinions are recorded in *Genesis Rabbah* (third to fourth century),[41] the 'first complete and systematic Judaic commentary to the book of Genesis'.[42] Although this text, *Genesis Rabbah*, appreciably postdates the 4G it may preserve some traditions that are earlier. Thus, a similar thought, the denigration of Enoch, may appear in John 3.13, whose author must have known about the Enoch apocalyptic traditions, and perhaps the books that

38. VanderKam concludes that the 'Jewish Enoch was originally fashioned in the likeness of the seventh Mesopotamian king Enmeduranki' (p. 188). See his *Enoch and the Growth of an Apocalyptic Tradition* (CBQ Monograph Series, 16; Washington, D.C.: Catholic Biblical Association of America, 1984).

39. Enoch is not named in WisSol; that is because the author deliberately avoids citing names. He rather wishes to break down the barrier between past and present and to affirm the universalism of an event and idea.

40. Barrett, *St John*, pp. 177–78 and F.H. Borsch (in *The Son of Man in Myth and History* [The New Testament Library; Philadelphia: Westminster Press, 1967], p. 272) rightly stress that the Fourth Evangelist is not interested in an ascent. They are close to arguing for a polemic against such a belief.

41. The translation used is the one by J. Neusner, *Genesis Rabbah* (3 vols.; Brown Judaic Studies, 104, 105, 106; Atlanta: Scholars Press, 1985); see 1.271.

42. These are Neusner's words in *Genesis and Judaism: The Perspective of Genesis Rabbah, an Analytical Anthology* (Brown Judaic Studies 108; Atlanta: Scholars Press, 1985), p. xi.

celebrate Enoch's ascent into the heavens and return with 'heavenly' wisdom for the elect (esp. *1 En.* and *2 En.*).

Probably against such Enoch traditions, the author of the 4G claimed that 'no one has ascended into heaven except he who descended from heaven, the Son of Man'.[43] The connection with Enoch in this gospel seems assured, since Enoch is hailed as the Son of Man in *1 En.* 71 and Jesus announces he is 'the Son of Man' in Jn 9.35-38.[44] This scenario seems possible, perhaps probable, since *1 En.* 37–71 is now judged to be Jewish and dated to the late first century BCE by most experts.[45]

The XXVII edition of Nestle-Aland's *Novum Testamentum Graece* lists the parallels to the 'Old Testament' found by scholars in the New Testament. Under *Loci citati vel allegati ex Vetere Testamento* are included passages found in the intracanonical and extracanonical Jewish compositions. One sees 57 references to *1 Enoch* in the New Testament. Passages in the Gospels of Matthew, Mark, and Luke are included:

1 En.	*the Gospels*
5.7	Mt. 5.5
15.6s	Mc 12.25
16.1	Mt. 13.39
22.9ss	Lk. 16.26
38.2	Mt. 26.24
39.4	Lk. 16.9
48.10	Mc 8.29
51.2	Lk. 21.28
51.4	Mc 12.25

43. Of course, until the Son of Man traditions are examined (some of the earliest strata in the GosJn) it is conceivable that other biblical figures, who reputedly ascended into heaven may have been intended by the Fourth Evangelist, including Adam, Abraham (esp. ApAb), Baruch (*2 Bar.* esp.), and Ezra (*4 Ezra*). Among them, however, only Enoch is hailed as the Son of Man (viz. *1 En.* 37–71; cf. *2 En.*, and later *3 En.*). I am convinced that we cannot study *1 En.* and the 4G and ignore the complex literary history of each document (in contrast, Hare studies the function of the Son of Man in the extant 4G; Hare, *The Son of Man Tradition*, p. 79). The Fourth Evangelist is not suggesting that the Son of Man had ascended into heaven; he, as Jesus is clearly from above (ἄνωθεν). In 3.14 he stresses Jesus' ascension (lifting up) is on the cross and to Mary Magdalene Jesus intimates that he is about to ascend to the Father (20.17).

44. The expression 'that Son of Man' in *1 En.* 71, if it goes back to an Aramaic or Greek text that would have been known to the Fourth Evangelist, may explain the otiose use of 'that' (ἐκεῖνός) in Jn 9.37 [which is usually not represented in modern translations; also see Jn 9.36].

45. See Charlesworth, 'The Date of the Parables of Enoch'; J.C. Greenfeld and M.E. Stone, 'The Enochic Pentateuch and the Date of the Similitudes', *HTR* 70 (1977) 51–66; Chrys C. Caragounis, *The Son of Man* (WUNT 38; Tübingen: Mohr [Siebeck], 1986) pp. 84–94; and G.W.E. Nickelsburg, *1 Enoch 1*, edited by K. Baltzer (Hermeneia; Minneapolis: Fortress Press, 2001). Nickelsburg is convinced that *1 En.* 37–71 is 'the latest of the Enochic texts and probably dates to the late first century BCE' (p. 7). He means 'the latest of the Enochic texts' in *1 En.*; this is not to be confused with *2 En.*, *3En*, or the Coptic fragments of Enoch books. M. Black changed his mind on the dating of *1 En.* 37–73; finally, he advocated a date in 'the early Roman period, probably pre-70 CE'. Black, *The Book of Enoch*, p. 188. M.A. Knibb still prefers a pre-70 CE date; see Knibb's review of Black's *The Book of Enoch* in *JSJ* 17, pp. 86–92; esp. p. 88.

1 En.	*the Gospels*
61.8	Mt. 25.31
62.2s	Mt. 25.31
63.10	Lk. 16.9
69.27	Mt. 25.31, 26.64
94.8	Lk. 6.24
97.8–10	Lk. 12.19
103.4	Mt. 26.13.

Not one passage in the 4G is noted.

Is that accurate? Have the traditions in *1 Enoch* not helped to shape the present form of the 4G? Eighteen passages in the *Parables of Enoch* or *1 En.* 37–71 are listed as paralleled in the New Testament documents, so the failure to include the 4G in the list cannot be due to the uncertainty of the Jewishness or earliness of this composition, which was a discussion held during the SNTS congress in Tübingen in 1977.[46] Today, many scholars would consider it rather remarkable if no parallels were found between *1 Enoch* and the 4G.[47] Long ago, in his classical work, *The Apocrypha and Pseudepigrapha of the Old Testament*, R.H. Charles pointed to similarities between *1 Enoch* and John 5.22, 12.36, and 14.2; he did so after stressing that '*1 Enoch* has had more influence on the *New Testament* than has any other apocryphal or pseudepigraphic work'.[48]

R.H. Charles missed the influence from *1 Enoch* on the 4G that I am bringing now into central focus. The reasons are twofold. He wrote at a time when only positive influences were examined. We have been discerning negative – even polemical – influences. When the Fourth Evangelist argues that και οὐδεὶς ἀναβέβηκεν εἰς τὸν οὐρανὸν 'no one has ascended into heaven' (3.13), he is arguing against those who claim someone has ascended into heaven.[49] The οὐδεὶς is a strong contradiction; as F.J. Moloney states, the force of the sentence is to reject any validity in the claims that 'the great revealers of Israel had been to heaven to learn the secrets they eventually revealed…'.[50] That is why the Fourth Evangelist then adds the emphatic positive (as in Isa 45.23 [LXX] and MSS F and G in Rom. 14.11)[51]: εἰ μὴ ὁ ἐκ τοῦ οὐρανοῦ καταβάς, 'except the one who

46. See Charlesworth, '1977 (Tübingen; Eberhard-Karls Universität): The Books of Enoch', in *The Old Testament Pseudepigrapha and the New* Testament (SNTS Monograph Series, 54; Cambridge, New York: Cambridge University Press, 1985), pp. 102–106.

47. S. Chialà draws attention to numerous parallels between the concept of the Son of Man in the *Parables of Enoch* and in the 4G. See Chialà, *Libro delle parabole di Enoch* (Studi Biblici 117; Brescia; Paideia Editrice, 1997), pp. 327–29.

48. Charles (ed.), *The Apocrypha and Pseudepigrapha of the Old Testament*, 2.180.

49. Borsch claims that behind Jn 3.13 is a Man myth; 'he has functions or roles both in heaven and yet on earth through the one who represents him'. *The Son of Man*, p. 274 (also see p. 277). As is well known, the identity of the implied speaker of 3.13 is unclear; it may be Jesus or the Fourth Evangelist. I agree with R.A. Culpepper that we should grasp that we are confronted with 'a classic instance of the blending of the narrator with Jesus' voice' (p. 42). Culpepper, *Anatomy of the Fourth Gospel* (Philadelphia: Fortress Press, 1987).

50. F.J. Moloney, *Belief in the Word* (Minneapolis: Fortress Press, 1993), p. 117.

51. See, esp., N. Turner, *Syntax* in J.H. Mouton's *A Grammar of New Testament Greek* (Edinburgh: T&T Clark, 1963), p. 333.

surely descended from heaven'.[52] Then to underscore the point he adds the identity and title of this individual: ὁ υἱὸς τοῦ ἀνθρώπου (which is an epexegetical clarification of 'he who descended from heaven). And to drive the point home more clearly (he or)[53] some scribes have added that the Son of Man is ὁ ὢν (ὃς ἦν, e, sy^c^) ἐν τῷ οὐρανῷ (viz. A (*), Θ, Ψ, syr^c.p.h^), 'the one who is in (or whose being resides in) heaven', or ὁ ὢν ἐκ τοῦ οὐρανοῦ (pc sys), 'the one being (or whose being is defined as coming) from heaven'. Only the Son of Man – namely Jesus – can reveal Wisdom and the way to eternal life (the intentionality of 3.13–17).[54]

Thus, when the Fourth Evangelist has Jesus declare that he is the Son of Man this declaration seems to have polemical overtones. E.M. Sidebottom correctly pointed out that only in the 4G is the Son of Man portrayed as descending;[55] this may be the Fourth Evangelists mixing influences from the Jacob cycle (the ascending and descending motif) and the Enoch cycle (the Son of Man concept that is developed beyond Daniel). Brown has added the insight that *1 Enoch* 48.2-6 'portrays the Son of Man as pre-existent in heaven (and this seems to be implied in John), but does not speak of his descent' (1.133). These observations – including the possibility that the preexistence of the Logos presented in John is indebted to *1 Enoch* – lead me to speculate that Jn 3.13 seems directed against the Enoch groups and their claim that Enoch is the one who ascended into heaven to obtain the wisdom that they alone possess and the one who has been named 'the Son of Man'. The Wisdom motive clearly raises the question of the source of the Jewish traditions regarding Wisdom that have influenced the evolutionary shaping of the 4G.

Second, Charles lived before the study of the 4G was enriched by sociological studies of the community behind the 4G, notably in the publications by W. Meeks, J.L. Martyn, R.E. Brown.[56] The studies of ἀποσυνάγωγος in the 4G reveal the polemical ambience of the document; the Johannine Jews are in a life-and-death

52. Jn 3.13 is an *ellipsis*, as Sidebottom, Ruckstuhl, Moloney, Hare, and others have claimed; hence, I suggest this rendering of 3.13, 'And no one has ascended into heaven (and returned with τὰ ἐπουράνια) except the one who descended from heaven (and alone is able to reveal τὰ ἐπουράνια)'. See E. M. Sidebottom, *The Christ of the Fourth Gospel* (London: SPCK, 1961); E. Ruckstuhl, 'Die johanneische Menschensohnforschung, 1957–1969', *Theologische Berichte*, edited by J. Pfammatter and F. Furger (Einsiedeln: Benziger, 1972), pp. 171–284; Ruckstuhl, *Jesus im Horizont der Evangelien* (Stuttgarter Biblische Aufsatzbände 3; Stuttgart: Verlag Katholisches Bibelwerk, 1988), pp. 288–90; F.J. Moloney, *The Johannine Son of Man* (Rome: Las, 1976); Hare, *The Son of Man Tradition*, pp. 86–87.

53. Lagrange, Boismard, Wikenhauser, and some scholars judge these words to be authentic. Brown (1.133) rightly states that 'the phrase is so difficult that it may well have been omitted in the majority of manuscripts to avoid a difficulty'. This is clear, but if one weighs the manuscript evidence, the phrase seems redactional.

54. The connection between Jn 3.13 and 3.14 is often lost, because scholars do not grasp the positive symbolic meaning of the serpent. Jesus, as the upraised serpent, brings life through his death and resurrection and he is also the wisest of all (see Gen. 3.1 esp. in the LXX).

55. Sidebottom, 'The Ascent and Descent of the Son of Man in the Gospel of St. John', *ATR* 39 (1957), pp. 115–22.

56. See esp. R.E. Brown, *The Community of the Beloved Disciple* (New York: Paulist Press, 1979).

struggle with the Jews who control the synagogue.[57] As M. Hengel states, many Johannine experts have come to the conclusion that

> die 'johanneische Gemeinde' bzw. den Evangelisten in eine erbitterte Auseinandersetzung mit dem sich nach der Katastrophe von 70 unter pharisäischer Führung wieder neu formierenden palästinischen Judentum verwickelt sehen und dieses Judentum als den eigentlichen Gegner der Gemeinde betrachten.[58]

Thus, the polemical ambience of the 4G has been clarified by other studies that are unrelated to the search for influences from the Jewish apocryphal works on the 4G. Apparently, the Jews with whom the Johannine Jews were struggling were not only those who 'owned' the synagogue, but also those who revered Enoch as the Son of Man who had the secret of Wisdom and life (and perhaps some Jews in the synagogue may also have held such views).

Another link between the Enoch traditions and the 4G should be stressed. According to *1 Enoch* the Son of Man is the judge. Note this section from *1 Enoch*:

> And they had great joy, and they blessed and praised and exalted because the name of that Son of Man (*we'etu walda 'eguâla 'emma ḥeyâw*)[59] had been revealed to them. And he sat on the throne of his glory, and the whole judgement was given to the Son of Man (*walda 'eguâla 'emma ḥeyâw*), and he will cause the sinners to pass away and be destroyed from the face of the earth. (69.26-27; Knibb; underlining mine)

> And there was great joy amongst them,
> And they blessed and glorified and extolled
> Because the name of that Son of Man had been revealed unto them.
>
> And he sat on the throne of his glory,
> And the sum of judgement was given unto the Son of Man,
> And he caused the sinners to pass away and be destroyed
> from off the face of the earth,
> And those who have led the world astray. (69.26–27; Charles in 1912)[60]

Charles' translation brings out the poetic structure of the passage. The Righteous One is clearly identified with the Chosen One in *1 En.* 53.6 and the Chosen One seems to be also the Son of Man, since in 61.8-10 he is the enthroned one who judges. Charles claimed that the one who 'sat on the throne of glory' according to 69.26 is 'the Messiah', and he pointed out the parallel between the 'sum of judgement, i.e. all judgement' and Jn 5.22 πᾶσαν τὴν κρίσιν. This parallel is important, since according to Jn 5.27 Jesus is the judge because he is the Son of

57. See Charlesworth, 'The Gospel of John: Exclusivism Caused by a Social Setting Different from That of Jesus (Jn 11.54 and 14.6)', in R. Bieringer, *et al.* (eds.), *Anti-Judaism and the Fourth Gospel* (Jewish and Christian Heritage Series, 1; Assen: Royal van Gorcum, 2001), pp. 479–513.

58. M. Hengel, *Die Johanneische Frage* (WUNT, 67; Tübingen: Mohr [Siebeck], 1993), p. 288.

59. Knibb, *The Ethiopic Book of Enoch*, 1.207 [fol. 9ra]. Those who are not familiar with Ethiopic grammar may need to know, when studying the photographs of *1 En.*, that Ethiopic is defective in the sense that a doubled consonant is not indicated by the script. The collective *'eguâla 'emma ḥeyâw* denotes 'humankind'; it is composed of *'eguâla* (which specifies the young of an animal or human), *'emm* (which means 'mother'), and *ḥeyâw* (which denotes 'the living' [from the verb *ḥaywa*, 'to live']).

60. Charles, *The Book of Enoch or 1 Enoch I* (Oxford: Clarendon Press, 1912), pp. 140–41.

Man: The Father has given him authority to execute judgment, 'because he is the Son of Man (ὅτι υἱὸς ἀνθρώπου)'. The Fourth Evangelist brings out his own theology, which is a polemic against the Jewish documents that claim God is the judge: 'The Father judges no one, but has given all judgment to the Son' (5.22; cf. 5.27, 30; 8.16).

Before proceding further we must pause to contemplate the presence of the term 'the (that or this) Son of Man' in *1 (Ethiopic) Enoch*. The Ethiopic translator(s) chose three expressions to represent 'the Son of Man' in *1 Enoch*:

(1) *zeku* (or *zentu*) *walda sab'*, 'that (or this) Son of Man' (46.2 [B and C], 3, 4; 48.2; cf. 60.10 [without the demonstrative adjectival pronoun and addressed to Enoch]);

(2) *zeku* (or *we'etu*) *walda 'eguâla 'emma ḥeyâw*, literally 'that (or this) son of the offspring of the mother of the living (or Eve)'[61] (62.7 [without the demonstrative], 9, 14; 63.11; 69.27 [26 in Knibb], 29; 70.1; 71.17);

(3) *we'etu walda be'si*, 'this Son of Man' (62.5;[62] 69.29; 71.14 [without the demonstrative]; cf. the variant *walda be'sit*, 'son of woman'[63] in Eth. II at 65.2).[64]

Black concluded, 'All three expressions clearly go back to an original בן־האדם (Aram. בר־[א]נשא, ὁ υἱὸς τοῦ ἀνθρώπου).[65] The *Untertext* of the translation is far from clear. N. Schmidt concluded that three Aramaic expressions had been translated with three Ethiopic terms.[66]

walda sab'	=	בר נשא
walda be'si	=	ברה דגברא
walda 'eguâla 'emma ḥeyâw	=	ברה דבר נשא

It is impossible to ascertain the *Vorlage* of *Ethiopic Enoch*; the translators seem to have used not only Aramaic but also Greek.[67] Since we do not have *1 En.* 37–71

61. See Isaac's philological notes in *OTP* 1.43 note j.

62. N.B. the variant 'that Son of a Woman', cf. Knibb, *The Ethiopic Book of Enoch*, p. 2.151 and note to 62.5.

63. The noun *be'sit* (from *be'si*, see the earlier note) means not only 'woman' but also 'wife'.

64. Due to the corruption caused by orality and the relative recent date of the manuscripts of Enoch, there are numerous scribal errors in Ethiopic manuscripts. On manuscript errors, see T.O. Lambdin, *Introduction to Classical Ethiopic (Ge'ez)* (Harvard Semitic Studies, 24; Ann Arbor: Scholars Press and Edwards Brothers, Inc, 1978), pp. 13–14.

65. *Book of Enoch*, p. 206.

66. N. Schmidt, 'The Original Language of the Parables of Enoch', in R.F. Harper, *et al.* (eds.), *Old Testament and Semitic Studies in Memory of William Rainey Harper* (Chicago: The University of Chicago Press, 1908), pp. 2.329–49; Schmidt, 'The Apocalypse of Noah and the Parables of Enoch', in C. Adler and A. Ember (eds.), *Oriental Studies Dedicated to Paul Haupt* (Baltimore, Leipzig: Johns Hopkins Press, 1926), pp. 111–13; 'Recent Studies on the Son of Man', *JBL* 45 (1926), pp. 326–49; Schmidt, 'Was *bar nash* a Messianic Title?' *JBL* 15 (1986), pp. 36–53.

67. E. Ullendorf claims that the Ethiopic translator made direct use of Aramaic (and perhaps had access also to a Greek text); see Ullendorf, 'An Aramaic 'Vorlage' of the Ethiopic Text of Enoch?' in *Atti del convegno internazionale di studi etiopici: Accademia Nazionale dei Lincei* (Problemi Attuali di Scienza e di Cultura; Rome: Accademia Nazionale dei Lincei, 1960), pp. 259–67 [reprinted in his

in Aramaic (or Syriac and Greek) we have no textual basis to make a sure judgment. We need to remember, however, when comparing so-called *1 Enoch* with the 4G to remember that, if the Fourth Evangelist knew the Enoch text or tradition, he would probably have known it in Aramaic. Thus, the New Testament scholar must allow for some flexibility in comparing the two texts (or traditions).

Surely, it seems likely that we need to be open to the possibility of influences from the Enoch traditions on the 4G.[68] Yet, the commentators have not been interested in examining a relation between the traditions in *1 Enoch* and the 4G.[69] While S. Schulz indicated the early nature of the Son of Man passages in the 4G, and argued that they are pre-Johannine,[70] R. Schnackenburg, who affirms strong affinities between Qumran and John and claims that the Son of Man sayings are probably of 'apocalyptic' origin, prefers to imagine that the Fourth Evangelist obtained the Son of Man concept from 'Judaeo-Christian circles' and perhaps the Synoptics.[71] The latter possibility ebbs in light of the growing awareness that the 4G seems to be independent of the Synoptics.[72]

Ethiopia and the Bible (London: British Academy, Oxford University Press, 1968), pp. 61–62]; Ullendorf, 'An Aramaic Vorlage of the Ethiopic Text of Enoch', *Is Biblical Hebrew a Language? Studies in Semitic Languages and Civilizations* (Wiesbaden: Harrassowitz, 1977), pp. 172–80. Knibb is surely correct, because of translation errors in the Ethiopic that can be explained by the supposition of a Greek *Untertext* (esp. in 101.4), to conclude that the translator(s) of *Ethiopic Enoch* used, most likely, Aramaic and Greek manuscripts. See Knibb, *The Ethiopic Book of Enoch*, 2.38–46.

68. J.J. Collins, of course, thinks that *1 En.* 71 is a redactional addition. His argument is attractive but not convincing, since the flow of *1 En.* 69.26–71 makes sense within the apocalyptic genre (as M. Hooker claimed in *The Son of Man in Mark* [Montreal: McGill University Press, 1967], esp. pp. 41–42). See Collins, 'The Heavenly Representative: The 'Son of Man' in the Similitudes of Enoch', in J.J. Collins and G.W.E. Nickelsburg (eds.), *Ideal Figures in Ancient Judaism* (SBL Septuagint and Cognate Studies, 12; Chico, CA: Scholars Press, 1980), pp. 111–33; see esp. pp. 121–24. Also, Collins mentions manuscript variants, but we are confronted rather with Charles' emendation in 70. J. Ashton rightly suggests that 'the reaction could equally well have been from the Christian, and specifically the Johannine side' (p. 360). That is what I am arguing in the present publication. See Ashton, *Understanding the Fourth Gospel* (Oxford: Clarendon Press, 1991).

69. R. E. Brown refers numerous times to Elijah, for example, but not to Enoch. See Brown, *The Gospel According to John* (2 vols.; The Anchor Bible; Garden City, NY: Doubleday, 1966), pp. 47–50, 101–102. K. Barrett discusses Abraham and Moses but not Enoch; see Barrett's *The Gospel According to St John* (London: SPCK, 1965 [I use this edition because it was my *vade mecum* in seminary]), esp. pp. 291–92, 300–301 [Barrett does imply that Jn 1.35-51 should be read in light of *1 En.* 105.2; see p. 155]. Barrett doubts that *1 En.* 7.2 and 7.1 'really illuminates John's thought which has no room for such an ascent' (pp. 177–78); the influence seems, however, to be negative –the Fourth Evangelist would be arguing against it. C.H. Dodd saw numerous parallels between *1 En.* and the 4G but he did not focus on the Son of Man traditions; see Dodd, *The Interpretation of the Fourth Gospel* (Cambridge: Cambridge University Press, 1960), esp. pp. 144–45, 231–32. E. Haenchen concentrated only on the Wisdom motif in *1 En.* 42 and the 4G; see his *John* (2 vols.; trans. R.W. Funk; Hermeneia; Philadelphia: Fortress Press, 1984), see esp. vol. 1, pp. 101, 125, 126, 138.

70. S. Schulz, *Untersuchungen zur Menschensohn-Christologie im Johannesevangelium* (Göttingen: Vandenhoeck & Ruprecht, 1957)

71. R. Schnackenburg, *The Gospel According to St John* (3 vols.; trans. K. Smyth; New York: Crossroad, 1987), I, pp. 128–29.

72. See esp. D.M. Smith, *John Among the Gospels* (Columbia: University of South Carolina Press, 2nd edn, 2001), see esp. p. 241, 'It is reasonable to take seriously the Gospel's claim to represent a

In seeking to discern possible influence from *1 En.* on the 4G it is pertinent to draw attention to the *Odes of Solomon.* A section of *Ode* 36 – composed *ex ore Christi* – celebrates Christ as the Son of Man and the Son of God:

> (The Spirit) brought me forth before the Lord's face.
> And because I was the Son of Man (ܒܪ ܐܢܫܐ),
> I was named the Light (ܢܗܝܪܐ), the Son of God (ܒܪܗ ܕܐܠܗܐ). (*Ode* 36.3)[73]

This passage is obviously reminiscent of *1 En.* 48.2–4 (cited previously):

> At that hour, that Son of Man was given a name, in the presence of the Lord of the Spirits, the Before-Time; even before the creation of the sun and the moon, before the creation of the stars, he was given a name in the presence of the lord of the Spirits. ... He is the light of the gentiles and he will become the hope of those who are sick in their hearts.[74]

Since the *Odes of Solomon* are clearly linked somehow with the 4G, it is unwise to dismiss the Jewish thoughts preserved in *1 Enoch* as possible sources of influence on perhaps our most Jewish gospel, the Fourth Gospel.[75]

Why have New Testament scholars shied away from digging deeply into the theology of *1 Enoch* and following the lead of R.H. Charles by exploring how and in what ways, if at all, the books collected into the *Books of Enoch* have impacted the authors of the New Testament documents? The main reasons are somewhat obvious. First, J.T. Milik claimed that the most important section for New Testament specialists, *1 En.* 37–71, is a Christian composition and dates from the third century CE.[76] His position is now no longer tenable. The *Parables of Enoch* are certainly Jewish. They most likely antedate Hillel and Jesus; it is evident that this claim, well known to the members of the international Enoch seminar, is shocking to some New Testament experts.[77] Recently, the leading scholars have come to a dating of the last section of *1 Enoch* that is similar to that advocated by R. Laurence in 1835, even though he was unaware of the composite nature of the *Enoch Books*: 'The reign of Herod was of considerable duration, extending to four and thirty years; at some period of whose reign, probably at an early one, the Book of Enoch seems to have been written'.[78]

separate and independent witness...'. Also, see P. Borgen, 'The Independence of the Gospel of John', *Early Christianity and Hellenistic Judaism* (Edinburgh: T&T Clark, 1996), pp. 183–204.

73. For the Syriac and translation, see Charlesworth, ed., *The Odes of Solomon* (Oxford: Clarendon Press, 1973), pp. 126–27.

74. E. Isaac in *OTP* 1.35.

75. Surprisingly, in *De Structuur van de Henoch-Traditie en Het Nieuwe Testament*, C.P. Van Andel discusses the concept of the Son of Man in Mt., Mk, and Lk., but not in Jn; see pp. 91–99.

76. J.T. Milik: 'In conclusion, it is around the year A.D. 270 or shortly afterwards that I would place the composition of the Book of Parables' (p. 96). Milik, *The Books of Enoch* (Oxford: Clarendon Press, 1976).

77. B. Lindars lived when the tide had turned and it was clear that the *Parables of Enoch* postdated the gospels. See Lindars on this point and his announcement that 'the assumption that the Son of Man could be recognized as a title of an eschatological figure in Jewish thought', has 'now been demolished'. He was adamant, 'no such myth existed in the setting in which the gospels were composed'. See Lindars, *Jesus: Son of Man* (Grand Rapids: Eerdmans, 1983), pp. 7–8, 151.

78. R. Laurence, *The Book of Enoch* (Oxford: J.H. Parker, 2nd enlarged edn, 1833), p. xxvii.

Second, New Testament scholars labor with the misconception that the relation between the Son of Man, the Messiah, the Righteous One, and the Elect One are confused and misleading in the *Books of Enoch*. Research on the *Parables of Enoch* was seriously hindered by R.H. Charles emendation of *1 En.* 71.14. J.C. VanderKam, M. Black, and I have shown that these terms appear to be synonymous in the thought of the author.[79]

Third, New Testament specialists shy away from the *Parables of Enoch* because they are not extant in Greek, Latin, or Aramaic – the languages New Testament scholars master; they are extant only in Ethiopic. This language factor is major; but today there are excellent translations in English, German, Italian, French, and Spanish.[80] Most experts on *1 Enoch* today conclude that the *Parables of Enoch* had been composed by the time when the 4G was composed. Hence, the major reasons for ignoring the importance of the *Books of Enoch* for the developing thoughts in the New Testament writings are no longer valid.

The present reflections have served us well if they stimulate more scholars to explore how and in what ways the Enoch literature, especially *1 En.* 37–71, may have shaped the formation of the 4G. To discover a polemic that relates *1 Enoch* and the 4G is not to suggest that the Son of Man in the 4G is explained by the Son of Man in *1 Enoch*. Nowhere in the 4G, or in the New Testament, are we to assume Jesus is portrayed as declaring that he is categorically the Son of Man. The identity of Jesus is linked with God (not with the Son of Man); the Son is progressively revealed in the story, which is the good news about the incarnation of the Son on earth and his return to the Father.[81]

Long before Origen relegated the book, Tertullian considered *1 Enoch* (not *Ethiopic Enoch*, of course) inspired (usually as a witness to Jesus as the Christ, '*Sed cum Enoch eadem scriptura etiam de Domino praedicavit,*[82] *a nobis quidem nihil omnino rejiciendum*[83] *est, quod pertineat ad nos. Et legimus omnem scripturam aedificationi habilem divinitus inspirari.*[84] If *1 Enoch* was known to the author of Jude, and used by him to support prophecy, then why presume that the Fourth Evangelist could not have known it?

79. See our contributions in Charlesworth (ed.), *The Messiah* (Minneapolis: Fortress Press, 1992).

80. All these modern translations have been cited in the present publication.

81. Hare wisely contends that it is 'incarnation that distinguishes the Son of man from Gabriel, Michael, and other angels whose itinerary is superficially the same as his. *Ho katabas ek tou ouranou* is thus John's shorthand way of referring to the incarnation'. Hare, *The Son of Man Tradition*, p. 87. I would add to his list of 'angels' Enoch, who obtains angelic status. R. Kysar rightly states, 'The story of Jesus that the evangelist will sketch out for us is indeed a story of a human on the plane of history; but it is at the same time the story of one who comes from beyond the world and from the beginning of all existence' (p. 18). Kysar, *John's Story of Jesus* (Philadelphia: Fortress Press, 1989).

82. This is probably an error for *praedicarit*.

83. This today would be *reiciendum*.

84. Tertullian, *Opera* [now, see *de cultu feminarum* I.3]; as cited by Laurence, *The Book of Enoch*, p. xvii [I do not represent the words put into italics by Laurence: *de Domino* and *divinitus inspirari*]. An English translation of Tertullianis' *Opera* by S. Thelwall appears in AFN 4.16, 'But since Enoch in the same Scripture has preached likewise concerning the Lord, nothing at all must be rejected *by* us which pertains *to* us; and we read that 'every Scripture suitable for edification is divinely inspired'. [Italics his; the quotation, or allusion, derives from 2 Tim. 3.16].

One might object to my argument by claiming that the Fourth Evangelist treats those whom he rejects differently than this alleged rejection of Enoch in 3.13. Some experts might contend that he treats Moses and Abraham differently; hence, there is probably no polemic here against Enoch.[85] The objection is miscast or misinformed. John 3.13 is a polemic, 'no one has ascended into heaven', but the Fourth Evangelist did not polemicize against Moses or Abraham. He affirmed that the Torah (Law) came through Moses (1.17). He also portrayed Jesus arguing against those who claimed to have Abraham as their ancestor; he did not polemize against Abraham (cf. 8.39–58).

3. *Conclusion*

It seems that the Fourth Evangelist was influenced by Jewish apocalypticism. He even polemicizes against the apocalyptic claim that one, like Enoch, Abraham, Levi,[86] Isaiah, Baruch, and Ezra, has ascended into heaven.[87] In the early half of the twentieth century Hugo Odeberg offered the sage suggestion that Jn 3.13 'seems to imply the rejection of the traditions of ascensions into heaven made by the great saints, patriarchs and prophets of old...such as Enoch, Abraham, Moses, Elijah, Isaiah, and also of the views of those who at the time maintained that they could ascend to heaven and obtain knowledge of Divine Things and therefore had no need of the Son of Man'.[88] More recently in 'Some Jewish Exegetical Traditions', P. Borgen points out the polemic in Jn 3.13. For Borgen it is 'a polemic against the ascents of Moses and all others who are said to have ascended into heaven'.[89]

In light of the growing recognition of the power and prestige of the Enoch groups before Bar Kokhba (the books show up in the Qumran caves), perhaps the above conclusion now may be refined. What cycle of Jewish apocalyptic traditions was perhaps in the mind of the Fourth Evangelist?

The most likely target of the Johannine polemic is the Enoch group within Second Temple Judaism. They celebrated Enoch as the only one who ascended into heaven and was then exalted as the 'Son of Man'. Since ὁ υἱὸς τοῦ ἀνθρώπου in

85. This objection, or one similar to it, was voiced and discussed when this paper was read at the 'Pseudepigrapha and Christian Origins' seminar of the *Studiorum Novi Testamenti Societas* in Durham, England, August 2002.

86. Cf. T. Levi 2.5–12.

87. H. Odeberg rightly argued 'that Jn 3^{13} cannot primarily be directed against the Jewish conceptions of the descent and ascent of the *Šᵉkînâ*'. Odeberg, *The Fourth Gospel* (Uppsala and Stockholm: Almqvist & Wiksells Moktryckeri – A.-B, 1929), p. 94. Of course, Paul, according to 2 Cor. 12, claims to have ascended into the third heaven and obtained heavenly knowledge. Paul's polemic is also subtle; knowledge of Christ is superior to all knowledge and claims to revelation.

88. Odeberg, *The Fourth Gospel*, pp. 97–98.

89. P. Borgen, 'Some Jewish Exegetical Traditions as Background for Son of Man Sayings in John's Gospel [Jn 3,13–14 and context]', M. de Jonge (ed.), *L'Évangile de Jean* (BEThL, 44; Gembloux and Leuven: J. Duculot [c. 1977]), p. 243. Also, see W. Meeks, *The Prophet-King: Moses-Traditions and the Johannine Christology* (New Testament Suppl. 14; Leiden: Brill, 1977), p. 141; and S. Schulz, *Untersuchungen zur Menschensohn-Christologie im Johannesevangelium*, p. 105.

Jn 3.13 is an epexegetical clarification of 'he who descended from heaven', this intriguing possibility is enhanced. Clearly, the Fourth Evangelist contrasts Jesus' teachings with those of other Jews, represented by 'a leader of the Jews', Nicodemus. The Evangelist is eager to stress the uniqueness of Jesus': only through him, as the Son of Man, who alone is from above and has returned there, is it possible to be born ἄνωθεν (anew, indeed from above). The 4G, thus, is defined by the canon's claim; in the words of an admired exegete, this 'limited canon' contains numerous claims to 'be a testimony of God's unique revelation through which his general intent, his all-embracing grace, and the deepest structure of his creation may be discovered'.[90]

90. P. Pokorný, *Jesus in the Eyes of His Followers* (Dead Sea Scrolls and Christian Origins Library 4; North Richland Hills, TX: BIBAL, 1998), p. 84.

CHRIST THE SON AND THE FATHER–FARMER IN THE IMAGE OF THE VINE (JN 15.1–11, 12–17)

Stanislaw Pisarek

The relation of the Son and the Father is expressed by the image of vine (ἡ ἄμπελος)[1] and the verb *to remain* + in (μένειν ἐν)[2] and thus the two matters are closely related. The second one can be called immanence (Latin *maneo, manere* + in comes from Greek μένω). The two problems have been discussed in my two studies: 'The relation of the vine (Christ the Son of God) and the father–farmer (God the Father) in the image of the vine (Jn 15.1–11)' and ''Εγώ είμι ἡ ἄμπελος ἡ ἀληθινή, καί ὁ πατήρ μου ὁ γεωργός ἐστιν (Jn 15.1) and the immanence in the pericope Jn 15.1–17'. This paper presents the contents of the first article.[3]

1. Nine times in the Old Testament – three times in the pericope: 15.1; 15.4; 15.5.
2. Forty times in St John's Gospel: 15.4.4.5.6.7.7.9.10.10.16 – in the full version of the pericope 15.1-16.
3. S. Pisarek, *The image of the vine in St John's Gospel* (Lublin: typescript, 1967). Doctoral dissertation under the supervision of Professor F. Gryglewicz. It has also been published in some specialist periodicals and in celebratory volumes (Festschriften) with updating:

1.1. 'The context of the pericope about the vine (Jn 15.1–11)', *Theological-Canonical Annuals 15* (1968), pp. 77–96.
1.2. 'Le context de la péricope du cep de la vigne (Jn 15.1–11)', pp. 94–96 (Résumé).
2.1. 'The image of the vine in St John's Gospel (Jn 15.1–11). The stage of the research work carried out on the pericope' *SESHT*, 2, 1969), pp. 19–30.
2.2. 'La vigne dans l'Évangile selon saint Jean (15.1–11)', pp. 29–30 (Résumé)
3.1. 'Literary genre of the pericope about the vine (Jn 15.1–11)', *SESHT*, 4, 1971), pp. 15–22.
3.2. 'Le genre littéraire de la péricope sur le vigne (Jn 15.1–11)', p. 22 (Résumé).
4. 'The love of Jesus (Jn 15.9–17)', *GN* LXX (1993) no 37 from 12 Sept., p.7 (The series: Reading and understanding the Bible).
5. 'The true vine (Jn 15.1–8)', *GN* LXXII (1996) no 13 from 31 March, p. 6 (The series: Reading and understanding the Bible).
6. 'The disciple and his joy in the pericope about the vine Jn 15.1–11', *Collectanea Theologica. Theological Review. Polish Theologians Quarterly Magazine* LXVIII (1998), 4, pp. 21–29.
7.1. 'Christ's disciple according to the pericope about the vine (Jn 15.1–11: καρπὸν φέρειν)', in: *Diliges Me? Pasce*, Vol. I (Pontifica Academia Theologica Cracoviensis, Facultas Theologica, Studia VI, Analecta Excellentissimo Episcopo, Prof V. Swierzawski oblata; Sandomierz: Hodie Publishers, 1999), pp. 236–63.
7.2. English summary in the above mentioned art., pp. 260–61.

For a researcher, studying the speech about the vine and the grapes, the historical-religious problem seems at first to be of great importance. It concerns the source of the image of grapevine. Who did use it originally: was it St John or Jesus of Nazareth himself? And were there any earlier patterns? There are some analogies in the Old Testament, Jewish literature, Dionysius cult, Mandaean religion[4] and oriental myths about the tree of life. A. Wikenhauser assumed that the associations with oriental myths[5] are quite probable and R. Bultmann seems to be convinced that this is the right explanation.[6] J. Behm is more reserved in that respect, although he also accepts the possibility of a parallel between Jn 15 and Dionysian and Mandaean texts.[7]

But perhaps, there is no need to look for so far into the past. The Old Testament texts, e.g. Jer. 2.21; Ps. 80/79.8.14; Hos. 10.1, reveal that the people of Israel were called 'vine' and this is the most probable background of the pericope in St John's Gospel. Later on, the Messiah is called ἄμπελος in (Syriac) Apocalypse of Baruch, chapter 36, where there is a vision of a forest, a vine, springs and cedar trees. God speaks to the prophet, explaining to him the real sense of the vision: 'Then the reign of the anointed will be revealed and it will be

7.3. 'Jünger Christi sein nach der Pericope vom Weinstock (Jn 15.1–11)', in the above, pp. 261–63 (Zusammenenfassung).

7.4. 'To be Christ's Disciple according to the pericope about the vine (Jn 15.1–11)', in the above, p. 263.

7.5. Summary (in the above), p. 810.

8.1. 'The relation with the vine (Christ the Son) and the father-farmer (God the Father) in the image of the vine (Jn 15.1–11)', *SESHT* 32 (1999), pp. 37–44.

8.2. 'Bindung mit dem Weinstock (Christus Sohn) und mit dem Vater-Bauer (Gott Vater) im Bild des Weinstocks (Jn 15.1–11)', in the above, p. 44 (Zusammenfassung).

9.1. 'Immanence in the pericope Jn 15.1–17', in: *Sanctificetur Nomen Tuum (Mt 6,9)* (commemorative book dedicated to Professor Janusz Czerski on his 65th birthday and the 38th anniversary of his engagement in research; edited by B. Polok, K. Ziaja (Opole:The Faculty of Theology at the Opole University, 2000), pp. 237–55.

9.2. 'Die Immanenz in der Perikope Jn 15.1–17. Zusammenfassung', pp. 254–55.

See also R. Borig, *Der wahre Weinstock. Untersuchungen zu Joh 15,1–10* (München: Kösel Verlag, 1967); F. Gryglewicz, 'Jesus as the vine', in *idem* (ed.), *Exegesis of St John's Gospel* (Lublin: RW KUL, 1976), pp. 49–57; *The Speeches of Jesus in the fourth Gospel* (Cracow, 1986), pp. 149–56. This vision depicted in the Old Christian art: C. Leonardi, *Ampelos. II simbolo della vite nell' arte pagana e paleocristiana* (Bibliotheca Ephemerides Liturgicae, Sectio Historica 21; Rome, 1947).

4. See A. Baum, *The Mandaeans,* in: *The Practical Dictionary of the Bible* (edited by A. Grabner-Haider; Warsaw, 1995), col. 699; complete information about this Gnostic group together with bibliography: K. Rudolph, Mandaeism, in D.N. Freedman (ed.), *The Anchor Bible Dictionary*, 4 (Garden City, NY: Doubleday, 1992), pp. 500–502.

5. A. Wikenhauser, *Das Evangelium nach Johannes* (Regensburg: Pustet, 3rd edn, 1961), p. 283; Regensburger Neues Testament 4.

6. R. Bultmann, *Das Evangelium des Johannes* (Berlin: EVA, 17th edn, 1963), p. 407. Bultmann follows E. Schweizer's assumptions that this image comes from the Mandaeans. Compare E. Schweizer, *Ἐγώ εἰμι* (FRLANT.NF 38; Göttingen: Vandenhoeck & Ruprecht, 1939), pp. 39–41.

7. Ἄμπελος, in: *Theologisches Wörterbuch zum Neuen Testament*, I, pp. 345–46.

like a spring and a vine'.[8] In Eccl. (24.17) the personified God's wisdom is presented as a vine and therefore it was easy to identify Messiah as the vine and the disciples as the grapes.[9]

The Mandaean scriptures come from the eighth century, some parts of them dating back to 400–600 CE. It is quite unlikely that there is any kind of relation between St John's Gospel and the Mandaean scriptures.[10] Since S. Schulz's opinion on the matter,[11] new Mandaean texts were published due to philological research by E.S. Drower[12] (from Oxford) and M. Macuch[13] (from Teheran), but the results have not changed the basic approach to the analysis of the Mandaean texts after 1953 and there is no need to verify the already established views on that subject matter.[14] S. Schulz carried out detailed studies on Mandaeism and he concluded that it could not be definitely decided, which traditions in Mandaean literature were oldest. Therefore, he recommended caution and moderation in defining the relation between the early Mandaean tradition and St John's Gospel.[15]

We may take the religious-historical problem of the origin of the vine image in St John's Gospel for already solved. The main chapter of R. Borig's doctoral dissertation (under the supervision of Professor R. Schnackenburg from Würzburg)[16] presents a thorough discussion on the subject. Having analysed in detail the Mandaean, Gnostic and Qumran texts, the Apocrypha of the Old Testament, as well as the works of Philo of Alexandria and the Old Testament testimonies with regard to the origin of the vine image, he came to the conclusion that the Old Testament was the source of St John's pericope. The fact that the reference to the vine has originated in the Old Testament is of great importance for christology and ecclesiology of St John.

8. P. Riessler, *Altjüdisches Schrifttum ausserhalb der Bibel* (Augsburg: Dr Benno Fischer Verlag, 1928), pp. 75, 78. The Syrian text of Baruch's Apocalypse is a translation from Greek, the Greek version was translated from Hebrew. The original part of the apocryphon probably comes from pre-Christian times. However it was compiled as a whole soon after 70 CE. Cf. P. Riessler, quotations, p.1270. Compare also *The Baruch's Apocalypse* (Syrian), in *The Apocrypha of the Old Testament* (analysis and introduction by Ryszard Rubinkiewicz SDB; Warsaw: Vocatio, 2nd edn, 2000), pp. 405–42; 419–20: *The image of the vine and the forest.*

9. Compare B. Schwank, 'Ich bin der wahre Weinstock: Joh. 15,1–17', *Sein und Sendung* 28 (1963), VI, p. 247.

10. Compare S. Schulz, *Komposition und Herkunft der Johanneischen Reden* (Stuttgart: Kohlhammer, 1960), p. 172.

11. *Op.cit.*, pp. 2, 176.

12. *Diwan Haran Gawaitha* (Diwan of the great Revelation), Studi e Testi; Città del Vaticano 1953; 176. Compare C.K. Barrett and C-J Thornton (eds.), *Texte zur Umwelt des Neuen Testaments* (Tübingen: Mohr-Siebeck, 2nd edn, 1991), pp. 145–50; J. Leipoldt and W. Grundmann (eds.), *Umwelt des Urchristentums. I. Darstellung des neutestamentlichen Zeitalters* (Berlin: EVA, 3rd edn, 1971), pp. 396–401.

13. *Alter und Heimat des Mandäismus nach neuerschlossenen Quellen*, Theologische Literaturzeitung, 83 (1957), pp. 401–408.

14. Compare F. Porsch, ἄμπελος, Weinstock, in H. Bolz und G. Schneider (eds.), *Exegetisches Wörterbuch zum Neuen Testament*, I (Stuttgart: Kohlhammer, 1980), col. 172–73.

15. S. Schulz, *op.cit.*, p.182.

16. R. Borig, *op.cit.*, pp. 135–94.

The vine, commonly grown in Palestine,[17] is an image of the people of Israel in the Old Testament. The motif of a vineyard in Isaiah (5; 27.2–6) is of lesser importance for the interpretation of the Johannine pericope; there is just a similar motif of vine.[18] Isaiah always speaks about ὁ ἀμπελών (vineyard) and only once uses ἄμπελος (a single vine) which, however, sometimes can have the same meaning as ἀμπελών (as in Ap. 14.18), whereas the image in Jn 15 is one of a single vine. It is rather St Matthew who mentions the vineyard in 20.1; 21.8.33, as well as St Mark and St Luke in the parallel texts. The Septuagint texts Hos. 10.1; Joel 1.7; Jer. 6.9 and 2.21 speaking about Israel as a vine seem to sufficiently explain St John's image of vine.

The vine, grapes, bearing fruit, and plentiful fruit, are common elements in Hos. 10.1 and Jn 15. Beautifully spread vine is an image of the people of Israel growing in number; the members of the nation are described as grapes.

Joel 1.7 presents Israel being attacked by the enemy (1.6) with use of the image of vine (Israel). The expressions *grapevine* and *cut off* are related to Jn 15.6. The devastated vine and branches that had been cut off the fig tree are images of those who died at war.[19]

The adjective *true* used by Jer. in 2.21 appears in Jn 15. There is also the image of vine and bearing fruit. The adjective ἀληθινή refers to fulfilling God's commandments and acting truthfully.[20] Israel, however, was unfaithful or, to put it figuratively: the vine disappointed the farmer who had planted it.

The negative image of vine punished by burning flames (Jn 15.6), had developed in Ezek. 15. The vine was punished for disloyalty (Ezek. 15.8) and thrown into a fire – both its trunk and the grapes.

In Ps. 80.9–12 it is said that although the vine was not faithful to Yahweh, it will be reborn again because of the Son of Man (18–20). A. Jaubert thinks that there is an allusion in the text to Christ's death and His resurrection, as the Son of Man means the King-Messiah.[21] C.H. Dodd expresses the opinion that the Son of Man is almost identified with the vine[22] at the end of Psalm 80. The Jews in the Old Testament believed that the Messiah – the vine – would restore Israel to the new life. We can see that the image of vine was used as a metaphor either for Israel or for the Messiah. The image of the vine-Messiah may be found also in *2 Bar.* 36.2–11 and 39.2–8.[23]

17. F.H. Wight, *The Customs of Biblical Countries* (Warsaw: Vocatio, 1998), pp. 166–173.

18. A. Jaubert, L'image de la Vigne (Jean), in F. Christ, *OIKONOMIA. Heilsgeschichte als Thema der Theologie* (Hamburg-Bergstedt: Reich, 1967), p. 93.

19. The Italian Ecumenical Bible (Torino: Bibbia TOB, 2nd edn,1995, 1111), gives Is 5.1 as an example of a parallel to Nah. 2.2, and in the footnote it is explained that the vine and the fig tree are symbols of peace and happiness, compare l Kgs 5.5; Mic. 4.4; Zech. 3.10. Their destruction is a sign of the forthcoming catastrophe.

20. A. Jaubert, *op.cit.* p.93.

21. *Op.cit.*, p. 94.

22. C.H. Dodd, *The Interpretation of the Fourth Gospel* (Cambridge: University Press, 1963), p. 411.

23. The text (in German) and explanations (pp. 1266–1339), in: *Altjüdisches Schrifttum außerhalb der Bibel* (übersetzt und erläutert von Paul Riessler; Augsburg: Filser, 1928), pp. 40–54 (Greek, chs. 1–17); pp. 55–113, (Syrian, chs. 1–87); pp. 75–78. Rubinkiewicz, *op. cit.*, pp. 419–20.

The Old Testament has offered some fundamental motives with regards to the vine in St John's pericope. The most significant of them refer to the chosen vine, looked after and protected by God (parallel to God the Father in Jn 15.1); to the true vine that will bear fruit; to the fire punishment for infertile branches of the vine, to the role of the Son of Man who will return life to the grapes in Messiah times. The image of sap (the *evergreen cypress* and its fruit of *Ephraim*) that brings Israel to life is also present in Hos.14.9. Israel is called 'tree' and 'holy seed' in Isa. 6.13. The concept of a *holy sap*[24] that cannot vanish because of its origin in God[25] was developed in the times of early Judaism. The Law (Covenant?), the Word and Wisdom[26] are the sap, the element that restores life to the vine (Israel).

So is the Johannine pericope about the vine widely based on the elements from the Old Testament. The concept of vine is explicit in vv. 1, 4 and 5, whereas in the vv. 2, 4, 6 it is rather the concept of grapes and in the vv. 2, 4, 8, 16 the concept of bearing fruit.

In the vv. 1, 4 and 5 the definite article is used before the noun ἄμπελος. Whenever St John or Jesus speak about truth, light or life and there is a definite article before these nouns, a perfection is emphasized. Thus St John underlines the fact that Jesus is *the* Truth, *the* Light and *the* Life, hence any other truth, light and life lose significance and are not worthy to be called *the* truth, *the* light and *the* life.[27]

Similarly, the use of the article (ἡ) before the word ἄμπελος implies that the vine is exceptional and perfect and all other vines are not worthy of the name. Hence the word ἡ ἄμπελος indicates the god-like, divine reality. The qualifier ἡ ἀληθινή, added to the subject and preceded by the article, indicates that here the features of the grapevine are embodied perfectly. The phrase τὸ φῶς τὸ ἀληθινόν in the prologue (Jn 1.9) and in St John's First Letter (2.8) is similar to the term ἡ ἄμπελος ἡ ἀληθινή. Also the tabernacle of the Old Testament was only a figure and a type in comparison to the New Testament tabernacle, qualified by the same ἡ ἀληθινή[28] at two occasions in the Letter to Hebrews. The vine with its grapes called true, stands for Christ and His worshippers, for which Yahweh's vine (i.e. the chosen nation) in the Old Testament was the type.

The Father is compared to a farmer and not to a vinedresser (ἀμπελουργός), but that is rather accidental, because in other parts of the New Testament the

24. There are but a few phrases in the New Testament mentioning juice; liquid (τὸ γλεῦκος, ου) is used for defining young vine and it is a *hapax legomenon*. In Mk 13.28 there is the adjective ἁπαλός added to κλάδος (succulent branch), referring to the fig tree, refreshing juice is mentioned in Rom. 11.17. This juice was made of olive tree roots (ἡ πιότης = greasiness and nutrition with reference to plants, also a *hapax legomenon* in New Testament). Mk 14.25ff. suggests that juice or wine made of vine (τὸ γένημα, fruit) was offered by Jesus at the Last Supper. A presence of juice and its circulation in the vine and the grapes is assumed in Jn 15.1–11.

25. A. Jaubert, *op.cit.*, p. 94.

26. A. Jaubert, *op.cit.*, p. 95.

27. M. Zerwick, *Graecitas Biblica* (Rome: Pontificio Instituto Biblico, 4th edn, 1960), p. 55.

28. F. Zorell, *Lexicon Graecum Novi Testamenti* (Rome: Pontificio Instituto Biblico, 3rd edn, 1961), col. 64. Compare Heb. 8.2; 9.24.

word vinedresser is used, e.g. the parable of the infertile fig-tree (Lk. 13.7), and γεωργός can also mean vinedresser (Mk 12.1-2).

Philo in *De plantatione* I[29] makes a distinction between the farmer and the vinedresser. The concept of God the farmer was known in ancient times and it can be found in miracle plays (mystery religions?),[30] in magic Greek papyri[31], in Philo[32], in the New Testament Apocrypha[33] and the writings of Ignatius of Antioch[34]. Jesus used this concept that was common in his time, to express His (the vine) attitude to Father the Farmer (cultivating the vine). The use of the article (ὁ) before the word γεωργός underlines the full sense of the meaning of the word 'vinedresser' (farmer), i.e. Yahweh Himself.

In vv. 15.1 and 15.5, the formula ἐγώ εἰμι,[35] a characteristic introduction of a divine revelation, indicates that Christ is the one who has been long awaited[36]. From the grammatical point if view, the pronoun ἐγώ has the function of predicate, εἰμι is a joining verb and ἡ ἄμπελος is subject. The context indicates that the pronoun is strongly stressed because in that sentence Christ (the vine) is contrasted to Israel (the vineyard) from the Old Testament. The literal translation of the phrase would be: 'I am the one who is the true vine' – the pronoun is

29. Sometimes, both words γεωργός and ἀμπελουργός can be translated as 'vinedresser', e.g. Jn 15.1 and Lk. 13.7 in *The Bible – The Scriptures of the Old and New Testament and the Apocrypha. New translation from Hebrew and Greek* (Warsaw: The British and Foreign Bible Society, 1990 [18th edition with the apocrypha i.e. the deutero-canonical books in the Roman Catholic Bible for the first time]), pp. 1370, 1328. Some dictionaries have a *vine-grower* instead of vinedresser (Z. Abramowiczówna, *The Greek-Polish Dictionary*, vol. I [Warsaw: PWN, 1958]), p. 114; R. Popowski SDB, *The Greek-Polish Dictionary of the New Testament* (KUL; Warsaw: Vocatio, 1997, p. 20: 'vine gardener, gardener') – it seems to sound quite artificial and the expression 'vinedresser' is more appropriate. *The Polish Dictionary*, vol. III (Warsaw: PWN, 1983), does not have such entry. Jakub Wujek gives 'ploughman' for γεωργός in Jn 15.1 (*The New Testament* [trans. Jakub Wujek; introduction by Władyslaw Smereka; Cracow: The Polish Theological Association, 1966], p. 366: Lk. 13.7: ἀμπελουργός – 'wine-maker', p. 250; *The Bible* [trans. Jakub Wujek, 1599]; 'B' type transcription of the original text from the 16th century and introductions by Janusz Frankowski [Warsaw: Vocatio, 1999], has in Lk. 13.7 – 'vineyard manager', p. 2078).

30. W. Scott, *Hermetica* 9,6; 14,10; compare Barrett/Thornton, *op.cit*, pp. 123–34.

31. K. Preisendanz (ed.), *Papyri Graecae Magicae* (Die Griechischen Zauberpapyri; Stuttgart: Teubner, 1973), I, p. 26; compare Barrett/Thornton, *op.cit.*, pp. 33–43.

32. Philo, *De plantatione* 1,39; 2,73.94; *De confusione linguarum* 61, 1966.

33. *Acta Thomae* 10, p. 114,13; *Acta Philippi* 119, p. 84,12; E. Hennecke, *Neutestamentliche Apokryphen in deutscher Übersetzung* (ed. W. Schneemelcher; Tübingen: Mohr-Siebeck, 3rd edn, 1964), II, pp. 312–13.

34. Ignatius of Antioch, *The Letter to Trallians* 11,1; 6,1; *The Letter to Phildelphians* 3,1; *The Letter to Ephesians* 10,3; *The First Witnesses*, in The Selection of the Oldest Christian Scriptures (Cracow: Znak, 1988), pp. 154, 152–53; p. 164; pp. 137–38.

35. The formula ἐγώ εἰμι has been discussed in many books and articles. It can be found in St John's writings: 6.35.41.51; 8.12; 10.7.9.11.14 and in 15.1.5. Compare F. Gryglewicz *I am* in St John's Gospel, in: *KUL – Some additional materials for lectures on the Bible*, II. (Collective work edited by S. Łach, M. Filipiak, H. Langkammer; Lublin: RW KUL, 1977), pp. 219, 231.

36. R. Bultmann, *op.cit.*, pp. 167–68, 406. This type of formula for expressing the revelation has been called by him the formula of authentication, confession (Rekognitionsformel).

stressed and there is a contrast in the sentence.[37] The close relationship between Christ-Messiah and his people is the one of a trunk with its branches (τὰ κλήματα, 15.2.4.5.6; only here in the New Testament); they are animated by the sap from the trunk; the Father-farmer takes care of them and even punishes them in order to purify them – all this indicates immanence in Christ-the vine.

So there are references to God the Father in the pericope (15.1: the father/the farmer) and to the Son (15.1: the vine, my father). Acting of the Holy Spirit is assumed by the fact that fruit is born (καρπὸν φέρειν – appears eight times in Jn 15.1–16). In the preceding (14.16.26) and following (15.26; 16.7) context Paraclete's activity (ὁ παράκλητος) is mentioned – and that is a name of the Holy Spirit.[38] The love of Jesus to his disciples that continues the love of the Father to Him in 15.9 also seems to be allusion to the Spirit; the construction is similar to that in 15.1: ἡ ἀγάπη ἡ ἐμή. The love that is so determined must surely be referring to the Holy Spirit.[39] These issues, however, require a separate analysis and reflection, taking into consideration the history of exegesis of the vine in Jn 15.1–11. To the further investigation should also be left the question, whether Jn 15.1–16 has ever been or perhaps could nowadays be interpreted under the aspect of the Trinity.[40] So far, it remains open.[41]

37. Compare H. Van den Bussche, *Le discours d'adieu de Jésus* (Tournai: Casterman, 1959), p. 12.

38. Compare Augustyn Jankowski, O.S.B., *The Holy Spirit in the New Testament* (The Outlines of New Testament Pneumatology; Tyniec-Kraków: Wydawnictwo Benedyktynów, 3rd expanded edn, 1998), pp. 55–67. Out of Jn 15.1-16 only verse 15 is mentioned (p. 601).

39. Compare J.-M. Lagrange O.P., *Évangele selon Saint Jean* (Paris: Gabalda, 1925), pp. 401–409. He explains in the comments to 15.9: What was the man's existence in Jesus? It was (and still is) the existence in His love, His love to the disciples, in the same way as the Father loves Him. Since then, Father's love to His Son has always been expressed in the present tense (3.35; 5.20; 10.17); it will be also expressed in the aorist (17.24.26). The verse does not have the meaning of love of the Father to the Son, when He brings Him to life in eternity – since it is the matter of the Son's obedience – but just the love of the Father: *ad hoc scilicent ut simul esset Deus et homo* (St Thomas Aquinas: Thom. 2^0; *S. Thomae Aquinatis expositio in evangelium Johannis* [Paris: Vives, 1876]). Jesus loved his disciples in the same way before He had chosen them. They ought to be in that love which is His, not their love, as it is more clearly expressed in the next verse. The concept of the first love gives a better understanding of *to be* in the love (1 Jn 4.10ff.).

40. R. Borig sees a relationship between the Holy Spirit (πνεῦμα) in Jn 15 and the immanence (μένειν), *op.cit.*, pp. 223–25. *Lexicon Biblicum*, III (published by M. Hagen S.I., Parisiis, 1911), col. 1221–23 (Trinitas) where only 5.17ff.; 10.28ff.; 14.23 etc; 14.17,26; 3.5 were quoted from St John. However, what did he mean by etc?

41. W. Breuning, 'Trinität' in *Lexikon der katholischen Dogmatik* (Freiburg im Breisgau: W. Beinert, 2nd edn, 1988), pp. 517–19: Jesus Christ's worshippers have been included into the relation of God's inner life by adoration of Jesus for His resurrection. This happens because of the Holy Spirit's activity as the bond of love between the Father and the Son, and comes to its full form (Jn 7.37–39; 14.1–16.15). Jn 15.1–16 is also included in the above mentioned work.

INCARNATUS EST?
CHRIST AND COMMUNITY IN THE JOHANNINE FAREWELL DISCOURSE

Kari Syreeni

'I am going to speak about something that I basically do not understand', conceded Ernst Käsemann in introducing his 1966 Yale lectures on Jesus' last will according to John 17.[1] As one committed to the hermeneutical quest, I partly make that confession my own. Hermeneutics is the human attempt to understand something one ultimately cannot fully understand. The hermeneutical *law* of being dictates that one cannot understand the other as one does oneself. At the same time, the possibility of understanding, if only otherwise, is given with the communality of life, customarily called 'a life-relation to the subject matter'.

The subject matter of this essay is the problem of incarnation in the Johannine farewell discourse, as it appears from the relationship between Jesus and the community of believers.[2] Käsemann's provocative thesis was that John presents a naive docetism rather than a theology of incarnation. Of the many responses to Käsemann, Pokorný's 1984 article on the earthly Jesus in John is among the most persuasive counter-positions.[3] Pokorný is in good company in defending the incarnatory interpretation. Käsemann knew well that this understanding was not only widespread but pregnantly formulated by Rudolf Bultmann in his New Testament theology.[4] After the decades since the original debate, one is obviously

1. Ernst Käsemann, *Jesu letzter Wille nach Johannes 17* (Tübingen: J.C.B. Mohr [Paul Siebeck], 1966), p. 9.

2. In theological vocabulary, this perspective on incarnation addresses the Johannine conception of *Christus pro nobis* and *in nobis*. Hermeneutically, the issue is the *significance* of Jesus.

3. Petr Pokorný, 'Der irdische Jesus im Johannesevangelium', *NTS* 30 (1984), pp. 217–28, repr. in Petr Pokorný and Josef B. Souček, *Bibelauslegung als Theologie* (WUNT, 100; Tübingen: Mohr Siebeck, 1997), pp. 327–39. (The page numbers below refer to the original publication.) For an early critical response (observed by Käsemann in the third edition of his book), see Günther Bornkamm, 'Zur Interpretation des Johannes-Evangeliums: Eine Auseinandersetzung mit Ernst Käsemanns Schrift 'Jesu letzter Wille nach Johannes 17', in *idem*, *Geschichte und Glaube* I (Gesammelte Aufsätze III; München: Chr. Kaiser Verlag, 1968), pp. 104–21. For a good mainstream defence of the 'humanity' of the Johannine Jesus, see Marianne Meye Thompson, *The Incarnate Word: Perspectives on Jesus in the Fourth Gospel* (Peabody, MA: Hendrickson, 1988).

4. Rudolf Bultmann, *Theologie des Neuen Testaments*, 9. Aufl. (Tübingen: J.C.B. Mohr [Paul Siebeck], 1984), p. 392: 'Das Thema des ganzen Johannes-Evangeliums ist der Satz: ὁ λόγος σὰρξ ἐγένετο'.

expected to go beyond old positions from a specific angle,[5] but I doubt that we can do so by pushing the whole issue out of the biblical battlefield[6] or by replacing one theological label (incarnation theology) with another (theology of the cross).[7] Rather we should delve deeper into the *hermeneutical* depth of the multiple Johannine layers of textualized life.[8]

1. *The Glory of Jesus: Tracing the Origins and Development of Johannine Christology in Jn 1–12*

Käsemann addressed the problem of incarnation in the framework of Jn 17 in order to confirm his interpretation of the prologue.[9] Käsemann observed that Jn 13–17 is patterned after a 'testament', but it is crucial for his interpretation that John's application of this literary model is a deliberate *contradictio in adiecto*.[10] If the dominant idea is not the Word's becoming flesh, but the earthly manifestation of Christ's everlasting glory, then his suffering and death are in some sense only apparent. The farewell speech is not really a testament, but the abiding will of one who is just going home. I agree that the literary form of the testament is indeed noteworthy, but of course, *all* the canonical (and most extra-canonical) Gospels hold that the earthly Jesus now lives with God. Mk 13, which Käsemann mentions as the closest parallel in the Gospels, has Jesus say, 'Heaven and earth will pass away, but my words will not pass away' (Mk 13.31). That Jesus did not depart like the patriarchs and that his words have everlasting significance are not ideas unique to the fourth Gospel. What Käsemann is heading for

5. James Dunn, 'Let John be John – A Gospel for Its Time', in Peter Stuhlmacher (ed.), *Das Evangelium und die Evangelien* (FS Otto Betz; WUNT, 28; Tübingen: J.C.B. Mohr [Paul Siebeck], 1983), pp. 309–39; p. 313, reminds us that continuing the Bultmann-Käsemann debate risks 'asking the right questions, but against too broad a background'.

6. Jürgen Becker, 'Ich bin die Auferstehung und das Leben: Eine Skizze der johanneischen Theologie', *ThZ* 39 (1983), pp. 138–51; p. 139, suggests that the controversy is *theologiegeschichtlich* rather than exegetical. He immediately adds a number of *exegetical* (literary-critical) arguments to the effect that 1.14 does not represent the main christological schema in John. The ease with which Becker rejects the notion of incarnation as an interpretative key (p. 140: 'Das ist rundweg zu verneinen. Diese Verneinung ist zudem gar nicht schwer zu begründen…') indicates that he does not attend to the *hermeneutical* problem.

7. A suggestive case for a Johannine *Kreuzestheologie* is Herbert Kohler, *Kreuz und Menschwerdung im Johannesevangelium* (*AThANT*,72, Zürich: Theologischer Verlag, 1987).

8. Since the tradition-historical and literary layers are still visible in the final text, a proper synchronic analysis can also illuminate the hermeneutical quest. Konrad Haldimann, *Rekonstruktion und Entfaltung: Exegetische Untersuchungen zu Joh 15 und 16* (BZNW, 104; Berlin/New York: De Gruyter, 2000), pp. 412–30, offers a perceptive discussion of incarnation in his linguistic study of the second farewell speech.

9. See Käsemann, 'Aufbau und Anliegen des johanneischen Prologs', in *Libertas Christiana* (FS F. Delekat; *BEvTh* 26; München: Chr. Kaiser, 1957), pp. 75–99; reprinted in *Exegetische Versuche und Besinnungen II* (Göttingen: Vandenhoeck & Ruprecht, 1965), pp. 155–80.

10. Käsemann, *Jesu letzter Wille*, p. 15: 'Ein Testament im Munde des Lebenfürsten ist aber zweifellos höchst sonderbar, und man kann sich nicht vorstellen, dass der Evangelist darüber nicht reflektiert haben sollte'.

is, firstly, that in comparison with the Synoptics a far more advanced but very different *christological schema* dominates John's Gospel, and secondly, that behind this schema there is a notably different experience (or lack of it) about the Christ-event, which distinguishes the language of the fourth Gospel as *dogmatic* rather than kerygmatic.[11]

As to its christology, John is no doubt special. The pre-existence of the divine pervades the whole Gospel, surfacing, e.g., in 8.58: 'Before Abraham was, I am'. Neither Matthew nor Luke comes close to Johannine high christology, despite the fact that both evangelists describe the virginal birth of Jesus *and* (!) offer a genealogy to prove his Davidic descent. The Johannine authors may be aware of these innovations,[12] but they did not need their assistance in order to shape a very distinctive christology. Käsemann discerned in John a traditional 'sending' christology with the idea of the Son's obedience to his Father,[13] and he noted that the idea of Christ's pre-existence is not unique to John. In spite of these common traits, the Johannine concept differs remarkably from the kenosis-exaltation schema of Phil. 2.6–11. Jesus' earthly life did not empty, but manifested his glory; exaltation is not the result of Jesus' obedience.[14] Käsemann could easily give examples of the divine posture of the earthly Jesus in John. Certainly the question can be posed in what sense he who walks on the sea and through closed doors, feels no physical thirst or hunger at the well in Samaria, and so on, can be human 'flesh'.[15] However, while such traits illustrate the glory of Jesus (1.14c–e), this is not sufficient proof that the fourth Gospel is *not* trying to tackle the problem of Jesus' becoming a human being (1.14a). The intimate *juxtaposition* of these two aspects in the prologue should warn us against premature conclusions. While the

11. The second assumption surfaces, e.g., on p. 47: 'Mit dem christologischen Geheimnis verbindet sich, was spätere Zeiten das innertrinitarische Geheimnis nennen wird. Ist das jedoch richtig, hat die im 4. Evangelium angewandte Mythologie nicht mehr nur wie sonst im Neuen Testament die Aufgabe, die heilsgeschichtliche und weltweite Dimension des christologischen Ereignisses zu *proklamieren*. Sie ist dann zugleich Ausdruck der beginnenden *dogmatischen* Reflexion im strengen Sinne des Wortes und eröffnet der altkirchlichen Christologie den Weg' (my italics). Cf. also p. 91 ('dogmatics in the guise of a Gospel').

12. Pokorný, 'Der irdische Jesus', p. 223.

13. Recent research tends to regard the notion of the divine messenger as *the* Johannine christological pattern. To some extent this is justified, but Becker's reasoning ('Ich Bin', *passim*) is difficult to follow at some points. If incarnation was considered a Hellenistic commonplace at the time of John's Gospel, how did it become the main christological dividing line in 1 Jn 4.1–3? If the culturally obvious and transparent idea of God's obedient messenger exhausts Johannine high christology, one might imagine Jesus either as a prophet or an apostle, but hardly as one accused of blasphemy (Jn 10.33). In practice, though, Becker's description of the dualistic 'sending' christology matches Käsemann's interpretation of the divine Word's temporary visit on earth. Käsemann, too, realized that John's christology does not conform to a *theios aner* imagery, and that the sending and return of the Son is a vital part of the christological-soteriological schema.

14. Käsemann, *Jesu letzter Wille*, p. 25.

15. Käsemann, *Jesu letzter Wille*, pp. 22–23. But Jesus walks on the sea already in Mark, and goes through closed doors in John only after the resurrection. The difference between John and the synoptics is not *quite* as vast as the caricature suggests.

translation of 1.14a as the Word's being '*made* flesh' (vg: *factum est*) is an over-interpretation, it is not clear that the Johannine authors thought of the 'becoming' merely as a contingent manifestation or epiphany.[16]

Käsemann's second point is basically a question of the Johannine writers' 'life-relation to the subject matter'. Käsemann seems to deny the existential authenticity of John: language and experienced reality have fallen apart.[17] Here Käsemann and Pokorný disagree most fundamentally. For Pokorný, the fourth Gospel is still an authentic expression of Christian faith-experience and is thus communicable with other contemporary articulations of faith.[18] This is a vital hermeneutical problem, but also one that is difficult to approach exegetically, since we cannot ascertain the tradition-historical and social lineage from the earliest Jesus movement to the Gospel of John. It is a plausible working hypothesis, however, that the origins of the specifically Johannine strand of tradition – often considered the contribution of 'the evangelist' – are to be sought in Hellenistic Jewish Christian milieu. Of special interest is Käsemann's reference to the 'enthusiastic' experience that the believers' resurrection is a present reality. This pneumatic strand was familiar to Paul, who refashioned it in a more futuric direction in Rom. 6 and confronted it in 1 Cor. 15. It probably originated in a baptismal setting, as reflected in Col. 2.12–13 and Eph. 2.5–6, but was eventually banned as heresy in 2 Tim. 2.18. In John, Käsemann argues, the ritual background is removed and the tradition is placed in the service of christology.[19]

Käsemann's tradition-historical hypothesis is still worth considering. There is, I think, enough to suggest a connection between Johannine theology and Pauline left-wing enthusiasm. Besides the presentic understanding of resurrection, there is the peculiar theology of glory in 2 Cor. 3. Here, in v. 12, Paul seems to re-accentuate, in terms of hope, a tradition which compares the different grades or degrees of the glory of Moses and Christ. Here also, two dispensations are outlined in a way not far from Jn 1.17. Furthermore, 2 Cor. 3 describes the glory of Christ as permanent (v. 11), and as one that 'we' behold face to face (v. 18).[20] Paul's

16. Käsemann, *Jesu letzter Wille*, p. 41, speaks of incarnation and death as a 'Wechsel des Raums' which did not change anything in Christ's 'nature'. The notion of *Ortswechsel* is the main object of Kohler's (*Kreuz und Menschwerdung*) critique. Against it, he postulates an interpretation in terms of a theology of the cross: the flesh of Jesus, more particularly, the crucified body of Jesus, is the 'place' where God and man are united.

17. Cf. Käsemann's remark on 'die eherne Kälte des angeblichen Apostels der Liebe' (*Jesu letzter Wille*, p. 113).

18. Pokorný, 'Der irdische Jesus', pp. 224–25: 'Die johanneische Christologie, die die ganze Wirklichkeit realistisch und zugleich total im Lichte Gottes sieht, ist ein wirklich elementarer Ausdruck christlicher Glaubenserfahrung und ihre tiefe Reflexion, die mit den anderen, z.T. sogar älteren neutestamentlichen Reflexionen über den Glauben in einer gewissen Spannung zwar steht, aber in ihrer Tiefe und Authentizität der Grundeinstellung fähig ist, mit ihnen zu kommunizieren'.

19. Käsemann, *Jesu letzter Wille*, pp. 32–33, 48–49. I am inclined to accept the main lines of Käsemann's tradition-historical thesis but would not assume that the Johannine development involves a breakdown (and a late revival) of the ritual connection. The possible addition in Jn 6.51c–58 hardly introduces a radically new thought or practice.

20. Further points of contact between early Pauline and Johannine enthusiastic traditions include the stress laid on *the Spirit* and *freedom* (2 Cor. 3.17 etc., cf. Jn 8.36), Jesus as the *Son sent by God*

emphasis on the believers' spiritual 'sonship' (e.g., Rom. 8.14–17) and its radically otherworldly nature (e.g., 1 Cor. 2.10–12) also parallel Jn 1.13–14. The prologue may show an affinity with the deutero-Pauline ecclesiological accent of the Christ-event: the community has received 'grace', i.e. spiritual gifts, from the 'fullness' of the Word (1.16; cf. Col. 1.19, Eph. 4.7).[21] However, while Jn 1.14–18 breathes the presence of a community of believers, no advanced ecclesiology or church structure seems suggested.

Once we recognize the ultra-Pauline component in the Johannine concept of glory, it is hard to regard the prologue as a late invention. Rather it points to the *origins* of John's high christology.[22] The general outlook of the prologue is on par with an enthusiastic Pauline type of spirituality centred on Christ's resurrectional, ever-present glory. The soteriological tie between Christ and the believers is found in a pneumatic unity through becoming God's children and taking part in his fullness. Such spirituality need not be too concerned with Jesus' physical absence. If the divine realm (the kingdom of God, 3.3) is a pneumatic entity, and if both Jesus and the believers are 'from above', it is basically irrelevant where Jesus goes: 'The wind blows where it wills, and you hear the sound of it, but you do not know whence it comes and whither it goes (ποῦ ὑπάγει, 3.8)'.

The 'pneumatic' stratum can be detected throughout in the revelatory speeches that accompany Jesus' signs, and it seems to have informed the composition of Jn 1–12 in a decisive way. In fact, everything promised in the prologue finds a symbolic fulfilment here.[23] At Cana, the new era of fullness and abundance that

and the believers' *sonship* (or adoption, υἱοθεσία) through the Spirit (at baptism), eschatological *joy* and brotherly *love*, and, socially, the relatively prominent role of women. Other, in part overlapping traditions seem to come from the Baptist movement, the early Hellenistic Jewish mission (the 'Hellenists' in Acts 6–8) and Samaria (Jn 4; 8.48). Cf. Raymond E. Brown, *The Community of the Beloved Disciple: The Life, Loves, and Hates of an Individual Church in New Testament Times* (London: Geoffrey Chapman, 1979), pp. 36–58. Michael Goulder, 'The Two Roots of the Christian Myth', in John Hick (ed.), *The Myth of God Incarnated* (London: SCM Press, 1977), pp. 64–86, stretches the evidence in speaking of 'the Samaritan gnostic myth' (p. 65) as the root of Johannine christology.

21. Already Paul applied the 'charismatic' tradition to legitimate his apostleship, cf. Rom. 1.5 (δι' οὗ ἐλάβομεν χάριν καὶ ἀποστολὴν κτλ.).

22. A rather different procedure is argued by Michael Theobald, *Die Fleischwerdung des Logos: Studien zum Verhältnis des Johannesprologs zum Corpus des Evangeliums und zu 1 Joh* (*NTA NF* 20; Münster: Aschendorff, 1988). Theobald regards the prologue (and the whole of John 1) as a late preface to the Gospel with a polemical (anti-docetic) purpose. I find this literary *Sichtung* unconvincing, but it is interesting that Theobald, while trying to show that Jn 2–12 does not presuppose the prologue, nevertheless assumes that the final summary in 12.44–50, by the latest redactor, does. As for tradition-history, I find it improbable that a piece from the contemporary adversaries' reservoir has been reworked in the prologue. Instead, the prologue's Logos christology may have nurtured gnosticizing interpretations in the community, so that Jesus' baptism was interpreted in analogy with the believers' pneumatic partaking of divinity (divine sonship through baptism, ecstatic visions, etc.). The Johannine main christology developed along other lines (the *sending* of the Son/Word, the *unity* of Father and Son, the *glorified* Son of Man) and avoided speculations about Jesus' divine adoption or insemination.

23. The *symbolic* nature of many Johannine scenes is well known. The post-Easter *perspective* and the *transparency* of some features of the story *vis-à-vis* the community's contemporary

supersedes the Mosaic worship of God is inaugurated. Jesus shows his glory to his disciples who believe in him (2.11; cf. 1.14c). A new spiritual temple is then foreshadowed (2.13–21; 4.19–21), and further signs and relevatory speeches are given to highlight Jesus as the goal and end of all Jewish (temple-related and calendaric) rituals (chs. 5–10). The account of Jesus' superior glory reaches its climax in the raising of Lazarus and is crystallized in Jesus' answer to Mary (11.25–26): 'I am the resurrection and the life'. Toward the close of chapter 12, the narrative tide turns back to themes presented in the prologue. The *light* was disappearing (12.35–36). Jesus had come *to his own people*, who *rejected* him, as Isaiah foretold (12.37–40) having seen his *glory* (12.41). A later hand has added Jesus' final cry (13.44–50) to summarize the gospel of glory.[24] The Markan transfiguration narrative (Mk 9.2–9) would have been misleading in Jn 1–12, where the *whole* of Jesus' ministry manifests his glory that 'dwelled among us'.

At an early stage, the *manner* of Jesus' 'going away' from the sight of the unbelievers seems unspecified. There are traces of ascent imagery in John, not least in chapter 17, and the earliest resurrection appearance tradition in John depicts Jesus on the way back to his father (ἀναβαίνω, 20.17). However, in the present form of Jn 1–12 this 'high' christology has undergone further development, in part due to acquaintance with and reflections on a synoptic type of passion narrative. Thus, the glory of Jesus is described as his *glorification* and the crucifixion as the *lifting up* of *the Son of Man*.[25] His crucial *hour*, which was in the passion tradition a dreadful sign of abandonment and betrayal (cf. Mk 14.41), became in Johannine reinterpretation the moment of the Son's glorification.[26] But

situation are also obvious. Yet neither the Gospel as a whole nor chs. 1–12 can be interpreted in a straightforward manner as a 'two-level drama' (thus J. Louis Martyn, *History & Theology in the Fourth Gospel*, 2 [Nashville: Abingdon Press, revised and enlarged edn, 1979), and still less can it be assumed that the author was 'analytically conscious' of this design (thus John Ashton, *Understanding the Fourth Gospel* [Oxford: Clarendon Press, 1991], p. 419). See Adele Reinhartz, *Befriending the Beloved Disciple: A Jewish Reading of the Gospel of John* (New York-London: Continuum, 2001), pp. 48–53.

24. 12.44–50 is often described as a 'compendium' of Jn 1–12. Martinus C. de Boer (*Johannine Perspectives on the Death of Jesus* [Kampen: Pharos, 1996], p. 119) notes that there is no mention of Jesus' death here or in an earlier summary in 3.31–36. His conclusion (*ibidem*) is that 'at one level of the Gospel's thought it is not immediately evident how, or even if, this death is relevant or necessary to Jesus' identity as the life-giving envoy from above'. Theobald (*Die Fleischwerdung des Logos*, p. 329 n.151) observes the personified use of λόγος in 12.48, which connects the résumé to the prologue, but also distinguishes Jesus from his Logos. This, I think, might indicate a modification of the Logos christology. Further steps are taken when the word(s) of Jesus are accentuated as his (new) commandment(s) in 13.34 and 14.15 (cf. 1 Jn).

25. The witty 'lifting up' imagery stresses that precisely crucifixion (rather than stoning) was the proper mode of death for the Messiah, or actually (cf. 12.34), for the descending-ascending Son (of Man). All the Son of Man sayings seem later additions. See de Boer (*Johannine Perspectives*, pp. 102–105; 147ff.), who also shows how the Son of Man sayings proceed from those describing ascent (1.51; 3.13; 6.62) through those that speak of lifting up (3.14–15; 8.28; 12.34) to the final statements of the glorification of the Son of Man (12.23; 13.31), so that 'there is a spiral-like progression' (p. 158).

26. Cf. the secondary references to the 'hour' that is 'not yet' (2.1; 7.6.8.30; 8.20).

the life-giver's *death* implied that the relationship between the pneumatically ever-present Christ and his community had to be refashioned. This painstaking literary and theological process resulted in the farewell section Jn 13–17.

2. *Death as the Glorification of Jesus: Tracing the Ideation of Jn 13–17*

Käsemann's choice of Jn 17 as a second proof-text was clear-sighted, as several traits in the farewell prayer might lend themselves to a docetic or gnostic interpretation. Here the sovereign but obedient Son is presented before his passion but no longer in the world (οὐκέτι εἰμὶ ἐν τῷ κόσμῳ, v. 11a; but cf. v. 11c and 13). His mission in the world appears completed (τὸ ἔργον τελειώσας, v. 4). It would seem (were it not for vv. 24–26) that his own have already received his δόξα (v. 22). There is an unmistakable deterministic bent in the prayer: Jesus' own were from the beginning in God's hand (v. 6) and were fully protected by Jesus, except for the evil one whom the scripture determined to betray him (v. 12).

However, as suggested above, the notion of *glorification* (17.1) points to a novel interpretation of Jesus' glory. To be sure, 17.24 refers back to 1.14c, but the δόξα of Jesus is no longer his earthly appearance but his 'protological' glory that those who are his own *will* see in the future. To be able to appreciate this new theological reflection, we need to interpret Jn 17 in its present form and context.[27] Jn 13–17, as we have it, is a purposefully designed unit, and its themes are, in spite of much editorial effort, remarkably different from those of chs 1–12. 'The disciple whom Jesus loved' is first introduced in 13.23.[28] The Paraclete appears for the first time in 14.15–17. The concept of (*eternal*) *life*, which was prominent in parts of Jn 1–12, is not used in the farewell discourse apart from the framing elements at 14.6 and 17.2.3.[29] The overloaded and repetitive verses 13.1–4 mark a clear hiatus in the Gospel.

27. The final prayer may have undergone more reworking than is usually thought before becoming the present John 17. By way of example, see Sara C. Winter, 'Little Flags: The Scope and Reconstruction of the Signs Gospel', in Robert T. Fortna and Tom Thatcher (eds.), *Jesus in Johannine Tradition* (Louisville: WJK, 2001), pp. 219–35 (I doubt, however, the existence of SG).

28. 'The beloved disciple' is hardly suggested in Jn 1.35–37, see Ismo Dunderberg, 'The Beloved Disciple in John: Ideal Figure in Early Christian Controversy', in Ismo Dunderberg, Christopher Tuckett and Kari Syreeni (eds.), *Fair Play: Diversity and Conflicts in Early Christianity, Essays in Honour of Heikki Räisänen* (Leiden/Boston/Cologne: Brill, 2002), pp. 243–69; (243 n.1). Dunderberg shows the ideational proximity of the figure to the various favourite disciples in Gnostic and related texts. I assume that the beloved disciple is a late creation. The peculiar description in 13.23 (ἐν τῷ κόλπῳ τοῦ Ἰησοῦ) is a relecture of 1.18 and reveals the figure's ideological function as a witness of Jesus and a guarantor of the Gospel's trustworthiness. The figure is too late and literary to be a legendary folktale character (as suggested by T. Thatcher). It may refer to an authoritative real person, but he cannot be an eye-witness. The church-political import of the figure is to mark the Johannine community's superiority *vis-à-vis* Petrine authority, a function discharged in ch. 21. There is some functional affinity between the beloved disciple and the Paraclete, insofar as both are means of authorization and legitimation. This affinity also implies some rivalry (Becker, *Johannesevangelium II*, pp. 523, 568), but since the former is a narrative device and the latter only appears in the farewell discourse, there is no real conflict. Instead, it is noteworthy that the beloved disciple has a crucial function as witness in the Johannine *passion story*.

29. Dettwiler, *Die Gegenwart des Erhöhten: Eine exegetische Studie zu den johanneischen*

The farewell scene[30] is introduced in 13.1 as the site of *Jesus' love for his own who are in the world* (ἀγαπήσας τοὺς ἰδίους τοὺς ἐν τῷ κόσμῳ). In comparison with the prologue, where οἱ ἴδιοι (1.11) must refer to Jews, this is a striking reformulation – and at the same time a community-oriented relecture of 3.16 – but coheres well with the farewell prayer, as does also 13.3 (πάντα ἔδωκεν αὐτῷ ὁ πατὴρ εἰς τὰς χεῖρας, cf. 17.2). These framing elements come close to creating the illusion of a post-resurrectional commissioning scene (cf. Mt. 28.16–20), yet unmistakably marking the farewell discourse as part and continuation of the last supper (the supper 13.2, end of speeches and moving to a new place 18.1). The notion of glorification and the solemn third-person style (13.31; 17.1) tie the beginning and end of the farewell discourse formally together,[31] with 13.(33)34–35 and 17.24–27 creating a thematic *inclusio*.[32]

The farewell setting is clearly employed to prefigure the significance of Jesus' death. The introduction to the farewell scene stresses that Jesus' death is indeed the final part of his mission. The seemingly redundant remark in 13.1 εἰς τέλος ἠγάπησεν αὐτούς anticipates and deepens the two ensuing interpretations of the symbolic act of footwashing: only the τέλος (death) of Jesus ensures a μέρος (v. 8) in him and substantiates his ὑπόδειγμα (v. 15) of love. Thus, seen in the context of the whole farewell scene, 17.2–3 gains a fuller meaning than the concluding prayer alone would necessitate. The τέλος is reached at death. Jesus will not simply go home, nor does the eternal life consist merely of knowing God and the one he has sent. Since the glorification of the *Son of Man* (13.31)[33] is the immediate consequence of Judas' betrayal, it refers to Jesus' death.[34]

Abschiedsreden (Joh 13,31–16,33) unter besonderer Berücksichtigung ihres Relecture-Characters, Göttingen (*FRLANT*, 169; Göttingen: Vandenhoeck & Ruprecht, 1995), p. 165 n. 206, emphasizes the word-statistical difference of the occurrences of ζωή in Jn 1–12 and 13–20.

30. My terminology is as follows: Jn 13–17 is the farewell *section*, 13.1–30 introduces the farewell *scene*, 13.31–16.33 is the farewell *discourse*, 13.31–38 is the *introduction* to the farewell discourse, chapter 14 (+ 13.33*) is the *first* farewell speech, chs. 14–15 are the *second* farewell speech, and ch. 17 is the farewell *prayer*. For the terminological diversity, see Christina Hoegen-Rohls, *Der nachösterliche Johannes: Die Abschiedsreden als hermeneutischer Schlüssel zum vierten Evangelium* (WUNT, 2/84; Tübingen: J.C.B. Mohr [Paul Siebeck], 1996), pp. 82–86.

31. Hoegen-Rohls, *Der nachösterliche Johannes*, p. 231.

32. Markku Kotila, *Umstrittener Zeuge: Studien zur Stellung des Gesetzes in der johanneischen Theologiegeschichte* (*AASF Diss*. 48; Helsinki: Suomalainen Tiedeakatemia, 1988), p. 190.

33. The gradual shift in the terminology seems purposeful. Jn 13.31 is the last occurrence of the Son of Man epithet. It served in 3.14–15, 8.28 and 12.34 as a vehicle for expressing Jesus' being 'lifted up' to the cross. In 12.23 and 13.31 the death of Jesus is described as the 'glorification' of the Son of Man. Thus, at 17.1 the 'glorification' of the Son is subtly described as including his death. At the same time, the expressions used in 13.1 mix allusions to 'going home' (μεταβαίνω, πρὸς τὸν πατέρα) and death / crucifixion (ὥρα, εἰς τέλος), so that there is a smoother transition to ch. 17. In addition, μεταβαίνω is not 'ascension' language but rather a term for moving from the world to the divine realm (Jn 5.4; 1 Jn 3.4), and the expression 'to sanctify oneself on behalf of (ὑπέρ)' in 17.19 is suggestive of self-sacrifice.

34. Margaret Pamment, 'The meaning of *doxa* in the Fourth Gospel', *ZNW* 74 (1983), pp. 12–16; p. 14. Pamment's interpretation that δόξα in John is used as a near synonym to 'God's love' is one-sided, however.

These observations do not invalidate the standard literary-critical hypothesis[35] that chs 15–16 and 17 were inserted into an earlier farewell scene, but show that the redaction, where the comprehensive new block of material was added, focused very decidedly on the farewell setting. The great insertion had a double impact, however. On the one hand it made the occasion of Jesus' farewell supper the hermeneutical centre of the emerging new Gospel. On the other hand, this centre assumed such a key role that it exceeded its narrative limits, anticipating the completion of Jesus' mission in the world and reaching forward to the time to follow. The farewell scene became a *mythic* place, a merger of the divine Word's eternal pre-history (17.5) and future role as the community's interlocutor before the Father (14.12–14). From a literary point of view, much of the mythic value was naturally given with the literary form of the farewell speech.

Whence did the idea for this scene come? The Old Testament and intertestamental valedictory addresses provided a flexible literary model[36] with some general *topoi*.[37] Much suggests that settings derived from the synoptic storyline gave additional impulses to Johannine reflection. The last supper was one of the last occasions during the earthly life of Jesus on which a 'testament' could reasonably be delivered, as also the Synoptics recognized. Especially Luke employed this scene for Jesus' final teaching to the disciples (Lk. 22.7–38).[38] Some features in the farewell section may echo the synoptic eschatological discourse, such as the refrain 14.29 (cf. Mk 13.23), the notion of the world's hatred (cf. Mk 13.13) and the strongly reinterpreted theme of Jesus' *parousia*. There are signs that the Gethsemane story, narrated in Mark (14.32–43) with considerable passion and force, gave a further impetus to the ideation of the Johannine farewell discourse. The Johannine authors seem troubled by a Markan kind of Gethsemane tradition. It is not enough that the Gethsemane scene is absent from John; the very name of the place is avoided in 18.1.

Nevertheless, the waves of the exploded Gethsemane narrative are seen in John and go as far back as (11.33 and) 12.27 and forward to 18.11. In the

35. See, e.g., Jürgen Becker, 'Die Abschiedsreden Jesu im Johannesevangelium', *ZNW* 61 (1970), pp. 215–46; pp. 215–18.

36. For the genre of 'literary testament', see Jürgen Becker's excursus in his commentary (*Das Evangelium nach Johannes*, 3. Aufl. [*ÖTK* 4/2], pp. 523–29); Martin Winter, *Das Vermächtnis Jesu und die Abschiedsworte der Väter: Gattungsgeschichtliche Untersuchung der Vermächtnisrede im Blick auf Joh. 13–17* (*FRLANT* 161; Göttingen: Vandenhoeck & Ruprecht, 1994), pp. 45–213. Dettwiler, *Die Gegenwart des Erhöhten*, pp. 20–27, compares John 13–17 with the Gnostic dialogical Gospels, noting that the import of the comparison is mainly phenomenological and perhaps *wirkungsgeschichtlich*.

37. The vocative τεκνία 13.33, coming from the oldest stratum of the first discourse, is a typical feature in valedictory speeches, characterizing the addressees as 'children' of the departing patriarch or divine wisdom. This is in some tension with the final form of the Johannine discourse but resonates well with the 'orphans' in 14.18. The farewell pattern therefore seems to have been employed from early on in the development of 14–17. However, the generic features do not as such *explain* the details of Jn 13–17; e.g., the successor topos is not a sufficient explanation for the fact that the beloved disciple is not introduced before Jn 13 (contra Winter, *Das Vermächtnis Jesu*, p. 306).

38. For Lk. 22.7–38 and Jn 13–17 as 'testaments', see Klaus Berger, *Formgeschichte des Neuen Testaments*, Heidelberg: Quelle & Meyer, 1984, pp. 78–80.

farewell section, not only is there the disturbing remark ἐγείρεσθε, ἄγωμεν ἐντεῦθεν (14.31), but even the formulations in 14.1 and 14.27 echo (while reversing) the Gethsemane theme,[39] which therefore must be considered part of the ideational background for the first farewell speech. It is not excluded either that the original idea for Jn 17 was to provide a proper prayer of Jesus to his Father (instead of the Markan petitions).[40] If so, the concluding prayer need not be regarded tradition-historically as later than the rest of the farewell discourse. There are hints that the end of the second farewell speech in ch. 16 develops themes from Jn 13 and the first speech (as is often recognized) and presupposes the final prayer (which is rarely assumed).[41] Such observations may indicate that the formation of the farewell speech is in some respects utterly complex.[42]

If the Johannine author is thinking of the Gethsemane tradition, we can better appreciate, firstly, the peculiar *shift of roles* that takes place in the farewell section. In Gethsemane, Jesus is the one who feels anxiety. The Johannine Jesus is beyond such sentiments, even though he is not untouched (cf. 11.33, 38; 12.27; 13.21). Instead, it is the *disciples* who are distressed and need consolation (14.1.27). Secondly, we can understand better the inserted passage 12.23–34, where the Gethsemane tradition is already reworked to interpret the Son of Man's fate. Jesus will not simply go home. He must *die* (12.24) in order that 'his own' may have eternal life, i.e., his original followers and the new (12.20; cf. 17.20) people. This is the ultimate relecture of the hymnic credo of 1.14.

3. *The 'Presence' of the Departed: Christ and Community in the Farewell Discourse*

If the farewell section is about the significance of Jesus' departure, it is hermeneutically about his *absence*,[43] or theologically, about his *presence* with the

39. See Haldimann, *Rekonstruktion und Entfaltung*, pp. 7–8. Haldimann points out that in all these cases an existing Gethsemane tradition has been *reworked* and *displaced* in a very complex way.

40. Cf. Hans Windisch, 'John's Narrative Style' (original 1923 title 'Der Johanneische Erzählungsstil') in Mark W.G. Stibbe (ed.), *The Gospel of John as Literature: An Anthology of Twentieth-Century Perspectives* (Leiden-New York/Cologne: Brill, 1993), pp. 25-64; p. 53: 'The divine Christ's high-priestly prayer now replaces the prayer-struggle of the synoptic Jesus'.

41. Consider Jn 16.29–32. The disciples' understanding and confession of faith (16.29–30) prepares for 17.7–8. At the same time this tradition is modified in 16.31–32: complete understanding is a matter of the future, *now* (in the narrative to follow) is the time that Jesus will be left alone (but not quite alone, because the Father is with him). I am inclined to see 16.32 in a rather lenient light, as an elaboration of the 'sending' pattern of 17.18: while Jesus returns to his Father, the disciples go, 'every man to his (new earthly) dwelling place'.

42. The seam at 14.30–31 suggests that the original first farewell speech was included in a (rudimentary) 'passion' narrative. Subsequently, however, the farewell section must have been developed as a more independent unit, as the distinctive frames in 13.1–3 and 17.24–27 indicate, until it was inserted into the main narrative (of the present Gospel). This procedure complicates a detailed literary *Schichtung*, but on the other hand it seems that chs 15–16 can be treated as one (composite) insertion.

43. I concur with Dettwiler, who argues that the basic issue of the Johannine farewell discourse is 'die nach der *Abwesenheit Jesu*' (*Die Gegenwart des Erhöhten*, p. 299). Dettwiler also regards

community of those who believe in him. There are several modes in which this continuing 'presence' of the exalted Christ asserts itself in the farewell section. Assessing these modes may help us understand how the once 'dwelling' in the world of the Logos/Son was interpreted in the Johannine community. Some lines of development and shifts of emphasis are traceable in the farewell section, but, as always in John, the earlier and the later sediments are part of the same soil.

Ritual enactment is one of the basic ways of assuring continuity, and it is especially apt in a mythic scene like that of Jn 13–17.[44] It is not surprising, then, that the farewell scene is opened with the narrative of the rite of *footwashing*. Regrettably, this ritual is usually not recognized as such, because it is is not included among the principal sacraments of the church. Even the 'properly' sacramental traits in Johannine theology have been evaluated in opposite ways. Bultmann and Käsemann agreed, as do many scholars even today, that baptismal and eucharistic notions play a minor role for the 'evangelist' and only surface with the final redaction of the Gospel.[45] This seems too schematic a view. The footwashing episode in Jn 13 reveals a ritual interest both in the pre-Gospel tradition and in the latest redaction, and it is risky to postulate an evangelist paying no attention to such fleshly matters. In view of the Johannine passion chronology (and 1.29; 19.36)[46], it is hardly accidental that the last supper is not described as a eucharistic meal. However, eucharistic connotations may well be present in 13.18 (cf. Mk 14.18) and 13.26 (cf. 6.51; Mk 14.22 parr.). It is also probable that ὁ λελουμένος, in 13.10 includes a baptismal allusion. In fact it would be quite conceivable that 13.10 discusses an urgent theological and practical problem in the community at that time concerning the possibility of post-baptismal sins (and thus the necessity of footwashing) – a moot issue in 1 John.[47]

Rather than deplore the omission of the eucharistic words, we should thus appreciate that the institution of the rite of footwashing is narrated. Obviously we are being introduced to the community's actual *praxis*: 'For I have given you an example, that you also should do as I have done to you' (13.15).[48] That

the evolution of the farewell speeches as a successive reflection and *relecture* on the ecclesiological implications of Jn 1–12.

44. Windisch, 'John's Narrative Style', p. 53, describes the dramatic flow of Jn 13–17 as follows: sacramental action–expulsion of the impure–sermon–prayer. This literary structure may reflect the Johannine community's ritual practice at the sacred meals.

45. See Robert Kysar, *The Fourth Evangelist and His Gospel: An examination of contemporary scholarship* (Minneapolis: Augsburg, 1975), pp. 249–63.

46. For a detailed discussion of these passages, see de Boer, *Johannine Perspectives*, pp. 270–83. While the passages may come from the latest redaction, the image of Jesus as a Passover lamb is probably earlier (cf. 1 Cor. 5.7). As de Broer points out, the idea of the expiation of sins is not necessarily implied in these passages. Bruce W. Longenecker, 'The Unbroken Messiah: A Johannine Feature and its Social Function', *NTS* 41, pp. 428–41, hypothesizes on the theme of unity (unbrokenness) at Jn 6 and 19.31–36; this concern seems more plausible in a late *Sitz im Leben* with intra-community strifes.

47. See de Boer, *Johannine Perspectives*, pp. 283–92.

48. This being so, it seems futile to discard the well-attested longer text in v. 10 (εἰ μὴ τοὺς πόδας νίψασθαι). Rightly Alan R. Kerr, *The Temple of Jesus' Body: The Temple Theme in the*

footwashing is of real concern for the narrator[49] is evident, since this symbolic act is interpreted, not once but *twice*. The two interpretations are often referred to as 'soteriological vs. paradigmatic'[50] or 'sacramental vs. moralistic'[51] and are sometimes regarded as competitive.[52] Obviously, the interpretations were originally independent of each other, but in the present context both serve the thematic development of the farewell section. The first interpretation focuses on Jesus' death, whereas the second gives expression to the disciples' mutual love. At the fusion point of both interpretations is the notion of *self-sacrificial love*, and precisely this combination is made in 1 Jn 3.16 and 4.10–12. This soteriological-ethical theme is probably the latest stratum in Jn 13–17, being emphasized in the frames of the whole section (13.1, 17.24–27).[53]

For Käsemann, the dominant Johannine thought represents a radical *theology of the Word*. The community of believers is 'die Gemeinde unter dem Wort'.[54] If that sounds dubiously Protestant, and if some commentators' interpretation of Jn 13.10 ('you are clean') in light of 15.3 ('you are already made clean by the word which I have spoken to you') so as to undermine the importance of the ritual act[55] seems unduly spiritual, it remains true that the final form of the farewell discourse does emphasize the 'word' (λόγος, 17.14, 17) and 'words' (ῥήματα, 17.8) of Jesus. To know this word of revelation is to *believe* in God and Jesus (14.1). The revelation consists of the fact that to see Jesus is to see God, as an insertion into the earliest version of the first farewell speech hammers home (14.7.8–11). The risk of 'empty revelation' that Bultmann (agreed by Käsemann) saw is admittedly close at hand. However, besides the '*dass*' of revelation, there is an ethical imperative: the love commandment (ἐντολή, 15.12), which entails several commandments (ἐντολαί, 15.10). The redactor who inserted 13.34–35 and completed the introductory part of the farewell discourse

Gospel of John (JSNTSup, 220; London and New York: Sheffield Academic Press [Continuum], 2002), pp. 280–82, with reference to J.C. Thomas's previous work (JSNTSup, 61, 1991). Johannine scholars, however, more often than not opt for the shorter variant. 1 Tim 5.10 mentions the washing of the saints' feet as one qualification for a woman to be enrolled as a widow; obviously John's community had a less hierarchic praxis.

49. Contrary to, e.g., James Dunn, 'The Washing of the Disciples' Feet in Jn 13.1–20', *ZNW* 61 (1970), pp. 247–52; pp. 251–52: 'For it is in the essence of the symbolism (sign-ificance) of the whole incident that we are dealing here solely with spiritual cleansings – that is, cleansings which are not dependent on ritual actions'. However, symbolism and significance rather imply that there is a symbol or a sign to be interpreted.

50. De Boer, *Johannine Perspectives*, p. 284.

51. M-É. Boismard, 'Le lavement des pieds (Jn XIII, 1–17)', *PB* 71 (1964), pp. 5–24; p. 21.

52. For the spectrum of opinions, see Kohler, *Kreuz und Menschwerdung*, p. 193 n. 4.

53. This combination is not without tensions. Some ambivalance is palpable, e.g., in the second interpretation of the footwashing: 'You call me Teacher and Lord; and you are right, for so I am. If then I, your Lord and Teacher, have washed your feet…' Is Jesus here the glorious Master pretending to be a servant?

54. Käsemann, *Jesu letzter Wille*, pp. 53–100 (ch. 3). Käsemann agreed with Bultmann on this point (p. 74 n. 22).

55. Thus W.K. Grossouw, 'A Note on Jn 13.1–3', *NovT* 8 (1966), pp. 124–31; pp. 130–31.

(13.31–38) describes this ethical legacy as a 'new' commandment (ἐντολὴν καινὴν δίδωμι ὑμῖν, v. 34). The idea of a *nova lex Christi* is spelled out here in nuce.[56] To be sure, the content of the new Christian ethic seems scanty.

The seeming anaemia of moral instruction is, to a degree, compensated for by the perseverance of the insistence of brotherly love both in the farewell speech and in 1 John, and by the depth of its soteriological foundation (cf. 13.35–36.37–38; 15.13, 14; 1 Jn 3.16). In all cases, the lack of detailed moral guidance is a logical consequence of the *pneumatic* inheritance of Johannine theology. Like the Pauline Christians, the Johannine believers must have regarded themselves as θεοδίδακτοι, who by (divine) nature practiced brotherly love (cf. 1 Thess. 4.9). As τέλειοι in their knowledge of God (cf. 1 Cor. 2.6) they were in principle not in need of moral instruction. In practice, of course, the need existed. In Pauline Christianity, practical moral guidance was channelled through various instances and legitimized in a variety of ways: through dominical sayings or the apostle's dictum, with reference to 'nature', proper behaviour or simply 'the custom'. 1 John has a narrower repertoire. The only explicit commandment concerns brotherly love. More concrete advice is not given, because every believer should be under the Spirit's direct guidance and thus able to avoid sin.[57]

With the notion of *the Spirit* we are at the heart of the Johannine answer to the problem of Jesus' 'presence'. The figure of the *Paraclete* is a relatively late coinage but antedates 1 John.[58] It is introduced in the first farewell speech, in the expanded version we now have.[59] The formulation 'another Paraclete' in 14.16 implies that Jesus is the 'first' Paraclete. In the next verse, the same figure is described as 'the Spirit of truth'.[60] The Paraclete/Spirit is mentioned once more in the same speech, now called both the 'Paraclete' and 'the holy Spirit' (14.26). In the second speech, the Paraclete appears twice. In 15.26 he is again called 'the Spirit of truth', but this time he is sent by Jesus, whereas in 14.16 the Father gives him. The last mention of the Paraclete in 16.7–10 contains the most extensive description of his task and stresses – somewhat rationalistically – Jesus' departure as the precondition for the Paraclete's coming.

Irrespective of the religion-historical origin of the Johannine Paraclete, the occurrences in the farewell speech give a fairly clear picture of what is meant. The identity of the Paraclete is actually no mystery: it combines the holy Spirit and the resurrected/ascended Jesus. The first identification is articulated in 14.26, the latter is implied in 14.16 and stated in 1 Jn 2.1. Since the notion of the Paraclete is a relatively late invention in the tradition-history behind the fourth

56. Kotila, *Umstrittener Zeuge*, pp. 199, 212.

57. 1 John is deeply aware of the need of 'testing the spirits'. Two tests indicate whether it is God's spirit or not: keeping the commandments and confessing to Jesus who has come in flesh (4.2) and through water and blood (5.6).

58. 1 Jn 2.1, where Jesus is expressly identified as the Paraclete, suggests that the notion of the Paraclete as a *separate* identity is in decline.

59. The core of the first farewell speech is probably found in 13.33*, 14.1–3.18*, 27–31*.

60. In 4.23–24 'Spirit' and 'truth' are closely connected. The (later) coinage 'the Spirit of Truth' in 14.17 thus seems a natural Johannine development.

Gospel and seems rather unnecessary as a separate identity already in 1 John, the question is why it was invented in the first place. This figure has an important role in the farewell discourse, which may well be its literary birthplace. Yet the Paraclete is more than a literary device; namely, the means and the result of *hermeneutical reflection* on the mode of the 'presence' of the departed with his own. 'The Paraclete is the presence of Jesus while Jesus is absent', as Raymond E. Brown defines in an oft-quoted sentence.[61] At the same time, the notion of the Paraclete elaborates on the earlier concept of the Spirit, especially on the function of the Spirit as the tie between the exalted Christ and the believers.[62]

One of the tasks of the Paraclete is to guide the believers 'into all the truth' (16.13). This includes, besides things future, facts and incidents concerning the earthly Jesus. The repeated remarks in Jn 1–12 on how the disciples 'remembered' what had happened to Jesus are thus explained. The most peculiar example is 12.16, which justifies the whole inserted narrative 12.9–19, but the same literary strategy is used already in 2.21–22 to ensure the proper understanding of the gospel of Jesus' glory. The articulation of this new perspective is sometimes disturbing and tends to turn the symbolic narrative of Jesus' spirit-laden ministry into a mere prelude to his departure and the Spirit's coming.[63]

This remarkable turn is made explicit and motivated ecclesiologically in the expanded form of the first farewell speech, when Jesus promises that the believer will do 'greater works' than he had done on earth (14.12). The explanation is that when Jesus has gone to his Father, the disciples may ask anything in his name (v. 14) and the Father will give them, namely (as the traditional promise is now interpreted), the Paraclete (v. 16). The 'greater works' are those enabled by the Paraclete and thus works of the exalted Christ through the community of believers (cf. v. 14 'I will do it'). The later generations of believers are then actually in a better position than the historical disciples. According to Christian Dietzfelbinger, this bold programme of the Johannine 'evangelist' provides the most fully developed solution to the problem of Jesus' absence.[64]

However, by introducing the Paraclete and the 'greater works' that await the post-Easter community, the author is, in effect, only restating and enhancing his pneumatic-enthusiastic inheritance. What is new is the uneasy combination of

61. Brown, *The Gospel according to John* (*Anchor Bible* 29A, 1970), p. 643. Some users of this quote have detected a measure of (perhaps unintentional) 'postmodernism' in this terse formulation.

62. The idea of 'divine indwelling', which in the expanded form of the first farewell speech reinterprets the promise of Jesus' coming (cf. 14.23 with 14.3), is a further indication of the merging of Jesus and the Spirit, especially if read in the light of 2.19 and 4.21–24. Cf. Mary L. Coloe, *God Dwells with Us: Temple Symbolism in the Fourth Gospel* (Collegeville: The Liturgical Press [Michael Glazier], 2001), pp. 157–78; but some details in her interpretation may go too far.

63. In 7.39 Jesus calls to come to him and 'drink' (7.37) of the Spirit, but the editorial remark in 7.39 states bluntly: 'as yet there was no Spirit'.

64. C. Dietzfelbinger, 'Die grösseren Werke (Joh 14,12f.)', *NTS* 35 (1989), pp. 27–47, esp. pp. 38–42. Dietzfelbinger compares the Johannine solution to other early Christian responses to the problem of Jesus' absence: the *apocalyptic*, the *hymnic*, the *sacramental*, the *ecclesiological* and the *pneumatological* responses, as well as the grief reaction attested in Mk 2.18–22. In fact, the various Johannine answers include aspects of all these responses.

Jesus and the Spirit, so that the Paraclete *both* recalls the earthly Jesus *and* continues his work.[65] To the extent that the coming of the Paraclete is the parousia of Jesus (14.18–19) and the Paraclete-Jesus remains with his own εἰς τὸν αἰῶνα (14.16), the gain seems to be that realized eschatology (Jesus has returned to his own) and the 'sending' christology (Jesus has returned home to his Father) can be maintained at once.[66] Weighed against the resulting bifurcation of the exalted Jesus, it remains doubtful if this reasoning is superior to earlier and more recent ways of dealing with the 'presence' of Jesus. However, to the extent that this combination binds the Spirit to the Jesus tradition, it may function as a reminder of the earthly Jesus.[67] 'The Paraclete becomes the agent of memory, the spur generating the community's meaningful recollection of Jesus'.[68]

Whatever its merits, the programme of 14.12–17 was not the Johannine community's final answer, as the latest stratum in ch. 14 (e.g., the intrusive v. 15, stressing the commandments of Jesus) and the new discussion in 15–16 testify.[69] Rather than keeping to the strained spiritual vision that relativized the past, the community, or those within it whose testimony the latest material has preserved, adhered to 'what had been from the beginning'. The orientation to the life-giver's abiding *word* and ritual *presence* is evident in the extended metaphor of the vine and the branches (15.1–8). Its tone is slightly threatening,[70] emphasizing the danger of being cut off from the vine, but the promise of greater works still holds for those who abide in Christ and his words (v. 7). The waiting of the parousia was not extinguished. It was there from early on, as the opening of the first farewell speech indicates (πάλιν ἔρχομαι, 14:3). This is interpreted presentically as the 'seeing' of Jesus after a little while (μικρόν, viz., after exaltation, 14.19) and as a permanent divine 'indwelling' (14.23), but the traditional expectation probably surfaces again in the latest stratum of the farewell discourse; the extensive discussion and elaboration of the 'little while' in the second speech (16.16–22) seems to leave the door open to parousia.

65. The Paraclete as the fulfiller of Jesus' revelation stands in some tension with the idea of John 17 that the Son's revelation is complete. Cf. 17.4 with 16.12–14.

66. However, Udo Schnelle, 'Johanneische Ekklesiologie', *NTS* 37 (1991), pp. 37–50; p. 43 is right in saying that the sending of the Paraclete and the coming of Jesus are not 'einfach identisch'.

67. This aspect of the Paraclete is correctly emphasized by Dettwiler, *Die Gegenwart des Erhöhten*, p. 206. Hereby I am not taking sides in the *theological* debate between Dettwiler and Dietzfelbinger; cf. Johanna Rahner, 'Vergegenwärtigende Erinnerung: Die Abschiedsreden, der Geist-Paraklet und die Retrospektive des Johannesevangeliums', *ZNW* 91 (2000), pp. 72–90; pp. 78–79.

68. Arthur J. Dewey, 'The Eyewitness of History: Visionary Consciousness in the Fourth Gospel', in Robert T. Fortna and Tom Thatcher (eds.), *Jesus in Johannine Tradition* (Louisville: WJK, 2001), pp. 59–70; p. 67. In practice, the Johannine author's 'creative chemistry of remembrance' (Dewey, p. 70) stretches that which can reasonably be considered historical memory.

69. Dietzfelbinger, 'Die grösseren Werke', p. 47, ends his article prophetically by asking whether the community is able to become the receiver and doer of the promised 'greater works'. At least for the Johannine community the challenge was overwhelming.

70. De Boer, *Johannine Perspectives*, p. 204, rightly points out that the threat of being cut off and the idea of 'pruning' are issued in 15.2 before the more consoling discussion in the subsequent verses. 15.1–17 elaborates on the first interpretation of footwashing (cf. 15.3 and 13.10), but it is somewhat reductionist to regard this section as a mere *relecture* of 13.6–11.

In addition, the enigmatic, apocalyptical imagery of 16.21 depicting a woman's labour pains,[71] seems to carry a deeper meaning, where the Johannine understanding of incarnation takes an *anthropological* turn. Still after Easter, the *disciples* will have sorrow in the hostile world that seems to have got its way. But from an eschatological perspective the painful time appears as a process leading to the birth of a new human being (ἄνθρωπος). This will happen when *Jesus* 'sees again' the disciples, so that their hearts will be filled with joy. Why this *shift of roles*? Is Jesus here finally allowed to feel pain, even if highly ambiguously and metaphorically, as being somehow involved in the painful delivery of a new human being? In any case, the seeing is mutual and corresponds to the final transformation of God's children envisaged in 1 Jn 3.2. A similar metamorphosis of the believers was described in 2 Cor. 3: 'we' who are looking at Christ are transformed into the likeness of his superior glory (v. 18).[72] While in the early times this eschatological change was thought to have taken place in a spiritual birth into the divine sphere, the realities of life may have taught the Johannine community that they still lacked the final 'fullness' of Christ.

4. *It Is Finished (Jn 18–21): The 'Sein' and 'Schein' of the Johannine Jesus*

Käsemann may be right that the passion narrative – if that is a proper designation[73] – is less existentially engaging for the Johannine author(s) than the farewell section. However, if that is so, it may be because the problem of the death of the life-giver is by now theologically mastered. What remains is to narrate it. The Jesus we meet here is the sovereign of his destiny, as in Jn 1–12. He allows his enemies to arrest him, at the same time protecting his own from the hostile world. He carries his own cross, does not show pain, cares for his mother and the beloved disciple at the moment of his death. But in all that, he is Jesus of Nazareth, as the three short 'I am' sayings in Jn 18 emphasize.[74] Pilate's simple words *Ecce homo* (19.5) are not the storyteller's whole confession, but this piece

71. Francis J. Moloney, *Glory not Dishonor: Reading John 13–21* (Minneapolis: Fortress Press, 1998), pp. 92–93, presents succintly the features of 16.21 that make the reader look for a deeper meaning. His reader will 'suspect that something of messianic and final significance is being mooted', which for him would be Jesus' second coming. While not denying a reference to parousia, I think that the *birthing* imagery and the unexpected change to *Jesus* together signal the key idea. Fernando F. Segovia, *The Farewell of the Word: The Johannine Call to Abide* (Minneapolis: Fortress Press, 1991), p. 254, is on the right track: 'the disciples...are portrayed as undergoing a process of birth'. In Gal. 4.19 *Paul* describes himself as being in labour pains 'until Christ be formed in you'.

72. This idea is developed and corrected in 1 Cor. 13.8–12: the transformation is a gradual growth toward adulthood, and the immediate seeing is a matter of the future. In 1 Cor. 15.51–52, Paul refers to the eschatological change (ἀλλαγησόμεθα) as a profound mystery, stressing that it is a sudden future event.

73. Ashton, *Understanding the Fourth Gospel*, p. 489, sides with Käsemann: 'In the case of the Fourth Gospel 'passion' is a misnomer; Jesus controls and orchestrates the whole performance'.

74. Pokorný, 'Der irdische Jesus', pp. 222–23.

of Johannine irony does point out that Jesus was a human being.[75] And when Jesus is dying on the cross, the Johannine authors are fully alert to highlight the ecclesiological, pneumatological and sacramental significance of the event by every available narrative means.[76]

The Easter appearances are generous enough, yet they do not overshadow the farewell discourse as the site for Jesus' 'testament' to the community. No new teaching is given, the main intent is to confirm the fact of Jesus' corporeal death. Curiously, the risen One appears almost more human than the earthly Jesus: he is mistaken for a gardener, bears the wounds of crucifixion, and shares an early breakfast by a charcoal fire with some of his disciples. He is sovereign but not more glorious than in his earthly days. When the narrative curtain falls, he remains with his disciples: the divine Son's ascent is never told, he is only allowed to talk about it. Thus the Gospel narrative attaches the reading community to the glorious *but* earthly Jesus in like manner as the farewell discourse lets the community hear the earthly Jesus' words from the lips of the departed One.

How should we understand the 'Sein' and 'Schein'[77] of this Jesus? Certainly the fourth Gospel is perplexing, but Pokorný's insistence on its 'spiritual' nature seems feasible, even on Käsemann's premises. It is the product of a community where tradition was boldly interpreted in the light of the Spirit. Why should the faith experience it reflects be less authentic than that behind the Synoptics? Indeed, why should *Paul* be a more authentic witness, though he did not aspire to know the fleshly Jesus (2 Cor. 5.16)? If we feel uncomfortable with John, it may be because we moderns prefer to have myth and history separated, not mixed as in John. However, a humble Christ with cries and tears (Heb. 5.7), forsaken by God (Mk 15.34), may not be a less mythic construct. And has not the Johannine *community* in the end learned from what it suffered (cf. 16.20–22)?[78] I suggest, *pace* Käsemann, that 'John, the maverick Gospel'[79] be taken seriously on this one point, namely that Jesus gave a *farewell* speech. The hermeneutical law of incarnation is that what is born must die. The aspect of grace reminds us that through

75. Some manuscripts omit these words, and Pokorný's ('Der irdische Jesus', p. 224) interpretation is quite feasible that the scribes or their communities found the utterance disturbing.

76. The τετέλεσται in Jn 19.30 brings Jesus' mission to an end within the passion narrative. A later hand, possibly the same final redactor who in 13.1–3 anticipates the betrayal, now anticipates (ἤδη) the fulfilment in 19.28. This seems to take note of the preceding verses 26–27 (note εἰς τὰ ἴδια in v. 27, cf. 13.1). Everything was complete at the cross – not just *on* the cross but *at* it, with the new community being given birth. The sacramental interest is evident at 19.33, 36 (the unbroken legs of the Passover Lamb) and 19.34–35 (water and blood). A pneumatological interpretation of 19.30 (Jesus hands over the Spirit to the community) seems possible at earlier stages of the narrative, but the final redaction is not likely to stress it (cf. 20.22).

77. Kohler, *Kreuz und Menschwerdung*, p. 134, in reference to the Bultmann-Käsemann dispute.

78. Käsemann, *Jesu letzter Will*, p. 34, mentions an *unlearned* lesson: 'Die Johanneische Darstellung ... hat noch nicht wie Lukas gelernt, Jesu Auferweckung als ein individuelles, auf Jesus beschränktes Geschehen zu verstehen'. Should it have? Does not precisely the *participatory* trait – the legacy of apocalyptic enthusiasm – contribute to the continuing appeal of Johannine theology? Cf. Charlene P.E. Burns, *Divine Becoming: Rethinking Jesus and Incarnation* (Minneapolis: Fortress Press, 2002), esp. pp. 115–46 (a chapter entitled, 'The Incarnation as Participation').

79. The title of Robert Kysar's commentary (Louisville: WJK, new, enlarged ed. 1994).

transformation and participation, something can be born of that which must die (Jn 12.24). As exegetes, we know the law, and patiently unearth and gather the fragments of the Jesus who once was. John's Gospel may do little help in this historical task,[80] but it might teach us something about the grace of being.

80. Except for showing it (to an imaginative reader). Cf. J.D. Crossan, 'It is Written: A Structuralist Analysis of John 6', *Semeia* 26 (1983), pp. 3–21; p. 20: 'It is only of the bread that nothing must be lost, and the bread, with the fish quietly forgotten, becomes the discourse 'I' of Jesus. It is, then, the fragments of Jesus which must be gathered so that nothing may be lost'.

Part IV

THE BEGINNINGS AND LATER DEVELOPMENTS

WO BLEIBT DAS GERICHT?
EINE HISTORISCHE IMAGINATION ZU DEN ANFÄNGEN DER CHRISTOLOGIE

Christoph Demke

Die historische Imagination, die hier vorgestellt wird, soll dazu beitragen, zu verstehen, wie es zum Verständnis des Kreuzestodes Jesu als Heil schaffenden Sühnetod gekommen ist.

Ulrich Wilckens hat in seinem jetzt mit dem ersten Teilband vorliegenden opus magnum einer Theologie des Neuen Testamentes mit Vehemenz erklärt, es sei „historisch absurd", anzunehmen, daß dieses Verständnis des Kreuzestodes Jesu theologische Erfindung früher Christen sei. Er kündigt den Versuch an, „ein *historisch* besser begründetes Gesamtbild zu gewinnen durch eine Revision historisch ganz unwahrscheinlicher Vorurteile".[1] Auf seine Weise tritt er damit an die Seite, aber auch in Gegensatz zu der amerikanischen Jesusforschung, die sich selbst als „Third Quest" begreift und bezeichnet im Bestreben, die reale historische Dimension in der historischen Jesusforschung wiederzugewinnen. Während die „Third Quest" die theologisch-dogmatischen Fesseln, in die die einstmals „neue" Frage nach dem historischen Jesus verstrickt war und sich verstrickt hatte, sprengen will, will Wilckens die als Selbstverständlichkeiten ausgegebenen Dogmen der historisch-kritischen Wissenschaft, die die wirkliche Geschichte Jesu Christi verstellen, überwinden. Es ist deutlich: methodologische Fragen gewinnen in solcher Diskussion einen hohen Stellenwert.[2]

In der Tat muß man einräumen, daß die deutsche neutestamentliche Exegese Geschichte primär geistes- und ideengeschichtlich wahrgenommen hat.[3] In der sog. Traditionsgeschichte wirkt dieses Manko bis heute fort. Daran ändert auch eine differenziertere Wahrnehmung der jüdischen Umwelt zur Zeit Jesu und der ersten Gemeinden nicht viel. Sozialgeschichtliche Beobachtungen bringen schon eher eine Korrektur. Aber auch sie können nicht verhindern, daß die Fragestellungen

1. Ulrich Wilckens, *Theologie des Neuen Testamentes. I/1 Geschichte des Wirkens Jesu in Galiläa* (Neukirchen: Neukirchener, 2002), S. 34.

2. U.Wilckens sieht dafür in seinem Programm einen abschließenden III. Band vor (s. a.a.O., S. 59ff.) vgl. auf der anderen Seite z.B. Jens Schröter, *Jesus und die Anfänge der Christologie* (Neukirchen: Neukirchener, 2001), S. 37ff.

3. Die Begegnung mit Petr Pokorný war für mich von Anfang an auch dadurch anziehend, daß er sich – wohl auch in der Tradition tschechischer Geschichtswissenschaft – gegen diese Beschränkung wandte (s. z.B. nur P. Pokorný, *Der Epheserbrief und die Gnosis*, Berlin: EVA, 1965, S. 21f.).

und Interessen des Forschers bzw. Exegeten, ob sie nun theologisch-dogmatischer oder religionsgeschichtlicher oder sozialgeschichtlicher Natur seien, die geschichtliche Wirklichkeit verfremden, gerade auch dann, wenn sie Einzelheiten dieser Wirklichkeit erschließen.

Hier soll nun nicht das ganze hermeneutische Problem des Verhältnisses von Rekonstruktion, Interpretation und Fiktion erörtert werden. Ich denke, auch ohne solche Erörterung muß einsichtig sein: Die Geschichte Jesu wie der frühen Gemeinden geht hervor aus der Interaktion mindestens folgender Faktoren: Gott, Jesus, die Schrift, Jesu verschiedene Anhänger, seine verschiedenen Gegner usw. Die Reihe kann je nach Bedarf des Stoffes verlängert bzw. variiert werden. Wichtig ist nur, daß auch Gott und die Schrift als mitwirkende Faktoren der Geschichte im Blick bleiben. Wer Gott von vornherein zum Gottesverständnis oder Gottesgedanken o.ä. schrumpfen läßt, geht nicht besonders kritisch vor, sondern verbaut die Möglichkeit einer wirklichen historischen Imagination, denn für die Zeit Jesu waren Gott und die Schrift eben nicht nur Gedankeninhalte, sondern Partner, die man befragte, von denen man Antworten vernahm (oder auch nicht) usf.; man erlebte sie und lebte mit ihnen. Diesen Bereich der Interaktion aufzuklären, ist deswegen so schwierig, weil wir in den historischen Dokumenten meist nur die Ergebnisse solcher Kommunikationsprozesse finden.

Es ist zwar wichtig, daß die Wissenschaft die Fragen, mit denen sie ihre Stoffe angeht, methodologisch klärt. An erste Stelle aber gehört Klarheit darüber, daß die Fragen, die die seinerzeit handelnden Personen bewegten, den Vorrang vor den Fragen der Forschung bei der Suche nach einem Zugang zur wirklichen Geschichte erhalten müssen. Welche Fragen wurden durch ihr Erleben ausgelöst? Mit welchen Fragen nahmen sie die Schrift wahr? Welche Fragen stellten sich ihnen durch bestimmte Aussagen der Schrift? Welche Fragen steuerten die Aufnahme von oder das Desinteresse an bestimmten Traditionen? Diese Fragen schlagen sich in der Regel nicht im Quellenmaterial nieder. Sie können auch schwer aus dieser oder jener Einzelheit abgeleitet werden. Für die Entdeckung dieser Fragen ist der Historiker und Exeget auf seine Phantasie angewiesen.[4] Sie müssen sich dadurch bewähren, daß sie eine hinreichende Anzahl von Einzelbeobachtungen in einem einleuchtenden Zusammenhang sehen lassen. Der einleuchtende Zusammenhang muß sich nicht durch Einfachheit auszeichnen. Das mathematische Kriterium der Eleganz für die Bestimmung der „richtigen" Lösung (z.B. bei Gleichungen) ist auf geschichtliche Sachverhalte nicht ohne weiteres übertragbar. Dennoch ist die Erinnerung an dieses Kriterium in der Mathematik sinnvoll, weil sie deutlich machen kann, daß sich die Geschichtwissenschaft bei solchen Erwägungen nicht ihrer Wissenschaftlichkeit begibt.[5]

4. U.Wilckens bekräftigt dies nachdrücklich für eine „historisch geschulte Phantasie" (a.a.O., S. 32, A.46).

5. Die historische Forschung muß sich um möglichst präzise Beschreibung und Benennung ihrer Gegenstände bemühen; sie muß aber zugleich das Bewußtsein wachhalten, daß ihre Begriffsbildungen vor allem arbeitshypothetischen Wert haben; geschichtliches Leben richtet sich nicht nach den Unterscheidungen historischer Begriffsbildung, sondern verbindet oder vermischt nur allzu oft begrifflich streng zu Unterscheidendes.

Meine These lautet nun: Ein Teil der Jüngerschaft Jesu war auf Grund der Begegnungen Jesu mit ihnen nach seinem Tod von der Frage bewegt: Wo bleibt das verdiente Gericht Gottes? Unter dieser Frage wurde der Tod Jesu als „für uns" geschehen verstanden und schließlich das Lied vom Gottesknecht in Jes 52/53 als Gottes Interpretation der Geschichte Jesu und seines Todes entdeckt. Über diese Entdeckung hinaus ist diese Frage aber überhaupt für die Ursprungsgeschichte der Christologie von hervorragender Bedeutung.

Bevor diese These veranschaulicht werden kann, müssen einige Voraussetzungen klargestellt werden, die noch nicht selbstverständlich sind, sondern gern als historische Vorurteile verdächtigt werden:

1. Jesus hat sich um eine gesicherte, d.h. kontrollierte Rezeption seiner Worte und seiner Geschichte nicht gekümmert.[6] Das Vater-unser stellt in gewisser Weise eine Ausnahme dar.

Dieser Sachverhalt bedeutet aber: der Historiker muß prinzipiell von einer Mehrzahl von Rezeptionen ausgehen. Man darf nur nicht gleich von verschiedenen Konzeptionen, Entwürfen, geistesgeschichtlichen Horizonten usw. phantasieren. Aber so verschieden die Anhänger Jesu waren, so unterschiedlich war ihre Rezeption, war das Interesse, das sie an Jesus band bzw. mit ihm verband: einem ehemaligen Fischer war anderes wichtig als einem ehemaligen Johannesjünger, dem Weggenossen Jesu etwas anderes, als demjenigen bzw. derjenigen, in deren Haus er einkehrte,[7] einem ehemaligen Zöllner etwas anderes als einem bisherigen Pharisäer.

Also gilt prinzipiell für die Jesusüberlieferung: Am Anfang steht eine Vielfalt, die z.T. sehr schnell, z.T. nach und nach zu relativen Einheiten zusammengeführt wurde, so daß es zu Überlagerungen, Ergänzungen und verschiedenen Interferenzen kommt. Erst dann kann es zu so etwas wie einem Stammbaum der Überlieferung kommen, der es erlaubt, zeitliche Ordnungen vorzunehmen („schon" oder „noch nicht" oder „nicht mehr").

Diese Überlegungen zeigen, wie wenig wir von den Überlieferungsanfängen wissen und auf welchem Hintergrund Wahrscheinlichkeitsurteile abgegeben werden.

6. Bei Matthäus ist entschlossene Traditionspflege erkennbar, wenn er z.B. alle Stellen korrigiert, in denen bei Markus durchklingt, daß Jesus noch anderes als im Markus-Evangelium erhalten, gelehrt hat (vgl. z.B. Mk 4,33 mit Mt 13,34) und das Jüngerunverständnis insoweit (und nur insoweit!) beseitigt als dadurch die Integrität der Überlieferung fraglich werden könnte (vgl. Mk 8,17–21 mit Mt 16,9–12, bs. V.11f., dazu 13,51); er erhebt den Anspruch, alles, was Jesus geboten hat, in seiner Schrift zu präsentieren, denn nur so ist ja auch der Missionsbefehl Mt 28,20a ausführbar. Ein anderes Interesse der Traditionssicherung belegt Lk 1,1–4. Die Freiheit, mit der beide die Überlieferung verarbeiten, zeigt aber, daß sie noch nicht auf eingespielte Verfahren der Traditionssicherung zurückgreifen können.

7. Das lukanische Symposion (14,1–24) dürfte nicht zu Unrecht das Tischgespräch als Rahmen für Worte Jesu (vielleicht besonders die ausgeführten Gleichnisse) darstellen. Welche Rezeption fand da statt? Hängt der so auffallende Milieuunterschied in den großen Gleichniserzählungen des lukanischen Sondergutes auf der einen Seite und des matthäischen Sondergutes auf der anderen Seite mit unterschiedlichen Rezeptionsmilieus und Rezeptionsorten zusammen?

Analoges gilt auch für die Ostererlebnisse; auch hier muß von einer Mehrzahl unterschiedlich artikulierter Begegnungen Jesu mit seinen Anhängern[8] ausgegangen werden. Das Gegenteil wäre nur dann anzunehmen, wenn Petrus durch die ihm zuteil gewordene Ersterscheinung prägend auf die Artikulierung aller weiteren Erscheinungen gewirkt hätte. Dergleichen ist aber nicht erkennbar. Denn das Wissen, daß Petrus als Erster eine Begegnung mit Jesus nach seiner Kreuzigung hatte, hinterläßt in verschiedenen Überlieferungssträngen seine Spuren (l. Kor 15,5; Lk 24,34; Joh 20,6). Aber die Suche nach einer Erzählung, in der dieses Erlebnis seinen Niederschlag gefunden hat (Lk 5,1–11; Mk 9,2–8; Joh 21), hat zu keinem anerkannten Ergebnis geführt. Dieser „Befund" wird auch durch folgende Beobachtung bestätigt: Die Leitungsaufgabe des Petrus, die ihm wohl auf Grund dieser Erstbegegnung zukam, wird von jedem Evangelisten anders gezeichnet, nämlich je nach dem, was der jeweilige Verfasser als wesentlich für Kirchenleitung ansah (Lukas: Mission und Seelsorge – 5,10; 22,32; Matthäus: Lehre und Disziplin – 16,19; Johannes: Kybernese und Einheit – 21,15ff.). Daran aber wird erkennbar: Sie hatten keinen Stoff und schon gar keinen „Text", den sie variieren konnten[9].

Also muß es bei der größeren Wahrscheinlichkeit einer Unterschiedlichkeit am Anfang bleiben. Wer auf einem „Urbekenntnis" besteht, besteht auf einer historischen Unwahrscheinlichkeit[10] und muß dann die entsprechend gewichtigen

8. Ich formuliere möglichst offen (Erlebnis, Begegnung mit Jesus), um die Artikulierung des Geschehens nicht zu präjudizieren. Methodologisch behält W. Marxsen, *Anfangsprobleme der Christologie* (Gütersloh: Gerd Mohn, 1958), mit der Unterscheidung zwischen Widerfahrnis und Interpretament Recht, nicht aber mit seiner Unterscheidung zwischen einem funktionalen Interpretament (beauftragt zur Fortsetzung der Verkündigung Jesu und seiner Sache) und einem reflexiven Interpretament (auferweckt von den Toten), das sich der nachträglichen Reflexion auf die Voraussetzungen, von denen her das Erlebnis überhaupt möglich war, verdankt. Die Herabstufung des zweiten Interpretamentes zur bloßen Hilfsvorstellung übersieht, daß die Möglichkeit, vom Ostererlebnis zu sprechen, zusammenhängt mit der jeweiligen Möglichkeit vom Kreuzestod Jesu zu sprechen. Aber das wäre Gegenstand einer eigenen Untersuchung; hier sei nur die Vermutung geäußert, daß das Verständnis des Kreuzestodes Jesu als Sühnetod und die Rede von Jesu Auferweckung durch Gott, wenn nicht von Anfang an zusammenhängen, so sich doch zumindest angezogen und stabilisiert haben. Hier ist nur die Feststellung wichtig: Ein erstes Interpretament war zur Stelle mit der Artikulation des Erlebnisses, aber es gibt keinen Grund zu der Annahme, daß diese von vornherein einhellig und einstimmig war.

9. Auch Paulus hat allem Anschein nach sein Damaskuserlebnis nicht zum Gegenstand einer formulierten Überlieferung gemacht (vgl. 1. Kor 9,1 mit Gal 1,12–16); die Wirkung dieses Erlebnisses war ja unübersehbar (Gal 1,23f.). Schließt man von da aus auf die österliche Erstbegegnung zurück, so könnte auch dort die unübersehbare Verhaltensänderung, nämlich Rückkehr nach Jerusalem, den Ort der Hinrichtung Jesu, mit dem Risiko der Verfolgung, jede Erlebnisschilderung erübrigt haben.

10. Insofern ist der Sicht der urchristlichen Geschichte bei H. Köster und J.M. Robinson (*Entwicklungslinien durch die Welt des frühen Christentums* [Tübingen: Mohr-Siebeck, 1971], darin besonders H.Köster, Gnomoi diaphoroi. Ursprung und Wesen der Mannigfaltigkeit in der Geschichte des frühen Christentums, S.106–46, in englischer Sprache zuerst 1965, deutsch in *ZThK* 1968, S.160ff.) grundsätzlich zuzustimmen, auch wenn die inhaltlichen Aufstellungen zu revidieren sind (s.z. B. J. Schröters Auseinandersetzung mit H. Köster in *Jesus und die Anfänge der Christologie*, Neukirchen: Neukirchener, 2001, S.180ff.).

Argumente vorbringen und zwar sowohl im Blick auf den einzelnen Stoff als auch im Blick auf den Überlieferungsgang.

2. Eine weitere Voraussetzung im oben beschriebenen Sinne ist: Jesus hat seine Person nicht zu einem Gegenstand seiner Lehre und Verkündigung gemacht. Allerdings ist es sehr wahrscheinlich, daß die Frage, wer Jesus sei, schon zu seinen Lebzeiten eine Rolle gespielt hat. Seine Nähe zum Täufer und Hochachtung für den Täufer auf der einen Seite und der deutliche Unterschied zum Verhalten des Täufers auf der anderen Seite scheint diese Frage verursacht zu haben. Spuren davon sind, wie auch immer es mit der Historizität der Texte im Einzelnen bestellt sein mag, in Mk 8,27ff.; Mk 6,14f.; Mt 11,2ff. und Mk 11,27ff. erkennbar. Hätte Jesus auf die Frage nach seiner Person, die schon zu seinen Lebzeiten gestellt worden sein muß, eine klare Antwort gegeben, dann müßte sie sich in der Überlieferung als ein gewichtiges und unumstößliches Fundament jedes späteren Bekenntnisses und aller späteren Glaubenslehre niedergeschlagen haben.[11] Das eben ist nicht erkennbar. Im Gegenteil: es gibt hinreichende Anzeichen dafür, daß Jesus die Antwort vermieden hat.[12] Trotz größter Achtung für den Täufer legt Jesus dessen Rolle oder Titel nicht fest (Mt 11,9 par. vgl. das „mehr als Jona" und „mehr als Salomo" in Mt 12,42f. par.). Auch die Rede vom Menschensohn ist in der Jesusüberlieferung eher verhüllend als offenbarend. Nimmt man die Verweigerung einer Antwort auf die Vollmachtsfrage (Mk 11,27ff. vgl. die Verweigerung einer Antwort auf die Zeichenforderung Mk 8,11–13 parr.) dazu und beachtet, wie Jesus die wohlwollende Unentschiedenheit gegenüber dem Täufer getadelt hat (Mt 11,7–9 und wieder Mk 11,27ff. vgl. auch 11,16–19), dann unterstreicht das den Entscheidungsruf Jesu (Mt 11,6 par. und z.B. Mk 8,38).[13]

3. Eine dritte Voraussetzung muß noch erläutert werden. Ich setze voraus, daß Jesus seinen möglichen Tod nicht zu einem Gegenstand besonderer Sinndeutung und deren Verkündigung gemacht hat. Freilich deutet auch nichts darauf hin, daß er sich über die Möglichkeit seines Todes getäuscht hat. Wenn Bultmann diese

11. Eine Antwort auf eine ausdrückliche Frage hinterläßt andere Spuren in der Rezeption und folglich der späteren Überlieferung als eine gelegentliche Andeutung usw.

12. Wenn das zutrifft, dann müssen sich diejenigen, die dahinter zurückfragen möchten – was als historische Neugier verständlich oder sogar notwendig sein mag –, klar darüber sein, daß sie den Willen Jesu unterlaufen. P. Stuhlmacher konstatiert freilich, die Annahme, Jesus habe auf die naturgemäß sich einstellende Frage, wer er sei, nicht geantwortet, „macht den irdischen Jesus zu einem wandelnden historischen Rätsel" (*Jesus von Nazareth – Christus des Glaubens* [Stuttgart: Calwer, 1988], S. 28). Das Rätselhafte mag für Stuhlmacher so sein, bestätigt dann aber, daß seine Erwartungen unangemessen waren. Jedenfalls ist Stuhlmachers Feststellung nicht an Textbefunden orientiert.

13. Dieses scheint mir der näherliegende Zusammenhang gegenüber der Vermutung von U.Wilckens: „Zwar hat Jesus es offensichtlich vermieden, sich selbst als den Messias zu bekennen, denn die Messiaserwartung war damals das Herz der immer stärker werdenden antirömischen Bewegung, die er nicht teilte. So ist von Jesus selbst her zu begründen, daß das Messiasprädikat nachösterlichen Ursprungs ist" (a.a.O., S. 34). Gibt es in der Jesusüberlieferung wirklich Anhaltspunkte für so taktische Überlegungen und solche Sorge, nicht mißverstanden zu werden, die auch G.Theißen/A. Merz, *Der historische Jesus* (Göttingen: Vandenhoeck & Ruprecht, 1997), S. 469, vermutet?

Möglickeit mit einer gewissen Inbrunst[14] behauptet, so ist das nicht einfach Ausdruck historischer Skepsis oder eines historistischen Dogmas, sondern ihn leitet dabei ein theologisch-dogmatisches Interesse: der Glaubende soll seine Gewißheit nicht auf vermeintliche historische Sicherheiten gründen, die doch immer wieder in Zweifel gezogen werden können. Darum läßt sich Bultmann auch gar nicht auf Einzelerörterung des Materials zu dieser Frage in der Jesusüberlieferung ein. Tut man dies, so kann man das Folgende feststellen: Die Bejahung der Begrenztheit des Lebens, die nicht dem menschlichen Willen unterworfen ist, verbindet Jesus mit der Weisheit (Lk 12,27; 16–20).

Worte wie Mt 10,29–31par.[15] und Lk 17,33par. vgl. Mk 8,35parr.[16] zeigen, daß Jesus seine Jünger auf die Bedrohtheit ihres Lebens einstellte und ihnen gerade dafür die Zuwendung Gottes zusprach.

Ein termingebundenes Verständnis der Nähe der Gottesherrschaft, das ihn bewogen haben könnte, mit dessen Anbruch vor seinem Lebensende zu rechnen, ist nicht festzustellen.[17]

Die kompakte Direktheit, mit der Jesus auf die Sadduzäerfrage Mk 12,26f. parr. mit dem Verweis auf die Selbstoffenbarung Gottes als Gott Abrahams, Isaaks und Jacobs antwortet,[18] entspricht nicht nur seiner Gottesgewißheit, sondern muß man auch für sein Verhalten zur Möglichkeit seines Sterbens bei jeder historischen Betrachtung als grundlegend ansehen. Heinz Schürmann hat in diesem Zusammenhang sehr treffend von der „grundsätzlichen Offenheit, mit der Jesus den Ratschlüssen und Schickungen des Vaters gegenüberstand“,[19] gesprochen.

14. In seinem Vortrag vor der Heidelberger Akademie der Wissenschaften: „Das Verhältnis der urchristlichen Christusbotschaft zum historischen Jesus“ 1959, in dem er sich mit der „neuen“ Frage nach dem historischen Jesus bei seinen Schülern auseinandersetzte, abgedruckt in Rudolf Bultmann, *Exegetica* (Tübingen: Mohr-Siebeck, 1967), S. 445–69, hier besonders S. 452f.

15. Dabei ist das Besondere dieses Spruches, daß der negative Entscheid mit Gott in Verbindung gebracht wird (kein Vogel geht in die Falle ohne Gott). Für die Kühnheit, so die Zusage der Zuwendung Gottes zu veranschaulichen, ist mir keine Parallele bekannt.

16. Lk 17,33 kommt sicherlich bei der Frage nach Authentizität der Vorrang zu. Auch demjenigen, der sein Leben verliert (von verlieren *wollen* oder Leben opfern usw. wie in manchen Parallelfassungen ist hier nicht die Rede), wird Leben zugesagt Johannes 11,25 („…der wird leben, auch wenn er stirbt“) ist nicht weit entfernt.

17. S. besonders W. Vogler, Die „Naherwartung“ Jesu, *Theologische Versuche* 16 (1986), S. 57–71.

18. S. die gründlichen Erörterungen bei J. Ringleben, *Wahrhaft auferstanden* (Tübingen: Mohr-Siebeck, 1998), S. 11–27.

19. H. Schürmann, *Jesus. Gestalt und Geheimnis* (Paderborn: Bonitatius, 1994), S. 174. S. schon ders., *Jesu ureigener Tod*, Freiburg 1974. Schürmanns Arbeiten zu den von mir ja nur resümierten Fragen verbinden in besonderer Weise Interpretation und historische Rekonstruktion. Ich folge ihm vor allem in der dialogischen Auffassung des Gottesverhältnisses Jesu im Blick auf den Fortgang von Jesu Geschichte und Geschick. Seine interpretatorischen Rekonstruktionsversuche legen aber nahe, im Verlauf und Zustand der Überlieferung die Bestätigung zu sehen, daß Jesus seinen Tod nicht als Sühnetod zu verstehen lehrte. Nicht die Frage, ob Jesus seinem Sterben einen Heilssinn gegeben hat, ist zunächst von Interesse, sondern im Duktus des Auftretens Jesu und der Erfahrung, daß Israel seinem einladenden Ruf in die Gegenwart der Herrschaft Gottes nicht folgte, ist mit der Frage bei Jesu Anhängern zu rechnen, ob Gott nun doch das Gericht über Israel verhängt.

Aus dem allen kann nur gefolgert werden, daß Jesus die Möglichkeit seines Todes sehr wohl vor Augen gestanden haben wird. Aber es wird zugleich deutlich, daß diese Möglichkeit nicht zum Gegenstand einer besonderen Sinndeutung seines Todes werden mußte. Wer mit dem Psalmisten sagen kann: „Meine Zeit steht in deinen Händen" (Ps 31,16), wird von der Frage nach dem Sinn seines Sterbens nicht beunruhigt und muß seinen Lebensausgang nicht deuten.[20]

Zu diesen Feststellungen paßt die Beobachtung, daß das Verständnis des Todes Jesu als „für uns" geschehenen Sühnetod keineswegs so generell den Bestand der Überlieferung beherrscht, wie man es erwarten müßte, wenn er selbst dieses Verständnis unter seinen Anhängern geltend gemacht hätte. Das apokalyptische *dei*, das vor allem in der Menschensohnüberlieferung zur Wirkung kam, scheint eher das Rätsel des Todes Jesu dem Verdacht der Sinnlosigkeit entreißen zu sollen.

Einer eigenen Erörterung bedürfte die Frage, wie Jesus die Erfahrung der überwiegenden Ablehnung durch Israel in seinem Gegenüber zu Gott verstanden und bestanden hat.[21] Die Imagination, die hier vertreten wird, hat auch ohne eine hinreichend einleuchtende Beantwortung dieser Frage Bestand. Ja, sie kann zur Erörterung und Klärung dieser Frage hoffentlich beitragen.

Es sei nur angedeutet: Jesus hat auf die Erfahrung der Ablehnung allem Anschein nach nicht mit einer Veränderung seines Zeitverständnisses und mit der Ankündigung des unausweichlichen Gerichtes über Israel[22] reagiert, sondern er hat seinen Tod als Bestätigung seines Zeitverständnisses und der von ihm praktizierten zuvorkommenden Gnade verstanden. Das kommt bei dem hervorgehobenen Abschiedsmahl Jesu, an dessen Historizität nicht gezweifelt werden kann,[23] im sogenannten Deutewort zum gemeinsamen Becher, durch den dieses

20. So formuliere ich in bewußtem Gegensatz zu J. Jeremias: „Wenn er sich als der Gottesbote wußte, der die abschließende Botschaft bringen sollte, und wenn er mit seinem gewaltsamen Tod gerechnet hat, dann mußte ihn die Frage nach dem Sinn und der sühnenden Wirkung seines Todes beschäftigen" (*Neutestamentliche Theologie I* [Berlin: EVA, 1973], S. 274). Daß er sich damit beschäftigt hat, mag sein, nur wissen wir darüber nichts Gewisses. Daß er sich damit beschäftigten mußte, ist ein Urteil, das von einer unausgewiesenen Psychologie ausgeht, die m.E. nicht der von Schürmann treffend beschriebenen Offenheit des Gehorsams Jesu gegenüber Gott, dem Vater hinreichend Rechnung trägt.

21. Hier haben die Untersuchungen Schürmanns ihren Schwerpunkt; im Zusammenhang dieser Problematik hat sich wohl für Jesus auch die Sinnfrage gestellt, durch deren Beantwortung auch Licht auf die Möglichkeit seines Sterbens fallen kann. Das ist aber etwas anderes, als zu unterstellen, Jesus habe sich mit dem Sinn seines möglichen Sterbens beschäftigt.

22. Dagegen sprechen weder die Tempelreinigung noch die Ankündigung der Zerstörung des Tempels: „Auch der Konflikt Jesu mit dem Tempel ist ein Konflikt im Judentum – nicht ein Konflikt mit dem Judentum" (Theißen/Merz [s. Anm. 13], 1997), S. 383).

23. Ich gehe dabei von den vorsichtigen Rekonstruktionen G.Theißens (G.Theißen/A.Merz, a.a.O., S. 359–86) aus, halte aber das Verständnis des Sterbens Jesu als Bundesopfer bei Jesus für möglich. Die traditionsgeschichtliche Feststellung, daß die Tradition vom neuen Bund nicht mit dem Opfergedanken verbunden sei (s. Theißen a.a.O., S. 372), kann ja nicht ausschließen, daß auf Grund der Situation Verbindungen entstehen, die in der Tradition nicht vorgegeben waren (s. im übrigen H. Geses Studie, „Psalm 22 und das Neue Testament" in: *Vom Sinai zum Zion* [München: Chr. Kaiser, 1974], S. 200). Eine regelrechte Einsetzung des Mahles als Ersatz für den Tempelkult

Mahl im äußeren Vorgang von anderen Mahlzeiten unterschieden ist, zum Ausdruck.

Nachdem diese Voraussetzungen klargestellt sind, kann die oben genannte These weiter entfaltet und beschrieben werden.

Will man „imaginieren", welche Fragen für die Anhänger Jesu durch die Ostererlebnisse entstanden, so muß man versuchen, ihre Situation zu verstehen, in der ihnen Jesus begegnete. *In der Struktur* trifft immer noch die Feststellung J. Moltmanns zu: „Die Situation der Osterzeugen war (also) bestimmt: 1. durch die Verkündigung Jesu und ihre Nachfolge, 2. durch Jesu Kreuzigung, ihren darin zerstörten Glauben und erst 3. durch die Motive und Symbole der allgemeinen apokalyptischen Naherwartung des von den Römern beherrschten Judentums ihrer Zeit".[24]

Ich greife zunächst den zweiten Punkt heraus: Wie bestimmte die Hinrichtung Jesu die Situation der Anhänger Jesu, in der ihnen Jesus neu begegnete und in deren Horizont diese Begegnung von ihnen erfahren wurde? Geht man von der Flucht der Jünger aus und ihrer Rückkehr nach Galiläa (Mk 14,50),[25] so ist die Frage, was sie zur Flucht bzw. Heimkehr bewog. Sehr wahrscheinlich war da Angst, auch noch ergriffen zu werden, im Spiel. Moltmanns Antwort, daß der Glaube der Jünger zerstört, durch die Kreuzigung, „diese harte Tatsache, widerlegt" war (ebenda), kann als common sense angesehen werden. Sie wird oft mit theologisch-dogmatischem Nachdruck vertreten. Das Skandalon des Kreuzes soll so historisch anschaulich werden.[26] Bei dieser Problemstellung wird aber ganz übersehen, daß Jesu Verkündigung und Verhalten gerade Hoffnung für von aller Hoffnung Ausgeschlossene bedeutete, und zwar nicht durch die Propagierung bestimmter Vorstellungen über die Zukunft, sondern durch Einholung in diese schon angebrochene Zukunft. Jesu Verkündigung hatte wie alle Zeitansagen performativen Charakter. Für den, der sich darauf einließ, brachte sie Zukunft.

(G. Theißen: „Das Abendmahl als kultstiftende Symbolhandlung") kann ich nicht erkennen; sie würde die Variabilität der Abendmahlfeiern zum Rätsel machen. Es sind keine Spuren dafür vorhanden, daß die Mahlfeier, ihre Gesten und Worte zur Brücke wurden, die über die Anfechtung durch die Hinrichtung Jesu hinübertrug. Vielmehr wird das Mahl zur Brücke von Ostern aus.

24. *Der gekreuzigte Gott* (München: Chr. Kaiser, 2. Aufl., 1973), S. 153.

25. Diskussionswürdige Argumente gegen die Historizität kenne ich nicht, allerdings wird man bezweifeln müssen, daß alle Jünger nach Galiläa flohen; einige der Frauen blieben bekanntlich; Anhänger aus Judäa und Jerusalem werden sich nach Hause zurückgezogen haben, wo sie leicht „untertauchen" konnten.

26. S. z.B. mit besonderem Nachdruck, G. Bornkamm, *Jesus von Nazareth* (Stuttgart: Kohlhammer, 2. Aufl., 1957), S. 158, wo er schon im Blick auf das Leben Jesu von „einer Bewegung zerbrochener Messiaserwartungen" spricht. Die Osterzeugen sind „mit dem, was sie bis dahin geglaubt haben, gescheitert" (S.169). Das theologische Interesse der breiten Ausmalung dieses Sachverhaltes bei Bornkamm wird sichtbar in dem Satz: „Nein, sie sind nicht selber auferstanden" (ebenda). Zu Recht hat E. Fuchs in seiner Kritik geltend gemacht, daß nicht der Glaube zerbrach, sondern Glaubensvorstellungen sich als unangemessen erwiesen und korrigiert wurden (E. Fuchs, Glaube und Geschichte im Blick auf die Frage nach dem historischen Jesus. Zu G. Bornkamms Buch über Jesus von Nazareth, in: *Zur Frage nach dem historischen Jesus* [Tübingen: Mohr-Siebeck, 1960], S. 174, 188).

Bei der Beschreibung des Kreuzes als Skandalon geht auch die historische Forschung in der Regel abstrakt und dogmatisch vor, weil sie sich mit der Widersprüchlichkeit oder Kompatibilität von Vorstellungen und Konzepten beschäftigt und die handelnden Personen nur als Träger solcher Vorstellungen und Konzepte würdigt. Sicherlich hat es auch so etwas wie zerbrechenden Glauben, Hoffnungen, die sich nicht erfüllten, Vorstellungen, die gegenstandslos wurden, gegeben.[27] Daneben – und wahrscheinlich in überwiegender Zahl – hat es Anhänger Jesu gegeben, die an dem, was sie durch ihn erfahren hatten,[28] nicht irre wurden. Vom Leiden und Sterben des Gerechten, den Gott schließlich retten wird, wußte man aus den Gebeten der Psalmen. So konnte z.B. Ps 22 zur Sprachhilfe für die Passionsgeschichte werden. Daß Verfolgung und Leiden gerade die gottgesandten Propheten treffen, war nichts Neues. Gewiß wird mit diesem Wissen auch die Hoffnung verbunden gewesen sein, daß jetzt endlich diese ständige Wiederholung durchbrochen wird als Durchbruch zum Heil. Aber gerade dann konnte die Erfahrung der Hinrichtung Jesu erst recht in Verzweiflung stürzen: Was wird Gott jetzt tun? Wenn der Jesus, der die Nähe Gottes gelebt und zugesprochen hat, hingerichtet wird, dann wird sich Gott entfernen, abwenden; dann kommt das Gericht. Mit dieser Reaktion[29] unter den Anhängern muß mindestens auch, wahrscheinlich aber in erster Linie gerechnet werden. Vielleicht ist sie auch der Hintergrund für die Jüngerflucht: das Gericht beginnt ja bekanntlich zuerst am Hause Gottes (s. nur Ez 9). Vor allem aber mußte sich diese Frage mit hoher Wahrscheinlichkeit einstellen, weil sie schon im Übergang von Johannes dem Täufer,[30] der den unmittelbar bevorstehenden Gerichtsschlag Gottes (und seines Beauftragten?) angedroht hatte und zur Bußtaufe rief, zu Jesus, der ganz anders auftrat als der Täufer und in seinem Verhalten so entschieden die Zuwendung des Heiles in Wort und Tat praktizierte, in der Luft lag,

27. Wer dies als einzige Möglichkeit annimmt, muß freilich unterstellen, daß Jesus generell mißverstanden worden ist.

28. Man muß sich hier unbestimmt ausdrücken, denn das wird durchaus Verschiedenes gewesen sein, wobei das Gewicht der durch Jesus gewährten Gemeinschaft in keinem Fall unterschätzt werden sollte. Die „Pro-Existenz" Jesu (H.Schürmann, der übrigens im Blick auf in Prag und Budapest immer wieder aufgeworfene Fragen vermutete, „eine eigenständig eingefärbte Theologie" und Spiritualität „in der Kirche des ‚Ostens' ... könnte um den Begriff der ‚Pro-Existenz' versammelt werden und damit Gehalte in den Blick stellen, in denen alle Theologien Zukunft haben könnten", *Jesus, Gestalt und Geheimnis*, S. 286).Die Frage nach den christologischen Titeln – soll sie wirklich geschichtlich untersucht werden – darf nicht abgesehen von der existentiellen Bedeutung für die Rezepienten erörtert werden.

29. H. Gollwitzer hat in einer mehr erbaulichen Auslegung der Emmaus-Geschichte diese Dimension sehr eindringlich zur Sprache begracht (*Jesu Tod und Auferweckung nach dem Bericht des Lukas* [Theologische Existenz heute 77; München: Chr. Kaiser, 1941]). Andeutungsweise E. Jüngel, *Paulus und Jesus* (Tübingen: Mohr-Siebeck, 1962), S. 281: „ Mit dem Tode Jesu wurde Jesus den Lebenden als Lebender entzogen. Damit wurde seine eschatologische Bedeutung in Frage gestellt, insofern die Nähe Gottes zur Geschichte sich wiederum in die Ferne Gottes zur Geschichte zu verwandeln drohte (Mk 15,34)."

30. Wieviele „Überläufer" es gab, wissen wir nicht, aber daß beide, Johannes und Jesus, auch bei Unbeteiligten zusammen im Blick waren, zumal Jesus solche Zusammenschau aufnahm (s. Mk 6,14 parr. Mk 8,27 parr. Mt 11,16f.f. par. Mk 11,27ff.parr.).

zumal Jesus an der Autorität des Täufers mit hohen Worten festhielt. Wo bleibt das von Johannes angekündigte Gericht? Bis heute macht es bei der Interpretation Schwierigkeiten, hier Übereinstimmung und Unterschied zwischen Johannes und Jesus zu beschreiben,[31] weil es so schwer ist, bei Jesus das Zusammengehören von Gericht und Heil zu bestimmen.[32] Denn Jesu, ihn vom Täufer unterscheidendes Zeitverständnis, brachte die Ordnung der Vorstellungen und vor allem den Grundsatz apokalyptischen Denkens, daß das Alte erst vergehen muß, damit das Neue kommen kann (4 Ezra 4,26–29), durcheinander. Im Alten brach das Neue herein. Die Wolke, in der sich der Regen ankündigt, war schon zu sehen; der Südwind, den die Hitze voranschickt, war schon zu spüren. „Ihr Heuchler, das Aussehen von Erde und Himmel wißt ihr zu prüfen, wieso prüft ihr nicht diese Zeit?" (Lk 12,54–56). Das ist also die Frage: Aus welcher Zukunft kommt die Gegenwart?[33] Muß man darauf antworten, daß die Gegenwart aus der Zukunft der Gottesherrschaft kommt und Jesus davon Gebrauch macht, so daß sie in seinem Wirken nicht nur zu erkennen, sondern auch zu ergreifen ist, dann überholt diese Nähe der Herrschaft Gottes das Gericht. Gott kommt sich selbst zuvor.

Ein so überraschendes und verwirrendes Zeitverständnis ist in der biblischen Überlieferung nicht ohne Parallele. Im 3. Jesaja findet sich die Verheißung: „Bevor die Schwangere gekreist, bevor die Wehen (apokalyptischer terminus technicus) über sie kamen, hat sie einen Sohn geboren. Wer hat so etwas je gehört? Wer hat derartiges schon gesehen?" (Jes 66,7f.). Die Verwirrung, die solche Sicht anrichtet, zeigt sich daran, daß später diese Verheißung (Jes 66,7–14) mit einer Gerichtsepiphanie gerahmt (V. 6 und 15f.) und damit gewissermaßen eingebunden worden ist.[34]

Diese kurze Charakterisierung des Zeitverständnisses Jesu mag genügen, um zu veranschaulichen, daß die Frage: „Wo bleibt das Gericht?" schon zu Jesu Lebzeiten in seiner Anhängerschaft lebendig gewesen sein wird, so daß dann die Hinrichtung Jesu bei vielen die erschreckende Gewißheit brachte: „Jetzt wird Gottes Gericht hereinbrechen!" und zur Flucht aus Jerusalem bewog. Dabei mag es zwei Ausformungen dieser Gewißheit gegeben haben, einmal die Erwartung des Gerichtes über Israel und „uns", die wir selbst ihn verraten und verlassen haben, zum anderen die Erwartung des Gerichtes über die Feinde, Juden und

31. S. z.B. Jürgen Becker, *Johannes der Täufer und Jesus von Nazareth* (Biblische Studien 63; Neukirchen: Neukirchener, 1972), einerseits und U.B. Müller, *Johannes der Täufer* (Leipzig: EVA, 2002) andererseits; dazu M. Reiser, *Die Gerichtspredigt Jesu* (NTA 23; Münster: Aschendorf, 1990).

32. „Zwei Seiten einer Medaille"; „Das Gericht ist die Kehrseite des Heils und seine notwendige Voraussetzung" Reiser, S. 241 aufgenommen von Müller, S. 65. Gerade die letzte Formulierung zeigt die Verlegenheit der Interpretation.

33. An diesem Bildwort ist deutlich, daß sich Jesus nicht als der Bringer der Gottesherrschaft verstand, sondern als ihr Exponent (s. Jüngel, *Paulus und Jesus* [Tübingen: Mohr-Siebeck, 1962], S. 187f.). Deswegen sollte man auch nicht mit Selbstverständlichkeit auf eine grundlegende Berufungserfahrung Jesu rekurrieren (s. G. Theißen, *Der historische Jesus*, S. 196f.).

34. So jedenfalls die Analyse von C. Westermann, *Das Buch Jesaja 40 – 66* (ATD 19; Berlin: EVA, 1968), S. 332; er sieht in dieser Rahmung „den ersten Schritt von der nachexilischen Heilsprophetie Tritojesajas in die beginnende Apokalyptik".

Heiden, von denen wir als Freunde Jesu durch seine Berufung geschieden sind.

Auf diesem Hintergrund konnte dann die neue Begegnung Jesu mit ihnen in den Ostererlebnissen als ein Ereignis neuer Zuwendung und also der Vergebung verstanden werden. Wußte man sich auf Grund eigenen Schuldiggewordenseins in Solidarität mit Israel, so wurde darin eine Vergebung erfahren, die nun auch Israel als Ruf zur Umkehr alsbald bekannt zu machen ist, so daß diese Jünger, zu denen sicherlich Petrus gehört hat, nach Jerusalem zurückkehrten. Wußte man sich durch die Zugehörigkeit zu Jesus schon zu seinen Lebzeiten heilvoll von allen Gegnern geschieden, so konnte das Ostererlebnis in erster Linie als Bestätigung früherer Erwählung erfahren werden; eine Rückkehr nach Jerusalem legte sich dann nicht unbedingt nahe.[35]

In dem „Jerusalemer Zweig" dieser imaginierten Entwicklung wurde auf Grund der Erfahrung des Ostererlebnisses als Ereignis der Vergebung die Frage „Wo bleibt das Gericht?" erneut lebendig. Ihre Beantwortung hat sich sicherlich in mehreren Schritten vollzogen. In der Erinnerung an die erfahrene Pro-Existenz, die den Anhängern Jesu so schmerzlich entzogen war und sich nun in den neuen Begegnungen Jesu mit ihnen erneuerte, konnte auch der Tod Jesu in dieses Licht rücken und dann unter Zuhilfenahme unterschiedlicher Vorstellungen als „für uns" geschehen ausgesagt und schließlich mit Hilfe von Jesaja 53 zur Sprache gebracht werden.

Diese Beantwortung der Frage nach dem ausgebliebenen Gericht war freilich durch die Interpretation des Todes Jesu als „ für uns" bzw. „für viele" geschehen nicht erledigt, sondern blieb einerseits in der Frage lebendig, wie der so verstandene Tod Jesu auf das bevorstehende Endgericht „ausstrahlt" (bei Paulus besonders 1 Thess. 5, 9f.; Röm 5,6–10) und führte andererseits in den großen zeitgeschichtlichen Krisen[36] zu Identifikationen des Gerichtes Gottes mit solchen zeitgeschichtlichen Ereignissen, insbesondere mit der Zerstörung Jerusalems und des Tempels.

Auch bei dieser Imagination bleibt ein Rätsel – oder wird sogar erst recht zum Rätsel –, warum Jesaja 53 erst so spät ausdrücklich zitiert und in welchen Teilen es zitiert wird.

35. Sicherlich muß man auch mit anderen Fragen rechnen, die für einige Anhänger beim Erleben seiner Hinrichtung unabweislich waren: So wird die Frage, wer Jesus sei, sicherlich durch die Kreuzesinschrift neu belebt. Für andere mag entscheidend gewesen zu sein: Ist sein Vollmachtsanspruch widerlegt durch Gott angesichts seines Endes am Fluchholz? Diese Frage wird in der Interpretation häufig unter Verweis auf Dt 21, 23 als die Kernfrage, die sich den Anhängern Jesu stellte, angesehen. Aber zu Recht hat Ernst Käsemann darauf hingewiesen, daß die Anhänger Jesu aus dem am haarez kommend schwerlich so schriftgelehrt auf die Gesetzesproblematik gestoßen sind (Käsemann, *Exegetische Versuche und Besinnungen II* [Göttingen: Vandenhoeck & Ruprecht, 1964], S. 113f.). Doch damit kann diese Möglichkeit des Verstehens nicht völlig ausgeschlossen werden; denn der Kreis der Anhänger Jesu war durchaus heterogen. Das Argument Käsemanns schränkt aber die Breite, die diese Möglichkeit in der Forschung einnimmt, zu Recht ein.

36. S. dazu G. Theißen, *Lokalkolorit und Zeitgeschichte in den Evangelien* (Göttingen: Vandenhoeck & Ruprecht, 1989).

The Witness of the Seer of Patmos

John M. Court

On the staircase wall at my home hangs an original oil painting by a contemporary priest/artist whose name is Robin Bradbury. This painting is entitled *Outlook from Patmos* (1998). Because it hangs by the staircase I see it several times a day from different viewpoints relative to the picture, as I stand above, below or on a level with it. The twilight of the scene shades from golden brown to black. The cliff-top, crowned with buildings resembling a modern cityscape, stands silhouetted against the effect of the sun, while the sky is shot through with brilliant white, orange, crimson and purple. On the cliffs a venerable figure of a man appears to stand, gazing into the distance and clasping a book. I say that he 'appears' to stand because at some times of day, and in certain lighting conditions, he is not visible to me as I walk by. At other times he emerges boldly from the canvas, almost as clearly as the strong colours that surround him.

The Seer of Patmos, the 'author' of the canonical Book of Revelation, is a visionary who seeks to communicate his vision to others. We would like to know more about him as a person; but, as in Robin Bradbury's painting, he is evanescent. Now we see him; now we don't.

The only evidence we have about him is in his text, the text of his book. This tells us particular things, but can hardly be said to constitute an autobiography. The comparison is with another New Testament personality, Saul/Paul of Tarsus, where we are fortunate in having at least two perspectives, in the Acts of the Apostles and from Paul himself (e.g. in his letter to the Galatians). By contrast, the text of the Book of Revelation begins with a promise to reveal the story of 'what must soon take place' (1.1), and then proceeds to confuse the reader completely. In Alan Garrow's words:

> This situation is not unlike that of someone who buys a flat-pack bedside cabinet from a furniture store, takes it home in great excitement, only to find that the assembly instructions are missing. The hapless assembler knows that the various pieces must fit together so as to create a useful unit, but which bit does what, and what bit fits where? Without the instructions various random attempts at assembly result in frustration. Ultimately it is concluded that this is not a bedside cabinet at all, but an abstract piece of sculpti-furniture which expresses its form in terms of furniture-like themes and elements, while remaining intentionally non-functional.[1]

Garrow, for his part, makes a bold attempt to identify the essential contents and line of the story in the Book of Revelation. He has to argue with those who

1. Alan Garrow, *Revelation* (New Testament Readings; London: Routledge, 1997), p. 20.

see the action going round and round in circles, recapitulating the same point; and he will also take issue with those who identify pauses and flashbacks in the storyline. But the most important principle is to recognize that Revelation uses different kinds of material to tell the story, and that different materials have different functions. The best illustration is that of the hymns scattered through the book; their function is rather like the chorus in Greek tragedy, to comment on the action, and here to affirm the abiding truths of the Christian faith. The mixed nature of the literary material in the book used to trigger source critical analyses, resolving the supposed problem by assigning the different genres of the composite work each to their own origins, and even providing the basis for value judgements as to which were the 'truly Christian' parts of the work. Nowadays the literary variety is simply a feature of the work's description, and this mixture of genres makes a positive rather than a negative contribution to analysis.

What we are told about the Seer of Patmos, among the materials of his book, includes:

1. his sense of authority – commissioned like an Old Testament prophet;
2. something about his historical situation;
3. that he is a visionary, and has the capacity to communicate those visions;
4. that he is a theologian of the Church, seeing its past, its present and its future;
5. as an individual Christian prophet his overriding concern is with the concept of witness (the practical implications, including martyrdom, as well as the theological role).

I propose to look briefly at each of these aspects in turn.

1. *Authority*

The mixture of literary genres in the book is immediately apparent at the very beginning and at the conclusion of the work. It is both an apocalypse and a circular letter: introduced as an apocalypse in 1.1–3, and as a letter in 1.4–8; there is an epistolary conclusion at 21.21, and immediately before that a series of final guarantees and solemn warnings, appropriate for an apocalyptic work, at 22.6–20. Both literary genres are likely to set up distinctive relationships between the author and the readers. The underlying difference between the authority of a prophet/seer and the authority of a pastor inevitably seems to set up tensions in the way the work will be received.

The authority claimed in the apocalyptic introduction is uncompromising. In management terms there is a 'hot line' from God himself to Jesus Christ, and then to Christ's angel, and on 'to his servant John'. It is only the 'Revelation of John' insofar as he does not deviate from the message which he has received, ultimately, he claims, from God. There is more than a suggestion of a clash of rival authorities in the background here, which would be the reason for so outspoken and direct a claim to be the mouthpiece of God. The language of 'prophecy' is used here to enhance the sense of a direct commission from God, analogous to that of the canonical prophets of the Hebrew Bible. To secure the immediate impact and effectiveness of this Christian prophecy, measures are taken in the concluding verses to make the message directly accessible, but to prevent any tampering or modification, with the direst threats against those tempted to interfere (Rev. 22.10, 18–19).

The juxtaposition of apocalyptic and epistolary openings may ultimately soften the hardest edge of the authority claim. If we think in terms of the Johannine community, there are mixed signals. The opening of 1 John, transcending the normal opening of a letter, does so in order to emphasize the fundamental conformity of the message with the very beginnings of Christianity ('We declare to you what was from the beginning'). From the contents of the Johannine correspondence, we recognize the polemic with those who thought differently and indeed left the community because of it (e.g. 1 Jn 2.19). But within the community itself, in the relations between the brethren and the pastor, the pattern is one of unity and reciprocality, modelled on the relationship between God and Christ (cf. 1 Jn 4 and Jn 17). In the same way, in Revelation the emphasis is on relationship, such as that between Christ and his Church, in the imagery of the New Jerusalem (Rev. 21).

2. *The Historical Situation*

> *Revelation* comes from a situation of actual (or threatened) persecution of Christians by the local Roman imperial authorities in Asia Minor towards the end of the first century.[2]

This much can still be claimed, and possibly asserted more strongly now, after a fashion for doubting the reality of any threatened imperial persecution has come and receded again. But the scholar still needs to be cautious in the face of a circular argument, if the book of Revelation supplies almost the only data for the persecution of Christians by the Romans in the first century CE. There may be more evidence for targeted persecution by Jews of individual Christians, as a result of the partings of the ways, especially if all the texts relating to the Johannine community are taken together. Either the book of Revelation is a database for the persecution of Christians from one or more directions, or it is a projection (well-founded or neurotic) of the possibility (the threat) of persecution. We must ask quite seriously what effect does it have on the way the book is regarded, depending on which of these alternatives is the true one.

Revelation 6 shows the saints waiting for an expected future transformation. 'Sovereign Lord, holy and true, how long will it be…?' (6.10). The letters to the seven churches in chapters 2 and 3 may offer us a realistic glimpse of the Asia Minor communities during this time of waiting. The formulaic structures of the individual messages may remind us of the realistic but brief observations from holiday postcards, or we may conclude from the same structural evidence that

2. 'Revelation of John', in R. J. Coggins and J. L. Houlden (eds.), *A Dictionary of Biblical Interpretation* (London: SCM Press, 1990), p. 593.

these are stereotypes, the main function of which is to demonstrate the relationship of these communities to the ideal church of the End Time. Such a demonstration works in the way that particular promises are collated and fulfilled in the description of the New Jerusalem.

> 'In Revelation John depicts the glories of the reigning Christ who holds the churches in his hands. His sovereignty is a reality now. But, as always, the sovereign Lord expresses his sovereignty, not by bypassing our minds and wills, but by working through them. To the mind which is uninformed by the gospel this is a contradiction. Many Christians show that they have not brought the gospel to bear on their thinking when they reject, for example, the sovereign predestination of God as being incompatible with human responsibility.'[3]

Once again the extent to which reality, as opposed to theological theory, is recognized in these texts, will affect the way the book is interpreted and then is applied to modern church situations. As Goldsworthy acknowledged, 'John's first concern is not to minister to armchair prophets in some far-off age, but to the battlers of his own day who struggle to reconcile the fact of their suffering with the fact of Christ's victory over sin.' Do the seven letters then offer ethical recommendations appropriate for actual situations? In the past, theological scholarship in Germany, for example, has emphasized the divide between apocalyptic and ethics, to the neglect of apocalyptic. To see Roman political power as satanic, and to issue harsh calls for repentance in the face of judgement, seem to form as unpromising a foundation for ethics as do the current relationships between Israel and the Palestinians. Jürgen Kerner[4] sought to redress the balance and demonstrate that apocalyptic was compatible with serious ethical thought, by concentrating on the themes of endurance in the face of persecution and of the eschatological destiny of the individual, in the book of Revelation. He clarified these themes in comparison with *4 Ezra*, using the Ten Commandments, and discussing concepts of sin, and the relationship between imperatives and indicatives within the language of salvation. The options for the Christian, according to the text of Revelation, then seem to be an enduring confidence (or hope against hope), a vindictive reaction that rejoices at the downfall of enemies, or a hymnic celebration of the divine order of heaven, over against the chaos of earth.

3. *The Seer as Visionary*

After the apocalyptic and epistolary introductions of the opening verses of Revelation, the reader is immediately immersed in a visionary experience: 'I, John, ...was on the island called Patmos... I was in the Spirit on the Lord's day' (1.9–10). Not so much a wandering attention during a church service, but rather a profound and mystical religious experience seems to be described. The question for the interpreter concerns the reality of this visionary experience and its sequels

3. Graeme Goldsworthy, *The Gospel in Revelation* (Exeter: Paternoster Press, 1984), pp. 79–80.

4. Jürgen Kerner, *Die Ethik der Johannes-Apokalypse im Vergleich mit der des 4.Esra* (BZNT, 94; Berlin/New York: W. de Gruyter, 1998).

throughout the book. To what extent are the Old Testament echoes, as well as the detail of the imagery, evidence rather for a literary construction within the genre of vision? These alternatives are not mutually exclusive. It is obvious that someone who has spontaneous experiences of a visionary kind will see through eyes and mind that are culturally conditioned, and afterwards will reconstruct those experiences in traditional form and image. So early Christians will perceive the relationship with the Hebrew Bible in general, and texts like Daniel and Ezekiel, Joel and Isaiah in particular. If this is true of the Christian community at large, it is even more true of the early Christian prophet and seer.

It is defensible to claim that the visions derive from authentic religious experiences, while giving full credit to the literary structure which is the foundation of the book and can be seen to unite the text at just those points where its wealth of bizarre imagery risks confusing and disorientating the reader. So the visionary experience of the Risen Christ, translating the theology of Resurrection into the immanence of worship experience, draws the reader, by the literary structure of the book, into the practical question of how such belief and experience should be applied in the day-to-day patterns of church life. Just as the texts derived from the vision introduce each message like a sermon, so the climax of each message will draw the reader on to the ultimate stage of the book, the promise of existence in the New Jerusalem.

The final stage of this visionary experience is recorded in ch. 21, with the descent of the New Jerusalem in the context of a new heaven and a new earth. The scholar cannot overlook the traditional elements of this picture, reflected in many Jewish apocalyptic texts. But the uniqueness of the Seer's vision must also be acknowledged: here alone is the holy city caught in the process of descent (21.2), as the new reality comes about. Equal attention should be paid to the relation of this literary description to the prophetic imagery of the rest of the book, to the ultimate details of this author's symbolism and to the psychological impact of this climactic visionary experience as a reassurance to the saints who suffer, as well as to the Seer himself. David L.Barr[5] has raised the tantalizing question, as to whether the end of this apocalyptic text ever really comes. But equally for its psychological, theological and literary purpose, a vision which anticipates the real end will serve just as well.

The point can be seen in a slightly different way, in relation to one of a number of possible hypotheses as to the book's historical setting.[6] If the book of Daniel is possibly to be regarded as a re-run of the formative historical experience of the Exodus from Egypt and the Settlement in Canaan, re-presenting this theological scenario in terms of the later realities of the Exile to Babylon and the subsequent Restoration, then is it equally possible to see the book of Revelation (on analogy with this) as having its historical and theological focus on the Fall of Jerusalem

5. David L.Barr, 'Waiting for the End that Never Comes: The Narrative Logic of John's Story' in Steve Moyise (ed.), *Studies in the Book of Revelation* (Edinburgh/New York: T&T Clark, 2001), pp. 101–12.

6. Based on George Wesley Buchanan, *The Book of Daniel* (Mellen Biblical Commentary, Old Testament 25; Lewiston: Mellen Biblical Press, 1999).

(at the end of the Jewish War) and therefore only achieving completion with the descent of the New Jerusalem as the ultimate restoration? An hypothesis of this kind certainly serves to show the psychological importance of completion, and how this can be achieved by a prophetic vision, whereas a literary construction or a theoretical compensation by themselves would prove inadequate.

4. *The Seer as Theologian*

The Seer's theological insights are best appreciated by stepping back a few paces from the text and recognizing the wider view. His work encompasses both God's creation and the re-creation of the world, both the incarnation of Christ and his ascension, both the gift of the Spirit of God and his role as prosecutor, condemning the world. In the final phase, with the descending of the New Jerusalem, what the Seer stresses is the essential relationship (the theological marriage) between Christ and his Church. The Seer as theologian of the Church, essentially to be compared with the writer of Ephesians and with the Acts of the Apostles, sees the complementary dimensions of past, present and future of the cosmic Church. As with Paul's letters, there is an important correlation between the separate local communities of worshippers and their identification within the universal church (as its local representatives).

M. Eugene Boring[7] analysed the theology of Revelation as a response to three fundamental questions in the mind of the Church:

Who, if anyone, rules in this world?

What, if any, is the meaning of the tragic events which comprise our history?

If there is a good God who is in control of things, why doesn't he do something about present evil?

The Seer's answer is: 'He *will*, for history is a unified story which is not yet over.' This note of reassurance is conveyed by the interlocking relationship between the components of his visionary text, and particularly by the hymns which are sung repeatedly within the worship of heaven. God has already acted. Christ is the Lord and will come as the rider on the white horse. God will go on acting consistently within his underlying purpose. The Kingdom of God is not a matter of uncertain speculation as to when (or if) and how it will come. The coming of the Kingdom was combined with the Christological confession of Jesus' Lordship. God is Almighty (the *pantocrator* of all time sequences – see 1.8; 4.8; 11.17; 15.3; 16.7,14; 19.6,15; 21.22). The local Church is invited to join in the heavenly worship: 'Hallelujah! For the Lord our God the Almighty reigns' (19.6).

5. *The Witness of the Seer*

Witness, or testimony, is a key idea in Revelation, which leads practically (and etymologically as well) towards martyrdom. The Greek words for this concept

7. *Interpretation* 40/3 (1986), pp. 257, 260. Cf. M. Eugene Boring, *Revelation* (Interpretation Bible Commentary; Louisville: John Knox Press, 1989).

(*martys / martyria*) evolve in their meaning within the context of this book of the New Testament. It becomes a complex idea, as Elisabeth A. Castelli describes it, 'of martyrdom as death and as witness (a telling) and as victory (an inversion of contemporary power relations, repression becoming exaltation)'.[8] The visions of ch. 11 indicate how this witnessing is effective. Witness is an activity in the closest relation to Christ (an Imitation of Christ) on the path from suffering to glory (see 1.5; 11.8). Revelation demonstrates a significant chain of witness, from God to Christ, to the angel, to the prophet John, to the churches, to the world (see 1.1–2). God's reign is seen as universal in power, but it works towards its culmination through human agencies and representative individuals. Those who hold the testimony are those who preserve the witness entrusted to them by Jesus, declare their witness to Jesus in witnessing to the world, and are prepared to suffer and to die for that witness. What they declare is what Jesus himself reveals: the judgements and the sovereign authority of God.

Testimony/evidence is not simply what one has gained, like an investigative detective, and which one then holds onto, as the vital clue. It is something that needs to be communicated, because, like the prophet of old, one cannot keep it to oneself. But the role of Christian witness also evolves from the original job-description, in the act of presenting the message to the world. As Jean-Pierre Jossua OP writes:

> 'Something of what one wants to bear witness to emerges only in the act of witnessing. … The word of God is only grasped in its meaning for today…by expressing itself and acting as a word of salvation, of pity, of hope for specific human beings, at a given time.'[9]

Greg Carey has recently drawn out the significance of witnessing as part of the Seer's use of identification markers in his intention to share his own status with his audience, so crossing or blurring the lines of authority which would otherwise divide:

> 'Christ is *the* 'faithful witness' (1.5) and the 'faithful and true witness' (3.14). Antipas is also a 'faithful witness' (2.13), and John performs the same function: his vision is 'faithful and true' (22.6), and he has narrated all that he saw (1.2). Other faithful witnesses include the unnamed martyrs of 6.9–11 and of 11.3–13. In principle, all members of John's audience may become faithful witnesses (12.11). Likewise, John is both a prophet and a slave [a sign of status, as in 'slave of Christ'] (1.1–3; cf.10.9; 22.7, 10, 18–19). But even this status links him to the audience, for 'the testimony of Jesus is the spirit of prophecy' (19.11; cf.11.6), while God's slaves are 'all who fear [God], the small and the great' (19.5) and God's slaves will worship God in the new city (22.3). In short, John offers his audience the possibility of joining him as a slave and a prophet; they may even join John and Christ as faithful witnesses.'[10]

8. Elisabeth A. Castelli, *Imitating Paul: A Discourse of Power* (Louisville: Westminster/ John Knox Press, 1991), p. 47.

9. Jean-Pierre Jossua OP, *The Condition of Witness* (London: SCM Press, 1985), p. 64 (French original, Paris: Cerf, 1984).

10. In Steve Moyise (ed.), *Studies in the Book of Revelation* (Edinburgh/New York: T&T Clark, 2001), pp.176–77.

6. *Conclusions*

By examining these five categories of evidence about the Seer of Patmos, the intention has been to seek clarification of the book in its context, while remaining aware of the potential application of these ideas in the modern Church. Hopefully the figure of the Seer, while not crystal clear, is not as evanescent as he was at the start. It may be that the visions take on a new (and awful) clarity in the aftermath of 11 September 2001 (Nine/Eleven) and the War on Terror.

Difficult though these apocalyptic visions and interpretations undoubtedly are, we need to remember that the worldwide Church, in obedience to the Seer's commission and example, did indeed adopt and communicate these insights, and lodge them within the canon of the New Testament. This is not to understate the problems they encountered here. The Early Church did not always find it easy to cope with this sort of visionary material. (The Jewish tradition had experienced similar problems with the prophecy of Ezekiel). Accordingly there was much discussion as to whether Revelation belonged properly in the New Testament. There is no certain trace of the Apocalypse in the writings of the Apostolic Fathers. In the Second century, however, it was all but universally accepted in Asia Minor, Western Syria, North Africa, Rome and South Gaul. In this century there were two protests against its Johannine authorship and validity, associated with Marcion and with the Alogi. Dionysius of Alexandria (247–265 CE) re-opened the question of Revelation's authenticity. As a result of his criticisms the book of Revelation was rejected for a time by the Syro-Palestinian Church and by the Churches of Asia Minor. For some centuries it was ignored or unknown in the Eastern-Syrian and Armenian Churches. It was always accepted in Western Christendom, and gradually came to be acknowledged also in the East.

Over the centuries, it has probably been the visionary artists and the spiritual saints who have found it easier than most to tune in to the wavelength of the seer's message. The wealth of artistic interpretation in many formats and in many centuries bears witness to this. William Blake is one of the most striking of English exponents of this imagery.[11] And it was also quite deliberate on my part that the present exploration of the Seer should begin with the work of a modern artist, Robin Bradbury.

In a critical age, such as that of Post-Modernism, we certainly need to ask the awkward question about such visionary material and how relevant it might be for later centuries than the Seer's own time. As part of this critical questioning, we might glance at the example of Joanna Southcott (1750–1824).[12] She was a domestic servant in Exeter when, in 1792, she announced the Second Coming of Christ (= Shiloh). Her message, claimed to be written at the Spirit's dictation,

11. See Christopher Rowland, 'Blake and the Bible: Biblical Exegesis in the Work of William Blake', in J.M. Court (ed.), *Biblical Interpretation: The Meanings of Scripture – Past and Present* (London: T&T Clark International, 2003), pp. 168–84.

12. See J.M. Court, *The End of the World: A Short History of Christian Millenarianism* (in preparation).

was largely ignored by the Church of England and the Methodist Church, but her followers rapidly became an influential sect. Her prophecies were kept sealed until such time as a gathering of church and political leaders would agree to open the box. Joanna Southcott used the language of the Book of Revelation extensively in her prophecies. She saw herself as the 'woman clothed with the sun' (Rev. 12.5). The question for us is whether her message represented the truth of the Seer for her time, or was it merely a pale imitation and parody, or possibly simply a clever fraud?

EAST AND SOUTH OF CHALCEDON

Paul Ellingworth

This brief study does not claim to be an original contribution to the academic study of christology. It is, first and foremost, a grateful personal tribute to my old friend Professor Pokorný, in particular for his gracious chairmanship of the United Bible Societies' Europe Middle East Subcommittee on Translation (EUMESCOT) from 1991 to 1996.

We shall offer a report on two contrasting areas of christological development which appear to be largely or wholly independent of the Chalcedonian definition. The first is a corpus of eighth- and ninth-century Chinese Christian texts which have been called 'the Jesus Sutras' (sutra = 'sacred text'). The second is a small selection of modern African writings on christology.

It is not surprising that the first of these corpora should have made little or no impact on western christological thought, since they were discovered only in 1907. They have been recently retranslated, in the context of a wide-ranging popular survey, in Martin Palmer's *The Jesus Sutras: Rediscovering the lost religion of Taoist Christianity*.[1] It is rather more surprising that western theologians should have taken so little account of the rapidly growing amount of christological reflection by African theologians. Its scope is suggested for example by Grant LeMarquand's 170-page annotated 'Bibliography of the Bible in Africa',[2] which includes much material of relevance to christology.

*

The extant 'Jesus sutras' comprise:

(a) Four early scrolls, the first dated 641,[3] and the others slightly later. The

1. M. Palmer, *The Jesus Sutras: Rediscovering the lost religion of Taoist Christianity* (New York: The Ballantine Publishing Group; London: Judy Piatkus [Publishers] Ltd, 2001).

2. In Gerald O. West and Musa W. Dube (eds.), *The Bible in Africa: Transactions, Trajectories, and Trends* (Boston and Leiden: Brill, 2001, henceforward West and Dube), pp. 631–800. See also Josiah U. Young III: *African Theology: A Critical Analysis and Annotated Bibliography* (Westport, CT and London: Greenwood Press 1993). This book is no. 26 in the series Bibliographies and Indexes in Religious Studies. No. 12 in the same series is Arland J. Hultgren's *New Testament Christology: A Critical Assessment and Annotated Bibliography* (1988), which mentions J.S. Rhee, 'Writings on Christology in Korea', *Northeast Asia Journal of Theology* 2 (1969), pp. 111–16 – a very rare reference to a non-western publication.

3. Apparently the first known use of the 'Christian era' dating.

first three are translations into Chinese from lost originals; the fourth was written in Chinese. We refer to these as *S1–S4*.

(b) Four liturgical scrolls, all originally written in Chinese. The first was composed in 720; the others, by a monk named Jingjing, c. 781. We refer to these as *L1–L4*.

(c) A pillar erected in 781, known as the stone sutra (*SS*).

Our remarks on the christology of these documents is based on the translation by Martin Palmer and his Chinese colleagues. Allowance must be made for the fact that in some cases, as just indicated, the English texts are translations of translations. Large parts of the documents are not concerned with christology; parts of *S4*, for example, are based on the Ten Commandments, and *SS* is largely a history of the Chinese church from its beginnings in 635 until 781.

Parts of the sutras are based quite closely on biblical texts, notably Mt. 6–7 (*S1*) and the Ten Commandments (*S4*), other passages on non-biblical texts such as the *Didascalia Apostolorum*. Titles given to persons of the Trinity vary; it is occasionally unclear which person is referred to. The Father is called 'the World-Honoured One', 'the Heavenly Ruler above', 'your Father, the Compassionate One' (all *S4*, some also elsewhere), and 'Allaha' (*L1*). The Son is most often called 'the Messiah', also 'a Visitor' (*S2*).

The Trinity is sometimes named 'the Father, the Son, and the Pure Wind' (*S4*). The second liturgical sutra begins:

> Let us praise Allaha – Great Father and Mysterious One
> Let us praise the Messiah – his Supreme Son
> Let us praise the Holy Spirit, who witnesses divinity (*L2.2–4*).[4]

In at least one place, the distinction of the persons is clearly affirmed: 'the Messiah is not the Honoured One' (*S4*). *S4.5* describes the life of Jesus in some detail, with particular stress on his birth and infancy, and on his death ('the Holy Event'), resurrection, and saving work.

> ...[A]t this time the One was born in the city of Wen-li-shish-ken [Jerusalem] in the orchard of But Lam [Bethlehem]. After five years had passed the Messiah began to talk. He did many miraculous and good things while teaching the Law. When he was twelve he assumed the Holy Word and began teaching. (*S4.5.10–13*)
>
> The Messiah gave up his body to the wicked ones for the sake of all living beings. (*S4.5.41*)

Jesus is represented as telling a story of a sick man, clearly a representative of humanity, whose friends cut steps in the side of a mountain so that he could be carried to its summit and be healed. He then explains:

> [T]he Compassionate Knowing One...is the scaling ladder and the steps cut in stone
> By which they can find the true Way, freed of their weight forever. (*L3.39*)

The death and resurrection of Jesus are described in rather ambiguous terms, which may perhaps be attributed to mistranslation into Chinese:

4. We follow Palmer's numbering of divisions and verses.

> While his Five Attributes[5] passed away, he did not die but was released again after his death. (*S1.4.20*)

In selecting quotations from the sutras, one may overstress points of contact with the New Testament and other Christian teaching. The documents as a whole are clearly marked by non-Christian traditions, especially Taoism and to a lesser extent Buddhism.[6] To redress the balance, one may quote a passage from the third liturgical sutra which has a strangely postmodern ring:

> Now, what are the Four Essential Laws of the Dharma?...
> The fourth is no truth. Don't try to control everything.
> Don't take sides in arguments about right and wrong.
> Treat everyone equally, and live from day to day.
> It's like a clear mirror which reflects everything anyway ...
> What does the mirror do? It reflects without judgment.
> And you – you should do likewise,
> Then true Peace and Happiness will flow from your heart. (*L3.5.1,23–30*)

Perhaps enough has been said to indicate the freshness, and in many places the originality, of these documents. In a concluding section, we shall tentatively suggest possible criteria for the assessment of this and other non-Chalcedonian christologies.

*

As already indicated, African christology is expanding as rapidly as African Christianity itself. For our present purpose we shall consider relevant contributions to three symposia, West and Dube's *The Bible in Africa* (n. 2), *Paths of African Theology*, edited by Rosino Gibellini (henceforward Gibellini),[7] and *Faces of Jesus in Africa*, edited by Robert J. Schreiter (henceforward Schreiter).[8] Several contributions to these symposia include surveys of other writing.

One's first impression, even of this restricted corpus, is of its extreme diversity. We shall use, as an approximate criterion of classification, a modified form of the distinction between christologies 'from above' and 'from below'.[9] Christologies 'from above' are those which stress the divine initiative in the incarnation, while those 'from below' take as their starting-point the earthly life of Jesus. We shall

5. Apparently the Five Skandas, elsewhere defined as 'form, perception, consciousness, action, and knowledge' (S2.3.1).

6. See Palmer, ch. 5, 'The Multicultural World of Seventh-Century China'.

7. West and Dube, *The Bible in Africa*. II. *Paths of African Theology* (ed. Rosino Gibellini; London: SCM Press, 1994).

8. West and Dube, *Faces of Jesus in Africa* (ed. Robert J. Schreiter; London: SCM Press; Maryknoll, NY: Orbis Books, 1991).

9. This distinction has a long and somewhat tortuous history. According to J. Macquarrie, *Christology Revisited* (London: SCM Press, 1998), p. 70, Paul of Samosata, finally condemned as a heretic and deposed in 268/9, 'was probably the first to introduce the language of "from above" and "from below" into christological discourse. He is reported to have said, "The Word is from above, Jesus Christ is a man from below" '; cf. Macquarrie, *Jesus Christ in Modern Thought* (London: SCM Press; Philadelphia: Trinity Press, 1990), pp. 55–59; Eusebius, *Hist. Eccl.* 7.30. Our use of the expressions 'from above' and 'from below' is not intended as a value judgment on either.

also use these expressions in order to distinguish African christologies which predominantly use categories drawn from African traditional religions (in that modified sense 'from above') from those whose point of departure is the contemporary African situation ('from below'). We fully recognize, however, that neither distinction is absolute. On the one hand, every christology based on New Testament data must include, in differing proportions, elements 'from above' and 'from below'; while in African traditional religions, the borderline between (what westerners would call) the natural and the supernatural is often blurred.

As we apply this flexible criterion to the writings in our small corpus, two essays immediately stand out as representing christology 'from above'. J.A. (Bobby) Loubser[10] appeals to the ancient Coptic representation of Christ as Pantokrator, Christ crucified who 'reigns as Lord of the church and the world' – a representation which, though technically 'south of Chalcedon', is related, if only by negative reaction, to the Definition of 451.

In a quite different way, Charles Nyamiti's own reflection,[11] fully aware of both traditional and contemporary western christologies, tends predominantly towards a christology 'from above'. His suggested outline of a seminary course on African christology, clearly intended for advanced students, includes for example references to 'christological *perichoresis*' and to the events of Jesus' life as 'ancestral, onomastic, initiatory, liberative, and vitalistic mysteries'. In another survey,[12] Nyamiti points out that christologies of inculturation, in which 'an effort is made to incarnate the Gospel message in the African cultures on the theological level' ('from above'), were at the time of writing (1991) generally more numerous and more developed than christologies of liberation ('from below'). Nyamiti insists that christology in Africa should not be separated from teaching about the Trinity and the church. He concludes, however, with the significant admission: 'With the exception, perhaps, of Black christology in South Africa, none of the existing African christologies has had any appreciable influence in the life of the African churches'.[13] This suggests that Nyamiti also favours christological development 'from above' in a different sense, namely from the seminary to the churches. He does, however, also call for more field research into 'African nonsystematic christologies', notably among the African independent churches.

Traditional African categories generally tend to support christologies 'from above'. Justin S. Ukpong[14] refers to John Mbiti's use of the images of Jesus as miracle worker and risen Lord to show him as the conqueror of evil spirits,

10. 'How Al-Mokattam Mountain was Moved. The Coptic Imagination and the Christian Bible', in West and Dube, pp. 103–26, here 109–10.

11. Gibellini, in 'Contemporary African Christologies: Assessment and Practical Suggestions', pp. 62–77, here 74–75.

12. Schreiter, in 'African Christologies Today', pp. 3–23, here 3, 18.

13. 'African Christologies Today', p. 18, quoted in 'Contemporary African Christologies', p. 76.

14. 'Developments in Biblical Interpretation in Africa: Historical and Hermeneutical Directions', in West and Dube, pp. 11–28, here 18, referring to John S. Mbiti, 'Some African Concepts of Christology', in George F. Vicedom (ed.), *Christ and the Younger Churches* (London: SPCK 1972), p. 54.

disease and death. Although such images may support a picture of Christ as a divine and supernatural figure, they also have clear points of contact, both with the earthly life of Jesus, and also with African traditional society. For example, Gomang Seratwa Ntloedibe[15] compares Jesus' role as a divine healer with that of the traditional *Ngaka* as 'saviour, liberator and balance-keeper' among the Setswana. Similarly, Cécé Kolié's 'Jesus as Healer'[16] examines the role of healers, primarily among the Kpélé of Guinea; describes the culture clash between traditional and colonial views of health and healing; asks in what sense the crucified Christ can be a symbol of healing; relates the resurrection of Christ to African funeral rituals; but concludes that 'the fact of Christ in Africa today is more that of the ill than of a healer'.

Ukpong's own approach, following a survey of other options, claims to be a 'biblical approach', built up inductively from historical critical study of the gospel records, and thus predominantly a christology 'from below'. A study of Jesus' preaching, his attitude to the Torah, his parables and his miracles leads to the conclusion that 'in evangelizing the Jewish culture from within... Jesus left a model of approach to evangelization that was to be applied in all cultures to the extent any model can be applied to particular situations'.[17]

Several writers refer more directly to contemporary African situations. Grant LeMarquand quotes Allan Boesak as one who sees 'Jesus himself...as one who shares the black experience of poverty'.[18] Eliud Wabukala and Grant LeMarquand[19] describe how, in the Revival among the Babukuso of Western Kenya and Eastern Uganda, 'preaching about Christ's death by hanging has immediate appeal'.

Jean Claude Loba Mkole[20] discusses the translation of ὁ υἱὸς τοῦ ἀνθρώπου (always an intractable problem) in Kiswahili, and incidentally in Lingala. In these languages, as in many others, the problem is compounded by the absence of a definite article. Mkole rejects the messianic interpretation given to the title in some African translations (more precisely, in their explanatory notes), preferring to interpret the title as meaning 'a human being', and sometimes as a circumlocution for 'I'. Many other scholars share this view, but Mkole's conclusion that 'a son of man' refers to 'an important human component of the understanding of Jesus' person' could perhaps be misunderstood as an attempt to rehabilitate the old equation: 'son of man = human nature; Son of God = divine nature'.

15. '*Ngaka* and Jesus as Liberators: a Comparative Reading', in West and Dube, pp. 498–512, here 502.

16. Schreiter, pp. 128–50, here 149.

17. *Art. cit.*, p. 56.

18. Grant LeMarquand, 'New Testament Exegesis in Modern Africa', in West and Dube, pp. 76–102, here 82, quoting Allan Boesak, *Farewell to Innocence: A Socio-Ethical Study of Black Theology and Black Power* (Kampen: Kok, 1976), p. 43.

19. Eliud Wabukala and Grant LeMarquand, 'Cursed be Everyone who Hangs on a Tree: Pastoral Implications of Deuteronomy 21.22 and Galatians 3.13 in an African Context', in West and Dube, pp. 350–9, here 357.

20. J.C. Mkole, 'The Kiswahili *Mwana wa Mtu* and the Greek *Ho huios tou anthrôpou*', in West and Dube, pp. 557–66, here 562.

Perhaps closest to the proverbial 'grass roots', and thus to a christology 'from below' is Efoé Julien Pénoukou's 'Christology in the Village'.[21] He begins by recording his Mina great-uncle's response to the question: 'Uncle, you are a Christian. Who is Jesus for you?'. It deserves quotation in full.

> Jesus
> is really someone [an identifiable person]
> for me,
> saviour (*hlwengan*)
> in solidarity and saviour of the world,
> come to tell us that God, who has created us,
> has sent him for us.
> We had once been on the road
> to perdition,
> in the devil's hands.
>
> He showed us the whole road to follow
> to be saved.
> We are sure of this;
> we have placed our faith in it;
> we have learned and understood it
> in this way.
> He came to witness to truth here,
> and not the lie
> as the devil does.
> He is the person of truth.

Pénoukou is thus concerned less with 'the identity or entity of Jesus Christ' than with 'the kind of relationship that his coming establishes with the human being'. He thus agrees with Nyamiti that '[christology] will be primarily trinitarian and ecclesial'. He draws extensively on 'the Ewe-Mina view of human existence and destiny'. An African christology, he believes, is not a matter of adapting Christian truth to African religious aspirations, but rather of 'going to the depths of their meaning, thereupon to lead them to maturity in the love of the triune God'. Pénoukou's article emphasizes the point that the distinction between christologies 'from above' and 'from below' is not one of content but of starting-point.

Other contributions arising from African contemporary situations include Douglas W. Waruta's 'Who is Jesus Christ for Africans today? Prophet, Priest, Potentate'.[22] He explores African parallels to the threefold office of Christ, maintaining that it 'provide[s] for the African people the most perfect model for them', and that, rightly understood, it offers an effective antidote to authoritarian excesses. Similarly, Wablon Nthamburi's 'Christ as seen by an African'[23] argues for a christology starting from the gospel witness to the historical Jesus. 'The only way in which we can understand Christ is through concrete historical

21. Schreiter, 'African Christologies Today', pp. 24–51, here 24–25, 36, 50. The confession quoted on pp. 24–25 has been translated from Mina through French.

22. Schreiter, 'African Christologies Today', pp. 52–64, here 63.

23. Schreiter, 'African Christologies Today', pp. 65–69, here 69.

experience of God's action which is always a liberating experience'. Anne Nasimyu Wasike's 'Christology and an African Woman's Experience'[24] responds to various christological models, especially that of Christ as liberator and healer.

Already in 1988 Arland Hultgren[25] was noting that research into christological titles 'may not be an area of scholarship in the future to the degree it has been up to recent times'; yet several writers in our corpus relate New Testament titles to traditional names and functions in African society. The second part of Schreiter's symposium is devoted to these. Anselme T. Sanon's 'Jesus, Master of Initiation'[26] begins and ends as a meditation on the christological hymn in Colossians 1.15–20, but embraces also the place of Christ in African liturgy and art, and offers a translation of the hymn into Madarè, a language of Burkina Faso.

François Kabasélé's 'Christ as Chief'[27] begins by pointing out that the Luba now use, for liturgical purposes, the word *Mulaba*, 'anointed', as a translation of 'Christ', thereby raising the questions: 'With what is this person 'anointed'? And why?' He explores the christology of the Luba Missal, in which 'Latin prayers are no longer merely "translated into Luba"; they are rewritten, with one eye on the texts of the day, and another on the culture of those who pray…'. In a second contribution,[28] Kabasélé explores the significance of 'Christ as Ancestor and Elder Brother', maintaining that the traditional invocation of ancestors finds its place in African Christian faith as a 'subordinate mediation'.

Further christologies 'from below' are presented by two other writers. Laurent Magesa's 'Christ the Liberator and Africa Today'[29] arises out of the oppression of the colonial period and the disappointments of the following decades. He calls for 'a christology of social betterment and human uplift' which 'views [Jesus] most prominently as herald of the Good News, healer, and liberator'.

In a similar vein, John M. Waliggo's 'African Christology in a Situation of Suffering'[30] 'tries to respond to the question: Who is Christ to the suffering people of Africa?' Responses to a questionnaire completed by theological students at Gaba National Seminary in Uganda showed: 'The majority emphasised an image of Christ who is irrelevant and passive, remote and unconcerned with the situations of suffering', while '[m]any expressed an image of Christ who rewards the victims of suffering only in the life hereafter… Among the positive images of Christ, informants stressed the Suffering Servant, a "black Christ, economically poor and from a poor family" … "that mysterious God who cannot be manipulated', 'a mysterious Christ who is not understood but who is always very reliable".' Africans, Waliggo believes, need a Christ who is healer and liberator. 'The theology of the rejected stone is the theology of the historical Jesus, while the theology of the cornerstone is that of the risen Christ. When the two

24. Schreiter, 'African Christologies Today', pp. 70–81.
25. *Op. cit.*, p. 13.
26. Schreiter, 'African Christologies Today', pp. 85–102.
27. Schreiter, 'African Christologies Today', pp. 103–15, here 103.
28. Schreiter, 'African Christologies Today', pp. 116–27, here 126.
29. Schreiter, 'African Christologies Today', pp. 151–63, here 162.
30. Schreiter, 'African Christologies Today', pp. 165–80, here 176, 177.

theologies are put together we get the one theology for all the rejected people of the world who, if they have faith in God and themselves, must one day become a key people'.

*

It is time to draw these disparate threads together, as far as may be, and to suggest criteria for a possible assessment of christological formulations.

First (though some readers may think too late) a definition of christology: 'that branch of theology which treats of the nature and person of Christ' (*Chambers English Dictionary*). It is already clear from this almost tautological definition that christology is metalanguage, language about language; in this case, linguistic reflection on what people have said or written about Jesus Christ. As J.D.G. Dunn has put it: '"Christology" of course is a narrowing of the complete wholeness of the "Christ-event" – a reduction to mere words of the much more than verbal impact of the historical figure and the risen Lord...'[31] If what the New Testament itself says of Christ is understood as 'an intense period of innovation and of development in what we now call "christology",'[32] then later christological reflection must be placed *historically* at a further remove from the Christ-event.

Second, there appears to be a radical difference, a change of gear, between New Testament christological statements and later developments, towards Chalcedon and beyond. Theologians from patristic times to the present day have mostly been preoccupied with the problem of relating the divine and human natures of Christ, or in more recent times that of relating the Jesus of history to the Christ of faith. Typical in this respect is J.L. Houlden's admirable *Jesus: A Question of Identity*,[33] which devotes successive chapters to 'Jesus and History', 'Worship and Belief', and then 'Problems and Solutions' concerning the relation between the two previous areas of discussion. In the New Testament itself, however, the two are inextricably fused, and this from the earliest recoverable confessional statements[34]: 'Jesus is Lord' (1 Cor. 12.3); 'Christ died for our sins' (1 Cor. 15.3) – and even the juxtaposition 'Jesus Christ', until 'Christ' became in the gentile world just another name for Jesus. The onion has no kernel. However valuable in itself the successive quests for the historical Jesus may be, they are all of necessity abstractions from the New Testament writings, potentially as far removed from those original witnesses as (in the opposite direction) the Definition of Chalcedon. The answer to John Macquarrie's question 'How do we know Jesus Christ?'[35] can never be purely historical. '[W]e should not distinguish too sharply between the knowledge that we have from the testimony of the past and the knowledge that we have in present experience. (...) If we read the Gospels primarily in a critical

31. J.D.G. Dunn, *Christology in the Making* (London: SCM Press, 2nd ed. 1989), p. ix.

32. Dunn, *Christology*, p. xii.

33. J.L. Houlden, *Jesus: A Question of Identity* (London: SPCK, 1992).

34. On which see P. Pokorný, *The Genesis of Christology* (Edinburgh: T&T Clark, 1987), pp. 63–72.

35. J. Macquarrie, *Christology Revisited*, ch. 5, here p. 85.

way, we are not likely to be encountered by Christ in them'. If this is so, it may provide an initial criterion for the assessment of christologies, whether Chalcedonian, Chinese, or African.

This raises, thirdly, the question of the point of reference for particular christologies. Is it Chalcedon? – by wide but not universal ancient consent the summary and culmination of patristic reflection on the person of Christ. What criteria, if any, may be considered 'normative' for christology? Possible options, in chronological order, include: (a) Jesus' own self-understanding[36]; (b) the historical Jesus; (c) the New Testament writings; (d) the Chalcedonian Definition; (e) later dogmatic, for example Tridentine, formulations; (f) some set of modern, for example existential, or postmodern approaches or presuppositions. Of these, (a) and (b) are critical reconstructions, and (d) to (f), however powerful and illuminating in certain sociohistorical settings, require constant verification against (c), the primary sources. If this appeal to the primary sources appears simplistic, even fundamentalist, it should be remembered that the New Testament writings are both creatively diverse among themselves, and also offer an inexhaustible field for secondary constructions. This point merits a little elaboration.

All major branches of the Christian church, whether or not they require acceptance of the historic creeds or other formulations, in principle attribute to them lower authority than to Scripture. Yet the more closely one examines the christological data of the New Testament, the more one is astonished by the freedom with which these data were handled. Among many examples, one may mention the primitive church's almost total indifference to preserving Jesus' (presumably Aramaic) *ipsissima verba*; the Fourth Gospel's radical recasting of the story of Jesus' ministry; the unembarrassed recycling of (ὁ) Χριστός as a proper name in the area of the Gentile mission; the immediate abandonment, in that area, of the meaningless title ὁ υἱὸς τοῦ ἀνθρώπου; and Paul's relative lack of interest in Jesus' earthly life.[37] The New Testament writings' flexibility may thus prove a stimulating rather than a constricting influence on christological reflection in other cultural areas.

This is by no means to question the value of other christologies; it is merely to warn against the pervasive tendency to think of the New Testament materials as mere raw materials or building blocks, providentially intended for some coherent piece of architecture. On the contrary, the relation between the primary sources and later formulations may be compared to that between the Greek text of the New Testament, and translations of it to which one may refer as secondary resources in the course of preparing a new version.

Other possible criteria are more difficult both to define and to use. One may think, for example, of the capacity of a christology to speak (especially but not

36. On which see P. Pokorný, *The Genesis of Christology*, pp. 38–62.

37. A feature which W.L. Petersen ('The Genesis of the Gospel', in A. Denaux (ed.), *New Testament Textual Criticism and Exegesis. Festschrift J. Delobel* [Leuven: Leuven University Press 2002]), has found also in Christian writings of about 90–180. The other side of this flexibility, however, is the conservatism with which all the canonical gospels, in different ways and to different extents, preserve traditional material such as the title ὁ υἱὸς τοῦ ἀνθρώπου.

exclusively to Christians) across barriers or time, geography and culture. A strong christology, in this sense, may be compared to a classic work by Beethoven or Shakespeare, capable of communicating worldwide and across generations. Conversely, a weak christology could be compared with an ephemeral piece of music or literature. But the analogy is difficult to sustain. A Chinese or an African christology, like Chinese music or African dance, may speak powerfully to a particular, even a very large, group, but not normally to others; it may even elicit that immediacy of reaction which characterizes New Testament confessions of faith.

John Macquarrie's great contribution to christological reflection has been largely developed in a western, specifically European setting. But we end this survey with a quotation which may find a wider resonance, in Africa and perhaps also in China:

> [F]rom the beginning Christ the incarnate Word was there in the counsels of God, and even his humanity, like the humanity of us all, was taking shape in the long ages of cosmic evolution.[38]

38. J. Macquarrie, *Christology Revisited*, p. 114.

New Testament Christology in the Creed, in Preaching and in Christian Life

Zdeněk Sázava

1. *Introduction*

Christology belongs to the most important parts of the New Testament Theology and to the rudiments of the Christian faith. There are perhaps thousands of books devoted to this topic, written in different languages and forms, to be found in the libraries all over the world. It is sometimes a long way, however, from a scholarly work to what is practised in the Christian churches and what forms the everyday life of Christians. At the same time, the biblical christology, as can be 'scientifically' described, is incomplete without such practice – as well as is the practical life of the church without critical reflection of its theological and christological fundaments. I will offer some reflections on this.

2. *Jesus Christ in the Apostles' Creed*

The Apostles' Creed is an important declaration of Christian faith. It has been recognized in the ecumenical movement that it is indispensable for the very existence of the church as unity: 'The coming together of all Christians in an authentic communion of faith, evangelical life and mission requires the common confession of the apostolic faith… Christians cannot be truly united unless they recognize in each other the same apostolic faith which is witnessed in word and in life'.[1] That is not to say that in the creeds one could find all important information about the Christian faith. We read there nothing about the Bible and its significance for the modern readers, nothing about the sacraments, nothing about the relationship between the faith and reason (science), nothing about the ecumenical variety of the church. But even what is mentioned there, is mentioned only in a basic form. That is true of christology, too: Christ's nativity, death and resurrection are noticed, together with the most important titles, but nothing is reported about Jesus' teaching, e.g. his 'sermon on the mount'. Only the fundamentals are recorded there, and it is interesting to see what they are!

One of the Gospel texts that belong to the 'golden treasure' of the New Testament is certainly Jn 3.16–18. One can come across it as an inscription on the

1. *Confessing the One Faith. An Ecumenical Explication of the Apostolic Faith as it is Confessed in the Nicene-Constantinopolitan Creed (381)* (Faith and Order Paper No. 153; Geneva: WCC Publications), p. viii. English text of the NC and Apostles' Creeds on pp. 10–14.

inside walls of the protestant churches, it has become a popular theme of Christian art, youngsters learn it by heart for confirmation. This popular usage often leads to neglecting the context of the saying, i.e. the dialog between Jesus and Nicodemus in a dark night. To this dialogue the saying builds a climax: the inner motivation of Jesus' earthly work, the inner meaning of the whole of his career, of his witness, crucifiction and resurrection, is the love of God. And it is addressed to all people.

John pays special attention to the present of his readers. The salvation has come already with the first advent of Christ. The Light has come. This affirmation, however, brings about questions pointed to those who claim to belong to him, to the visitors of the divine services, the communicants at the eucharist. Are we really his? That means: are we full of his *agape*, is our house ready to receive Jesus as visitor? Is our heart and our private life open for him? Are we already today brothers and sisters, living in the Light of Jesus Christ? It is not enough to comment on the creeds or on the biblical texts, as they call us to a personal response, not only of words, but also of life. We should not forget that this applies not only to a 'layman' in the church, but also to theologians, ministers and bishops.

Here the Johannine text meets with the general character of christology in the classical creeds: of fundamental importance is what Christ *is* and what he is for us, not what he says or what can be said about him. It is particularly in this sense, that we may recall Karl Barth's perspective on the place of christology in the creed: although it comes only in the second place, it is a fountain of light, illuminating both the first and the third part.

3. *Jesus Christ and His Residence according to John*

In Jn 1.35–46 we find questions, answers and appeals that are very important for our theme. First to the questions. Jesus asks two of his future disciples: 'What are you looking for?' And these two men then ask Jesus: 'Where are you staying, Rabbi?' And thirdly, there is the question of Nathanael: 'Can anything good come from Nazareth?' The answers to these questions are only indirect and they come in an unexpected form. The appeals, on the contrary, are simple and as plain as the sun on one's face. Jesus calls: 'Come and see!' and then: 'Follow me!' Philip's appeal to Nathanael is identical: 'Come and see!'

Now, we have to understand ourselves as the addressees of this message. Jesus comes to us, too, with the question: 'What are you looking for?' Our answers are often little wise. We wish to get various things, we are interested in various kinds of knowledge, but we often forget to ask the most important thing: 'Where are you staying, Rabbi?' The question of Jesus' presence has been an important problem in theology over the centuries, but only rarely it was asked in such a plain and straightforward manner and with the awareness, that it is for us to go and see, *following* Jesus, that it may be somewhere else than where we are. Is it necessarily in our churches of stones and bricks? Is it in our fellowship, our sacraments, our families?

In the Johannine text we see a very rapid movement. No such 'No hurry, plenty of time' that we are so used to. Initially, there are three disciples here: Andrew, Peter and Philip. But Philip very quickly finds another one. This is important: it brings new life to the church. After all, we too have this experience: somebody had found and invited us. There are no motionless spectators here. Jesus attracts people through other people.

Of course, our problem is what it means today, 'to lead to Jesus'. As we have said: he does not necessarily reside, where we are. We can hardly bring someone to him, when we are not ourselves ready to follow him, or even to seek him. In this respect, it will be crucial for the church and for each Christian today to realize anew the importance of prayer. And secondly: when confronted with our half-empty churches, we often think hard about the ways and means, how to bring people back in. But maybe, we should rather think about how to introduce the Spirit of Christ into our 'secular' surroundings. Maybe our families are the important places, where the Lord's residing should be – and could be – clearly visible. This is where faith as permeating friendship and relationships of love could be demonstrated. To come to Jesus is similar to, but yet different from what expresses the well-known *veni, vidi, vici*: the last part has to be modified, as the victory belongs to Jesus, the goal of the movement is to be overcome by him.

Jesus resides neither in the New Testament, nor in the creed. But they are indispensable aids for seeking the way to him.

4. *Jesus as the Prominent Guest*

Personally, my favourite gospel is Luke. Why? Mainly because of his special stories: the Good Samaritan, the Parable of the Prodigal Son and the nice story of Mary and Martha. Perhaps, these are the best known and most loved of all the teachings of Jesus, justly appreciated for their exquisite literary grace and penetrating delineation of characters, as well as for their assurance with divine mercy, surpassing all expectation. Here I would like to pay attention to the story of Mary and Martha.

This story has often been misinterpreted. In the middle ages, for instance, it was argued from there in favour of superiority of the contemplative to the active life. The respective sisters have been taken as types of certain attitude. This leads to the unresolved question of what is more important: to listen to Jesus' words or to engage in active service? Is the story really meant to renounce care and service in the christian existence?

In my view, this difficulty arises from overlooking the fact that the central figure of the story is neither Martha (who is most active in it, moving in the foreground, as it were), nor Mary (who is praised by Jesus), but Jesus himself. The story tells us what the women make of Jesus' presence, maybe that both of them feel it as a unique moment, a unique opportunity. Martha takes the opportunity to offer to the Lord all she can. Mary, on the contrary, is ready to receive from him. She understands better that he has come to serve and not to be served. This is the most important in his presence: to accept his service, to listen to him. So Mary 'has chosen the better part'.

That is not to say, however, that Martha's service was (and is) of no value. It was probably she who invited Jesus. It has its value, when the church collects money, organizes help to those who are in need of it, builds houses for its meetings, etc. But all this can only have sense and real value, when we are able to recognize the primary necessity of Jesus' presence and of his service.

Luke has introduced Jesus to us as indeed a prominent guest. Will we be able to recognize the right nature of his prominence? When Jesus comes and is received, a great change and deep peace arrives. Are we ready for it? It is the common goal of our scholarly research on the New Testament and our commitment in the church. We should take all effort that the way from one to the other be as short and straight as possible.

SELECT BIBLIOGRAPHY OF PETR POKORNÝ[1]

I. *Monographs*

1. *Der Epheserbrief und die Gnosis,* Berlin: Evangelische Verlaganstalt 1965, p. 154.
2. *Der Kern der Bergpredigt,* Hamburg-Bergstedt: H. Reich 1969. English summary: 'The Core of the Sermon on the Mount', in *Studia evangelica VI* (Texte und Untersuchungen zur Geschichte der altchristlichen Literatur 112; Berlin: Akademie-Verlag, 1973), pp. 429–33.
3. *Der Gottessohn. Literarische Übersicht und Fragestellung* (Theologische Studien, l09; Zürich: Theologischer Verlag 1971).
4. *Die Hoffnung auf das ewige Leben im Spätjudentum und Frühchristentum* (Aufsätze und Vorträge zur Theologie und Religionswissenschaft, 70; Berlin: Evangelische Verlagsanstalt, 1978).
5. *Die Entstehung der Christologie. Voraussetzungen einer Theologie des Neuen Testaments* (Berlin: Evangelische Verlagsanstalt, 1985; published also in Stuttgart by Calwer Verlag).

5A. *The Genesis of Christology. Foundations for the Theology of the New Testament* (Edinburgh: T&T Clark, 1987; 2nd paperback edition, 1997).

6. *Der Brief des Paulus an die Kolosser* (Theologischer Handkommentar zum Neuen Testament, 10/1; Berlin: Evangelische Verlagsanstalt, 2nd edition, 1990 [1987]).

6A. *Colossians. A Commentary* (Peabody, MA: Hendrickson, 1991).

7. *Die Zukunft des Glaubens. Sechs Kapitel über Eschatologie* (Stuttgart: Calwer Verlag, 1992).
8. *Der Brief des Paulus an die Epheser* (Theologischer Handkommentar zum Neuen Testament, 10/2; Leipzig: Evangelische Verlagsanstalt, 1992).
9. (together with Josef B. Souček) *Bibelauslegung als Theologie* (WUNT, 100; Tübingen: Mohr-Siebeck, 1997).
10. *Theologie der lukanischen Schriften* (FRLANT, 174; Göttingen: Vandenhoeck & Ruprecht, 1998).
11. *Jesus in the Eyes of His Followers* (Dead Sea Scrolls and Christian Origins Library, 4; North Richland Hills, TX: BIBAL Press, 1998).
12. (Edited with Jan Roskovec), *Philosophical Hermeneutics and Biblical Exegesis* (WUNT, 153; Tübingen Mohr-Siebeck, 2002).

1. Included are only the titles published in languages other than Czech.

II. *Articles and Shorter Studies*

1. 'SOMA CHRISTOY im Epheserbrief', *EvTh* 20 (1960), pp. 456–64.
2. 'Das Magische in den Attismysterien', *LF* 85 (1962), pp. 51–56.[2]
3. 'Der Epheserbrief und gnostische Mysterien', *ZNW* 53 (1962), pp. 160–94.
4. (together with J. L. Hejdánek) 'Jesus, Glaube, Christologie', *ThZ* 18 (1962), pp. 268–82.
5. 'Das sog. Evangelium Veritatis und die Anfänge des christlichen Dogmas', *LF* 87 (1964), pp. 51–59.[2]
6. 'Der Ursprung der Gnosis', *Kairos* 7 (1967), pp. 94–105; also in K. Rudolph (ed.), *Gnosis und Gnostizismus* (Wege der Forschung, 262; Darmstadt: Wissenschaftliche Buchgesellschaft, 1975), pp. 749–67.
7. 'Die Worte Jesu nach der Logienquelle im Lichte des zeitgenössischen Judentums', *Kairos* 9 (1969), pp. 172–80.
8. Gnosis als Weltreligion and als Häresie, *Numen* 16 (1969), pp. 51–62.
9. Die Romfahrt des Paulus und der antike Roman, *ZNW* 64 (1973), pp. 233–44.
10. Der Theologe J. B. Souček, *EvTh* 32 (1972), 241–51; also in *CV* 15 (1972), pp. 161–72.[3]
11. 'Der soziale Hintergrund der Gnosis', in K.W. Tröger (ed.),*Gnosis und Neues Testament* (Berlin: Evangelische Verlagsanstalt, 1973; also published in Gütersloh by G. Mohn), pp. 77–87.
12. 'The Temptation Stories and Their Intention', *NTS* 20 (1973–74), pp. 115–27.
13. 'Die Bedeutung der griechischen Mystik', *Helikon* 11–12 (1971–72), pp. 507–13.
14. '„Anfang des Evangeliums." Zum Problem des Anfangs und des Schlusses des Markusevangeliums', in R. Schnackenburg, J. Ernst and J. Wanke (eds.), *Die Kirche des Anfangs* (FS H. Schürmann; Leipzig: St. Benno Verlag, 1978; also published in Freiburg i. Br. by Herder Verlag), pp. 115–32.
15. 'Über die sog. individuelle Eschatologie der Gnosis', in P. Nagel (ed.), *Studien zum Menschenbild in Gnosis und Manichäismus* (Wissenschaftliche Beiträge 1979/39/K 5/; Halle [Saale]: Martin-Luther Universität, 1979), pp. 127–37.
16. 'Das Wesen der exegetischen Arbeit', *CV* 23 (1980), pp. 167–78.[3]
17. 'Christologie et baptême à l'époque au christianisme primitif', *NTS* 27 (1980–81), pp. 368–80.
18. 'Der Begriff der Person und die Auslegung des Neuen Testaments', in *De servitute gratiosa* (FS L. M. Pákozdy; A Raday Kolleguim Kyadvaniai II-4; Berlin: Ref. Akademie in Budapest, 1981), pp. 58–78 (rotaprint).
19. 'Probleme biblischer Theologie', *ThLZ* 106 (1981), 1–8; also in *The Bible in Cultural Context* (Brno: ČSSN, 1994), pp. 239–45.
20. 'Der irdische Jesus im Johannesevangelium', *NTS* 30 (1984), pp. 217–28.
21. 'Greek Philosophy in the Apostle Paul's Letter to the Colossians', in: *Concilium Eirene XVI/1* (Prague: Kabinet pro studia řecká, římská a latinská ČSAV, 1983), pp. 286–91.
22. 'Das theologische Problem der neutestamentlichen Pseudepigraphie', *EvTh* 44 (1984), pp. 486–96.
23. 'Die gnostische Soteriologie in theologischer und soziologischer Sicht', in J. Taubes (ed.), *Religionstheorie und politische Theologie II: Gnosis und Politik* (Paderborn/Vienna/Zürich: W. Fink Verlag & Verlag F. Schöningh, 1984), pp. 154–62.
24. 'Das Markusevangelium. Literarische Einleitung mit Forschungsbericht', in H. Temporini and W. Haase (eds.), *ANRW* II/25/3 (Berlin-New York: Walter de Gruyter, 1985), pp. 1969–2035.

2. *LF* = Listy filologické (Folia philologica), published in Prague (since 1874) by the Institute of Classical Studies of the Czech Academy of Sciences.

3. *CV* = Communio viatorum, published by the Protestant Theological Faculty of Charles University in Prague.

25. 'Zur Entstehung der Evangelien', *NTS* 32 (1986), pp. 393–403.
26. 'Lukas 15,11–32 und die lukanische Soteriologie', in K. Kertelge, T. Holtz und C.P. März (eds.), *Christus bezeugen* (FS W. Trilling; Erfurter theologische Studien Bd. 59; Leipzig: St. Benno Verlag, 1989; also published in Freiburg i. Br. by Herder Verlag), pp. 179–92.
27. 'Die Herrenworte im Thomasevangelium und bei Paulus. Ein Bericht zur Überlieferungsgeschichte der Sprüche Jesu', in P. Nagel (ed.), *Carl-Schmidt-Kolloquium* (Wissenschaftliche Beiträge, 1990, 23 /K 9/; Halle [Saale]: Martin-Luther-Universität, 1990), pp. 157–64.
28. 'Neutestamentliche Ethik und die Probleme ihrer Darstellungen', *EvTh* 50 (1990), pp. 357–71.
29. 'Strategies of Social Formation in the Gospel of Luke', in Ch. W. Hedrick, J.T. Sanders and H.D. Betz (eds.), *Gospel Origins and Christian Beginnings* (FS J. M. Robinson; Sonoma, CA: Polebridge Press, 1990), pp. 106–19.
29A. 'Die soziale Strategie in den lukanischen Schriften', *CV* 34, 1992, pp. 9–19.[3]
30. 'Das Neue Testament – seine Erforschung und Deutung', in *Informationes Theologiae Europae* (Frankfurt am Main etc.: Peter Lang, 1992), pp. 59–77.
31. 'The Problem of Biblical Theology', *Horizons in Biblical Theology* 15 (1993), pp. 83–94.
32. 'Griechische Sprichwörter im Neuen Testament', in *Tradition und Translation* (FS C. Colpe; Berlin/New York: W. de Gruyter, 1994), pp. 336–43.
33. 'Die Bedeutung des Markusevangeliums für die Entstehung der christlichen Bibel', in T. Fornberg and D. Hellhom (eds.), *Texts and Contexts* (FS L. Hartman; Oslo/Copenhagen/Stockholm/Boston: Scandinavian University Press, 1995), pp. 409–27.
34. '„...bis an das Ende der Erde"', in *Landgabe* (FS J. Heller; Prague: OIKOYMENE, 1995), pp. 198–210.
35. '"From a Puppy to the Child". Some Problems of Contemporary Exegesis Demonstrated from Mark 7.24–30 par.', *NTS* 41 (1995), pp. 321–34.
36. 'Antigone und Jesus – Opfer und Hoffnung', in *Geschichte–Tradition–Reflexion III* (FS M. Hengel; Tübingen: Mohr-Siebeck, 1996), pp. 49–62.
37. '„Ihr Männer von Athen!" Apg 17,16–34 und die Rolle der theologischen Fakultät im Rahmen der Universitätswissenschaften', in I.9, pp. 87–97.
38. 'Was ist (die biblische) Exegese?', in *Wege zum Verständnis* (FS Ch. Demke; Leipzig: Evangelische Verlagsanstalt, 1997), pp. 227–37.
39. 'Jesus als Gleichnis Gottes. Möglichkeiten und Grenzen einer These', *EvTh* 57 (1997), pp. 401–409.
40. 'Lukas 1,1–4 als Prolog zum lukanischen Doppelwerk', in *Warszawskie studia theologiczne* 10 (FS K. Romaniuk; Warszawa: Akademia Teologii Katolickiej, 1997), pp. 271–76.
41. Die Bergpredigt/Feldrede als supraethisches System, in: K. Wengst, G. Sass (ed.), *Ja und Nein. Christliche Theologie angesichts Israels* (FS W. Schrage; Neukirchen-Vluyn: Neukirchener Verlag, 1998), pp. 183–93.
42. 'St. John's Revelation: Structure and Message', in *1900th Anniversary of the Book of John's Revelation* (Symposion at the University of Athens 1995; Athens: Monastery St John at Patmos, 1999), pp. 499–512.
43. 'Römer 12,14–21 und die Aufforderung zur Feindesliebe (Q 6,27 Par.)', in *Dummodo Christus annuntietur* (FS J. Heriban; Roma: LAS, 1999), pp. 105–12.
44. '„Wo zwei oder drei versammelt sind in meinem Namen..." (Mt 18,20)', in *Gemeinde ohne Tempel – Community without Temple. Zur Substituierung und Transformation des Jerusalemer Tempels* (Konferenz Greifswald 1998; WUNT, 116; Tübingen: Mohr-Siebeck, 1999), pp. 477–88.
45. 'Postmodernes Ostern im Neuen Testament', in *Ehrenpromotion John Barton – Petr Pokorný* (Bonner Akademische Reden 82; Bonn: Bouvier, 1999), pp. 28–40.

46. 'Justification and Sanctification according to the Scriptures', in *Justification and Sanctification in the Traditions of the Reformation* (Studies from WARC; Geneva, 1999), pp. 11–17.
47. 'Die soziale Rolle der Alten Kirche', in E. Noort (ed.), *Geschichte und Geschichtlichkeit* (Rijksuniversiteit Groningen, 2000), pp. 43–56.
48. 'Religionsfreiheit – ein Thema des Neuen Testaments?', in G. Frank, J. Haustein and A. de Lange (eds.), *Asyl, Toleranz, Religionsfreiheit* (Bensheimer Hefte 95; Göttingen: Vandenhoeck & Ruprecht, 2000), pp. 40–49.
49. 'Matth 25,31–46 und die Globalisierung christlicher Ethik', *CV* 43 (2001), pp. 153–58.[3]
50. '„Dies Geheimnis ist groß". Epheser 5,21–33: Theologische Voraussetzungen und hermeneutische Folgen einer paränetischer Aussage', *BThZ* 19 (2002), pp. 175–82.
51. 'Luk. 17,33par. und ein (damals) bekanntes Sprichwort', in H.-G. Bethge, St. Emmel, K. L. King and J. Schlatterer (eds.), *For the Children, Perfect Instruction* (FS H.-M. Schenke; Nag Hammadi and Manichean Studies, 54; Leiden/Boston: Brill, 2002), pp. 387–98.
52. 'Der Evangelist Lukas und die theologische Bedeutung seines Werkes', in G. Leonardi, F.G.B. Trolese (ed.), *San Luca Evangelista – testimone della fede che unisce I* (Atti del congresso internazionale, Padova 2000; Fonti e ricerche di storia ecclesiastica padovana 28; Padova: Istituto per la storia ecclesiastica, 2002), pp. 255–64.
53. 'Philosophische Hermeneutik und biblische Exegese (Introduction)', in I.12, pp. 1–4.
54. 'Christliche Verkündigung als Modell des hermeneutischen Prozesses nach 1Kor 14,23–25', in I.12, pp. 245–51.
55. 'Jesus von Nazareth als Problem der historischen Forschung und ihrer theologischen Interpretation', *CV* 44 (2002), pp. 137–38.[3]
56. 'Stilistische und rhetorische Eigentümlichkeiten der ältesten Jesustradition', in J. Schröter and R. Brucker (eds.), *Der historische Jesus. Tendenzen und Perspektiven der gegenwärtigen Forschung* (BZNW, 114; Berlin/New York: de Gruyter, 2002), pp. 393–408.
57. 'Jesus' Message in the Eyes of His Opponents (Q 7.33f.)', in preparation for FS G. Galitis.

III. *Reviews*

1. *Theologische Literaturzeitung.*

E. Gaugler, *Der Epheserbrief*, 92 (1967), p. 427.
H. Binder, *Der Glaube bei Paulus*, 95 (1970), pp. 102–103.
P. Stuhlmacher, *Das paulinische Evangelium I*, *ibidem*, pp. 202–204.
J.N.D. Kelly, *A Commentary on the Epistle of Peter and of Jude*, *ibidem*, pp. 351–52.
J. Mánek, *Ježišova podobenství* (The Parables of Jesus), 98 (1973), pp. 588–89.
D. L. Tiede, *The Charismatic Figure as Miracle Worker*, 100 (1975), pp. 40–41.
H. Merklein, *Das kirchliche Amt nach dem Epheserbrief*, *ibidem*, pp. 122–24.
Studies in New Testament Language and Text (FS G.D. Kilpatrick), 103 (1978), pp. 353–54.
W. Thissen, *Erzählung der Befreiung*, 104 (1979), pp. 578–80.
J. M. Derrett, *Studies in the New Testament I-II*, *ibidem*, pp. 905–906.
U. Berner, *Die Bergpredigt*, 106 (1981), pp. 186–88.
B.H.M. Standaert, *L'évangile selon Marc*, *ibidem*, pp. 256–57.
C.R. Kazmierski, *Jesus, the Son of God*, *ibidem*, pp. 337–38.
B. Byrne, *Sons of God – Seed of Abraham*, 107 (1982), pp. 46–47.
K. Koschorke, *Die Polemik der Gnostiker gegen das kirchliche Christentum*, *ibidem*, pp. 112–14.

W. Telford, *The Barren Temple and the Withered Fig Tree*, *ibidem*, pp. 675–76.
J. Gray, *The Biblical Doctrine of the Reign of God*, *ibidem*, pp. 722–24.
G. Strecker, *Eschaton und Historie*, *ibidem*, pp. 738–39.
O. Ogawa, *L'historie de Jésus chez Matthieu*, 109 (1984), pp. 194–94.
J. Ernst, *Das Evangelium nach Markus*, 110 (1985), pp. 448–50.
J.M. Derrett, *Studies in the New Testament III*, *ibidem*, pp. 527–28.
O. Cullmann, *Einführung in das Neue Testament*, 111 (1986), pp. 23–24.
J.M. Derrett, *The Making of Mark*, *ibidem*, pp. 360–61.
W.M. Thompson, *The Jesus-Debate*, *ibidem*, pp. 620–22.
J.D. Kingsbury, *The Christology of Mark's Gospel*, *ibidem*, pp. 818–19.
D. Lührmann, *Auslegung des neuen Testaments*, 112 (1987), pp. 106–108.
J.A.T. Robinson, *Wann entstand das Neue Testament?*, *ibidem*, pp. 435–37.
D.G. Meade, *Pseudonymity and Canon*, 113 (1988), pp. 101–102.
H. Baarlink, *Die Eschatologie der synoptischen Evangelien*, *ibidem*, pp. 347–48.
F. Mußner, *Die Kraft der Wurzel*, *ibidem*, pp. 523–25.
J. Schreiber, *Der Kreuzigungsbericht des Markusevangeliums*, *ibidem*, pp. 673–74.
M. Reiser, *Syntax und Stil des Markusevangeliums im Lichte der hellenistischen Literatur*, *ibidem*, pp. 893–95.
D.O. Via, *The Ethics of Mark's Gospel*, 114 (1989), pp. 525–26.
K. Usami, *Somatic Comprehension of Unity*, *ibidem*, pp. 732–33.
L.J. Magness, *Sense and Absence. Structure and Suspension in the Ending of Mark's Gospel*, *ibidem*, pp. 884–85.
W. Weiß, *„Eine neue Lehre im Vollmacht". Die Streit- und Schulgespräche des Markusevangeliums*, 115 (1990), pp. 105–107.
R. Hoppe, *Epheserbrief – Kolosserbrief*; N.T. Wright, *The Epistles of Paul to the Colossians and to Philemon*, *ibidem*, pp. 272–73.
S.E. Dowd, *Prayer, Power, and the Problem of Suffering*, *ibidem*, pp. 891–92.
J.M. Robinson, *Messiasgeheimnis und Geschichtsverständnis*, 116 (1991), pp. 283–84.
C.K. Barrett, *Das Evangelium nach Johannes*, 117 (1992), pp. 120–21.
B. Witherington, *The Christology of Jesus*, *ibidem*, pp. 277–78.
K.P. Donfried (Hg.), *The Romans Debate*, *ibidem*, pp. 754–55.
J.K. Elliott (Hg.), *The Language and Style of the Gospel of Mark*, 119 (1994), pp. 986–87.
J. Becker, *Das Urchristentum als gegliederte Epoche*, 120 (1995), pp. 517–18.
J.B. Gibson, *The Temptations of Jesus*, 121 (1996), pp. 659–60.
H. Hübner, *An Philemon. An die Kolosser. An die Epheser*, 124 (1999), pp. 174.
S.J. Roth, *The Blind, the Lame, and the Poor*, *ibidem*, pp. 286–88.
M. Karris, *Jesus Christus im Neuen Testament*, *ibidem*, pp. 740–41.
B.D. Schildgen, *Crisis and Continuity. Time of the Gospel of Mark*, 125 (2000), pp. 169–70.
Bas M.F. van Iersel, *Marc*, *ibidem*, pp. 284–85.
E.K. Broadhead, *Naming Jesus*, *ibidem*, pp. 1155–56.
M. Böhm, *Samarien und Samaritai bei Lukas*, 126 (2001), 922–23.
R. Feneberg, *Der Jude Jesus und die Heiden. Biographie und Theologie Jesu im Markusevangelium*, *ibidem*, pp. 1267–69.
N. Dahl, *Studies in Ephesians*; R.J. Jeal, *Integrating Theology and Ethics in Ephesians*, 127 (2002), pp. 394–95.
Ben Witherington III, *The Gospel of Mark*, 127 (2002), pp. 918–19.
J. Schröter, *Jesus und die Anfänge der Christologie*, 128 (2003), pp. 891–92.

2. *Folia philologica (Listy fiologické)*

R. Merkelbach, *Roman und Mysterium in der Antike*, 86 (1963), p. 336.
U. Berner, *Origenes*, 105 (1982), pp. 121–22.
K.H. Schelkle, *Paulus*, *ibidem*, pp. 183–84.
K. Beyschlag, *Grundriß der Dogmengeschichte*, 107 (1984), pp. 56–57.
S.S. Averincev, *Ot beregov Bospora do beregov Evfrata*, 112 (1989), pp. 52–53.

3. *Deutsche Literaturzeitung*

K.W. Tröger, *Mysterienglaube und Gnosis in CH XIII*, 93 (1972), 376–78.

4. *Archiv Orientální*

T.O. Lambdin, *Introduction to Sahidic Coptic*, 58 (1990), p. 94
H.-M. Schenke, H.-G. Bethge, V.V. Kaiser (eds.), *Nag Hammadi Deutsch I.*, 70 (2002), pp. 95–96.

5. *Evangelische Kommentare*

Bekenntnis zum Juden Jesus. F.-W. Marquarts Christologie, 24 (1991), pp. 237–39.

IV. *Lexica etc.*

1. W. Beltz (ed.), *Lexikon der letzten Dinge* (Augsburg: Pattloch, V., 1993): Lemmata: Eros in der Gnosis; Eschatologie in der Gnosis; Pneuma.
2. *Theologische Realenzyklopädie* (Berlin/New York: de Gruyter), Art: Pseudepigraphie I, Altes und Neues Testament, Vol. XXVII (1997), 645–55.
3. *Religion in Geschichte und Gegenwart* (Tübingen: Mohr-Siebeck, 4th edn, 2001), Art. Jesus Christus I. Name und Titel. 2. Jesus als Christus, Vol. III (2002), pp. 467–70.

V. *Editor*

1. 1980–83 and 1993–96 *New Testament Studies* (Cambridge): editorial board member.
2. Since 1990 chairman of the editorial board of the Czech Bible Dictionary.
3. Since1993 editorial board member of *Religio* (Czech Revue for Religious Studies), published by Masaryk University in Brno.
4. Since 1998 editorial board member of the *Journal of Greco-Roman Christianity and Judaism*, Los Angeles.
5. Since 2001 coeditor of the series 'Knihovna rané křestanské literatury' – Library of Early Christian Literature.

INDEXES

INDEX OF REFERENCES

BIBLE

Index of Authors